EXCEPTIONS FROM EU FREE MOVEMENT LAW

This collection of essays brings together contributions from judges, legal scholars and practitioners in order to provide a comprehensive assessment of the law and practice of exceptions from the principle of free movement.
It aims:

- to conceptualise how justification arguments relating to exceptions to free movement operate in the case law of the Court of Justice of the European Union and national courts;
- to develop a comprehensive and original account of empirical problems on the application of proportionality;
- to explore the legal and policy issues which shape the interactions between the EU and national authorities, including national courts, in the context of the efforts made by Member States to protect national differences.

The book analyses economic, social, cultural, political, environmental and consumer protection justifications. These are examined in the light of the rebalancing of the EU constitutional order introduced by the Lisbon Treaty and the implications of the financial crisis in the Union.

Volume 66 in the Series Modern Studies in European Law

Modern Studies in European Law
Recent titles in this series:

EU International Relations Law Second Edition
Panos Koutrakos

Fundamental Rights in the EU: A Matter for Two Courts
Edited by Sonia Morano-Foadi and Lucy Vickers

What Form of Government for the European Union and the Eurozone?
Federico Fabbrini, Ernst Hirsch Ballin and Han Somsen

The UK and European Human Rights: A Strained Relationship?
Edited by Katja S Ziegler, Elizabeth Wicks and Loveday Hodson

The European Union in International Organisations and Global Governance: Recent Developments
Edited by Christine Kaddous

Nudge and the Law: What Can EU Law Learn From Behavioural Sciences?
Edited by Alberto Alemanno and Anne-Lise Sibony

Fundamental Rights in EU Internal Market Legislation
Vasiliki Kosta

Uniformity of Customs Administration in the European Union
Kathrin Limbach

The Impact of Union Citizenship on the EU's Market Freedoms
Alina Tryfonidou

Equal Citizenship and Its Limits in EU Law
Päivi Johanna Neuvonen

The European Union's External Action in Times of Crisis
Edited by Piet Eeckhout and Manual Lopez-Escudero

The Legitimacy of Family Rights in Strasbourg Case Law: Living Instrument or Extinguished Sovereignty?
Carmen Draghici

Strengthening the Rule of Law in Europe: From a Common Concept to Mechanisms of Implementation
Edited by Werner Schroeder

For the complete list of titles in this series, see 'Modern Studies in European Law' link at www.hartpub.co.uk/books/series.asp

Exceptions from EU Free Movement Law

Derogation, Justification and Proportionality

Edited by
Panos Koutrakos, Niamh Nic Shuibhne
and Phil Syrpis

•HART•
OXFORD • LONDON • NEW YORK • NEW DELHI • SYDNEY

HART PUBLISHING
Bloomsbury Publishing Plc
Kemp House, Chawley Park, Cumnor Hill, Oxford, OX2 9PH, UK

HART PUBLISHING, the Hart/Stag logo, BLOOMSBURY and the Diana logo are trademarks of Bloomsbury Publishing Plc
First published in Great Britain 2016

First published in hardback, 2016
Paperback edition, 2019

A catalogue record for this book is available from the British Library.

Library of Congress Cataloging-in-Publication Data

Names: Koutrakos, Panos, editor. | Nic Shuibhne, Niamh, editor. | Syrpis, Phil, editor.

Title: Exceptions from EU free movement law : derogation, justification, and proportionality / edited by Panos Koutrakos, Niamh NIC Shuibhne, and Phil Syrpis.

Description: Oxford [UK] ; Portland, Oregon : Hart Publishing, 2016. | Series: Modern studies in european law ; volume 66 | Includes bibliographical references and index.

Identifiers:LCCN2016034347(print)|LCCN2016035223(ebook)|ISBN9781849466202 (hardback) | ISBN 9781509900350 (Epub)

Subjects: LCSH: Freedom of movement—European Union countries. | Free choice of employment—European Union countries. | Proportionality in law—European Union countries.

Classification: LCC KJE5170 .E99 2016 (print) | LCC KJE5170 (ebook) | DDC 342.2408/2—dc23

LC record available at https://lccn.loc.gov/2016034347

ISBN: HB: 978-1-84946-620-2
PB: 978-1-50992-886-6
ePDF: 978-1-50990-034-3
ePub: 978-1-50990-035-0

Series: Series Modern Studies in European Law, volume 66

Typeset by Compuscript Ltd, Shannon

To find out more about our authors and books visit www.hartpublishing.co.uk. Here you will find extracts, author information, details of forthcoming events and the option to sign up for our newsletters.

Foreword

This book on exceptions from free movement rights will be a welcome contribution to a field which does not easily lend itself to clear-cut or well-structured answers. In fact, the articles bring out the difficulties in obtaining a structured overview of the case law of the European Court of Justice and in seeing great coherence in that case law. The same might perhaps also be said of the articles themselves … Different approaches and explanations seem to emerge.

Is this a great sin? I do not think so. The terrain and material are simply so broad and diverse that an overall and clear picture may be difficult, if not impossible, to attain. Let me mention a few considerations which, from the perspective of a judge, seem to play a role when assessing whether a restriction on free movement may be justified or not.

It may be useful to start by noting that not all free movement rights will necessarily play out in the same way. This is because the relevant texts differ in terms of both status and content. To take an obvious example, Article 21(1) TEU, unlike the other relevant provisions, makes the right to move and reside freely within the territory of the Member States subject to the limitations and conditions laid down not only in the Treaties but also 'by the measures adopted to give them effect'. And with respect to all the free movement rights, the scope and content of such secondary law may vary greatly. It may come as a surprise to some but the judges of the Court of Justice do take legal texts seriously and the wording and context of a provision are often decisive whilst the importance of the teleological method is sometimes exaggerated in doctrinal commentaries.

Apart from the text of the applicable provisions, obvious factors to take into account are the gravity of the restriction on free movement that the national measures imply, including whether they are discriminatory or not, and the importance that the Court attaches to the public interest invoked. Serious environmental or health concerns, for instance, may more easily justify restrictions than some other concerns (but here, again, the wording of the relevant provisions of primary law attests to the importance attached to environment and health). And economic considerations will not suffice as a justification unless it can be reasonably argued that there is a serious threat to public finances so that preserving a certain national system (such as a national health care system) would be jeopardised if the restriction were to be discarded.

Moreover, as judges are there to resolve cases rather than to construe doctrine, the facts of each case, the applicable national rules as well as the arguments of the interested parties are of crucial importance. This also applies to the preliminary ruling procedure, even if it is not the task of the Court of Justice to establish the facts or to interpret national law. When dealing with requests for preliminary rulings, the Court often devotes some time and energy to obtaining as accurate a picture as possible of the factual situation and the national legal context.

As to the arguments of the interested parties, it goes without saying that the Court pays much attention to the arguments presented by the Member State that applies an alleged restriction in order to deny the existence of a restriction and/or to justify it on the basis of an explicit derogatory clause or a so-called mandatory requirement. If such arguments are based on objectively verifiable facts such as the *travaux préparatoires* of the relevant national legislation, the chances of success may be greater than if it becomes obvious that a certain public interest has been invoked at a later stage, for the purposes of the litigation in question. Arguments which remain at a general and abstract level will as a rule not turn out to be very successful. The invocation of several public interests at the same time may convey the perception of a 'shopping list' while one single public interest consideration backed up by solid and as concrete as possible information and plausible arguments as to the negative effects which would follow were the restriction to be lifted may well do the trick. And the chances of success are further enhanced if it is shown that alternatives which may be less restrictive have been considered and that the solution finally opted for has been chosen after careful reflection, taking into account the principle of proportionality.

As to this principle, the Court should probably somewhat streamline the way it is formulated, referred to and used in the reasoning of judgments. That said, the actual outcome will probably not depend on such factors. Here is an example where the result of reconciling, or as the case may be, balancing of different interests will not depend so much on the actual formulation used in the judgment but rather on perceptions among the sitting judges of what is fair and reasonable, based on an overall assessment of all relevant factors and whether the problem for the proper functioning of the internal market is deemed to be minor or more serious. It almost goes without saying that the final outcome could be different had the case been decided by another chamber of the Court than the one to which the case has been referred.

It is my impression that, since the 1990s, the Court has in some areas become somewhat more understanding of national rules which may be susceptible to restrict free movement rights. On the other hand, it is equally my impression that the Court remains vigilant vis-à-vis restrictions which could erode the free movement principles and would not hesitate to strike such restriction down, including in the area of free movement of citizens.

And let me in this context end by refuting the claim that the Court would be focusing solely on the economic aspects of the internal market, to the detriment of a 'social Europe'. Let me take the example of the famous, for some infamous, judgment in *Laval un Partneri* (Case C-341/05). The Court here took a critical eye at what it perceived as Swedish protectionism (hindering posted Latvian workers from working on a building project) and in fact upheld the interests of these workers to earn more than they would have in their home State (whilst the action of the Swedish trade unions caused the bankruptcy of the Latvian company).

A social Europe should mean just that, rather than simply a bundle of national social markets.

And what about Ms Dano (Case C-333/13) and her son, Romanian nationals who, according to the Court, could be denied certain 'special non-contributory benefits' in Germany although those benefits were granted to German nationals? Here the outcome is explained by the link which is made in Directive 2004/38 on the free movement of EU citizens between the requirement for persons not seeking employment to have sufficient resources as a condition of residence and the concern not to create a burden on the social assistance system of the host State. As Ms Dano did not work or seek work, nor did she have sufficient resources, she could not claim a right of residence. She was accordingly not residing in Germany on the basis of the Directive and could not claim the benefits in question. To decide otherwise would have rendered the condition of sufficient resources more or less meaningless (economically inactive non-nationals would in that case be able first to obtain full social assistance and then, on that basis, claim that they have sufficient resources). We may deplore this requirement established in the Directive but the Court is not empowered to remove it, unless it was held that it is in violation of Article 21 TFEU. Given the wording of that Article, such a result would be far from obvious, to say the least.

So we are back to my starting point: The text of applicable primary and secondary law does matter. This does not, of course, mean that judges should be blind to context and objectives, or that they should forget about considerations of fairness and reasonableness. And we may also remember what a friend of mine, the late Finnish Permanent Representative to the EU, Ambassador Satuli, used to say: 'Even in the EU, the use of common sense is not prohibited.'

Allan Rosas
Judge at the European Court of Justice

Preface

This collection of essays is based on a workshop hosted by City, University of London in February 2014. The project began in a café in Bristol. We did have a piece of paper, so did not have to resort to making plans on the back of a napkin; though we did have to borrow a pen.

Our primary aims are to adjust the analytical filter away from the concept of a restriction in EU free movement law, and to provide a comprehensive assessment of the law and practice of derogation and justification. For example, in the free movement of goods, academic attention has focused largely on how quantitative restrictions and measures having equivalent effect are defined, through the Court of Justice's journey from *Dassonville* to *Keck* and now to *Trailers*. This leaves the justification stage, in our view, underexplored. Moreover, the application of an extremely broad market access test means that almost any national law or practice can be conceived as a restriction of the Treaty freedoms. In consequence, States have to justify an increasing range of national measures. Academics, lawyers and judges therefore need to think more about this stage of the free movement paradigm.

The contributions in this book—addressing various derogation and justification arguments, and framed by thematic chapters that aim to link the individual discussions together—reflect (at heart) on whether the in-built function of justification receives appropriate weight in the free movement framework, and thus whether the line between market-making uniformity and the accommodation of diversity is in the right place. An important question in that regard is how we should evaluate what the 'right' place actually means. In our view, the lack of a clear normative framework in EU primary law does not enable States to navigate between the competing poles of integration and autonomy effectively. The generic derogation categories in the Treaty have in many ways outlived their functionality—for example, when drafted in the 1950s, concern for consumer protection or for the environment was absent. In this collection, we present the justification arguments that tend to be put forward by Member States in a more thematic way: economic; political; social; cultural; moral; and wellbeing. Some of these categories are well established; others seek to innovate—for example, our idea of 'wellbeing' encapsulates both consumer and environmental protection, enabling more complete consideration of ethical factors shaping global development at present. Furthermore, some of our categories are contested—for example, the Court consistently rejects the idea in principle that economic reasons constitute valid justification arguments, but contributions in this volume investigate case law that suggests otherwise.

Even where it can be established that a national measure is justifiable in principle, its proportionality must also be defended. Proportionality is therefore one of the most important—yet also problematic—principles in EU free movement law. There is little coherence in terms of the Court's empowerment of national courts in its preliminary ruling judgments. Sometimes, the Court hands the decision back to the national court with clear guidance on proportionality; sometimes, it appears to decide this question itself; and there are instances of 'handing back' but with virtually no useful guidance at all. The Court also varies its approach to the distinctiveness of the justification and proportionality stages, sometimes blending them together in an unhelpful blurring of the *why* and *how* aspects of public interest arguments. Finally, there are specific questions to be addressed around the Court's inconsistent exploration of the 'least restrictive measure' concept, since this can amount, in effect, to the substitution of judicial in place of legislative assessments. In this respect, the role of national courts and their assessment of the proportionality of national restrictions are central to the process of striking the balance between integration and autonomy. The manner in which national courts exercise this role raises questions similar to those that underpin the Court's approach to the interpretation and application of the free movement exceptions.

There are also strong policy imperatives for greater clarity about the law and practice of justifying free movement restrictions. Continuing uncertainty for Member States about what they can legitimately regulate for themselves (and how they should demonstrate this) threatens the credibility and stability of the polity at a time when neither the Union nor its market can afford any deepening fractures. The entry into force of the Lisbon Treaty raised fresh questions about the (re) ordering of EU norms: how do free movement rights sit alongside an expanded range of 'competing' EU-level public interest values in the Treaties themselves and the strengthened legal status of the Charter of Fundamental Rights? The instinct of isolationism intensifying both internationally and domestically since the global financial crisis was triggered in 2008 raises distinct dangers for the EU internal market and for the premises of freedom on which it is based. In order to safeguard their own economic and social stability, the protectionist reflexes of Member States are heightening.

It is essential for the long-term survival of the European project that Member States are afforded appropriate space to pursue their policy priorities, and that they are given appropriate guidance about whether and how they might be able to advance public interests. The law on free movement was designed precisely to accommodate this. More recently, the energy of the Union institutions is focused on safeguarding the Eurozone and responding to migration challenges, testing their appetite for further consolidation of the internal market—all the more in light of a credible threat at the time of writing that the UK may withdraw from the EU altogether. The Treaty on Stability, Coordination and Governance illustrated a shift towards subsuming national economic choices to centralised EU control. This Treaty, and reactions to it, also affected the balance between market integration and national diversity in other areas of activity. Additionally, the focus of the book on interactions between the Court of Justice and national courts addresses the role of the former at a time when it is viewed with increasing suspicion in both political and legal circles.

A further objective for the project was to integrate academic thinking with the experience and insights of practitioners of EU law. From that perspective, and reflecting on how justification arguments are constructed, challenged, and evaluated, we benefitted greatly from the contributions of Malcolm Jarvis, Professor Sir David Edward, Sally Langrish, Aidan O'Neill QC, and Judge Allan Rosas at our 2014 workshop. We owe thanks to Peter Aggar who helped with the organisation of that event. We also very much appreciate the funding provided by all three of our home institutions—Bristol, City and Edinburgh Universities. At Hart Publishing, we are grateful to Richard Hart, who embraced the project right from the start. Finally, thanks to Tom Daly at the University of Edinburgh and Edward Dean at City, University of London for exceptional research assistance at the final stages.

PK, NNS, PS
1 February 2016

Contents

Foreword v
Preface ix
List of Contributors xv
Table of cases xvii

1. The Exceptions to the Four Freedoms: The Historical Context 1
David Edward

2. Economic Justifications and the Role of the State 12
Jukka Snell

3. Citizenship: Reallocating Welfare Responsibilities to the State of Origin 32
Eleanor Spaventa

4. (Dis)Enfranchisement and Free Movement 53
Aidan O'Neill

5. Social Justifications for Restrictions of the Right to Welfare Equality: Students and Beyond 80
Sara Iglesias Sánchez and Diego Acosta Arcarazo

6. The Worker Protection Justification: Lessons from Consumer Law 106
Catherine Barnard

7. Cultural Policy Justifications 131
Bruno de Witte

8. Morality, Free Movement and Judicial Restraint at the European Court of Justice 143
Dimitrios Doukas

9. The Constitutional Dimension of Public Policy Justifications 170
Daniel Thym

10. Public Security Exceptions and EU Free Movement Law 190
Panos Koutrakos

11. Free Movement, the Quality of Life and the Myth that the Court Balances Interests 218
Gareth Davies

12. Justification, Proportionality and Consumer Protection 240
Stephen Weatherill

13. The Proportionality Test: Constructive Dialogue between the English and Scottish Courts 265
Malcolm Jarvis

14. EU Secondary Legislation and its Impact on Derogations from Free Movement 278
Phil Syrpis

15. Primary Laws: Judging Free Movement Restrictions after Lisbon 297
Niamh Nic Shuibhne

Index 319

List of Contributors

Diego Acosta Arcarazo is Senior Lecturer at University of Bristol.

Catherine Barnard is Professor of Law at University of Cambridge.

Gareth Davies is Professor of EU Law at Free University of Amsterdam.

Bruno De Witte is Professor of EU Law at Maastricht University.

Dimitrios Doukas is Reader at University of Manchester.

Sir David Edward is Emeritus Professor at the University of Edinburgh and former Judge at the European Court of Justice.

Sara Iglesias Sánchez is Legal Secretary at the European Court of Justice.

Malcolm Jarvis is barrister at 20 Essex Street.

Panos Koutrakos is Professor of EU law and Jean Monnet Professor of EU Law at City, University of London.

Niamh Nic Shuibhne is Professor of European Union Law at University of Edinburgh.

Aidan O'Neill is barrister at Matrix Chambers.

Allan Rosas is a Judge at the European Court of Justice.

Jukka Snell is Professor of EU Law University of Turku and Swansea University.

Eleanor Spaventa is Professor of EU law at Durham University.

Phil Syrpis is Professor of EU Law at the University of Bristol.

Daniel Thym is Professor of Public, European and International Law at University of Konstanz.

Stephen Weatherill is Jack Delors Professor of EU Law at University of Oxford.

Table of cases

European Union

Case 7/61 *Commission v Italy* EU:C:1961:31 .... 14, 172
Case 48/65 *Lütticke* EU:C:1966:8 6
Case 7/68 *Commission v Italy* EU:C:1968:51 135
Case 13/68 *Salgoil* EU:C:1968:54 6
Joined Cases 6 and 11/69 *Commission v France* EU:C:1969:68 190
Case 11/70 *Internationale Handelsgesellschaft* EU:C:1970:114 315
Case 155/73 *Sacchi* EU:C:1974:40 135
Case 2/74 *Reyners* EU:C:1974:68 6
Case 8/74 *Procureur du Roi v Dassonville* EU:C:1974:82 .... 4–5, 16, 24–25, 294, 311
Case 33/74 *Van Binsbergen* EU:C:1974:131 .... 6, 311
Case 36/74 *Walrave and Koch* EU:C:1974:140 .... 24, 274
Case 41/74 *Van Duyn* EU:C:1974:133 .... 149, 155, 172, 181, 229, 297
Case 67/74 *Bonsignore* EU:C:1975:34 203
Case 36/75 *Rutili* EU:C:1975:137 153
Case 104/75 *De Peijper* EU:C:1976:67 266
Case 35/76 *Simmenthal* EU:C:1976:180 .... 172, 192
Case 46/76 *Bauhuis* EU:C:1977:6 172
Case 71/76 *Thieffry* EU:C:1977:65 .... 6, 293
Case 5/77 *Tedeschi v Denkavit* EU:C:1977:144 192
Case 30/77 *Bouchereau* EU:C:1977:172 .... 153, 172, 181, 203, 297
Case 15/78 *Koestler* EU:C:1978:184 .... 160, 163
Case 120/78 *Rewe Zentrale v Bundesmonopolverwaltung fur Branntwein* EU:C:1979:42 .... 28, 108, 146, 148, 173, 223, 230, 240, 244, 311
Case 153/78 *Commission v Germany* EU:C:1979:194 152
Case 251/78 *Denkavit* EU:C:1979:252 192
Case 15/79 *Groenveld* EU:C:1979:253 .... 6, 16
Case 34/79 *Henn and Darby* EU:C:1979:295 .... 146, 149, 163
Case 140/79 *Chemial* EU:C:1981:1 193
Case 788/79 *Gilli and Andres* EU:C:1980:171 .... 7, 223
Case 53/80 *Eyssen* EU:C:1981:35 242
Case 155/80 *Oebel* EU:C:1981:177 .... 107, 121
Case 279/80 *Webb* EU:C:1981:314 .... 107, 112, 122
Joined Cases 62 and 63/81 *Seco v EVI* EU:C:1982:34 .... 112, 115
Joined Cases 115/81 and 116/81 *Adoui and Cornuaille* EU:C:1982:183 .... 149, 151, 153, 155–56
Case 261/81 *Walter Rau* EU:C:1982:382 247
Case 283/81 *CILFIT v Ministry of Health* EU:C:1982:335 294
Case 40/82 *Commission v United Kingdom* EU:C:1984:33 241

Case 202/82 *Commission v France* EU:C:1984:67 120
Case 227/82 *Van Bennekom* EU:C:1983:354 241
Case 238/82 *Duphar* EU:C:1984:45 .... 16, 87
Case 286/82 *Luisi e Carbone* EU:C:1984:35 33
Case 15/83 *Denkavit Nederland* EU:C:1984:183 270
Case 72/83 *Campus Oil* EU:C:1984:256 .... 17, 152, 172, 176, 192–93
Case 229/83 *Leclerc v Au blé vert* EU:C:1985:1 135
Case 240/83 *ADBHU* EU:C:1985:59 7
Case 248/83 *Commission v Germany* EU:C:1985:214 198
Case 288/83 *Commission v Ireland* EU:C:1985:251 172
Joined Cases 60 and 61/84 *Cinéthèque* EU:C:1985:329 137
Case 178/84 *Commission v Germany* EU:C:1987:126 .... 120, 182, 223, 230, 245
Case 222/84 *Johnston v Chief Constable of the Royal Ulster Constabulary* EU:C:1986:206 .... 198, 208
Case 121/85 *Conegate* EU:C:1986:114 .... 146, 150, 164
Case 316/85 *Lebon* EU:C:1987:302 46
Case 407/85 *3 Glocken* EU:C:1988:401 .... 182, 223
Case 57/86 *Greece v Commission* EU:C:1988:284 190
Case 90/86 *Zoni* EU:C:1988:403 120
Case 222/86 *UNECTEF v Heylens* EU:C:1987:442 65
Case 286/86 *Deserbais* EU:C:1988:434 .... 223, 248
Case 302/86 *Commission v Denmark* EU:C:1988:421 .... 8, 244, 252
Case 81/87 *Daily Mail* EU:C:1988:456 294
Case 127/87 *Commission v Greece* EU:C:1988:331 190
Case 186/87 *Cowan* EU:C:1989:47 224
Case 379/87 *Groener* EU:C:1989:599 .... 256, 309
Case 382/87 *Buet* EU:C:1989:198 249
Case 145/88 *Torfaen Borough Council v B & Q* EU:C:1989:593 .... 152, 234
Case 331/88 *ex p FEDESA* EU:C:1990:391 .... 258, 267
Case C-23/89 *Quietlynn* EU:C:1990:300 150
Case T-51/89 *Tetra Pak Rausing SA v Commission* EU:T:1990:41 265
Case C-113/89 *Rush Portuguesa* EU:C:1990:142 111–13
Case C-154/89 *Commission v France* EU:C:1991:76 .... 137, 245
Case C-180/89 *Commission v Italy* EU:C:1991:78 137
Case C-198/89 *Commission v Greece* EU:C:1991:79 137
Case C-205/89 *Commission v Greece* EU:C:1991:123 241
Case C-221/89 *Factortame and Others* EU:C:1991:320 190
Case C-260/89 *ERT* EU:C:1991:254 .... 229, 254, 276
Case C-288/89 *Stichting Collectieve Antennevoorziening Gouda* EU:C:1991:323 .... 112, 137, 148
Case C-292/89 *Antonissen* EU:C:1991:80 33
Case C-312/89 *Conforama* EU:C:1991:93 .... 191, 234
Case C-314/89 *Rauh* EU:C:1991:143 223
Case C-332/89 *Marchandise* EU:C:1991:94 .... 121, 191, 234
Case C-350/89 *Sheptonhurst Ltd v Newham Borough Council* EU:C:1991:151 150
Case C-367/89 *Criminal proceedings against Aimé Richardt and Les Accessoires Scientifiques SNC* EU:C:1991:376 .... 152, 193, 195, 197

Joined Cases C-1 and 176/90 *Aragonesa* EU:C:1991:327 270
Case C-2/90 *Commission v Belgium* EU:C:1992:310 312
Case C-76/90 *Säger* EU:C:1991:331 146
Case C-159/90 *Grogan* EU:C:1991:378 ....146, 154
Case C-344/90 *Commission v France* EU:C:1992:328 161
Case C-370/90 *Singh* EU:C:1992:296 236
Case C-65/91 *Commission v Greece* EU:C:1992:388 8
Case C-169/91 *Stoke on Trent and Norwich City Councils v B & Q plc* EU:C:1992:519 ....191, 234, 260
Joined Cases C-267 and 268/91 *Criminal proceedings against Keck and Mithouard* EU:C:1993:905 ....30, 150, 234, 249, 260, 267
Case C-320/91 *Corbeau* EU:C:1993:198 18
Case C-17/92 *FEDICINE* EU:C:1993:172 136
Case C-19/92 *Kraus v Land Baden Württemburg* EU:C:1993:125 9
Case C-275/92 *Schindler* EU:C:1994:119 ....147, 155, 162–63
Case C-315/92 *Clinique* EU:C:1994:34 109
Joined Cases C-401 and 402/92 *Tankstation 't Heukste & JBE Boermans* EU:C:1994:220 260
Case C-43/93 *Van der Elst* EU:C:1994:310 ....111, 115, 125
Case C-51/93 *Meyhui NV v Schott Zwiesel Glaswerke* AG EU:C:1994:312 270
Case C-279/93 *Schumacker* EU:C:1995:31 172
Case C-324/93 *Evans Medical* EU:C:1995:84 15
Case C-384/93 *Alpine Investments* EU:C:1995:126 ....16, 160, 163
Case C-392/93 *British Telecommunications* EU:C:1996:131 194
Case C-415/93 *Bosman* EU:C:1995:463 ....148, 252
Case C-470/93 *Mars* EU:C:1995:224 ....109, 206, 248
Case C-473/93 *Commission v Luxembourg* EU:C:1996:80 314
Case C-55/94 *Gebhard* EU:C:1995:411 ....9, 148, 224, 231
Case C-70/94 *Fritz Werner Industrie-Ausrustungen GmbH v Germany* EU:C:1995:328 193–94
Case C-83/94 *Criminal Proceedings against Peter Leifer and Others* EU:C:1995:329 193–95
Case C-120/94 *Commission v Greece* EU:C:1995:109 ....208, 210
Joined Cases C-163, 165 and 250/94 *Sanz de Lera* EU:C:1995:451 294
Case C-233/94 *Germany v Parliament and Council* EU:C:1997:231 20
Case C-237/94 *O'Flynn v Adjudication Officer* EU:C:1996:206 33
Case C-272/94 *Guiot* EU:C:1996:147 ....111, 115
Case C-1/95 *Gerster* EU:C:1997:452 198
Case C-3/95 *Reisebüro Broede v Gerd Sanker* EU:C:1996:487 243
Case C-120/95 *Decker* EU:C:1998:167 ....17, 87, 148, 190
Case C-124/95 *Centro-Com* EU:C:1997:8 190
Case C-189/95 *Franzén* EU:C:1979:194 ....152, 163
Case T-219/95 R *Danielsson, Largenteau and Haoa v Commission* EU:T:1995:219 265
Case C-265/95 *Commission v France* EU:C:1997:595 236

Case C-344/95 *Commission v Belgium* EU:C:1997:81 46
Case C-368/95 *Familiapress* EU:C:1997:325 ....194, 244, 275
Case C-398/95 *SETTG* EU:C:1997:282 ....16, 32
Case C-1/96 *ex p Compassion in World Farming Ltd* EU:C:1998:113 152
Joined Cases C-64 and 65/96 *Ücker and Jacquet* EU:C:1997:285 56
Case C-67/96 *Albany International* EU:C:1999:430 107
Case C-85/96 *Martinez Sala* EU:C:1998:217 ....36–37, 40, 43, 81
Case C-114/96 *Kieffer and Thill* EU:C:1997:316....270
Case C-158/96 *Kohll* EU:C:1998:171 ....17, 87, 191
Case C-184/96 *Commission v France* EU:C:1998:495....223
Case C-210/96 Gut *Springenheide* EU:C:1998:369 121
Case C-264/96 *ICI v Colmer* EU:C:1998:370 ....15, 190
Case C-348/96 *Calfa* EU:C:1999:6 ....151, 153, 156
Joined Cases C-369 and 376/96 *Criminal proceedings against Jean-Claude Arblade and Arblade & Fils SARL and Bernard Leloup, Serge Leloup and Sofrage SARL* EU:C:1999:575 ....115, 127
Case C-110/97 *Netherlands v Council* EU:C:2001:620 258
Case C-124/97 *Läärä and Others* EU:C:1999:435.... 155, 160, 161, 164, 166, 253
Case C-273/97 *Sirdar v The Army Board and Secretary of State for Defence* EU:C:1999:523 197
Case C-303/97 *Kessler* EU:C:1999:35 121
Case C-378/97 *Wijsenbeek* EU:C:1999:439 24
Case C-394/97 *Heinonen* EU:C:1999:308 ....153, 158
Case C-414/97 *Commission v Spain* EU:C:1999:417 213
Joined Cases C-49, 50, 52 to 54 and 68 to 71/98 *Finalarte* EU:C:2001:564 ....106, 126
Case C-67/98 *Zenatti* EU:C:1999:514 ....151, 155, 160, 164–66
Case C-165/98 *Criminal proceedings against André Mazzoleni and Inter Surveillance Assistance SARL* EU:C:2001:162....115
Case C-179/98 *Mesbah* EU:C:1999:549....65
Case C-190/98 *Graf* EU:C:2000:49 107
Case C-220/98 *Estée Lauder* EU:C:2000:8....121
Case C-224/98 *D'Hoop* EU:C:2002:432 .... 33, 36, 40, 65, 85, 86
Case C-281/98 *Angonese* EU:C:2000:296 24
Case C-285/98 *Kreil* EU:C:2000:2 198
Case C-367/98 *Commission v Portugal* EU:C:2002:326....24, 27
Case C-368/98 *Vanbraekel* EU:C:2001:400 24
Case C-376/98 *Germany v Parliament and Council* EU:C:2000:544....231
Case C-379/98 *Preussen Elektra* EU:C:2001:160....244, 252
Case C-398/98 *Commission v Greece* EU:C:2001:565 195
Case C-405/98 *Gourmet* EU:C:2001:135.... 173, 187, 194
Case C-473/98 *Kemikalieinspektionen v Toolex Alpha AB* EU:C:2000:379 121
Case C-45/99 *Ambulanz Glöckner* EU:C:2000:273 18
Case C-54/99 *Scientology* EU:C:2000:124 ....149, 154, 156
Case C-157/99 *Smits and Peerbooms* EU:C:2001:404 ....24, 87, 191

Case C-164/99 *Portugaia Construções* EU:C:2002:40 114–15
Case C-184/99 *Grzelczyk* EU:C:2001:458 .... 34, 36–37, 81, 104, 235
Case C-268/99 *Jany* EU:C:2001:616 .... 146, 149, 151, 154–55
Case C-413/99 *Baumbast* EU:C:2002:493 .... 24, 35, 37, 40, 97, 235, 295
Case C-493/99 *Commission v Germany* EU:C:2001:578 .... 115, 117, 127
Case C-503/99 *Commission v Belgium* EU:C:2002:328 193
Case C-12/00 *Commission v Spain* EU:C:2003:21 223
Case C-14/00 *Commission v Italy* EU:C:2003:22 223
Case C-60/00 *Carpenter* EU:C:2002:434 235
Case C-112/00 *Schmidberger* EU:C:2003:333 .... 182, 236, 254, 261
Case C-123/00 *Bellamy* EU:C:2001:214 .... 224, 231
Case C-208/00 *Überseering* EU:C:2002:632 .... 122, 173
Case C-279/00 *Commission v Italy* EU:C:2002:89 .... 115, 117
Case C-294/00 *Deutsche Paracelsus Schulen* EU:C:2002:442 243
Case C-6/01 *Anomar* EU:C:2003:446 155
Case T-26/01 *Fiocchi* EU:T:2003:248 213
Case C-79/01 *Payroll Data Services* EU:C:2002:592 .... 116, 122–23
Case C-95/01 *Greenham and Abel* EU:C:2004:71 .... 161, 183
Case C-100/01 *Olazabal* EU:C:2002:712 151
Case C-168/01 *Bosal Holding* EU:C:2003:479 15
Case T-168/01 *GlaxoSmithKline Services v Commission* EU:T:2006:265 109
Case C-186/01 *Dory* EU:C:2003:146 198
Case C-189/01 *Jippes and Others* EU:C:2001:420 .... 267, 271
Case C-192/01 *Commission v Denmark* EU:C:2003:492 242
Case C-243/01 *Gambelli* EU:C:2003:597 .... 147, 151, 163–65, 183
Joined Cases C-482 and 493/01 *Orfanopoulos and Oliveri* EU:C:2004:262 .... 154, 156
Case C-491/01 *ex p British American Tobacco (Investments) and Imperial Tobacco* EU:C:2002:741 .... 148, 267
Case C-14/02 *ATRAL SA* EU:C:2003:265 241
Case C-36/02 *Omega* EU:C:2004:614 .... 149, 154–55, 160, 163, 181, 221, 225, 228, 244, 255–56, 261, 297, 314
Case C-41/02 *Commission v Netherlands* EU:C:2004:762 242
Case C-42/02 *Lindman* EU:C:2003:613 .... 161, 165
Case C-138/02 *Collins* EU:C:2004:172 .... 36, 81, 86
Case C-148/02 *Garcia Avello* EU:C:2003:539 .... 33, 224–25
Case C-200/02 *Zhu and Chen* EU:C:2004:639 .... 42, 235
Case C-224/02 *Pusa* EU:C:2004:273 .... 65, 93
Case C-262/02 *Commission v France* EU:C:2004:431 .... 160, 163, 183, 243
Case C-334/02 *Commission v France* EU:C:2004:129 190
Case C-429/02 *Bacardi France* EU:C:2004:432 243
Case C-434/02 *Arnold André* EU:C:2004:800 .... 267, 270–71
Case C-442/02 *Caixabank France* EU:C:2004:586 .... 232, 300
Case C-456/02 *Trojani* EU:C:2004:488 .... 36, 38, 40, 43
Case C-60/03 *Wolff & Müller* EU:C:2004:610 115
Case C-86/03 *Greece v Commission* EU:C:2005:769 258

Case C-140/03 *Commission v Greece* EU:C:2005:242 ....224, 230–31
Case C-147/03 *Commission v Austria* EU:C:2005:427 ....85–86, 103, 224, 230
Case C-209/03 *Bidar* EU:C:2005:169 .... 22, 36, 38, 86, 88, 291
Case C-210/03 *Swedish Match* EU:C:2004:802 270–71
Case C-408/03 *Commission v Belgium* EU:C:2006:192 ....37, 42
Case C-445/03 *Commission v Luxembourg* EU:C:2004:655 ....113–15, 117, 124–25, 127
Case C-446/03 *Marks & Spencer* EU:C:2005:763 190
Case C-470/03 *AGM-COS.MET* EU:C:2007:213....274
Joined Cases C-94 and 202/04 *Cipolla* EU:C:2006:758 173
Case C-145/04 *Spain v United Kingdom* EU:C:2006:543 59
Joined Cases C-154 and 155/04 *Alliance for Natural Health* EU:C:2005:449 ....257, 270–71
Joined Cases C-158 and 159/04 *Alfa Vita* EU:C:2006:562 223
Case C-168/04 *Commission v Austria* EU:C:2006:595....113, 117, 125
Case C-170/04 *Rosengren* EU:C:2007:313....163, 243, 263
Case C-174/04 *Commission v Italy* EU:C:2005:350 28
Case T-234/04 *Netherlands v Commission* EU:T:2007:335....289
Case C-244/04 *Commission v Germany* EU:C:2006:49 .... 114, 117, 124, 127
Case C-258/04 *Ioannidis* EU:C:2005:559 85–86
Case C-260/04 *Commission v Italy* EU:C:2007:508 164
Case C-300/04 *Eman and Sevinger* EU:C:2006:545....60–61, 70
Joined Cases C-338, 359 and 360/04 *Placanica* EU:C:2007:133 .... 147, 151, 163–65, 177, 182
Case C-372/04 *Watts* EU:C:2006:325....24
Case C-406/04 *De Cuyper* EU:C:2006:491 .... 33, 51, 65, 85, 96
Case C-434/04 *Ahokainen and Leppik* EU:C:2006:609.... 150, 242–43, 261, 263, 270
Case C-441/04 *A-Punkt Schmuckhandels* EU:C:2006:141....250
Case C-490/04 *Commission v Germany* EU:C:2007:430 ....116–17, 127
Case C-513/04 *Kerckhaert and Morres* EU:C:2006:713 17
Case C-519/04 P *Meca-Medina and Majcen v Commission* EU:C:2006:492 252
Case C-524/04 *Test Claimants in the Thin Cap Group litigation* EU:C:2007:161 190
Case C-40/05 *Lyyski* EU:C:2007:10 85
Case C-76/05 *Schwarz and Gootjes-Schwarz* EU:C:2007:492 ....65, 96
Case C-94/05 *Emsland-Stärke* EU:C:2006:185....258
Case C-110/05 *Commission v Italy* EU:C:2009:66 ....183, 270, 318
Case C-112/05 *Commission v Germany* EU:C:2007:623 ....114, 117, 122
Case C-142/05 *Mickelsson and Roos* EU:C:2009:336 260
Case C-152/05 *Commission v Germany* EU:C:2008:17 85
Case C-192/05 *Tas-Hagen* EU:C:2006:676....65, 86, 89
Case C-212/05 *Hartmann* EU:C:2007:437 91
Case C-213/05 *Geven* EU:C:2007:438 ....91, 97
Case C-284/05 *Commission v Finland* EU:C:2009:778....213
Case C-287/05 *Hendrix* EU:C:2007:196....99
Case C-294/05 *Commission v Sweden* EU:C:2009:779 213–14
Case C-337/05 *Commission v Italy* EU:C:2008:203 213

Case C-341/05 *Laval un Partneri* EU:C:2007:809 .... vi, 29, 116, 126, 186, 237, 274, 286, 301
Case C-372/05 *Commission v Germany* EU:C:2009:780 213–14
Case C-378/05 *Commission v Italy* EU:C:2006:581 213
Case C-409/05 *Commission v Greece* EU:C:2009:782 213–14
Case C-415/05 P *Kadi* EU:C:2008:30 205–06
Case C-438/05 *The International Transport Workers' Federation and The Finnish Seamen's Union* EU:C:2007:772 .... 20, 126, 182, 190, 237, 274
Joined Cases C-439 P and 454/05 P *Land Oberösterreich and Austria v Commission* EU:C:2007:510 289
Case C-461/05 *Commission v Denmark* EU:C:2009:783 213–14
Joined Cases C-11 and 12/06 *Morgan and Bucher* EU:C:2007:626 .... 45, 65–66, 82, 85–86, 88, 100
Case C-157/06 *Commission v Italy* EU:C:2008:530 213
Case C-210/06 *Cartesio* EU:C:2008:723 294
Case C-239/06 *Commission v Italy* EU:C:2009:784 213
Case C-244/06 *Dynamic Medien* EU:C:2008:85 .... 160–61, 181, 244, 297
Case C-250/06 *United Pan-Europe Communications Belgium* EU:C:2007:783 252
Case C-265/06 *Commission v Portugal* EU:C:2008:210 246
Case C-346/06 *Rüffert* EU:C:2008:189 .... 126, 151, 284–85
Case C-409/06 *Winner Wetten* EU:C:2010:503 315
Case C-499/06 *Nerkowska* EU:C:2008:300 .... 85–86, 89
Case C-500/06 *Corporación Dermoestética* EU:C:2008:421 151
Case C-518/06 *Commission v Italy* EU:C:2009:270 232
Case C-42/07 *Liga Portuguesa de Futebol Professional and Bwin International* EU:C:2009:519 .... 147, 157, 162, 166, 253
Case C-158/07 *Förster* EU:C:2008:630 .... 39, 85–86, 90, 99, 291
Case C-169/07 *Hartlauer* EU:C:2009:141 .... 17, 151, 157
Joined Cases C-171 and 172/07 *Apothekerkammer des Saarlandes and Others* EU:C:2009:316 .... 151, 157, 311
Case C-213/07 *Michaniki* EU:C:2008:544 314
Case C-219/07 *Nationale Raad van Dierenkwekers en Liefhebbers and Andibel* EU:C:2008:353 244
Case C-221/07 *Zablocka-Weyhermüller* EU:C:2008:681 .... 85–86, 89, 94
Case C-222/07 *UTECA* EU:C:2009:124 .... 139–40, 309
Joined Cases C-316, 358, 359, 360, 409 and 410/07 *Stoß and Kulpa* EU:C:2010:504 .... 162, 164–66
Case C-518/07 *Commission and European Data Protection Supervisor v Germany* EU:C:2010:125 54
Case C-531/07 *Fachverband der Buch- und Medienwirtschaft v LIBRO* EU:C:2009:276 252
Case C-558/07 *SPCM and Others* EU:C:2009:430 258
Joined Cases C-22/08 and C-23/08 *Vatsouras and Koupatantze* EU:C:2009:344 .... 35, 39, 100

Case C-46/08 *Carmen Media* EU:C:2010:505....166
Case C-51/08 *Commission v Luxembourg* EU:C:2011:336....314
Case C-58/08 *Vodafone and Others* EU:C:2010:321....258, 271
Case C-64/08 *Engelmann* EU:C:2010:506....161, 166
Case C-73/08 *Bressol* EU:C:2010:181....85, 87, 93
Case C-96/08 *CIBA* EU:C:2010:185....28
Case C-135/08 *Rottmann* EU:C:2010:104....60, 64–65, 73, 229
Case C-153/08 *Commission v Spain* EU:C:2009:618....161
Case C-165/08 *Commission v Poland* EU:C:2009:473....152
Case C-203/08 *Betfair* EU:C:2010:307....162, 164, 166
Case C-212/08 *Zeturf* EU:C:2011:437....162, 164–66
Case C-219/08 *Commission v Belgium* EU:C:2009:599....127
Case C-258/08 *Ladbrokes* EU:C:2010:308....162, 164–66, 225, 253
Case C-271/08 *Commission v Germany* EU:C:2010:426....310
Case C-310/08 *London Borough of Harrow v Ibrahim* EU:C:2010:80....33
Case C-400/08 *Commission v Spain* EU:C:2011:172....10, 173, 224, 231
Joined Cases C-436 and 437/08 *Haribo Lakritzen* EU:C:2009:17....15
Joined Cases C-447 and 448/08 *Sjöberg and Gerdin* EU:C:2010:415....162
Case C-515/08 *Santos Palhota* EU:C:2010:589....29, 111, 127
Case T-565/08 *Corsica Ferries France v Commission* EU:T:2012:415....310
Case C-20/09 *Commission v Portugal*, EU:C:2011:214....32
Case C-28/09 *Commission v Austria* EU:C:2011:854....252, 312
Case C-34/09 *Ruiz Zambrano* EU:C:2011:124....35, 45, 56, 74, 235
Case C-52/09 *TeliaSonera Sverige* EU:C:2011:83....109
Case C-108/09 *Ker-Optika* EU:C:2010:725....266
Case C-137/09 *Joseman* EU:C:2010:774....147, 149, 151, 156–57, 177, 316
Case C-145/09 *Tsakouridis* EU:C:2010:708....43, 201, 203, 207, 306
Case C-208/09 *Sayn-Wittgenstein* EU:C:2010:806....181, 221, 225, 256, 297, 316
Case C-213/09 *Chabo* EU:C:2010:372....271–72
Case C-236/09 *Association belge des Consommateurs Test-Achats and Others* EU:C:2011:100....309
Case C-338/09 *Yellow Cab* EU:C:2010:814....21
Case C-343/09 *Afton Chemical* EU:C:2010:419....267
Case C-347/09 *Dickinger and Ömer* EU:C:2011:582....162, 165–66, 202
Case C-348/09 *PI* EU:C:2012:300....43–44, 177, 182, 201, 203, 306
Case C-391/09 *Runevič-Vardyn and Wardyn* EU:C:2011:291....139–41, 173, 256, 309
Case C-503/09 *Stewart* EU:C:2011:500....44, 82, 86, 89, 98
Case C-542/09 *Commission v Netherlands* EU:C:2012:346....22, 82, 84–86, 90–91, 97, 100
Case C-34/10 *Brüstle* EU:C:2011:669....153
Joined Cases C-72 and 77/10 *Costa and Cifone* EU:C:2012:8....165
Joined Cases C-244 and 245/10 *Mesopotamia* EU:C:2011:607....158
Case C-309/10 *Agrana Zucker* EU:C:2011:531....267, 271
Case C-393/10 *O'Brien* EU:C:2012:110....315
Case C-400/10 PPU *McB* EU:C:2010:582....203
Joined Cases C-424 and 425/10 *Ziolkowski and Szeja* EU:C:2011:866....40
Case C-544/10 *Deutsches Weintor* EU:C:2012:526....310

Case C-571/10 *Kamberaj* EU:C:2012:233 309
Case C-577/10 *Commission v Belgium* EU:C:2012:814 .... 110, 113, 117, 125
Case C-615/10 *Insinööritoimisto InsTiimi* EU:C:2012:324 213
Case C-171/11 *Fra.bo* EU:C:2012:453 26
Case C-172/11 *Erny* EU:C:2012:399 310
Case C-176/11 *HIT hoteli* EU:C:2012:454 162
Joined Cases C-186 and 209/11 *Stanleybet* EU:C:2013:33 164–66
Joined Cases C-197 and 203/11 *Libert and Others*
EU:C:2013:288 85
Case C-202/11 *Las* EU:C:2013:239 .... 111, 124, 139–40, 256, 309
Case C-256/11 *Dereçi* EU:C:2011:734 .... 35, 74
Case C-283/11 *Sky Österreich* EU:C:2013:28 309
Case C-300/11 *ZZ* EU:C:2013:363 204
Case C-367/11 *Prete* EU:C:2012:668 86
Case C-379/11 *Caves Krier Frères* EU:C:2012:798 .... 66, 82, 85, 100
Case C-399/11 *Melloni* EU:C:2012:600 314
Case C-470/11 *Garkalns* EU:C:2012:505 164
Joined Cases C-523 and 585/11 *Prinz and Seeberger* EU:C:2013:524 .... 21, 45, 65, 82, 86, 98, 100
Case C-529/11 *Alarape and Tijani* EU:C:2013:290 33
Case C-539/11 *Ottica New Line di Accardi Vincenzo* EU:C:2013:591 310
Case C-577/11 *DKV Belgium* EU:C:2013:146 250
Case C-628/11 *International Jet Management* EU:C:2014:171 32
Case C-639/11 *Commission v Poland* EU:C:2014:173 280–82
Joined Cases C-660/11 and 8/12 *Biasci and Rainone* EU:C:2013:550 .... 162, 165–66
Case C-20/12 *Giersch and Others* EU:C:2013:411 .... 37, 47, 82, 85–86, 91, 94, 97
Case C-46/12 *N* EU:C:2013:97 46
Case C-86/12 *Alokpa* EU:C:2013:645 .... 35, 41, 45
Joined Cases C-105 to 107/12 *Essent* EU:C:2013:677 19
Case C-140/12 *Brey* EU:C:2013:565 .... 21, 35, 43, 48–50, 82, 88, 101
Case C-220/12 *Thiele Meneses* EU:C:2013:683 .... 22, 45–46, 82, 85–86, 90, 100
Case C-265/12 *Citroën Belux* EU:C:2013:498 250
Case C-275/12 *Elrick* EU:C:2013:684 .... 45, 85, 94
Joined Cases C-293 and 594/12 *Digital Rights Ireland* EU:C:2014:238 .... 58, 294
Case C-367/12 *Sokoll-Seebacher* EU:C:2014:68 243
Case C-370/12 *Pringle* EU:C:2012:756 295
Case C-378/12 *Onuekwere* EU:C:2014:13 43–44
Case C-385/12 *Hervis Sport- és Divatkereskedelmi* EU:C:2014:47 21
Case C-390/12 *Pfleger* EU:C:2014:281 .... 164, 166, 253
Case C-400/12 *G* EU:C:2014:9 43–44
Case C-456/12 *O and B* EU:C:2014:135 .... 35, 40
Case C-457/12 *S and G* EU:C:2014:136 .... 33, 235–36
Case C-483/12 *Pelckmans Turnhout* EU:C:2014:304 260
Case C-557/12 *KONE and Others* EU:C:2014:45 310
Case C-573/12 *Ålands Vindkraft* EU:C:2014:2037 .... 173, 183
Case C-138/13 *Dogan* EU:C:2014:2066 98

Joined Cases C-144, 154 and 160/13 *VDP Dental Laboratory* EU:C:2014:2163 313
Case C-156/13 *Digibet* EU:C:2014:1756 ....162, 315
Case C-268/13 *Petru* EU:C:2014:2271 18
Case C-302/13 *flyLAL-Lithuanian Airlines* EU:C:2014:2319 181
Case C-315/13 *De Clercq and Others* EU:C:2014:2408 113
Case C-333/13 *Dano* EU:C:2014:2358 ....vii, 21–22, 39, 41, 82, 102, 292
Case C-359/13 *Martens* EU:C:2015:118....66, 85–86, 90, 98
Case C-463/13 *Stanley International Betting* EU:C:2015:25 ....162, 166, 297
Case C-549/13 *Bundesdruckerei* EU:C:2014:2235 ....113, 116, 284
Case C-650/13 *Delvigne* EU:C:2015:648....61
Case C-44/14 *Spain v Parliament and Council* EU:C:2015:320....313
Case C-67/14 *Alimanovic* EU:C:2015:597....39
Case C-98/14 *Berlington* EU:C:2015:386 ....162, 164–66
Case C-115/14 *RegioPost* EU:C:2015:760.... 284–86
Case C-299/14 *García-Nieto and Others* [2014] OJ C315/38....102
Case C-333/14 *Scotch Whisky Association* EU:C:2015:845....261
Joined Cases C-340 and 341/14 *Trijber and Harmsen* EU:C:2015:641....146, 159
Case C-362/14 *Schrems* EU:C:2015:650....58

Opinions of the Court

Opinion 2/13 of the Court (Full Court) EU:C:2014:2454....308

United Kingdom

Stoke-on-Trent City Council v B & Q plc [1991] Ch 48 11
Smith New Court Securities Ltd v Scrimgeour Vickers (Asset Management) Ltd [1997] AC 254 143
R v Shayler [2002] UKHL 11, [2003] 1 AC 247 275
Three Rivers District Council and Others v Governor and Company of the Bank of England (No 3) [2003] 2 AC 1 143
Wolfgang Schmelz v The Immigration Appeal Tribunal [2004] EWCA Civ 29 207
R (Countryside Alliance) v Attorney General [2007] UKHL 52, [2008] 1 AC 719 ....169, 260, 275
R (Mabanaft Limited) v Secretary of State for Energy and Climate Change [2009] EWCA Civ 224 196
R (Petsafe Ltd) v The Welsh Ministers [2010] EWHC 2908 (Admin), [2011] Eu LR 270....275
R (Quila) v Secretary of State for the Home Department [2011] UKSC 45, [2012] 1 AC 621....71
R (Sinclair Collis Ltd) v Secretary of State for Health [2011] EWCA Civ 437, [2012] QB 394....265, 268, 275
R (Daha Essa) v Upper Tribunal (Immigration and Asylum Chamber) & anr [2012] EWCA Civ 1718 207

R (G1) v Secretary of State for the Home Department [2012] EWCA Civ 867, [2013] QB 1008 60
FV (Italy) v Secretary of State for the Home Department [2012] EWCA Civ 1199, [2013] 1 WLR 3339 207
R (Preston) v Wandsworth LBC [2012] EWCA Civ 1378, [2013] QB 687 68–69
Bank Mellat v HM Treasury (No.2) [2013] UKSC 39, [2013] 3 WLR 179 .... 72, 272, 275
R (Chester) v Secretary of State for Justice/McGeoch v Lord President of the Council [2013] UKSC 63, [2014] AC 271 .... 58–59, 61, 67, 70, 79
Gibraltar Betting & Gaming Association Ltd v The Secretary of State for Culture, Media & Sport [2014] EWHC 3236 (Admin), [2015] 1 CMLR 28 270–71
Kennedy v Charity Commission [2014] UKSC 20, [2014] 2 WLR 808 272
Lumsdon v Legal Services Board [2014] EWCA Civ 1276, [2014] HRLR 29 .... 268, 269, 270, 272
Moohan v Lord Advocate [2014] UKSC 67, [2015] AC 901 64
R (Nicklinson) v Ministry of Justice [2014] UKSC 38, [2014] 3 WLR 200 272
R (Rotherham Borough Council) v Secretary of State for Business, Innovation and Skills [2014] EWCA Civ 1080, [2015] 1 All ER 242 272
ZZ (France) v Secretary of State for the Home Department [2014] EWCA Civ 7, [2014] QB 820 206
Pham v Home Secretary [2015] UKSC 19, [2015] 1 WLR 1591 .... 56, 72, 76
R (Tomescu) v Lord President of the Council [2015] EWHC 3293 (Admin), [2016] ACD 1 57

Northern Ireland

In the Matter of Applications by Siegnerella Elaine Flaneur and Siegnette Elaine Flaneur for Judicial Review [2011] NICA 72 207

Germany

2 BvE 2/08 *Treaty of Lisbon*, Judgment of 30 June 2009 229

France

Conseil d'Etat 8 April 1998 *Sté SERC Fun Radio*, (1999) Revue française de droit administratif 209 138

UN Human Rights Committee reports

Gillot and others v France (UN Doc CCPR/C/75/D/932/2000, Communication No. 932/2000, 15 July 2002) 71–72

ECHR

Application No. 5493/72 *Handyside v UK* [1976] Series A No. 24 169

Scotland

Macnaughton v Macnaughton's Trustees [1953] SC 387 10
Petition for Judicial Review by Scotch Whisky association and others (Court of Session, 2013) http://www.scotcourts.gov.uk/opinions/2013CSOH70.html 261
Sinclair Collis Ltd v Lord Advocate (2013) SC 221; [2013] SLT 100 (Court of Session (Inner House, Extra Division)) 265, 269
Scotch Whisky Association v Lord Advocate [2014] CSIH 38 .... 261, 272

EFTA Court

Case E-8/97, *TV1000 Sverige AB v The Norwegian Government*, Advisory Opinion of 12 June 1998, [1998] 3 CML Rev 318 <http://www.eftacourt.int/uploads/tx_nvcases/8_97_Advisory_Opinion_EN_01.pdf> 159

United States of America

Edwards v California 314 US 160 (1941) 23

Other

Permanent Court of International Justice, Advisory Opinion No. 4 of 17 August 1923, *Nationality Decrees Issued in Tunis and Morocco (French Zone)* PCIJ Ser B No. 4 at 23 172

1

The Exceptions to the Four Freedoms: The Historical Context

DAVID EDWARD

THIS BOOK IS concerned with the exceptions to the Treaty rules governing the four freedoms, discussing the question: What restrictions or limits can be placed on the right of freedom of movement for goods, persons, services and capital? The relevant provisions, now contained in Part 3, Titles I, II and IV of the Treaty on the Functioning of the European Union (TFEU), remain largely unchanged since they were written almost 60 years ago. Yet they were written for a very different world—a world of slow communication (largely by post) and slow travel (largely by land or sea) where state frontiers were, in every respect, seen and unseen, barriers to freedom of movement. They were conditioned by the political, social and economic context of the time and by the international agreements that were already in place or under negotiation.

Use of the expression 'four freedoms' in the Treaty context was inspired by President Roosevelt's State of the Union message on 6 January 1941, where he spoke of the four fundamental freedoms: freedom of speech and expression; freedom of worship; freedom from want; and freedom from fear. As a way of summarising the aims and ideals of the Treaty, 'the four freedoms' was excellent. From a legal point of view, it has been misleading in so far as it suggests that the Treaty provisions on each of the four topics (goods, persons, services and capital) are of the same character and follow parallel tracks. In fact they deal with different forms of economic activity, and were conceived in different ways and for different reasons.

Development of the law has been beset by four problems:

— the absence of the implementing legislation envisaged in the Treaty;
— changes in public preoccupations and priorities over the years;
— the limits of the procedural scheme within which the European Court of Justice (ECJ) (now the Court of Justice) has to operate; and
— tracing an acceptable line of demarcation between the functions of the judiciary and those of the legislature.

The following chapters discuss these and other issues. The aim of this chapter is to provide the historical context which is often overlooked: the Treaty-makers in 1956–57 did not start from scratch.

The contracting Member States of the Treaty establishing the European Economic Community (EEC) were already signatory States of the General Agreement on Tariffs and Trade (GATT 1947) and of the Organisation for European Economic Co-operation (OEEC 1948). The GATT was the forerunner of the World Trade Organisation but, at that stage, dealt only with trade in goods, being 'directed to the substantial reduction of tariffs and other barriers to trade and to the elimination of discriminatory treatment in international commerce'.[1]

The OEEC (forerunner of the Organisation for Economic Co-operation and Development (OECD)) was originally set up in 1948 to administer the Marshall Plan. Robert Marjolin, who led the French delegation in the negotiations for the EEC Treaty and was one of the first commissioners, was its first Secretary General. The interests of the OEEC were wider than those of the GATT and included matters that fall within the scope of the Treaty chapters on capital, establishment and services. A Code of Trade Liberalisation, adopted in 1950, was extended in 1951 to include invisible current account operations, especially those related to economic activities and international trade. Negotiations went on during the 1950s for a Code of Liberalisation of Capital Movements, eventually realised in 1959.

In addition, there were the precedents of the Belgium–Luxembourg Economic Union dating back to 1921, and the Benelux Customs Union, originally devised by the governments in exile in London, which came into force in 1948. The Belgian government in exile included Paul-Henri Spaak, who later chaired the Committee whose report formed the basis of the drafting convention for the new EEC Treaty (the Spaak Report).[2]

All the negotiators of the new EEC Treaty were conscious that its terms must, as regards goods, be compatible with the GATT and, as regards goods and capital, be consonant with the direction of travel of the OEEC. The programme set out in the Spaak Report envisaged the creation of a Common Market based on a customs union with no internal tariffs and a common external tariff.

The significance of the customs union as the economic bedrock of the EU tends, at this distance of time, to be overlooked. But it was only within the context of a functioning customs union that the complete fusion of markets implied in a Common Market could be achieved. Since the creation of a customs union necessarily involved a difference of treatment as between goods of internal and external origin, Article XXIV of the GATT required that any new customs union be completed (a) according to a plan or schedule submitted for consideration to the other Contracting Parties and (b) within a reasonable time.[3]

[1] Preamble to the GATT 1947.

[2] *Rapport des Chefs de Délégation aux Ministres des Affaires Étrangères*, Brussels, 21 April 1956. A shorter English text was published as *The Brussels Report on The General Common Market* in June 1956.

[3] Article XXIV 7(b).

The rules of the Treaty therefore constituted the required 'plan or schedule', while Article 8(7) EEC provided that 31 December 1969 (the end of the transitional period) was to 'constitute the latest date by which all the rules laid down must enter into force and all the measures required for establishing the common market must be implemented'. This explains why Pierre Pescatore, who had been one of the Luxembourg negotiating team and was later a Judge of the ECJ, denounced the Single European Act, with its legislative programme for completion in 1992 (23 years late), as inconsistent with the Community's obligations under the GATT.[4]

In 1956–57, the most contentious issues in the course of the negotiations concerned the conditions for creation of the customs union, the progressive elimination of internal quotas, and the conditions of trade in agricultural products. These were the subject of detailed provisions—mainly programmatic—which have now disappeared from the Treaty, leaving the general rules set out in Articles 30, 34–37 and 110 TFEU. (Agriculture has always been dealt with separately.)

The basic rules on free movement of goods within the customs union were taken directly from the GATT. Article XI.1 (General Elimination of Quantitative Restrictions) stated the general rule:

> No prohibitions or restrictions other than duties, taxes or other charges, whether made effective through quotas, import or export licences or other measures, shall be instituted or maintained by any contracting party on the importation of any product of the territory of any other contracting party or on the exportation or sale for export of any product destined for the territory of any other contracting party.

Article XX of the GATT (General Exceptions) provided, so far as relevant for present purposes:

> Subject to the requirement that such measures are not applied in a manner which would constitute a means of arbitrary or unjustifiable discrimination between countries where the same conditions prevail, or a disguised restriction on international trade, nothing in this Agreement shall be construed to prevent the adoption or enforcement by any contracting party of measures:
>
> (a) necessary to protect public morals;
> (b) necessary to protect human, animal or plant life or health;
> (c) …
> (d) necessary to secure compliance with laws or regulations which are not inconsistent with the provisions of this Agreement, including those relating to customs enforcement, the enforcement of monopolies operated under paragraph 4 of Article II and Article XVII, the protection of patents, trade marks and copyrights, and the prevention of deceptive practices;
> (e) …
> (f) imposed for the protection of national treasures of artistic, historic or archaeological value; …

[4] P Pescatore, 'Some Critical Remarks on the Single European Act' (1987) 24 *CML Rev* 9.

Article XXI provided for exceptions on grounds of national security.

The aim of the Treaty-makers was to establish a code, compliant with the GATT, setting out the basic rules and limited exceptions. Comparison of the Treaty texts with those of the GATT helps to explain two points where the more telegraphic wording of the Treaty has given rise to perplexity.

First, the expression 'quantitative restrictions … and all measures having equivalent effect', used in Articles 34 and 35 TFEU (30 and 34 EEC), seems to imply that it is only measures having effect equivalent to *quantitative* restrictions that are struck at. By contrast, Article XI.1 of the GATT clearly strikes at *all* restrictions *made effective* through quotas, licences *or* other measures. This explains the wide interpretation given to 'measures of equivalent effect' in *Dassonville*.[5]

Second, Article 36 TFEU (36 EEC), having stated in the first sentence that certain prohibitions or restrictions on imports, exports or goods in transit are permitted, goes on in the second sentence to say that they 'shall not constitute a means of arbitrary discrimination or a disguised restriction on trade between Member States'. It is not obvious how these sentences fit together. Article XX of the GATT makes it clear that the distinction to be drawn is between the adoption and enforcement of the permitted prohibitions and restrictions and the *manner of applying* them. It is the latter which may constitute an 'arbitrary or unjustifiable discrimination' or 'disguised restriction on trade'.

The Spaak Report envisaged that the customs union and the single internal market in goods would be part of a Common Market covering all aspects of economic activity. But apart from trade in tangible goods, there was no code, such as the GATT, to be followed. An obvious distinction could be drawn between the economic activities of human beings, those of entities such as companies which have legal personality, 'invisible' monetary transactions, and the provision of 'services' considered in the abstract. But there was no particular sanctity about any method of classification nor any firm precedent.

In the Spaak Report, free movement of the liberal professions was treated, first, as an aspect of services, but later, as regards the professionals themselves (and almost as an afterthought), as analogous to free movement of wage- and salary-earners ('workers'). The financial and non-personal aspects of establishment, such as the acquisition of premises, opening factories and offices, and moving fixed plants were mentioned under the general heading of free movement of capital.

In the Treaty, the various forms of economic activity are classified, in the heading of Title III, under the three heads of Persons, Services and Capital, but the operative provisions are arranged, confusingly, under four heads: Workers, Establishment, Services and Capital. There is no particular problem about treating free movement of workers and capital as distinct categories, but this is less so as regards establishment and services which cover the activities of natural persons (human beings), legal persons (companies, partnerships, etc.) and 'invisible' services. However, as

[5] Case 8/74 *Procureur du Roi v Dassonville* EU:C:1974:82.

noted at the beginning, the Treaty was written in an era of slow travel and slow communication. In the 1950s moving from one country to another to establish a business would normally involve physically uprooting oneself from one's country of origin, and even the temporary provision of services would normally require the physical movement of the provider to the recipient or *vice versa.*

The Chapter on capital was programmatic, rather than prescriptive, with the exception of Article 67(2) EEC on 'current payments', which followed the existing approach of the OEEC. The provisions of this Chapter are now very different from those originally enacted.

By contrast, the Chapters on workers, establishment and services remain very much the same. There is a degree of uniformity in approach, providing for (a) a general rule of freedom of movement to be achieved by the end of the transitional period, (b) a standstill clause prohibiting the introduction of *new* restrictions, and (c) the adoption of regulations or directives to remove any *existing* obstacles by the end of the transitional period. In outline, this scheme was similar to that for free movement of goods, and the Article 36 exceptions on grounds of public policy, public security and public health were adapted for workers, establishment and services by Articles 48(3), 56(1) and 66 (applying Article 56 to services). But the subject matter, and the method of dealing with it, was substantially different in detail.

As we now know, the programme for completion by the end of 1969 was hopelessly optimistic. Quite apart from the legislative stalemate created by the Luxembourg Compromise, the Treaty-makers had gravely underestimated the nature and extent of the task involved in drawing up the necessary 'rules' and 'measures'—a task that became all the greater with the accession of the UK, Ireland and Denmark. (In 1985, the Cockfield White Paper estimated that over 300 new legislative measures would still be necessary to complete the internal market.)

As far as goods were concerned, the Commission sought to clarify the (as yet) uncertain scope of 'measures of equivalent effect' by adopting Directive 70/50/EEC on 22 December 1969 (that is, just before expiry of the transitional period). The Directive was 'based on the provisions of Article 33(7), on the abolition of measures which have an effect equivalent to quantitative restrictions on imports and are not covered by other provisions adopted in pursuance of the EEC Treaty'.[6] Its compatibility with the peremptory terms of Article 30 was later questioned by Advocate General Capotorti in his Opinion in *Cassis de Dijon.*[7] But in any event, the Directive very soon lost its importance when the Court provided its wide-ranging and all-inclusive definition in *Dassonville*[8] (albeit the Court has

[6] Commission Directive 70/50 [1970] OJ L13/29. See also Commission Directives 66/682/EEC and 66/683/EEC [1966] OJ P220/3745.

[7] Case 120/78 *Rewe-Zentral AG v Bundesmonopolverwaltung für Branntwein* EU:C:1979:3, paras 669–71.

[8] Case 8/74 *Dassonville* (n 5). It is instructive to read the report of the Commission's submissions at pages 846–47. If that wording had been more closely followed in the judgment, some of the problems that led to *Keck* might have been avoided.

complicated matters by adopting a narrower approach to restrictions on exports as compared with imports).[9]

The legislative vacuum resulting from the failure to put all the legislation in place by the end of the transitional period (or stages of it) was, to some extent, overcome by the Court's decisions in *Alfons Lütticke*[10] and *Salgoil*[11] that, on the expiry of the time limit, the basic rules guaranteeing free movement must have direct effect. The logic of this approach, later followed in *Reyners*[12] and *Van Binsbergen*,[13] is explained by the need to stick to the Treaty schedule in order to comply with Article XX of the GATT.

That did not mean, however, that all national restrictions on free movement—other than those expressly provided for in Articles 36, 48, 56 and 66—were thereby rendered unenforceable. Article 57 EEC had provided for a programme of directives to deal with problems specific to establishment and services generally, such as mutual recognition of qualifications, and especially those of the medical, allied and pharmaceutical professions. As the Court explained in *Thieffry*,

> [Article 57] is ... directed towards reconciling freedom of establishment with the application of national professional rules justified by the general good, in particular rules relating to organization, qualifications, professional ethics, supervision and liability, provided that such application is effected without discrimination.[14]

A similar formula, adapted to the very different character of the market in goods, was used three years later in *Cassis de Dijon*:

> Obstacles to movement within the Community resulting from disparities between the national laws relating to the marketing of the products in question must be accepted in so far as those provisions may be recognized as being necessary in order to satisfy mandatory requirements (*exigences impératives*) relating in particular to the effectiveness of fiscal supervision, the protection of public health, the fairness of commercial transactions and the defence of the consumer.[15]

The same point was made, perhaps even more clearly, a year later in *Gilli and Andres*:

> In the absence of common rules relating to the production and marketing of the product in question it is for Member States to regulate all matters relating to its production, distribution and consumption on their own territory subject, however, to the condition that those rules do not present an obstacle, directly or indirectly, actually or potentially, to intra-Community trade.
>
> It is only where national rules, which apply without discrimination to both domestic and imported products, may be justified as being necessary in order to satisfy imperative

[9] Case 15/79 *Groenveld v Produktschaap voor Vee en Vlees* EU:C:1979:253.
[10] Case 48/65 *Alfons Lütticke v Hauptzollamt Saarlouis* EU:C:1966:8.
[11] Case 13/68 *Salgoil v Italian Ministry for Foreign Trade* EU:C:1968:54.
[12] Case 2/74 *Reyners v Belgium* EU:C:1974:68.
[13] Case 33/74 *Van Binsbergen v Bestuur van de Bedrijfsvereniging voor Metaalnijverheid* EU:C:1974:131.
[14] Case 71/76 *Thieffry v Conseil de l'Ordre des Avocats à la Cour de Paris* EU:C:1977:65, para 12.
[15] Case 120/78 *Rewe* (n 7), para 8.

> requirements relating in particular to the protection of public health, the fairness of commercial transactions and the defence of the consumer that they may constitute an exception to the requirements arising under Article 30.[16]

A sub-theme of all these judgments was the idea that was gradually developed as the principle of proportionality (discussed below).

Following the judgments in *Cassis de Dijon* and *Gilli and Andres*, the Commission issued a Communication which summarised the consequences for application of the free movement rules:

> Any product imported from another Member State must in principle be admitted to the territory of the importing Member State if it has been lawfully produced, that is, conforms to rules and processes of manufacture that are customarily and traditionally accepted in the exporting country, and is marketed in the territory of the latter.
>
> This principle implies that Member States, when drawing up commercial or technical rules liable to affect the free movement of goods, may not take an exclusively national viewpoint and take account only of requirements confined to domestic products. The proper functioning of the common market demands that each Member State also give consideration to the legitimate requirements of the other Member States.
>
> Only under very strict conditions does the Court accept exceptions to this principle; barriers to trade resulting from differences between commercial and technical rules are only admissible:
>
> — if the rules are necessary, that is appropriate and not excessive, in order to satisfy mandatory requirements (public health, protection of consumers or the environment, the fairness of commercial transactions, etc.);
> — if the rules serve a purpose in the general interest which is compelling enough to justify an exception to a fundamental rule of the Treaty such as the free movement of goods;
> — if the rules are essential for such a purpose to be attained, i.e. are the means which are the most appropriate and at the same time least hinder trade.[17]

It is significant that the Commission put into the same category 'protection of consumers or the environment and the fairness of commercial transactions', none of which figured in the Treaty as permissible limits on free movement, and 'public health', which did. Moreover, the addition of 'etc.' was a tacit indication that other concerns might justify exceptions to the four freedoms.

Environmental protection was explicitly recognised as 'one of the Community's essential objectives' (and therefore a 'mandatory requirement')[18] in '*ADBHU*'.[19] By

[16] Case 788/79 *Gilli and Andres* EU:C:1980:171, paras 5–6.

[17] Communication from the Commission concerning the consequences of the judgment given by the Court of Justice on 20 February 1979 in Case 120/78 ('Cassis de Dijon') [1980] OJ C256/2.

[18] It is regrettable that this absurd expression became part of the vocabulary of Community law rather than 'imperative requirements', which was used in *Gilli and Andres*.

[19] Case 240/83 *Procureur de la République v Association de défense des brûleurs d'huiles usagées* EU:C:1985:59, para 13.

the time of *Danish Bottles*[20] three years later, the Single European Act had added 'Environment' to the Treaty as a 'Policy of the Community'.

Since that time, the Treaty-makers have added greatly to the list of 'policies', 'objectives' and 'aims' that must be taken into account. Although some parts of the Treaty have begun to look like a politically correct wish-list rather than a legal text, it is inevitable that, over the 60 years since the EEC Treaty was drafted, public and political priorities and preoccupations have changed and developed, especially as the Union has grown from six to 28 Member States.

Yet it is regrettable that the Treaty-makers have made no attempt to tell us which of their new policies, objectives and aims are to be regarded as *exigences impératives*; nor, if they are, whether they justify restrictions across the whole range of free movement rights or only some of them; nor how they are to be reconciled with the practical exercise of the four freedoms; nor, in cases where they may conflict, which of these political desiderata is to take priority. So it is important, when considering the case law on the exceptions to the rules of free movement, to recognise that the Court has, from the beginning, been forced to map out uncharted territory with inadequate and increasingly confusing navigational aids.

The task has not been made easier by the procedural scheme within which the Court has to operate. By far the largest number of cases on the exceptions to free movement has come before the Court under the preliminary reference procedure (now Article 267 TFEU). This procedure presupposes that issues of fact are for the national court making the reference and not for the Court of Justice. In many cases the questions(s) referred cannot be answered without making assumptions as to the underlying facts, or making some attempt to find them by putting questions to the parties or interveners. Neither method is entirely satisfactory. Quite often, the party with the closest knowledge of the facts may not be represented at the oral hearing; and because of the language régime, the representative of the Commission presenting the case may not be as familiar with the underlying facts as the official in charge of the file.

Fact-finding is only marginally easier in direct actions under Article 258 TFEU where the Commission alleges that a Member State has unlawfully restricted free movement rights. The exchange of pleadings may consist of little more than charge and counter-charge, and the accuracy of the facts in issue depends on the assiduity and impartiality of the Commission's investigations and the honesty of the defendant State.[21]

[20] Case 302/86 *Commission v Denmark* EU:C:1988:421.

[21] Case C-65/91 *Commission v Greece* EU:C:1992:388 is a particularly egregious example, where the damning appearance of the letter Delta on application forms (mentioned in paragraph 9 of the judgment) went unnoticed until the oral hearing.

Moreover, the fact/law distinction, so familiar to common lawyers, is less marked in other legal systems, and in any event is easier to draw in theory than in practice.[22] This is perhaps particularly so when it comes to applying the principle of proportionality which has drawn attention to profound differences in legal culture.

As Jürgen Schwarze explains in his magisterial survey of European Administrative Law, the principle of proportionality was well developed in German jurisprudence and academic writing going back to the end of the nineteenth century. He identifies three factors that govern the applicability of the proportionality principle in German law:

1) First, the state measures concerned must be *suitable* for the purpose of facilitating or achieving the objective pursued.
2) Second, the suitable measure must also be *necessary*, in the sense that the authority concerned has no other mechanism at its disposal which is less restrictive of freedom. … [I]t is not the method used which has to be necessary, but 'the excessive restriction of freedom involved in the choice of method.'
3) Finally, the measure concerned may not be *disproportionate* to the restrictions which it involves (proportionality *in stricto sensu*).[23]

This is broadly the approach that has been adopted in EU law, though not always under the general heading of proportionality. In *Kraus*, the Court of Justice formulated the principle to be applied in this way:

> Articles 48 and 52 preclude any national measure … where that measure, even though it is applicable without discrimination on grounds of nationality, is liable to hamper or to render less attractive the exercise by Community nationals … of fundamental freedoms guaranteed by the Treaty. The situation would be different only if such a measure pursued a legitimate objective compatible with the Treaty and was justified by pressing reasons of public interest. … It would however also be necessary in such a case for application of the national rules in question to be appropriate for ensuring attainment of the objective they pursue and not to go beyond what is necessary for that purpose.[24]

In *Gebhard*, the Court adopted a briefer, all-purpose formulation:

> National measures liable to hinder or make less attractive the exercise of fundamental freedoms guaranteed by the Treaty must fulfil four conditions: they must be applied in a non-discriminatory manner; they must be justified by imperative requirements in the general interest; they must be suitable for securing the attainment of the objective which they pursue; and they must not go beyond what is necessary in order to attain it.[25]

[22] See D Edward, 'Article 177—The Problem of Fact-finding' in Henry G Schermers, TMC Asser Institute (eds), *Article 177 EEC: Experiences and Problems* (Amsterdam, North-Holland, 1987) 216–20.

[23] Jürgen Schwarze, *European Administrative Law* (London, Office for Official Publications and Sweet & Maxwell, 1992, revised 2006) 685–92, especially 687.

[24] Case C-19/92 *Kraus v Land Baden Württemburg* EU:C:1993:125, para 32.

[25] Case C-55/94 *Gebhard v Consiglio dell' Ordine degli Avvocati e Procuratori di Milano* EU:C:1995:411, para 6 of the Operative Part.

In *Commission v Spain*, Advocate General Sharpston summarised the case law together with an indication of the sort of evidence that must be adduced to justify a derogation from a fundamental freedom:

> [W]here a restriction results from a measure which does discriminate on grounds of nationality, Article 46(1) EC allows it to be justified on grounds of public policy, public security or public health. Where there is no such discrimination, the restriction may also be justified by overriding requirements relating to the general interest, provided that the restrictions are appropriate for securing attainment of the objective pursued and do not go beyond what is necessary for attaining that objective. The reasons invoked by a Member State in order to justify a derogation from the principle of freedom of establishment must be accompanied by an analysis of the appropriateness and proportionality of the restrictive measure adopted by that Member State, and by precise evidence enabling its arguments to be substantiated.[26]

Commission v Spain was, of course, a direct action where the Court of Justice has jurisdiction to assess the analysis and the evidence. The position is different in references, where the national court is the judge of fact. As a way of overcoming the problem of fact/law jurisdiction, the Court resorts fairly frequently to the pretext of 'providing a useful/helpful answer' to justify performing the assessment of proportionality itself. This technique has been questioned as an illegitimate overreach of jurisdiction, and it is certainly not helpful or useful if the Court turns out to have given the wrong answer to the wrong question.

On the other hand, protracted judicial ping-pong between the Court of Justice and national courts serves no good purpose, and critics should bear in mind the old maxim, *interest reipublicae ut sit finis litium*—it is in the public interest that there be an end to litigation. The procedures of the Court of Justice are already criticised as unduly lengthy and, as a wise Scottish judge observed, 'the Courts are neither a debating club nor an advisory bureau'.[27] In general, litigants expect the courts to provide them with answers without undue delay or unnecessary expense, and it is reasonable that the Court of Justice should attempt to do this where possible.

A more fundamental and important issue was raised by Mr Justice (later Lord) Hoffmann in the ill-starred Sunday Trading cases in 1991, where he questioned whether—or at least, to what extent—the assessment of proportionality could properly be the province of the judiciary:

> In my judgment it is not my function to carry out the balancing exercise or to form my own view on whether the legislative objective could be achieved by other means. These questions involve compromises between competing interests which in a democratic society must be resolved by the legislature. The duty of the court is only to inquire whether the compromise adopted by the United Kingdom Parliament, so far as it affects community trade, is one which a reasonable legislature could have reached. The function of the court is to review the acts of the legislature but not to substitute its own policies or values.

[26] Case C-400/08 *Commission v Spain* EU:C:2011:172, para 36.
[27] Lord Justice Clerk Thomson in *Macnaughton v Macnaughton's Trustees* 1953 SC 387, 392.

> This is not an abdication of judicial responsibility. The primacy of the democratic process is far more important than the question of whether our Sunday trading laws could or could not be improved.[28]

It is true that judicial attitudes and practice in the United Kingdom have changed and developed in the intervening years—accelerated by incorporation of the European Convention on Human Rights in the Human Rights Act 1998. Nevertheless, there remains an underlying tension between asserting as a matter of principle that restrictions to the four freedoms must be shown to be legitimate and proportionate and the practical exercise of deciding *how and by whom* that principle is to be applied in the concrete case.

That is only one of the many problems and uncertainties that are discussed in this book. Essentially, they centre upon the role of one of the institutions—the Court of Justice—and its case law. The reason for stressing the historical context is to show that the dominant role of that institution has been due to the failure of the others to fulfil the obligations assigned to them by the Treaty. So it is important, not only to consider the merits and defects of the Court's case law, but also to ask whether the original scheme of the Treaty was really workable, and what might have been the result if the Court had been less 'active'.

[28] *Stoke-on-Trent City Council v B & Q plc* [1991] Ch 48, 69.

2

Economic Justifications and the Role of the State

JUKKA SNELL*

I. INTRODUCTION

THE LAW OF justifications for restrictions on EU free movement rights is an area that is difficult to teach to students. The law seems messy and casuistic. Rulings tend to be intimately tied to their precise facts and their wider applicability is often doubtful. There are various more or less amorphous principles, but rules are few and far between. One of the few things that are seemingly clear-cut is that purely economic reasons cannot be relied upon to justify restrictions on free movement. This has been established both for the written exceptions found in provisions such as Article 36 TFEU and for the doctrine of mandatory or overriding requirements developed in the case law. It applies to all freedoms.[1]

Unfortunately, in this chapter I suggest that even here things are not that simple. When the Court of Justice rules that a reason is purely economic, whatever that might mean, it is defining the functions that states may pursue. This is of great constitutional significance. As a result, many difficult questions have been encountered. There are cases where the Court seems unsure how to proceed and has come up with conflicting rulings. There are also situations where the restrictive measure does not emanate from a Member State, but either from a private party or from the European Union (EU) legislature, and this has caused further complications.

The chapter begins at macro-level by discussing some of the different functions that states have performed, how those functions have changed, and how this is connected to the question of economic justifications. It then moves to micro-level and charts the Court's case law, arguing that there are in essence six categories of

* Earlier versions of this paper were presented at City University London in February 2014, at Swansea University in February 2014, and at a joint seminar of University of Turku and Vrije Universiteit Brussel in June 2014. I would like to thank all participants, as well as the editors of this book and Peter Oliver, for their helpful comments.

[1] See generally, eg C Barnard, *The Substantive Law of the EU: The Four Freedoms* (Oxford, Oxford University Press, 2013) and N Nic Shuibhne, 'Exceptions to the Free Movement Rules' in C Barnard and S Peers (eds), *European Union Law* (Oxford, Oxford University Press, 2014).

relevant cases and analysing the strategies the Court has employed in its jurisprudence. Finally, it will attempt to draw some meso-level conclusions and argue that the difficulties that the Court is encountering are partly of its own making, and that the task of drawing the line between the economic and the non-economic is likely to get harder.

II. THE CONSTITUTIONAL DIMENSION

This section considers the significance of the doctrine of inadmissibility of economic reasons at the macro-level. It links the case law to the changing role of the state, and argues that the legal doctrine is a part of and contributes to much larger constitutional phenomena.

It is important to note how fundamental a finding that something is of purely economic nature is. While a finding of a restriction or disproportionality represents only the start or a part of the discussion, a ruling that a reason is of purely economic nature ends it. A restriction can still be justified, and a disproportionate rule can simply be recast so that the same aim is achieved by methods that are less restrictive. By contrast, the finding that an interest is economic means that the aim itself cannot be legally pursued. The state is not told to explain itself, as in the case of restriction, or to try again, as in the case of disproportionality—instead it is ordered to cease and desist.

A ruling that an interest is purely economic thus allocates the concern away from the realm of politics and into the sphere of markets. The Court of Justice decides that states can no longer protect that interest, at least if this means restricting free movement. Given how wide the reach of the internal market is today and how broadly the notion of restriction has been interpreted,[2] this can significantly curtail the ability of Member States to promise to protect the economic security of their citizens. This can be seen as a part of a wider phenomenon, namely the transformation of the nature of states that some constitutional scholars such as Philip Bobbitt have detected.[3]

The nation state of the twentieth century was to a large extent based upon and legitimated by the objective of protecting its citizens. The state ensured their external security by maintaining permanent and sizeable armed forces that could deter and defeat external threats. It protected their internal security with police and criminal courts. Their physical well-being was protected by systems of public healthcare and laws on health and safety. Their economic security was protected by welfare systems and various interventions in the market place to provide greater security of employment and to oppose unfair competition. The keys to much of

[2] See generally, eg, Barnard and Peers (n 1), chs 11–15.

[3] P Bobbitt, *The Shield of Achilles: War, Peace and the Course of History* (London, Penguin, 2002), in particular at 213–42. The next three paragraphs draw on Bobbitt.

this were tightly controlled state borders and nationally determined policies. It was this promise of security that was meant to attract the loyalty of citizens and to legitimise the state itself.

The states of the twenty-first century have found it difficult to offer similar guarantees, ultimately because of technological change including international communications and increasingly powerful computers. Phenomena such as international terrorism, computer viruses and hacking, the spread of weapons of mass destruction and missile technology, and international criminal organisations raise questions about whether nation states can credibly promise to stop security threats at the border. The same applies to the danger of global pandemics and environmental threats. As for economic security, in a global, interconnected and financialised economy, shocks travel rapidly across borders. The promise of nation states to protect their citizens rings hollow.

As a result, it has been argued that a new source of legitimacy needs to be found. The promise of opportunities could provide this. Instead of protection, the state would offer its citizens individual choice and opportunities. It would facilitate and enable them. This could range from offering them opportunities to sell, buy and move internationally to offering retraining and education to those whose jobs have been lost in international competition. Bobbitt calls this a market-state.[4]

The EU is a complex and multifaceted part of this phenomenon. On the one hand, it might offer some collective protective capacity that small nation states can no longer provide on their own,[5] for example in the context of environmental threats. On the other hand, it reduces the ability of individual nation states to offer protection, especially against economic insecurity, by imposing on them rules on free movement and undistorted competition.[6] Even more profoundly, could the EU itself gain legitimacy as a new type of polity that offers opportunities rather than protection?

This is where the doctrine of the inadmissibility of purely economic justifications comes into play. By drawing the line between economic and non-economic, the Court limits the ability of states to offer protection against economic risks and directs them towards enabling citizens instead. It could be argued that there is nothing new in this. The inadmissibility of economic justifications has been a part of EU law for decades.[7] That is true. Yet the connection between it and the role of

[4] ibid, 228.

[5] See also the classic argument in AS Milward, *The European Rescue of the Nation-State* (London, Routledge, 2000) 3: 'The European Community has been ... an indispensable part of the nation-state's post-war construction. Without it, the nation-state could not have offered to its citizens the same measure of security and prosperity which it has provided and which has justified its survival.'

[6] The impact of the opening of markets on economic stability was recognised already in the Spaak Report (Report of the Heads of Delegation to the Foreign Ministers at the Messina Conference, 21 April 1956), which on the one hand proposed the suppression of national protections creating obstacles and distortions of competition, and on the other hand sought to ensure conditions for common growth, inter alia by envisaging assistance to businesses in adjusting to competition and modern production methods.

[7] Case 7/61 *Commission v Italy* EU:C:1961:31, para 329.

the state has arguably become more important for at least three reasons. First, the reach of EU law has increased. It now captures many more areas of Member State activity than in earlier decades, with the Court policing, for example, national systems of direct taxation and healthcare. Second, the pressure of international competition has grown as a result of technological change. For example, many services that were previously considered non-tradable can now be imported and exported. Factually, there are many more cases where free movement rules are relevant. Third, the law is now working together with the general trend of globalisation that is forcing states to reassess their functions.

In sum, the discussion of what the purely economic considerations that cannot be relied upon are goes to the heart of the role of the state in our societies and economies. A particularly important aspect of this is the state's ability to protect its citizens against economic risks, which is ultimately connected to its very legitimacy.

III. THE CASES

The analysis now moves from macro-level to micro-level, and considers the details of the case law of the Court of Justice. Given the broad reach of free movement law and the fundamental constitutional significance of the dividing line between economic and non-economic, it is not surprising that the Court has struggled to draw it in practice, let alone clearly articulate the reasons for its choices. The case law can be divided into six rough clusters.[8] The first three concern the way the Court has treated particular justifications, the last three involve particular areas where the Court's approach may differ from its usual one.

A. Particular Justifications

The first cluster is the cases where the Court has always unhesitatingly deemed an aim to be purely economic. This set of cases ranges from micro-reasons, such as the protection of a particular undertaking,[9] to macro-reasons, such as avoiding the loss of tax revenue[10] or the erosion of the tax base.[11]

[8] See for an earlier analysis, dealing with a narrower class of cases but in more detail, J Snell, 'Economic Aims as Justification for Restrictions on Free Movement' in A Schrauwen (ed), *Rule of Reason: Rethinking Another Classic of European Legal Doctrine* (Groningen, Europa Law Publishing, 2005).

[9] See eg Case C-324/93 *Evans Medical* EU:C:1995:84.

[10] See eg Case C-264/96 *ICI v Colmer* EU:C:1998:370. In the field of free movement of capital, the same applies also in the context of restrictions on capital movements between EU Member States and third countries. See eg Joined Cases C-436 and 437/08 *Haribo Lakritzen* EU:C:2009:17, para 126.

[11] See eg Case C-168/01 *Bosal Holding* EU:C:2003:479.

The second cluster concerns borderline cases where it has been genuinely difficult for the Court to classify an aim.[12] Compare here two cases concerning the protection of a national market: *Alpine Investments*, where the Court allowed the aim of protecting the reputation of the national market;[13] and *SETTG*,[14] where the aim of protecting the national market against industrial unrest was not accepted. In the former case, the Netherlands was able to maintain a rule that banned certain methods of marketing financial services. The rule had been adopted to ensure that the reputation of the Dutch financial services sector would not be damaged by mis-selling scandals. In the latter case, Greece was prevented from insisting on a rule that all tourist guides be in a relationship of employment. The rule had been adopted to end industrial disputes that had damaged the tourism sector. The Court did not explain why the protection of the national market was a non-economic aim in the first case but economic in the second one. Yet what was ultimately at stake in both instances was the State's attempt to support its general economy by safeguarding a particular sector.[15]

The third cluster involves cases where the Court has always wished to allow the national rule to stand, but has been unsure how to achieve this. The best example is a set of decisions that concerns health care. These rulings demonstrate the three different strategies that the Court has employed. I call the strategies avoidance, denial and linkage.

The strategy of avoidance can be seen in the case of *Duphar*.[16] At issue were national rules designed to control health care spending. The Court held that Article 36 TFEU 'relates to measures of a non-economic nature. That provision cannot therefore justify a measure whose primary objective is budgetary inasmuch as it is intended to reduce the operating costs of a sickness insurance scheme.'[17] However, all was not lost. The Court held that the rules would only fall within the free movement of goods in the first place if they were discriminatory. In other words, it allowed the national court to avoid the stage of justification altogether, by only applying a discrimination test rather than the more common and demanding restriction test.[18]

[12] See S Arrowsmith, 'Rethinking the approach to economic justifications under the EU's free movement rules' (forthcoming) for an accurate and detailed examination of the many borderline cases.

[13] Case C-384/93 *Alpine Investments* EU:C:1995:126. The Court held at para 44 that '[m]aintaining the good reputation of the national financial sector may … constitute an imperative reason of public interest' without even mentioning the possibility that the justification could be considered economic.

[14] Case C-398/95 *SETTG* EU:C:1997:282. The Court held at para 23 that 'maintaining industrial peace as a means of bringing a collective labour dispute to an end and thereby preventing any adverse effects on an economic sector, and consequently on the economy of the State, must be regarded as an economic aim which cannot constitute a reason relating to the general interest.' The ruling in *Alpine Investments* was not mentioned by the Court.

[15] In *SETTG*, AG Lenz was (at para 62) prepared to consider the maintenance of industrial peace a general interest objective, but he objected to it as a means of protecting national economic interests.

[16] Case 238/82 *Duphar* EU:C:1984:45. Case 15/79 *Groenveld* EU:C:1979:253 can be seen as another example.

[17] *Duphar*, ibid, para 23.

[18] Case 8/74 *Dassonville* EU:C:1974:82.

The strategy of denial was at work in the cases of *Decker* and *Kohll*.[19] Again the cases concerned national rules aimed at controlling health care spending. This time the Court did not avoid the justification stage but instead denied that the aim was economic. It held that while purely economic aims cannot justify restrictions, 'it cannot be excluded that the risk of seriously undermining the financial balance of the social security system may constitute an overriding reason in the general interest capable of justifying a barrier of that kind'.[20] In other words, the Court simply reclassified (serious) health care budget reasons from economic to non-economic.

Finally, the strategy of linkage can be seen, for example, in yet another case on controlling health care costs, *Hartlauer*.[21] Here the Court neither avoided the issue nor denied the economic nature of the justification, but instead linked the intermediate economic aim with a final public interest aim. It held that the objective of preventing the risk of serious harm to the financial balance of the social security system was simply an element in the protection of public health. Without planning aimed at controlling costs and reducing wastage, the ultimate public health goal could not be attained. The economic consideration was a means to reach a non-economic end.

In all three cases, the same result was achieved: the national rule could be upheld. This was done in the first instance by avoiding the assessment of the national rule; in the second, by denying that the criterion of assessment was economic; and, in the third, by linking the intermediate economic aim with the ultimate non-economic aim. The three strategies of avoidance, denial and linkage can be found elsewhere in the case law as well. However, they do not sit easily together but suggest a chaotic state of the law, as it is not at all clear why the Court chooses one line of reasoning in one case but an entirely different one in the next. The very same budgetary aim has variously been seen as economic, as non-economic, and as a part of a broader public health aim.

The avoidance strategy could be fine in principle, but it creates problems of coherence when other national rules with similar effects are found to be restrictive. It should not be thought that it is a thing of the past. Today, the Court is much more reluctant to find restrictions in the field of tax law than in other areas.[22] It examines whether national tax rules discriminate; it does not object to them purely on the basis of their dissuasive effects, as it does in its case law on non-fiscal barriers. Most notably, double taxation is not seen as a restriction at all,[23] while double regulation has been one of the main targets of internal market law for decades. One possible explanation for this is that the Court is seeking to avoid the

[19] Case C-120/95 *Decker* EU:C:1998:167 and Case C-158/96 *Kohll* EU:C:1998:171.

[20] *Decker*, ibid, para 39; *Kohll*, ibid, para 41.

[21] Case C-169/07 *Hartlauer* EU:C:2009:141. See also eg Case 72/83 *Campus Oil* EU:C:1984:256.

[22] For discussion, see J Snell, 'Non-Discriminatory Tax Obstacles in Community Law' (2007) 56 *ICLQ* 339.

[23] Case C-513/04 *Kerckhaert and Morres* EU:C:2006:713.

justification stage entirely. Since tax rules tend to exist for economic reasons, they would typically be impossible to justify and would have to be disapplied in the name of the four freedoms, something the Court is reluctant to do. As a result, the Court has chosen not to see them as restrictions in the absence of discrimination, thus avoiding the need to consider their justification at all.

The denial strategy is unsatisfactory in that it may have the effect of reclassifying justifications that have previously been treated as economic suddenly as non-economic, putting the consistency of the case law in serious doubt. The Court has attempted to rationalise this with the suggestion that the seriousness of the consequences might transform the nature of a justification to a non-economic one. Yet there are a number of reasons why this is not helpful. Seriousness is a quantitative rather than a qualitative issue—it concerns the intensity of the effects, not their nature—and analysis of this type is logically a matter of proportionality and better suited for that stage,[24] if carried out at all. The differentiation between 'ordinary' harm that counts as economic and 'serious' harm that does not is difficult and unpredictable, and seems incapable of consistent application in practice. In any event, the idea has been rejected in the case law on tax restrictions, where the intensity of the economic consequences has not affected the analysis. In *Bosal*, for example, both the Commission and the affected state, the Netherlands, argued that the relevant national tax rule was justified by 'the aim of avoiding an erosion of the tax base going beyond mere diminution of tax revenue'.[25] In other words, they claimed that the seriousness of the consequences transformed the justification from economic to non-economic. The Court responded laconically by stating that the risk of erosion of the tax base 'does not differ in substance from that concerning the risk of a diminution in tax revenue'.[26]

The linkage strategy has some advantages. In practice, it maintains the ability of Member States to continue to provide public goods under acceptable economic conditions.[27] While it is possible in theory to say that a state should not impose restrictions in the name of the health care budget, as any shortfalls can be covered by increases in general taxation, in the real world this is unlikely to be practicable or desirable. The linkage strategy also aligns with the law of Article 106(2) TFEU on undertakings entrusted with the operation of services of general economic interest. Here the case law has permitted Member States to grant exclusive rights if they are necessary to allow the relevant undertaking to operate the service of general economic interest in acceptable economic conditions.[28] For example, in *Corbeau*,[29] Belgian legislation

[24] But see the concerns expressed by Arrowsmith (n 12).

[25] *Bosal* (n 11), para 42.

[26] ibid.

[27] See, for an extreme example, the Opinion of AG Cruz Villalón in Case C-268/13 *Petru* EU:C:2014:2271.

[28] See generally JL Buendia Sierra, *Exclusive Rights and State Monopolies under EC Law* (Oxford, Oxford University Press, 1999).

[29] Case C-320/91 *Corbeau* EU:C:1993:198. The approach was confirmed, eg in Case C-45/99 *Ambulanz Glöckner* EU:C:2000:273 paras 56–57.

gave Régie des Postes an exclusive right to collect, carry and distribute mail, but also imposed on it a universal service obligation, under which it was required to provide services throughout Belgium at uniform tariffs. The Court accepted that the exclusive right and the universal service obligation were two sides of the same coin. Due to the exclusive rights, Régie des Postes made profits that could not be competed away by other undertakings. However, its universal service obligation forced it to carry mail at the same price even to remote locations, imposing losses on it. The exclusive right was an intermediate economic means for the ultimate aim of universal postal service.[30]

However, the linkage strategy is not without its weaknesses. Its basic logic is suspect.[31] If a Member State is allowed to safeguard the financial balance of its health system, should it not also be allowed to combat the reduction of tax revenue? A financially balanced health system contributes to public health, while high tax intake allows the Member State to provide all kinds of public goods. The standard answer is that there needs to be a close connection between the economic and the non-economic,[32] as in the case of avoiding the wastage of scarce health resources and public health, and that the connection between tax revenue and public goods is not sufficiently direct. Unfortunately this raises further questions. Why do we need a direct connection? For example, assume a ring-fenced or hypothecated tax the revenues of which are directed to a particular public interest cause. Under the linkage approach, it would seem acceptable to combat the loss of revenue for such a tax, but not for general taxation. Why? And in any event, how can such directness be assessed in a reliable way? For example, in *Essent*,[33] a case that will be considered in more detail later, Advocate General Jääskinen argued that there was no clear connection between the relevant Dutch rules on gas and electricity distribution, which were designed for the economic objectives of transparency and the prevention cross-subsidies on the domestic energy market, and the justifications of public security and consumer protection. By contrast, the Court considered that these economic objectives served the intermediate goals of undistorted competition, and investment in electricity and gas distribution systems, which in turn ultimately contributed to the general interest objectives of consumer protection and public security. Which approach one prefers depends entirely on the degree of directness needed, an issue that seems hard to answer in a principled way. Altogether, the multitude of strategies and unanswered questions suggest that the case law is more of a series of ad hoc reactions to particular fact patterns than a consistent application of coherent principles.

[30] See in more detail on the case law V Hatzopoulos, *Regulating Services in the European Union* (Oxford, Oxford University Press, 2012) 91–92.

[31] See also G Davies, '"Any Place I Hang My Hat?", or: Residence Is the New Nationality' (2005) 11 *European Law Journal* 43 at 47–49, as well as Arrowsmith, n 12 above, for a particularly withering critique.

[32] See the Opinion of AG Mancini in *Duphar* (n 16), para 4.

[33] Joined Cases C-105 and 107/12 *Essent* EU:C:2013:677, para 88 of the Opinion and paras 58–66 of the judgment.

B. Particular Areas

The fourth cluster of cases is where the restriction does not emanate from a Member State but a private actor. The famous case of *Viking* is the *locus classicus*.[34] In issue was collective action taken by trade unions to oppose the reflagging of a vessel from Finland to Estonia. The action was deemed to constitute a restriction on the freedom of establishment, but the trade unions argued that 'the right of trade unions to take collective action to preserve jobs is a fundamental right'[35] recognised by EU law. The Grand Chamber of the Court accepted that the right to take collective action for the protection of workers is a legitimate interest and that the protection of workers has been accepted as an overriding reason in the case law. However, it then stated that 'even if that action—aimed at protecting the jobs and conditions of employment of the members of that union liable to be adversely affected by the reflagging of the Rosella—could reasonably be considered to fall, at first sight, within the objective of protecting workers, such a view would no longer be tenable if it were established that the jobs or conditions of employment at issue were not jeopardised or under serious threat'.[36] In the end, the Court left the matter for the referring national court to determine.

The *Viking* case again exemplifies the strategy of denial. The Court accepts that the protection of jobs from serious threats can serve to justify restrictions under the banner of protection of workers. Just like with *Decker* and *Kohll*, the Court hedges its reasoning with qualifiers such as 'even if ... at first sight' and explicitly refers to the issue of seriousness. Yet this seems wordplay.[37] Ultimately free movement will threaten jobs at inefficient companies that are exposed to international competition. If these jobs can now be protected by restrictive measures, free movement can be stopped the moment its impact is felt. This seems to be the purest of economic reasons—protectionism.[38]

There is a fifth set of cases that again does not concern the typical situation of a Member State measure, but rather the case of the EU legislature restricting free movement for economic reasons. The classic example is the *Deposit Guarantee* ruling,[39] where in issue was the legality of the Deposit Guarantee Directive,[40] and in particular the 'export prohibition' found in its Article 4(1). The Directive provided that national deposit guarantee schemes were to cover also the depositors in

[34] Case C-438/05 *Viking* EU:C:2007:772.

[35] ibid, para 24.

[36] ibid, para 81.

[37] W-H Roth, 'Economic Justifications and the Internal Market' in M Bulterman et al (eds), *Views of European Law from the Mountain: Liber Amicorum Piet Jan Slot* (Alphen aan den Rijn, Kluwer, 2009) 88.

[38] See also K Lenaerts and JA Gutiérrez-Fons, 'The Constitutional Allocation of Powers and General Principles of EU Law' (2010) 47 *CML Rev* 1629, who talk of 'protectionist, albeit socially legitimate, claims' at 1666.

[39] Case C-233/94 *Germany v European Parliament and Council* EU:C:1997:231.

[40] European Parliament and Council Directive (EC) 94/19 on deposit-guarantee schemes [1994] OJ L135/5.

the foreign branches of domestic banks. However, the maximum cover was set at the level of the country hosting the branch, not at the home state level. This was done to ensure that depositors in a country with a low level or narrow scope of cover would not flock to the branches of banks from Member States with a more generous system. In other words, the objective was the protection of the banking sectors of some of the Member States against competition from abroad in the name of avoiding market disturbances. The Court upheld the legality of the Directive, following Advocate General Léger. It rejected Germany's argument that the prohibition of the export of cover levels was a disproportionate infringement of the right of establishment, reasoning that the EU legislature was free to decide on a system that ruled out any market disturbance whatsoever. It is very difficult to imagine that the Court would allow an individual Member State to neutralise the competitive advantage of foreign companies under the banner of avoiding market disturbances that could result from domestic companies losing custom. Surely, in the case of an individual Member State, this would be deemed a purely economic consideration.[41]

A more recent and an even clearer example is offered by *Yellow Cab*.[42] The Third Chamber of the Court explicitly stated that, under an EU Regulation,[43] transport services may be denied authorisation if they were to compromise the existence of already authorised regular services. However, outside the EU regulatory framework, similar objectives cannot justify restrictions on the right of establishment.[44] In other words, a Member State could not rely on the same justification as the EU legislature. I will return to the position of private parties and the EU legislature in the next section.

The final cluster concerns cases that deal with EU citizenship and is partially connected to the previous cluster. The case law affords Member States a significant degree of freedom to protect their public finances,[45] and in fact the Court has explicitly stated that the protection of public finances is a legitimate interest.[46] In this, the case law is in strong tension with the cases on tax restrictions where combatting the loss of tax revenue or the restoration of budgetary balance have been held to be purely economic considerations.[47] However, the context of the citizenship case law is different. There is a Directive that allows Member States to limit

[41] Similarly, W-H Roth, 'Case Note on *Germany v European Parliament and* Council' (1998) 35 *CML Rev* 459, 478.

[42] Case C-338/09 *Yellow Cab* EU:C:2010:814.

[43] Council Regulation (EEC) 684/92 on common rules for the international carriage of passengers by coach and bus [1992] OJ L74/1, as amended.

[44] ibid, para 52.

[45] See for analysis the Opinion of AG Sharpston in Joined Cases C-523 and 585/11 *Prinz* EU:C:2013:524 and the Opinion of AG Wathelet in Case C-333/13 *Dano* EU:C:2014:2358.

[46] Case C-140/12 *Brey* EU:C:2013:565, para 55 states that 'the exercise of the right of residence for citizens of the Union can be subordinated to the legitimate interests of the Member States—in the present case, the protection of their public finances'.

[47] See recently eg Case C-385/12 *Hervis Sport- és Divatkereskedelmi* EU:C:2014:47.

free movement within certain parameters.[48] The restrictions do not arise purely from national legislation but have an EU background.[49] Further, the wording of Article 21 TFEU explicitly states that the right of free movement and residence is 'subject to the limitations and conditions laid down in the Treaties and by the measures adopted to give them effect'. This sets citizenship apart from the provisions on the economic freedoms, which list acceptable grounds of justification and do not refer to secondary legislation.[50]

In practice, the Court has made a sharp distinction between workers and non-economically active citizens in the context of budgetary reasons put forward by Member States to justify restrictions. For example, in *Commission v Netherlands*,[51] the Second Chamber of the Court rejected an attempt to rely on the ruling in *Bidar* in the context of migrant workers.[52] In *Bidar*, the Court had accepted that Member States have an interest in safeguarding the financial balance of their social security system and can therefore require an applicant for student financing to demonstrate sufficient integration into the society of the host state. By contrast, in the context of migrant workers and their family members, the Court in *Commission v Netherlands* refused to accept that a similar justification amounted to an overriding reason at all.[53]

The tolerance of the Court towards rules that allow Member States to oppose an inflow of undesirable foreigners on grounds of avoiding unreasonable burdens on national social systems is a cause of mixed feelings. One the one hand, free movement of indigents could trigger a race to the bottom, with Member States responding to real or perceived threats of benefit tourism by cutting the level of social protection to reduce expenditure and to render themselves less attractive destinations.[54] On the other hand, it can be questioned whether it is appropriate to restrict free movement at all in the context of countries that participate in a currency union, in other words within the eurozone. Free movement of persons

[48] European Parliament and Council Directive (EC) 2004/38 on the right of citizens of the Union and their family members to move and reside freely within the territory of the Member States [2004] OJ L158/77. According to the ruling in Case C-333/13 (n 45) para 74, an objective of the Directive is to prevent 'Union citizens who are nationals of other Member States from becoming an unreasonable burden on the social assistance system of the host Member State', and the Directive is to be read in the light of this objective.

[49] Contrast here the approach adopted in *Brey* (n 46) where the Directive was applicable, with that in Case C-220/12 *Thiele Meneses* EU:C:2013:683, in particular paras 35 and 43.

[50] See eg Art 36 TFEU. The derogations from economic freedoms do of course refer to the potentially broad notion of 'public policy', but it has to be noted that other language versions use terms that seem narrower, such as 'ordre public', and the ECJ has always taken a very restrictive view of this ground of derogation. See generally, T Corthaut, *EU Ordre Public* (Alphen aan den Rijn, Kluwer Law International, 2012).

[51] Case C-542/09 *Commission v Netherlands* EU:C:2012:346.

[52] Case C-209/03 *Bidar* EU:C:2005:169.

[53] Case C-542/09 *Commission v Netherlands* (n 51), para 69.

[54] For example, the danger to the overall level of student assistance was recognised in *Bidar* (n 52) para 56.

provides critical economic flexibility that was lost with the unification of monetary policies,[55] in particular as the unemployed or students often enter the labour force once they have settled in the host country. It should not be forgotten that in the US, some of the seminal cases on the right of personal free movement under the US Constitution were decided against the background of the Great Depression of 1930s and concerned the free movement of indigents. In particular, in *Edwards v California*[56] in issue was a Californian anti-Okie law that criminalised the bringing of a pauper into the state of California. Edwards, a Californian, had driven his unemployed brother-in-law from Texas to California, and was sentenced to six months' imprisonment. The Californian law was held unconstitutional by a unanimous Supreme Court. In the words of Mr Justice Byrnes, no single State may 'isolate itself from difficulties common to all of them by restraining the transportation of persons and property across its borders … [A] State might gain a momentary respite from the pressure of events by the simple expedient of shutting its gates … But "the peoples of the several States must sink or swim together, and … in the long run, prosperity and salvation are in union, and not division"'.[57] Despite the creation of an economic and monetary union and citizenship in Europe, the law of the EU has not embraced a similar conception of a common economic destiny. Of course, for Europe a particular complication is that the internal market and citizenship cover all the Member States, yet the importance of the free movement of natural persons is particularly pronounced between those countries that have adopted the single currency.

In sum, I hope that the description and analysis of the cases has shown a complex, not entirely coherent landscape, where broadly right results are achieved with casuistic, fact-sensitive decisions. The Court is struggling to strike sensible balances among difficult to reconcile interests against the messy background of the real world, in a situation where major constitutional consequences follow from its rulings.

IV. THE BIGGER PICTURE

The present section moves from the micro-level to the meso-level, and seeks to tease out and examine the lessons that emerge from the two previous sections. It will consider the role of the Court and will seek to offer ways to develop the law in a more rational direction.

The case law analysed above shows that the Court is facing an almost impossible mission of finding appropriate balances in an environment of complexity

[55] See the seminal article by RA Mundell, 'A Theory of Optimum Currency Areas' (1961) 51 *The American Economic Review* 657.

[56] *Edwards v California* 314 US 160 (1941).

[57] ibid, 173–74, partly quoting Mr Justice Cardozo.

and high stakes. My sympathy towards the Court is limited, however. The reason some of these balances need to be struck at all is due to the relentless expansion of the reach of the freedoms by the Court. To a large extent, it is the author of its own injury. It was the Court that decided that national measures may fall within the Treaty free movement provisions even in the absence of discrimination.[58] The Court found that health services are covered by the Treaty even in the context of public healthcare systems, despite the different view of a number of Advocates General, who relied on the wording of Article 56 TFEU which speaks of only services 'normally provided for remuneration' benefiting from free movement.[59] It was the Court that decided that private parties are caught by the free movement provisions.[60] It was the Court that gave free movement of citizens its direct effect, despite contrary arguments based on the wording of the Treaty.[61]

It should not come as a surprise that the expansion of the jurisdiction of the Court to rule on justifications and proportionality has presented it with delicate dilemmas and difficulties in maintaining the coherence of its jurisprudence. In fact, the Court can perhaps be compared to an inexperienced but optimistic homeowner who decides to renovate the bathrooms while getting a new kitchen installed and having the windows fixed at the same time. Unforeseen problems and complications are likely to arise.

Recently, the Grand Chamber of the Court continued this trend of expanding the reach of free movement in the case of *Essent*,[62] contrary to the advice of Advocate General Jääskinen. It held that Dutch rules prohibiting the privatisation of electricity and gas distribution system operators amounted to a restriction on free movement of capital. This was despite the fact that Article 345 TFEU provides that '[t]he Treaties shall in no way prejudice the rules in Member States governing the system of property ownership', laying down a principle of neutrality. This principle had previously been thought to protect public ownership from scrutiny under free movement law,[63] but now the Court held that it did not allow the Netherlands

[58] Case 8/74 *Dassonville* (n 18).

[59] Contrast the Judgments in Case C-157/99 *Smits and Peerbooms* EU:C:2001:404 and Case C-372/04 *Watts* EU:C:2006:325 with the Opinion of AG Ruiz Jarabo Colomer in *Smits and Peerbooms* and the Opinion of AG Saggio in Case C-368/98 *Vanbraekel* EU:C:2001:400.

[60] Case 36/74 *Walrave and Koch* EU:C:1974:140 and Case C-281/98 *Angonese* EU:C:2000:296.

[61] Case C-413/99 *Baumbast* EU:C:2002:493. At paras 78–79, the UK and German Governments, as well as the Commission, argued that the limitations in the wording of Art 21(1) TFEU meant that it was not a freestanding provision that could assist a person without a residence right arising from another source. In Case C-378/97 *Wijsenbeek* EU:C:1999:439 AG Cosmas, who supported direct effect, summarised the contrary argument as follows at para 79: 'It is contended that Article 8a [now 21] of the Treaty does not in itself have autonomous regulatory scope and that it is no more than a general declaration of no legal value which recapitulates in a non-binding manner the contents of other specific provisions of primary and secondary Community law regarding the free movement of persons. According to this point of view, there can be no question of this article producing direct effects.'

[62] n 33.

[63] See eg the Opinion of AG Ruiz-Jarabo Colomer in Case C-367/98 *Commission v Portugal* EU:C:2002:326. For analysis, see B Akkermans and E Ramaekers, 'Article 345 TFEU (ex Article 295 EC), Its Meanings and Interpretations' (2010) 16 *European Law Journal* 292.

to disregard the rules on free movement of capital. As a result, the Court was again immediately faced with difficult questions concerning the justification of the rules, which could potentially be characterised as pursuing economic aims.[64]

The implications of this ruling are far reaching. Prohibition of privatisation is now a restriction in need of justification, which already goes beyond the previous case law on Golden Shares.[65] This is radical enough, but can perhaps be taken even further. Would the mere fact that a state owns significant stakes in a company now constitute a restriction on free movement of capital, since Article 345 does not offer protection? After all, the effect on capital movements of a law prohibiting privatisation and the factual long-term holding of shares by a state are the same, and the four freedoms have always focused on the effects rather than the form.[66] If so, public ownership would now need to be justified by reference to non-economic aims of general interest. This would undoubtedly both engender more disputes over what constitutes an economic aim and further limit the role of the state in the economy.[67]

The sensitivity and importance of public ownership is highlighted by recent research in the field of economics, in particular by Mariana Mazzucato, which has emphasised the role of the public sector in innovation.[68] It is argued that the states' involvement in innovation is much greater than traditional economics has allowed for. For example, it is pointed out that all the technologies that make an Apple smartphone smart were developed with public funding. The same is true for the search algorithm of Google. These examples highlight the problem. Significant risks and costs have been borne by the public sector, while the rewards have gone to the private sector. There is a worry that losses are socialised, while profits are privatised. To deal with the issue, reform of the current model might be necessary. For example, some public ownership of companies might be seen as a sensible way to ensure that the state captures some of the rewards from the innovation it has supported, rather than an aberration in conflict with the normal functioning of the market economy.[69] But how would this square with the law on economic justifications, in particular with *Essent*, which starts from the premise that public ownership is problematic in the internal market?

How could more rigour and coherence be brought to the law of economic justifications in general? A good starting point would be the *explicit* recognition that Member States, private entities, and EU institutions are to be treated differently.[70] Attempting to impose the same standards on them would be inappropriate to and

[64] The Court employed the linkage strategy and found that the ultimate aims were non-economic.

[65] n 63.

[66] Case 8/74 *Dassonville* (n 18), para 5.

[67] See further P van Cleynenbreugel, 'No Privatisation in the Service of Fair Competition? Article 345 TFEU and the EU Market—State Balance after *Essent*' (2014) 39 *EL Rev* 264, especially 272–74.

[68] M Mazzucato, *The Entrepreneurial State: Debunking Public vs. Private Sector Myths* (London, Anthem Press, 2013).

[69] ibid, ch 9.

[70] See also Roth (n 37) 87–90.

incoherent with the different positions and political contexts they occupy. Ultimately the law of economic reasons is about the roles and functions that different actors may play and pursue, and states, private parties and the EU are simply not the same in this respect.

The rulings on actors other than Member States, cluster four in the typology adopted in the previous section, attempt to strike reasonable compromises but raise further questions. It seems correct to take into account the status of the party imposing restrictions.[71] For private parties, such as trade unions, an inability to rely on economic justifications would make a mockery of their private autonomy, which is a value recognised in the constitutions of some Member States. Private parties do not aim to protect the public interest—that is what public bodies are for. Instead, they pursue their private economic interests, or those of their members. To admit only general interest justifications would impose an impossible expectation on their conduct. This has always been recognised in competition law, where undertakings are, for example under Article 101(3) TFEU, explicitly allowed to justify their anticompetitive actions by economic reasons, provided that a fair share of the benefits is passed on to consumers.[72]

In the case of the EU legislature, cluster five in the previous section, it is again sensible to tolerate that which would be intolerable in the case of Member States. In the case of states, a protectionist motive for any action must always be suspected. That is simply the reality of a political process dominated by insiders where those outside the polity do not have a say. Nationals can vote, foreigners cannot, and therefore the results will favour the former.[73] Further, producer interests are often able to exert a dominant influence, as they are concentrated, have high stakes, and may find it easy to organise. By contrast, diffuse national consumer interests may struggle to get their voice heard.[74] When compared with a national process, the EU legislature is much less likely to adopt rules motivated by state protectionism. All interests are represented and well-organised groups calling for protection may be matched by equal groups that see more trade and competition in their interest. As a result, a deferential approach towards EU legislation seems warranted. This would also potentially allow the Union to offer some of the protections against economic insecurity that Member States can no longer individually provide.

[71] See also the Opinion of AG Trstenjak in Case C-171/11 *Fra.bo* EU:C:2012:453, paras 38–39.

[72] See on the detailed application of the law, Commission Communication, 'Guidelines on the Application of Article 81(3) of the Treaty' [2004] OJ C101/08. Similar principles have been put forward for Article 102 TFEU in Commission Communication, 'Guidance on the Commission's Enforcement Priorities in Applying Article 82 of the EC Treaty to Abusive Exclusionary Conduct by Dominant Undertakings' [2009] OJ C45/7, in particular at para 30.

[73] See generally eg M Poiares Maduro, 'Europe and the Constitution: What if This Is as Good as It Gets?' in JHH Weiler and M Wind (eds), *European Constitutionalism beyond the State* (Cambridge, Cambridge University Press, 2003) 83–86.

[74] See M Olson, *The Logic of Collective Action: Public Good and the Theory of Groups* (Cambridge, MA, Harvard University Press, 1965).

In other words, what is needed is not a massive change in the law but that the Court's sensitivity to the identity of the defendant should be expressed more clearly in the reasoning, in particular in the case of private parties. The attempt to deny in *Viking*[75] that the protection of jobs was an economic reason and to transform the issue into one of worker protection was disingenuous. Further, the test according to which only a serious threat to jobs can be opposed by collective action, which must be proportionate, seems challenging to operate in practice.[76]

Another possible way to further clarify the case law would be to consider whether protectionism was at play.[77] After all, normatively it is easy to condemn national protectionism,[78] while it is more difficult to say why Member States should not be allowed to pursue economic aims more generally; for example, what is objectionable about economic policy goals such as the strengthening of the competitive structure of the market or modernising and increasing the efficiency of means of production?[79] This avenue was examined by Advocate General Jääskinen in his Opinion in *Essent*,[80] although the Court ultimately did not follow this line of reasoning. According to the Advocate General, a number of decisions of the Court in the fields of capital and establishment can be explained by the implicitly protectionist goals of the national rules.

The same line of analysis might help more generally in explaining the rulings in the field of taxation. It has been remarked in the previous section that the case law on taxation, where revenue loss and the erosion of tax base have been seen as purely economic considerations, sits uneasily with the case law where the financial balance of the social security system and protection of public finances more generally have been admitted as legitimate interests. Protecting revenue and limiting expenses seem two sides of the same coin, and it is not easy to say why one is purely economic while the other is not. However, there is an important background factor. The case law on tax restrictions has targeted discriminatory rules[81] and has explicitly held that double taxation does not constitute a restriction.[82] This is a

[75] n 34.

[76] See eg S Weatherill, 'From Economic Rights to Fundamental Rights' in S de Vries, U Bernitz and S Weatherill (eds), *The Protection of Fundamental Rights in the EU after Lisbon* (Oxford, Hart Publishing, 2013) 28. For suggestions on how to modify the approach, see C Barnard, 'A Proportionate Response to Proportionality in the Field of Collective Action' (2012) 37 *EL Rev* 117.

[77] Arrowsmith (n 12) provides a sustained argument in support of this approach.

[78] See eg G Davies, 'The Court's Jurisprudence on Free Movement of Goods: Pragmatic Presumptions, Not Philosophical Principles' (2012) 2 *European Journal of Consumer Law* 25 and J Snell, 'Free Movement of Services and the Services Directive: The Legitimacy of the Case Law' in J van de Gronden (ed), *The EU and WTO Law on Services: Limits to the Realisation of General Interest Policies within the Services Markets?* (Alphen aan den Rijn, Kluwer, 2009) 44–49.

[79] These aims were condemned in Case C-367/98 *Commission v Portugal* (n 63) para 52.

[80] n 33, paras 89–97.

[81] Snell (n 22). See also K Banks, 'The Application of the Fundamental Freedoms to Member State Tax Measures: Guarding against Protectionism or Second-Guessing National Policy Choices?' (2008) 33 *EL Rev* 482.

[82] n 23.

very different approach from that adopted for regulatory obstacles, where non-discriminatory rules have been routinely examined by the Court and where the suppression of double regulation has been one of the key targets of the case law.[83] Perhaps the differing approaches to the notion of restriction have had an effect on justifications. It seems natural to condemn a rule that seeks to maximise revenue by discriminating on the basis of nationality,[84] while condemning revenue maximisation in the case of a truly even-handed rule would be a very different exercise. In other words, because in the tax field the rules that are caught are discriminatory, the Court is right to see economic goals as protectionist, while in the regulatory field where non-discriminatory rules are also caught, a consideration with an economic flavour might not be tainted by protectionism.

However, while the anti-protectionism reading is attractive, it is not without its problems. First, the Court does not use the term protectionism. In fact, it is very difficult to find any recent decisions of the Court in the field of the four freedoms that have been reasoned in these terms, even if the parties have raised the issue.[85] It may well be that protectionism is an underlying unstated concern, but the Court certainly does not articulate this in its rulings. Second, anti-protectionism fits poorly with the general thrust of the case law. The Court considers that national measures *prima facie* violate the four freedoms as soon as they have a dissuasive effect on free movement, even if they have an equal impact on purely domestic actors and circumstances.[86] It is difficult to see why the Court should throw the net of free movement so wide as to catch truly even-handed rules if its real target is national protectionism. Third, protectionism is not a self-defining concept. As discussed in the previous section, the Court does accept, for example, the protection of national hospitals against competition from hospitals in other Member States. If we were to use the concept of protectionism as a lodestone, we would need to engage in a discussion of its precise meaning.[87]

In the end, the law of economic justifications is ultimately and unavoidably about what functions a state can perform. As a result, the quest for a more rigorous and coherent law requires us to consider and find a degree of agreement on what the proper role of the state is in today's Europe. This is going to be difficult in a Union of 28. Yet, the law of free movement will inevitably have an impact on this. When does the competition that the internal market brings become unfair, allowing Member States to restrict it, for example by insisting that service providers

[83] Case 120/78 *Rewe-Zentral v Bundesmonopolverwaltung für Branntwein* EU:C:1979:42 (Cassis de Dijon).

[84] See eg Case C-96/08 *CIBA* EU:C:2010:185, para 48.

[85] See eg Case C-174/04 *Commission v Italy* EU:C:2005:350, where the Commission argued (at para 24) that the national measures were 'of strictly protectionist character' but the issue of possible protectionism was not mentioned by the Court.

[86] See eg J Snell, 'The Notion of Market Access: A Concept of a Slogan?' (2010) 47 *CML Rev* 437 and the sustained analysis in N Nic Shuibhne, *The Coherence of EU Free Movement Law: Constitutional Responsibility and the Court of Justice* (Oxford, Oxford University Press, 2013).

[87] See Arrowsmith (n 12) for an important contribution.

from other Member States adhere to local conditions of employment?[88] More broadly, should a Member State be able to protect the economic security of its citizens, or should its role simply be limited to enabling them and offering them opportunities?

It seems to me that answering these questions has become harder, not easier. The recent analyses of the internal market point to a general disenfranchisement among citizens: a feeling that the social dimension has lagged behind the economic one.[89] It is not clear that the majority of Europeans wish to be enabled rather than protected. The hostile public reactions to the Services Directive[90] and to rulings such as *Viking* and *Laval*[91] suggest that when the EU attempts to offer its citizens opportunities at the expense of national protective systems, this damages rather than enhances its legitimacy.

The changes incorporated into the Lisbon Treaty are of limited help. They provide ammunition for those who argue for a new, more protective approach. For example, Advocate General Cruz Villalón called in *Santos Palhota* for particular sensitivity for the social protection of workers and wrote that: '[t]o the extent that the new primary law framework provides for a mandatory high level of social protection, it authorises the Member States, for the purpose of safeguarding a certain level of social protection, to restrict a freedom, and to do so without European Union law's regarding it as something exceptional and, therefore, as warranting a strict interpretation.'[92] In the same way, the Commission's Communication 'Towards a Single Market Act' states that '[t]he Lisbon Treaty, and the affirmation of the concept of a "highly competitive social market economy" as one of its key objectives, require us to adopt a more all-embracing view of the single market.'[93] Yet the Treaty hardly offers clear guidance.[94] It is now committed to a 'highly competitive social market economy'—a concept that is far from self-defining and may

[88] See eg Case C-341/05 *Laval un Partneri* EU:C:2007:809, paras 74–75, in the context of European Parliament and Council Directive (EC) 96/71 concerning the posting of workers in the framework of the provision of services [1997] OJ L18/1.

[89] M Monti, 'A New Strategy for the Single Market: At the Service of Europe's Economy and Society' 9 May 2010, available at http://ec.europa.eu/bepa/pdf/monti_report_final_10_05_2010_en.pdf, eg at 26.

[90] European Parliament and Council Directive (EC) 2006/123 on services in the internal market [2006] OJ L376/36. See eg K Nicolaïdis and SK Schmidt, 'Mutual Recognition "On Trial": The Long Road to Services Liberalization' (2007) 14 *Journal of European Public Policy* 717.

[91] n 88. The rulings played a role in the Irish debates on the Lisbon Treaty; see Houses of the Oireachtas, Joint Committee on European Affairs, 'Seventh Report: The Lisbon Treaty and Workers' Rights' (September 2009) 11–12.

[92] Case C-515/08 *Santos Palhota* EU:C:2010:589, para 53 of the Opinion.

[93] Commission Communication, 'Towards a Single Market Act for a highly competitive social market economy: 50 proposals for improving our work, business and exchanges with one another' COM (2010) 608 at 23. Commission Communication, 'Single Market Act: Twelve levers to boost growth and strengthen confidence' COM (2011) 206/4 emphasises the importance of the social dimension, eg at 5 and 16–17, citing Art 9 TFEU and the Charter of Fundamental Rights.

[94] Similarly Weatherill (n 76) 29–35.

not be free from internal tensions.[95] It contains both the rules on the internal market and a cross-cutting commitment to a high level of employment and adequate social protection. In the binding Charter of Fundamental Rights, it puts forward fundamental social rights, but also, for example, the freedom to conduct a business. The balance between the differing interests is not set in the Treaty, but needs to be established in political and judicial arenas.[96]

Ultimately, the Court seems to be caught in a trap of its own making. In general, it tries to chart a third way in the field of internal market law.[97] On the one hand, it does not wish to second-guess the rationality of all national policies, as seen, for example, in its case law on the regulation of selling arrangements.[98] On the other hand, it has expanded free movement law beyond protectionism and chosen to apply it also in sectors, such as health care, where market logic may not be predominant. This forces the Court to decide the legality of a very large number of national rules without a clear theory to guide it. Any incoherence on economic justifications may at least partly be a consequence of and reflect the unresolved broader questions about the nature of the four freedoms. And to make matters worse, the stakes are high: in the end these decisions are inevitably not just about internal market law, rather they contribute to defining the role and legitimacy of the state.

V. CONCLUSION

In this chapter, it has been argued that the case law on economic justifications serves to define the role of the states. In particular, it limits their ability to protect the economic security of their citizens. Due to the profound effects of a ruling that a particular interest is purely economic, it is not surprising that the Court's case law has sometimes lacked coherence, especially given the wide reach of free movement law. It has been suggested that clearer differentiation between cases that involve private restrictions, restrictions emanating from EU institutions, and national restrictions could provide clarity, as could the consideration of whether protectionism was involved. Ultimately, however, only a degree of consensus on the legitimate role of the state in the internal market can provide a foundation for rational law.

[95] According to European Convention final report of Working Group XI on Social Europe CONV 516/1/03 REV 1 para 17 the purpose of the phrase 'social market economy' was to 'underline the link between economic and social development and the efforts made to ensure greater coherence between economic and social policies'. See C Joerges and F Rödl, '"Social Market Economy" as Europe's Social Model?' EUI Working Paper LAW No 2004/8 for a pessimistic account.

[96] See for assessment eg E Szyszczak, 'Building a Socioeconomic Constitution: A Fantastic Object?' (2012) 35 *Fordham International Law Journal* 1364.

[97] Snell, n 86 above, 470–71.

[98] Joined Cases C-267 and 268/91 *Keck* EU:C:1993:905.

There is a further question, and that concerns the role of the EU, which is again affected by the case law that defines the aims that can be pursued lawfully. Is the EU simply a great enabler whose function is to provide Union citizens opportunities, for example to engage in commerce and consumption free of the barriers that states have imposed? Or is it to have a protective role as well, ultimately offering Union citizens protection against physical or economic risks that small nation states can no longer provide? Does it work to accelerate the general trends that technological change and globalisation entail or does it offer shelter from them? How these questions are answered is likely to have a major impact on the fragile and contested legitimacy of the EU. It is therefore important to recognise that the seemingly technical rulings on economic justifications are ultimately of great constitutional significance.

3

Citizenship: Reallocating Welfare Responsibilities to the State of Origin

ELEANOR SPAVENTA*

I. INTRODUCTION

FREE MOVEMENT ORTHODOXY teaches us that Member States cannot rely on economic justifications in relation to rules that are directly discriminatory;[1] and that economic reasons can be taken into account in order to justify rules that are not directly discriminatory provided that the aim pursued by the measure is not solely economic. This approach is entirely consistent with the premises of an internal market where protectionism should be eradicated, but where Member States should still be allowed to pursue public policy aims which, quite naturally, might carry budgetary constraints. In this respect, the greatest challenge for the interpreter concerns rules that are both economic and inherently territorial, such as tax rules: in those cases, eliminating discrimination without impinging on the integrity of the tax system has not always been easy to achieve. Similarly, the application of internal market rules to fields, such as health care, that are particularly resource-sensitive has not been entirely straightforward. Jukka Snell, in Chapter 2 of this collection, analyses the extent to which the 'no economic justification' rule is actually supported by a more careful reading of the case law on the free movement provisions. In this contribution, on the other hand, I want to explore how far those hermeneutic guidelines can be transposed to one particular area of free movement, that of citizens. In particular, my contention is

* I am very grateful to the participants in the workshop for a very fruitful discussion on these issues, and to the editors for very useful suggestions; the usual disclaimer applies. This contribution was completed in the summer of 2015 and it has been updated only insofar as possible given editorial constraints.

[1] See, recently, Case C-628/11 *International Jet Management GmbH* EU:C:2014:171, para 70; see also Case C-398/95 *SETTG* EU:C:1997:282, para 23, and Case C-20/09 *Commission v Portugal* EU:C:2011:214, para 65. See generally the contribution to this volume by J Snell, 'Economic Justifications and the Role of the State'.

that in the field of Union citizenship, the migration of citizens with no connection to the internal market can be limited on economic grounds; and, further, that this tells us something important about what Union citizenship is (or, more precisely, what Union citizenship is not).

I will start by analysing the case law on incoming migration of non-economically active Union citizens. I will then turn to the Court's approach to outward movement; and to citizens that, whilst not economically active, have some internal market 'credentials'. I will conclude that the Court's approach to justifications shapes Union citizenship to reinforce the allocation of welfare responsibilities along traditional lines, so that Union citizens are primarily the economic and social responsibility of their State of nationality, regardless of the actual links existing between citizen and state of residence and state of nationality.

II. NON-ECONOMIC MIGRATION, THE WELFARE STATE, AND ECONOMIC JUSTIFICATIONS

The interpretative tools developed in the context of the internal market, especially in relation to free movement rights—such as the notion of discrimination and the notion of obstacles—have been to a certain extent transposed to the interpretation of Union citizenship.[2] Given the fact that an important part of the internal market relates to migration of individuals, this is not surprising: after all, the Court had always made clear that the free movement provisions pursued a social as well as an economic aim and should therefore be so interpreted. If the worker was not to be seen merely as a factor of production, so that she would gain extensive rights from a liberal interpretation of free movement rights,[3] and if the individual was protected also when simply seeking employment,[4] and to a certain degree when receiving economic services,[5] then the extension of interpretative tools developed in the context of the economic freedoms to cover movement of non-economic actors is perfectly understandable.

[2] See eg Case C-224/98 *D'Hoop v Office national de l'emploi* EU:C:2002:432; Case C-148/02 *Garcia Avello v Belgium* EU:C:2003:539; Case C-406/04 *De Cuyper v Office National de l'Emploi* EU:C:2006:491.

[3] See for the extensive rights to equal treatment in relation to social and tax advantages, eg Case C-237/94 *O'Flynn v Adjudication Officer* EU:C:1996:206; for the derived rights of family members, including the derived right of the separated spouse who is the parent of a child in education in a host State (also when the EU worker has left the host territory), eg Case C-310/08 *London Borough of Harrow v Ibrahim* EU:C:2010:80 and Case C-529/11 *Alarape and Tijani* EU:C:2013:290; and for the derived right of residence of family members of frontier workers in the home Member State, eg Case C-457/12 *S & G* EU:C:2014:136.

[4] Case C-292/89 *Antonissen* EU:C:1991:80.

[5] Case 286/82 *Luisi e Carbone v Ministero del Tesoro* EU:C:1984:35.

And yet, it hardly needs repeating, economic and non-economic integration are radically different, both in aims and in ambition. Economic integration is (or possibly was) premised on the benefits arising from movement of factors of production: ideally, migration would allow for a better allocation of skills and resources, so that migrants would move from regions with higher unemployment to those which could afford more work opportunities. Receiving countries would benefit not only by hosting a workforce that would fill labour or skill shortages,[6] but also because migration of those who are economically engaged has overall positive effects on the receiving country's economy. EU economic migrants might draw on the host State welfare provision, but they also pay into it through general and ad hoc contribution. It is for this reason that economic justifications cannot be relied upon in the internal market: protectionism is to be eradicated, not encouraged. In this context, the purposive and generous interpretation of the free movement rights of economic actors is entirely consistent: there is a clear mandate in the Treaty; and there is a clear narrative that can be used to explain the benefits of economic migration (although that narrative is increasingly coming under strain).[7]

Not so in the case of non-economic migrants: there, we have no clear *telos*, and no clear narrative. On the one hand, the language of citizenship naturally resonates with state-like ideals of communities based on a sense of shared belonging, if not values; on the other hand, the Union sense of 'togetherness' is still, if existing at all, at a very incipient state.[8] Furthermore, Union citizenship almost crept in on the Member States; it would be naïve to think that in establishing Union citizenship in the Maastricht Treaty the Member States were intending to establish a supranational welfare community. In fact, it is likely that most (if not all) Member States did not want to establish anything new at all.[9] It comes as no surprise then that the balance between belonging to a supranational community and national welfare states is one of the two fields, together with migration rights

[6] See the latest (2013) Eurostat statistics on intra-EU migration (http://ec.europa.eu/eurostat/statistics-explained/index.php/File:Employed_persons_aged_15_and_older_taking_up_residence_in_an_EU_Member_State_other_than_their_countr_yof_citizenship_of_from_outside_the_EU_within_the_last_two_years,_by_nationality,_2011_and_2013_-_new.png) and note an unsurprising direct link between the extent to which a country has been hit by the economic crisis and the extent to which it is a migration target (eg Italy –32.5%; Spain –47.8%; Germany +63.5%).

[7] See eg D Cameron (UK Prime Minister at the time), Letter to the *Financial Times* 26 November 2013; on the same lines, Mr Cameron's letter to the *The Daily Telegraph* 15 March 2014. Economic migration is considered to have played a major role in the outcome of the UK referendum on membership of the EU.

[8] It is sufficient here to recall the reactions to the economic problems in Greece and the Greek bailouts.

[9] See eg the submissions of the Member States in Case C-184/99 *Grzelcyck v Centre public d'aide sociale d'Ottignies-Louvain-la-Neuve* EU:C:2001:458 where, with the exception of Portugal, Member States argued against using Union Citizenship to grant meaningful rights to equal treatment.

for third country national family members,[10] where the battle for citizenship is more strongly felt.

If, at the very beginning, Member States did not intend for Union citizenship to be innovative, or even to have direct effect, with the adoption of Directive 2004/38 they accepted that Union citizenship would change, at least to some extent, the relationship between economically inactive migrants and host Member States.[11] However, pursuant to the provisions of Directive 2004/38, membership of the host welfare community, and the consequent potential to make claims, is very limited: the economically inactive migrant shall not become a 'burden on the social assistance system' of the host State;[12] and the short-term visitor shall not become an 'unreasonable burden'[13] on the social assistance system of the host State, so that during the first three months of residence Union citizens are not entitled, as a matter of Union law, to equal treatment in relation to social assistance,[14] though recourse to the latter cannot lead to automatic expulsion.[15] Similarly, work-seekers can (in principle) be excluded from social assistance,[16] both in the first three months of residence and for the longer period of their stay when they continue looking for employment.[17]

Economic justifications, then, are at the very heart of the regime foreseen by Directive 2004/38 in relation to non-economically active migrants.[18] Member States are allowed to discriminate on grounds of nationality against non-economically active migrants in two instances: first of all, in relation to short-term

[10] See eg the cases relating to third country national parents of Union citizens, eg Case C-413/99 *Baumbast and R v Secretary of State for the Home Department* EU:C:2002:493, Case C-34/09 *Ruiz Zambrano v ONEm* EU:C:2011:124, Case C-256/11 *Dereci and others* EU:C:2011:734, Case C-86/12 *Alokpa v Ministre du Travail, de l'Emploi et de l'Immigration* EU:C:2013:645; and the cases relating to family members of own citizens, eg Case C-456/12 *O and B* EU:C:2014:135.

[11] Directive 2004/38 on the right of citizens of the Union and their family members to move and reside freely within the territory of the Member States [2004] OJ L158/77 (hereinafter Directive 2004/38).

[12] Directive 2004/38, Art 7(b).

[13] ibid, Art 6(1).

[14] ibid, Art 24(2).

[15] ibid, Art 14(3).

[16] Social assistance was first interpreted in a narrow way, so that benefits intended to facilitate access to the labour market were also available to migrant work-seekers who had established a sufficient link with the host employment market (see Joined Cases C-22 and 23/08 *Vatsouras* and *Koupatantze* EU:C:2009:344). However in Case C-66/14 *Alimanovic* ECLI:EU:C:2015:597, the Court redefined 'social assistance' and de facto excluded most (if not all) monetary subsidies to workseekers from the scope of the principle of equal treatment.

[17] Directive 2004/38, Art 24(2).

[18] See eg Case C-140/12 *Brey* EU:C:2013:565, para 55 (discussed in Section V below). Directive 90/364 on a general right to residence [1990] OJ L180/26, Directive 90/365 on retired persons [1990] OJ L180/28, and Directive 93/96 on students [1993] OJ L317/59, precursors to Directive 2004/38, were also, and not surprisingly, preoccupied with the potential effects on the welfare systems of host States of economically inactive individuals, students and pensioners, and therefore also specified that such individuals should not become a burden on the social assistance system of the host States (see Art 1 of the relevant Directives).

visitors by excluding them from social assistance *tout court*;[19] second, in relation to medium-term visitors by making their residence rights conditional upon the fulfilment of economic requirements, in the form of a minimum income and comprehensive health insurance.[20] The reason why Member States can engage in such discriminatory treatment is to limit the economic burden arising from non-economic migration between Member States. Therefore, unlike in the case of economic free movement provisions, Member States *are* entitled to erect absolute barriers (no residency rights for those who do not possess sufficient resources and comprehensive health insurance) as well as discriminatory conditions (no access to social assistance to short-term migrants) *only* in order to protect their public finances.[21]

This said, whilst Directive 2004/38 sought to clarify the case law of the Court as it was at the time of drafting, in more recent times there has been a perceptible shift in the Court's interpretation.

In the first wave of cases, those rooted in the Treaty provisions, the Court was trying to define the rights of Union citizens, starting from the premise that the introduction of citizenship had been a game-changer in EU law, so that it was to be considered the 'fundamental status' of Union citizens.[22] In this first wave, much as it is the case in the free movement of economic actors, direct discrimination could not be saved by budgetary considerations alone, so that a Member State could not deny equal treatment to foreign citizens on the sole grounds that to allow membership of the welfare community to foreigners would be too expensive. As a result, and insofar as the Union citizen was lawfully resident by virtue of *either* national *or* EU law,[23] then she would be entitled to equal treatment, save for the possibility for Member States either to terminate residence on the grounds that the Union citizen no longer satisfied the requirements provided for in EU law;[24] or to justify *indirect discrimination* on grounds which might have also been pursuing economic considerations, but which are not 'exclusively' economic in nature. Thus, the protection of the welfare state from *unwarranted* claims, whilst based on the banal assumption that welfare resources are limited, aims to determine who should be admitted to the circle of solidarity.[25]

[19] Directive 2004/38, Art 24(2).

[20] Arts 7(1)(b) and (c) Directive 2004/38; pursuant to Art 8(4) Directive 2004/38, Member States are not allowed to lay down a minimum amount that they regard as 'sufficient resources', rather having to take into account the personal situation of the claimant.

[21] See *Brey* (n 18).

[22] Case C-184/99 *Grzelcyck* (n 9), para 31.

[23] Case C-85/96 *Martínez Sala v Freistaat Bayern* EU:C:1998:217; Case C-184/99 *Grzelcyck* (n 9).

[24] Case C-184/99 *Grzelcyck* ibid; Case C-456/02 *Trojani v Centre public d'aide sociale de Bruxelles*, EU:C:2004:488.

[25] eg Case C-224/98 *D'Hoop v Office national de l'emploi* EU:C:2002:432; Case C-209/03 *Bidar v London Borough of Ealing and Secretary of State for Education and Skills* EU:C:2005:169; Case C-138/02 *Collins v Secretary of State for Work and Pensions* EU:C:2004:172.

This is not the same as accepting an economic justification *tout court*. Rather, it is premised on the idea that welfare societies are based on links of belonging which might be presumed for certain individuals (for example, nationals); and might be acquired by others (through contribution to the economic life of the host State;[26] or simply by virtue of the passage of time/contribution to the host society). Thus, in this phase of development of Union citizenship, budgetary considerations are relevant only insofar as they allow Member States to limit the class of claimants to those who have established a meaningful 'link' with the host welfare society.[27]

Furthermore, the rights in secondary legislation were seen as merely complementing/detailing the rights granted by the Treaty: hence, the limitations and conditions provided for therein had to be interpreted in accordance with the general principles of Union law, and particularly the principle of proportionality.[28]

Thus, for instance, in *Martínez Sala*, a case that would arguably be decided in a very different way nowadays, the Court explicitly held that since the discrimination at issue was direct, it could not be justified.[29] In *Grzelcyck* the Court, whilst accepting that an excessive burden on the welfare resources of the host State might be a reason to terminate the residency rights of an economically inactive Union citizen, also clarified that the residency directives[30] (precursors to Directive 2004/38) had 'accepted a certain degree of *financial solidarity* between nationals of a host Member State and nationals of other Member States, particularly if the difficulties which a beneficiary of the right of residence encounters are temporary'.[31] In *Baumbast*,[32] having found that Article 21(1) TFEU was directly effective, the Court proceeded to assess whether Mr Baumbast could be denied a residence permit because he did not possess emergency health insurance so that his insurance cover was not 'comprehensive'.[33] Here the Court accepted that the rights conferred

[26] See recently Case C-20/12 *Giersch and others v Luxembourg* EU:C:2013:411, para 63: 'In that regard, it should be noted that the Court has already held that migrant and frontier workers, since they have participated in the labour market of a Member State, have in principle created a sufficient link of integration with the society of that State, allowing them to benefit from the principle of equal treatment, as compared, respectively with national workers and resident workers. The link of integration arises, in particular, from the fact that, through the taxes which they pay in the host Member State by virtue of their employment there, migrant and frontier workers also contribute to the financing of the social policies of that State'.

[27] On the rather nebulous notion of 'real link', see eg C O'Brien, 'Real links, abstract rights and false alarms: the relationship between the ECJ's case law and national solidarity' (2008) 33 *EL Rev* 643; PJ Neuvonen, 'In search of (even) more substance for the "real link" test: comment on *Prinz and Seeberger*' (2014) 39 *EL Rev* 125.

[28] See eg Case C-413/99 *Baumbast and R v Secretary of State for the Home* Department EU:C:2002:493 and Case C-408/03 *Commission and Belgium* (sufficient resources) EU:C:2006:192, para 39.

[29] Case C-85/96 *Martínez Sala* (n 23), para 64.

[30] Directive 90/364 on a general right to residence [1990] OJ L180/26; Directive 90/365 on retired persons [1990] OJ L180/28; Directive 93/96 on students [1993] OJ L317/59.

[31] Case C-184/99 *Grzelcyck* (n 9), para 44 (emphasis added).

[32] Case C-413/99 *Baumbast* (n 10).

[33] Although it is not clear whether Mr Baumbast was not in fact covered by the provisions of then Regulation 1408/71, see para 89 of the ruling.

by the Treaty could be limited to avoid an 'unreasonable burden on the *public finances* of the Member States',[34] and yet, by requiring a personal assessment, one based on the particular situation of *that particular* claimant, the Court excluded the absolute relevance of *mere* budgetary considerations in determining the rights of Union citizens: rather a balancing act is required to determine whether the burden on public finances imposed by the claimant is reasonable or not. In turn, whether the burden is reasonable or not depends on non-economic criteria, such as the personal circumstances of the claimant, her family ties, her link with the host society and so on.

In *Bidar*, the Court examined the extent to which a lawfully resident Union citizen could rely on the Treaty in order to obtain a maintenance loan for his studies; here the United Kingdom, whose rules were under attack, attempted to rely on two grounds of justification. First of all, it was legitimate to ensure that 'the contribution made by parents or students through taxation is or will be sufficient to justify the provision of subsidised loans'.[35] Second, it was argued, '[i]t is also legitimate to require a genuine link between the student claiming assistance to cover his maintenance costs and the employment market of the host Member State'.[36] It is then interesting to note that the Court ignored the first issue, of a purely budgetary nature, to focus exclusively on the need to ensure the existence of a genuine link between claimant and host State: only the existence of said genuine link would justify that degree of financial solidarity mentioned in *Grzelcyck*. Again, the Court found that a single rule which excluded the possibility for a student – who had resided in the UK for a significant time and had undergone a part of his secondary education there – to demonstrate such a link in other ways was incompatible with the Treaty. Furthermore, the Court refused the request, put forward by the UK, Austria and Germany, to limit the temporal effects of the ruling, thus pointing at the fact that even the cumulative effect of such claims would not be a good enough reason to limit the rights of Union citizens who had established a real link with the host State to receive support for their university education. In *Trojani*, the Court clarified again that once the Union citizen was lawfully resident in the host State, despite not fulfilling the criteria listed in the residency directives, he was entitled to equal treatment in relation to social assistance so that the only course open to the host State would be that of terminating the right to reside (subject to the principles of Union law, including and especially that of proportionality).[37]

Directive 2004/38, by not excluding medium-term residents from the scope of the principle of equal treatment, then codifies this case law: whilst it can be taken

[34] ibid, para 90 (emphasis added).
[35] ibid, para 55.
[36] Case C-209/03 *Bidar* (n 25), para 55.
[37] Case C-456/02 *Trojani v Centre public d'aide sociale de Bruxelles* EU:C:2004:488.

for granted that stays of three months or less are not sufficient to establish a link with the host community that justifies access to social assistance, that is not the case for economically inactive individuals residing for a longer period pursuant to Article 7(1)(b) of Directive 2004/38. The budgetary considerations in relation to access to host welfare states are resolved, similarly to the case law of the Court, by virtue of the conditional rights of residence of those migrants who do not engage, and do not wish to engage, in an economic activity. It is the comprehensive health insurance/sufficient resources criteria that act as a break for benefit tourism; not a variation of the principles informing equal treatment between national and non-nationals in EU law.

In a second wave of case law, that immediately following the adoption of Directive 2004/38, this approach is broadly speaking maintained, although the Court accepts the further limitation imposed by Article 24(2) of Directive 2004/38 to the effect that economically inactive migrant students can legitimately be excluded from maintenance grants and other subsidies for higher education awarded by the host State until such time as they have established a genuine link with the host society. A requirement of five years' residency before being eligible for any form of maintenance grant for studies, consistent with Article 24(2) of Directive 2004/38, is seen as a reasonable way to ensure the existence of such a link.[38] In relation to work-seekers, the Court, in this stage of the case law, departed from the compromise espoused in the Directive to restate the centrality of a purposive interpretation of the free movement provisions, so that benefits which sought to aid the individual to gain access to the employment market were not to be considered 'social assistance' for the purposes of Article 24(2) and were therefore also available to migrant work-seekers.[39]

In a third wave of case law, the Court's interpretation shifts so as to adopt a more rigid approach: those who do not derive the right to reside from Directive 2004/38 cannot rely on Article 24(1) of the Directive. More importantly, though, the rights detailed in the Directive cannot be supplemented by the rights conferred in the Treaty: rather, at least in relation to the relationship between economically inactive migrants and the host State, the Directive becomes the floor and the ceiling of the rights granted by Union law.[40] It is to this more recent case law that we shall now turn our attention.

[38] Case C-158/07 *Förster* EU:C:2008:630.

[39] Joined Cases C-22 and 23/08 *Vatsouras and Koupatantze* EU:C:2009:344, 'this has now been superseded by the Court's interpretation in Case C-67/14 Alimanovic, ECLI:EU:C:2015:597; and Case C-299/14 Garcia Nieto, ECLI:EU:C:2016:114.

[40] And, in fact, stays which are not in pursuance to Directive 2004/38 seem to exclude the claimant from the scope of application of EU law (regardless of Art 21 TFEU); see eg Case C-333/13 *Dano* ibid, and also the exclusion of the relevance of the Charter of Fundamental Rights in that case. On the 'new' relationship between primary and secondary law see P Syrpis, 'The relationship between primary and secondary law in the EU' (2015) 52 *CML Rev* 461.

III. THE MORE RECENT CASE LAW OF THE COURT: ECONOMIC JUSTIFICATIONS AND ALLOCATION OF RESPONSIBILITIES BETWEEN MEMBER STATES

We have mentioned above that the Court's case law evolves (and regresses) over time. The first and most notable change in the case law relates to the relevance of Articles 21 and 18 TFEU when assessing the rights of Union citizens who reside or seek to reside in another Member State: in the first instance, and as mentioned above, the residence directives were seen as a limitation to Treaty rights which therefore needed to be interpreted pursuant to the principles of necessity and proportionality. This was partially due to the fact that the secondary legislation applicable predated the introduction of Union citizenship; the Court therefore felt empowered to reinterpret the residency directives in the light of the Treaty changes.[41] As a result of the primacy of the Treaty rights over the pre-existing secondary legislation, a migrant fell within the scope *ratione personae* of the Treaty even when she did not satisfy (all of) the conditions contained in secondary legislation;[42] or when she was residing in the host State pursuant to national law rather than the Directive.[43] In this first phase, then, the traditional scheme regarding justifications pursuing also an economic aim is maintained: economically inactive citizens derive their rights from the Treaty, and as a result limitations to their rights must be justified. The need to preserve the welfare system is at this stage considered a mixed economic/social objective, so that the mere aim to avoid welfare claims by non-nationals is insufficient to deny rights to Union citizens. Furthermore, and because the Union citizen's claim rests directly on the Treaty, the justification must in any case be interpreted in a proportionate way, which means taking into account the citizen's factual circumstances.

This is no longer true in more recent case law: the rights of economically inactive Union citizens are now (primarily) those conferred by Directive 2004/38,[44] and are limited accordingly. Thus, residence pursuant to national law becomes immaterial to the enjoyment of rights conferred not only by the Directive,[45] but also to the right of equal treatment granted by Article 18 TFEU.[46] The 'limitations

[41] Directive 90/364 on a general right to residence [1990] OJ L180/26; Directive 90/365 on retired persons [1990] OJ L180/28; Directive 93/96 on students [1993] OJ L317/59.

[42] eg Case C-413/99 *Baumbast* (n 10).

[43] Case C-85/96 *Martínez Sala* (n 23); Case C-224/98 *D'Hoop* (n 25); Case C-456/02 *Trojani* (n 24).

[44] The Treaty provisions remain relevant when Directive 2004/38 does not apply, especially in relation to claims brought by Union citizens against their Member State of nationality; this said, the Court has indicated that in those instances Directive 2004/38 applies, mutatis mutandis, by analogy; see Case C-456/12 *O and B* (n 10), annotated by E Spaventa, 'Family rights for circular migrants and frontier workers: *O & B* and *S & G*' (2015) 52 *CML Rev* 753.

[45] For instance, the cases relating to which 'residence' is relevant in order to establish the five years of lawful and continuous residence required for permanent residence; eg Joined Cases C-424 and 425/10 *Ziolkowski and Szeja* EU:C:2011:866.

[46] See Dano (n 39).

and conditions' contained in Directive 2004/38, primarily the sufficient resources/ comprehensive health insurance requirements, no longer need to be interpreted having regard to the principle of proportionality; and a migrant who does not satisfy the criteria of sufficient resources/comprehensive health insurance required by Directive 2004/38 falls, for that reason, outside the scope of Union law.[47] This is the case even when she is residing in the host State lawfully pursuant to national law.[48]

Thus, for instance, in the case of *Alokpa*,[49] the claimant was the Togolese mother of two minor French citizens residing in Luxembourg. Ms Alokpa applied for a residence permit and a work permit as the mother of Union citizens: she had already secured a job that would allow her to provide for her children and hence satisfy the requirements of Directive 2004/38. However, lacking a work permit, which in turn depended on her residence status, she could not take up the job offer, and was therefore left without resources. The Court found that, lacking resources, Ms Alokpa could not derive residency rights from her children, despite the fact that she had arguably formed a real link with the host society since she had resided there for over three years and her children, who had been born severely premature in Luxembourg, had been cared for in that State. In this case, the Treaty provisions were not used to supplement Ms Alokpa's rights and, as a result, Luxembourg—the host Member State—did not need to justify the denial of residency rights.

Similarly, in *Dano*, we see a shift in relation to the 'origin' of the resources relevant in order to satisfy Article 7(1)(b) of Directive 2004/38.[50] In this case, the claimant was a Romanian national living with her sister in Germany; her sister provided for both Ms Dano and her child, who had been born in Germany. When Ms Dano applied for a benefit, she was denied it on the grounds that she was not 'lawfully resident' for the purposes of Union law, although she was lawfully present pursuant to national law.[51] The Court then had to clarify the extent to which Ms Dano could rely on either Article 18 TFEU (general principle of equal treatment) or on Article 24 of Directive 2004/38 in order to claim access to the benefit in question. The Court held that the general equal treatment right was given specific expression in Article 24(1) of the Directive. As a result, this was the only equal treatment provision that was found to be relevant. Further, given that Article 24 only applies to those resident

[47] For a positive assessment of this development, in terms of democratic legitimacy of legislation vis-à-vis Treaty interpretation see Syrpis (n 40).

[48] See eg Case C-333/13 *Dano* (n 39) and the exclusion of the relevance of the Charter therein.

[49] Case C-86/12 *Alokpa* (n 10).

[50] Case C-333/13 *Dano* (n 39); the ruling in *Dano* has already given grounds to a fertile academic debate; see eg H Verschueren, 'Preventing "benefit tourism" in the EU: a narrow or broad interpretation of the possibilities offered by the ECJ in *Dano*?' (2015) 52 *CML Rev* 363; and D Thym, 'The elusive limits of solidarity: residence rights of and social benefits for economically inactive Union Citizens' (2015) 52 *CML Rev* 17.

[51] On this aspect see D Thym, 'When Union Citizens turn into illegal migrants: the *Dano* case' (2015) 40 *EL Rev* 249.

pursuant to the Directive, the Court assessed whether Ms Dano satisfied the conditions contained therein and, in particular, the 'sufficient resources' condition.

In this respect, it might be useful to recall that in *Chen*, the Court accepted that, in order to comply with the sufficient resources criterion, it was enough for the citizen 'to have' sufficient resources, regardless of the origin of such resources.[52] As a result, the sufficient resources requirement was satisfied also when the funds were not the citizen's own, rather being provided by a family member. In *Commission v Belgium* the Grand Chamber went a step further:[53] funds could be provided also by a third party who was not (legally speaking) a family member of the Union citizen. Faced with the objection that the support granted by a third party not having a legal link with the Union citizen might increase the risk of such resources being withdrawn, so that the Union citizen might become a burden on the social assistance system of the host State, the Court found that such a risk was inherent in the possibility of circumstances changing, regardless of the source of the income. In *Dano*, however, the Court focuses exclusively on the resources of the claimant: the fact that Ms Dano was hosted by her sister, who provided for Ms Dano and her son 'materially' (including lodging), was not taken into any consideration by the Court in assessing whether Ms Dano had sufficient resources pursuant to Directive 2004/38. As a result, Germany found itself exempted from providing any justification in relation to its rules: Article 18 TFEU was declared irrelevant; and Article 24(1) of Directive 2004/38 did not apply since Ms Dano did not fall within the personal scope of the Directive.

Leaving aside any more critical assessment of this case law, and of its compatibility with the hierarchy of sources as elaborated by the Court in a consistent jurisprudence,[54] this shift in interpretation also has repercussions for our reflection on economic justifications. The Court's new approach means that if, before, secondary legislation provided the floor of the rights conferred by Union law and the Treaty provided the ceiling, now Directive 2004/38, in most cases,[55] exhausts the rights conferred on non-economically active migrants. In this way, the Directive has become the floor *and* the ceiling of rights conferred by Union law. As a result, a national rule which is consistent with the Directive is consistent with Union law, and the necessity and proportionality assessment no longer plays a role. This is crucial given that, as said above, the rights of movement of economically inactive migrants are limited primarily by the desire to protect the welfare state from claims by those extraneous to the welfare community. While the Treaty provisions remained the main focus, it was open to the Union citizen to argue that she was in fact part of *that* welfare community. Furthermore, it was for the Member State

[52] Case C-200/02 *Chen* EU:C:2004:639.

[53] Case C-408/03 *Commission and Belgium* (sufficient resources) EU:C:2006:192.

[54] On this issue, see N Nic Shuibhne, 'Limits rising, duties ascending: the changing legal shape of Union citizenship' (2015) 52 *CML Rev* 889.

[55] The Treaty provisions are still relevant when the Directive does not apply, such as in the case of challenges to rules imposed by the Member State of nationality to outward and circular migration, although in the latter case the Directive applies by 'analogy'. See n 44.

to prove that satisfying that claim would transform the claimant into an 'unreasonable burden', not necessarily an easy task given that a single claim will never have any effect on the welfare budget of the host State; and that the effect of cumulative claims is almost impossible to assess,[56] not least since there seems to be a paucity of relevant statistical data. Similarly, a defence based on the threat of welfare tourism is also difficult to sustain given that there is little if any evidence that welfare tourism is a motive for migration.[57]

The shift from Treaty assessment to a straightforward application of Directive 2004/38 therefore allows the 'economic justification' to be internalised: the assessment made by the legislature as to the risks to national welfare communities from the migration of economically inactive people has been accepted by the Court, which no longer requests from the Member States an ad hoc assessment of the impact of the single claim on the welfare state. Here, just compare the earlier case of *Martínez Sala*—a claimant lawfully resident in Germany by virtue of national law and entitled to full equal treatment in relation to benefits[58]—to the above-mentioned, and more recent, case of *Dano*—a claimant lawfully present in Germany but somehow excluded from the protection of both Treaty and Directive.

Furthermore, and given the lack of any statistical information, it should be queried whether the need to protect the welfare resources of the host State is the only driver behind Directive 2004/38. In other words, it could be argued that the Directive, as recently interpreted by the Court, is as much about protecting unwarranted claims as it is about apportioning the allocation of welfare responsibilities in a more integrated EU. And that allocation is made along traditional national citizenship lines: it is the state of nationality that bears primary responsibility for the welfare claims of non-economically active individuals in need of support.[59] This is the case even for those citizens who have established genuine links with the host society, for instance, by having resided there for a long time.[60] Unless those individuals have

[56] In Case C-140/12 *Brey* (n 18), the Court held that in order to ascertain the burden on the national social assistance system of granting a benefit to a pensioner 'it may be relevant ... to determine the proportion of the beneficiaries of that benefit who are Union citizens in receipt of a retirement pension in another Member State' (para 78).

[57] See *A fact finding analysis on the impact on the Member States' social security systems of the entitlements of non-active intra-EU migrants to special non-contributory cash benefits and healthcare granted on the basis of residence*. Report prepared on behalf of DG Employment Social Affairs and Inclusion via DG Justice Framework Contract (14 October 2013, revised 16 December 2013).

[58] Case C-85/96 *Martínez Sala* (n 23); see also Case C-456/02 *Trojani* (n 24).

[59] On these issues see further E Spaventa, 'Earned Citizenship—Understanding Union Citizenship Through its Scope' in D Kochenov (ed), *Citizenship and Federalism in the European Union: the Role of Rights* (Cambridge University Press, 2015, forthcoming).

[60] And the case law on the public policy/security derogations seems to point at the continued responsibility of the State of nationality for the misbehaviour of their citizens, even when the latter have spent most of their lives in another Member State. See eg Case C-145/09 *Tsakouridis* EU:C:2010:708; Case C-348/09 *PI* EU:C:2012:300; on the idea of a 'qualitative' element to integration, see Case C-378/12 *Onuekwere v Secretary of State for the Home Department* EU:C:2014:13; Case C-400/12 *Secretary of*

also satisfied the conditions provided for in the Directive (inextricably linked to wealth),[61] they continue to be excluded from the host welfare society.[62]

IV. THE MEMBER STATE OF NATIONALITY AND ITS RESPONSIBILITIES

The fact that more recent Union citizenship cases simply reinforce the allocation of responsibility of the Union citizen to the welfare community of origin is shown also, and possibly especially, by the case law concerning the responsibilities of the Member State of nationality. Here, the full force of the traditional *modus interpretandi* of the Court results in the non-economic migrant being able to challenge restrictions to their right to movement even when budgetary considerations might be paramount. In other words, whilst the Court accepts that it is legitimate for Member States to require that the (migrant) claimant continues to have a real link with the welfare community of origin, the mere desire to reduce the welfare bill is not sufficient to justify a barrier to movement of the economically inactive citizen. Hence, in this context, economic justifications are again not permitted: the link of belonging to the welfare community is not severed by absence from the national territory. For instance, in *Stewart*,[63] a young person with Down's syndrome made a claim for incapacity benefits; however, the claim was refused on the ground that Ms Stewart was not present in the UK, and had not been so for at least 26 weeks in the 52 weeks immediately prior to the claim. The Stewart family had in fact been living in Spain for more than 10 years, albeit the father had worked in the United Kingdom during that time; moreover, Ms Stewart had been able to receive disability living allowance from the UK whilst living in Spain.

The Court found, inter alia, that the minimum presence requirement was a barrier to Ms Stewart's right to move, in that it might naturally deter her from moving abroad. The UK claimed that the rules were justified on two grounds: first of all, in order to ensure that there is a genuine link between claimant and Member

State for the Home Department v MG EU:C:2014:9. On these issues, see E Spaventa, 'Once a foreigner always a foreigner: who does not belong here anymore? Expulsion Measures' in H Verschueren (ed), *Residence, Employment and Social Rights of Mobile Persons* (Intersentia 2016), 89.

[61] S de Mars, 'Economically inactive EU migrants and the United Kingdom's National Health Service: unreasonable burdens without real links?' (2014) 39 *EL Rev* 770, analyses the Commission's claim that the NHS, the UK's National Health Service, which is free at the point of use, satisfies the condition of comprehensive health insurance. Thus, economically inactive migrants coming to the UK would only have to possess sufficient resources in order to obtain a residence permit.

[62] Furthermore, the Court has superimposed on the Directive some qualitative criteria in order to be able to benefit from the enhanced protection deriving from having stayed for a considerable time in the host State; see Case C-378/12 *Onuekwere* (n 60); Case C-400/12 *MG* (n 60). The Court has also given a very broad interpretation of the 'imperative grounds of public security' which, pursuant to Art 28(3) Directive 2004/38, are the only grounds that can justify the expulsion of a Union citizen who has resided in the host State for more than 10 years, see Case C-348/09 *PI* (n 60). On 'imperative grounds of public security', see also Ch 10 in this volume.

[63] Case C-503/09 *Stewart v Secretary of State for Work and Pensions* EU:C:2011:500.

State; and, second, to guarantee the financial balance of the national social security system. The Court found both aims to be, in theory, compatible with the Treaty: yet, the legislation was incompatible with EU law insofar as it did not allow the claimant to prove a 'real link' with the UK welfare community in ways alternative to past presence. The Court then gave instructions as to the elements which might be relevant to such an assessment: Ms Stewart was already receiving disability living allowance and national insurance contributions were credited to her account in the UK; her parents were both in receipt of retirement pensions from the UK and her father had worked there; and Ms Stewart had been born and had spent a significant part of her life in the UK. The Court then found that the same considerations also applied in relation to the aim to guarantee the financial balance of the national social security system; and it concluded that 'the necessity of establishing a genuine and sufficient connection between the claimant and the competent Member State enables that State to *satisfy itself that the economic cost of paying the benefit at issue in the main proceedings does not become unreasonable*'.[64]

This notion of continued responsibility of the State of origin is visible also in other strands of the case law. In the above-mentioned case of *Alokpa*,[65] the Court also relied on the fact that Ms Alokpa could have gone to France, the state of nationality of her children, where she would have (probably) enjoyed a derived right of residence.[66] This was the case even though neither Ms Alokpa nor her children had any emotional or actual link with that Member State. It is the Member State of nationality which therefore bears primary responsibility for its nationals.

Similarly, in relation to students wishing to go and study in another Member State, the Court has been generous in finding that Member States may not impose criteria for eligibility for financial support for studies abroad which are indirectly discriminatory[67] or unduly penalise those who have taken advantage of their free movement rights.[68] In these cases, the Court falls just short of admitting that, in most cases, the real link between awarding-state and beneficiary will be satisfied by the latter possessing the nationality of the former. For instance, in the *Thiele Meneses* case,[69] the issue related to a permanent residence condition required in order to be able to export an education grant to another Member State. The claimant in that case had never resided in Germany, even though he possessed German

[64] ibid, para 103 (emphasis added).

[65] Case C-86/12 *Alokpa* (n 10).

[66] In France she would presumably be protected (through her children's right to stay in the territory of the EU) by EU law: see Case C-34/09 *Ruiz Zambrano* (n 10). The result is rather bizarre since even though EU law theoretically does not apply to purely internal situations, the Alokpa family would be protected when static but not when migrating.

[67] See eg Case C-275/12 *Elrick v Bezirksregierung Köln* EU:C:2013:684; Joined Cases C-11 and 12/06 *Morgan and Bucher* EU:C:2007:626.

[68] eg Case C-359/13 *Martens v Minister van Onderwijs, Cultuur en Wetenschap* EU:C:2014:2240.

[69] eg Joined Cases C-523 and 585/11 *Prinz and Seeberger* EU:C:2013:524; Case C-220/12 *Thiele Meneses v Region Hannover* EU:C:2013:683.

nationality and had moved there only for the purposes of tertiary education. After six months, he decided to transfer his degree to the Netherlands and applied for an education grant, which was denied since he resided in Turkey rather than Germany as required by the relevant rules. The Court found that the rules at issue constituted a barrier to movement since they were likely to discourage students from exercising their right to move and study in another Member State. In examining the justification issue, the Court of Justice stated:

> The Court has recognised that it may be legitimate for a Member State, in order to ensure that the grant of assistance to cover the maintenance costs of students from other Member States does not become an unreasonable burden which could have consequences for the overall level of assistance which may be granted by that State, to grant such assistance only to students who have demonstrated a certain degree of integration into the society of that State, and *if a risk exists of such an unreasonable burden, theoretically*, similar considerations may apply as regards the award by a Member State of education or training grants to students wishing to study in other Member States.[70]

It is therefore much more difficult for the Member State of nationality to rely on economic considerations in order to justify a restriction on the free movement rights of economically inactive citizens than it is for the host State.

V. ACCESS TO WELFARE BENEFITS: THE ECONOMIC LINK AND THE SENSE OF BELONGING

If economically inactive citizens remain the responsibility of their Member State of origin, so that host Member States are able to erect barriers to access to the host welfare society which are justified on economic grounds, whilst Member States of nationality are prevented from hindering movement through measures intended to reduce the overall welfare bill, the situation is very different in relation to those migrants who establish an economic link. In this respect, the link with a past or present economic activity allows the individual mobility also across welfare societies (at least to a certain extent), although the weaker the link with the economic activity the easier it is for the Member State to justify restricting welfare entitlement.

Thus, for instance, in the case of *N*,[71] the Court restated that the reasons why a Union citizen takes up employment are immaterial to her gaining the rights conferred by Treaty or secondary legislation, as the case might be. Article 24(2) of Directive 2004/38 excludes a duty to ensure equal treatment in relation to maintenance grants for migrant students who have yet to gain the right to permanent residency. However, once an individual has triggered one of the economic free

[70] Case C-220/12 *Thiele Meneses* ibid, para 35 (emphasis added).

[71] Case C-46/12 *N v Styrelsen for Videregående Uddannelser og Uddannelsesstøtte* EU:C:2013:97, especially para 47.

movement provisions, and even when she has done so for the sole purpose of gaining eligibility to maintenance grants,[72] she benefits from the full right to equal treatment. Similarly, in *Giersch*,[73] the Court was asked to determine the compatibility with the free movement of workers (specifically, Article 45 TFEU and Article 7(2) of Regulation 1612/68) of a residence requirement for eligibility to a study grant. The claimants were children of frontier workers employed in Luxembourg who were denied a study grant on the grounds of residence. The economic implications of the case were considerable since, at the time of referral, there were another 600 cases pending in front of the national court on the same issue just for the 2010/11 year. In examining whether the residence requirement, undoubtedly indirectly discriminatory, was justified, the Court of Justice explicitly excluded the possibility of relying on budgetary considerations; it held:

> As regards the justification based on the additional burden which would result from non-application of the residence requirement, it should be borne in mind that, although budgetary considerations may underlie a Member State's choice of social policy and influence the nature or scope of the social protection measures which it wishes to adopt, *they do not in themselves constitute an aim pursued by that policy* and cannot therefore justify discrimination against migrant workers.[74]

The Court then found that the aim of increasing the percentage of resident population with a higher education degree was a legitimate objective and that whilst, in principle, a residence requirement was appropriate to achieve that aim, its blanket application, especially to the claimants in the case at issue, was disproportionate. Again, then, when there is a link with the internal market the Court is more likely to demand a careful scrutiny of the rules limiting entitlement to benefits, including a scrutiny over the personal circumstances of the actual claimants. Broad-brush rules, even when justified in theory, might be incompatible with EU law in practice.

Finally, it seems that pensioners might also benefit from some preferential treatment, possibly because of their connection with the internal market.[75] In *Brey*, the Court was faced with the compatibility with the Treaty of Austrian rules which had the effect of excluding pensioners from other Member States from a compensatory supplement. Application for the benefit implied, in fact, that the claimant did not possess sufficient resources to establish lawful residence in Austria. Mr Brey, a German national in receipt of a German pension, applied for the benefit and was refused it on those grounds. The Court of Justice therefore had to decide whether the rules at issue were compatible with the provisions of Directive 2004/38, and in particular with Article 7(1)(b), which stipulates that Union citizens wishing to

[72] And *cf Dano*, where the Court held that Member States must maintain the right to refuse social benefits to economically inactive citizens that move 'solely in order to obtain another Member State's social assistance' (para 78).

[73] Case C-20/12 *Giersch and others v Luxembourg* EU:C:2013:411.

[74] ibid, para 51 (emphasis added).

[75] Regulation 883/2004 on the coordination of social security systems [2004] OJ L166/1.

reside in another Member State must have sufficient resources so as not to become a burden on the social assistance system of the host Member States, interpreted in the light of Article 14(3) of the same Directive, which provides that an expulsion measure shall not be the automatic consequence of a citizen's recourse to the social assistance system of the host Member State.

The Court found, first, that the conditional rights provided by the Directive to economically inactive citizens are based on the subordination of those rights to the 'legitimate interests' of the Member States, in that case the '*protection of their public finances*'.[76] It then turned to provide a broad interpretation of 'social assistance' for the purposes of Directive 2004/38, as all assistance that can be claimed by those who do not have sufficient resources to meet their basic needs.[77] The Court acknowledged that the fact that an individual who is not economically active needs to receive a benefit to supplement her pension might be an indication that she does not have sufficient resources to avoid becoming a burden on the social assistance system of the host State. But the Court then adopted the same interpretation that characterised its earlier case law: free movement rights derive directly from the Treaty; any limitation must be necessary and proportionate; and blanket rules are not compatible with that requirement but rather the relevant authority must make an assessment based on the personal circumstances of the claimant. In order to determine whether the claim would in fact impose a burden on the social assistance system, the national authority must make 'an overall assessment of the *specific burden* which granting that benefit would place on the social assistance system as a whole'[78] by reference to the personal circumstances of the claimant. And 'in order to ascertain more precisely the extent of the burden which that grant would place on the national social assistance system, it may be relevant … to determine the proportion of the beneficiaries of that benefit who are Union citizens in receipt of a retirement pension in another Member State'.[79]

The Court in *Brey* therefore requires the national authorities to carry out a very precise assessment of the burden on the social assistance system—one that might in practice be almost impossible to make, especially by lower courts. In this respect, and as said before, *Brey* falls within the more traditional interpretation of the Treaty (and the Directive as 'implementation' of the Treaty rights); and, consequently, the right of Member States to rely on an economic justification to justify limiting a free movement right is interpreted extremely narrowly. In this respect, it is useful juxtaposing the rulings in *Brey* and *Dano*. Both cases related to economically inactive individuals, that is, people whose right of residence would be established pursuant to Article 7(1)(b) of Directive 2004/38.

[76] Case C-140/12 *Brey* (n 18), para 55 (emphasis added).
[77] ibid, para 61.
[78] ibid, para 77 (emphasis added).
[79] ibid, para 78.

First of all, Mr Brey's income was very low, given the fact that his wife was entirely dependent on him. They relied on earnings of €1,089.75 before tax, approximately half of which went on rent. This left the couple with a disposable income of less than €560, through which they had to pay all living expenses including utilities. Ms Dano, on the other hand, was living free of charge with her sister (so possibly we could estimate that contribution at around a minimum of €300), who also provided for her and her son's maintenance. On top of this, Ms Dano was receiving €307 in child maintenance benefits, entitlement to which had not been called into question by the German authorities. It seems therefore that, as a matter of fact, there was no huge difference in the resources available to Mr Brey and those available to Ms Dano, with Ms Dano having possibly slightly more disposable income in real economic terms.

Secondly, Mr Brey had no apparent connection to the host State, besides a decision to reside in the latter rather than in his state of nationality; Ms Dano, on the other hand, had joined a family member in the host State and had been present within its territory for a considerable period of time (three years or more, with her son actually having been born there). It could be presumed, then, that Ms Dano's connection to Germany was stronger than Mr Brey's connection to Austria.[80]

Yet, despite the above, both the mode of reasoning of the Court and the results achieved in the two cases are very different. Both rulings related, basically, to whether an economically inactive citizen is entitled to subsistence benefits of any sort, or whether recourse to such benefits de facto indicates lack of sufficient resources. In both cases, the claimants were in possession of a certificate issued by the public authorities; in both cases, the claimants were denied the benefits applied for (directly or indirectly) on the grounds that they did not fulfil the sufficient resources criterion, so that even though their presence might have been lawful it was not relevant to establishing legal residence for the purposes of accessing the benefits in question. In *Brey*, however, the Court starts from the premise of a Union citizen's entitlement: if the Union citizen is exercising her Treaty right, then any limitation to this right, including the sufficient resources requirement, must be interpreted narrowly and assessed in relation to the principle of proportionality.[81] A rule which simply excludes economically inactive Union citizens from a certain benefit is inconsistent with said principle insofar as the personal circumstances of the claimant cannot be taken into account.

[80] The Court makes repeated references to the fact that Ms Dano had moved to Germany to receive benefits; however, there is nothing in the ruling or in the Opinion to suggest that was actually the case; rather the expression seems directly borrowed from the German legislation under consideration that excluded the benefits at issue for foreign work-seekers and those foreign nationals who had entered the national territory 'in order to obtain social assistance' (see *Dano* ruling para 26).

[81] See Case C-140/12 *Brey* (n 18), para 70: 'Lastly, it should be borne in mind that, since the right to freedom of movement is—as a fundamental principle of EU law—the general rule, the conditions laid down in Article 7(1)(b) of Directive 2004/38 must be construed *narrowly* … and in compliance with the limits imposed by EU law and the principle of *proportionality*' (emphasis added).

In *Dano*, the approach is turned on its feet: this time, the rights conferred on Union citizens (and primarily the right to equal treatment) are subsumed in the rights granted by Article 24 of Directive 2004/38, which, being *lex specialis*, applies with preference/instead of the Treaty rights. But Article 24(1) can only be actioned within the scope of the Directive and since, in the eyes of the Court, Ms Dano did not meet the requirements provided for in Article 7(1)(b) of that measure, she was then not entitled to equal treatment.

It is difficult to reconcile the two rulings; whilst *Dano* was a Grand Chamber ruling, and therefore might carry more weight, it did not overrule *Brey*. Advocate General Wathelet in *Dano* suggested that the two cases could be distinguished having regard to the national rules at issue: in *Brey*, anyone who applied for the benefit in question would be failing the sufficient resources hurdle, and therefore would not be able to establish lawful residence. In *Dano*, the benefit would be refused to those 'whose right of residence is based on the sole objective of seeking employment or obtaining social assistance'.[82] Thym, on the other hand, reads the two rulings as expressions of different models of transnational solidarity, one based on territorial presence and the other on promoting social cohesion.[83]

Without prejudice as to the question of whether the two rulings can in fact be reconciled, to me the two rulings are symptomatic of the Court's preference for certain (good) citizens: pensioners and students are both 'good'.[84] The former have contributed to the economy (and the internal market more generally even when they have not migrated), the latter are well positioned to make a contribution to the economy in the future. Both categories therefore fit in the economic paradigm which remains the core of the European Union project. The same is true for those who are attempting to enter the labour market of another Member State: by definition, work-seekers are doing what European integration suggests they should do: move from one market to the other to ensure a better fit between supply and demand for labour. On the other hand, that is not true for those with no connection to the internal market: the Danos, but also the Trojanis, of this world continue to be left out of the integration project. Possibly this is both inevitable, given the fact that the EU only possesses very limited redistributive power, and consistent with the dominant political mood post-recession, since there seems to be very little appetite for pure transnational solidarity.[85] But, the repatriation of welfare

[82] AG Wathelet's Opinion in Case C-140/12 *Brey* (n 18), para 123.

[83] D Thym, 'The elusive limits of solidarity: residence rights of and social benefits for economically inactive Union Citizens' (2015) 52 *CML Rev* 17.

[84] On the good/bad citizen see also L Azoulai, 'The (Mis)Construction of the European Individual. Two Essays on Union Citizenship Law', EUI Working papers, 2014/14 http://cadmus.eui.eu/bitstream/handle/1814/33293/LAW_WP_%202014_14.pdf?sequence=1.

[85] See eg 'Angela Merkel dashes Greek hopes of rescue bid', *The Guardian*, 11 February 2010; 'Merkel reaches her overdraft limit' *Spiegel Online International* (www.spiegel.de/international/germany/merkel-reaches-her-overdraft-limit-greek-bailout-could-push-german-debt-through-the-roof-a-691802.html), 28 April 2010; also F de Witte, 'Transnational Solidarity and the Mediation of Conflicts of Justice in Europe' (2012) 18 *European Law Journal* 694.

responsibilities almost exclusively to the State of nationality might signal the failure of the Union citizenship experiment, in that it seems clear that the latter is far from being an innovative form of supranational citizenship allowing its beneficiaries multiple, and more nuanced, links of belonging. Rather it reinforces the link between citizen and her State of nationality, also by strengthening that link so that absences to other EU states do not necessarily terminate the welfare responsibilities of the home state.

VI. CONCLUSIONS

The first preliminary conclusion is that there is no absolute 'dogma' whereby economic justifications are incompatible with EU law. Rather, whether they are, or are not, compatible with the Treaties will depend very much on the aims pursued by integration in a given area. In the case of the internal market, one of the main aims of integration is to dispose of economic protectionism; economic justifications for discriminatory measures would allow Member States to engage in protectionist policies and are therefore inconsistent with the very raison d'être of the internal market. Conversely, non-discriminatory measures might be legitimately justified by policy considerations even when economic factors form part of that policy: public budgets are unfortunately finite, and most policies require funding. Economic considerations are therefore legitimate in pursuing other public policy aims. In relation to inward migration of non-economic actors with no link to the internal market, on the other hand, economic justifications are accepted by both the legislature and the Court: thus, the limits and conditions prescribed by Directive 2004/38, as more recently interpreted in the case law, ensure that Member States can shelter their welfare communities from economically inactive Union citizens.

The second conclusion is that whilst economic considerations seem to be paramount in relation to claims made by non-economically active citizens to the host welfare society, they become close to irrelevant in relation to claims made by migrants vis-à-vis their Member States of origin. This means that, on the one hand, the Court has become more sensitive to the political compromise made in Directive 2004/38, a compromise which clearly excluded a meaningful notion of transnational solidarity beyond the internal market. On the other hand, though, the Court engages in a close scrutiny of the reasons justifying the refusal, by the Member State of origin, of the possibility to export benefits in another Member State. In this way, it might fill a gap:[86] if solidarity is not provided for by the host Member State then, where possible,[87] it might have to be provided by the Member State of origin, and

[86] Although possibly opening another gap in relation to co-ordination of social security benefits, see H Verschueren, 'Preventing "Benefit Tourism" in the EU: A Narrow or Broad Interpretation of the Possibilities offered by the ECJ in *Dano*' (2015) 52 *CML Rev* 363.

[87] See eg Case C-406/04 *De Cuyper* (n 2).

the economic burden of so doing is close to irrelevant. After all, had the claimant not moved to another Member State, she would have been able to draw (unchallenged) upon the welfare resources of her State of nationality.

The third conclusion is that this variable relevance of economic considerations might tell us something about the very nature of Union citizenship. The more recent case law demonstrates that its potential has imploded, so that we witness a reallocation of welfare responsibilities along traditional nationality lines, at least when there is no internal market/economic dimension. The transformative effect of Union citizenship is much more limited than earlier case law might have suggested: it empowers citizens to move also when economically inactive merely by calling into question the link between benefit entitlement and residence in the national territory. It is possible that in the current political climate this is as good as it gets; whether this amounts to 'supranational' citizenship is, however, open to debate.

4

(Dis)Enfranchisement and Free Movement

AIDAN O'NEILL

I. INTRODUCTION

THIS CHAPTER CONSIDERS the issue of disenfranchisement operating as a possible disincentive to the exercise of free movement rights. It looks at whether and how Member States' rules of electoral law can fall within the ambit of EU law and, if so, how they might be justified for their compatibility with EU law. The particular situation examined is the disenfranchisement from national elections and constitutional referendums in their Member State of origin for those who have exercised their free movement rights within the EU, with particular focus on the situation in relation to the UK's Brexit referendum. The chapter highlights that the individuals arguably most affected by the result of this referendum are British citizens who have exercised their free movement rights and now live elsewhere in the EU (some 2.2 million people) and separately nationals of other Member States who have exercised their EU free movement rights to move to the UK (some 2.3 million people). But the franchise for the Brexit referendum denies the vote to British nationals living abroad (if they have been away for more than 15 years) and excludes all and any EU citizens living in the UK from the right to vote, unless they happen to hold Irish, Cypriot or Maltese nationality. Non-EU Commonwealth citizens resident in the UK are given the right to vote, despite the fact that the result of the referendum has no effect on their rights or status, since they have no rights which they can claim directly under EU law. The Brexit referendum franchise, then, seems both over-inclusive (in covering Commonwealth citizens who will be unaffected by it) and under-inclusive (in excluding non-Commonwealth EU citizens and British nationals who are long-term resident elsewhere in the EU, whose rights and status will be directly affected). The question raised in this chapter is whether the Brexit referendum franchise might be said to be unlawful as a matter of EU law because it is disproportionate and/or discriminatory.

II. THE EUROPEAN UNION AS A UNION OF DEMOCRACIES AND AS A DEMOCRATIC UNION

The Grand Chamber of the Court of Justice has stated that

> the principle of democracy forms part of European Community law and was expressly enshrined in Article 6(1) EU as one of the foundations of the European Union. As one of the principles common to the Member States, it must be taken into consideration when interpreting acts of secondary law.[1]

Democracy is, then, a governing principle of the idea, and the ideals, of the European Union. Article 2 of the Treaty on European Union (TEU) provides that

> [t]he Union is founded on the values of respect for human dignity, freedom, democracy, equality, the rule of law and respect for human rights, including the rights of persons belonging to minorities. These values are common to the Member States in a society in which pluralism, non-discrimination, tolerance, justice, solidarity and equality between women and men prevail.

Only democracies can become Member States of the European Union and Article 7 TEU makes it clear that if a Member State is in serious and persistent breach of any of Article 2 TEU then its rights (but not its obligations) under the Treaties may be suspended.

Article 10 TEU affirms that:

> 1. The functioning of the Union shall be founded on *representative democracy*.
>
> 2. Citizens are *directly represented* at Union level in the European Parliament. Member States are represented in the European Council by their Heads of State or Government and in the Council by their governments, themselves *democratically accountable* either to their national Parliaments, or to their citizens.
>
> 3. Every citizen shall have the right to *participate in the democratic life of the Union*. Decisions shall be taken as openly and as closely as possible to the citizen.
>
> 4. Political parties at European level contribute to forming European political awareness and to expressing the will of citizens of the Union.

III. THE RIGHT TO VOTE AND THE EXERCISE OF FREE MOVEMENT IN THE EUROPEAN UNION

Classically, democratic States have regulated the entitlement to vote within the national polity based on a combination of nationality and residence. The central case for entitlement to vote in a democratic polity is for an individual to be both

[1] Case C-518/07 *Commission and European Data Protection Supervisor v Germany* EU:C:2010:125, para 41.

a national of that State, and to be resident within it. It is, however, consistent with international law norms for a democratic State to choose, by operation of law, to restrict or deny the right to vote whether to lawfully resident aliens or to non-resident nationals, or alternatively to extend the right to vote beyond its own citizens and, indeed, beyond its borders.

A central pillar of the European Union has, from the outset, been the right of free movement of workers across the Member States. EU law therefore encourages the creation of a class across the Member States of lawfully resident aliens/non-resident nationals. The paradox is that the exercise of these EU law rights (of free movement) results in a (potential) loss of democratic rights. This is because the class of persons who exercise their EU free movement right might find themselves, as a matter of national law, losing their right to vote in their Member State of origin and nationality (because no longer resident there) and yet, as a matter of national law, not gain any right to vote in the Member State to which they have moved because they have the status there of lawfully resident aliens.

There has been increasing awareness that it would be inconsistent with the self-understanding of the European Union as itself a democratic union if individuals' exercise of free movement within the EU were to have their disenfranchisement as an attendant consequence. Thus in late January 2014 the then EU Justice Commissioner and Vice President of the Commission Viviane Reding made a speech to the following effect (emphasis in the original):

> EU citizens who lose the right to vote in national elections and they *do not receive a corresponding right* in their country of residence (as they do in European or local elections) … are *disenfranchised entirely—left without the right to vote, anywhere in the EU.*
>
> *In a certain way such practice is punishing EU citizens for exercising their right to free movement* in the EU.
>
> Disenfranchisement practices such as these have *created in fact—a group of second class citizens* from whom something essential has been taken away from their home country.
>
> …
>
> [W]e have *issued guidance* to those Member States applying disenfranchisement policies. *Five countries* are concerned: *Cyprus, Denmark, Ireland, Malta and the United Kingdom.* I am asking these countries to show *greater flexibility* so that their own nationals are *not automatically denied* their vote after a certain period … We believe these citizens should have the *option of applying to remain* on the electoral roll … This is about empowering EU citizens, who feel strongly about their country and making sure they *are not automatically denied the fundamental democratic right of voting.*
>
> *Never should the right to free movement lead to a loss of rights.*[2]

[2] V Reding, Vice-President of the European Commission, EU Justice Commissioner *Disenfranchisement: defending voting rights for EU citizens abroad* (Midday Statement/Brussels 29 January 2014) (Speech 14/73).

IV. EU CITIZENSHIP: SQUARING THE CIRCLE BETWEEN DEMOCRACY AND FREE MOVEMENT?

The concept of EU citizenship is one attempt to resolve this dilemma and reconcile the principle of democracy in the public square with the continued free circulation of people across the EU. Article 9 TEU states that:

> In all its activities, the Union shall observe the principle of the equality of its citizens, who shall receive equal attention from its institutions, bodies, offices and agencies. Every national of a Member State shall be a citizen of the Union. Citizenship of the Union shall be additional to national citizenship and shall not replace it.

Article 20(1) TFEU confirms the establishment of the concept of EU citizenship which supplements their national citizenship rights in the following terms:

> Citizenship of the Union is hereby established. Every person holding the nationality of a Member State shall be a citizen of the Union. Citizenship of the Union shall be additional to and not replace national citizenship.

Significantly, Article 20(2) TFEU mentions both the right to vote and the rights of free movement under the umbrella concept of EU citizenship. It specifies that:

> 2. Citizens of the Union shall enjoy the rights and be subject to the duties provided for in the Treaties. They shall have, *inter alia*:
>
> (a) the right to move and reside freely within the territory of the Member States;
> (b) the right to vote and to stand as candidates in elections to the European Parliament and in municipal elections in their Member State of residence, under the same conditions as nationals of that State …

The general rule is that the Treaty protections consequent upon free movement do not apply to situations which are wholly internal to a Member State.[3] The reference in Article 20(2)(b) TFEU to voting and standing in elections 'under the same conditions as nationals of that State' seems to imply that the right to vote which is protected under EU law is, in some sense, dependent on the exercise of free movement rights.

On the other hand, the CJEU's constant refrain has been that EU citizenship 'is intended to be the fundamental status of nationals of the Member States'. And there is a growing body of case law—which has not been universally welcomed by courts in the UK[4]—which allows for the EU citizenship rights afforded to individuals to be lawfully be prayed in aid against their Member State of origin regardless of whether free movement rights have in fact been exercised.[5]

[3] Joined Cases C-64 and 65/96 *Ücker and Jacquet* EU:C:1997:285, para 23.

[4] The approach of the CJEU to the interplay of EU citizenship and Member State rules on nationality has been questioned in *Pham v Home Secretary* [2015] UKSC 19, [2015] 1 WLR 1591. See notably Lord Mance at paras [84]–[85], [90].

[5] Case C-34/09 *Zambrano v ONEm* EU:C:2011:124, para 41.

V. THE EU CITIZEN'S RIGHT TO VOTE IN MEMBER STATES' MUNICIPAL ELECTIONS

Enshrining in the Treaties the right of EU citizens to stand and vote in the municipal elections of Member States represents both a significant development and a significant compromise. It is a significant *development* in that, as a matter of EU law, 'resident aliens' who are EU citizens and who have exercised their free movement rights by moving to another Member State, are given rights of democratic participation in their Member State of residence. It is a significant *compromise* in that the right of democratic participation does *not* extend to general elections to the central legislature or government of the Member States.[6]

Further, the Treaty does not itself provide any definition of what is meant by 'municipal elections'. Directive 94/80/EC (the Municipal Elections Directive) is the provision of secondary EU law intended by the EU legislature to give flesh to the implementation of this primary Treaty right to vote. The Municipal Elections Directive notes in its preamble that 'the way in which local government operates in the different Member States is a reflection of different political and legal traditions and is characterized by an abundance of structures'. The preamble continues: 'the term "municipal election" does not mean the same thing in every Member State'. In order, therefore, to clarify its object and extent, a definition is given within the body of Directive 94/80/EC of 'municipal elections' as meaning elections 'at the level of basic local government units and their subdivisions' and which is intended to cover 'elections by direct universal suffrage both to representative councils of municipalities and of members of a municipal executive'.

Article 2(1)(a) of the Municipal Elections Directive defines 'basic local government units' as

> the administrative entities listed in the Annex which, in accordance with the laws of each Member State, contain bodies elected by direct universal suffrage and are empowered to administer, at the basic level of political and administrative organization, certain local affairs on their own responsibility.

So the list of 'basic local government units' sets out the scope of the Directive but leaves it to Member States to tell the Commission what it considers to be its 'basic local government units' and hence what the scope of the Directive is to be within the territory of the Member State. This is an unusual provision for EU law in appearing to delegate to each Member State the decision as to how far EU law extends. And this reference to 'basic local government units and their subdivisions' does not appear in the Treaty. But because the EU citizen's right to vote in Member States' 'municipal elections' is a matter of *primary* EU law—being set out in Article 20(2)(b) TFEU and picked up and repeated in Article 40 of the EU Charter of Fundamental Rights (CFR)—the substance of this rights cannot be

[6] See *R (Tomescu) v Lord President of the Council* [2015] EWHC 3293 (Admin), [2016] ACD 1.

cut down or limited by any provisions of *secondary* EU law, or by any national implementing measures.[7]

There has, to date, been no litigation before the CJEU on the issue as to whether or not the Municipal Elections Directive's reference to 'basic local government units'—which the Directive then leaves for the Member State to specify—correctly reflects and transposes the substance the EU citizen's Treaty right under Article 20(2)(b) TFEU to vote in municipal elections in the Member State where they reside. It is, however, clearly essential for the proper working of the Municipal Elections Directive 94/80/EC that the Member States duly notify the Commission and keep the list of its 'basic local government units' up to date. The United Kingdom has, however, failed to do so. The Annex to the consolidated Directive 94/80/EC continues to list the following bodies as being covered by its provisions in the United Kingdom:

> counties in England; counties, county boroughs and communities in Wales; *regions and Islands in Scotland*; *districts in England, Scotland* and Northern Ireland; London boroughs; parishes in England; the City of London in relation to ward elections for common councilmen.

But regions, islands and district authorities were abolished in Scotland as local government units as long ago as 1 April 1996, when the Local Government (Scotland) Act 1994 came into force and replaced them with new unitary authorities. Further, the Scotland Act 1998 came into force from May 1999, and since then there have been elections by direct universal suffrage to the Scottish Parliament (and also to the Welsh Assembly and to the Northern Ireland Assembly). The United Kingdom has simply failed to bring these significant constitutional changes in the government of the United Kingdom to the attention of the Commission, however. The out-of-date Annex to Directive 94/80/EC therefore gives no proper indication to EU citizens as to precisely the extent to which EU law protects their voting rights within the UK.

Some discussion of just what is protected by the Treaty/Charter right to vote in municipal elections appears in *R (Chester) v Secretary of State for Justice/McGeoch v Lord President of the Council* where it was argued on behalf of Scottish appellant, Mr McGeoch, that the Treaty vested in all EU citizens as a matter of EU law the right to vote in all elections within the Member States other than general elections and therefore could be relied upon to vindicate an EU law protected right to stand and vote in elections to the devolved Scottish Parliament. The argument was complicated by the fact that, contrary to the requirements of Article 2(2) of Directive 94/80/EC, this Annex had *not* been updated to reflect the reorganisation of local government in the UK since 1994 and/or the introduction of devolution in the UK, leaving it unclear whether or not, as a matter of EU law, EU citizens can claim a right to vote in elections to the Scottish Parliament and/or to the Welsh

[7] Joined Cases C-293 and 594/12 *Digital Rights Ireland* EU:C:2014:238, para 69 and Case C-362/14 *Schrems v Data Protection Commissioner* EU:C:2015:650, para 95.

and Northern Irish Assemblies. In *R (Chester)/McGeoch* Lord Mance just thought the answer to this matter was 'obviously not', noting:

> European Union law refers in various contexts, which have already been set out in this judgment, to voting in European parliamentary elections and in 'municipal' elections, and to no other elections. It is *obvious* that Scottish parliamentary elections fall within neither category ... That municipal elections are local government elections *at a lower level of government, closer to people and with a more direct responsibility for service delivery*, is furthermore consistent with the nature of the units found (though in the case of Scotland, not yet updated) in the annex to Council Directive 94/80/EC of 19 December 1994, which lays down detailed arrangements for the exercise of the right to vote and stand in municipal elections by Union citizens residing in a member state of which they are not nationals.[8]

Quite where Lord Mance divined his test of 'municipal elections' as referred to in Article 20(2)(b) TFEU and Articles 40 CFR as 'obviously' meaning, for the purposes of EU law, 'elections at a lower level of government, closer to people and with a more direct responsibility for service delivery' than the devolved legislatures is not known. It certainly does not appear in the Treaty itself. As we have seen the UK originally listed in the Directive's Annex *all* council and local government elections in the UK, excluding only elections to the Westminster Parliament. And, since devolution, UK law has continued to recognise in its national law the right of EU citizens to vote in elections to the devolved Parliaments and Assemblies as if they were a further tier of local government. The UK therefore acts *as if* the phrase 'municipal elections' in the UK means, for the purposes of EU law, elections to the Scottish Parliament and to the Welsh and Northern Irish legislative assemblies.

VI. THE EU CITIZEN'S RIGHT TO VOTE IN ELECTIONS TO THE EUROPEAN PARLIAMENT

It is clear that the conferring on individuals of rights associated with national citizenship remains wholly within the exercise of the sovereign power of the Member States. Thus in *Spain v United Kingdom*[9] the Grand Chamber confirmed the lawfulness of the UK conferring voting rights for the European Parliament on Commonwealth citizens who were resident in Gibraltar but who were not also EU citizens.

But, once national citizenship has been conferred by the law of the Member States, the CJEU Grand Chamber has held that the Member State's *withdrawal* of these national citizenship rights or status may bring matters within the ambit of EU law (and the supervision of the CJEU) because of its possible adverse effects on the

[8] *R (Chester) v Secretary of State for Justice/McGeoch v Lord President of the Council* [2013] UKSC 63, [2014] AC 271 per Lord Mance at [45].

[9] Case C-145/04 *Spain v United Kingdom* EU:C:2006:543.

individual's EU law rights *qua* EU citizen.[10] Accordingly a Member State's undoubted power—in exercise of its powers as a sovereign State in international law—to lay down the conditions for the possible loss or deprivation of that of nationality also requires to be exercised with due regard to the principles of EU law. The fact that such issues fall centrally within the legal competence of the Member States does *not* preclude the concurrent application of EU law in this area.[11] Because the exercise of that Member State's power against its own national *also* directly affected the rights conferred on that Member State's national *qua* EU citizen, the matter was held by the CJEU in *Rottmann v Bavaria* to fall within the ambit of EU law.

In *Eman and Sevinger v Netherlands*[12] the CJEU Grand Chamber ruled that the (European) Netherlands Government was *obliged* as a matter of EU law to make provision for Dutch nationals living outside the (European) Netherlands but still inside the Kingdom of the Netherlands (namely, in Aruba and the Netherlands Antilles) to vote for the European Parliament.[13] This decision established the principle that, as a matter of EU law, the right to vote in elections to the European Parliament could be prayed in aid, and directly relied upon, by EU citizens against the Member State of which they were nationals regardless of whether they had exercised their free movement rights within the EU (or indeed had left the EU altogether). Article 14(3) TEU now enshrines the principle of direct universal suffrage in respect of elections to the European Parliament. It provides:

> The members of the European Parliament shall be elected for a term of five years by *direct universal suffrage* in a free and secret ballot.[14]

The UK's Declaration 64 on the franchise for elections to the European Parliament which is appended to the Lisbon Treaty states that:

> The United Kingdom notes that Article 14 of the Treaty on European Union and other provisions of the Treaties *are not intended to change the basis for the franchise for elections to the European Parliament.*

[10] Case C-135/08 *Rottmann v Bavaria* EU:C:2010:104.

[11] This claim was strongly doubted in the Court of Appeal in *R (G1) v Secretary of State for the Home Department* [2012] EWCA Civ 867, [2013] QB 1008 per Laws LJ at paras [38]–[39], [43].

[12] Case C-300/04 *Eman and Sevinger v Netherlands* EU:C:2006:545.

[13] Dutch constitutional law in the form of the *Statuut voor het Koninkrijk der Nederlanden* ('Charter for the Kingdom of the Netherlands'), as amended in 2010, provides that the Kingdom of the Netherlands consists of the (European) Netherlands, Aruba, Curaçao and Saint Maarten. Only the Netherlands is within the EU. Aruba, Curaçao and Sint Maarten are defined under the Treaties as overseas countries and territories subject to subject to the specific association arrangements with the EU. The Netherlands and the other entities forming part of the Kingdom of the Netherlands share a single nationality, head of State, foreign policy and defence. However, areas such as the franchise remain autonomous, although co-operation is possible. This means that, as a matter of Dutch constitutional law, citizens of Aruba share a common Dutch nationality with the citizens of the other constituent countries of the Kingdom of the Netherlands. But conditions relative to the *franchise* are, under Dutch constitutional law, a matter for each independent constituent country making up the Kingdom of the Netherlands.

[14] Emphasis added.

In *Delvigne v Commune de Lesparre Médoc and Préfet de la Gironde*[15] the CJEU considered the case of a French national, who following his conviction of a serious crime (punishable by at least five years' imprisonment) was, by operation of a general French law, also automatically and indefinitely deprived of his civic rights in France, including his right to vote in the European Parliament. Detention clearly also deprives an individual of the possibility of his exercising free movement rights. In its judgment in *Delvigne* the CJEU confirmed that the right to vote in elections to the European Parliament was a substantive right which was protected under and in terms of EU law and which an EU citizen could rely upon against his own Member State regardless of whether he or she had exercised free movement rights (in any event, a difficult condition to fulfil for the imprisoned). While limitations might be imposed on the exercise of this fundamental right by Member States, these national limitations would be compatible with EU law only if and insofar as they complied with the EU law requirements of proportionality. Because French law allows a person in Mr Delvigne's situation to apply for, and obtain, reinstatement of the civic rights lost following his conviction and imprisonment, the CJEU considered that the national legislation at issue survived its scrutiny for EU law compatibility.

The decision in *Delvigne* appears to be a fairly routine application of EU law which appears to have been established in *Eman and Sevinger v Netherlands.*[16] In *R (Chester)*[17] Lord Mance, somewhat controversially, had denied that EU law accorded individuals the right to vote in the European Parliament. He opined that the CJEU in *Eman and Sevinger* had ruled only that 'voting by nationals residing outside their own member state' fell within the scope of EU law. Only in that context, he said, was the principle of equal treatment applied by the CJEU to rule that the Netherlands could not lawfully discriminate in the voting rights to the European Parliament which it chose to afford to those of its nationals who were resident outside the EU. Lord Mance also asserted (at paragraph 84) that his conclusions on EU law were *acte clair* and so required no preliminary reference to the CJEU despite the UKSC being the national court of final instance. This somewhat strained reading of *Eman and Sevinger* cannot, however, survive the CJEU decision in *Delvigne*, which makes it clear beyond peradventure that the franchise to the European Parliament falls within the scope of EU law. The protections of EU law in this regard are independent of the exercise of free movement rights and can be prayed in aid by a national against his or her Member State.

[15] Case C-650/13 *Thierry Delvigne v Commune de Lesparre Médoc and Préfet de la Gironde* EU:C:2015:648.

[16] Case C-300/04 *Eman and Sevinger* (n 12).

[17] *R (Chester) v Secretary of State for Justice* (n 8).

VII. THE UK'S EU REFERENDUM FRANCHISE AND EU LAW

The European Union Referendum Act 2015 (EURA) sets out the basic principles governing the referendum on whether the United Kingdom should remain a member of the European Union. Section 1 specifies that the question appearing on the ballot papers for its referendum (which had to be held before 31 December 2017) is

> Should the United Kingdom remain a member of the European Union or leave the European Union?

The answers to that question which are to appear on the ballot papers as alternatives are:

> Remain a member of the European Union
>
> or
>
> Leave the European Union.

Section 2 EURA makes the following provision on entitlement to vote in the referendum:

(1) Those entitled to vote in the referendum are –
  (a) the persons who, on the date of the referendum, would be entitled to vote as electors at a parliamentary election in any constituency
  (b) the persons who, on that date, are disqualified by reason of being peers from voting as electors at parliamentary elections but –
    (i) would be entitled to vote as electors at a local government election in any electoral area in Great Britain,
    (ii) would be entitled to vote as electors at a local election in any district electoral area in Northern Ireland, or
    (iii) would be entitled to vote as electors at a European Parliamentary election in any electoral region by virtue of section 3 of the Representation of the People Act 1985 (peers resident outside the United Kingdom), and
  (c) the persons who, on the date of the referendum –
    (i) would be entitled to vote in Gibraltar as electors at a European Parliamentary election in the combined electoral region in which Gibraltar is comprised, and
    (ii) fall within subsection (2).

(2) A person falls within this subsection if the person is either –
  (a) a Commonwealth citizen, or
  (b) a citizen of the Republic of Ireland.

(3) In subsection (1)(b)(i) 'local government election' includes a municipal election in the City of London (that is, an election to the office of mayor, alderman, common councilman or sheriff and also the election of any officer elected by the mayor, aldermen and liverymen in common hall).

By basing the EU referendum franchise on the electoral register used for UK parliamentary general elections to the House of Commons (and then making specific provision for enfranchising members of the House of Lords and some residents of Gibraltar), the classes of people who have a vote in this matter include the following:

(i) British citizens resident in the UK;
(ii) British citizens who have lived overseas for less than 15 years;[18]
(iii) members of the British armed forces, employees of the British Council and other Crown servants posted abroad, no matter the length of their residence abroad;[19]
(iv) Commonwealth citizens[20] who either have leave to remain in the UK or do not require such leave, and who are resident in the UK or in Gibraltar;
(v) citizens of the Republic of Ireland who are resident in the UK or in Gibraltar.

Among the class of individuals who are *not* afforded a vote in this referendum are:

(vi) EU citizens, no matter how long they have been resident in the UK, from Member States other than Ireland, Malta, or Cyprus. This is because the UK has traditionally afforded the right to vote in UK general elections to citizens of the Irish Republic, and to citizens of Commonwealth countries (among which are Malta and Cyprus);
(vii) British citizens who have resided outside the UK for more than 15 years, whether or not in exercise of their EU free movement rights.

In the course of the debates in the Westminster Parliament on the exclusion of these two classes from the EU referendum franchise it was noted that 'there are 2.3

[18] The general ban on non-resident voting in UK General Elections was lifted in 1985 but the right to vote was limited to those who had lived outside the country for less than five years. This five-year cut-off was increased to 20 years in 1989 and then reduced to 15 years in 2000.

[19] Service declarations are a means for certain people to register to vote when, because of the nature of their jobs (or the jobs of their spouses or civil partners), they may not be considered resident at an address in the UK. The following people can make a service declaration for the purposes of registering for the EU referendum: members of the armed forces and their spouses or civil partners; some Crown servants posted outside the UK; employees of the British Council posted outside the UK; and spouses or civil partners who are residing outside the UK to be with those Crown servants or British Council employees.

[20] Schedule 3 to the British Nationality Act 1981 sets out the list of relevant countries whose citizens are regarded in UK law as 'Commonwealth citizens' for the purposes of having an entitlement to vote, if lawfully resident in the UK, both in UK general elections and in UK national referendums (including the EU referendum): Antigua and Barbuda; Australia; The Bahamas; Bangladesh; Barbados; Belize; Botswana; Brunei; Cameroon; Canada; Republic of Cyprus; Dominica; Fiji; Ghana; Grenada; Guyana; India; Jamaica; Kenya; Kiribati; Lesotho; Malawi; Malaysia; Maldives; Malta; Mauritius; Mozambique; Namibia; Nauru; New Zealand; Nigeria; Pakistan; Papua New Guinea; Rwanda; Saint Christopher and Nevis; Saint Lucia; Saint Vincent and the Grenadines; Seychelles; Sierra Leone; Singapore; Solomon Islands; South Africa; Sri Lanka; Swaziland; Tanzania; Tonga; Trinidad and Tobago; Tuvalu; Uganda; Vanuatu; Western Samoa; Zambia; and Zimbabwe.

million EU citizens living in the UK, and 2.2 million British citizens living in the other 27 EU countries'.[21]

The exclusion from the EU independence franchise of this significant number of individuals who fall into these two classes might be said to engage EU law on the following grounds, among others:

(i) In the case of British nationals who have moved elsewhere in the European Union and have been non-resident in the UK for more than 15 years, their non-inclusion in the EU independence referendum could be understood as acting as a *disincentive from*, or *penalty for*, their exercising their EU free movement rights.
(ii) For non-Irish, Maltese or Cypriot EU nationals resident in the UK they have been excluded from the franchise *despite* having exercised their EU free movement rights to live and work in another Member State.
(iii) If a majority of the current franchise votes in this referendum to leave the European Union, negotiations will be commenced between the UK and the rest of the EU to provide for the UK no longer to be part of the European Union.[22]
(iv) Once the UK leaves the EU, British nationals will no longer be EU citizens and nationals of other Member States would no longer have EU free movement rights to live and work in the UK.
(v) It is clear, therefore, that the result of the independence referendum has a direct impact on the current acquired rights and legal status of EU citizens from other Member States who are currently resident in the UK and those British nationals who have exercised their EU free movement rights to live and work elsewhere in the EU.

The freedom of movement for workers has been described by the Court of Justice as 'one of the fundamental objectives of the Treaty' and 'free access to employment

[21] House of Commons *Hansard* 18 June 2015 Column 515 per Mike Gapes MP.

[22] Compare *Moohan v Lord Advocate* [2014] UKSC 67, [2015] AC 901. In rejecting a challenge to the lawfulness of the blanket ban on convicted prisoners voting in the Scottish independence referendum, Lord Hodge observed at [23]:

> [I]t must be borne in mind that a 'yes' vote in the referendum would not itself determine the citizenship of the appellants or other people born in Scotland. The Scottish Government and UK Government would have to negotiate the terms of Scotland's secession from the UK and it is not possible at this time to say whether people may be empowered to elect to retain United Kingdom citizenship. While the Scottish Independence Bill, if enacted as currently drafted, would end the UK citizenship of a Scottish-born citizen, that Bill might be amended in the light of the negotiations. It would not have been the independence referendum but legislation that followed those negotiations and also negotiations between the Scottish Government and the governments of European Union Member States which might have given rise to a withdrawal of EU citizenship. The judgment of the Court of Justice of the European Union in Case C-135/08 *Rottmann v Freistaat Bayern* [2010] QB 761 may be distinguished on the basis that the Scottish Parliament in enacting the Franchise Act to provide for the franchise of the referendum was not exercising powers in the sphere of nationality in a way which affected the rights conferred or protected by the EU legal order.

is a fundamental right which the Treaty confers individually on each worker in the Community'.[23] Nationals of non-EU countries, even if lawfully resident and working in the EU on the basis of an Association Agreement between their country of origin and the EU, do not thereby obtain the right to free movement within the EU.[24]

The CJ case law is clear that Member States must not act in any way which might discourage or penalise their own nationals for exercising their free movement rights under the Treaties.[25] National legislation which places at a disadvantage certain of the nationals of the Member State concerned simply because they have exercised their freedom to move and to reside in another Member State constitutes a restriction on the freedoms conferred by Article 21 TFEU on every citizen of the Union.[26] Indeed, the CJ has ruled that the opportunities offered by the Treaty in relation to freedom of movement for citizens of the Union cannot be fully effective if a national of a Member State may be deterred from availing himself of his free movement rights by obstacles placed in the way of his stay in another Member State by legislation of his State of origin which effectively penalises the mere fact that he has used those opportunities of free movement under the Treaty.[27]

Thus, insofar as it affects the possible or actual exercise of their nationals' rights under EU law, a Member State's exercise of its otherwise sovereign powers is open to review in the light of EU law.[28] British nationals who have left the UK and moved elsewhere in the EU can do so on the basis of their status, and in exercise of their rights, as EU citizens. Similarly nationals of other Member States who have moved to live and work in the UK can do so on the basis of their status, and in exercise of their rights, as EU citizens. EU citizens can undoubtedly pray in aid EU law in relation to those actions of the Member States (even those of which they are nationals) which may curtail or threaten their continued or future enjoyment of their EU law protected rights, notably their rights associated with free movement.[29]

For example, in *Prinz v Region Hannover*[30] the Court of Justice ruled that the principles of EU free movement law preclude national legislation which purported

[23] Case 222/86 *Union Nationale des Entraineurs et Cadres Techniques Professionnels du Football (UNECTEF) v Heylens* EU:C:1987:442, paras 12, 14.

[24] See eg Case C-179/98 *Mesbah* EU:C:1999:549, para 35.

[25] Case C-192/05 *Tas-Hagen v Raadskamer WUBO van de Pensioen- en Uitkeringsraads* EU:C:2006:676, para 22; Case C-76/05 *Schwarz v Finanzamt Bergisch Gladbach* EU:C:2007:492, para 87; Joined Cases C-11 and 12/06 *Morgan v Bezirksregierung Köln* EU:C:2007:626, para 23.

[26] See Case C-406/04 *De Cuyper v Office National de l'Emploi (ONEM)* EU:C:2006:491, para 39; Case C-192/05 *Tas-Hagen* ibid, para 31; Joined Cases C-11 and 12/06 *Morgan v Bezirksregierung Köln* EU:C:2007:626, para 25.

[27] See, to that effect, Case C-224/98 *D'Hoop v Office National de l'Emploi* EU:C:2002:432, para 31; Case C-224/02 *Pusa v Osuuspankkien Keskinäinen Vakuutusyhtiö* EU:C:2004:273, para 19; and Joined Cases C-11 and 12/06 *Morgan* ibid, para 26.

[28] Case C-135/08 Rottmann (n 10), para 48.

[29] See Case C-192/05 *Tas-Hagen* (n 25), para 19; Joined Cases C-11 and 12/06 *Morgan* (n 26), para 22.

[30] Joined Cases C-523 and 585/11 *Prinz v Region Hannover* EU:C:2013:524.

to make the award of an national education grant for studies lasting over a year in another Member State subject to a sole condition that the applicant must have had a permanent residence in (German) national territory for at least three years before commencing studies abroad. The CJEU held that a sole condition of uninterrupted residence of three years was too general and exclusive, and went beyond what was necessary to achieve the objectives pursued. It was therefore disproportionate. The rationale for the Luxembourg Court's decision was that a pure residence condition for eligibility to a student grant risked excluding from funding students who, despite not having resided for an uninterrupted period of three years in Germany immediately prior to studying abroad, were nevertheless to be regarded as sufficiently connected to German society. Accordingly this rule could not be used to deny German funding to one student who, although born in Germany in 1991, had lived with her family for 10 years in Tunisia where her father was employed by a German company, returning to Germany in January 2007 until August 2009, when she commenced studies at a university in the Netherlands, or to another German-born student who lived in Germany with his German national parents for the first 11 years of his life and then moved with them to Spain for the next 11 years when his parents returned to Germany and he, after residing with them there for two and a half years, returned to Spain to commence a university course there.

This line of case law confirms that national legislation which places certain nationals at a disadvantage simply because they have exercised their freedom to move and to reside in another Member State constitutes a restriction on the freedoms conferred by Article 21(1) TFEU on every EU citizen.[31] Indeed, the opportunities offered by the Treaty in relation to freedom of movement for EU citizens would not be fully effective if a national of a Member State could be dissuaded from using them by obstacles or disadvantages placed upon him by legislation of his State of origin which, in effect, penalises him for having moved to another Member State.[32]

The UK undoubtedly has the legal competence to fix the terms of the franchise in the EU referendum. Even if EU law does not impose any express provision obliging Member States to allow its non-resident nationals to vote or to allow resident non-nationals to vote, where a Member State has provided for such a system it then has an obligation, as a matter of EU law, to ensure that the detailed rules concerning the franchise do not themselves create unjustified restrictions on the exercise of EU free movement rights. Such national rules can only be justified in the light of EU law if they can be shown, to the courts' satisfaction, to be proportionate and non-discriminatory. A measure is proportionate if, while appropriately seeking to achieve a legitimate objective in a 'consistent and systematic manner', it does not go beyond what is necessary in order to attain it.[33]

[31] Joined Cases C-11 and 12/06 *Morgan* (n 26), para 24 and the case law cited therein.

[32] See Case C-359/13 *Martens v Minister van Onderwijs, Cultuur en Wetenschap* EU:C:2015:118.

[33] Case C-379/11 *Caves Krier Frères Sarl v Directeur de l'Administration de l'emploi* EU:C:2012:798, para 48 and the case law cited.

Accordingly, in making provision for the EU referendum franchise, the UK may be said to be obliged as a matter of EU law to avoid (unjustified) discrimination among EU citizens resident in the UK and avoid penalising British nationals who have exercised their EU free movement rights yet have maintained a connection with the UK. It is difficult to envisage just what sufficient and lawful justification might be offered by the UK authorities for the Brexit franchise rules were this matter to come before the national courts or the CJEU.

In January 2014 a formal Recommendation was issued by the Commission to Member States on the issue of automatic disenfranchisement from national elections by Member States of those of their nationals who would exercise their free movement rights.[34] In it, the European Commission noted that:

> (12) The rules currently applicable in certain Member States may lead to a situation where Union citizens residing in other Member States could lose their right to vote solely on the ground that they have been residing abroad for a certain period of time. This is based on the presumption that residence abroad of a given duration means that the connection with the political process in the home country is lost. This presumption is, however, not correct in every individual case. Therefore, it might be appropriate to give citizens who risk becoming disenfranchised the possibility to demonstrate their continuing interest in the political life in the Member State of which they are nationals.
>
> (13) Union citizens residing in another Member State can maintain lifelong and close ties with their country of origin and may continue to be directly affected by acts adopted by the legislature elected there. The widespread access to television broadcast across borders and the availability of internet and other web-based and mobile communication technologies make it easier than ever to follow closely and take part in social and political developments in the home Member State.
>
> (14) The rationale of policies that disenfranchise citizens should be reassessed in the light of current socioeconomic and technological realities, the current trend towards inclusive political participation and the present state of European integration, along with the prime importance of the right to participate in the democratic life of the Union and the right to free movement.
>
> (15) A more inclusive and proportionate approach would consist in ensuring that citizens who make use of their right to free movement and residence in the Union can retain their right to vote in national elections when they demonstrate a continuing interest in the political life in the Member State of which they are nationals.
>
> (16) A positive action on the part of the individuals such as their application to remain registered on the electoral roll of their Member State of origin should be considered as an appropriate criterion—and the simplest means—for the purposes of demonstrating a continuing interest in the national political life, without prejudice to the possibility for those Member States to request their citizens to renew such applications at appropriate intervals, so confirming the persistence of such an interest.

[34] In *R (Chester) v Secretary of State for Justice* (n 8) Lord Mance observed (at [58]): 'There is no sign that the European Commission has ever sought to involve itself in or take issue with voting eligibility in member states'. This observation no longer holds true.

The Commission accordingly recommended to Member States that:

> Where Member States' policies limit the rights of nationals to vote in national elections based exclusively on a residence condition, Member States should enable their nationals who make use of their right to free movement and residence in the Union to demonstrate a continuing interest in the political life in the Member State of which they are nationals, including through an application to remain registered on the electoral roll, and by doing so, to retain their right to vote.[35]

This reference to a test of being able to 'demonstrate a continuing interest in the political life in the Member State of which they are nationals' broadly aligns with the approach taken by the Court of Appeal of England and Wales in *R (Preston) v Wandsworth LBC* in considering a challenge to the EU law compatibility of national provisions which resulted in the disenfranchisement from UK general elections for individuals after 15 years of non-residence in the UK, even if that residence was in another Member State of the EU in exercise of the individual's Treaty free movement rights. The Court of Appeal observed that, in one sense, the right to vote in national general elections fell outside the scope of EU law since that franchise existed solely by virtue of the domestic legislation of Member States and it was not the express creation of any of the articles in the TFEU. However, the Court of Appeal went on to hold that it did not follow from the fact that the right to vote was created and conferred by domestic law that Member States could lay down in their electoral law the conditions of the UK parliamentary franchise without any regard to the impact that the conditions might have on the exercise of fundamental rights that existed by virtue of the TFEU. Thus the Court of Appeal ruled that, even in areas falling within their national sovereignty such as voting rights in general elections, the exercise of competence by a Member State was subject to the applicable provisions of EU law, in particular the provisions that conferred fundamental rights. One such right was that of moving and residing freely in the territory of Member States. If the conditions for the UK parliamentary franchise laid down in national legislation restricted the exercise of the right of free movement and residence, the courts of the Member States were bound to address the question whether those conditions were objectively justified. On the facts of the case before it the Court of Appeal held that the 15-year non-residence rule had the legitimate aim of testing the strength of a British citizen's links with the United Kingdom over a significant period of time by measuring past commitment to the United Kingdom and seeing whether it was sufficiently diminished or diluted to justify removal of the right to vote in UK parliamentary elections. That aim was legitimate for the purpose of confining the parliamentary franchise to those citizens with an ascertainable, continuing, close and objective connection with the United Kingdom, whose government made decisions and whose

[35] Commission Recommendation of 29 January 2014 addressing the consequences of disenfranchisement of Union citizens exercising their rights to free movement (2014/53/EU) [2014] OJ L32/34 at Recitals 12–16 and Recommendation 1.

parliament passed laws that most directly affected those British citizens resident in the United Kingdom. The Court of Appeal further considered that the country of residence of a citizen was not an arbitrary measure of connection with a country; it was a relevant, rational and practicable criterion for assessing the closeness of the links between an EU citizen and a Member State. Accordingly the Court of Appeal concluded that the 15-year rule was proportionate to the legitimate aim of testing the strength of a British citizen's links with the United Kingdom over a significant period of time. The length of the period was noted to represent three full Parliamentary terms. The current rules provided a substantial opportunity for continued voting by British citizens who had moved to reside in another Member State. While accepting that the loss of franchise after 15 years' non-residence in the UK could be said to be proportionate and hence objectively justified as a matter of EU law, the Court of Appeal accepted that a lesser period of non-residence resulting in disenfranchisement could infringe the free movement principles of EU law. As Mummery LJ observed in a judgment with which the other members of the court agreed in full:

> It is not difficult to devise hypothetical examples of extreme conditions, which, though very unlikely to occur in practice, could affect the right to vote and could deter freedom of movement, but could not possibly be justified. No Member State is likely to deny the right to vote to a citizen for residing for more than one month a year in another Member State, but if it did, that would obviously constitute an unjustified restriction on freedom of movement.[36]

A different focus of argument might be made in the present case precisely because of direct impact which the result of the EU referendum might have on the rights of British nationals who have exercised their free movement rights. Indeed it might be argued that the impact upon those Britons who have been resident in other Member States for 15 years or more is going to be *greater*, since there has been even stronger reliance upon their EU free movement rights to place down roots in other Member States. There is all the more reason, then, for their being concerned about the result of, and therefore legitimately to be involved in the franchise for, the EU referendum because of its direct and immediate impact upon them. In these circumstances the failure in the EU Referendum Act 2016 to make a differentiation for the purposes of entitlement to vote between those British citizens who have left the UK for places outside the EU compared to those who have settled as EU citizens within other Member States wrongly treats unlike cases alike. Surprisingly, some support for this analysis may actually be found in the judgment of Lord Mance in *Chester*, where he states:

> 63 It is however a general principle of Strasbourg law under article 14 of the Convention that additional rights falling within the general scope of any Convention right for which the state has voluntarily decided to provide must in that event be provided without

[36] *R (Preston) v Wandsworth LBC* [2012] EWCA Civ 1378, [2013] QB 687 per Mummery LJ at [72].

discrimination: *Belgian Linguistic Case (No 2)* (1968) 1 EHRR 252, 283, *R (Clift) v Secretary of State for the Home Department* [2007] 1 AC 484, §§ 12, 17–18.

This principle in my opinion clearly underlies Case C-300/04 *Eman and Sevinger v Netherlands* [2006] ECR I-8055. As the court noted (at § 53) article 19 EC (now article 22 TFEU) only covered nationals resident in another member state. But the Dutch legislator had chosen to extend the right to vote to its nationals resident outside any member state—but not in the Dutch Antilles or Aruba. There was no justification for this different treatment of comparable situations in *a context which fell within the scope of European law, that is voting by nationals residing outside their own member state.*[37]

In relation to the exclusion from the EU referendum franchise of the nationals of other EU Member States who have moved to and reside in the UK, this might be challenged as being inconsistent and unsystematic (and so unlawful) precisely because it would allow the vote to some Member State nationals (those from Ireland, Malta and Cyprus) while denying it to the nationals of the remaining Member States. This appears to be treating like cases differently, and once again breaches the EU principles of equality and, indeed, the express provision of Article 18 TFEU which states that 'within the scope of application of the Treaties, and without prejudice to any special provisions contained therein, any discrimination on grounds of nationality shall be prohibited'.

No reasoned justification seems to have been essayed before the Westminster Parliament by the UK Government promoters of the EU Referendum Bill for this failure to differentiate in the franchise arrangement between British nationals who reside elsewhere in the EU abroad in exercise of their EU free movement rights and those who have left the EU, or for the decision to treat Maltese, Cypriot and Irish EU citizens residing in the UK differently from nationals of the other Member States who have similarly exercised their EU free movement rights to move to the UK. The UK Government appears simply to have paid no regard to the requirements of EU law in this matter, although they could not but be aware of the impact of this measure on individual EU free movement rights.[38]

[37] *R (Chester) v Secretary of State for Justice* (n 8) per Lord Mance at [63].

[38] See House of Commons *Hansard* 18 June 2015 Column 523–24 per Tom Brake MP:

> In relation to the franchise for EU citizens, currently 2.3 million citizens of other European member states live and work in the United Kingdom. In the regional and local elections that will be held across Britain and Northern Ireland next year, all EU citizens living in the UK will be entitled to vote, yet, as clause 2 stands, EU citizens living abroad in the UK will not be entitled to vote in the referendum. To respond to the point made by the Opposition spokesman, the right hon. Member for Wolverhampton South East (Mr McFadden), I do not think the fact that other countries have not allowed EU citizens to take part in similar referendums means that that is the path that the UK Government should follow.
>
> I said earlier that EU citizens will not be entitled to vote, but of course, as several hon. Members have said today, a number of EU citizens will be able to vote in the referendum, because there is no consistency. Citizens of Ireland, Cyprus and Malta living in the UK will be able to vote in the referendum, but citizens from all other EU member states will not. As the hon. Member for Ilford South (Mike Gapes) said, it is clear that non-British EU citizens living in the UK have a very big stake in this election. If Britain leaves the EU, those men and women will

The UK Government bears the onus of establishing that the failure to enfranchise individuals, whether EU citizens resident in the UK or British nationals who have resided elsewhere in the EU for more than 15 years, pursues a legitimate aim and is proportionate to that aim.[39]

But it is simply not clear what the aim of such disenfranchisement might be, since no aim was articulated in the promotion and passage of the EU Referendum Bill through the Westminster Parliament. All that appears to have been said on behalf of the Government is, in effect, that is how we have always done things.[40] One may contrast in this regard the approach taken to the lawfulness of the franchise conditions for the independence referendum of the territory of New Caledonia considered by the UN Human Rights Committee under reference to Article 1 and Article 25 of the International Covenant on Civil and Political Rights in *Gillot and others v France*:

> 13.5 … [T]he Committee observes, as the State party indeed confirms, that the criteria governing the right to vote in the referendums have the effect of establishing a restricted

still be EU citizens â unlike their UK counterparts, who will lose their EU citizenship rights – but they will no longer have the automatic right to live and work in the UK.

[39] *R (Quila) v Secretary of State for the Home Department* [2011] UKSC 45, [2012] 1 AC 621 [44].

[40] See House of Commons *Hansard* 18 June 2015 Column 554 where the Parliamentary Secretary, Cabinet Office (John Penrose MP) summed up the House of Commons debate in which amendments on this issue were proposed (and rejected on a Division of Ayes 71, Noes 514)) with the following remarks:

> As a vote of national importance, the Bill starts with the parliamentary franchise. It extends it to Commonwealth citizens in Gibraltar … and to Members of the House of Lords, who do not vote in general elections … [I]t would be neither principled nor right to change the franchise to try to get a certain result. Instead, *we should follow the precedent set in 1975 and again in 2011 when UK-wide votes on membership of the European Economic Community and on the alternative vote were put to the parliamentary franchise. This is the franchise that we use for big questions that will determine the future of our nation*—I am talking about not just for referendums but for who should form the Government and lead the country. It is right that we apply it again here … A few EU citizens have long been able to vote in UK parliamentary elections. Citizens of Malta, Cyprus and Ireland are already able to vote if they are resident in the UK, because of our historical connections to those countries and their citizens. But for the rest of the EU, British citizens living abroad do not have voting rights in their national elections. The only exceptions of which I am aware are in Ireland, where voting rights here are reciprocated, and in the upper chamber of Slovenia's Parliament—I suspect that not many people here knew that they had that right. I doubt anyone will be dashing over there to set up residence in Slovenia, but if they do, they are of course welcome to vote when they get there. I am not aware of any national referendum in the EU that allowed citizens from other member states to take part … *It would be lopsided indeed if we were to take a different approach for our nationals than has been done elsewhere in the EU. As I was saying, British citizens were not entitled to vote in the Dutch or French referendums*. Finally, switching from the parliamentary to the local elections franchise would block British citizens living abroad from voting at all, because they are not entitled to vote at local elections. The net effect of the amendments would be to deny British citizens living abroad the right to vote on their own country's future while giving that right to other Europeans who are living here but have chosen not to become citizens. That strikes me as fundamentally unfair and inequitable. I hope that the hon. Members will withdraw their amendments when the time comes.

> electorate and hence a differentiation between (a) persons deprived of the right to vote, including the author(s) in the ballot in question, and (b) persons permitted to exercise this right, *owing to their sufficiently strong links with the territory whose institutional development is at issue.*
>
> The question which the Committee must decide, therefore, is whether this differentiation is compatible with article 25 of the International Covenant on Civil and Political Rights.
>
> *The Committee recalls that not all differentiation constitutes discrimination if it is based on objective and reasonable criteria and the purpose sought is legitimate under the International Covenant on Civil and Political Rights.*[41]

In deciding whether a measure is proportionate to its aim:

> it is necessary to determine (1) whether the objective of the measure is sufficiently important to justify the limitation of a protected right, (2) whether the measure is rationally connected to the objective, (3) whether a less intrusive measure could have been used without unacceptably compromising the achievement of the objective, and (4) whether, balancing the severity of the measure's effects on the rights of the persons to whom it applies against the importance of the objective, to the extent that the measure will contribute to its achievement, the former outweighs the latter.[42]

It is difficult to see how, applying these tests, the exclusion of a class of persons whose rights are going to be directly and immediately affected dependent upon the outcome of the referendum could be said to be proportionate. As we have seen, the franchise chosen by the UK Government and passed by the Westminster Parliament allows some EU citizens resident in the UK to vote, but not others. This is, on its face, discrimination on grounds of particular EU nationality. And it has no regard to the different situation (and the impact that the result of the referendum will have) on different classes of non-resident British nationals (those who have exercised free movement right within the EU compared to those who have left the EU altogether). It is difficult to see how this might be said to be a proportionate restriction or interference as regards the actual, or possible intended future, exercise of free movement rights.

Indeed, the franchise for the referendum appears to be both over and under-inclusive. It enfranchises complete categories of persons who are not EU citizens

[41] *Gillot and others v France* (UN Doc CCPR/C/75/D/932/2000, Communication No 932/2000, 15 July 2002) para 13.5.

[42] *Bank Mellat v HM Treasury (No 2)* [2013] UKSC 39, [2013] 3 WLR 179 per Lord Reed at [74]. See too *Pham v Home Secretary* (n 4) per Lord Reed at [120]–[121]:

> 120 The present case concerns the Secretary of State's power under section 40(2) of the British Nationality Act 1981 to deprive a person of a citizenship status if satisfied that deprivation is conducive to the public good. *Given the fundamental importance of citizenship, it may be arguable that the power to deprive a British citizen of that status should be interpreted as being subject to an implied requirement that its exercise should be justified as being necessary to achieve the legitimate aim pursued.*
>
> 121 If the question of proportionality under EU law is raised before SIAC, it may well be that the answer is the same as it would be under domestic law.

and who have no direct EU law rights which might be affected by the result of the EU referendum (Commonwealth non-EU citizens) while disenfranchising categories of persons whose rights and status will be directly affected by a leave vote in the referendum (UK nationals who are long-term residents of other Member States and non-Commonwealth EU citizens resident in the UK). In his Opinion in *Rottmann v Bavaria* Advocate General Poiares Maduro observed (with emphasis added) that:

> 23. … [A]lthough it is true that nationality of a member state is a precondition for access to Union citizenship, it is equally true that the body of rights and obligations associated with the latter cannot be limited in an unjustified manner by the former. In other words, it is not that the acquisition and loss of nationality (and, consequently, of Union citizenship) are in themselves governed by Community law, but *the conditions for the acquisition and loss of nationality must be compatible with the Community rules and respect the rights of the European citizen.*
>
> …
>
> 26. … [A]s *possession of the nationality of a member state determines possession of Union citizenship and, hence, the enjoyment of the rights and freedoms which are expressly linked to it by the Treaty, and also the receipt of social benefits which it makes it possible to claim* the obligation to have due regard to Community law in the exercise of the member states' competence in the sphere of nationality cannot be denied some effect.
>
> …
>
> 28 And it would also be wrong to assume that, owing to the specific characteristics of the law of nationality, only certain Community rules—essentially the general principles of law and the fundamental rights—are capable of being invoked against the exercise of state competence in this sphere. In theory, *any rule of the Community legal order may be invoked if the conditions for the acquisition and loss of nationality laid down by a member state are incompatible with it.*
>
> …
>
> 30 Other rules capable of restricting the legislative power of the member states in the sphere of nationality include the provisions of primary Community legislation and the general principles of Community law. Thus, mention has been made … by the Hellenic Republic in its observations, of *the Community principle of sincere co-operation laid down by article 10EC [now Article 4(3) TFEU], which could be affected if a member state were to carry out, without consulting the Commission or its partners, an unjustified mass naturalisation of nationals of non-member states.*[43]

In its decision in *Rottmann v Bavaria* the Grand Chamber of the CJEU confirmed the analysis of the Advocate General and ruled that the exercise by current EU

[43] Case C-135/08 *Rottmann* (n 10) EU:C:2010:104 per Advocate General Poiares Maduro at paras 23, 26 and 28 of his Opinion.

Member State authorities of legal powers in the area of national citizenship and associated political rights:

> in so far as it affects the rights conferred and protected by the legal order of the Union … is amenable to judicial review carried out in the light of European Union law … [I]t is, however, for the national court to ascertain whether the withdrawal decision at issue in the main proceedings *observes the principle of proportionality so far as concerns the consequences it entails for the situation of the person concerned in the light of European Union law*, in addition, where appropriate, to examination of the proportionality of the decision in the light of national law.[44]

Given that the result of the EU referendum could 'affect the rights conferred and protected by the legal order of the Union'—and, separately, impact upon the conditions for 'the genuine enjoyment of the substance of the rights conferred by virtue of his status as a citizen of the Union'[45]—the conditions for the participation in the referendum by persons whose EU citizenship and separately whose EU law based rights would have been directly affected by its result must be amenable to judicial review carried out in the light of EU law.

VIII. *R (ON THE APPLICATION OF SHINDLER AND ANOTHER) V CHANCELLOR OF THE DUCHY OF LANCASTER AND ANOTHER*

Many of the foregoing arguments were essayed before the UK courts in *R (on the application of Shindler and another) v Chancellor of the Duchy of Lancaster and another*. In an oral decision given after hearing argument on 24 May 2016[46] a unanimous Supreme court (Lady Hale, Lord Mance, Lord Sumption, Lord Hughes and Lord Reed) refused to grant two British expatriates permission to appeal against the Court of Appeal's (Lord Dyson MR, Elias and King LLJ)[47] refusal of their appeal against a Divisional Court's (Lloyd Jones LJ and Blake J)[48] dismissal of their challenge to section 2 EURA, which excluded them from voting in the referendum because they were last registered to vote in the UK more than 15 years ago.

The applicants for leave to appeal were two British nationals who had exercised their right of free movement and moved to Italy and Belgium, respectively. The first applicant's name had last appeared in the UK register of electors in 1982, while the second applicant's name had last appeared in 1987. They applied for judicial review, claiming that their exclusion from voting under Section 2 EURA

[44] ibid, paras 48, 53.

[45] See Case C-34/09 *Zambrano* (n 5), paras 41–42 and Case C-256/11 *Dereçi and others v Bundesministerium für Inneres* EU:C:2011:734, para 74.

[46] https://www.supremecourt.uk/watch/uksc-2016-0105/240516-am.html.

[47] *R (on the application of Shindler and another) v Chancellor of the Duchy of Lancaster and another* [2016] EWCA Civ 469 [2016] HRLR 14 (20 May 2016).

[48] *R (on the application of Shindler and another) v Chancellor of the Duchy of Lancaster and another* [2016] EWHC 957 (Admin) [2016] HRLR 12 (28 April 2016).

constituted an unjustified restriction of their EU law rights of free movement. The Divisional Court held that, contrary to the UK Government's argument, Section 2 EURA fell within the scope of EU law; however, the Divisional court concluded that the provision was not a restriction on the applicants' rights of free movement, but if it was, it was objectively justified as a proportionate means of achieving the legitimate objective of testing the strength of a British citizen's links with the UK over a significant period of time. The Court of Appeal held that Section 2 EURA did fall within the scope of EU law by virtue of article 50(1) of the Treaty on European Union (TEU), and it agreed with the Divisional Court the 15-year rule did not interfere with the right of free movement. The applicants sought leave from the Supreme Court to appeal against that decision.

The applicants submitted that the Court of Appeal had wrongly upheld the two preliminary arguments of the UK Government which, somewhat paradoxically and ironically, were to the effect that EU law meant that EU law could not be prayed in aid by the applicants to challenge any aspect of the referendum. The UK Government's first argument had relied upon TEU, art 50, which says that any decision by a Member State to withdraw from the EU should be made in accord with its own constitutional requirements; and their second argument had relied upon a line of case law from the Court of Justice of the European Union (CJEU) which said that where the national measure at issue could not reasonably be said to have the effect of deterring people from exercising their free movement rights, then it could not be subject to a further proportionality review under EU law and the respondents had no obligation to show it to be justified as a matter of EU law.

Before the Supreme Court, the applicants contended that these EU law arguments as upheld by the Court of Appeal were disputable and certainly not *acte clair* from the case law of the CJEU. Accordingly, in the normal run of things, were it not for the urgency of matters, the Supreme Court would be obliged to make a preliminary reference to the CJEU under article 267(3) of the Treaty on the Functioning on the European Union (TFEU) if, as a court of final instance, it felt that a preliminary ruling was necessary for the resolution of the issues before it. However, rather than refer matters to the CJEU, which would lead to the referendum being postponed until the CJEU ruled, the applicants proposed that the clearer route for the Supreme Court would be simply for it to consider and rule on the proportionality of excluding them from voting in the referendum by considering the exclusion's compatibility with EU law free movement rights and, at common law, with respect for the fundamental constitutional right of citizens to vote in elections and national referendums. Such a course would avoid any question of the need to make a TFEU, art 267 reference since the test for proportionality as a matter of EU law was clearly set out by the Supreme Court in its decision in *Lumsdon and others) v Legal Services Board*[49] and the test for proportionality at

[49] *See R (on the application of Lumsdon and others) v Legal Services Board* [2015] UKSC 41 [2016] AC 697 (24 June 2015).

common law has also been recently considered and decided upon by the Supreme Court in *Pham v Secretary of State for the Home Department*.[50]

The applicants strongly argued that there was no proper proportionality defence for Section 2 EURA (which is why the UK Government was so keen to dispose of the challenge on preliminary issues and thus avoid any proportionality examination—this being the course they persuaded the Court of Appeal to follow). The applicants said it was clear that their disenfranchisement had the following effects:

- Penalised them for having exercised their free movement rights for more than 15 years
- Offered an incentive to them to cease exercising their free movement rights and move back to the UK to take up residence there by 8 June 2016 because that would be the only way for them to regain their right to vote and be able to vote specifically in this referendum
- Deterred them from continuing to exercise their free movement rights in the way that they had to date

The applicants argued there was no legitimate aim which could justify their disenfranchisement. They were British citizens exercising free movement rights who were relying every day on their British citizenship since it was that citizenship which gave them rights as EU citizens to be treated in the same fashion as the nationals of the Member States where they resided and gave them substantive and procedural legal rights allowing them to challenge the decisions of public authorities of those Member States insofar as they were incompatible with respect for EU law.

The applicants argued that the UK Government's reliance on the European Court of Human Rights' case law, which allowed for residence requirements to be imposed in respect of the right to vote in national elections to the legislature, was inept as the Strasbourg court has made it clear that the right to vote conferred by article 3 of Protocol 1 of the European Convention on Human Rights does not extend to the right to vote in referendums. And, in any event, the justification offered by the Strasbourg court to say that residence requirements in respect of the right to vote in national elections to the legislature might be proportionate (day-to-day knowledge of the issue being voted upon, being directly affected by the decision resulting from the vote etc.) did not apply to this referendum as it was, in effect, about whether British citizens should be able to retain or lose the rights associated with being EU citizens. Therefore, the Strasbourg court's case law did not justify the disenfranchisement of British citizen free movers who were relying day-to-day on those very rights of EU citizenship which the referendum might take away.

The applicants noted that UK Government Ministers had repeatedly and publicly (both within and outside Parliament) said that the disenfranchisement of

[50] *Pham v Secretary of State for the Home Department* [2015] UKSC 19 [2015] 1 WLR 1591 (25 March 2015).

British expats was 'arbitrary' and that the Government was committed to repealing it. The only reason this avowedly arbitrary rule was retained for this referendum was because of a political compromise within the Conservative party between supporters and opponents of the UK's continued membership of the EU. From a point of view of political expediency, it had been thought better not to rock the boat too much by re-considering and re-arranging the franchise for this referendum to allow the applicants and those like them to vote. Even so, the franchise for the Brexit referendum does not mirror the terms of the franchise for Westminster elections, or for any other elections ore referendums in the UK. For example, peers get the vote, and Irish (but not Spanish or any other Member State's) citizens lawfully resident Gibraltar get the vote, but not the appellants. The applicants argued that the result of this political compromise (which they said could not constitute a valid reason to infringe the fundamental common law constitutional right to vote or to impact upon their EU law guaranteed free movement rights) was that non-British Commonwealth citizens who happened to be lawfully resident in the UK as at the date of the referendum (e.g. a student from Malaysia or Australians on a limited two-year work visa) got a vote on the question of whether British citizens should retain or lose EU citizenship, whereas British citizens such as themselves, who were directly reliant upon their continued EU citizenship, got no say. So in sum, there was no legitimate aim to the exclusion of the applicants from the franchise. And there was no rational connection between the avowed aim of the referendum, which was to give the British people the final say on the UK's continued membership of the EU, and what was in fact legislated for, which allowed two million or so non-British Commonwealth and Irish citizens resident in the UK or in Gibraltar being entitled to vote, while the two million or so long-term British free movers living elsewhere in the EU were excluded from the vote.

The Supreme Court refused permission and so declined to rule on any of these arguments. Its reason for refusing permission was that, on the assumption EU law could be prayed in aid in this matter (i.e. without ruling on or endorsing the Court of Appeal's finding on the meaning of TEU, art 50), it considered that the disenfranchisement did not impact upon free movement rights such as to require to be justified as under EU law. But the decision does not in any sense clarify the law but leaves it in quite an unclear state. By refusing permission, the Supreme Court has left standing a decision of the Court of Appeal on the meaning, as a matter of EU law and international law, of TEU, art 50 which is novel and unsupported by anything in the *travaux préparatoires*. This is a matter which in any normal circumstances should have been referred to the CJEU for its authoritative decision. It also leaves standing the Court of Appeal's decision that disenfranchisement does not, and cannot, interfere with free movement. This finding rests on dubious factual assumptions and questionable legal propositions. Again, the issue of whether the future or potential deterrence effect on others—as opposed simply to the fact of penalising or disadvantaging these individual applicants for exercising free movement—was a necessary part of the test before a national measure could be subject to proportionality review under EU law should, in the normal run of things and had it not been for the urgency of matters and the general desire not to postpone the referendum, have been referred to the CJEU.

IX. CONCLUSION

A Commission Communication on *A new EU framework to strengthen the rule of law*, which was issued in March 2014, stated as follows:

> The rule of law is the backbone of any modern constitutional democracy. It is one of the founding principles stemming from the common constitutional traditions of all the Member States of the EU and, as such, one of the main values upon which the Union is based. This is recalled by Article 2 of the Treaty on European Union (TEU), as well as by the Preambles to the Treaty and to the Charter of Fundamental Rights of the EU. This is also why, under Article 49 TEU, respect for the rule of law is a precondition for EU membership. Along with democracy and human rights, the rule of law is also one of the three pillars of the Council of Europe and is endorsed in the Preamble to the European Convention for the Protection of Human Rights and Fundamental Freedoms (ECHR).
>
> …
>
> [R]espect for the rule of law is intrinsically linked to respect for democracy and for fundamental rights: there can be no democracy and respect for fundamental rights without respect for the rule of law and vice versa. *Fundamental rights are effective only if they are justiciable. Democracy is protected if the fundamental role of the judiciary, including constitutional courts, can ensure freedom of expression, freedom of assembly and respect of the rules governing the political and electoral process.*[51]

The above cases illustrate how the rules of EU law might, in principle, be prayed in aid to challenge the legitimacy of restrictions on the national franchise imposed by parliaments within the Member States. Against that background, the particular exclusion from the Brexit referendum franchise of British nationals who have settled for more than 15 years in other Member States in exercise their free movement rights, and of EU citizens (other than Irish, Cypriot and Maltese nationals) who have moved to live and work in the UK calls out for justification. But the only justification which appears to have been essayed before the UK Parliament is that the exclusion of these classes of individuals is not particularly intended or sought but is simply a consequence of its adoption for the Brexit referendum of the current UK General election franchise rules. That does not appear to be a sufficient justification to satisfy the requirements of proportionality or non-discrimination.

It might even be suggested that not only is the current definition in the EURA franchise wanting in terms of its proportionality, but it would fail even the higher hurdle of such general principles of EU law as respect for the rule of law and

[51] Commission Communication on *A new EU framework to strengthen the rule of law* COM(2014) 158 final (Brussels, 11 March 2014) 2, 4 (emphasis added).

for the fundamental democratic principles governing the political and electoral process within the EU as a democratic Union.

But there is a paradox and an irony in seeking so to rely upon EU law in this context given that EU law itself has, at its heart, a certain democratic deficit. Perhaps then it was too much to expect UK judges—or the Commission—to use (undemocratic and supra-national) EU law as the means to defend the ideals of democracy against the settled and express will and legislation of democratically elected and accountable national legislatures. But as Lady Hale has reminded us:

> Of course, in any modern democracy, the views of the public and Parliamentarians cannot be the end of the story. Democracy is about more than respecting the views of the majority. It is also about safeguarding the rights of minorities, including unpopular minorities. 'Democracy values everyone equally even if the majority does not': *Ghaidan v Godin-Mendoza* [2004] 2 AC 557, § 132. It follows that one of the essential roles of the courts in a democracy is to protect those rights.
>
> ...
>
> If the current franchise unjustifiably excludes certain people from voting, it is the court's duty to say so and to give them whatever remedy is appropriate. More fundamentally, Parliamentarians derive their authority and legitimacy from those who elected them, in other words from the current franchise, and it is to those electors that they are accountable. They have no such relationship with the disenfranchised. Indeed, in some situations, they may have a vested interest in keeping the franchise as it is.[52]

[52] *R (Chester) v Secretary of State for Justice* (n 8) per Lady Hale at [88]–[89].

5

Social Justifications for Restrictions of the Right to Welfare Equality: Students and Beyond

SARA IGLESIAS SÁNCHEZ* AND DIEGO ACOSTA ARCARAZO

I. INTRODUCTION

THE IMPACT OF European integration on national welfare systems is one of the most crucial issues concerning the regulatory autonomy of Member States.[1] In particular, the widening of the scope of the free movement of persons,[2] and its later transformation into the most fundamental EU citizenship right,[3] has added to the tensions already present in the interaction between free movement law and national social protection. With the introduction of the citizenship of the Union, not only did free movement and its concomitant principle of equality become a potential universal right for nationals of the Member States,

* The opinions expressed are purely personal to the author.

[1] On these tensions, see E Spaventa and M Dougan (eds), *Social Welfare and EU Law* (Oxford, Hart Publishing, 2005); G de Búrca (ed), *EU Law and the Welfare State. In Search of Solidarity* (Oxford, Oxford University Press, 2005).

[2] See Council Directive 93/96/EEC of the Council of 29 October 1993 on the right of residence for students, 1993 OJ L317/59; Council Directive 90/364/EEC of 28 June 1990 on the right of residence, 1990 OJ L180/26; Council Directive 90/365/EEC of 28 June 1990 on the right of residence for employees and self-employed persons who have ceased their occupational activity, 1990 OJ L180/28.

[3] D Kochenov and R Plender, 'EU Citizenship: From an Incipient Form to an Incipient Substance? The Discovery of the Treaty Text' (2012) 37 *EL Rev* 369. Significantly, the debate after Maastricht turned to the rights of citizenship as constitutional or fundamental rights. In this sense, Advocate General Cosmas underlined that '[I]t follows that the new regime of freedom of movement introduced by Article 8a differs from the previous regime not only by reason of the extent of the category of persons benefiting from this freedom. In other words, Article 8a does not simply enshrine in constitutional terms the acquis communautaire as it existed when it was inserted into the Treaty and complement it by broadening the category of persons entitled to freedom of movement to include other classes of person not pursuing economic activities. Article 8a also enshrines a right of a different kind, a true right of movement, stemming from the status as a citizen of the Union, which is not subsidiary in relation to European unification, whether economic or not', Opinion of AG Cosmas in Case C-378/97 *Wijsenbeek* EU:C:1999:144 point 85. According to Advocate General Wathelet, '[t]he right to move and work is a fundamental and absolute freedom of EU law', Opinion of Advocate General Wathelet in Case C-67/14 *Alimanovic* EU:C:2015:210.

but also the material scope of EU law became de-compartmentalised, with the result that the principle of equal treatment is now applicable to EU citizens in general and not only to economic actors.[4]

In this scenario of extended and reinforced equality through EU citizenship, the possibility of introducing measures that derogate from the equal treatment principle, or that allow restrictions in the field of welfare, through the doctrine of 'public interest requirements' or 'objective justifications', is of utmost interest to the Member States.

Justification arguments are a legitimate feature of the construction of market freedom rules. Nonetheless, in this sphere, the line between the legitimate interests of Member States and protectionism—which is against the very foundations of the single market—is often blurred. Indeed, in the field of free movement of persons and EU citizenship, the practice of social justifications may be seen as a purely technical device by which Member States determine which individuals are entitled to particular social rights within their borders. The political discourse presents, however, a more complex background, heightened not only by the alleged fiscal impact of mobility on the budgets of receiving States, but also by considerations of belongingness, merit and solidarity.[5] Hence, whereas EU citizenship possibly represents in itself the most paradigmatic example of the development of a form of citizenship beyond the State,[6] its restriction through the lack of access to certain rights and, indeed, the debates on supposed forms of 'welfare tourism', are representative of a countering and exclusionary trend.[7] In this regard, political and legal debates are closely intertwined. As the paradigm of this development, the idea of the prevention of 'benefit tourism', strongly entrenched in the political discourse in certain Member States, is making its way into the legal arena as a forceful argument.[8]

Against this background, the particular legal framework of free movement and equal treatment in primary and secondary law frames the practice of justifications. The constitutional construction of free movement as a citizenship right under Article 21 TFEU refers, since the Treaty of Maastricht, to the limitations and conditions laid down not only in the Treaties, but also in legislation. The legislator has established conditions for the right to reside in other Member States based on the sufficiency of the citizen's economic resources, and has also limited the principle

[4] See Case C-85/96 *Martinez Sala* EU:C:1998:217; Case C-184/99 *Grzelczyk* EU:C:2001:458; Case C-138/02 *Collins* EU:C:2004:172. For a critique, see C Tomuschat, 'Case C-85/96, *Maria Martinez Sala v Freistaat Bayern*' (2000) 37 *CML Rev* 449.

[5] E Guild, S Carrera and K Eisele, *Social Benefits and Migration: A Contested Relationship and Policy Challenge in the EU* (Brussels, Centre for European Policy Studies, 2013).

[6] Y Soysal, *Limits of Citizenship: Migrants and Postnational Membership in Europe* (Chicago, University of Chicago Press, 1994) 1.

[7] D Acosta Arcarazo and J Martire, 'Trapped in the Lobby: Europe's Revolving Doors and the Other as Xenos' (2014) 39 *EL Rev* 362.

[8] See the discussion on Directive 2004/38/EC of the European Parliament and of the Council of 29 April 2004 on the right of citizens of the Union and their family members to move and reside freely within the territory of the Member States, OJ [2004] L 158/77.

of equal treatment with regard to social assistance and maintenance grants for studies in Article 24(2) of Directive 2004/38.[9] This provision states that, by way of derogation from the principle of equal treatment, 'the host Member State shall not be obliged to confer entitlement to social assistance during the first three months of residence or, where appropriate, the longer period provided for [job seekers] nor shall it be obliged, prior to acquisition of the right of permanent residence, to grant maintenance aid for studies, including vocational training, consisting in student grants or student loans to persons other than workers, self-employed persons, persons who retain such status and members of their families'. Thus, through secondary law, the legislator has introduced new elements into the discussion on social justifications, replacing within the realm of Article 24(2) the previous case-by-case approach of fixed residential requirements. This has led to one of the most problematic episodes of interaction between Treaty law and secondary law, and between the judiciary and the legislator.[10] Indeed, through the operation of the Directive, the reference in Article 21 TFEU to 'limitations and conditions laid down in the Treaties and by the measures adopted to give them effect' has been framed as marking, 'an exception to the normal rule that secondary law cannot adjust primary law'.[11]

The case-by-case analysis of social justifications had occupied a crucial place in the case law of the Court of Justice before the entry into force of Directive 2004/38. This importance continues with regard to cases in which the derogations from and limitations of Articles 7(1)(b) and 24(2) of the Directive are not applicable (for example, regarding workers),[12] or cases that fall outside the Directive's personal scope of application (for example, when citizens are claiming benefits from their own States).[13] However, the role of proportionality, intrinsic to the methodological approach to the analysis of objective justifications, is still doubtful in the framework of the Directive, as the cases of *Brey*, *Dano* and *Alimanovic* make apparent.[14]

Against that background, this chapter aims to understand what is meant by social justifications, what social objectives Member States may legitimately pursue in order to limit free movement, and how proportionality is assessed in such

[9] The prevention of 'benefit tourism' had already been portrayed as a legitimate objective by Advocate General Geelhoed (Opinion in Case C-209/03 *Bidar* EU:C:2004:715 point 66) and has explicitly been recognised as such within the terms of Directive 2004/38 (Case C-333/13 *Dano* EU:C:2014:2358 paras 79–80).

[10] See P Syrpis (ed), *The Judiciary, the Legislature and the EU Internal Market* (Cambridge, Cambridge University Press, 2012).

[11] N Nic Shuibhne, 'Exceptions to the free movement rules' in C Barnard and S Peers (eds), *European Union Law* (Oxford, Oxford University Press, 2014) 478.

[12] Cases C-379/11 *Caves Krier Frères* EU:C:2012:798; C-542/09 *Commission v Netherlands* EU:C:2012:346; C-20/12 *Giersch and others* EU:C:2013:411.

[13] Joined Cases C-11/06 and 12/06 *Morgan and Bucher* EU:C:2007:626; and Cases C-503/09 *Stewart* EU:C:2011:500; C-523/11 and 585/11 *Prinz & Seeberger* EU:C:2013:524; C-220/12 *Thiele Meneses* EU:C:2013:683.

[14] Cases C-333/13 *Dano* EU:C:2014:2358; C-140/12 *Brey* EU:C:2013:565 and Opinion of AG Wathelet in Case C-67/14 *Alimanovic* (n 3).

cases. For these purposes, the chapter analyses the cases resolved on the basis of the citizenship provisions of the Treaty, where a 'justification' approach has been adopted, with a focus on students case law. The chapter is organised as follows. Section II explores the notion of 'social justifications', mapping the legitimate objectives of social content that have been accepted by the Court. Section III analyses the problematic issue of the overlapping content of social and economic justifications. Section IV examines the emergence of an 'integration objective' and its interaction with the objective to avoid an unreasonable burden on national welfare systems. Section V explains the practice of justifications aimed at preserving the elements of national systems of social provision, such as welfare payments or access to education, with a focus on the particularities that affect the analysis of the appropriateness and necessity of State measures. Finally, the chapter will conclude with some remarks on the tensions between the impact of European integration, destined to lead progressively to a transformation of the assumptions that underlie national rules governing access to grants and social benefits, and the strategies that Member States may still use to retain a certain degree of control, as exemplified by the recent cases.

II. SOCIAL JUSTIFICATIONS AND THE SOCIAL MANDATES OF THE TREATY

The practice of justification relies on the existence of certain objectives related to public interest concerns that Member States consider worthy of preservation from the liberalising effects of market freedoms. It becomes clear, from a reading of the case law, that differences in treatment or restrictions on the freedoms conferred by the Treaty can only be justified if they are based on objective considerations independent of the nationality of the persons concerned and if they are proportionate to their legitimate aim. This indeterminate and elastic notion of objective considerations has found a breeding ground in the social field, with multiple references to the protection of welfare and social services having been accepted by the Court.[15] Indeed, it is easy to frame a public policy measure in terms of its ultimate social purposes, all the more so where the Court has been relatively lenient, in this particular field, to accept financial or budgetary concerns as legitimate objectives.[16] Member States are therefore often successful at the stage of proving the legitimate nature of an objective. This can be considered as an indicator of the openness of the Court towards considerations of social content.

[15] C Barnard, 'Derogations, Justifications and the Four Freedoms: is the State Interest Really Protected?' in C Barnard and O Odudu (eds), *The Outer Limits of European Union Law* (Oxford, Hart Publishing, 2009) 279, referring, eg, to objectives such as preserving the financial balance of a social security scheme, preventing fraud on the social security system, or the obligation of solidarity.

[16] Indeed, as Snell posits, '[t]he case law affords Member States a significant degree of freedom to protect their public finances, and in fact the Court has explicitly stated that the protection of public finances is a legitimate interest'. See J Snell, 'Economic Justifications and the Role of the State', ch 2 in this volume.

The doctrine of justifications is not premised upon the need that the public interests raised by the States are also protected as a Union interest, as is the case with regard to express Treaty derogations.[17] Nonetheless, in the specific case of social justifications, the recognition of a legitimate interest of the States converges with the need to ensure the protection and promotion of values that are placed among the core objectives of the Union itself. The Treaties confirm their attachment to fundamental social rights and to the social progress of the peoples of the Member States,[18] and set as an objective the promotion of their well-being. The functioning of the internal market shall be based on 'a highly competitive social market economy aiming at full employment and social progress' and the Union shall promote social justice and protection.[19] Moreover, the Union shall take into account the requirements linked to the guarantee of adequate social protection, the fight against social exclusion and a high level of education when defining and implementing its policies and activities.[20] Other specific objectives which are usually labelled as 'social', such as the promotion of student mobility,[21] also converge with Treaty objectives.

Alongside the express social mandates contained in the Treaties, social and welfare objectives are particularly relevant in their role as justifications. In fact, the Union has to rely on Member States to pursue the above-mentioned objectives and values, given that it does not have competences as a welfare provider. It is in light of this 'symbiotic relationship' between EU law and national law[22] that we have to understand the variety and breadth of justifications ultimately connected with social purposes that have been accepted by the case law. Within the specific field of citizenship case law, the fact that a wide array of justifications has been admitted as legitimate unveils the tensions intrinsic to the delicate balance between the objective to foster the exercise of the fundamental right of free movement, and the need to preserve State welfare functions.[23]

Against this background, three types of objective considerations can be discerned in the case law of the Court. A first type of justification seeks to preserve State measures that set in motion different incentives to change or promote certain behaviours

[17] N Nic Shuibhne, 'Exceptions to the free movement rules' in C Barnard and S Peers (eds), *European Union Law* (Oxford, Oxford University Press, 2014) 481.

[18] Preamble to the TEU.

[19] Article 3(1) and (3) TEU.

[20] Article 9 TFEU.

[21] Article 165(2) TFEU. See Case C-542/09 *Commission v The Netherlands* EU:C:2012:346.

[22] This notion is taken from S O'Leary, 'Solidarity and Citizenship Rights in the Charter of Fundamental Rights of the European Union' in G de Búrca (ed), *EU Law and the Welfare State. In Search of Solidarity* (Oxford, Oxford University Press, 2005) 58.

[23] For a critique concerning the case law of the Court concerning economically inactive free movers, see K Hailbronner, 'Union Citizenship and Access to Social Benefits' (2005) 42 *CML Rev* 1245. For a discussion on the impact of free movement case law on social rights, see N Reich, 'Free Movement v Social Rights in an Enlarged Union—the Laval and Viking Cases before the ECJ' (2008) 9 *German Law Journal* 125. To explore that question in terms of the distinct approach to economically active and non-economically active citizens, see ch 3 in this volume.

of the members of a given society in order to attain specific outcomes or to protect specific values that may be positive for the public interest. Indeed, Member States have often resorted to 'promotion measures' that aim at fostering student mobility,[24] encouraging the recruitment of workers of a certain age,[25] increasing the proportion of residents holding a higher education degree,[26] or promoting the building of dwellings in order to ensure an adequate supply of housing.[27] Other measures aim at the preservation of features that are considered, per se, desirable as a policy choice such as having an open and democratic university system,[28] maintaining a balanced high-quality medical service open to all,[29] ensuring high standards of university education,[30] the preservation or improvement of the education system,[31] or guaranteeing sufficient housing for the low-income or otherwise disadvantaged sections of the local population.[32] In many cases, the objectives have mixed purposes, and their purported aim is a means for a more general socio-economic objective.[33]

A second kind of justification, which can be considered as functional to the first one, concerns measures having organisational or administrative purposes that are instrumental to the correct functioning of welfare benefits.[34] This includes the convenience of avoiding duplication of aids,[35] or the need to monitor the employment and/or family situation of a beneficiary.[36]

Finally, the third and most common type of objective is linked to the general need to preserve the financial viability of national welfare schemes through the restriction of the potential circle of beneficiaries. For this purpose, Member States avail themselves of various restrictive criteria to make the entitlement to benefits dependent on residence requirements,[37] on the fact of being a child of a migrant worker,[38] on the country in which studies have been accomplished,[39] on specific features of the quality or length of the studies to be pursued,[40] or on the length

[24] Case C-542/09 *Commission v Netherlands* (n 12); Case C-220/12 *Thiele Meneses* (n 13).

[25] Case C-379/11 *Caves Krier Frères* (n 12).

[26] Case C-20/12 *Giersch* (n 12).

[27] Case C-152/05 *Commission v Germany* EU:C:2008:17. It is to be noted that, in this case, the Court did not explicitly state that the objective was legitimate since it considered that 'on any view' the measure was disproportionate.

[28] Case C-73/08 *Bressol* EU:C:2010:181; Case C-147/03 *Commission v Austria* EU:C:2005:427 para 66.

[29] Case C-73/08 *Bressol* ibid, para 62.

[30] Opinion of AG Sharpston in *Bressol* EU:C:2009:396, point 102.

[31] Case C-40/05 *Lyyski* EU:C:2007:10 para 39.

[32] Joined Cases C-197/11 and C-203/11 *Libert e.a.* EU:C:2013:288.

[33] For example, that students complete their courses in a short period of time, therefore contributing to the financial equilibrium of the educational system. See Joined Cases C-11/06 and 12/06 *Morgan and Bucher* EU:C:2007:626 para 36.

[34] Somek refers to these justifications as 'administrative objectives'. See A Somek, 'Solidarity Decomposed: Being and Time in European Citizenship' (2007) 32 *EL Rev* 787.

[35] Joined Cases C-11/06 and 12/06 *Morgan and Bucher* (n 13).

[36] Cases C-406/04 *De Cuyper* EU:C:2006:491; C-499/06 *Nerkowska* EU:C:2008:300; C-221/07 *Zablocka-Weyhermüller* EU:C:2008:681.

[37] Cases C-158/07 *Förster* EU:C:2008:630; C-359/13 *Martens* EU:C:2015:118.

[38] Case C-258/04 *Ioannidis* EU:C:2005:559 para 33.

[39] Cases C-258/04 *Ioannidis* ibid para 31; C-224/98 *D'Hoop* EU:C:2002:432 para 39.

[40] Case C-275/12 *Elrick* EU:C:2013:684.

of time of studies in the provider Member State.[41] In this regard, the most widely employed reasoning is that of avoiding an unreasonable burden on national welfare systems through the requirement of criteria that determine the existence of a 'real' or 'genuine' link with the Member State in question—which we will refer to as the 'integration objective' and which, as explained in Section V, is developing into an 'independent objective'. The social or economic nature of this objective is widely disputed, and will be discussed below in Section III. Here, it suffices to note that the Court has accepted that it is legitimate for a State to wish to ensure that there exists a real link between jobseekers and the labour market of a Member State in order to grant them benefits related to access to employment,[42] to grant assistance only to students who are sufficiently integrated in the society of the host State,[43] or to limit the obligation of solidarity to war victims that have a connection with a certain population.[44]

III. ECONOMIC CONSIDERATIONS AS A FUNCTION OF SOCIAL OBJECTIVES?

The material basis of 'social' justifications is the framing of a State measure in terms that show that its inspirational foundations are connected to the promotion or protection of a social objective. This criterion is ultimately very broad and indeterminate, and embraces a wide panoply of considerations, which are intertwined with basic state functions.[45] Thus, the identification and isolation of a truly social objective, independent from economic justifications—which are, in principle,[46] excluded from being considered legitimate objectives[47]—presents significant difficulties from a conceptual point of view.

[41] Case C-367/11 *Prete* EU:C:2012:668.

[42] Eg in Cases C-224/98 *D'Hoop* (n 39); C-138/02 *Collins* (n 4); C-258/04 *Ioannidis* (n 38); C-367/11 *Prete* ibid. Nonetheless, integration into society should also play a role for jobseekers; see, eg, the Opinion of AG Cruz Villalón in *Prete* EU:C:2012:501 at point 39: 'Among the objectives legitimately pursued by States, the Court emphasised in that judgment the existence of "a connection between persons who claim entitlement to such an allowance and its employment market [that of the host Member State]". Consequently, the case-law allows a host State to require job seekers from other Member States to demonstrate a degree of integration. This may be the integration that exists between the job seeker and the labour market, but it may also be the connection between the job seeker and the host society, whether through the existence of family or emotional ties with nationals of the host State or through a prolonged period of residence.'

[43] Cases C-209/03 *Bidar* EU:C:2005:169; C-158/07 *Förster* (n 37); C-11/06 and 12/06 *Morgan and Bucher* (n 13); C-503/09 *Stewart* EU:C:2011:500; C-542/09 *Commission v Netherlands* (n 12); C-147/03 *Commission v Austria*; C-523/11 and 585/11 *Prinz & Seeberger* (n 13); C-20/12 *Giersch* (n 12); C-220/12 *Thiele Menese* (n 13) and C-359/13 *Martens* (n 37).

[44] Case C-192/05 *Tas-Hagen* EU:C:2006:676; and Cases C-499/06 *Nerkowska* and C-221/07 *Zablocka-Weyhermüller* (n 36).

[45] See ch 2 in this volume.

[46] Case C-542/09 *Commission v Netherlands* (n 12) para 69.

[47] It is to be noted that Article 27 of Directive 2004/38 states, as a general principle, that 'Member States may restrict the freedom of movement and residence of Union citizens and their family members, irrespective of nationality, on grounds of public policy, public security or public health'. However, '[t]hese grounds *shall not be invoked to serve economic ends*.'

Among the different types of legitimate objectives enunciated in Section II, the objective on which Member States most often rely is the need to avoid an unreasonable burden on their social assistance systems. This acceptance of economic justifications is not exclusive to the field of citizenship, as Chapter 2 in this volume explains.[48] However, the economic objective is not framed in purely protectionist terms, but is rather directly connected to a 'higher' end. As Roth puts it, even if it is evident that all the elements considered can be regarded to have an economic component, 'it should be made clear that the economic aim is not accepted as an end in itself, but only as *instrumental* towards safeguarding public health [or another social justification] as the final *non-economic objective*'.[49]

This flexible approach towards economic considerations, the ultimate purpose of which can be somehow traced back to a social aim, lends legitimacy to economic objectives related to the financial sustainability of welfare and public provision schemes. As one of the potential fields to help unveil the 'social ideal' of the Court of Justice, Schiek has pointed to the case law aimed at 'maintaining collective mechanisms (for example, through insurance) for protection against risks such as ill health, old age, unemployment and permanent need of care, as well as dire poverty for other reasons';[50] that is, 'public provision of social welfare in classical functions'.[51] This strategy, analysed in Chapter 2, is limited by the difficulty of demonstrating in a given case the real impact of national measures on the overall financial balance. Moreover, this reasoning bears with it the risk of becoming generalised to all cases in which welfare benefits or access to public services are at stake. As Advocate General Sharpston notes, the acceptance by the Court of these objectives as overriding reasons in the public interest 'may, in part, reflect the inescapable fact that every public service provided by our welfare states is dependent on there being sufficient budgetary means to finance it'.[52] The need to demonstrate a real risk for the balance and survival of the system whose sustainability is advanced as an objective of public policy is indeed very difficult to assess at the

[48] In the field of free movement of goods and services with regard to reimbursement of medical expenses, several cases have already advanced in this direction. Even though budgetary considerations intended to reduce operating costs of a sickness insurance scheme were rejected in *Duphar* as economic objectives (Case 238/82 EU:C:1984:45), in *Decker* (Case C-120/95 EU:C:1998:167) and *Kohll* (Case C-158/96 EU:C:1998:171), the Court stated that the risk of seriously undermining the financial balance of the social security system could constitute an overriding reason in the general interest, even though in the cases at issue the national measure was not justified, since it had no actual effect on the financing or balance of the social security system. The Court finally accepted budgetary reasons as justifications in more explicit terms in *Geraets-Smits and Peerbooms* (Case C-157/99 EU:C:2001:404). This idea has proliferated in latter cases.

[49] W-H Roth, 'Economic Justifications and the Internal Market' in M Bulterman, L Hancher, A McDonnell and H Svenster (eds), *Views of European Law from the Mountain. Liber Amicorum Piet Jan Slot* (Amsterdam, Wolters Kluwer, 2009) 81 (emphasis added).

[50] D Schiek, 'Is there a Social Ideal of the European Court of Justice?' in U Neergaard, R Nielsen and L Roseberry (eds), *The Role of Courts in Developing a European Social Model* (Copenhagen, DJOF Publishing, 2010) 78.

[51] W-H Roth, 'Economic Justifications and the Internal Market' (n 49).

[52] Opinion of AG Sharpston in Case C-73/08 *Bressol* (n 30) para 91.

stage of the determination of the legitimacy of the objective, and belongs rather with the analysis of the proportionality.

In this regard, the danger of overgeneralisation intrinsic to the reasoning of budgetary justifications has materialised through its acceptance in secondary legislation. Indeed, the budgetary objective is explicitly acknowledged by the legislator through the conditions laid down in Articles 7 and 14 of Directive 2004/38, according to which Union citizens who do not have worker or self-employment status must have sufficient resources, as well as by the derogations enshrined in Article 24(2) of the Directive. In *Brey*, the Court underlined that the first of these provisions is precisely intended 'to prevent such persons becoming an unreasonable burden on the social assistance system of the host Member State', which is based 'on the idea that the exercise of the right of residence for citizens of the Union can be subordinated to the legitimate interests of the Member States [such as] the protection of their public finances'.[53]

IV. TOWARDS A COMMUNITARIAN APPROACH TO SOLIDARITY? THE CENTRALITY OF INTEGRATION REQUIREMENTS

Despite the clear acceptance of the 'financial objective' through legislation and case law, the legitimacy of budgetary considerations often comes coupled with the expression of the desire of Member States to require proof of a certain degree of integration or a genuine connection with their societies. Indeed, national measures aimed at ensuring a certain degree of integration into or a link with the society of a Member State have commonly been put forward as a means to allow for a reasonable limitation of the circle of beneficiaries, with the ultimate (legitimate) goal of avoiding an unreasonable burden on the national welfare system. Therefore, initially, the notion of integration was a function of the financial soundness objective. This formulation was explicitly put forward in *Bidar*, where the Court stated that, with regard to non-economically active citizens,

> it is permissible for a Member State to ensure that the grant of assistance to cover the maintenance costs of students from other Member States does not become an unreasonable burden which could have consequences for the overall level of assistance which may be granted by that State.[54]

It is for this reason that it was legitimate to limit the benefit in question only to those students 'who have demonstrated a certain degree of integration into the society of that State'.[55] According to this formulation, the final objective, which is considered as justified by the Court, is precisely to prevent negative consequences for the overall level of assistance in the State concerned. For this purpose, the State may use the 'integration link' as an instrumental connector, which may help to

[53] Case C-140/12 *Brey* (n 14) paras 54 and 55.
[54] Case C-209/03 *Bidar* (n 43) para 56.
[55] ibid, para 56. See also Joined Cases C-11/06 and 12/06 *Morgan and Bucher* (n 13) para 43.

limit the potentially large number of individuals that may claim assistance. Thus, in purely conceptual terms, the existence of an 'integration link' would not be considered in itself as an overriding reason in the public interest, but it would merely constitute the content of a type of measure that may help to attain the actual objective of preserving the financial sustainability of a welfare scheme.[56]

Nevertheless, this functional approach to integration requirements has disappeared in other cases, giving the impression that a new and independent legitimate objective has emerged. The progressive autonomy of the requirement of 'a certain degree of integration' can be traced back to the cases concerning job seekers, where the notion of a 'real link with the employment market' was first developed (*D'Hoop*, *Collins*, *Ioannidis* and *Prete*).[57] In all these cases, the 'integration link' is considered *in itself* as a justification, without expressing the underpinning 'financial balance' objective. In the same vein, the case law concerning benefits for war victims also expresses the national wish to limit the obligation of solidarity to those victims who had links with the concerned population as a legitimate and objective consideration of public interest, without considering its actual incidence in the financial sustainability of such a scheme.[58] This evolution of the 'integration' or the 'real link' criterion towards the status of an independent 'legitimate objective' seemed to have reached completion in *Stewart*, a case concerning the refusal by the British authorities to grant a short-term incapacity benefit to a British national living in Spain. In its ruling, the Court referred to two apparently different objectives. On the one hand, the first concern was to establish a genuine link between the claimant and the Member State. On the other hand, the second objective, presented distinctly, was 'to preserve the financial balance of the national social security system'.[59]

This debate came once more to the fore in *Prinz*, where Advocate General Sharpston discussed the interpretative possibilities of the integration requirement as a means to achieving the economic objective *or* as an objective in itself. In this sense, she explicitly posited the need to clarify whether the integration objective constitutes a 'separate legitimate objective capable of justifying a restriction on the right of freedom of movement'; whether both objectives 'represent interests that are linked and that should therefore be considered as part of a single objective'; or whether the degree of integration criterion is 'merely a means to achieve the economic objective'.[60] Indeed, as the Advocate General explains, the need for clarification arises out of the fact that this confusion projects into the assessment

[56] See, in this regard, the Opinion of AG Sharpston in Case C-542/09 *Commission v the Netherlands* EU:C:2012:79, point 78.

[57] In *D'Hoop* (n 39) at para 38, the Court stated that 'it is legitimate for the national legislature to wish to ensure that there is a real link between the applicant for [an] allowance and the geographic employment market concerned'. This formula was restated in *Collins*, *Ioannidis* and *Prete*.

[58] Case C-192/05 *Tas Hagen* (n 44); and Cases C-499/06 *Nerkowska* and C-221/07 *Zablocka-Weyhermüller* (n 36).

[59] Case C-503/09 *Stewart* (n 13) para 90.

[60] Opinion of Advocate General Sharpston in Case C-523/11 *Prinz & Seeberger* EU:C:2013:90.

of proportionality of measures (as we will see in Section V): '[t]he ambiguity as to whether a restriction such as the residence requirement contained in the three-year rule can be justified on the basis of the economic objective or the integration objective appears to have resulted in false logic when it comes to assessing the proportionality of such a restriction. The Member States appear to invoke the economic objective in order to justify a restriction but then submit that the measure is proportionate by reference to the integration objective'.[61]

Despite the apparent evolution towards an autonomous and fully fledged integration objective, the judgment of the Court in *Prinz* seemed to have reinstated the validity of the financial requirement as the underpinning goal of the integration objective: 'in order to ensure that the grant of assistance to cover the maintenance costs of students from other Member States does not become an unreasonable burden which could have consequences for the overall level of assistance which may be granted by that State', it is legitimate for Member States to grant such 'assistance only to students who have demonstrated a certain degree of integration into the society of that State'.[62] However, again, in the recent case of *Martens*,[63] also concerning students who claim portable benefits against their state of nationality, Member States argued exclusively in terms of integration, and the Court did not consider underlying financial considerations, acknowledging the virtue of integration as an objective in itself. These cases demonstrate the ductile nature of integration considerations, which can be used as an objective on its own, and/or at the same time, as a privileged proxy for financial objectives.

The idea of integration as an autonomous objective extends to the regulatory framework of Directive 2004/38, as can be induced from the Court's reasoning in *Förster*.[64] In this case, despite the fact that the Directive was not applicable *ratione temporis*, the Court declared that a condition of five years' uninterrupted residence—which coincides with the length of residence that leads to the acquisition of permanent residence, provided for in the Directive, with regard to study and maintenance grants—was appropriate for the purpose of guaranteeing that the applicant for the maintenance grant at issue was integrated into the society of the host Member State and did not go beyond what was necessary in order to attain that objective. Therefore, following this rationale, we can also identify the same 'integration philosophy' in Article 24(2) of Directive 2004/38.

Finally, and to close the circle, the 'integration objective' has also been introduced in cases concerning economically active citizens. The Court was very careful in *Commission v Netherlands* to rule out the possibility of applying justifications based on unreasonable financial burdens in cases where the rights of workers are at stake.[65] However, even though the Court insisted on the differences between

[61] ibid point 77.
[62] ibid para 36. See also, Case C-220/12 *Thiele Meneses* (n 13).
[63] Case C-359/13 *Martens* (n 37).
[64] Case C-158/07 *Förster* (n 37).
[65] Case C-542/09 *Commission v Netherlands* (n 12) para 65.

student cases per se (particularly, *Bidar* and *Förster*) and cases concerning students who are the children of migrant workers, it went on to state that the Member States' power to require nationals of other Member States to show a certain degree of integration is not limited to situations in which the applicants are economically inactive.[66] The Court found that the existence of a residence requirement to prove the required degree of integration is 'in principle' inappropriate when the persons concerned are migrant workers or frontier workers.[67] The Court explains why workers are deemed to be integrated—they pay taxes so they contribute to the financing of social policies.[68] As a consequence, financial considerations, mediated through the universalised requirement of integration, are fully applicable to economically active citizens, but the need for their examination in a given case is waived, 'in principle', by the 'rebuttable presumption'[69] that the exercise of economic activities entails an acceptable level of integration.[70] Indeed, in *Giersch*, the Court followed the approach in *Hartmann and Geven* – the 'game changer' case for frontier workers[71]—where it had stated that 'the frontier worker is not always integrated in the Member State of employment in the same way as the worker who is a resident in that State'.[72] As a result, no European citizen is absolutely immune from the consideration of their level of integration, but different degrees of integration demonstrated by different means, and with regard to different kinds of benefits, are required for the various categories of (thus far) workers, migrant student citizens, students who are the children of migrant workers, students who are the children of frontier workers, and home State students who want to study abroad.

Recourse to integration may seem logical in this connection. Through this case law, '[the Court] has conceded that financial and social realism make it unavoidable that some benefits are only available to society's "members"; that is, to those with "a certain degree of integration" in that society'.[73] Certainly, this rationale seems to establish some kind of rule of reason based on the connection of individuals with a society in order to make them deserving of the protection of the State, transforming the very nature of the formerly quasi-economic objective into

[66] ibid para 63.

[67] ibid.

[68] ibid paras 65 and 66.

[69] O'Leary, 'The curious case of frontier workers and study finance: a new "Luxembourg compromise" or a new exception to the free movement of persons?' (Annotation of C-20/12, Giersch) (2014) 51 *CML Rev* 601.

[70] Hoogenboom states in this regard that 'the "fitting in" of migrant Union workers into the genuine link case law is an important conceptual clarification, although the repeated use by the CJEU of the words "in principle" suggests that the Court is still developing this issue'. A Hoogenboom, 'Export of Study Grants and the Lawfulness of Durational Residency Requirements Comments on Case C-542/09, *Commission v Netherlands*' (2012) 14 *European Journal of Migration and Law* 417, 436.

[71] Case C-213/05 *Geven* EU:C:2007:438; Case C-212/05 *Hartmann* EU:C:2007:437. See O'Leary (n 69) 609.

[72] On this discussion see O'Leary, 'Developing an Ever Closer Union Between the Peoples of Europe? A Reappraisal of the Case-law of the Court of Justice on the Free movement of Persons and EU Citizenship' (2008) 27 *Yearbook of European Law* 167.

[73] D Chalmers, C Hadjiemmanuil, G Monti and A Tomkins, *EU Law* 2nd edn (Cambridge, Cambridge University Press, 2006) 456.

an objective that seems to foster a communitarian notion of solidarity. Thus, the idea of making solidarity coextensive to those with substantial links to a community departs from the functional legitimate objective of safeguarding the financial balance of welfare systems, to introduce considerations of membership and worthiness. All in all, the underlying idea is that the 'link' is considered as an element that makes foreigners 'comparable' to citizens.[74]

However, the central role of integration in the justifications debate transforms the whole rationale that underlies the principle of inter-State equal treatment as the paramount vehicle to achieve the integration of free movers. If, traditionally in free movement law, integration of the migrant citizen in the host State is considered as the ultimate objective of equal treatment, the emergence of integration as a legitimate objective entails that equal treatment is an entitlement to be only granted to those who have already previously integrated.[75] As a result, the central role of the notion of 'integration' reinstates European citizens in their quality of 'foreigners'.

V. PROPORTIONALITY ASSESSMENT: THE ROLE OF INTEGRATION AND OF DIRECTIVE 2004/38

Despite the openness of the Court towards objective considerations of social content, and notwithstanding the pervasiveness of integration considerations, the number of citizenship cases where the Court has accepted a national measure as appropriate and necessary is significantly low. Among the examined cases falling into the categories enunciated in Section II of this chapter, the Court has declared State measures proportionate to the 'organisational' objective in only one case: in *De Cuyper*, the residence requirement for unemployment benefits was found to be appropriate and necessary to fulfil the need to monitor the employment and family situation of unemployed persons. As to 'integration'-related objectives, in *Collins*, the Court found the residence requirement as appropriate to prove the connection with the labour market for a jobseeker's allowance, but it left the appreciation of the necessity of the measure to the national court. In *Förster*, the Court considered a residence requirement of five years as proportionate to achieve the objective of granting maintenance assistance only to integrated students, in light of Directive 2004/38.

As a result, it is evident that the more rigorous assessment in the proportionality stage countervails the openness that the Court has shown towards the

[74] On this discussion, see K Lenaerts, 'European Union Citizenship, National Welfare Systems and Social Solidarity' (2011) 18 *Jurisprudence* 397; C O'Brien, 'Real links, abstract rights and false alarms: the relationship between the ECJ's "real link" case law and national solidarity' (2008) 33 *EL Rev* 643.

[75] On this debate, D Thym, 'The Elusive Limits of Solidarity: Residence Rights of and Social Benefits for Economically Inactive Union Citizens' (2015) *CML Rev* 17. For this debate in the field of the common migration policy, K Groenendijk, 'Legal Concepts of Integration in EU Migration Law' (2004) 6 *European Journal of Migration and Law* 111.

consideration of the legitimacy of State objectives and constitutes a development that can be observed with regard to the four freedoms more generally too.[76] In this connection, the intensity of review varies according to the pervasiveness of EU competences with regard to a given matter,[77] and 'areas of particular sensitivity tend to attract a less intensive degree of review'.[78]

The following discussion focuses on the different stages of the proportionality analysis in citizenship cases and, in particular, on the difficulties that arise out of an 'integration link' as either a means towards an economic objective or as an objective on its own, and on the impact of Directive 2004/38 in the practice of justifications.

A. Appropriateness Assessment

The assessment of appropriateness relies on the consistency of State arguments with their purported objective. At this stage, the Court unmasks vague arguments or disingenuous claims, showing that the objective justifications put forward by States, even if legitimate, are not really driving the contested measure. The Court analyses the inspiring rationale of the measures, sometimes taking into account the *travaux préparatoires*,[79] but also their actual connection with the objective in connection with which Member States try to justify the restrictive measure and the suitability of the methods applied in order to achieve it.

Often, the Court exposes clear cases of inconsistency between the purported legitimate objective and the measure at issue, even showing that some measures run counter to the goals alleged. For example, in *Pusa*, the Court found that the measure defended by Finland (calculation of pension subject to attachment, without taking into account taxes paid in another Member State) ran counter to the objective of guaranteeing the debtor a minimum income.[80] In *Morgan and Bucher*, the Court found that the 'first-stage studies' condition was not appropriate either to prevent the duplication of entitlements or to ensure that students completed their courses in a short period of time (thus contributing to the financial

[76] See, in this regard, Barnard, 'Derogations, Justifications and the Four Freedoms' (n 15).

[77] For example, in *Tas-Hagen and Tas*, the Court explicitly noted that in those areas in which the benefit in question falls outside the scope of application of EU law, the Member States should enjoy a wide margin of appreciation.

[78] N Nic Shuibhne, 'Exceptions to the free movement rules' (n 17) 496. See further ch 12 in this volume.

[79] In Case C-73/08 *Bressol* (n 28) one of the justifications put forward by the Belgian Government for the limitations on access in the system of secondary legislation was to avoid excessive burdens on the financing of higher education. Nonetheless, it appeared that this had not been an essential reason for the adoption of the rules in question, and that the financing system did not vary depending on the total number of students. This finding of inappropriateness prevented the Court from examining whether the objective of the 'financial burden' should be available if at all for cases not concerning the payment of student benefits, but access of education itself. On this issue, see the Opinion of AG Sharpston in this case, paras 91 et seq.

[80] Case C-224/02 *Pusa* EU:C:2004:273.

equilibrium of the education system): the condition could even bring about an increase in the overall duration of studies and was therefore inconsistent with the stated objective. In the same vein, in *Elrick*, the Court stated that it was not clear how the objective of subsidising only courses studied abroad which improve students' chances on the labour market could be attained by requiring that the course in question be of at least two years' duration, irrespective of the nature and the content of the course, whereas a course that did not satisfy this condition was subsidised when it was studied in Germany.[81] In *Zablocka-Weyhermüller*, the requirement of domicile in specific Member States with regard to benefits granted to surviving spouses of war victims was also considered as not meeting the objective of providing suitable benefits, taking into account the differences in costs of living, income, and average level of available social benefits.[82]

The assessment of the appropriateness of measures that attempt to ensure the 'integration' objective presents some difficulties nonetheless, the notion of integration being a highly subjective concept. Indeed, the difficulties relating to the 'integration objective' are common to the difficulties of assessing the impact of a national measure that aims at pursuing social objectives influencing the behaviour of citizens or economic operators. In this field, the Court is called to engage in a sociological analysis, where the line between objective factors and subjective assumptions is often difficult to draw. For example, in *Giersch*, a case regarding frontier workers, with regard to a State where this reality is of utmost importance—and where the composition of the population makes it a very particular laboratory of European integration—the Court upheld the assumption that students already resident in Luxembourg are more likely to come back, with the result that a residence condition is considered as appropriate to attain the objective of increasing population with university studies.[83] In this regard, it could be argued that reliance on a purely economic objective would somehow facilitate an 'empirical' assessment of the suitability of certain measures to impact on state finances, so as to prove appropriateness vis-à-vis the justified goal of avoiding unreasonable burdens. Nonetheless, this would lead to complex assessment of national budgets, which in turn opens important questions on the position of courts to carry out assessments of economic policy.[84] In a way, reliance on the 'genuine link' or integration objective as an independent concept allows the Court

[81] Interestingly, the Court did not pronounce itself about the legitimacy of that objective. Case C-275/12 *Elrick* (n 40).

[82] Case C-221/07 *Zablocka-Weyhermüller* (n 36).

[83] Indeed, the Court found that 'students who are resident in Luxembourg when they are about to embark on their higher education studies may be more likely than non-resident students to settle in Luxembourg and become integrated in the Luxembourg labour market after completing their studies, even if those studies were undertaken abroad' (Case C-20/12 *Giersch* (n 12) para 67). For a critical comment on the standard of evidence used in this regard, see O'Leary, 'The curious case of frontier workers' (n 69).

[84] In this regard, see at length N Nic Shuibhne and M Maci, 'Proving Public Interest: The Growing Impact of Evidence in Free Movement Case Law' (2013) 50 *CML Rev* 965.

to bridge these complexities. However, the complexities intrinsic to an examination of the appropriateness of a given measure, in order to show a real connection or a sufficient degree of integration, should not be underestimated. The need for careful consideration of all the elements in play in the circumstances of the case will often entail that the most adequate stage to carry out this analysis will be the examination of the necessity of the measure.

The assessment of necessity and appropriateness can, however, appear as somehow blurred when it comes to proving the proportionality of State measures with regard to the integration objective. The thin line between the tests is shown in two cases concerning residence requirements with regard to a benefit and a pension for civilian war victims. On the one hand, in *Nerkowska*, the Court observed that a residence requirement constituted a criterion capable of showing that there is a connection with the society of the Member State, but that this requirement went beyond what was necessary to attain the objective of preserving the obligation of solidarity to those with links to Polish society. On the other hand, in *Tas-Hagen and Tas*, the Court stated that the condition that a national of a Member State should be resident in that Member State at the specific time of the application for a benefit was not appropriate to the legitimate objective put forward, since it was not a satisfactory indicator of the degree of attachment to the population of the Netherlands. In the same vein, in *Stewart*, the Court established that a condition of presence in the territory of the Member State at the time of application for an invalidity benefit was appropriate neither to establish a genuine link nor to the objective of financial balance of the national social security system. Following the reasoning of these cases, it seems that the justification put forward is to be rejected at the appropriateness step only in cases where the requirement in question is absolutely disconnected from its capability of proving any degree of integration. Indeed, from these cases, we can draw the conclusion that requirements of residence or presence which are not durational, but that merely refer to a point in time, are not an appropriate proxy for integration.

B. Necessity Assessment

Whatever the conceptual classification of integration might be—as a privileged proxy for the financial objective or as an independent objective—it often serves as the reference for the necessity assessment of the measure. For example, despite the fact that the Court found in *Prinz* that the objective pursued was the avoidance of an unreasonable burden to public finance, the reasoning devoted to the analysis of appropriateness and necessity in this judgment does not reveal a consideration of the actual financial impact of the measures at issue, but rather examines the proportionality of the residence requirement as a connector to German society. As this case highlights, in both instances (when integration works as a proxy for the financial objective, or as an objective on its own), the practical implications are similar: the centrality of integration considerations spares Member States the need to demonstrate the real impact of the granting of a particular benefit on the sustainability of welfare finances. This point has already been put forward by Advocate General Sharpston, in her Opinion in *Commission v the Netherlands*. She warned that a superficial reading of the case law on the 'integration requirements' might be read as indicating that:

> Member States can set a residence requirement, irrespective of whether its purpose is to ensure that making available a social advantage does not adversely affect the stability of its public finances or the pursuit of any other legitimate objective justified by overriding reasons of public interest. On that basis, Member States might seek to justify less favourable treatment of (both economically active and inactive) EU citizens in terms of social policy (integration) by applying access criteria such as length of residence, marital and family status, language, diplomas, employment, and so forth, without ever explaining why the availability of a social benefit should be limited in that way.[85]

Against this background, and having in mind the central role that integration has acquired in the practice of social justifications, it is of utmost importance to define an EU law approach to this concept that would rationalise its use as a proxy or as a legitimate objective, without falling into purely subjective considerations. In this regard, the case law of the Court of Justice already provides for some useful indicators.

In the first place, it has to be noted that the necessity test is not met when a national measure makes it impossible for a citizen of the Union to have access to the benefit at issue under any circumstances and notwithstanding his real level of integration. This was the case in *Bidar*, since students were excluded by the relevant national legislation from ever being regarded as legally 'settled' in the national territory.

In the second place, the necessity of a measure will be examined having in mind alternative regulatory approaches. For example, in *Schwarz and Gootjes-Schwarz*, the Court found that the refusal of a tax relief for school fees incurred in other Member States was not necessary, since less stringent methods than refusing the tax advantage altogether could be found.[86] In this regard, it has to be noted that the assessment of the possible less restrictive measures that would be suitable to attain the legitimate objective is gaining importance. The parties, and the Court, often engage in legal creativeness in this regard, suggesting to Member States what they could do instead. This analysis closely follows the nature of the benefit scheme at issue. For example, with regard to measures pursuing 'organisational objectives', in *de Cuyper*, the Court rejected that less restrictive means, such as the production of certificates, would meet the need to monitor compliance with the requirements for the retention of the entitlement to unemployment benefits;[87]

[85] Point 85 of the Opinion of Advocate General Sharpston in Case C-542/09 *Commission v Netherlands* (n 56).

[86] Case C-76/05 *Schwarz and Gootjes-Schwarz* EU:C:2007:492.

[87] Considering mostly the specificity of the unemployment benefit system and that the effectiveness of monitoring measures depend on the fact that the monitoring is unexpected by the beneficiary of the unemployment (Case C-406/04 *De Cuyper* (n 36) para 45).

however, in *Nerkowska* the Court enumerated several alternative measures that could lead the Member State to attain the legitimate objective of verifying that the recipient continues to satisfy the conditions for the grant of the benefit.[88] In another case, where the 'behavioural' social objective was to increase the proportion of residents holding higher education degrees, the creative legal reasoning of the Court went as far as to put forward the possibility of making student finance conditional upon the return to work and residence of the claimant in the Member State granting the aid.[89]

With regard to the 'integration objective', in the majority of cases in which the States put forward measures that allegedly attempted to ensure the existence of a real connection with the employment market or with the society of that State, the Court found that they went beyond what was necessary to attain the objective. At this point, instead of identifying less stringent measures, the Court often finds that the measures adopted were too general and exclusive or unduly favoured one element to the exclusion of other representative elements relevant to determining a certain level of integration. Indeed, when national law treats a single element as the only possible criterion to demonstrate a 'real link' with that society, it is bound to fail and be deemed disproportionate by the Court.[90] It was Advocate General Geelhoed who first verbalised this in his Opinion in *Bidar*. Indeed, when discussing the criteria and conditions that Member States could impose in order to be eligible for social assistance, he insisted that

> it should also be possible to apply them with sufficient flexibility to take account of the particular individual circumstances of applicants, where refusal of such assistance is likely to affect what is known in German Constitutional law as the 'Kernbereich' or the substantive core of a fundamental right granted by the Treaty, such as the rights contained in Article 18 (1) EC [Article 21 (1)TFEU].[91]

This approach can be traced back to the early cases on EU citizenship, such as *Baumbast*,[92] and can consistently be found in rulings regarding economically inactive citizens (students and jobseekers) when States relied on a sole condition (place of the diploma of education in *D'Hoop* and *Ioannidis*; the first stage studies condition in *Morgan and Bucher*; or the six years of studies condition in *Prete*). For example, in *Morgan and Bucher*, the Court considered that it was disproportionate not to take into account the fact that the applicants had been raised in Germany and completed their schooling there, regardless of the fact that they had not completed at least one year of their university course in Germany.[93] As Dougan argues,

[88] Indeed, the Court stated that Member States could request the recipient to go back in order to comply with administrative and medical checks.

[89] Judgment in Case C-20/12 *Giersch* (n 12) para 79.

[90] See eg Case C-213/05 *Geven* (n 71).

[91] Opinion of AG Geelhoed in Case C-209/03 *Bidar* EU:C:2004:715 point 32.

[92] Case C-413/99 *Baumbast* EU:C:2002:493 paras 92–93.

[93] Similar reasoning has been applied in other cases; see, eg, Case 542/09 *Commission v Netherlands* or Case C-20/12 *Giersch* (n 12).

Morgan and Bucher is important in two respects. First, there is a clear instruction 'to take into account the claimant's individual circumstances'; second, Member States 'are obliged in all cases to give appropriate weight to both economic and non-economic links with the national community'.[94]

Nonetheless, the difficulties attached to some of these judgments derive from the fact that the Court does not mention what these other elements might be, but it merely determines 'negatively … the legislative means which is overbroad and too exclusionary with regard to attaining' the particular objective.[95] Useful guidance can be found in recent cases that examine the denial of certain benefits to a State's own nationals due to the introduction of residence or past residence conditions. Remarkably, in *Stewart*, the Court stated that a condition of past presence for access to invalidity benefits was too exclusive in nature, and pointed at other elements to establish that connection: the relationship between the claimant and the social security system; family circumstances (in this case, a person dependent on parents who are retired but had worked in that Member State); the fact of having been present in that Member State for a significant part of the claimant's life; and, why not, *nationality*.[96] This holistic approach to integration is confirmed in *Prinz*, where the Court established that some students that do not fulfil a requirement of uninterrupted residence for three years may be nonetheless connected to German society, particularly 'where the student is a *national* of the State concerned and was educated there for a significant period or on account of other factors such as, in particular, his family, employment, language skills or the existence of other social and economic factors'.[97] In the same vein, the Court has emphasised in *Martens* the need 'to take account of other factors which may connect such a student to the Member State providing the benefit, such as the *nationality* of the student, his schooling, family, employment, language skills or the existence of other social and economic factors'.[98]

All in all, it can be stated that the Court looks at the overall situation of the person involved, amounting to what can be referred to as a 'personalized analysis of proportionality'[99] (a method that has been labelled by others as 'the personal circumstances approach').[100] As a result, it has become clear that the Court tends

[94] M Dougan, 'Expanding the Frontiers of Union Citizenship by Dismantling the Territorial Boundaries of the National Welfare States?' in C Barnard and O Odudu (eds), *The Outer Limits of European Union Law* (Oxford, Hart, 2009) 161.

[95] A Somek, 'Solidarity Decomposed: Being and Time in European Citizenship' (2007) 32 *EL Rev* 787, 804.

[96] Case C-503/09 *Stewart* (n 13) para 101.

[97] Joined Cases C-523/11 and C-585/11 *Prinz and Seeberger* (n 13) para 38 (emphasis added).

[98] Case C-359/13 *Martens* (n 37) para 41 (emphasis added).

[99] Interestingly, this personalised proportionality test has also been extended by analogy to third country nationals. In the case of *Dogan* (C-138/13 EU:C:2014:2066), which concerned family reunification rights for a Turkish national, the Court found that proportionality was not respected because 'the absence of evidence of sufficient linguistic knowledge automatically leads to the dismissal of the application for family reunification without account being taken of the specific circumstances of each case' (para 38).

[100] M Dougan, 'Expanding the Frontiers of Union Citizenship' (n 96) 162.

to emphasise the importance of individually assessing the circumstances of the person concerned, among which nationality is also positively considered.

Nonetheless, it has also been argued that this personalised analysis of proportionality may lead to problems concerning legal certainty. Advocate General Kokott has expressed some anxieties in this regard: within the context of mass administration with a large number of applications from individuals, 'it must be considered legitimate to rely solely on the criterion of place of residence even if in individual cases, for example with regard to frontier workers, other factors might also play a role'.[101] This type of reasoning seems to have played an important part in *Förster*, where the Court, referring to Directive 2004/38—which was not applicable to the case—stressed the legal certainty and transparency provided by a five-year residence requirement. This was not, however, the view of the Advocate General, who concluded that such a blanket rule would be disproportionate.[102] In Nic Shuibhne's view, this ruling exemplifies the tension between achieving 'maximum certainty' versus obtaining 'maximum justice' through scrutiny of the proportionality of the measure.[103] This dilemma constitutes the central challenge for the interpretation and application of Article 24(2) of Directive 2004/38.

C. Proportionality and Directive 2004/38

Beyond the gains in legal certainty, the impact of Directive 2004/38 is highly controversial, with Article 24(2) establishing that host Member States are not obliged to confer either social assistance during the first three months of residence (or the longer period provided for jobseekers) or, prior to acquisition of the right of permanent residence, maintenance aid for students. The constitutionality of the requirements imposed by secondary law on the free movement of citizens who are not economically active, and their submission to the principle of proportionality, has haunted free movement law since the 1990s residence directives.[104] This debate was intensified by Directive 2004/38, which modified the rules affecting the way in which States can derogate from the equal treatment principle regarding access to social benefits. It is well known that this derogation is at odds with the genuine integration test put forward by *Bidar*, and developed thereafter, since it merely takes into account one element (that of duration of residence) to the exclusion of other possible important elements. Here, secondary law abandons the traditional view according to which 'conditions relating to residence are, as a matter of principle, "suspect" under EU law'.[105]

[101] Opinion of AG Kokott in Case C-287/05 *Hendrix* EU:C:2007:196 point 73.
[102] Opinion of AG Mazak in Case C-158/07 *Förster* point 130.
[103] N Nic Shuibhne, 'The Third Age of EU Citizenship. Directive 2004/38 in the Case Law of the Court of Justice' in P Syrpis (ed), *The Judiciary, the Legislature and the EU Internal Market* (n 10) 358.
[104] On this question, O'Leary, 'Solidarity and Citizenship Rights' (n 22) 70.
[105] Opinion of AG Cruz Villalón in Case C-503/09 *Stewart* EU:C:2011:159 point 36.

The endorsement that Article 24(2) of the Directive received in *Förster* entails a radical revision of the approach to proportionality in this field, leading to the result that one sole condition of residence is appropriate and necessary to ensure the existence of a 'genuine link', giving rise to a long-standing discussion of the effects of legislation on the constitutional interpretation of the Treaty. The judgment in *Vatsouras and Koupatantze* did not put an end to this controversy, since the audacious solution in that case was focused on the finding that financial benefits intended to facilitate access to the labour market 'cannot be regarded as constituting "social assistance" within the meaning of Article 24(2) of Directive 2004/38'.[106] However, that case already pointed at the need to read the derogation enshrined in this provision in accordance with the free movement provisions of the Treaty.[107]

As a result, it appears that the analysis of restrictions to equal treatment that fall within the category of the derogation provided for by the Directive are not subject to the traditional approach to social justifications. This entails a clear-cut fragmentation regarding the possibility of taking into account particular personal circumstances of citizens, and confers a very different value on residence requirements, which does not seem justified on objective differences. Granted, the exclusion of residence requirements with regard to migrant or border workers (or their children) can be regarded as self-evident,[108] due to the established approach to economic free-movers (whose need to *prove* actual social integration is forfeited). However, the application of Article 24(2) of the Directive has fragmented the regime applicable to citizens on the same position on the basis of nationality. Indeed, in as much as Directive 2004/38 only governs EU citizens who reside in the territory of a Member State the nationality of which they do not enjoy,[109] the general—and personalised—approach to justifications and proportionality will still apply with regard to those who claim benefits towards their Member State of nationality, as *Prinz and Seeberger*, *Thiele Meneses*, *Morgan and Butcher* or *Martens* highlight.[110] In a globalised educational system, it is not surprising that Member States also apply the idea of the 'genuine link' to their own nationals, even though, by definition, they should be regarded as having a legitimate connection. In this regard, the Court has consistently considered that a sole residence requirement is not proportionate when it comes to assessing the entitlement to benefits of home State students.[111]

[106] Joined Cases C-22/08 and C-23/08 *Vatsouras and Koupatantze* EU:C:2009:344 para 45.

[107] ibid, para 44.

[108] In Case C-542/09 *Commission v Netherlands* (n 12) after stating that the 'three out of six' residence requirement was appropriate for the legitimate objective of promoting student mobility (para 79), the Court reintroduced the basic element of the 'integration' rationale as a benchmark to assess the proportionality of the student mobility objective. Indeed, the Court stated that the contested rule prioritised 'an element which is not necessarily the sole element representative of the actual degree of attachment between the party concerned and that Member State' (para 86). See also, Case C-379/11 *Caves Krier Frères* (n 12).

[109] Joined Cases C-11/06 and 12/06 *Morgan and Bucher* (n 13) para 35.

[110] In this regard, see the Opinion of AG Sharpston in Case C-523/11 and 585/11 *Prinz & Seeberger* (n 60).

[111] See eg Joined Cases C-11/06 and 12/06 *Morgan and Bucher*, Case C-523/11 and 585/11 *Prinz & Seeberger* (n 13) and C-220/12 *Thiele Menese* (n 13).

These developments leave those who fall within the exceptions of Article 24(2) of Directive 2004/38 in a situation of isolation from the consideration of their real circumstances and from their actual degree of integration in a given society. In this connection, the reintroduction of a proportionality assessment within the application of Article 24(2) has been a topic for discussion since the adoption of the Directive, as the Opinion of Advocate General Geelhoed in *Bidar* makes evident.[112] The consolidation of a thorough integration examination in cases where EU citizens claim benefits against their own State speaks for the reintroduction of a proportionality assessment, taking into account the particular circumstances at issue, in the interpretation and application of Article 24(2) of the Directive. Indeed, such an approach would be suitable to reconcile this provision with the consistent approach to justifications under the Treaty, having in mind that 'legislation can shape the exercise of the primary free movement rights, but it cannot go as far as to undermine the very existence of those rights'.[113] Such an approach would, moreover, make possible a more coherent and equitable approach to the real link or integration of EU free movers as a criterion suitable to determine access to benefits notwithstanding the direction of their movement and the State with regard to which they intend to make their claim.

In this regard, we have to welcome the development in *Brey*, a case concerning access to a complementary supplement to a retirement pension for a German national residing in Austria for less than three months. The Court found incompatible with EU law a 'mechanism whereby nationals of other Member States who are not economically active are automatically barred by the host Member State from receiving a particular social security benefit, even for the period following the first three months of residence referred to in Article 24(2) of Directive 2004/38' since it did not 'enable the competent authorities of the host Member State, where the resources of the person concerned fall short of the reference amount for the grant of that benefit, to carry out—in accordance with the requirements under, inter alia, Articles 7(1)(b) and 8(4) of that directive and the principle of proportionality—an overall assessment of the specific burden which granting that benefit would place on the social assistance system as a whole by reference to the personal circumstances characterizing the individual situation of the person concerned'.[114]

However, the judgment of the Grand Chamber in *Dano* has not followed this approach. There, the Court ruled that Article 24(1) of Directive 2004/38, read in

[112] Indeed, the Advocate General in *Bidar*, when analysing Article 24(2) of Directive 2004/38, stated: 'in applying this condition, the fundamental rights conferred directly by the EC Treaty on EU citizens must be fully respected. This implies that the considerations set out above in respect of applying a residence requirement in individual cases are valid in respect of the application of a settlement requirement … and that account must be taken of all relevant factors in determining whether or not a genuine link exists with the educational system and the society of the host Member State. I do not consider that this amounts to an undermining of the requirement adopted by the Community legislature. Rather it is necessary to ensure that this requirement is applied in conformity with the fundamental provisions of the EC Treaty'. Opinion of AG Geelhoed in Case C-209/03 *Bidar* EU:C:2004:715 point 64.

[113] N Nic Shuibhne, 'Exceptions to the free movement rules' (n 11) 499.

[114] C-140/12 *Brey* (n 14) para 77.

conjunction with Article 7(1)(b), did not preclude national legislation excluding certain non-contributory benefits—generally awarded to nationals in the same position—from citizens of other Member States in so far as they did not have a right of residence under the Directive. By referring to the fulfilment of the residence conditions of Article 7(1)(b) as a prerequisite to being able to avail oneself of the equal treatment principle, the Court shied away from any specific consideration of the integration link.[115] This response entails that a direct connection between reliance on the welfare system of the host State, the absence of sufficient resources, and losing the right of residence—which had been carefully and long avoided in the previous case law—has been established. The current economic and political climate and the very specific circumstances of the *Dano* case are nonetheless very relevant factors to understanding this outcome.[116] The implications of *Dano* for jobseekers, pensioners or students are yet to be ascertained.[117] In this regard, the Opinion of Advocate General Wathelet in *Alimanovic* signals a development in the direction of reintroducing a 'genuine link' approach in the interpretation of the derogation contained in Article 24(2) of Directive 2004, since it states that it is contrary to EU law and to the principle of equal treatment to exclude automatically an EU citizen from a social assistance benefit beyond a period of involuntary unemployment of six months 'without allowing that citizen to demonstrate the existence of a genuine link with the host Member State'.[118]

VI. CONCLUDING REMARKS AND FUTURE PERSPECTIVES

In light of the evolution of the case law on access to benefits, the practice of justifications has entailed, for a considerable time already, a learning process for the Member States. In the particular field of social justifications in citizenship cases, the impact of European integration is destined to lead progressively to a transformation of the assumptions that underlie national rules governing access to grants and social benefits. Member States are required to take into account a different community of citizens as a reference point, namely, to consider that a part of the population may be fluctuant in a free area that escapes the jurisdiction of a given State. This places the national legislator in a situation similar to a Rawlsian 'veil of ignorance', in which legislation has to be produced for a citizen whose concrete circumstances cannot be discerned in advance.

[115] For a substantiated comment on this particular point, see D Düsterhaus, 'Timeo *Danones* et dona petentes. European Court of Justice (Grand Chamber), Judgment of 11 November 2014, Case C-333/13, *Elisabeta and Florin Dano v Jobcenter Leipzig*' (2015) 11 *European Constitutional Law Review* 121–39.

[116] The case concerned access to social benefits for a Romanian single mother living with her sister in Germany for more than three months, and who had never worked and did not show any intention to seek employment (Case C-333/13 *Dano* (n 14)).

[117] With regard to jobseekers, there are two pending cases: Case C-67/14 *Alimanovic and Others*, OJ C 142, 12.05.2014, 14; and Case C-299/14 *Garcia-Nieto and Others* [2014] OJ C315/38, both referred from courts in Germany.

[118] Opinion of AG Wathelet in Case C-67/14 *Alimanovic* (n 3) para 110. However, the Court did not follow this perspective in its final ruling.

It is also clear that this debate has an enormous impact on the capabilities of Member States in defining the rights of their citizens and in incentivising certain types of social outcomes. Somek analyses from this perspective the Austrian system of access to university, which was declared incompatible with the Treaty in *Commission v Austria*.[119] In this case, the Court pointed to an interesting conclusion: States cannot any more design generous schemes for their own nationals at the expense of excluding other EU citizens. Generosity has to be coupled with possibilities of access determined by fair criteria for all members of a supranational society. As a consequence, access to benefits and grants has to be designed not only for the 'traditional' citizen, born and raised within the national system, but also for the potential incoming free mover, as well as for the 'abandoning national', all of them European citizens. This pushes the State towards solutions that overcome the communitarian preconception of traditional assumptions inspiring the determination of beneficiaries of welfare payments, and brings it to legislate on the basis of objective considerations of fairness with regard to the multifarious ways in which an EU citizen can deploy a link to a given State.

In this context, the generalisation of the notion of the 'real link' or 'sufficient connection' as the concept of reference to assess the appropriateness and necessity of national measures restricting access to certain benefits relies on the assumption that any use by EU citizens of welfare resources has a potential impact on the sustainability of the system, since the response given in one case will have effects on a potentially unlimited—or at least unforeseeable—number of situations due to the dynamic nature of free movement trends. The 'integration approach' places the States and the Court in a situation in which they can probably escape the complex and burdensome evidence assessments that would accompany an examination of appropriateness and necessity of a measure in pure economic terms. However, it also inevitably leads to a more complex and detailed approach to the notions of 'real link' or 'sufficient connection', or 'integration', with conditions that are not necessarily clear and understandable as a place of diploma or residence requirement, and that oblige an assessment that is fraught with subjective elements and philosophical connotations. The introduction of the 'integration' rationale in frontier worker cases opens the door for an even wider spectrum of argumentative possibilities on potentially valid connections with the society and economy of a Member State. Therefore, a serious reflection on the concept of integration should be carried out by all relevant actors in order to set a clearer framework of reference for national regulatory authorities, and which could help citizens to manage their expectations in the course of the transnational lives they choose, in the promised land of free movement.

In this connection, the centrality of the notion of integration in the legitimacy analysis of State objectives, and in the assessment of the appropriateness

[119] Case C-147/03 *Commission v Austria*, n 28 above. A Somek, 'Solidarity Decomposed: Being and Time in European Citizenship' (2007) University of Iowa Legal Studies Research Paper No 07-13.

and necessity of State measures, bears challenges that should not be understated. Widespread recourse to integration should not amount to the use of an abstract tool that merely serves the escaping of complex and detailed assessment of the financial impact of a measure. The notion of integration is complex and difficult to assess, even more in a transnational modern society under construction. The subjective nature of integration bears the risk of turning it into a fluctuant notion, which can be relative and very vulnerable to ideological interpretations. This leads to a need for clear and tangible criteria, suitable to portray what integration is made of, and situates the debate in the sphere of the definition of a notion of integration. The case law of the Court of Justice is already engaging in this difficult task, pointing at a complex and holistic conception of integration in which the length of residence may play a limited role, together with other important factors such as family and social connections, economic activity, links to the social security system, as well cultural and linguistic links, and even nationality.

Against this background, the definitive interpretation of Article 24(2) of Directive 2004/38 seems to be still under construction. A blind interpretation of the derogations contained in this provision, which does not take into account the real links and connections of citizens with the host Member State, would entail a significant challenge to the legitimacy of the legislative construction of citizenship. This situation would also be somehow counterintuitive, because the Directive is supposed to encourage mobility and to overcome legal fragmentation between different groups of citizens. And yet, we see that the students who escape the scope of application of this Directive (those who claim the export of benefits from their own Member States to study abroad) are the ones who are getting more protection from the citizen's right to free movement. Indeed, and interestingly, in all these cases—*Prinz*, *Thiele Meneses*, *Morgan and Bucher*, *Elrick*, *Martens*—the Court has demonstrated a particular sensitivity towards the value of nationality in the supranational context, operating a revalorisation of the nationality link for non-residents towards their own Member State.[120] This was also the case in *Stewart*, where the Court stated that a condition of past presence for access to invalidity benefits was too exclusive in nature, and pointed at other elements to establish that connection, particularly to that of nationality. In this connection, the role of nationality in the assessment of integration also deserves further consideration. Additionally, in *Giersch*, relating to students who are children of migrant workers and also concerning the possibility of exporting scholarships, the Court conceded that students resident in a Member State are more likely to return to live in that State.

[120] See the arguments of France in Case C-184/99 *Grzelczyk* (n 4) reproduced in para 22 of the judgment: 'the idea that the principle of equal treatment in the matter of social advantages should be extended to all citizens of the Union … would amount to establishing total equality between citizens of the Union established in a Member State and nationals of that State, which would be difficult to reconcile with rights attaching to nationality'.

The revalorisation of nationality in the assessment of integration and the conservative views on the expected mobility behaviour of citizens convey a more modest appraisal of the EU citizen as a mover, abandoning a mechanical consideration of free movement in an abstract space. The preservation of a certain link of integration as a social objective may be a useful tool in a system based on inter-state equality with no legal harmonisation in the social benefits (and taxation) fields. However, reliance on such a ductile and evolving notion makes it difficult to find a definitive formula or a formalistic legal arrangement. Moreover, the crystallisation of the role of integration as a legitimate objective questions the legislative choices made in Directive 2004/38 and makes necessary a constant reconsideration of the value of elements such as residence or even nationality.

6

The Worker Protection Justification: Lessons from Consumer Law

CATHERINE BARNARD*

Overriding reasons relating to the public interest already recognised by the Court include the protection of workers.

European Court of Justice in *Finalarte*[1]

I. INTRODUCTION

A. The Problem

Much consideration has been given to the face of the consumer in EU free movement and competition law.[2] Much less time has been devoted to examining the face of the worker. This is surprising. The worker has been directly recognised by the Treaties since the inception of the EU, most obviously in respect of Article 45 TFEU on the free movement of workers and also Article 157 TFEU on 'equal pay for male and female workers'. Workers have also been recognised in other ways. They were the intended beneficiaries of the single market, as Article 117 EEC (now amended Article 151 TFEU) made clear:

> Member States agree upon the need to promote improved working conditions and an improved standard of living for workers ... They believe that such a development will ensue not only from the functioning of the common market ... but also from the procedures provided for in this Treaty.

* I am very grateful for the discussion with the participants in the seminar on justifications at City University in February 2014, as well as to those on the Czech Common Law Society Summer School, July 2014, to Niall O'Connor and to the editors of this volume for their careful comments.

[1] Joined Cases C-49/98, C-50/98, C-52/98 to C-54/98 and C-68/98 to C-71/98 *Finalarte* EU:C:2001:564 para 33.

[2] See eg A Albors-Llorens and A Jones, 'The images of the "Consumer" in EU Competition Law' in D Leczykiewicz and S Weatherill (eds), *The Images of the Consumer in EU Law: Legislation, Free Movement and Competition Law* (Oxford, Hart Publishing, 2016); S Weatherill, 'Consumer Policy' in P Craig and G de Búrca, *Evolution of EU Law* (Oxford, Oxford University Press, 2011).

Article 117 EEC was important for two reasons: first, it recognised that workers should enjoy (increasingly good) employment rights; and second, that *migrant* workers specifically, and the working population more generally, would benefit from the opportunities created by the common, now single, market.

Yet Article 117 EEC disguised a problem: how to reconcile the protection of social rights (largely delivered at national level) with the deregulatory push mandated at EU level by the four freedoms. For many years the Court of Justice was able to avoid adjudicating on this clash, usually by finding that EU law did not apply. So, for example, in *Oebel*,[3] the defendant, accused of breaching restrictions on night work limits, complained that those rules interfered with free movement of goods. The Court rejected his argument. It said that the national rules did not have the effect of restricting free movement of goods between Member States; and since trade within the EU remained possible at all times, there was no breach of Article 34 TFEU.[4]

Where avoidance techniques proved impossible, the Court created the 'worker protection' public interest requirement to allow states to justify their rules, which they could do relatively easily, at least in the early days. So, in *Webb*,[5] the Court found that the national rule, requiring temp agencies to be licensed, breached Article 56 TFEU, but could be justified on the grounds of worker protection. States could refuse licences where there was reason 'to fear that such activities may harm good relations on the labour market or that the interests of the workforce affected are not adequately safeguarded'.[6]

The accession to the EU of states such as Spain, Portugal, Greece and, more recently, the Eastern European states forced the Court to rethink its somewhat laissez-faire approach to states' justification of national laws on worker protection grounds. Workers in these new countries (and their employers) saw access to the (labour) markets of the wealthier countries in northern Europe as a way of improving their own standard of living. Barriers put in the way by host state laws on workers' rights potentially impeded these opportunities.

This changing context set up the conditions for a clash between, on the one hand, the interests of national workers (usually in the northern European states) who wanted to see their jobs, and terms and conditions of employment, protected and, on the other, the interests of migrant workers (usually from the Eastern and Southern states) who wanted freer (unrestricted?) access to the markets in those host northern European states.[7] The question for the Court was how to strike the balance between these two interests.

[3] Case 155/80 *Oebel* EU:C:1981:177.

[4] See also eg Case C-190/98 *Graf v Filzmoser Maschinenbau GmbH* EU:C:2000:49; Case C-67/96 *Albany International BV v Stichting Bedrijfspensioenfonds Textielindustrie* EU:C:1999:430.

[5] Case 279/80 *Webb* EU:C:1981:314.

[6] ibid para 19.

[7] C Barnard, 'The protection of fundamental social right after Lisbon: A Question of Conflicts of Interests' in S de Vries, U Bernitz and S Weatherill (eds), *The Protection of Fundamental Rights in the EU After Lisbon* (Oxford, Hart Publishing, 2013).

B. The Consumer Protection Case Law

Some, rather similar, battles had already been fought in the field of consumer protection, albeit with the Court working against a more incomplete canvas. Outside agriculture and competition law, consumers were not specifically recognised by the Treaty of Rome. Yet in the famous 1979 decision of *Cassis de Dijon*,[8] two years before its analogue in *Webb*, the Court said that states were, in certain circumstances, free to protect the interests of national consumers (despite the absence of any mention of consumers in Article 36 TFEU). *Cassis de Dijon* concerned German rules requiring fruit liqueurs to have a *minimum* alcohol content of 25 per cent. French cassis had an alcohol content of only 15–20%. The German Government justified its 25 per cent rule for various public health/consumer protection reasons, including the fact that the German consumer was less likely to get drunk on the *higher* alcohol (German) drink. The Court did recognise that Germany could, in principle, invoke the consumer protection justification to protect German consumers from the error of their ways. However, the combined application of the mutual recognition and proportionality principles resulted in a decision favouring market integration and the removal of barriers (the 25 per cent rule) which had been created by the host state in the name of consumer protection.

Cassis de Dijon and the subsequent case law forced the Court to address the question as to whether, and how, consumers should be protected. Some argued that the Court should adopt a restrictive interpretation of the four freedoms and so uphold paternalist national rules protecting consumers (such as the (not very bright) German consumers who risked drinking more of the lower alcohol fruit liqueur in the absence of the protective German rule). This paternalist approach supports the *consumer protection* model which, in turn, speaks to one of the objectives of EU law, namely ensuring a high level of consumer protection.[9] However, upholding the consumer protection justification leads to less free movement of goods and services and so less competition, resulting in (German) consumers having less choice of goods to purchase (that is they are denied the choice between the German fruit liqueur with 25 per cent alcohol or the French cassis with only 20 per cent). In other words, the aggregate welfare of consumers is reduced.

So, another school of thought argued that the Court should adopt an expansive reading of the free movement provisions, using them to strike down *national* rules drafted to protect consumers. This is done to ensure that the wider *EU* interest in securing the benefits of the single market for the consumer body as a whole. This wider interest is about consumers having greater choice of products and enjoying the benefits of greater competition between those products (cheaper prices and/or better quality goods). This, more liberal, reading of the Treaty provisions is described as embodying the *consumer welfare* approach.

[8] Case 120/78 *Cassis de Dijon* EU:C:1979:42.
[9] See eg Art 12 TFEU and Art 114(3) TFEU.

The genesis of the concept of *consumer welfare* lies in the field of competition law. For the Commission, 'consumer welfare' means the delivery of direct benefits to consumers through 'lower prices, better quality and a wider choice of new or improved goods and services'.[10] This approach has been endorsed by the General Court in *GlaxoSmithKline*[11] (albeit subsequent judicial decisions have clouded the water as to what precisely is the objective of EU competition law).[12]

A consumer welfare approach would suggest that any interference with the free movement principle by national legislation adopted on the grounds of consumer *protection* (that is, the paternalist approach) should be scrutinised very carefully. And this is the position the Court of Justice has generally taken. Usually, it finds that the (Union interest) in consumer welfare prevails over the national interest in consumer protection and thus the free movement principle trumps the paternalist state interest in consumer protection.[13] This may be due in part to a (neo)-liberal bias in the Court's judgments but it may also be due, as Poiares Maduro has argued, to wider EU control over Member State regulation in the common market.[14]

C. Worker Protection v Worker Welfare

This chapter draws on the consumer literature to develop a distinction between notions of (1) *worker protection* and (2) *worker welfare* as a way of analysing the outcomes of the Court's decisions in those cases where states have raised 'worker protection' as a public interest requirement to justify their rules. Where the Court recognises and upholds *worker protection* as a justification, it is essentially accepting that in the circumstance of this particular case the state's paternalist interest in ensuring decent working conditions takes precedence over the wider EU interest in the realisation of a single market.

By contrast, when the Court rejects the worker protection justification, it may be prioritising the Union interest in *worker welfare* (the term has been deliberately chosen to reflect the parallels with the consumer case law). To labour lawyers 'worker welfare' may be synonymous with 'worker protection' but that is not the

[10] See para 5 of the *Guidance on the Commission's enforcement priorities in applying Article 82 of the EC Treaty* [now Article 102 TFEU] *to abusive exclusionary conduct by dominant undertakings* ((OJ [2009] C 45/7).

[11] Case T-168/01 *GlaxoSmithKline Services v Commission* EU:T:2006:265 paras 118 and 121–22.

[12] Case C-52/09 *Konkurrensverket v TeliaSonera Sverige AB* EU:C:2011:83 para 22: 'the function of those rules [Article 102 TFEU] is precisely to prevent competition from being distorted to the detriment of the public interest, individual undertakings and consumers, thereby ensuring the well-being of the European Union'. See further Albors-Llorens and Jones (n 2).

[13] There are many examples but see eg Case C-315/92 *Clinique* EU:C:1994:34; Case C-470/93 *Mars* EU:C:1995:224.

[14] M Poiares Maduro, *We the Court: The European Court of Justice and the European Economic Constitution* (Oxford, Hart Publishing, 1998). See also IH Eliasoph, 'A "Switch in Time" for the European Community? Lochner Discourse and the Recalibration of Economic and Social Rights in Europe' (2010) *Columbia Journal of European Law* 468.

sense in which the term is being used in this chapter.[15] As used here, the term 'worker welfare' means allowing workers across the EU the opportunity to work in whichever state they choose and on the terms dictated by the market (unless EU social law intervenes to provide specific protection). In other words, where the Court rejects the worker protection justification it *may* be recognising that in the circumstances of this particular case, the Union interest in the realisation of a single market (with the opportunities this brings for workers from poorer states to improve their life chances in wealthier states) should take precedence over the host state's paternalist interest to protect (national) workers (and their jobs).

As we shall see, a strict quantitative approach to the cases suggests that the Court does indeed favour worker welfare over worker protection, just as it does consumer welfare over consumer protection (section III). However, as we shall also see, a more qualitative reading of the cases leads to more nuanced conclusions. When only the (non-migrating) employer stands to gain from invoking the free movement principle, there is some evidence the Court favours the state interest in worker protection (section IV). By contrast, when migrants are exercising their rights of free movement under Article 45 TFEU or where businesses are exercising their rights to freedom of establishment under Article 49 TFEU in a state with lower labour costs, or exercising freedom to provide services using posted workers under Article 56 TFEU, the Court is forced to balance the state interest in worker protection with the wider Union interest in worker welfare. It will be argued that in these cases the Court tends to favour worker welfare *unless* the host state raises a genuine worker protection concern and can show the measures it takes are proportionate. It will therefore be argued that while the presumption in the free movement case law is in favour of worker *welfare*, particularly where national rules are overtly or covertly protectionist, where there are genuine concerns for workers (both national and migrant/posted or just migrant/posted), the Court will uphold the worker *protection* justification or may do so in the future if the rules were modified in some way. So, a qualitative analysis of the case law shows that the Court's position is in fact less biased in favour of worker welfare than a pure quantitative analysis might suggest (section V).

This chapter concludes with the suggestion that while the consumer case law has helped to tease out some of the nuances as to when the worker protection justification is successfully invoked, it will be argued that the parallels are not as robust as would first appear (section VI).

[15] One other note for labour lawyers: the search of the Court's jurisprudence on '*worker* protection' did not reveal any cases which engaged with the question of who is a 'worker' for these purposes. This is a vexed question in national employment law and, increasingly, in EU substantive law because it raises the fundamental question of the personal scope of the protection. Under English law, for example, the term 'worker' is broader than 'employee'. Under Article 157 TFEU on equal pay, the term worker may also include the dependent 'self-employed'. Generally, these issues are not engaged with at all when it comes to considering the worker protection justification, albeit in Case C-577/10 *Commission v Belgium* EU:C:2012:814 the Court talked of the public interest requirement of 'protecting workers, including self-employed service providers'.

D. Methodology

The research question, then, is whether the Court's case law does lead to the prioritisation of worker welfare over worker protection, in much the same way as the Court's consumer case law generally prioritises consumer welfare over consumer protection. To help find an answer to this question, a simple methodology was used. A search was made in the Curia database[16] of all cases up to 1 July 2015 for the phrases 'worker protection' and 'employee protection', and analogous terms such as 'protection of workers' and 'protection of employees'. A search was also made for cases where the phrase 'social protection of workers' was used (this often came up in the posting of workers cases, which form the bulk of the cases in this data set), which seems to be a synonym for 'worker protection'.[17] This search did not, however, catch all the cases (most notable by their omission were the judgments in *Rush Portuguesa*[18] and *Van der Elst*,[19] known by the author to be important in this field). Therefore, a further check was made against the decisions cited in the worker protection case law that had come up in the Curia database search to ensure that all the main cases had been identified.

Having compiled a list of cases, each case was then considered. Those concerning the interpretation of EU social policy directives were discarded since they are not relevant to the enquiry about the use of the worker protection justification by states in the free movement context. This left 30 or so cases. These cases were then divided up into (1) Article 258 TFEU enforcement proceedings, where an outcome is clear; and (2) those involving an Article 267 TFEU reference, where it may be harder to determine an outcome due to the fact that it is the national court that makes the final decision on, say, the proportionality of the measure, and the final decision of the national court (if any) may not be subsequently reported/available. The Article 258 TFEU cases were then analysed to consider, where possible, if the state won or lost, and why. This quantitative analysis of the case law was then supplemented by a more qualitative analysis of the decisions.

II. THE WORKER PROTECTION JUSTIFICATION AND ITS LIMITS

In order to provide the context for the subsequent discussion, the chapter begins with a brief examination of the worker protection public interest requirement, the circumstances in which the term has been invoked, and the limitations on the use of the justification.

[16] http://curia.europa.eu/.

[17] See eg Case C-515/08 *Santos Palhota* EU:C:2010:589 paras 46–47. For an earlier example, see Case C-272/94 *Guiot* EU:C:1996:147 para 16. For an example in the field of workers, see Case C-202/11 *Las v PSA Antwerp NV* EU:C:2013:239 para 28.

[18] Case C-113/89 *Rush Portuguesa* EU:C:1990:142 para 18.

[19] Case C-43/93 *Van der Elst* EU:C:1994:310. This methodology may not have caught those cases where different terminology was used eg Case C-358/12 *Pascolo* EU:C:2014:2063, para 32 'proper conduct in relation to its employees'.

A. The Worker Protection Justification

i. Developing the Worker Protection Justification

As we saw in the introduction, the basic settlement at the time of the Treaty of Rome was that social policy was a value to be recognised by the EU[20] but actually delivered largely by the Member States. This meant it was inevitable that Member States would invoke worker protection as a justification to defend challenges on free movement grounds to their social legislation, and that the Court would eventually have to recognise that justification, as it did in *Webb*, considered above. By the early 1990s, the Court said in *Gouda*[21] that 'the protection of workers' was among the list of public interest justifications which it had already recognised:

> 14. In this respect, the overriding reasons relating to the public interest which the Court has already recognized include professional rules intended to protect recipients of the service ...; protection of intellectual property ...; the protection of workers (Case 279/80 *Webb* [1981] ECR 3305, paragraph 19; Joined Cases 62/81 and 63/81 *Seco v EVI* [1982] ECR 223, paragraph 14; Case C-113/89 *Rush Portuguesa* [1990] ECR 1-1417, paragraph 18);[22] consumer protection ...
>
> 15. Lastly, as the Court has consistently held, the application of national provisions to providers of services established in other Member States must be such as to guarantee the achievement of the intended aim and must not go beyond that which is necessary in order to achieve that objective. In other words, it must not be possible to obtain the same result by less restrictive rules.

Since *Gouda*, the 'worker protection' justification has been recognised by the Court in over 30 cases (see Tables 1–3 below). Its existence as an overriding reason in the public interest (ORPI) has also been confirmed by the Services Directive, where worker protection sits alongside the consumer protection justification:[23]

> The notion [ORPI] as recognised in the case law of the Court of Justice covers at least the following grounds: ... the maintenance of order in society; social policy objectives; the protection of the recipients of services; *consumer protection; the protection of workers, including the social protection of workers.*

[20] See specifically Title III on Social Policy.

[21] Case C-288/89 *Stichting Collectieve Antennevoorziening Gouda and others v Commissariaat voor de Media* EU:C:1991:323 paras 13–14.

[22] It is not entirely clear why the Court cited para 18 of *Rush Portuguesa* to justify the worker protection justification since the paragraph seems to say something different: 'Finally, it should be stated, in response to the concern expressed in this connection by the French Government, that [Union] law does not preclude Member States from extending their legislation, or collective labour agreements entered into by both sides of industry, to any person who is employed, even temporarily, within their territory, no matter in which country the employer is established; nor does [Union] law prohibit Member States from enforcing those rules by appropriate means.' Thus, this paragraph could mean that the application of labour law rules to migrant workers (i) does not amount to a restriction on free movement of services or (ii) that it is a restriction, but one which is (always) justified and proportionate.

[23] Directive 2006/123, OJ [2006] L376/36 Recital 40.

ii. Extending the Worker Protection Justification

Thus the early case law was clear: worker protection is an important public interest justification which was used by states in the way that labour lawyers would understand it: to justify national laws providing substantive protection to the weaker party (the employee). However, in subsequent cases defendant states tried their luck—or at the very least tried to stretch the contexts in which the worker protection justification could be invoked. For example, in Case C-577/10 *Commission v Belgium*,[24] Belgium tried to bring under the umbrella of the worker protection justification the need to protect the treasury as well as the need to create a level playing field. The Court was prepared, in principle, to accept the Belgian justification:

> the objective of combating fraud, particularly social security fraud, and preventing abuse, in particular detecting 'bogus self-employed persons' and combating undeclared work, can form part not only of the objective of the financial balance of social security systems, but also of the objectives of preventing unfair competition and social dumping and protecting workers, including self-employed service providers.

However, the Court stressed that any controls imposed had to comply with the limits imposed by EU law and could not render the freedom to provide services illusory.[25]

An even wider—and more controversial—reading of the worker protection justification[26] can be seen in Case C-445/03 *Commission v Luxembourg*,[27] where the host state, Luxembourg, argued that the worker protection justification included protecting the jobs of home state workers. Specifically, Luxembourg argued that its labour market needed to be protected from 'being disrupted by a flood of workers who are nationals of non-member countries'.[28] Somewhat surprisingly, given its long-stated opposition to the use of justifications to serve economic purposes,[29] the Court recognised this as an aspect of the worker protection justification:[30] 'the

[24] Case C-577/10 (n 15) para 45. See also Case C-549/13 *Bundesruckerei v Stadt Dortmund* EU:C:2014:2235, para 35; Case C-315/13 *De Clercq* EU:C:2014:2408 para 65.

[25] Case C-113/89 *Rush Portuguesa* (n 18) para 17.

[26] Luxembourg also ran a more traditional argument based on worker protection but this was rejected by the Court because the requirements imposed in connection with obtaining a licence were disproportionate (paras 29–36).

[27] Case C-445/03 *Commission v Luxembourg* EU:C:2004:655.

[28] Para 37. See also Case C-168/04 *Commission v Austria* EU:C:2006:595. In this way, the Court echoes the Spaak report: 'The European Commission will decide on the necessary protection measures in order to avoid an inflow of labor which would be dangerous for the standard of living or employment of workers in certain specified industries, without affecting the rights acquired by foreign workers.'

[29] For a full discussion of this subject see S Arrowsmith, 'Rethinking the Approach to Economic Justifications under the EU's free movement rules' (2015) 68 *Current Legal Problems* 307.

[30] The doubt relates to the fact that the Court cites para 13 of *Rush Portuguesa*, not para 18 (which was subsequently used as the authority for the worker protection justification), yet para 13 concerns Article 216 of the Act of Accession (ie a Treaty provision) which was 'intended to prevent disturbances on the employment market following Portugal's accession, both in Portugal and in the other Member States, due to large and immediate movements of workers'. The Luxembourg law dated from 1972; Portugal acceded to the EU in 1986.

desire to avoid disturbances on the labour market is undoubtedly an overriding reason of general interest'.[31] This point was picked up by the UK's (now defunct) New Settlement Decision:[32]

> If overriding reasons of public interest make it necessary, free movement of workers may be restricted by measures proportionate to the legitimate aim pursued. *Encouraging recruitment, reducing unemployment*, protecting vulnerable workers and averting the risk of seriously undermining the sustainability of social security systems are reasons of public interest recognised in the jurisprudence of the Court of Justice of the European Union for this purpose, based on a case by case analysis.

However, the Court is not generally sympathetic to such arguments, or finds ways around them on the facts, as it did in Case C-445/03 *Commission v Luxembourg* itself. In Case C-445/03 the Court said that 'workers employed by an undertaking established in a Member State and who are deployed to another Member State for the purposes of providing services there do not purport to gain access to the labour market of that second State, as they return to their country of origin or residence after the completion of their work'.[33] In other words, posted workers do not enter the Luxembourg labour market and so do not threaten national jobs, and therefore Luxembourg could not take action. In Case C-244/04 *Commission v Germany*,[34] the Court gave a similar reason to reject a German rule requiring at least one year's prior employment by the posting undertaking in order to ensure 'the protection of workers, the safeguarding of the Member States' prerogatives in respect of access to their employment market and the prevention of social dumping'.[35]

B. Limitations

As *Gouda* shows, even where the worker protection justification is successfully invoked, the steps taken must comply with the principle of proportionality (paragraph 15). Subsequent case law has elaborated on the limits on the use by the Member States of the worker protection justification, limitations which (unsurprisingly) reveal a number of commonalities with the general case law on justifications. They can be summarised as follows.

First, the Court (usually) requires evidence to support the justification: mere general assertions are not enough.[36] Second and relatedly, the Court requires that

[31] Para 38.

[32] The UK New Settlement Decision, 18–19 February 2016, section D.(1)(a). Emphasis added.

[33] ibid.

[34] Case C-244/04 *Commission v Germany* EU:C:2006:49.

[35] Para 57. *Cf* C-49/98 *Finalarte* (n 1) para 38 where the national court pointed out the protectionist aim behind the national law but the Court was not swayed: 'that declared intention is not conclusive'. See also Case C-164/99 *Portugaia Construções* EU:C:2002:40 para 27.

[36] Case C-112/05 *Commission v Germany (Volkswagen)* EU:C:2007:623 para 74.

there must be a direct link between the national law and the protection of the worker otherwise the justification is not made out; in other words, the national legislation must 'secure the protection of [posted] workers'.[37] So in *Seco*,[38] the Court said that an obligation requiring a provider of services to pay employers' contributions to the host State's fund could not be justified where those contributions conferred no social advantage on the workers concerned.[39] Similarly, in *Van der Elst*,[40] as in Case C-445/03 *Commission v Luxembourg*, the Court rejected the French argument that a Belgian company posting Moroccan workers had to have a French work permit for those Moroccan workers in order to regulate access to the French labour market for workers from non-member countries.[41] Since those workers did not intend to gain access the French labour market, the justification was not made out.[42]

Third, in the cases on free movement of services, the Court takes into account the protection already provided in the home state when assessing what (further) steps the host state can take.[43] So in *Guiot*, a case where the host state required the posting employer to pay employer's contributions to the state's social security fund, the Court said that the public interest of worker protection did not apply where the workers enjoyed 'the same protection, or essentially similar protection, by virtue of employer's contributions already paid by the employer in the Member State of establishment'.[44] Putting it another way, as the Court did in *Arblade*,[45] only if the employer's contributions to the host State's fund conferred on workers an advantage capable of providing them with real additional protection would it be possible to justify the payment of the contributions in question.[46]

There are other limitations on the use of the worker protection justification that the Court has referred to in the worker protection cases but can be found in most case law on justifications. They can be summarised as follows: considerations of a purely administrative nature cannot make lawful a restriction of the freedom to provide services justified on the grounds of worker protection;[47] nor can those of a purely economic nature (although as we have seen, the Court is increasingly ambivalent on this).[48] Measures taken to achieve the worker protection objective

[37] Case C-60/03 *Wolff & Müller GmbH & Co KG v José Filipe Pereira Félix* EU:C:2004:610 para 38; Case C-279/00 *Commission v Italy* EU:C:2002:89 para 22.

[38] Joined Cases 62/81 and 63/81 *Seco v EVI* EU:C:1982:34.

[39] Para 10.

[40] Case C-43/93 *Van der Elst* (n 19).

[41] Para 20.

[42] Para 21.

[43] Case C-165/98 *Criminal proceedings against André Mazzoleni and Inter Surveillance Assistance SARL* EU:C:2001:162 para 40.

[44] Case C-272/94 *Criminal proceedings against Michel Guiot and Climatec SA* EU:C:1996:147 paras 18–19.

[45] Joined Cases C-369/96 and C-376/96 *Criminal proceedings against Jean-Claude Arblade and Arblade & Fils SARL and Bernard Leloup, Serge Leloup and Sofrage SARL* EU:C:1999:575.

[46] Para 54.

[47] Case C-493/99 *Commission v Germany* EU:C:2001:578 para 21.

[48] Case C-164/99 *Portuguaia Construções* (n 35).

must also not discriminate between the public and private sectors,[49] must be consistent,[50] transparent,[51] and, of course, proportionate.

III. THE OUTCOME IN CASES WHERE STATES INVOKE WORKER PROTECTION

The case law considered so far already shows that there can be different understandings of the worker protection justification, and that the Court may or may not accept either the justification or the proportionality of the measures. We turn now to consider more systematically the outcomes in the cases where the worker protection justification has been raised by states.

There have been 31 cases identified in the data set where the state has invoked 'worker protection' or its analogues as a justification to restrict free movement. Of those 31 cases, there were nine enforcement proceedings (see Table 1) and 22 preliminary references (see Table 2). Of the nine enforcement proceedings in only one did the defendant Member State win (Case C-490/04 *Commission v Germany*) and there only in part. In all other cases the state lost because it offered no justification, or because the justification was not made out, or, more commonly, the state's actions were not proportionate (see Table 1, columns 3–6 (more than one X indicates more than one point)).

A simple win/lose analysis is harder to conduct in the case of the 22 Article 267 references since, by their very nature, the final decision on the compatibility of national law with EU law should be taken by the national courts. Nevertheless, sometimes the Court makes clear that the host state has won or lost, or at least sends a clear signal in that direction. In order to reflect this in the analysis, the cases were categorised as:

1. those cases where the Court made it very clear that the national rule was lawful ('state wins');
2. those where the Court gave an indication that the state rule was justified and proportionate ('likely state wins');
3. those cases where the Court made it clear that the state rule could not be justified ('state loses');
4. those where it gave a strong indication to that effect ('likely state loses'); and
5. those cases where the outcome was not clear.

The application of these categories can be seen in Table 3. A summary of the reasons given by the Court as to why the state lost (no justification offered, justification not made out, national measure not proportionate) can be found in Table 2.

[49] Case C-549/13 *Bundesruckerei v Stadt Dortmund* (n 24) para 32 but cf Case C-115/14 *RegioPost* EU:C:2015:249, paras 62–64.

[50] Case C-79/01 *Payroll Data Services* EU:C:2002:592 para 37.

[51] Case C-341/05 *Laval un Partneri* EU:C:2007:809.

Table 1: The outcome in Article 258 TFEU cases where the Member States raised worker protection as a justification

Case	**Freedom**	**State wins**	**State loses: No justification offered or available**	**State loses: Justification not made out**	**State loses: Measure Dispropor- tionate**
Case C-493/99 *Commission v Germany*	Services (posting) Establish- ment			X	X X
Case C-279/00 *Commission v Italy*	Services				X
Case C-445/03 *Commission v Luxembourg*	Services (posting)				X
Case C-490/04 *Commission v Germany*	Services (posting)	X (Commission produced no evidence) X	X		
Case C-112/05 *Commission v Germany*	Capital				X
Case C-244/04 *Commission v Germany*	Services (posting)				X X
Case C-168/04 *Commission v Austria*	Services (posting)				X
Case C-319/06 *Commission v Luxembourg*	Services		X (insufficient transparency)	X	
Case C-577/10 *Commission v Belgium*	Services				X

Table 2: The outcome in Article 267 TFEU references when states raised the worker protection justification

Case	State wins/ likely state wins	State loses: No justification offered or available	State loses: Justification not made out	State loses: Measure dispropor-tionate
Oebel	X			
Webb	X[52]			
Seco			X	
Rush Portuguesa			X	
Marchandise	X			
Van der Elst			X	[X]
Guiot			X	
Arblade	X		X	X
Mazzoleni				X[53]
Finalarte				
Toolex Alpha AB	X			
Portugaia Constr.		X		X
Überseering			X	
PDS				X
Wollf & Muller	X[54]			
Laval			X[55]	
Viking			X[56]	X[57]
Rüffert				X
Santos Palhota				X
Las				X
Bundesruckerei				X
De Clercq	X[58]			

[52] Although ultimately left to the national court to decide.
[53] Strong likelihood national rule not proportionate.
[54] Proportionality left to the national court, but with suggestion measure is lawful.
[55] Defendants were trade unions, not the state.
[56] Defendants were trade unions, not the state. Justification ultimately left to the national court to decide.
[57] Proportionality left to the national court to decide.
[58] Strong hint national measure proportionate.

Table 3: Summary of outcomes in the Article 267 TFEU cases

Outcomes	**Number of cases**
State wins	
State wins totally	3
State wins in part	1
Likely state wins	4
Likely state wins in part	1
Total	9
State loses	
State loses totally	13
State loses in part	1
Likely state loses	2
Total	16
Unclear	2

Table 3 shows us that, at its broadest, the states lost in 16 cases and won in 9. Table 3 shows that generally states lost either because they failed to substantiate the justification (approximately 8 cases) or the steps taken were not proportionate (approximately 9 cases). From this, we can say that the state loses in nearly double the number of cases than it wins. If, for reasons explained below, the goods cases are removed (*Oebel*, *Merchandise* and *Toolex Alpha*), the figure of 9 for 'state wins' is reduced to 6, as compared to 16 'state loses'. If we look at 'state wins totally' and add to this the figures for the state wins in enforcement proceedings, states win in 4 cases (three Article 267 TFEU references, one Article 258 TFEU enforcement proceedings) and lose in 22 cases (14 Article 267 TFEU cases, 8 Article 258 TFEU cases). This gives a win:lose ratio of 2:11. Putting it another way, states win in 15 per cent of cases and lose in 85 per cent of cases.

Although this analysis may seem crude, the raw data is overwhelming. The quantitative analysis supports the view that the Court is impatient when states raise the worker protection justification as a limitation on free movement rights.[59] Putting it another way, the quantitative data suggests that worker protection is being marginalised in favour of broader arguments based on worker welfare, although the Court has never made this point explicitly.

However, appearances can be deceptive. The discussion below suggests the reality is more complex. It will be argued that a distinction needs to be drawn between those cases where the justification is invoked to protect the national worker in

[59] Earlier research tends to support this view more generally in the field of justifications: C Barnard, Derogations, Justifications and the Four Freedoms: Is State Interest Really Protected?' in C Barnard and O Odudu (eds), *The Outer Limits of European Union Law* (Oxford, Hart Publishing, 2009).

the face of challenges to national rules, often by business using the four freedoms (section IV) and those where the worker protection justification is invoked in the context of migration, particularly by migrant workers under Article 45 TFEU or by companies providing services using posted workers under Article 56 TFEU (section V). In cases involving national workers and a more traditional labour law context (worker v employer) the Court seems more willing to uphold the worker protection justification than in the cases involving migration, provided there are genuine worker protection concerns. While the dynamic is more complex in cases involving migrant/posted workers even here the Court may be more willing to accept the worker protection justification where there are genuine concerns about ensuring that migrating workers enjoy employment protection.

IV. THE 'NATIONAL' WORKER CASES

A. Introduction

In this section, we look at those cases where the state is invoking the worker protection justification on behalf of (mainly) national workers against claims based on free movement (of goods, establishment, services and capital) brought by business (or by the Commission on behalf of business seeking to enjoy their free movement rights). It will be argued that in these more typical 'labour law' situations (business v national worker), provided a genuine argument is made out by the defendant state, the Court has broad sympathy with the worker protection justification and will prioritise it. The testing ground for this argument is the free movement of goods, where the earliest cases arose.

B. Free Movement of Goods

In respect of free movement of goods, when host states invoke national rules to protect national consumers from imports, the Court is generally sceptical. Most famously, as we saw in *Cassis de Dijon*, the Court rejected the German justification that consumers would be protected by a prohibition on the import of the weaker French cassis; access to those goods combined with adequate labelling would be a more proportionate response. In this way, consumer welfare would be increased given the greater choice that free movement of goods would bring to consumers. This is not an isolated example: rules limiting the ingredients in beer[60] and pasta,[61] all justified on the grounds of consumer protection/public health, were successfully challenged as being contrary to Article 34 TFEU, as were controls

[60] Case 178/84 *Commission v Germany* EU:C:1987:126.
[61] Case 202/82 *Commission v France* EU:C:1984:67; Case 90/86 *Zoni* EU:C:1988:403.

on advertising that claimed to protect consumers but were in reality placing unfair limits on competition.[62] In these cases consumer welfare prevailed over consumer protection.

By contrast, in the three free movement of goods cases where worker protection was at issue, the Court has favoured worker protection over worker welfare. First, in *Oebel*,[63] considered above, the Court ruled that the restriction on night-working did not breach Article 34 TFEU because the rules were non-discriminatory, and the restrictions on transport and delivery did not affect trade between Member States. The Court also noted the special nature of the sector: the prohibition in the bread and confectionery industry on working before 4 am was 'designed to improve working conditions in a manifestly sensitive industry, in which the production process exhibits particular characteristics resulting from both the nature of the product and the habits of consumers'.[64]

Second, *Marchandise*[65] concerned a French law prohibiting the employment of staff on Sundays after 12 noon. This case was part of the rather obscure series of decisions on Sunday trading which ultimately led to the *Keck* 'revolution'.[66] For the purposes of this chapter, the interesting point is that the Court emphasised the autonomy of the national social legislation:

> national rules governing the opening hours of retail premises reflect certain political and economic choices in so far as their purpose is to ensure that working and non-working hours are so arranged as to accord with national or regional socio-cultural characteristics, and that, in the present state of [Union] law, is a matter for the Member States.

The Court concluded that the 'restrictive effects on trade which may stem from such rules do not seem disproportionate to the aim pursued'.[67]

Third, *Toolex Alpha*[68] concerned national rules which included a general prohibition on the industrial use of trichloroethylene. The Court said the system of individual exemptions, granted subject to conditions, established by the Swedish regulation appeared 'appropriate and proportionate in that it offers increased protection for workers, whilst at the same time taking account of the undertakings' requirements in the matter of continuity'. The Court referred to a range of EU health and safety legislation to support its conclusion.[69]

These three cases suggest a prioritising of worker protection over the Union interest in creating the single market, although the sample size is too small to make such a generalisation with confidence. It should also be noted that in *Oebel* and

[62] Case C-210/96 *Gut Springenheide* EU:C:1998:369; Case C-303/97 *Kessler* EU:C:1999:35; Case C-220/98 *Estée Lauder* EU:C:2000:8.

[63] Case 155/80 *Summary proceedings against Sergius Oebel* EU:C:1981:177.

[64] Para 12.

[65] Case C-332/89 *Marchandise* EU:C:1991:94.

[66] N Reich, 'The "November revolution" of the European Court of Justice: *Keck*, *Meng* and *Audi* Revisited' (1994) 31 *CML Rev* 459.

[67] Para 13.

[68] Case C-473/98 *Kemikalieinspektionen v Toolex Alpha AB* EU:C:2000:379.

[69] Para 47.

Marchandise the facts hovered on the outer edges of EU law and *Toolex Alpha* concerned a product that raised serious health concerns. Nevertheless, we can say that in these few cases where worker protection has been raised, unlike in the field of consumer law, the Court seemed keen to protect the weaker party in the face of (aggressive?) single market challenges from business.

C. The Other Freedoms

The position is somewhat different in respect of the other freedoms. There are four cases—two on freedom of establishment (*Überseering*[70] and *Payroll Data Services (PDS)*[71]), one on capital (Case C-112/05 *Commission v Germany (Volkswagen)*[72]) and one on free movement of services (*Webb*)[73]—where the defendant state invoked worker/employee protection as a justification for its rules protecting national workers in the face of challenges by business/the Commission. In only one of the cases (*Webb*) did the Court suggest that the justification was made out.

In both *Überseering* and *Volkswagen*, the Court considered that the defendant state had failed to make out the link between the measure adopted and the justification alleged. *Überseering* concerned a German rule which denied legal capacity and, consequently, the capacity to be a party to legal proceedings, to a company properly incorporated in the Netherlands where it had its registered office. The Court said that such a measure was tantamount to an outright negation of the freedom of establishment conferred on companies by Articles 49 TFEU and 54 TFEU.[74] The Court said that 'It is not inconceivable that overriding requirements relating to the general interest, such as the protection of the interests of creditors, minority shareholders, *employees* and even the taxation authorities, may, in certain circumstances and subject to certain conditions, justify restrictions on freedom of establishment'[75] but this was not the case on the facts.[76]

Commission v Germany concerned the German Volkswagen law limiting the voting rights of every shareholder to 20 per cent of Volkswagen's share capital, requiring a majority of over 80 per cent of the shares represented for resolutions of the general assembly, and allowing, in derogation from the general law, the Federal State and the Land of Lower Saxony each to appoint two representatives to the company's supervisory board. The Court found these rules breached Article 63 TFEU. On the question of justification and proportionality, the Court said that Germany had been unable to explain, 'beyond setting out general considerations as to the need for protection against a large shareholder which might by itself

[70] Case C-208/00 *Überseering v Nordic Construction Company Baumanagement GmbH* EU:C:2002:632.
[71] Case C-79/01 *Payroll Data Services* (n 50).
[72] Case C-112/05 *Commission v Germany (Volkswagen)* (n 36).
[73] Case 279/80 *Webb* (n 5).
[74] Case C-208/00 *Überseering* (n 70) para 93.
[75] Emphasis added.
[76] Para 92.

dominate the company, why, in order to meet the objective of protecting Volkswagen's workers, it is appropriate and necessary for the Federal and State authorities to maintain a strengthened and irremovable position in the capital of that company'.[77]

In the third case, *PDS*,[78] the Court thought the host state's rules were out of date and inconsistent. National legislation required that undertakings with fewer than 250 employees, which wished to entrust the preparation and printing of their pay slips to data processing centres (DPCs), could have recourse only to those DPCs established and staffed exclusively by persons registered with certain professional bodies in Italy. This requirement did not apply where DPCs offered their services to undertakings with *more* than 250 employees. The Court said that 'since the tasks in question cannot be any less complex when the number of salaried staff concerned increases, the disputed provision goes, in any event, beyond what is necessary to attain its objective of protection'.[79]

In *Webb*, by contrast, as we saw above, the Court was sympathetic to the worker protection justification, particularly having emphasised (as in *Oebel*) the sensitivity of the sector (temp agencies).[80] Nevertheless, the Court required the national court to check that, in granting licences, the host state (1) did not discriminate on the grounds of nationality, and (2) took into account the evidence and guarantees already produced by the provider of the services for the pursuit of his activities in the home state.[81]

D. Preliminary Conclusions

Thus the tenor of *Webb* fits with the dominant worker protection theme found in the three cases on free movement of goods; the Court considered that there was a genuine concern about workers who needed protection. The failure of the worker protection justification in the establishment and capital cases can be explained more on the basis of the Court's general jurisprudence on limitations on the use of justifications field (see section II above) than by any outright rejection of the worker protection justification (namely, the states failed to make a proper case, to be consistent and to act proportionately). Taken as a whole, these seven cases (three goods, two establishment, one capital, one services) point to the provisional conclusion that, provided the thresholds outlined in section II are satisfied, the Court is broadly sympathetic to claims based on worker protection raised in standard labour law situations (business v national worker).

77 Para 74.

78 Case C-79/01 *Payroll Data Services* (n 50).

79 Para 37.

80 Para 18. This is still the case: agency work was excluded from the provisions of the Services Directive.

81 Para 21.

V. MIGRANT AND POSTED WORKER CASES

A. Prioritising of Worker Welfare

We now turn to focus on those cases where one group of workers' interests (generally poorer but ambitious migrant workers) are being pitted against another group (generally the immobile, possibly unionised, national workers). In these cases the host state may raise the worker protection justification ostensibly to protect the (migrant) workers' interests but in fact also as a cover to protect the national workers' interests, specifically their jobs. While the state's positon is understandable, the Court is sensitive to 'worker protection' being used either to obstruct free movement or, worse from an EU point of view, as a form of protectionism. In these cases, the Court will reject the state's justification and so deliver *worker welfare*, namely the opportunity for workers to improve their life chances through employment in other Member States, either as migrant workers under Article 45 TFEU or posted workers under Article 56 TFEU.[82]

Las[83] is a good example of worker protection being used to obstruct free movement by a migrant worker under Article 45 TFEU. The case concerned a Flemish law providing that only the Flemish text of a cross-border employment contract was authentic (and not, for example, a text in English). Belgium sought to justify its requirement on the basis of the need to ensure 'the protection of employees by enabling them to examine employment documents in their own language and to enjoy the effective protection of the workers' representative bodies and administrative and judicial bodies called upon to recognise those documents, and, finally, to ensure the efficacy of the checks and supervision of the employment inspectorate'. While the Court recognised worker protection as a justification, it found the rules disproportionate. The establishment of free and informed consent between the parties required those parties to be able to draft their contract in a language other than the official language of Belgium.[84]

In some of the cases involving posted workers under Article 56 TFEU the Court also seems to consider the worker protection justification as coming closer to protectionism. The Court therefore rejects the justification outright or finds the steps taken to be disproportionate. So, for example, the Court said that host state laws requiring the posted worker to have been employed by the service provider for at least six months in the case of Luxembourg[85] (a year in the case of Germany)[86]

[82] On the difficulties of balancing these competing interests and how the Charter has not, so far, been of much assistance, see C Barnard, 'The Silence of the Charter' in S De Vries, U Bernitz and S Weatherill (eds), *The EU Charter of Fundamental Rights as a Binding Instrument: Five Years Old and Growing* (Oxford, Hart Publishing, 2015).

[83] Case C-202/11 *Las* (n 17).

[84] Para 31.

[85] Case C-445/03 *Commission v Luxembourg* (n 27) paras 32–33.

[86] Case C-244/04 *Commission v Germany* (n 34).

were not lawful. A requirement for the posted workers to have individual work permits which were only granted where the labour market situation so allowed was also not compatible with the EU law.[87] The Court has also said that a requirement for the service provider to provide, for the purposes of obtaining a work permit, a bank guarantee to cover costs in the event of repatriation of workers at the end of their deployment was not permitted,[88] nor was a requirement that the work be licensed,[89] nor was a rule that in order for an EU posting confirmation to be issued, the posted worker had to have been employed by the sending company for at least a year previously and to have an indefinite contract with that company.[90]

Perhaps, the most extreme example of a state using 'worker protection' as a disguise for protectionism was Case C-445/03 *Commission v Luxembourg*[91] concerning a requirement that posted workers had employment contracts of indefinite duration in force for at least six months with their employer in the state of origin. Luxembourg argued that this rule addressed the risk of abusive exploitation of workers from non-member countries through the use of precarious and poorly remunerated contracts while also protecting against the dangers of distortion of competition through social dumping.[92] The Court rejected this argument. It said that the Luxembourg rule could not be regarded as constituting an appropriate means since it involved formalities and periods which were 'liable to discourage the free provision of services through the medium of workers who are nationals of non-member countries'.[93] Once again, worker welfare prevailed.

So far we have concentrated on posted workers cases but the Court's antennae for preventing the worker protection justification from being used as a cover for protectionism can be seen in other cases under Article 56 TFEU. So, in Case C-577/10 *Commission v Belgium*,[94] the Court found that a Belgian requirement imposing on migrant self-employed service providers the obligation to make a prior declaration breached Article 56 TFEU. The Court recognised that the 'objective of combating fraud, particularly social security fraud, and preventing abuse, in particular detecting 'bogus self-employed persons' and combating undeclared work, could form part not only of the objective of the financial balance of social security systems, but also of the objectives of preventing unfair competition and social dumping and protecting workers, including self-employed service providers'. However, the 'very detailed information' required was disproportionate.[95]

[87] Case C-445/03 *Commission v Luxembourg* (n 27) paras 42–43. See also Case C-43/93 *Van der Elst* (n 19).

[88] ibid, para 47.

[89] ibid, para 30.

[90] Case C-168/04 *Commission v Austria* (n 28).

[91] Case C-445/03 *Commission v Luxembourg* (n 27).

[92] Para 28

[93] Para 30.

[94] Para 45.

[95] Para 56.

Protecting national jobs was also the motivating force behind the trade unions' decisions to call their members out on strike in the well-known cases of *Viking*[96] and *Laval*.[97] In *Laval*, the Court recognised that 'the right to take collective action for the protection of the workers of the host State against possible social dumping may constitute an overriding reason of public interest'.[98] However, it said that on the facts the collective action could not be justified where the negotiations on pay formed part of a national context characterised by a lack of provisions, of any kind, which were sufficiently precise and accessible, rendering it impossible or excessively difficult in practice for such an undertaking to determine the obligations with which it was required to comply as regards minimum pay.[99] In *Viking*, the Court recognised the Finnish trade unions' right to take strike action to protest at the loss of jobs to Estonia but only where strict conditions were satisfied and the strike action was the last resort. These points were left to the national court to decide (the case was eventually settled) but there is a sense in the judgment that the unions were unlikely to make out either the justification or the proportionality test. Once again, it seems that in these cases worker welfare prevailed over state/trade union interest in worker protection.

B. A More Nuanced Approach

The general tenor of the cases considered so far in this section suggests that, unlike in the cases involving national workers (section IV), there is a suspicion by the Court of the worker protection justification being used as a cover for protectionism, with the result that worker welfare (of migrant or posted workers) is prioritised over worker protection. However, there are cases where the Court demonstrates, as it did in the national worker cases *Oebel* and *Webb*, an awareness that migrant and posted workers do in fact risk exploitation. So, for example, in *Guiot*, the Court talked of the social protection of workers in the construction industry [which] may, however, *because of conditions specific to that sector*, constitute an overriding requirement justifying a restriction on the freedom to provide services.[100] And given the risks facing posted workers in these sectors 'control

[96] Case C-438/05 *International Transport Workers' Federation and Finnish Seamen's Union* EU:C:2007:772.

[97] Case C-341/05 *Laval un Partneri* (n 51). There is now an enormous literature on these cases. For a good overview of the debate see M Freedland and J Prassl (eds), *Viking, Laval and Beyond* (Oxford, Hart Publishing, 2014).

[98] Para 103.

[99] Para 110. For further analysis of Directive 96/71 see Case C-346/06 *Rüffert v Land Niedersachsen* EU:C:2008:189. Cf more recently Case C-115/14 *Regiopost* EU:C:2015:760.

[100] Para 16 (emphasis added). See also C-71/98 *Finalarte* (n 1) para 69.

measures' such as inspection requirements, document checks and the like, may need to be put in place by the host state, as the Court recognised in *Arblade*:[101]

> The effective protection of workers in the construction industry, particularly as regards health and safety matters and working hours, may require that certain documents are kept on site, or at least in an accessible and clearly identified place in the territory of the host Member State, so that they are available to the authorities of that State responsible for carrying out checks, particularly where there exists no organised system for cooperation or exchanges of information between Member States as provided for in Article 4 of Directive 96/71.[102]

The importance of proportionate control measures is in fact a theme of a number of posted workers cases. For example, in Case C-244/04 *Commission v Germany*,[103] the Court said that the host state could insist that the service provider furnished a 'simple prior declaration certifying that the situation of the workers concerned is lawful', particularly in the light of the requirements of residence, work visas and social security cover in the Member States where the provider employs them.[104] In Case C-445/03 *Commission v Luxembourg*[105] the Court said that the host state could require the service provider to report beforehand to the local authorities on the presence, of one or more posted workers, the anticipated duration of their presence, and the provision or provisions of services justifying the deployment.[106] Further, in Case C-490/04 *Commission v Germany*,[107] the Court said that the host state could require a (reasonable) number of those documents concerning employees to be translated into German.

C. Preliminary Conclusions

In conclusion, the general tenor of the case law involving migrant and posted workers has been to favour worker welfare over worker protection, a view borne out by the quantitative analysis. This is particularly so in cases involving what the Court considers to be protectionism by the host state. It is also true that, in respect of cases involving antiquated national rules whose original rationale has been lost in the mists of time, the Court will reject the worker protection justification. We saw this in *Las* (considered above) and *Seco* (considered in section II). It can also be seen in Case C-493/99 *Commission v Germany* where German law said that companies could not provide trans-frontier services on the German market as

[101] Joined Cases C-369/96 and C-376/96 *Arblade* (n 45).

[102] Para 61.

[103] Case C-244/04 *Commission v Germany* (n 34), confirmed in Case C-219/08 *Commission v Belgium* EU:C:2009:599.

[104] However, the host state cannot require the declaration to be sent in advance so that a registration number can be issued without which the planned posting cannot take place: Case C-515/08 *Santos Palhota* (n 17).

[105] Case C-445/03 *Commission v Luxembourg* (n 27).

[106] Para 31.

[107] Case C-490/04 *Commission v Germany* EU:C:2007:430 para 76.

part of a consortium unless they had their seat, or at least an establishment, in Germany employing their own staff, and had concluded a company-wide collective agreement for those staff. The Court found that such rules constituted a clear breach of the Treaty provisions on free movement of services.

However, where there are genuine concerns about potential abuse or mistreatment of migrant or posted workers the Court will uphold proportionate control measures (mainly against the backcloth of the Posted Workers Directive 96/71,[108] which allows host states to insist on applying the substance of its rules, but does not cover control measures to ensure those rules and others are enforced).[109] Indeed, in its case law on control measures the Court comes close to providing a legislative catalogue as to what is—and is not—acceptable in the name of worker protection. Paradoxically, the decisions (considered in section V.A) which apparently favour worker welfare may go some way to promoting worker protection in future situations, not just of national workers but of migrant/posted workers. By giving a detailed consideration of, say, the proportionality criteria, the Court is essentially providing the host state with a template as to what it can lawfully do in the future to protect vulnerable posted workers. Thus, once again, in these cases the Court's approach upholds the function of labour law, protecting the weaker party (that is, the domestic or migrant worker). In these situations there is therefore not so much difference between the cases involving national workers (section IV) and those involving migrant/posted workers (section V). A qualitative analysis of the cases therefore suggests that the Court is trying to strike a careful balance between, on the one hand, protecting workers and, on the other, preventing protectionism. Putting it succinctly, in appropriate cases the Court does allow worker protection but not protectionism.

VI. CONCLUSIONS

The aim of this chapter has been to explore the 'face' of the worker in the Court's case law on 'worker protection' justifications. Drawing on the analysis of the Court's case law on the 'consumer protection' justification, the chapter has drawn a distinction between cases which support worker protection (that is, upholding paternalist national legislation protecting individual workers) and those which uphold worker welfare (that is, removing national legislation which protects workers in the name of allowing EU workers to benefit from free movement).

A bare statistical analysis suggests that the Court's case law does lead to the prioritisation of worker welfare over worker protection, in much the same way as the Court's consumer case law prioritises consumer welfare over consumer protection. The Court does have acute antennae for rules, justified in the name of

[108] OJ [1997] L18/1.

[109] *Cf* Directive 2014/67 on the enforcement of Directive 96/71 (OJ [2014] L159/11).

worker protection, which in fact have passed their sell-by date or are protectionist of the national market. It has therefore used the Euro-worker, in much the same way as it has the Euro-consumer, 'as a lever to prise open markets sheltered by national regulation'.[110]

However, a closer analysis of the case law suggests that, in fact in genuine cases, the Court is sensitive to the worker protection objectives of national legislation and will uphold the national rules (such as in cases involving particular types of work (eg construction) and, in respect of posted workers,[111] proportionate control measures) or will at least indicate how existing national rules can be made more proportionate to secure worker protection. It is therefore misleading to see all the cases where states 'lost' as a triumph of worker welfare over worker protection.

Thus while insights from the consumer literature have been helpful in unpacking what is actually going on in the Court's case law involving the worker protection justification, it is important to recognise the differences too between consumers and workers. The first concerns winners and losers. Consumers are the passive beneficiaries of the single market: they are either being protected from 'bad' goods produced elsewhere (consumer protection prevails) or they can have access goods produced elsewhere (consumer welfare prevails). By contrast, workers under Article 45 TFEU, and posted workers under Article 56 TFEU, are active beneficiaries of the single market. They are doing exactly what the Treaty envisages. For individual migrant/posted workers the worker welfare approach is advantageous; for weak, ill-educated individual consumers, the consumer welfare approach may be disadvantageous.

The second difference between the consumer and the worker case law concerns the social consequences of prioritising consumer/worker welfare. In the field of goods or services, there is an assumption of almost unlimited supply and that consumers are not competing with each other for particular products. This may not be the case with jobs, especially in a contracting economy. In the case of scarcity, the loss of a *product* may be upsetting to a consumer; the loss of a *job* may be devastating to (ex-) workers and their families. So the opening up of the fruit liqueur market in the name of consumer welfare is a win for consumers (although not necessarily in the longer term for the domestic manufacturers and their workers). By contrast, the opening up of the services market is a win for the migrant (posted) worker but may be a loss for the non-migrant (national) worker. These arguments of substitution are contested but they are politically and

[110] S Weatherill, 'Consumer Policy' in P Craig and G de Búrca (eds), *Evolution of EU Law* (Oxford, Oxford University Press, 2011) 843.

[111] Where the Court does uphold the worker protection justification raised by the host state, it allows states to protect not just national but also migrant/posted workers. With the consumer protection justification, the beneficiaries are mainly the national consumers.

psychologically resonant.[112] For this reason, when the Court prioritises worker welfare over worker protection there may be serious political consequences, as the aftermath of the judgments in *Laval* and *Viking* have shown and, more significantly, as the result of the UK's Brexit referendum has revealed.

The third difference between the consumer and worker case law concerns the regulatory consequences of a decision to prioritise consumer/worker welfare. The removal of regulatory barriers created by national consumer protection legislation in the name of consumer welfare can be serious but compensated for to a large extent by re-regulating at EU level. This is not the case with employment law and policy. The removal of any national social law in recent years has not been matched by re-regulation at EU level. Despite the expansion of EU competence in the social field, this has not been matched by an increased political will to use that increased competence.[113] As the Monti II[114] debacle has so clearly shown,[115] it is very difficult to reach agreement at EU level on new substantive social legislation (with the exception of legislation on enforcement).[116] So to proponents of the maintenance of national social models, the removal of any national social rules in the name of worker welfare is a further nail in the coffin of social structures which have been built up over decades as part of the fabric of national life. Sometimes, as in Spain and Italy, that fabric may become a straitjacket for adapting to modern conditions. In other countries, such as Germany, that infrastructure may be one of the explanations for its economic success.[117] The Court must tread carefully; this chapter shows that in many—but not all—cases it does.

[112] See eg J Kawalerowicz, 'Perception of immigration level, rather than actual change in local areas, explains the UKIP vote', LSE EUROPP http://blogs.lse.ac.uk/europpblog/2015/06/04/perception-of-immigration-levels-rather-than-actual-change-in-local-areas-explains-the-ukip-vote/?utm_source=feedburner&utm_medium=email&utm_campaign=Feed%3A+Europp+%28EUROPP+-+European+Politics+and+Policy+at+LSE%29.

[113] See C Barnard, *EU Employment Law* (Oxford, Oxford University Press, 2012) chs 1 and 2.

[114] COM(2012) 130.

[115] See further Freedland and Prassl (n 97) especially ch 5.

[116] Although *cf* the new proposal on Posted Workers: COM(2016) 128. Nine Member States have come out to say they are opposed to the measure.

[117] See P Hall and D Soskice, 'An Introduction to Varieties of Capitalism' in B Hancké (ed), *Debating Varieties of Capitalism: A Reader* (Oxford, Oxford University Press, 2009).

7

Cultural Policy Justifications

BRUNO DE WITTE

I. INTRODUCTION

ARE CULTURAL POLICY justifications legally distinct from other policy justifications that Member States may adduce to justify restrictions of the common market freedoms? The answer to that question not only depends on the European Court's views but also, and primarily, on the position of cultural policy within the EU's written constitutional framework (to be discussed in section II of this chapter). One of the major characteristics of that constitutional framework is its evolving nature: whereas culture was all but ignored in the original EEC Treaty text, the value of cultural diversity and the primacy of Member State competence in this field are now clearly affirmed in the text of the Treaties. This raises the question whether one can find a parallel evolution in the European Court's case law: has the way in which it considers cultural policy justifications changed over time, and has it echoed the changes taking place in the EU's constitutional documents? In order to answer that question, section III will examine the place of cultural policy justifications before and after the Treaty of Maastricht (the treaty which incorporated culture into primary EU law), and section IV will examine the most recent evolution of that case law since the Treaty of Lisbon, a treaty which made significant changes to the constitutional status of culture.

In terms of subject matter, this chapter adopts a rather narrow definition of what constitutes 'cultural policy' by focusing on national measures relating to the cultural industries and services, to cultural heritage and to the use of languages, whilst leaving to another chapter in this volume the discussion of national measures reflecting moral and ethical choices—even though the latter may also reflect the cultural traditions and values of a particular country or region, and may thus be seen as part of 'cultural policy' taken in a broader sense.[1] In the latter cases, the words 'culture/cultural' appear occasionally but neither the Court of Justice nor the parties involved in the cases tend to refer to 'cultural policy' as a ground for justifying restrictions to free movement.

[1] On moral and ethical diversity in free movement law, see P Kurzer, *Markets and Moral Regulation: Cultural Change in the European Union* (Cambridge, Cambridge University Press, 2001); F de Witte, 'Sex, Drugs & EU Law: The Recognition of Moral and Ethical Diversity in EU Law' (2013) 50 *CML*

II. THE CONSTITUTIONAL FRAMEWORK OF CULTURE AND EU LAW: FROM EXCLUDED FIELD TO CONSTITUTIONAL VALUE

The competences of the EU in the field of culture are defined, by the European Treaties, in a manner that places heavy emphasis on their subsidiary nature. According to Article 167 TFEU, action by the Union in relation to culture shall (only) be for 'supporting and supplementing' the action of the Member States. Moreover, the Union is not allowed to enact 'any harmonisation of the laws and regulations of the member states' in this field. In the three-level system of EU competences as codified by the Lisbon Treaty, culture is ranked in the lowliest category, namely the 'competence to carry out supporting, coordinating or complementary action' (Article 6 TFEU); in those areas, the main responsibility for defining and implementing policies clearly remains with the Member States.

Accordingly, the role of the EU is limited to taking so-called 'incentive measures' in order to achieve the cultural policy aims set out in Article 167. Whereas incentive measures may not amount to harmonisation, it is not clearly spelled out, in a positive way, what they are. In practice, they have taken the form essentially of multi-annual funding programmes through which the European Union supports projects proposed either by the Member State authorities or by private actors and organisations within the framework of policy objectives set at the European level. Under these funding mechanisms, a number of trans-national co-operation projects, set up between cultural operators established in different European countries, benefit from additional EU funding. That funding mainly relates to performing arts and cultural heritage projects, but also supports projects in the visual arts, books and translations. Its aim is to promote the creation of cross-national cultural networks and thereby to promote cultural interaction across intra-EU borders. The name of the cultural policy programme of the EU changed over time for no other reason, apparently, than to denote some idea of policy dynamism: it was called *Culture 2000* in the period between 2000 and the end of 2006,[2] then simply the *Culture Programme (2007–2013)* in the following seven-year period,[3] and since 1 January 2014 a new seven-year programme called *Creative Europe* is in operation and now also incorporates the previously separate *Media* programme (which funds the production and Europe-wide distribution of audio-visual material).[4] Despite the gradual increase of the sums allocated to those programmes, they continue to form a tiny part of the overall EU budget.[5]

Rev 1545. In this volume, see ch 8: D Doukas, 'Morality, free movement and judicial restraint at the European Court of Justice'.

[2] The programme was established by Decision 508/2000 of 14 February 2000 (OJ 2000, L 63/1).

[3] Decision 1903/2006 of 12 December 2006 (OJ 2006, L 378/22).

[4] Regulation 1295/2013 of 11 December 2013 establishing the Creative Europe Programme (2014 to 2020) (OJ 2013, L 347/221).

[5] The *Creative Europe* programme has a budget of €1.46 billion for its entire seven-year period of existence, which corresponds to an increase of 9% compared to the funding of its two predecessor programmes, *Culture* and *Media*, but still amounts to no more than 0.15% of the total EU budget.

The EU's funding programmes are, however, only the small visible part of the Union's policy relating to culture. There is a larger but hidden part represented by EU policy measures that may have an important cultural policy impact but are legally based on non-cultural Treaty articles. Paragraph 4 of Article 167 TFEU hints at the existence of this broader range of indirect cultural policies, by providing that '[t]he Union shall take cultural aspects into account in its action under other provisions of the Treaties, in particular in order to respect and to promote the diversity of its cultures'. In other words, European cultural policy measures can form part of laws and policies whose central aim is defined otherwise, for example the smooth functioning of the internal market, the promotion of external trade, regional development, and the regulation of migration.

When pursuing those policies with an ancillary cultural dimension, the EU institutions should 'take into account' (in the terms of Article 167) the need to respect cultural diversity. This requirement not only results from the language of Article 167(4), quoted above, but also, in the post-Lisbon era, from the wording of Article 3 TEU, which lists the EU's main policy objectives and includes among them respect for cultural and linguistic diversity, and the safeguarding and enhancement of Europe's cultural heritage. Moreover, the Lisbon Treaty gave the status of primary EU law to Article 22 of the Charter of Fundamental Rights, which makes respect of cultural diversity a duty for the EU institutions in *all* their actions (and also, incidentally, for the Member States when they implement EU policies).[6] The protection of cultural diversity should thus be 'mainstreamed' in all the policies of the EU, but there is little evidence of this; partly because this particular mainstreaming obligation is one of many that are imposed by the European Treaties so that their very multiplication strips each of them of much of its meaning, and partly because the cultural obligation is formulated less forcefully than those relating to environmental protection, gender equality or social protection, so that its neglect in day-to-day European policy making goes unnoticed and unsanctioned.[7]

A question arising from this constitutional framework is whether the two main choices expressed by the text of the European Treaties in respect of cultural policy (namely, that it should primarily remain a national competence and that cultural diversity should be respected by the EU) should have consequences also for the Court of Justice; for example, when it elaborates its case law on free movement. As regards the first choice, Jukka Snell made the convincing point that 'the notion of restriction could be interpreted in a more limited fashion or a softer version of proportionality could be applied in those areas where the primary responsibility

[6] See the commentary of this Charter article by R Craufurd Smith, 'Article 22' in S Peers, T Hervey, J Kenner and A Ward (eds), *The EU Charter of Fundamental Rights—A Commentary* (Oxford, Hart, 2014) 605.

[7] For an overall analysis of the cultural mainstreaming requirement and its translation into practice, see E Psychogiopoulou, *The Integration of Cultural Considerations in EU Law and Policies* (Leiden, Martinus Nijhoff, 2008); and the recent update by the same author: E Psychogiopoulou, 'Cultural Mainstreaming: The European Union's Horizontal Cultural Diversity Agenda and its Evolution' (2014) 39 *EL Rev* 626.

has been left to the Member States, so that EU law does not unduly hinder them in the performance of their tasks'.[8] Snell adds that there is some evidence for the Court taking this line in its case law on taxation and health,[9] but without adopting a principled and consistent approach. Should cultural policy, due to the limited nature of the EU's competence, be treated differently from other national policies that cover areas where the EU's law-making role is more clearly affirmed, such as consumer or environmental protection? As regards the second choice made by the authors of the Treaty, namely that cultural diversity should be a substantive value underpinning the EU's activities, it raises the question whether the Court confirms this value choice and gives special treatment to national policy measures that aim to protect cultural diversity, compared to national measures pursuing other aims of cultural policy.

Yet, before undertaking that assessment, it should be remembered that this constitutional framework emerged only gradually, with two key moments in that process, namely the Treaty of Maastricht and the Treaty of Lisbon. The Treaty of Maastricht introduced an article dealing with culture into the EC Treaty, but this seeming expansion of EC competence was made with the precise intention of restraining the EC's 'competence creep' in this field. The culture article included both the non-harmonisation clause and the mainstreaming clause. The latter was meant, by the authors of the Maastricht Treaty, not so much as encouragement to the EC institutions to develop cultural policies through the back door of other legal bases, but rather as a way to reduce the unwanted implications for national cultural policy of those other policies such as the internal market and competition. The Lisbon Treaty confirmed the Maastricht arrangements and almost literally reproduced the text of the culture article, which is now Article 167 TFEU; but it also gave a more prominent place to the value of cultural diversity by referencing it in Article 3 TEU as well as by making Article 21 of the Charter of Rights part of primary law. However, before all this happened, the Court of Justice had already been confronted, in its judicial practice, with the tension between market integration and national cultural policies. The Court developed its line of thinking in pre-Maastricht days, when the Treaty text did not offer any guidance in the matter. That early case law will be recalled in Section 3, since it set out the path the Court has continued to follow later on. In fact, the Treaty of Maastricht did not make any difference for the Court in this area, and the post-Maastricht cases will therefore be included in that same Section 3. However, the stronger constitutional position of culture in the Lisbon Treaty may have launched a new phase; in Section 4, we will examine the few post-Lisbon cases in this field to date in order to find out whether a significant change has occurred in the Court's attitude.

[8] J Snell, 'The Legitimacy of Free Movement Case Law: Process and Substance' in M Adams, H de Waele, J Meeusen and G Straetmans (eds), *Judging Europe's Judges. The Legitimacy of the Case Law of the European Court* (Oxford, Hart, 2013) 109, 123.

[9] Snell, ibid, 124.

III. THE CASE LAW BEFORE LISBON: CULTURAL POLICY AS AN 'ORDINARY' LEGITIMATE INTEREST

Although the original text of the Treaty establishing the European Economic Community did not mention the word 'culture', it soon became clear that the economic legal rules and principles contained in that Treaty could affect cultural products and activities to the extent that these had an economic dimension. The EEC Treaty could in fact be said to have had an implicit 'cultural programme' from the very beginning, namely the elimination of national obstacles to the *free flow of cultural goods and activities* within the common European market. Only one little phrase of the original text of the EEC Treaty revealed this, and only in an indirect way: Article 36 EEC (now Article 36 TFEU) allows the Member States to retain barriers to the free movement of goods when justified on grounds of 'protection of national treasures possessing artistic, historic or archaeological value'. There would have been no need for that derogation in favour of a limited category of cultural goods if the basic principle of free movement did not apply to all cultural goods in the first place. Indeed, the European Court of Justice confirmed at an early stage of the life of the European Community that all products forming the object of a commercial transaction (including works of art, music recordings, newspapers and books) came under the Treaty rules on free movement of goods.[10]

Cultural activities were similarly subsumed within broader economic concepts as regards the freedom to provide services, which includes, for example, the cross-border distribution of television programmes: thus, the ECJ held in 1974 in its *Sacchi* judgment[11] that the transmission of television (or radio) signals across an intra-Community border should be regarded as the provision of services in the sense of the EEC Treaty. The free movement of persons was similarly interpreted as granting a right to mobility and non-discrimination to economic operators, whether employed or self-employed, in the cultural sector. As a result of this approach, 'a range of culturally motivated regulations that many states would have expected to fall outside the scope of the TEEC were brought under judicial scrutiny'.[12]

When confronted with Member State restrictions based on cultural policy considerations, the Court employed its well-known distinction between discriminatory and indistinctly applicable restrictions. As regards the former category, the first judicial landmark concerning cultural policy was the *Leclerc* judgment of 1985.[13] The specific question submitted to the Court, by means of a preliminary reference, was whether the French legislation on book prices was compatible with the free movement of goods. The French statute imposed a system of

[10] Case 7/68 *Commission v Italy (Art Treasures)* EU:C:1968:51.

[11] Case 155/73 *Sacchi* EU:C:1974:40.

[12] R Craufurd Smith, 'The Cultural Logic of Economic Integration' in E Psychogiopoulou (ed), *Cultural Governance and the European Union* (Houndmills, Palgrave Macmillan, 2015) 7, 9.

[13] Case 229/83 *Leclerc v Au Blé Vert* EU:C:1985:1.

resale price maintenance for books, whereby prices were set by the publisher (for French books) or by the first distributor (for imported books). This meant that the Leclerc supermarkets and other non-traditional outlets could not purchase their own books from 'parallel' importers so as to set their own, lower, prices. The French Government, intervening in the case, admitted that the scheme might cause some restriction of the trade in goods, but tried to justify this by invoking the need to protect the consumer and by reasons of cultural policy: a fixed price for books, it argued, protects the existence of specialist booksellers and ultimately the diversity and quality of publishing.[14] The European Court did not question the existence of such cultural policy reasons, but refused to examine their merit. It rejected their relevance in the context of the case with the following words: 'Since it derogates from a fundamental rule of the Treaty, Article 36 [of the EEC Treaty] must be interpreted strictly and cannot be extended to cover objectives not expressly enumerated therein. Neither the safeguarding of consumers' interests nor the protection of creativity and cultural diversity in the realm of publishing is mentioned in Article 36. It follows that the justification put forward by the French government cannot be accepted.'[15] The situation resulting from *Leclerc* might seem rather unfair: on the one hand, the Court did not find difficulties in broadly interpreting the economic freedoms so as to cover cultural products and activities as well (*despite the fact* that they are not explicitly mentioned by the Treaty); on the other hand, it refused to accept cultural policy justifications for derogating from those freedoms, *because* such exceptions were not expressly listed in the Treaty.

This same strict approach to discriminatory restrictions was applied to the other common market freedoms as well. In the field of the free movement of persons and services, cultural exceptions were (and still are) entirely absent from the text of the Treaties. This led the Court to reject the possibility of justifying discriminatory restrictions to trade and mobility by cultural policy reasons. It did so most prominently in the *Fedicine* judgment of 1993, which dealt with a Spanish law requiring cinema distribution companies to schedule a minimum percentage of films produced in one of the languages of Spain. The Court rejected the argument of the Spanish Government that the distribution scheme pursued a cultural aim, namely to foster Spanish film production, as irrelevant because that aim was not among those mentioned in Article 56 EC Treaty (now Article 52 TFEU) and could thus not serve to justify a discriminatory restriction of the cross-border provision of film distribution services.[16] Yet, the Court failed to discuss why cultural policy could not be encompassed within a broadly defined concept of 'public policy', which was the term mentioned in Article 56.

When, on the other hand, a cultural policy restriction was not held to be discriminatory but applied equally to domestic products or services and to those

[14] ibid para 16.

[15] ibid para 30.

[16] Case C-17/92 *Federación de Distribuidores Cinematográficos (Fedicine) v The Spanish State* EU:C:1993:172 para 20.

from other EU countries, the Court adopted a more lenient test, based on the incorporation of those cultural policy considerations among the vast category of mandatory requirements. Cultural policy thus gradually emerged as a legitimate public interest in the Court's case law on the common market freedoms. The development started with a judgment of 1985 relating to the free movement of goods. In that *Cinéthèque* case, the Court avoided making a general reference to cultural policy justifications but recognised more narrowly that the 'encouragement of creation of cinematographic work' justified the barrier to intra-Community trade of videocassettes which resulted from a French law restraining the early exploitation on video of newly released films.[17]

This approach was confirmed in the 1991 *Tourist Guides* judgments dealing with the freedom to provide services, in which the Court included the proper appreciation of the artistic and historical heritage among the overriding requirements,[18] and was finally formulated in more general terms in the Dutch media law judgment of 1991. The Dutch Media Act, at that time, sought to preserve the existing public service television system against challenges by Dutch-language commercial broadcasters established abroad, under more liberal media regimes. It stated that the cable distribution of foreign TV programmes containing advertisements directed at the Netherlands was only allowed if those advertisements followed the Dutch model, as it applied at the time, that is: advertisements should be transmitted on behalf of an organisation which is separate from the broadcasting stations; the advertisements themselves must be clearly separated from the other programmes, could not cover more than 5 per cent of programming time and could not be transmitted on Sundays; and, finally, the advertising revenue should not be used for programming purposes. Although those rules did not entail a formal discrimination against foreign providers, they effectively protected the broadcasting system against commercial 'pirates' transmitting from abroad by requiring them to copy the Dutch model of advertising on television, which was sharply different from the normal business model of TV advertising as it existed elsewhere in Europe.

Despite the formal equal treatment of Dutch and foreign broadcasters, advertising directed at the Dutch public was actually made very difficult for foreign broadcasters. The Court of Justice did not treat the Dutch rules as being discriminatory but implicitly considered them to be indistinctly applicable to national and foreign broadcasters. It also accepted *in theory* that national laws which aim to preserve a pluralist and non-commercial public service television system were a form of 'cultural policy', which may 'constitute an overriding requirement relating to the general interest which justifies a restriction on the freedom to provide services'.[19] But the Court added that the provisions of Dutch law *in fact* pursued

[17] Joined Cases 60 and 61/84 *Cinéthèque v Fédération Nationale des Cinémas Français* EU:C:1985:329.

[18] Case C-154/89 *Commission v France* EU:C:1991:76; Case C-180/89 *Commission v Italy* EU:C:1991:78; Case C-198/89 *Commission v Greece* EU:C:1991:79.

[19] Case C-288/89 *Collectieve Antennevoorziening Gouda* EU:C:1991:323 para 23.

the economic goal of protecting the advertising revenue of the public broadcasters and therefore could not benefit from the cultural policy justification, so that there was not even a need to engage in a proportionality assessment.[20] The 1991 judgment was rightly criticised for failing to recognise the close connection existing between cultural policy goals and the financial means for attaining them, and thereby making it exceedingly difficult for the Member States to preserve a non-commercial public service broadcasting system against attacks by commercial stations operating from across the State border.[21]

The pattern established in the early 1990s was confirmed in the post-Maastricht era. The Court of Justice continued to accept cultural policy justifications for restrictions of economic trade and personal mobility on condition that those restrictions were not discriminatory and not disproportionate; but the outcome of those assessments was rather unpredictable and did not express a particular deference for the Member States' principal competence in cultural matters, despite the Maastricht Treaty's insistence on this.[22] This may have inspired some diffidence among national courts as to whether they should trust the European Court to strike the right balance and whether, therefore, they should send preliminary references on cultural policy issues. A clear example of this diffidence was the *Fun Radio* case, decided by the French *Conseil d'Etat* in 1998. It concerned the compatibility with EU law of the French radio quota regulation, according to which at least 40 per cent of songs broadcast on French radio stations must be *chansons d'expression française*. Similar types of linguistic requirement can, in fact, be found in many European countries. The French court acknowledged that this constituted a restriction of intra-European trade, both of the free movement of goods (namely, of music recordings) and of the free movement of services (namely, of pre-packaged music programmes). It held, however, that these restrictions were justified for reasons of national cultural policy, and that the 40 per cent requirement was not disproportionate. In doing so, the *Conseil d'Etat* formally applied the test formulated by the European Court of Justice for such situations, but it omitted to refer a question for a preliminary ruling to the ECJ (despite being a court of last instance), for fear probably that the ECJ would reach a different conclusion as to the necessity of the restriction.[23]

[20] ibid, para 29.

[21] R Mastroianni, 'Il ruolo del principio di sussidiarietà nella definizione delle competenze statali e comunitarie in materia di politiche culturali' (1994) 4 *Rivista italiana di diritto pubblico comunitario* 63, 73.

[22] For other discussions of the Court's pre-Lisbon case law in this field, see R Craufurd Smith, 'Community Intervention in the Cultural Field: Continuity or Change?' in R Craufurd Smith (ed), *Culture and European Union Law* (Oxford, Oxford University Press, 2004) 19, 28–40; and S de Vries, *Tensions within the Internal Market: The Functioning of the Internal Market and the Development of Horizontal and Flanking Policies* (Groningen, Europa Law Publishing, 2006) 85–96.

[23] Conseil d'Etat 8 April 1998 *Sté SERC Fun Radio* (1999) *Revue française de droit administratif* 209 (and the conclusions of the *commissaire* Sylvie Hubac, *Sté SERC Fun Radio*, 194).

IV. POST-LISBON CASE LAW: UNEVEN RECOGNITION OF NATIONAL REGULATORY CHOICES

The changes brought by the Lisbon Treaty to the constitutional framework of cultural policy did not escape the Court's attention and have been referred to in its post-Lisbon case law on free movement. In both the *Runevič-Vardyn* and *Las* judgments, the following sentence appears:

> According to the 4th subparagraph of Article 3(3) EU and Article 22 of the Charter … the Union must respect its rich cultural and linguistic diversity. Article 4(2) EU provides that the Union must also respect the national identity of its Member States, which includes protection of a State's official national language.[24]

Yet, the Court did not explicitly add that it counted itself among the Union institutions to which the Treaty message is addressed. The Court's post-Lisbon record so far is rather mixed, as one can see by examining three cases involving cultural policy restrictions of free movement. In *UTECA*, the Court left considerable room for manoeuvre to the Member State, whereas in *Las* it took a more rigid approach. In contrast with those two 'outcome' judgments,[25] the Court decided to 'sit on the fence' in *Runevič-Vardyn* and left it to the national court to balance the national cultural policy objective against the right to free movement. Those three judgments will now be considered in turn.

The *UTECA* case concerned a Spanish law compelling all Spanish TV stations to spend 3 per cent of their revenue on the acquisition of films originally produced in one of the languages of Spain. This law was challenged by an association of private broadcasters who argued that it interfered with their business choices by directing them towards the acquisition of films produced in Spain rather than films produced in other (European) countries, thus causing an unjustified restriction of the freedom to provide services. This issue was referred to the ECJ by the Spanish supreme administrative court. In its judgment, which was given when the Lisbon Treaty was already signed but had not yet entered into force, the European Court readily agreed that the Spanish law restricted the movement of services, but held that it was justified by the legitimate aim of defending and promoting the national languages of the country.[26] According to the Court, the fact that the

[24] Case C-391/09 *Malgožata Runevič-Vardyn, Łukasz Paweł Wardyn* EU:C:2011:291 para 86 and Case C-202/11 *Anton Las v PSA Antwerp NV* EU:C:2013:239 para 26.

[25] I take this term from the distinction proposed by Tridimas between different types of preliminary ruling: outcome cases, guidance cases and deference cases; see T Tridimas, 'Constitutional Review of Member State Action: The Virtues and Vices of an Incomplete Jurisdiction' (2011) 9 *International Journal of Constitutional Law* 737.

[26] Case C-222/07 *Unión de televisiones comerciales asociadas (UTECA) v Administración General del Estado* EU:C:2009:124. Among the commentaries of this judgment, see I Urrutia, 'Approach of the European Court of Justice on Accommodation of the European Language Diversity in the Internal Market: Overcoming Language Barriers or Fostering Linguistic Diversity?' (2012) 18 *Columbia Journal of European Law* 243, 265 ff; D Ferri, 'Il principio di protezione e promozione della diversità culturale quale parametro di legittimità delle misure a tutela delle lingue nazionali nel settore audiovisivo' (2009) *Diritto pubblico comparato e europeo* 1381.

language criterion operates, in practice, to the advantage of Spanish film producers, 'cannot, of itself, constitute proof of the disproportionate nature of the measure … without rendering nugatory the recognition, as an overriding reason in the public interest, of the objective … of defending and promoting one or several of its official languages'.[27] This comes close to accepting that the EU's commitment to the protection of cultural and linguistic diversity may go as far as justifying the discriminatory treatment of goods, services or persons from other EU countries; and the Court seems to have tacitly overruled its *Fedicine* judgment of the early 1990s (discussed above), where the legal facts were quite similar but the Court's verdict very different. Also, and unlike in the Dutch cases of the early 1990s, the Court refrained from scrutinising whether the Spanish law did, in fact, pursue economic (that is, protectionist) aims but rather accepted at face value the qualification of the measure as one of cultural policy.

The *Las* judgment of 2013 struck a rather different note. In this case, the Court examined employment legislation of the Flemish Community of Belgium imposing the exclusive use of the Dutch language (the official language of the region) for the conclusion of private employment contracts. This piece of legislation, dating from the early 1970s, was originally meant to protect employees against the practice of some employers who, although established in Flanders, sought to impose French as the language of communication within the firm. That original sociocultural concern is no longer pressing today, and the requirement now acts, arguably, as a nuisance in the cross-border mobility of persons: non-Dutch-speaking EU citizens might be puzzled by the requirement to conclude an employment contract whose terms they do not understand (although, in practice, informal translations of the contract can be made). Upon a preliminary reference by a Belgian labour court, the ECJ ruled that this legislative requirement was 'liable to have a dissuasive effect on non-Dutch-speaking employees and employers from other Member States and therefore constitutes a restriction on the freedom of movement of workers'.[28] When comparing with the facts of *Uteca*, this restriction of cross-border economic activity seems rather mild (would anyone really refrain from taking up a job in Flanders because they would be unable to understand the official version of the labour contract?) and economically less meaningful than the Spanish law on acquisition of films. And yet, although the Court of Justice explicitly referred to the recognition of cultural and linguistic diversity in Article 3(3) TEU and Article 22 of the Charter of Rights, and confirmed that Member States (or autonomous regions within them) may protect and promote their official languages,[29] it eventually struck down the Flemish law for imposing a disproportionately harsh restriction of free movement. The proportionality reasoning of this judgment was rightly criticised as open-ended and ad hoc, giving

[27] Case C-222/07 *UTECA*, ibid para 36.
[28] Case C-391/09 *Runevič-Vardyn* (n 24) para 22.
[29] Case C-202/11 *Las* (n 24) para 26 and 27.

little guidance for further cases involving conflicts between market integration and cultural diversity.[30]

From a comparative examination of the *Uteca* and *Las* cases, it appears that the Court of Justice does recognise, in principle, the importance of the value of cultural diversity, but that, when balancing that value against the conflicting requirements of free movement rights law under its proportionality review, the outcome varies and remains quite unpredictable. The uncertainty is further increased by the Court's common practice of shifting from giving 'outcome judgments' in which it basically decides the dispute in the main case (as in *Uteca* and in *Las*), to giving 'deference judgments', in which it leaves it to the referring court to balance free movement with the mandatory requirement. An example of the latter approach in the cultural policy field is the *Runevič-Vardyn* judgment of 2011.[31] The judgment dealt with a number of implications, from a European citizenship perspective, of the official spelling rules of Lithuania. A Lithuanian woman, when acquiring the family name of her Polish husband upon their marriage, had to adopt the spelling 'Vardyn' for her husband's name (and she was hence named Runevič-Vardyn); on the other hand, her husband's name was spelled 'Wardyn' both in his home country and in Lithuania. When the question was put whether this discrepancy in name-spelling could create a serious inconvenience for the couple and thereby breach their right to free movement under Article 21(1) TFEU, the Court preferred not to engage with the question and left it to the referring court to decide (i) whether there was effectively a restriction of free movement and (ii) if so, whether that restriction was justified by the need to protect the integrity of Lithuania's official language (which does not have the letter 'w'). At no point did the Court engage with the broader issue of the significance to be given to the Treaty value of respect for linguistic diversity where there is a tension between a country's official language policy and a claim for the protection of a minority language (namely the Polish language which was, in fact, Ms Runevič-Vardyn's mother tongue).[32]

So, on the whole, the Court does not seem to have fundamentally reconsidered its approach to cultural policy justifications in the post-Lisbon context. Arguably, national cultural policy should no longer be considered as a legitimate interest like any other. Now that respect for cultural diversity has become a norm of primary EU law with a legal status equivalent to free movement itself, the Court's traditional rule/exception reasoning should be replaced by a more deferential attitude to national cultural policy measures, at least when those measures can be shown to contribute to the protection of cultural diversity within Europe.

[30] E Cloots, 'Respecting Linguistic Identity within the EU's Internal Market: *Las*' (2014) 51 *CML Rev* 623, 640.

[31] C-391/09 *Runevič-Vardyn* (n 24).

[32] The latter point is made in the case comment by H van Eijken in 'Case C-391/09, Malgožata Runevič-Vardyn and Łukasz Paweł Wardyn v Vilniaus miesto savivaldybės administracija and Others' (2012) 49 *CML Rev* 809, 822.

V. CONCLUSION: HOW MUCH CULTURAL DIVERSITY IN THE EUROPEAN UNION'S INTERNAL MARKET?

Defining the rightful place of the value of cultural diversity in the context of the EU's market integration regime remains a controversial question. Recent Treaty reforms, in particular the Lisbon Treaty, have given more salience to cultural diversity, by inscribing it among the main objectives of the EU, in Article 3 TEU, and by including respect for cultural diversity in the (now binding) text of the EU's Charter of Fundamental Rights. This growing salience is perhaps more reflected in the *external* domain by the EU's conclusion and ratification of the UNESCO Convention on Cultural Diversity and by the increased attention to cultural co-operation clauses in the EU's external agreements. *Inside* the EU, though, cultural diversity plays a more ambiguous role. On the one hand, it is treated with due respect in Court judgments and policy documents of the EU institutions, and the Union's budget supports projects that favour the mutual exchange of cultural creations between the Member States. On the other hand, though, the pursuit by the Member States of their cultural or linguistic policies occasionally clashes with the principles of market integration, and when this occurs—and when the Court of Justice is called to balance both values—its case law remains, so far, rather uncertain and unpredictable, as it gives priority to national cultural policy objectives in one case, and to market integration in the next, without attempting to construct the kind of coherent doctrine which one might expect from the judicial organ which has the constitutional responsibility of ensuring the uniform application of EU law.[33]

[33] This lack of coherence characterises many other aspects of the Court's free movement case law. See N Nic Shuibhne, *The Coherence of EU Free Movement Law: Constitutional Responsibility and the Court of Justice* (Oxford, Oxford University Press, 2013).

8

Morality, Free Movement and Judicial Restraint at the European Court of Justice

DIMITRIOS DOUKAS

I. INTRODUCTION

LORD STEYN HAS famously noted that 'the law and morality are inextricably interwoven; to a large extent the law is simply formulated and declared morality'.[1] This interaction between law and morality may be particularly evident in the field of the EU internal market insofar as moral considerations may either inform the interpretation of the free movement provisions of the Treaty—on goods (Article 34 ff TFEU), persons (Articles 45 and 49 ff TFEU), services (Article 56 ff TFEU) or capital (Articles 63 and 65 TFEU)—and/or relevant secondary EU law, or serve as public interest grounds for justifying restrictions. In stark contrast to that statement, EU law on free movement is not by definition a simple formulation and declaration of morality, and can be readily distinguished as positive law from the concepts of moral or natural law that constitute the permanent underlying basis of all law, to which individuals feel themselves subject and to which all man's laws should conform as closely as possible.[2]

However, the impact of morality on the fundamental freedoms is indisputable as it may be relied upon by policy and law-makers, primarily at national but also at EU level, in order to exercise or maintain paternalist controls in the name of 'moral regulation'; such controls reflect a strong sense of moral direction over individuals who would otherwise not be deemed able to control or protect themselves, including persons exercising their free movement rights.[3] Moral arguments are unlikely to have any significant bearing on the application of the free movement provisions

[1] *Smith New Court Securities Ltd v Scrimgeour Vickers (Asset Management) Ltd* [1997] AC 254 at 279–80 (per Lord Steyn); cited in *Three Rivers District Council and Others v Governor and Company of the Bank of England (No 3)* [2003] 2 AC 1 at 163 (per Auld LJ).

[2] See J Law and EA Martin (eds), *Oxford Dictionary of Law* 7th edn (Oxford, Oxford University Press, 2009) 358 and 363.

[3] See A Littler, *Member States versus the European Union—The Regulation of Gambling* (Leiden/Boston, Martinus Nijhoff Publishers, 2011) 39–43. *Cf* LL Fuller, *The Morality of Law* (New Haven, Yale University Press / Universal Law Publishing, 1969, reprint 2006) 5–10.

in the first place except where an immoral act or practice is sanctioned by the law in its Member State of origin as illegal. In the absence of a uniform Europe-wide conception of public morals,[4] moral considerations are recognised as grounds for allowing Member States a margin of appreciation in restricting the fundamental freedoms, either by way of express derogations in the Treaty—or relevant EU legislation—such as public morality or public policy; or by way of public interest grounds that reflect a moral judgement or have an inherent moral dimension, which have been developed in the case law of the European Court of Justice.

Regardless of their legal (statutory or judge-made) basis, the concepts of public morality and public policy or public order may be distinguished from each other in that the former corresponds to an ethical order, consisting of the unwritten basic ethical rules applicable in a society, while the latter refer to the organisation of the State and the society or the markets by way of positive enactment of norms by the competent government or institutions. However, they clearly interact with one another, and may often be used interchangeably, inasmuch as most positive enactments may concur with societal ethics, while these ethics may also largely depend on the enacted political and economic system. A broader concept of public policy or *ordre public* may correspond to both the political and the social order and thus encompass public morality or other morally laden public interest objectives.[5]

A distinction is to be drawn between, on the one hand, the (substantive) questions of whether there is a restriction on any of the fundamental freedoms and, if so, whether such a restriction is justified and proportionate; and, on the other hand, the (formal) responsibility of the judiciary in ensuring that those questions are effectively addressed by balancing the fundamental freedoms with competing rights or public interest objectives in the best possible way. The latter includes judicial deference, which relates to institutional competence, and judicial restraint, which relates to constitutional legitimacy. Both deference and restraint interact with the review of proportionality and admit of degrees.[6] This supports the idea of a sliding scale of review of proportionality, whereby the appropriate intensity of review depends on the gravity of the interference with rights or freedoms or the significance of the competing public interest objectives in each case.[7] Thus, in parallel to a substantive principle or test of proportionality, which requires the seriousness of an interference to be weighed against the importance of a competing right or public interest objective, a formal principle or test of (variable)

[4] See S O'Leary and JM Fernández-Martín, 'Judicially-Created Exceptions to the Free Provision of Services' in M Andenas and W-H Roth (eds), *Services and Free Movement in EU Law* (Oxford, Oxford University Press, 2002) 163, 188–95. *Cf* G Letsas, *A Theory of Interpretation of the European Convention on Human Rights* (Oxford, Oxford University Press, 2007) 91.

[5] See T Corthaut, *EU Ordre Public* (London, Kluwer Law International, 2012) 21–22.

[6] *Cf* J Rivers, 'Proportionality and Variable Intensity of Review' (2006) 65 *Cambridge Law Journal* 174, 177, 191 and 195; and P Craig, 'Judicial Review, Intensity and Deference in EU Law' in D Dyzenhaus (ed), *The Unity of Public Law* (Oxford and Portland, Hart Publishing, 2004) 335, 342–47.

[7] See D Doukas, *Werbefreiheit und Werbebeschränkungen* (Baden-Baden, Nomos, 2005) 147–50, 156–60, 193–95, 220–23, 352–53 and 405–14.

intensity of review operates, which requires the importance or sensitivity of a competing public interest objective to be matched by increasing judicial deference and restraint with regard to the review of the justification and proportionality of the interference.[8]

As the main yardstick by which to evaluate whether Member States have overstepped the boundaries of their discretion, public interest grounds with a moral underpinning may be used by both the domestic and, in particular, the EU judiciary in order to relax the intensity of the scrutiny of restrictions on free movement; or they may support deference by the Court of Justice to the assessment by the domestic courts of the question whether such restrictions comply with EU law, and especially with the principles of proportionality and non-discrimination. This may be the case regardless of whether the relevant field of free movement has been subject to EU harmonisation or not, and irrespective of whether moral arguments rest on—or inform the interpretation of—explicit or judge-made public interest exceptions.

This chapter is structured in four sections. The first discusses the interaction of morality and legality in the application of the free movement provisions (section II). The second examines the Court of Justice's deference and restraint with regard to the express derogations of public morality and public policy, and their interaction (section III). The third analyses judicial deference and restraint with regard to judge-made, morally underpinned public interest exceptions to free movement, with the primary emphasis placed on the case law on gambling, whilst also comparing other fields where such exceptions have been judicially accepted, such as financial services or audiovisual media (section IV). The concluding section critically assesses the interaction between moral considerations and the decreasing intensity of the review by the Court of Justice of the question whether restrictions on free movement based on morality or public order grounds are justified or proportionate (section V).

II. THE INTERACTION BETWEEN MORALITY AND LEGALITY IN EU FREE MOVEMENT LAW

Moral considerations may primarily be relied upon by Member States in order to justify restrictions on the fundamental freedoms of the internal market, albeit subject to judicial control, and the ultimate scrutiny by the Court of Justice.[9] By contrast, they are unlikely to preclude the application of the free movement provisions in the first place; hence legality prevails over morality. To trigger the application of the Treaty, it suffices that a cross-border economic activity is lawfully exercised or a

[8] *Cf* Rivers (n 6) 177–78; and T Hickman, 'The Substance and Structure of Proportionality' (2008) *Public Law* 694, 697–700.

[9] See Corthaut (n 5) 119–21.

product is lawfully manufactured and/or marketed in its Member State of origin. The question whether the service or product may be morally questionable or even illegal in another Member State (the host Member State or the Member State of destination) is irrelevant at this stage.[10] It would go against the mutual recognition principle[11] to make the application of the Treaty dependent on an assessment—presumably by national courts and the Court of Justice—of the question whether particular activities or products are morally or socially desirable or not, for the list of such questionable activities or products might be endless: it might include abortions, infertility treatment, stem cell research, cosmetic surgery, animal experiments, sale of alcohol and tobacco, pornography, cars with high CO_2 emissions, financial products (including use of cold calling for promotion), sales at a loss or buy-one-get-one-free offers, to name but a few. The Court of Justice has rightly refused to get involved in such questions of a moral, political or economic nature.[12] Reliance on moral arguments cannot prevent the application of the free movement provisions unless immorality is coupled with illegality in the home Member State of the services, persons or goods in question; the latter could only benefit from the mutual recognition principle if they did not breach the law in their country of origin.

Thus, in *SPUC v Grogan*, medical termination of pregnancy, performed in accordance with the law of the Member State in which it was carried out, was regarded as service within the meaning of Articles 56–57 TFEU, which should, in principle, be open to recipients from other Member States, irrespective of whether abortion was unlawful or regarded as grossly immoral in the Member State where the recipients of the service were based.[13] The Court noted that it was not for itself to substitute its assessment for that of the legislature in those Member States where such activities were practised legally.[14] Similarly, in *Jany*, prostitution was regarded as service provided for remuneration and protected by freedom of establishment (Article 49 TFEU) notwithstanding its allegedly immoral nature;[15] and, in *Trijber and Harmsen*,[16] the operation of window prostitution businesses by letting rooms out in shifts to prostitutes was considered as falling within the scope of the Services Directive.[17] By the same token, the Court held that, although lotteries or other games of chance may be subject to strict regulation and close control by the various national authorities due to their harmful nature, they cannot be excluded from the scope of Article 56 TFEU as services insofar as they are not prohibited in

[10] See Case 34/79 *R v Henn and Darby* EU:C:1979:295 paras 12–13; and Case 121/85 *Conegate* EU:C:1986:114 paras 11 and 13.

[11] Case 120/78 *Cassis de Dijon* EU:C:1979:42 para 14; and Case C-76/90 *Säger* EU:C:1991:331 para 12.

[12] See A Arnull, 'Gambling with Competition in Europe's Internal Market' (2009) 30 *European Competition Law Review* 440, 443–44.

[13] Case C-159/90 *SPUC v Grogan* EU:C:1991:378 paras 19–20.

[14] ibid, para 21.

[15] Case C-268/99 *Jany* EU:C:2001:616 paras 50 and 56–57.

[16] Joined Cases C-340 and 341/14 *Trijber and Harmsen* EU:C:2015:641 paras 67–69.

[17] Directive 2006/123/EC of the European Parliament and of the Council of 12 December 2006 on services in the internal market [2006] OJ L 376/36.

all the Member States. Even if the morality of games of chance might be 'at least questionable', the Court has declined to substitute its assessment for that of the legislatures of the Member States where such games are lawful.[18] It thus dismissed the suggestion of AG Bot in *Bwin* that games of chance should not be subjected to the market freedoms because calling for tenders from service providers, which would necessarily lead them to offer even more attractive games in order to maximise profits, or making it easier for consumers to take part in lotteries organised in each Member State and bet on all the horse races or sporting events in the EU, would allegedly not produce the normal benefits of competition and fall outside the aims of the internal market.[19] As Arnull notes, this argument is not only untenable as a matter of principle but also difficult to reconcile with established case law, which protects the Court from accusations that it might be second-guessing policy choices made though the national political process.[20]

The basic premise is that a morally questionable cross-border activity cannot be excluded from the scope of the free movement provisions of the Treaty unless it has been sanctioned in its Member State of origin as illegal. Nevertheless, while the Court tries to avoid getting embroiled in a moral judgement when determining whether a national measure is in principle likely to restrict the fundamental freedoms, it has not always been consistent or successful in avoiding accusations of second-guessing national policy and moral regulation choices. This may be the exception at the stage of examining whether there is a restriction on free movement in need of justification, but seems to be the rule at the stage of assessing whether such a restriction could be seen as justified and proportionate with regard to the public interest objective(s) pursued. In the former case, should an activity or product be formally prohibited by the laws in all the Member States, underpinned by EU policy, there would in principle seem to be no restriction on free movement even if the relevant activity or product might exceptionally be tolerated in practice to a certain extent or in a certain form within their home Member State.[21] Thus, in *Josemans*, although the Court recognised that the sale of soft drugs such as cannabis in coffee-shops was tolerated in the Netherlands, it stressed that the marketing of drugs was supposed to be formally banned in all the Member States (except for drugs distributed through channels strictly controlled by the State for medical or scientific purposes);[22] and held that the prohibition by a Dutch local authority of the admission of persons other than residents in the Netherlands to such establishments did not constitute a restriction on the free movement of services as far as the distribution of cannabis was concerned.[23]

[18] Case C-275/92 *Schindler* EU:C:1994:119 paras 31–32. See also Case C-243/01 *Gambelli* EU:C:2003:597 and Joined Cases C-338, 359 and 360/04 *Placanica* EU:C:2007:133 (on the application of Arts 56 and 49 TFEU to betting).

[19] AG Bot in Case C-42/07 *Bwin* EU:C:2009:519 paras 245–46 and 248–49.

[20] See Arnull (n 12) 444.

[21] Case C-137/09 *Josemans* EU:C:2010:774 paras 41–43.

[22] ibid, paras 43, 74 and 77.

[23] ibid, paras 41–42 and 54.

The Court followed the suggestion of AG Bot that the exercise of fundamental freedoms would result in legitimising cross-border trade in narcotics, an activity that should be compared to human trafficking, prostitution of minors or child pornography; and banned as a breach of the rule of law.[24] This example illustrates how, despite the lack of uniform, EU-wide moral standards, a borderless internal market may invite a reassessment of the domestic and cross-border impact of divergent norms or practices in the various Member States, especially those which have traditionally pursued a more tolerant policy on morally questionable matters.[25] The Court's approach may, however, be criticised for arbitrarily insulating national moral, ethical or cultural norms from the dynamics of free movement.[26]

However, as a rule, moral arguments may be relied upon by national authorities or taken into account by domestic courts and the Court of Justice for the purpose of defending or assessing the compatibility with the Treaty of restrictions on free movement. As regards the potential justification of such restrictions, the Court has tried to strike a balance between achieving effective internal market integration and allowing for more localised regulatory diversity across the Member States in keeping with the constitutional mandate of an EU shared competence in this field.[27] It has supplemented the Treaty's express derogations from the free movement provisions with an open-ended list of judge-made public interest grounds capable of justifying restrictions provided that these are proportionate.[28] While express derogations can justify both distinctly and indistinctly applicable measures, the judge-made, mandatory[29] or overriding requirements or pressing reasons[30] in the public or general interest may, as a rule,[31] only justify indistinctly applicable—whether indirectly discriminatory or non-discriminatory—restrictions.[32] These requirements or reasons reflect a genuinely merits-based system and are an example of the Court's law-making powers and functional constitutionalism, as Member States have never regained constitutional ownership through a Treaty amendment.[33]

24 AG Bot in Case C-137/09 *Josemans* EU:C:2010:433 paras 105–06.

25 *Cf* P Kurzer, *Markets and Moral Regulation—Cultural Change in the European Union* (Cambridge, Cambridge University Press, 2001) 141–42.

26 See F De Witte, 'Sex, Drugs and EU Law: The Recognition of Moral and Ethical Diversity in EU Law' (2013) 50 *CML Rev* 1545, 1562–65.

27 Art 4(2)(a) TFEU; and Case C-491/01 *R v Secretary of State for Health, ex p British American Tobacco* EU:C:2002:741 para 179.

28 See N Nic Shuibhne, *The Coherence of EU Free Movement Law—Constitutional Responsibility and the Court of Justice* (Oxford, Oxford University Press, 2013) 25.

29 Case 120/78 *Cassis de Dijon* (n 11) para 8.

30 Case C-288/89 *Stichting Collectieve Antennevoorziening Gouda* EU:C:1991:323 paras 13–14; Case C-415/93 *Bosman* EU:C:1995:463 para 104; and Case C-55/94 *Gebhard* EU:C:1995:411 paras 35 and 37.

31 Contrast Case C-120/95 *Decker* EU:C:1998:167 paras 32, 39 and 44, where the Court did not rule out that a directly discriminatory restriction on free movement of goods might be justified not only by an express derogation (Art 36 TFEU) but also by a judge-made overriding requirement in the general interest.

32 See N Nic Shuibhne, 'Exceptions to the Free Movement Rules' in C Barnard and S Peers (eds), *European Union Law* (Oxford, Oxford University Press, 2014) 473, 479–84.

33 See Nic Shuibhne, *The Coherence of EU Free Movement Law* (n 28) 25–26.

Accordingly, moral justifications of restrictions on free movement are either explicitly prescribed by the Treaty or have been recognised in case law. The former category includes public morality as one of the express derogations from free movement of goods (Article 36 TFEU), but also morally laden considerations linked to public policy as an express derogation from free movement of persons (Articles 45(3) and 52(1) TFEU), services (Articles 52(1) and 62 TFEU) or capital (Article 65(1)(b) TFEU),[34] understood more broadly as *ordre public*.[35] The latter category, the development of judge-made mandatory or overriding requirements or pressing reasons in the public interest, which are underpinned by moral considerations, and may justify restrictions on the fundamental freedoms, has found fertile ground primarily in the case law on gaming and betting, including both games of chance and other games for entertainment,[36] but also, albeit to a lesser extent, in other fields, such as audiovisual media or financial services. The question is raised whether the standards applied by the Court of Justice to both the express and the judge-made morally laden derogations are comparable and consistent, or not.

III. MORALLY LADEN EXPRESS DEROGATIONS FROM FREE MOVEMENT

A. Public Morality as an Express Derogation

Although, as a rule, express derogations from fundamental freedoms are to be narrowly construed, the Court of Justice originally opted for a broad interpretation of public morality within the meaning of Article 36 TFEU, providing Member States with substantial latitude to justify restrictions on the free movement of goods. The only limit applied was the prohibition of arbitrary discrimination or any disguised restriction on cross-border trade (Article 36(2) TFEU), and the Court did not engage in a proportionality test. In *Henn and Darby*, an outright UK ban on importation of pornographic material from another Member State (the Netherlands) was found to be a quantitative restriction that could be justified on grounds of public morality and did not arbitrarily discriminate against imported goods.[37] The Court relied on the wide discretion that the Member States should in general enjoy in determining the requirements of public morality in the manner they see fit and setting their own standards of protection in accordance with their own scale of values. It was therefore held to be part of their 'reserved powers' to restrict

[34] See Case C-36/02 *Omega* EU:C:2004:614 paras 40–41; Case C-137/09 *Josemans* (n 21) paras 62–63, 65–66, 69 and 75. *Cf* Case 41/74 *Van Duyn* EU:C:1974:133 paras 19 and 23–24; Joined Cases 115 and 116/81 *Adoui and Cornuaille* EU:C:1982:183 para 8; Case C-268/99 *Jany* (n 15) paras 60–62; and Case C-54/99 *Scientology* EU:C:2000:124 paras 17–20.

[35] *Cf* Corthaut (n 5) 22, 50, 325–26, 422 and 430–31.

[36] See D Doukas and J Anderson, 'Commercial Gambling without Frontiers: When the ECJ Throws, the Dice is Loaded' (2008) 27 *Yearbook of European Law* 237; and D Doukas, 'In a Bet there is a Fool and a State Monopoly: Are the Odds Stacked against Cross-border Gambling?' (2011) 36 *EL Rev* 242.

[37] Case 34/79 *Henn and Darby* (n 10) para 22.

or totally prohibit the importation of indecent or obscene material, 'as understood by [their] domestic laws' for the whole of their territory.[38] What was decisive was the lack of any lawful domestic trade in the same goods within the UK at the time of the ban in question as domestic legislation sufficiently restrained the manufacture and marketing of pornography.[39]

Conegate marked a shift towards a more restrictive approach to public morality as a ground for justifying restrictions on free movement of goods.[40] Although the Court re-affirmed the prohibition of arbitrary discrimination as the only outer limit on the Member States' discretion,[41] it distinguished the case on the facts from *Henn and Darby* and reached the opposite conclusion. The then UK ban on imports of articles of erotic or sexual nature from another Member State (Germany) was found to be an unlawful quantitative restriction in breach of Article 34 TFEU, which could not be defended by the need to protect public morality as, at that time, the same products were lawfully manufactured and marketed in the UK, albeit within licensed outlets and subject to minimum age limits and marketing restrictions (including an absolute ban on delivery by post and a restriction on public display); such restrictions were not regarded as substantially equivalent to a ban on manufacture and marketing, and could equally be applied to goods imported from other Member States.[42] Subsequently, and already before the introduction of the *Keck* test with regard to selling arrangements,[43] the Member States' power to apply the same restrictions to the sale of any goods marketed in their territory, regardless of their origin, was acknowledged in *Quietlynn*; where a morally underpinned, indistinctly applicable prohibition on sale of lawful sex articles in unlicensed outlets in the UK was not found to be capable of having a disparate impact on the marketing of imported goods and was not caught in the net of Article 34 TFEU.[44]

While in *Conegate* the Court placed the emphasis on the prohibition of arbitrary discrimination, its reasoning strongly reflects a proportionality appraisal.[45] Although it acknowledged the Member States' freedom to make their own assessments of the indecent or obscene character of certain goods, the Court emphasised that the mere potential for causing offence could not be regarded as sufficiently serious to justify restrictions on free movement on grounds of public morality if the Member States did not adopt, with regard to the same goods manufactured or marketed on their own territory, criminal or other serious and effective measures intended to prevent their distribution.[46] This more restrictive approach to

[38] ibid, paras 15–17.

[39] ibid, paras 21–22.

[40] Case 121/85 *Conegate* (n 10) para 20.

[41] ibid, para 14.

[42] ibid, paras 16, 18 and 20–21.

[43] Joined Cases C-267 and 268/91 *Keck and Mithouard* EU:C:1993:905 paras 16–17.

[44] Case C-23/89 *Quietlynn Ltd and Richards v Southend Borough Council* EU:C:1990:300 paras 9 and 1–12. See also Case C-350/89, *Sheptonhurst Ltd v Newham Borough Council* EU:C:1991:151.

[45] See AG Poiares Maduro in Case C-434/04 *Ahokainen and Leppik* EU:C:2006:609 para 29.

[46] Case 121/85 *Conegate* (n 10) paras 15–16.

public morality (Article 36 TFEU) not only seems in line with the generally strict construction of the express derogation of public policy (Articles 36, 45(3), 52(1) and 65(1)(b) TFEU), which presupposes a genuine and sufficiently serious threat affecting one of the fundamental interests of society;[47] such a threat cannot be established if a Member State does not adopt, with respect to the same conduct on the part of its own nationals, repressive or other genuine and effective measures intended to combat such conduct.[48] The Court also seems to have sown the seeds of a consistency requirement, which emerged in connection with the express derogation of public policy,[49] and was consolidated as a fully fledged requirement a couple of decades later in the context of assessing the proportionality of restrictions on the free movement in the field of gaming and betting.[50]

Consistency has been taken as a proxy for genuineness in the pursuit of public interest objectives. Where a Member State attempts to defend restrictions of free movement on its territory, but takes no or less rigorous measures against similar domestic goods, services, capital or its home nationals, it undermines its own claim of threat to the public interest and defeats the intended purpose.[51] If national legislation or policy does not reflect a genuine concern to serve the public interest in a consistent manner, this compromises its effectiveness and, hence, the ensuing restriction on free movement cannot be regarded as suitable,[52] necessary,[53] or reasonable for the attainment of the relevant public interest objective.[54] Therefore, although the consistency requirement was originally read into the ban on arbitrary discrimination and regarded as a safeguard against misuse of express derogations, it has increasingly been applied as part of the principle of proportionality rather than the principle of non-discrimination.[55]

The curtailment of the Member States' margin of appreciation is based on the premise that the aim of an express derogation from free movement is not

[47] Case C-348/96 *Calfa* EU:C:1999:6 paras 21, 23 and 25. See generally, D Thym, 'The Constitutional Dimension of Public Policy Justifications', ch 9 in this volume.

[48] Joined Cases 115 and 116/81 *Adoui and Cornuaille* (n 34) paras 8–9; and Case C-268/99 *Jany* (n 15) paras 60–62.

[49] See Joined Cases 115 and 116/81 *Adoui and Cornuaille* (n 34) paras 8–9; and Case C-100/01, *Ministre de l'Intérieur v Aitor Oteiza Olazabal* EU:C:2002:712 para 42. *Cf* Case C-137/09 *Josemans* (n 21) paras 70 and 76.

[50] Case C-243/01 *Gambelli* (n 18) paras 67 and 69; Case C-67/98 *Zenatti* EU:C:1999:514 paras 36–37; and Joined Cases C-338, 359 and 360/04 *Placanica* (n 18) paras 53–55. See Doukas and Anderson (n 36) 247–49; and Doukas (n 36) 244, 247 and 256–59. See also section IV.B below.

[51] See D Chalmers, G Davies and G Monti, *European Union Law: Text and Materials* 3rd edn (Cambridge, Cambridge University Press, 2014) 903. *Cf* A Lippert, 'Das Kohärenzerfordernis des EuGH—Eine Darstellung am Beispiel der Rechtsprechung zum deutschen Glücksspielmonopol' (2012) 47 *Europarecht* 90, 92–93, where consistency is seen as an autonomous limit to restrictions on free movement, distinct from both non-discrimination and proportionality.

[52] Case C-169/07 *Hartlauer* EU:C:2009:141 paras 55–59; and Case C-500/06 *Corporación Dermoestética SA v To Me Group Advertising Media* EU:C:2008:421 paras 39–41.

[53] Case C-346/06 *Dirk Rüffert v Land Niedersachsen* EU:C:2008:189 paras 38–42.

[54] Joined Cases C-171 and 172/07 *Saarland* EU:C:2009:316 paras 42–51.

[55] See Chalmers et al (n 51) 901–11; and G Mathisen, 'Consistency and Coherence as Conditions for Justification of Member State Measures Restricting Free Movement' (2010) 47 *CML Rev* 1021–48.

to reserve certain matters to the Member States' exclusive jurisdiction but could only justify national measures if they were suitable to serve the public interest objective pursued and did not restrict cross-border trade more than is absolutely necessary;[56] this requires that the Court exercise some control over what a Member State regards as falling within the concept of public morality.[57] This substantive, albeit complementary and limited or minimal, review of national rules intended to protect public morality—especially in areas which traditionally lie at the heart of the public debate in most European societies—may be regarded as reflecting the Court's intention to ensure a degree of consistency within Member States with regard to their discretion to rely on this public interest ground, without judging values that may be specific to them;[58] and thus prevent the risk of national courts upholding unreasonable restrictions on free movement that serve aims which clearly cannot be a matter of public morality.[59] In a similar vein, the Court has suggested that a Member State could not rely on public morality to justify a general ban on genetically modified organisms (GMOs) in its territory, which breached EU harmonisation measures that authorised such products and allowed only limited derogations on health or environmental grounds, if the moral or religious concerns were not invoked independently as the primary justification but merely as an aspect relating to other public interest objectives, such as the protection of environment or health.[60]

Nevertheless, given the lack of an EU-wide uniform conception of public morality, Member States seem to maintain substantial discretion in protecting it, however constrained this may be by the principle of non-discrimination, the principle of proportionality, including its consistency component, or the degree of pre-emption of the relevant matter by EU legislation. This was made clear in *Heinonen*, where the Court held that EU harmonisation rules on duty-free allowances in international travel,[61] which presupposed the legality of importation of a given product but included a derogation comparable to Article 36 TFEU, should not preclude a Member State (Finland) from relying on non-economic public interest objectives, such as the protection of public order, morality or health,

[56] *Cf* Case 153/78 *Commission v Germany* EU:C:1979:194 para 5; and Case C-189/95 *Franzén* EU:C:1979:194 [76]–[77] (on public health); Case 72/83, *Campus Oil Ltd v Minister for Industry and Energy* EU:C:1984:256 para 32; and Case C-367/89 *Criminal proceedings against Aimé Richardt and Les Accessoires Scientifiques SNC* EU:C:1991:376 para 20 (on public security).

[57] See AG Van Gerven in Case C-145/88 *Torfaen Borough Council v B&Q* EU:C:1989:593 para 29, who argued that public morality was unlikely to cover the prevention of offence to religious convictions and justify a prohibition on Sunday trading.

[58] See Corthaut (n 5) 51–58 and 323–26.

[59] See AG Léger in Case C-1/96 *R v Minister of Agriculture, Fisheries and Food, ex p Compassion in World Farming Ltd* EU:C:1998:113 paras 95–104, who suggested that the UK prohibition on the 'veal crate system' of rearing calves should be regarded as a matter of public morality insofar as it was capable of unjustifiably causing harm to the life and health of domestic animals and did not seem manifestly contrary to Art 36 TFEU.

[60] Case C-165/08 *Commission v Poland* EU:C:2009:473 paras 54–59.

[61] Council Regulation (EC) 3285/94 of 22 December 1994 on the common rules for imports and repealing Regulation (EC) No 518/94 [1994] OJ L 349/53.

for the purpose of restricting or prohibiting private, non-commercial imports of alcohol from third countries for personal use, as part of a campaign against alcoholism.[62] While the appraisal of the proportionality of such measures was left to be determined by the national judges, the Court of Justice stressed that the latter should take into account the margin of discretion allowed to Member States in assessing which measures were capable of guaranteeing concrete results in the protection of the public interest objectives pursued, and in particular the social circumstances in which the measures were applied and the importance which the individual Member States attached to legitimate aims under EU law, such as the protection of the public order against criminality or disturbances linked to alcohol consumption.[63] Unlike AG Saggio, who questioned the proportionality of a total ban on imports of alcohol purchased for personal use in third countries following a journey lasting no more than 20 hours, and argued that the public interest could have been effectively protected by a less drastic measure such as an exclusion from duty-free allowances,[64] the Court concluded that such a ban would seem to be necessary and proportionate as there were no other effective alternatives.[65] Its reference to morality alongside the protection of other non-economic public interest objectives, such as public order or health, illustrates the strong interaction between public morality and public policy as two sides of the same coin—a broader concept of *ordre public*.[66]

B. The Interaction between Morality and Public Policy

The interaction between morality and public policy and the Court's reluctance to enter into an evaluation of fundamental values specific to a Member State have been striking features in case law despite the adoption—and subsequent codification for the free movement of persons[67]—of a narrow EU law definition of the scope of the express derogation of public policy (Articles 36(1), 45(3), 52(1) and 65(1)(b) TFEU); this requires that there is a genuine and sufficiently serious threat affecting one of the fundamental interests of society,[68] in addition to the perturbation of the

[62] Case C-394/97 *Heinonen* EU:C:1999:308 paras 30–34.

[63] ibid, para 43.

[64] AG Saggio in Case C-394/97 *Heinonen* EU:C:1999:10 paras 34–35.

[65] Case C-394/97 *Heinonen* (n 62) para 44.

[66] See also Case C-34/10 *Oliver Brüstle v Greenpeace* EU:C:2011:669 paras 30–38 and 46 on the exclusion of use of human embryos for industrial or commercial purposes from patentability as contrary to *ordre public* or morality under Art 6(2)(c) of Directive 98/44/EC of the European Parliament and of the Council of 6 July 1998 on the legal protection of biotechnological inventions [1998] OJ L213/13.

[67] See also Art 27(2) Directive 2004/38/EC of the European Parliament and of the Council of 29 April 2004 on the right of citizens of the Union and their family members to move and reside freely within the territory of the Member States ('Citizens' Rights Directive') [2004] OJ L 158/77 (as corrected in [2004] OJ L 229/35).

[68] Case 36/75 *Rutili* EU:C:1975:137 para 28; Case 30/77 *Bouchereau* EU:C:1977:172 para 35; Joined Cases 115/81 and 116/81 *Adoui and Cornuaille* (n 34) para 8; and Case C-348/96 *Calfa* (n 47) para 21.

social order, which any infringement of the law involves.[69] The Court's deference to the Member States' principal latitude to determine the requirements of their *ordre public* in the light of their own national needs or moral values was evident in *SPUC v Grogan*. The link between abortions carried out in clinics in another Member State (UK) and the activity of student associations distributing information on those clinics to the public in a Member State that banned such activities (Ireland), without however acting in co-operation with the clinics or on their behalf, was considered too tenuous for the prohibition on distribution of information in Ireland to be capable of constituting a restriction on free movement of services (Article 56 TFEU).[70] On the other hand, AG Van Gerven tied in the express derogation of public policy (Articles 52(1) and 62 TFEU) with judge-made, morally underpinned, imperative requirements of public interest, which could justify a restriction on free movement of services arising by the prohibition in Ireland of the provision of assistance with, or information about, abortions offered by clinics abroad. Given the protection of the unborn child by the Irish Constitution, and drawing an analogy with the construction of public morality under Article 36 TFEU, he emphasised that the public interest objective in question formed part of the fundamental principles of that Member State's society, and related to a policy choice of a moral and philosophical nature, the assessment of which was a matter for the Member States and in respect of which the latter should enjoy discretion in accordance with their own scale of values and in the manner they saw fit.[71]

The Court in fact read moral considerations into the interpretation of public policy (Articles 52(1) and 62 TFEU) in *Omega*, the only case to date in which this express derogation has been accepted as a valid ground for justifying restrictions on free movement in the gaming sector, concerning here the prohibition in Germany of the commercial exploitation of games simulating acts of homicide insofar as those games infringed human dignity.[72] The Court did not confine itself to reiterating that national authorities should be allowed a margin of discretion within the limits imposed by the Treaty, and subject to judicial review, as the specific circumstances which could justify reliance on the existence of a genuine and sufficiently serious threat to one of the fundamental interests of society might vary from one country to another and from one era to another.[73] Although the Court placed the emphasis on the protection of the fundamental right to human dignity as a general principle of EU law rather than on its guarantee in the national Constitution, it was reluctant to engage in a rigorous review of proportionality.[74]

[69] Joined Cases C-482 and 493/01 *Orfanopoulos and Oliveri* EU:C:2004:262 para 66; Case C-268/99, *Jany* (n 15) paras 60–62; and Case 54/99 *Scientology* (n 34) paras 17–20. See further the discussion in Thym (n 47).

[70] Case C-159/90 *SPUC v Grogan* (n 13) paras 24–27.

[71] Opinion of AG Van Gerven in Case C-159/90 *SPUC v Grogan* (n 13) para 26.

[72] Case C-36/02 *Omega* (n 34) paras 40–41.

[73] ibid, paras 30–31.

[74] ibid paras 32–36. See MK Bulterman and HR Kranenborg, 'What if Rules on Free Movement and Human Rights Collide? About Laser Games and Human Dignity: the *Omega* Case' (2006) 31 *EL Rev* 93, 98–99.

It held that the restrictions imposed by a Member State on the operation of games in its territory must not necessarily correspond to a common conception, shared by all the Member States, as regards the underlying moral, religious or cultural considerations, and in particular the precise manner in which the fundamental right or legitimate interest in question is to be protected.[75] Relying on established case law that the mere fact that a Member State has chosen for a system of protection different from that adopted by another Member State could not affect the assessment of proportionality,[76] the Court concluded that the prohibition in question was not disproportionate, not least because it corresponded to the level of protection of human dignity which the national Constitution sought to guarantee.[77] This reaffirms the Member States' substantial discretion to justify restrictions on free movement on the basis of their own evaluation or application of ethical or ideological standards in their territory,[78] and the Court's deference to their fundamental value judgements (*Grundurteile*) that underlie the law and are based on moral judgements, expressing—among other things—the principles of altruism and justice, which form standards of ethical or practical reason.[79] Conversely, as was emphasised in *Adoui and Cornuaille* and *Jany*, where an allegedly immoral activity, such as prostitution, was lawfully exercised by a Member State's own nationals, it could not be invoked to justify restrictions on free movement on grounds of public policy.[80] This marked a reversal of the Court's legal reasoning in its earlier *Van Duyn* case, according to which a Member State could rely on public policy in order to deny access to its territory to workers from another Member State if they were associated with an organisation that was merely regarded as socially harmful but was not illegal in the former Member State, where it was freely accessible to home nationals.[81]

Despite the outer limits set on the Member States' wide discretion by the narrowly construed concept of public policy, or general principles of law, and especially proportionality and its inherent requirement of consistency, the judicial review of restrictions on free movement in the light of the Treaty remains lax and

[75] Case C-36/02 *Omega* (n 34) para 37 dismissing any misreading of Case C-275/92 *Schindler* (n 18) para 60 as establishing a general, common standard for assessing the proportionality of any restriction on the exercise of an economic activity.

[76] Case C-124/97 *Läärä* EU:C:1999:435 para 36; Case C-67/98 *Zenatti* (n 50) para 34; and Case C-6/01 *Anomar* EU:C:2003:446 para 80. See also n 115 and n 140 below.

[77] Case C-36/02 *Omega* (n 34) paras 38–39. See N Nic Shuibhne, 'Margins of Appreciation: National Values, Fundamental Rights and EC Free Movement Law' (2009) 34 *EL Rev* 230, 243–45 and 253–54; and Thym (n 47).

[78] See S Kadelbach, 'Demokratische Legitimation als Prinzip zwischenstaatlichen Handels' in S Vöneky, C Hagedorn, M Clados and J von Achenbach (eds), *Legitimation ethischer Entscheidungen im Recht—Interdisziplinäre Untersuchungen* (Berlin, Heidelberg and New York, Springer, 2009) 147, 158–59.

[79] *Cf* M Mahlmann, 'New Trends of Cognitive Science in Ethical and Legal Reflection' in Vöneky et al, ibid, 15, 47–48.

[80] Joined Cases 115 and 116/81 *Adoui and Cornuaille* (n 34) para 8; and Case C-268/99 *Jany* (n 15) paras 60–62.

[81] Case 41/74 *Van Duyn* (n 34) paras 19 and 24.

minimal unless Member States have manifestly exceeded those outer limits. Thus, in both *Calfa* and *Orfanopoulos and Oliveri*, although the Court acknowledged that a Member State might consider that the personal use of drugs constituted such a sufficiently serious danger for society as to justify special measures against nationals from other Member States who breached its laws, in order to maintain public order, it held that an expulsion of foreign nationals that automatically followed a criminal conviction under national law could not be seen as a justifiable and proportionate restriction on free movement of services or persons if no account had been taken of the personal conduct of the offenders or of the danger which they represented for the requirements of public policy.[82] In a similar vein, in the *Scientology* case, the Court accepted that a system of prior authorisation of any direct foreign investment in a Member State (as was here the financing of the French branch of the Church of Scientology by its UK and US counterparts), which might be such as to constitute a genuine and sufficiently serious threat to public policy, might be regarded as a justifiable restriction on free movement of capital unless it did not provide for sufficiently clear and precise criteria according to which a foreign investment would represent such a threat (e.g. circumstances in which a religious organisation might be allegedly involved in fraud or tax evasion).[83] However, in this case, the French system was too general and thus contrary to the requirements of the general principle of legal certainty.[84]

Interestingly, in *Josemans*, the Court of Justice seems to have further relaxed its standards of assessment of the Member States' generally broad discretion to defend restrictions on free movement by relying on public policy.[85] Not only did it rule that the exclusion of residents of other Member States from accessing coffeeshops in the Netherlands did not constitute a restriction on the freedom to receive services as far as the distribution of soft drugs was concerned.[86] The Court went on to read into the express derogation of public policy (Article 52(1) TFEU) moral and social justifications relating to judge-made public interest objectives, such as the combating of drug tourism, and associated concerns about public nuisance and the maintenance of public order.[87] In addition, to the extent that such establishments also offered food and non-alcoholic drinks, the Court concluded that this directly discriminatory restriction on the freedom of nationals from other Member States to receive catering services in such establishments was justified and proportionate. In stark contrast to its otherwise narrow construction of public policy,[88] and although it generally acknowledged the need for consistency in

[82] Case C-348/96 *Calfa* (n 47) paras 22, 25 and 27–28; and Joined Cases C-482 and 493/01 *Orfanopoulos and Oliveri* (n 69) paras 67–68 and 71.
[83] AG Saggio in Case 54/99 *Scientology* (n 34) para 21.
[84] ibid, paras 19–23.
[85] See de Witte (n 26) 1563–65.
[86] Case C-137/09 *Josemans* (n 21) paras 41–42 and 54.
[87] ibid, paras 62–63, 65–66, 69 and 75.
[88] Joined Cases 115 and 116/81 *Adoui and Cornuaille* (n 34) paras 8–9.

the protection of the public interest,[89] it did not apply the consistency test to the present case.[90] It found that it was not inconsistent for a Member State to adopt appropriate measures in order to deal with a large influx of residents from other Member States who wished to benefit from the marketing of drugs, which was tolerated in that Member State, since those products were, 'by their very nature, prohibited from being offered for sale in all Member States';[91] other, less restrictive means, including the possibility of granting non-residents access to coffee-shops whilst refusing to sell cannabis to them, were regarded as ineffective.[92] The Court left it to the discretion of the Member States to adopt general rules, easily managed and supervised by their domestic authorities, for the purpose of combating drug tourism and related public nuisance.[93] The judgment, which went as far as to allow discriminatory treatment of foreign nationals, which should have otherwise been declared inconsistent and therefore disproportionate, was heavily influenced by the Opinion of AG Bot, who defended such measures as representing the expression not only of a Member State's right to maintain its internal public order, but also its obligation vis-à-vis other Member States to contribute to the maintenance of the European *ordre public*.[94] This approach has been criticised for ironing out the moral, ethical, social, cultural or public policy diversity in the different Member States and replacing it with a monolithic, unitary and autonomous new concept of European *ordre public*, which is based on majoritarian principles, tending to reflect solutions acceptable to the greatest number of Member States, without being capable of successfully accommodating any inherent nuances and premised on the presumption that the EU institutions may legitimately mediate between different views as to moral or ethical goods for the sake of uniform EU policy.[95]

The top-down approach to the interpretation of the public policy exception in *Josemans* allows a Member State to rely on the stricter norms or policies of other Member States in order to justify the application of double standards to the moral evaluation of the same activity in its territory, depending on whether this is exercised by home nationals or by nationals from other Member States who cross the borders. This stands in stark contrast to the Court's usual bottom-up approach, which is premised on deference to every Member State's margin of appreciation for the requirements of the domestic *ordre public* and the restraint of the judicial control over such fundamental value judgements in the light of the free movement provisions—unless the Member State has exceeded the outer limits of that discretion; most importantly those arising from the principle of proportionality,

[89] Case C-137/09 *Josemans* (n 21) para 70 citing Case C-169/07 *Hartlauer* (n 52) para 55, Joined Cases C-171 and 172/07, *Saarland* (n 54) para 42, and Case C-42/07 *Bwin* (n 19) paras 59–61. See also sections III.A and B above and IV.B below.

[90] Case C-137/09 *Josemans* (n 21) para 76.

[91] ibid, para 78.

[92] ibid, paras 80–81.

[93] ibid, paras 82–83.

[94] AG Bot in Case C-137/09 *Josemans* (n 21) para 124. See further the discussion in Thym (n 47).

[95] See de Witte (n 26) 1559–62.

and in particular its consistency component, or other general principles of law and, where applicable, EU legislation. Notwithstanding this incoherence in case law, regardless of whether public morality or public policy takes centre stage as a ground for justifying restrictions on free movement, the Court has otherwise been keen to defer, as a rule, to the Member States' own assessments of their domestic *ordre public*. It has only exceptionally relied on a deeper and uniform concept of an EU *ordre public* where the domestic *ordre public* serves the protection of moral, ethical or social values or fundamental rights and principles, which are common to the legal traditions of all the Member States, or where there are common minimum standards set out in EU legislation.[96]

Even in the latter case, Member States usually retain a broad discretion, as already demonstrated in *Heinonen* on the free movement of goods,[97] and also illustrated in the field of free movement of audiovisual services and minimum EU harmonisation standards relating to public policy or morality.[98] The Member States' discretion to derogate from the transmitting State principle,[99] and restrict the retransmission of TV programmes or other audiovisual media services transmitted by—not only domestic broadcasters but also—media service providers falling under the jurisdiction of another Member State if they manifestly, seriously and gravely infringe Article 6 and/or Article 27 of the AVMS Directive,[100] has not been subjected to a rigorous judicial scrutiny. The former provision concerns the prohibition of audiovisual media services that contain any incitement to hatred based on race, sex, religion or nationality; the latter provides for the exclusion or restriction of any programmes which are likely to (seriously) impair the physical, mental or moral development of minors, in particular programmes that involve pornography or gratuitous violence. This derogation has been used by the UK more often than any other Member State without any successful challenge.[101] In *Mesopotamia*, the Court construed the scope of the derogation in Article 6 of the AVMS Directive so broadly as to include TV programmes infringing the principles of international understanding.[102] An analogy can be drawn with the judicial restraint exercised by the EFTA Court in the *TV1000* case, where it found that, although (the predecessor to) Article 27(1) of the AVMS Directive[103] mentioned

96 See Corthaut (n 5) 323–26 and 426–27.

97 Case C-394/97 *Heinonen* (n 62) paras 30–34. See III.A above.

98 See Corthaut (n 5) 148–49.

99 Arts 2(1) and 4(6) Directive 2010/13/EU of the European Parliament and the Council of 10 March 2010 on the co-ordination of certain provisions laid down by law, regulation or administrative action in Member States concerning the provision of audiovisual media services (Audiovisual Media Services Directive) [2010] OJ L95/1 as corrected in [2010] OJ L263/15.

100 Directive 2010/13, ibid.

101 See C Barnard, *The Substantive Law of the EU—The Four Freedoms* 4th edn (Oxford, Oxford University Press, 2013) at 396–97.

102 Joined Cases C-244 and 245/10 *Mesopotamia* EU:C:2011:607 paras 39–44 and 46. *Cf* AG Bot in Joined Cases C-244 and 245/10 *Mesopotamia* EU:C:2011:284 paras 87–93.

103 Art 22 Council Directive 89/552/EEC of 3 October 1989 on the co-ordination of certain provisions laid down by law, regulation or administrative action in Member States concerning the pursuit of television broadcasting activities [1989] OJ L298/23, as amended by Directive 97/36/EC of the

pornography as content of a programme which might seriously impair the physical, mental or moral development of minors, Member States remained free to determine what is covered by the terms 'pornography' and 'likely to impair the development of minors' in accordance with their domestic legislation and moral standards; hence not all broadcasts of sexually explicit material would automatically be caught by that exception.[104]

A similar judicial restraint was exercised by the Court of Justice in the field of free movement of services harmonised by the Services Directive; this allows Member States to subject access to or the exercise of an economic activity to authorisation schemes based on criteria that are justified by overriding reasons relating to the public interest (including public policy).[105] In *Trijber and Harmsen*, a language rule prescribed by Dutch legislation, which made the grant of a licence for the operation of window prostitution businesses by letting rooms out conditional on the provider being able to communicate in a language which was understood by the recipients of the service, was found to be a proportionate restriction, justified by the need to protect public order and, in particular, prevent and monitor criminal offences against prostitutes—and, as such, compatible with the Directive.[106]

IV. MORAL JUSTIFICATIONS AS JUDGE-MADE PUBLIC INTEREST EXCEPTIONS TO FREE MOVEMENT

A. Judge-made Moral Grounds as Alternatives or Supplementary to Public Morality or Public Policy

Morally underpinned public interest objectives have been acknowledged in case law as overriding requirements or pressing reasons capable of justifying indistinctly applicable restrictions on the free movement provisions on persons (mainly establishment) and services—especially, albeit not exclusively, in the field of gaming and betting—in the absence of an express derogation in the Treaty relating to public morality, and to the extent that the relevant public interest objectives could not easily fit into the generally narrow EU law definition of the scope of the express derogation of public policy (Article 52(1) TFEU).[107] However, even in the field of goods, despite the existence of a public morality exception in the Treaty (Article 36 TFEU), public interest objectives of a moral nature have been

European Parliament and the Council of 30 June 1997 [1997] OJ L202/60, and by Directive 2007/65/EC of the European Parliament and the Council of 11 December 2007 [2007] OJ L332/27.

[104] Case E-8/97, *TV1000 Sverige AB v The Norwegian Government*, Advisory Opinion of 12 June 1998, [1998] 3 CMLR, Reports 318, www.eftacourt.int/uploads/tx_nvcases/8_97_Advisory_Opinion_EN_01.pdf paras 24–25.

[105] Arts 4(8), 9(1)(b)–(c) and 10(2)(b)–(c) Directive 2006/123, n 16 above.

[106] Joined Cases C-340 and 341/14 *Trijber and Harmsen* (n 17) paras 68 and 72–77.

[107] See section III.B above.

recognised as judge-made mandatory requirements to the extent that they could not be brought under the scope of that express derogation.

As regards the free movement of services, in *Koestler*, the Court first accepted the protection of the social order as a judge-made public interest objective capable of justifying the prohibition by a Member State's legislation of any legal action for recovery of debts arising from wagering, and in particular speculative stock-exchange time bargain contracts, which had been regarded by that State's courts as contrary to domestic public policy.[108] It found that such a restriction on the freedom to provide financial services was not incompatible with the Treaty (now Articles 56–57 TFEU) as long as it applied without discrimination to all services provided by any financial institutions operating in that Member State (Germany) irrespective of their place of establishment, including those established in another Member State, where similar debts were legally recoverable. This was the only limit set on the broad discretion allowed to a Member State in order to prevent a conflict of high-risk financial services with its domestic *ordre public*.[109]

More recently, in the field of goods, in *Dynamic Medien*, the Court recognised the need to protect children and young people against information and material injurious to their well-being as a judge-made ground for justifying restrictions on free movement.[110] In fact, it intertwined this public interest objective with moral, social or cultural considerations in order to relax the proportionality test to be applied.[111] The case concerned a prohibition in a Member State (Germany) on sale by mail order over the Internet of image storage media, which had not been examined, classified and labelled by the competent domestic authority with regard to their suitability for particular age groups, even if they had already been rated for audiences in their Member State of origin (for example, by the British Board of Film Classification in the UK). This was regarded as a lawful product requirement, not in breach of Article 34 TFEU.[112] Echoing its reasoning in *Omega*,[113] the Court held that restrictions imposed by a Member State to protect children's and young people's rights need not necessarily correspond to a conception shared by all Member States as regards the level and the detailed rules of protection; that conception might vary from one Member State to another, depending, among others, on moral or cultural views, and Member States should therefore enjoy a 'definite' margin of discretion.[114] In line with established case law,[115] the Court suggested that the mere fact that the host Member State had opted for a different or stricter

[108] Case 15/78 *Koestler* EU:C:1978:184 para 5.
[109] ibid, paras 2 and 5–6.
[110] Case C-244/06 *Dynamic Medien* EU:C:2008:85 paras 42–43 and 47.
[111] ibid, paras 40 and 44.
[112] ibid, paras 33–35 and 51–52.
[113] Case C-36/02 *Omega* (n 34) 37–38. See also section III.B above.
[114] Case C-244/06 *Dynamic Medien* (n 110) para 44.
[115] See Case C-384/93 *Alpine Investments* EU:C:1995:126 para 51; Case C-262/02 *Commission v France ('Loi Evin')* EU:C:2004:431 para 37; Case C-124/97 *Läärä* (n 76) para 36; Case C-67/98 *Zenatti* (n 50) para 34; and Case C-36/02 *Omega* (n 34) para 38. See also section IV.B below.

system of protection than the home Member State did not suffice to establish a breach of proportionality[116] unless it had manifestly exceeded the limits of its discretion. That would have been the case if the host Member State had prohibited all forms of marketing of 'unchecked' image storage media (including import and sale to adults by way of distribution channels involving personal contact between supplier and purchaser)—but it had not.[117] It was left to the national court to ascertain whether the classification procedure prescribed by the host Member State's legislation breached the principles of non-discrimination and transparency or could not be completed within a reasonable time.[118]

The Court's deference in both *Koestler* and *Dynamic Medien* to the Member States' margin of appreciation of the level of protection they wish to afford to morally underpinned, judge-made public interest objectives relating to their social or public order, and the judicial restraint therefore exercised in connection with the review of the ensuing restrictions on free movement in the light of the Treaty (and, in particular, the outer limits set on that discretion by the principles of non-discrimination and/or proportionality), fits more or less with the approach that the Court has generally taken to the express derogations of public morality and public policy.[119] Such an analogy is also apparent from an examination of the case law on games of chance, the only other—and most prominent—field where morally laden, judge-made public interest grounds have been accepted as capable of justifying restrictions on free movement of services or freedom of establishment.

B. Judge-made Moral Justifications for Restrictions in the Field of Gambling

In the field of cross-border gambling, the focus in case law has been on an analysis of whether the restrictions imposed by a Member State on free movement, mainly on services and/or establishment, can be supported by legitimate justifications, these being primarily judge-made overriding requirements or pressing reasons in the public interest. While express derogations such as public policy[120] or public health[121] have not been ruled out as potential defences especially for distinctly applicable restrictions, they have not in fact been applied yet given the generally narrow construction of their scope. Instead the emphasis has been placed on the open-ended list of broadly construed, judge-made public interest grounds, which are underpinned by moral considerations. These include the maintenance

[116] Case C-244/06 *Dynamic Medien* (n 110) paras 45 and 49.

[117] ibid, para 48.

[118] ibid, paras 50–52, citing Case C-344/90 *Commission v France* EU:C:1992:328 para 9, and Case C-95/01 *Greenham and Abel* EU:C:2004:71 para 35.

[119] See III.A and B above.

[120] Case C-64/08 *Engelmann* EU:C:2010:506 paras 37 and 39; and Case C-153/08 *Commission v Spain* EU:C:2009:618 paras 37 and 39.

[121] Case C-124/97 *Läärä* (n 76) paras 31–33; and Case C-42/02 *Lindman* EU:C:2003:613 paras 23 and 27.

of the public or social order, the protection of moral, cultural or religious factors or standards, the protection of consumers as recipients of services, and, in particular, the limitation of the exploitation of the human propensity for gambling, the prevention of incitement to squander money on gaming, the combating of addiction, the prevention of fraud and other criminal activities,[122] and the prevention of gambling from being a source of private profit.[123] Moral justifications weigh heavily on the Court of Justice's sliding scale of review of proportionality of restrictions on free movement in the field of games of chance. They seem to support a strong judicial deference to a wider margin of discretion enjoyed by the Member States' national authorities and their courts, and an increasing judicial restraint with the assessment of proportionality. The greater the weight attached to the morally laden public interest objective(s) at hand, the less rigorous the judicial scrutiny of the relevant restrictions seems to be in the light of EU law.[124]

According to the established line of case law, the acute sensitivity of gaming and betting from a moral, religious or cultural perspective, the inherently addictive nature of excess gambling, the morally and financially harmful consequences for individuals and society associated with such activity, and the risk of exploiting gambling passion for fraudulent or criminal purposes, may serve to justify a margin of discretion for the national authorities, sufficient to enable them to determine, in accordance with their own scale of values, what is required in order to protect players and society against such risks as addiction, squandering, crime or fraud.[125] This leaves Member States free, in principle, to set their own policy and determine the level of protection they wish to afford to the public interest objectives pursued.[126] In the absence of EU harmonisation[127] and the judicial exclusion of mutual recognition,[128] this 'substantial latitude', which was first recognised in *Schindler*, includes the Member States' discretion to organise, restrict or even prohibit, totally or partially, games of chance in their territory,[129] set up *de jure* or *de facto* State monopolies or oligopolies, and establish more or less stringent control mechanisms in this field.[130] This deference may be contrasted with the more rigorous scrutiny applied to the Nordic alcohol monopoly, which was based on both

[122] See Case C-463/13 *Stanley International Betting* EU:C:2015:25 paras 48–49.

[123] Joined Cases C-447 and 448/08 *Sjöberg and Gerdin* EU:C:2010:415 paras 42–43.

[124] See Doukas and Anderson (n 36) 247–253.

[125] Joined Cases C-316, 358, 359, 360, 409 and 410/07 *Stoß and Kulpa* EU:C:2010:504 para 76.

[126] Case C-212/08 *Zeturf* EU:C:2011:437 paras 39–40; Case C-42/07 *Bwin* (n 19) para 59; Case C-203/08 *Betfair* EU:C:2010:307 paras 23–28; Case C-258/08 *Ladbrokes* EU:C:2010:308 paras 15–20; Case C-156/13 *Digibet Ltd* EU:C:2014:1756 para 24; Case C-98/14 *Berlington* EU:C:2015:386 para 56; and Case C-176/11 *HIT hoteli* EU:C:2012:454 paras 34–35.

[127] Art 2(2)(h) Directive 2006/123 (n 16); and Art I.2 Commission Recommendation 2014/478/EU of 14 July 2014 on principles for the protection of consumers and players of online gambling services and for the prevention of minors from gambling online [2014] OJ L214/38.

[128] Joined Cases C-316, 358, 359, 360, 409 and 410/07 *Stoß and Kulpa* (n 125) paras 112–13; Case C-347/09 *Dickinger and Ömer* EU:C:2011:582 paras 47, 96 and 98–99; and Joined Cases C-660/11 and 8/12 *Biasci and Rainone* EU:C:2013:550 paras 40–43.

[129] Case C-275/92 *Schindler* (n 18) paras 59, 61–62.

[130] See Littler (n 3) 43–51.

medical and socio-ethical considerations.[131] Although the Court did not rule out that a State monopoly on retail sale of alcohol could in principle be justified by the need to protect public health, provided it applied without any discrimination, the prohibition of individuals from importing alcohol was regarded as a disproportionate restriction on free movement of goods inasmuch as it was attached to arbitrary conditions, or was not appropriate for limiting alcohol consumption or went beyond what was necessary for the protection of young persons against the harmful effects of alcohol abuse.[132]

On the contrary, originally, the only limit set to the Member States' latitude to regulate gambling activities in their territory was the requirement that the national rules apply without discrimination; the Court did not apply any proportionality test.[133] This has a clear parallel in the original approach taken to the express derogation of public morality in *Henn and Darby*,[134] and the judge-made public interest objective of the protection of the social order in *Koestler*.[135] Post-*Schindler*, and in line with its general judicial application to any exceptions from the fundamental freedoms, whether based on explicit or judge-made derogations,[136] the principle of proportionality was added as a second, and more crucial, limit to the Member States' wide margin of appreciation in the field of games of chance.[137] However, the strong emphasis placed on the serious risks and the harmful effects of such activity from a moral or social policy point of view can explain the Court's increasing deference and restraint: it generally avoids subjecting national licensing systems or other restrictions or bans on gaming and betting to a rigorous proportionality test.[138] This can be compared to the generally increasing judicial deference and restraint with regard to restrictions on free movement based on the express derogations of public morality and public policy or any other morally underpinned, judge-made public interest objectives.[139] As in other sensitive areas, such as financial services or the protection of health or minors,[140] the mere fact that a Member State opts for a different or stricter regulation of a gaming or betting activity than another Member State (e.g. the home Member State of the service or the provider) is not deemed sufficient as such to render the rules of

[131] See AG Elmer in Case C-189/95 *Franzén* (n 56) paras 112 and 121. *Cf* Kurzer (n 25) 73–96.

[132] Case C-189/95 *Franzén* (n 56) paras 41, 44, 57, 66 and 75–77; and Case C-170/04 *Rosengren v Riksåklagaren* EU:C:2007:313 paras 49–52 and 55–58.

[133] Case C-275/92 *Schindler* (n 18) paras 61–62.

[134] Case 34/79 *Henn and Darby* (n 10) paras 15–17 and 21–22. See also section III.A above.

[135] Case 15/78 *Koestler* (n 108) paras 2 and 5–6. See also section IV.A above.

[136] See C Barnard, 'Derogations, Justifications and the Four Freedoms: Is State Interest Really Protected?' in C Barnard and O Odudu (eds), *The Outer Limits of European Union Law* (Oxford and Portland, Hart Publishing, 2009) 273–305.

[137] Case C-243/01 *Gambelli* (n 18) paras 71–72; and Joined Cases C-338, 359 and 360/04 *Placanica* (n 18) paras 45 and 48–49.

[138] See Doukas and Anderson (n 36) 275–76; and Doukas (n 36) 243, 248, 253–54 and 261.

[139] See sections III.A and B and IV.A above.

[140] See Case C-384/93 *Alpine Investments* (n 115) para 51; Case C-262/02 *Commission v France ('Loi Evin')* (n 115) para 37; and Case C-36/02 *Omega* (n 34) para 38. See also section IV.A above.

the former disproportionate.[141] The objective of the maintenance of public order has in fact been so broadly construed as to include any—not necessarily moral—grounds of substantial impairment of the interests of the State or the residents of an administrative area or locality.[142]

While the Court normally leaves the identification of the public interest objectives and the level of protection actually pursued by national legislation,[143] and the ultimate decision on proportionality, to national judges,[144] it has tried to circumscribe the Member States' discretion in regulating such morally sensitive activities by drawing three main red lines. The primary red line is the requirement of consistency, as an essential component of the proportionality test, so that national laws should be regarded as disproportionate restrictions on free movement of services or freedom of establishment unless they are found to genuinely limit gaming or betting opportunities in a consistent and systematic manner.[145] This may be contrasted with the introduction of the idea of consistency as an inherent limit to the express derogation of public morality arising from the prohibition of arbitrary discrimination in *Conegate*.[146] But it has clear parallels in the application of consistency as an essential condition for the assessment of the question whether a restriction on free movement can be justified by the express derogation of public policy and whether it is proportionate.[147]

A secondary red line is the requirement of transparency, as an essential component of the principle of non-discrimination, which may however also have a bearing on the appraisal of proportionality,[148] so that national authorisation schemes for games of chance must be based on objective, non-discriminatory criteria, known in advance, and be transparent by providing, for instance, for a tendering procedure for the award or renewal of licences.[149] A final red line that cannot be crossed has to do with the burden of proof of the justification and the appropriateness of a Member State's regulation for the attainment of morally underpinned, public interest objectives. This may require that national laws be substantiated by concrete evidence about the gravity of risks associated with excess or problem gambling and the existence of a causal link between such risks and the participation (of that Member State's nationals or residents) in gambling services, especially those provided from

[141] Case C-124/97 *Läärä* (n 76) para 36; and Case C-67/98 *Zenatti* (n 50) para 34.

[142] Case C-470/11 *Garkalns* EU:C:2012:505 paras 45–48.

[143] Case C-390/12 *Pfleger* EU:C:2014:281 para 47; and Case C-98/14 *Berlington* (n 126) para 57.

[144] Case C-243/01 *Gambelli* (n 18) para 66, 72–73 and 75–76; Case C-212/08 *Zeturf* (n 126) paras 47–48; Case C-258/08 *Ladbrokes* (n 126) paras 27–29 and 33–38; and Joined Cases C-316, 358, 359, 360, 409 and 410/07 *Stoß and Kulpa* (n 125) para 107.

[145] Case C-243/01 *Gambelli* (n 18) paras 67 and 69; and Case C-67/98 *Zenatti* (n 50) paras 36–37.

[146] Case 121/85 *Conegate* (n 10) paras 15–16. See section III.A above.

[147] See section III.B above.

[148] Joined Cases C-338, 359 and 360/04 *Placanica* (n 18) paras 62–63; and Case C-260/04 *Commission v Italy* ('*Horse-race Betting*') EU:C:2007:508 paras 29–30 and 34.

[149] Case C-203/08 *Betfair* (n 126) para 50; Case C-470/11 *Garkalns* (n 142) para 42; and Joined Cases C-186 and 209/11 *Stanleybet International* EU:C:2013:33 paras 47–48.

other Member States.[150] It might also require that national authorities provide evidence of their intention to ensure a particularly high level of protection of the public interest in order to defend the introduction or the maintenance of a measure as restrictive as a public monopoly.[151] Nevertheless, the limits to the Member States' wide discretion seem to have been significantly relaxed or exempted from rigorous judicial scrutiny except where the Court found that national authorities had exceeded those limits in a manifestly discriminatory or disproportionate manner.[152]

First, the consistency requirement has been qualified since the *Placanica* case: the Court did not rule out that a national policy of 'controlled expansion' in games of chance might be wholly consistent—not with the objective of diminution of gambling opportunities,[153] but—with a competing morally underpinned objective, that is combating fraud and criminality by controlling the activities of operators, and thus drawing players away from clandestine to authorised and regulated gambling. The Court acknowledged that this objective could only be achieved if authorised operators represented a reliable and attractive alternative to illegal activities. This might necessitate the offer of an extensive range of games, advertising on a certain scale and the use of new distribution techniques.[154] The two competing, morally laden public interest objectives—curbing addiction and preventing squandering of money, on the one hand, and preventing the abuse of gambling for criminal or fraudulent purposes, on the other hand—were reconciled in *Stoss and Kulpa* and *Ladbrokes*, where the Court suggested that they should be regarded as two sides of the same coin, namely the protection of consumers and the preservation of the public and social order.[155]

Following the shift of emphasis away from the diminution of gambling opportunities to combating fraud and criminality, the Court has not ruled out that even a dynamic or expansive commercial policy pursued by the holder of a State monopoly or oligopoly might be regarded as consistent with the morally underpinned objective of channelling the propensity for gambling into authorised or regulated activities,[156] not least because of the significance of the scale of demand for unauthorised or clandestine gambling and the effectiveness of State supervision or control.[157] While the Court has not always applied the consistency test in

[150] Case C-42/02 *Lindman* (n 121) paras 25–26.

[151] See Case C-212/08 *Zeturf* (n 126) para 46.

[152] See Doukas (n 36) 243–44 and 248–49. See also Joined Cases C-72/10 and C-77/10 *Costa and Cifone* EU:C:2012:8 paras 60–64, 66 and 88–91; Joined Cases C-660/11 and 8/12 *Biasci and Rainone* (n 128) paras 32 and 37–38; and Case C-98/14 *Berlington* (n 126) paras 84–87 and 92.

[153] Case C-67/98 *Zenatti* (n 50) paras 35–36; and Case C-243/01 *Gambelli* (n 18) paras 62 and 67.

[154] Joined Cases C-338, 359 and 360/04 *Placanica* (n 18) paras 52–55 and 57.

[155] Joined Cases C-316, 358, 359, 360, 409 and 410/07 *Stoß and Kulpa* (n 125) paras 81–83 and 101–105; and Case C-258/08 *Ladbrokes* (n 126) paras 21, 24–26, 28–32 and 37.

[156] Case C-347/09 *Dickinger and Ömer* (n 128) para 67; and Case C-98/14 *Berlington* (n 126) paras 71 and 72–73.

[157] Case C-212/08 *Zeturf* (n 126) paras 41–42, 65 and 67–70; and Joined Cases C-186 and 209/11 *Stanleybet International* (n 149) paras 29–30 and 45.

an absolutely coherent manner,[158] it has indicated that the consistency requirement would be breached if the primary or exclusive objective of a Member State's policy on games of chance or the policy pursued by the holder of a State monopoly or oligopoly would be found not to be of a moral but of a purely economic nature; namely the maximisation of profits to the financial benefit of the public purse.[159] The redistribution of resulting profits by the State can only be legitimate so long as it is only an incidental or ancillary beneficial consequence.[160]

Second, as a result of its increasing deference to the Member State's margin of appreciation in protecting morally underpinned public interest objectives, the Court has qualified or undermined the requirement of transparency so that it does not necessarily presuppose a call for tenders but only a sufficient degree of publicity that would ensure competition or enable a review of the impartiality of the procedure for licensing of gambling activities.[161] In a similar vein, the Court has relaxed the burden of proof of the justification and the proportionality of national regulation of games of chance. Member States do not need to produce a concrete supporting study but only evidence of such a kind as to enable the domestic courts to be satisfied that the relevant restrictions are proportionate.[162] Last but not least, the Court generally presumes that the Internet has a higher risk potential from a moral point of view, and therefore allows Member States to subject remote gambling services to heavier restrictions than games of chance provided or marketed through traditional channels, or even total bans.[163]

The significance attached by the Court to judge-made, morally laden public interest objectives as grounds for justifying restrictions on free movement in the field of gambling is matched by its increasing deference and restraint with regard to the assessment of such restrictions in the light of the Treaty; and a significant relaxation of the limits set to the Member States' discretion by the principles of proportionality—especially the underlying requirement of consistency—and non-discrimination, or the burden of proof. The Court's attempt to reconcile competing public interest objectives of a moral nature, such as the diminution of

[158] Case C-46/08 *Carmen Media* EU:C:2010:505 paras 63, 66–68 and 71; and Case C-98/14 *Berlington* (n 126) paras 60–61.

[159] Joined Cases C-316, 358, 359, 360, 409 and 410/07 *Stoß and Kulpa* (n 125) paras 96 and 104–07; Case C-212/08 *Zeturf* (n 126) paras 58–62 and 71; and Joined Cases C-186 and 209/11 *Stanleybet International* (n 149) paras 31–35. See Doukas (n 36) 247, 256–59 and 261–62.

[160] Case C-67/98 *Zenatti* (n 50) para 36; Case C-124/97 *Läärä* (n 76) paras 33 and 37; Case C-212/08, *Zeturf* (n 126) paras 52–53; Case C-347/09 *Dickinger and Ömer* (n 128) para 55; and Case C-390/12 *Pfleger* (n 143) para 54.

[161] Case C-203/08 *Betfair* (n 126) paras 41, 44, 46–51, 54–55 and 58–62; Case C-64/08 *Engelmann* (n 120) para 50; Case C-463/13 *Stanley International Betting* (n 122) paras 39–41; Joined Cases C-660/11 and 8/12 *Biasci and Rainone* (n 128) paras 33 and 38; and Case C-98/14 *Berlington* (n 126) paras 84–87.

[162] Joined Cases C-316, 358, 359, 360, 409 and 410/07 *Stoß and Kulpa* (n 125) paras 70–72; and Case C-212/08 *Zeturf* (n 126) para 70.

[163] See Case C-42/07 *Bwin* (n 19) paras 69–70; Case C-212/08 *Zeturf* (n 126) paras 74–75; Case C-203/08 *Betfair* (n 126) paras 33–35; Case C-46/08 *Carmen Media* (n 158) para 101; and Case C-258/08 *Ladbrokes* (n 126) paras 41–46 and 54–56.

gambling opportunities and the prevention of crime and fraud, in order to relax the consistency test applied to State monopolies on gambling pursuing dynamic commercial policies, can be compared to the approach taken in *Josemans*, where the objective of combating cross-border drug tourism was given priority over the laxer moral standards applied domestically to the use of drugs.[164]

V. CONCLUSIONS

Moral arguments are unlikely to have any significant bearing on the application of the free movement provisions in the first place except where an immoral practice is sanctioned by the law in its Member State of origin as illegal. The Court seems generally—albeit not always consistently—to avoid getting embroiled in a moral judgement when determining whether a national measure is capable of restricting the fundamental freedoms. By way of exception, it has, however, suggested that should an activity or product be formally prohibited by the laws in (almost) all the Member States, underpinned by EU policy, the Treaty should not apply even if the relevant activity or product might exceptionally be tolerated in practice to a certain extent or in a particular form within their home Member State. Moral considerations play, however, a significant role as grounds for justifying restrictions on free movement, both in form of express derogations in the Treaty (or relevant EU legislation), mainly public morality and public policy, and in form of judge-made public interest objectives that reflect a moral judgement or have an inherent moral dimension.

In the absence of a uniform, EU-wide conception of public morality, and notwithstanding the generally narrow EU law definition of the scope of the express derogation of public policy, there is an increasing deference by the Court to the Member States' wide discretion in determining the level of protection they wish to afford to their domestic *ordre public*, whether on the basis of explicit or judge-made derogations. This goes hand in hand with an increasing judicial restraint with regard to the assessment of the question whether the ensuing restrictions on free movement are compatible with EU law, and in particular whether the Member States have exceeded the limits of their margin of appreciation. These limits arise mainly from the principles of non-discrimination and proportionality or, to a lesser extent, the degree of pre-emption of the relevant field by EU legislation.

A crucial role seems to be played by the requirement of consistency, which was originally applied as an inherent limit to the express derogations of public morality or public policy, arising from the prohibition of arbitrary discrimination, but seems to have been consolidated as an essential component of the principle of proportionality. Consistency is examined in particular in the assessment of the suitability or the reasonableness of restrictions that are capable of being justified

[164] See sections II and III.B above.

by either the express derogation of public policy or other, judge-made, morally underpinned public interest objectives, including the maintenance of the social order, the protection of the moral development of young people or minors or, especially in the field of gambling, the combating of addiction or the prevention of crime and fraud. Other limits may arise from the principle of transparency, which is often regarded as a corollary to the principle of non-discrimination, especially with regard to judge-made moral justifications, although it may also have a bearing on the proportionality test; or the principle of legal certainty, often applied to the express derogation of public policy in the field of capital.

Nevertheless, morality features high on the Court's sliding scale of review of proportionality. This seems to be the case irrespective of the (statutory or judge-made) ground of moral justifications or whether the relevant field of free movement is subject to some degree of EU harmonisation or not. As a rule, the Court has been keen to avoid exercising rigorous scrutiny and defers to the Member States' fundamental value judgements, which underlie their domestic law or policy and reflect moral considerations.

Although the Court—followed by the EU legislature—has narrowly construed the scope of the express derogation of public policy by setting a threshold for its application, it has only exceptionally relied on a uniform or autonomous concept of an EU *ordre public*. This is the case where there are minimum standards on public morality or public policy set out in EU legislation (such as on alcohol or audiovisual media); where the domestic *ordre public* serves the protection of moral, ethical or social values or fundamental rights and principles that are common to the legal traditions of all the Member States; or even, where a concept of a European *ordre public* may reflect standards that are common only to a majority of Member States. In all three cases, however, the Court's reliance on an autonomous concept of European *ordre public* has served the purpose of supporting, rather than containing, the Member States' margin of appreciation. It has strikingly even allowed the application by a Member State of double standards to the moral evaluation of the same activity in its territory, depending on whether this is exercised by home nationals or by nationals from other Member States who cross the borders.

This stands in stark contrast to the Court's usual bottom-up approach, which is premised on deference to every Member State's own assessment of its moral standards or the requirements of its domestic *ordre public* and the restraint of the judicial control over such fundamental value judgements in the light of the free movement provisions. Judicial restraint will decrease only where a Member State has manifestly exceeded the outer limits of that discretion, by pursuing policies that are arbitrarily discriminatory or blatantly inconsistent. That might especially be the case if the primary or exclusive aim of the restrictions is of an economic or protectionist—rather than moral—nature. However, because of its increasingly deferential approach, the Court has not always been successful in avoiding accusations of second-guessing national public policy and moral regulation choices at the stage of assessing whether restrictions on free movement are justified and proportionate. It has even tried—admittedly not always convincingly—to prioritise or reconcile competing or apparently conflicting non-economic public interest objectives within the broader concept of *ordre public* in order to relax the application of the consistency requirement.

A comparison may be made with the doctrine of margin of appreciation as applied by the European Court of Human Rights, which tends to consider national authorities and courts to be better placed to assess whether interferences with the fundamental rights protected by Articles 8 to 11 of the European Convention on Human Rights (ECHR) may be regarded as justified and necessary for the protection of public morals where there is no or little consensus among Member States on the matter.[165] Analogies may also be drawn with the 'conventional morality' theory of judicial review in the United States, according to which judicial review cannot properly be aimed at overturning the popular will or perception expressed in duly enacted laws and, hence, judges should refrain from substituting their own personal value judgements for commonly held beliefs and generally accepted standards; accordingly, in interpreting morally laden notions and standards, courts—including the US Supreme Court—may frequently refer to generally shared community values, and in particular, either explicitly appeal to, and make actual use of, conventional morality and community standards relevant to the issues before the court, or at least rest on community consensus about extra-legal values.[166] A similar approach has been adopted by the UK Supreme Court, which has held that the democratic process would be liable to be subverted if, on a question of moral and political judgement, opponents of domestic legislation achieved through the courts what they could not achieve in Parliament.[167]

Both the margin of appreciation and the conventional morality doctrines have clear parallels in the Court of Justice's increasing deference and restraint with regard to the assessment of questions of morality and *ordre public* in the field of free movement and the decreasing intensity of its scrutiny over the Member States' substantial discretion even where the Court may rely on a European—rather than domestic—*ordre public* concept, or get embroiled in moral judgements and second-guess national policy choices.

[165] See Application No 5493/72 *Handyside v UK* [1976] Series A No 24 paras 48–49, 52 and 57. See also Letsas (n 4) 88–95 and 120–26; and H Fenwick and G Phillipson, *Media Freedom under the Human Rights Act* 1st edn (Oxford, Oxford University Press, 2006) 410–22.

[166] W Sadurski, 'Conventional Morality and Judicial Standards' (1987) 73 *Virginia Law Review* 339, 340–41.

[167] *R (Countryside Alliance and Others) v Attorney General, and R (Derwin and Others) v Same* [2007] UKHL 52, [2008] 1 AC 719 per Lord Bingham paras 44–45 and 50 finding the UK ban on hunting and killing wild animals by recreation sports (Hunting Act 2004) to be compatible with Art 8 ECHR and Arts 34 and 56 TFEU.

9

The Constitutional Dimension of Public Policy Justifications

DANIEL THYM

I. INTRODUCTION

THE CONCEPT OF public policy justification is a classic notion of Union law. It is a central component of the fundamental freedoms and has been an essential element of the case law on the single market ever since the 1970s. It is explained to law students across Europe in introductory courses on EU law and, yet, the constitutional implications of the public policy justification are more unstable than many assume. Its configuration is not just a technical matter of doctrinal interpretation: it goes to the heart of the question what kind of Europe we are living in. This chapter traces the relative indecision of the doctrinal framework and shows that the ECJ case law exhibits changing constitutional visions. The argument proceeds from micro to macro by revisiting the doctrinal basics and conceptual foundations before embarking upon a constitutional analysis. In doing so, it will extrapolate two ideal types of how the interplay between domestic policies and the supranational polity can be structured: the federal solution and the conflicts of laws model.

More recent judgments exhibit a seemingly contradictory tendency when the Court embarks upon a pan-European definition of the public policy exception in light of normative value judgments in the EU legal order while, at the same time, granting Member States discretion in the application of the common standard. This apparent paradox can be explained by a change in the legal context as a result of which the fundamental freedoms apply primarily to subject areas not covered by extensive EU harmonisation measures nowadays. On this basis, this chapter will conclude with a discussion of theoretical arguments about why the Court should leave Member States leeway on how to apply the public policy justification, in particular in areas in which the EU legislature did harmonise domestic rules. It will be shown that, despite the preference among academics for clear-cut solutions, the ECJ's current approach of muddling through by focusing on the resolution of individual cases need not be the worst outcome.

II. DOCTRINAL BASICS AND CONCEPTUAL FOUNDATIONS

It is well known among experts and students of EU law that the 'public policy' justification features prominently in the wording of the fundamental freedoms constituting the single market. Ever since 1957, the free movement of goods, workers and services has embraced a 'public policy' exception in the same way as the freedom of establishment.[1] It is, therefore, very much a horizontal concept designating a limit to transnational free movement whose strict interpretation by the ECJ (II.A) can be explained by the historic context (II.B). Our examination of its constitutional impact should consider interaction with the counterpart: the concept of restriction, whose narrow or wide reading can have a knock-on effect on the treatment of the public policy exception (II.C), and also the relevance of the proportionality assessment (II.D). Similarly, the convergence of ECJ case law on goods and persons should not conceal potential cleavages between both areas of single market law (II.E).

A. Foundational Judgments

In the beginning, the common market was a vision to be achieved over a 12-year transitional period whose successful completion was no foregone conclusion. After initial achievements, the 1970s showed a proliferation of non-tariff barriers to trade hindering the smooth functioning of transnational economic activities within the European Economic Community of the time. This was the context of the foundational ECJ cases defining the contours of the public policy exception. They are an integral part of one of the most renowned episodes of European integration through law when judges in Luxembourg were instrumental in overcoming the alleged eurosclerosis by means of an innovative approach towards the fundamental freedoms as instruments of market integration.[2] Arguably, the ECJ's traditional approach to the public policy exception is a reaction to this context. Yet, it defines our understanding of the notion to this date, since the Court later retained the original doctrinal formulas despite a changing context.

The historic background shows that the Court was eager to prevent, during the 1970s, an interpretation of the public policy exception that would have presented Member States with a licence to do as they please. For that reason, it highlighted in the first *Simmenthal* judgment that matters of justification were no *domaine réservée* whose contours could be defined by Member States as being essentially

[1] See today's Arts 36, 45(3), 52(1) and 62 TFEU, which have not been modified substantively ever since the Treaty of Rome; by contrast, the corresponding exception for the free movement of capital in Art 65(1)(b) was amended a couple of times.

[2] See P Craig, 'The Evolution of the Single Market' in C Barnard and J Scott (eds), *The Law of the Single Market. Unpacking the Premises* (Oxford, Hart, 2002) 1, 6–9; and T Kingreen, 'Fundamental Freedoms' in A von Bogdandy and J Bast (eds), *Principles of European Constitutional Law* 2nd edn (Oxford, Hart, 2009) 515, 519–22.

within their domestic jurisdiction,[3] since today's Article 34 TFEU 'is not designed to reserve certain matters to the exclusive jurisdiction of Member States'.[4] The term 'public policy' belongs to the EU legal order and its interpretation pertains to the authority of the ECJ: 'its scope cannot be determined unilaterally by each Member State without being subject to control by the institutions of the [EU].'[5] Thus, the ECJ retains authority to decide in individual cases whether and if so to what extent national measures are covered by the exception.

It is widely known that the ECJ has defined, on this basis, the public policy exception to refer to 'a genuine and sufficiently serious threat … affecting one of the fundamental interests of society'.[6] It added that, for the resolution of individual cases, the public policy exception 'must be interpreted strictly', since it constitutes a derogation from the basic rule of free movement within the single market.[7] As a matter of principle, it cannot extend to cover economic considerations[8]—even though the distinction between (non-)economic considerations leaves room for a certain flexibility on the side of Member States to overcome the limitation by demonstrating the wider social or political impact of the policy concerned.[9] The potential thematic breadth of the formula becomes apparent when you consider that it applies, in the same way as the fundamental freedoms, to all areas of domestic law-making, including domains for which no EU legislation exists, since powers, such as direct taxation, 'retained by the Member States must nevertheless be exercised consistently with [Union] law'.[10]

B. Public Policy v Mandatory Requirements

The generic formula used by the Court for defining public policy is broad—and yet the Court considered it not to be broad enough when it decided in *Cassis de Dijon* to establish unwritten 'mandatory requirements', which complement the

[3] Remember that the concept of *domaine réservée*, enshrined in Article 2(7) UN Charter, is central to public international law and that its definition by international institutions, including courts, has always been controversial; *cf* Permanent Court of International Justice, Advisory Opinion No 4 of 17 August 1923, *Nationality Decrees Issued in Tunis and Morocco (French Zone)* PCIJ Ser B No 4 at 23.

[4] Case 35/76 *Simmenthal* EU:C:1976:180 para 14.

[5] Case 41/74 *Van Duyn* EU:C:1974:133 para 18.

[6] Case 30/77 *Bouchereau* EU:C:1977:172 para 3.

[7] See Case 46/76 *Bauhuis* EU:C:1977:6 para 12; this position can be defended as a doctrinal exercise of logical and systemic interpretation in the tradition of civil law jurisdictions.

[8] See Case 7/61 *Commission v Italy* EU:C:1961:31 at 720; and Case 288/83 *Commission v Ireland* EU:C:1985:251 para 28.

[9] See chs 2 and 14 in this volume; as well as N Nic Shuibhne and M Maci, 'Proving Public Interest' (2013) 50 *CML Rev* 965, 997–98; and, by way of example, for the consequences of an interruption in supplies of petroleum products, Case 72/83 *Campus Oil* EU:C:1984:256 para 35; see also chapters 2 and 3 in this volume.

[10] Case C-279/93 *Schumacker* EU:C:1995:31 para 21; see especially L Azoulai, 'The "Retained Powers" Formula in the Case Law of the European Court of Justice' (2011) 4 *European Journal of Legal Studies* 192–219.

public policy exception in so far as justifications of non-discriminatory national measures are concerned.[11] These unwritten grounds for justification can cover diverse objectives ranging from consumer protection and fairness of commercial transactions to environmental protection and the effectiveness of financial supervision. The thematic breadth of mandatory requirements becomes apparent when you consider their application to the free movement of services or persons where they can concern diverse questions such as town and country planning, the proper administration of justice, the protection of the interests of minority shareholders, or cultural and linguistic diversity.[12]

Readers may know that, in German legal education, we ask students to assume the role of a hypothetical judge and to present their knowledge by solving fictional cases. In my internal market class, this often results in the activation of the public policy exception in line with the Court's general formula for matters such as environmental protection or the well-being of children—and I have difficulties explaining why they should refer to mandatory requirements instead. Indeed, there is nothing in the broad definition of the term public policy with its reference to 'fundamental interests of society' which would prevent us from qualifying some if not all of the mandatory requirements as being related to a fundamental societal interest. Closer inspection of the case law shows that the ECJ occasionally struggles to delineate both concepts, in particular with regard to environmental protection[13] and matters of public health.[14] Similarly, the Charter of Fundamental Rights knows one category of justification only, which it designates as 'objectives of general interest' (in French: *objectifs d'intérêt général*).[15]

It seems, therefore, that the distinction between the written public policy justification and unwritten mandatory requirements is historically contingent in the sense that the ECJ did not want to call into question its more restrictive earlier case law on the narrow reading of the public policy exception when it established *Cassis*-style mandatory requirements at a time when the process of market integration had not advanced very far.[16] One should bear in mind that the *Cassis de Dijon* ruling was delivered less than five years after many of the foundational judgments establishing core assumptions about the interpretation of the public policy

[11] See Case 120/78 *Rewe-Zentral ('Cassis de Dijon')* EU:C:1979:42 para 8.

[12] See generally P Oliver (ed), *Oliver on Free Movement of Goods in the European Union* 5th edn (Oxford, Hart, 2010) ch VIII; and for the examples mentioned in the text, Case C-400/08 *Commission v Spain* EU:C:2011:172 para 80; Cases C-94/04 and C-202/04 *Cipolla* EU:C:2006:758 para 64; Case C-208/00 *Überseering* EU:C:2002:632 para 92; and Case C-391/09 *Runevič-Vardyn & Wardyn* EU:C:2011:291 para 36.

[13] See P Craig and G de Búrca, *EU Law. Text, Cases and Materials* 6th edn (Oxford, Oxford University Press, 2011) 702–03; and, more recently, Case C-573/12 *Ålands Vindkraft* EU:C:2014:2037 paras 77–82.

[14] While in *Cassis the Dijon* (n 11) para 10 the ECJ listed abstract public health concerns as a mandatory requirement, Case C-405/98 *Gourmet* EU:C:2001:135 para 26 referred to today's Art 36 TFEU.

[15] See Art 52(1) EU Charter.

[16] See F Mayer, 'Die Warenverkehrsfreiheit im Europarecht—eine Rekonstruktion' (2003) 38 *Europarecht* 793, 799.

exception. At the time, an extension of today's Article 36 TFEU to seemingly trivial issues, such as consumer protection, might have been perceived to open the floodgates for protectionism. As a matter of principle, however, there was and is nothing in the Court's definition of 'public policy' excluding such convergence of written und unwritten justifications.

C. Interplay between Justifications and Restrictions

Any justification is inherently connected to a rule which, in our case, concerns the fundamental freedoms. It would be misleading, therefore, to focus on matters of justification without due regard to the interplay between the justification and the general rule. This interaction is particularly relevant when the theoretical concept underlying the rule is subject to protracted uncertainty. Such arguments have accompanied the economic freedoms from the beginning and gained a renewed prominence more recently when the ECJ called into question the fundamental distinction between discriminatory rules and non-discriminatory measures, in particular selling arrangements, that had defined its approach towards the free movement of goods for more than 20 years.[17] This debate about the fundamental freedoms more broadly holds the potential for important knock-on effects on our understanding of the public policy exception.

In essence, the debate concerns the concept of 'restriction' constituting a decisive hurdle for any application of the fundamental freedoms to transnational economic activities. It revolves around the economic and constitutional rationale pursued by the notion of restriction, which is perceived as an instrument against protectionism by some and as an economic due process rule with deregulatory effects by others.[18] On closer inspection, the various twists and adaptations that can be observed in the case law of the ECJ in relation to goods, services and persons over past decades do not side unequivocally with either standpoint. In particular, the notion of market access which gained a renewed prominence in a number of more recent cases does not fully subscribe to an anti-protectionist reading of the free movement provisions. In short, the ECJ tends to fluctuate between different visions of the concept of restriction: there seems to be no uniform theoretical groundwork for the case law from Luxembourg.[19]

It had been argued that the theoretical distinction, in the original ECJ case law, between discriminatory and non-discriminatory measures explained the

[17] See I Lianos, 'In Memoriam *Keck*: the Reformation of the EU Law on the Free Movement of Goods' (2015) 40 *EL Rev* 225, 235 et seq; and S Dietz and T Streinz, 'Das Marktzugangskriterium in der Dogmatik der Grundfreiheiten' (2015) 50 *Europarecht* 50–72.

[18] See M Poiares Maduro, *We, the Court. The European Court of Justice and the European Economic Constitution* (Oxford, Hart, 1998) chs 2, 5; and Kingreen (n 2) 532–42.

[19] See J Snell, 'The Notion of Market Access: A Concept or a Slogan?' (2010) 47 *CML Rev* 437–72; Lianos (n 17) at 231–42; and G Davies, 'Understanding Market Access: Exploring the Economic Rationality of Different Conceptions of Free Movement Law' (2010) 11 *German Law Journal* 671–704.

distinction between mandatory requirements and the public policy exception, since non-discriminatory measures were deemed generally not to be suspicious for questions of market access and could be justified more easily as a result.[20] However, it is difficult to rationalise ECJ case law along these lines, since the latter tends to fluctuate between different economic rationales mentioned above. Moreover, the Court does not always pay much attention, in individual cases, to the abstract separation of discriminatory rules and measures applicable without distinction, although this difference had guided the delineation of public policy objectives and mandatory requirements in the beginning when only the former could be relied upon in situations of direct or indirect discrimination.

This imprecision on the side of the Court has implications for our topic, since justifications are related to a general rule by definition. If that general rule is defined narrowly, the justification will be invoked less often and can potentially be applied more strictly, since only highly suspicious rules will have to be justified in the first place. By contrast, a broad understanding of the general rule may require a generous approach to questions of justifications in order to prevent too many less suspicious rules from being struck down. Arguably, this rule of thumb motivated the original introduction of unwritten mandatory requirements in the *Cassis de Dijon* ruling. It may explain, moreover, why the distinction between the public policy exception and mandatory requirements has lost much of its initial significance in recent years in light of the Court's ambiguous approach to the concept of restriction. This indecision is an important indicator that it might be better not to distinguish categorically between a strict or lenient reading of both the concepts of restriction and justification. In practice, the different theoretical models beneath this argument tend to be blurred; matters of restriction and justification are intertwined.

D. The Significance of Proportionality

It is in the nature of the fundamental freedoms that they can be invoked by individuals before domestic courts to challenge domestic legislation. They assume, therefore, a quasi-constitutional function as a yardstick for the judicial review of domestic legislation. This entails that many of the arguments discussed in constitutional theory about non-majoritarian judicial review can be applied to the fundamental freedoms mutatis mutandis. More specifically, the classic dispute between a liberal approach to constitutional adjudication conceptualising rights as trumps, epitomised by the work of Ronald Dworkin and Jürgen Habermas, and the Republican focus on balancing in the writing of Robert Alexy can be relied upon to rationalise our understanding of the fundamental freedoms

[20] See J Snell, *Goods and Services in EC Law. A Study on the Relationship between the Freedoms* (Oxford, Oxford University Press, 2002) 172–81, who hints at the distinction.

and corresponding justifications.[21] For our purposes, this means that the public policy exception is inherently connected to the proportionality assessment that any justification entails.

The basic principles underlying the proportionality test which applies when justifying restrictions to the fundamental freedoms are well known. It is settled case law that exceptions to the free movement of goods laid down in Article 36 TFEU 'must be interpreted in such a way that its scope is not extended any further than is necessary' and that they 'must not create obstacles to imports which are disproportionate to these objectives'.[22] On this basis, the ECJ has incorporated a variant of the German principle of proportionality into its case law on the fundamental freedoms, although its practice tends to fluctuate between different attitudes to the proportionality assessment.[23] There is ample case law illustrating the significance of proportionality for resolving disputes about free movement whose outcome often hinges on the balancing exercise.[24]

In light of the practical significance of the proportionality test, some observers maintain, under recourse to constitutional theory, that internal market law is structurally biased against the Member States.[25] That reprimand may often be correct: there are ample examples of a structural bias in the case law of the Court as regards the proportionality assessment of domestic laws which it considered to be covered, in principle, by written or unwritten justifications.[26] At the same time, however, this strictness need not be pursued consistently by the ECJ, which often grants Member States much leeway in the same policy fields where it had been strict previously.[27] In short, we may observe the Court oscillating between different approaches to proportionality mirroring the indecision over restrictions.[28] That is not to say that one cannot distil a certain typology of different scenarios in the application of the proportionality principles.[29] All I mean is that balancing does not necessarily entail stricter standards for Member States.[30] It seems,

[21] See T-I Harbo, 'The Function of the Proportionality Principle in EU Law' (2010) 16 *ELJ* 158, 160–70; and C Barnard, 'Restricting Restrictions: Lessons for the EU from the US?' (2009) 68 *Cambridge Law Journal* 575–606.

[22] Case 72/83 *Campus Oil* (n 9) para 37.

[23] See T Tridimas, *The General Principles of EC Law*, 2nd edn (Oxford, Oxford University Press, 2007) ch 3.

[24] See D Chalmers, G Davies and G Monti, *European Union Law. Text and Materials* 3rd edn (Cambridge, Cambridge University Press, 2014) 899–924.

[25] See Barnard (n 21) 575–606.

[26] See, in relation to access to social benefits by migrant EU citizens, M Dougan, 'The Bubble that Burst' in M Adams et al (eds), *Judging Europe's Judges* (Oxford, Hart, 2013) 127, 136–38; and D Thym, 'Towards "Real" Citizenship?' in ibid, 155, 160–62.

[27] See, again with regards to social benefits, D Thym, 'The Elusive Limits of Solidarity' (2015) 52 *CML Rev* 17, 27–32; and Dougan, ibid, 140–45.

[28] See Harbo (n 21) at 171 et seq.

[29] See N Reich, 'How Proportionate is Proportionality?' in H-W Micklitz and B de Witte (eds), *The European Court of Justice and the Autonomy of the Member States* (Antwerp, Intersentia, 2012) 83, 94–107; and F de Witte, 'Sex, Drugs & EU Law' (2013) 50 *CML Rev* 1545, 1556–77.

[30] Along similar lines, K Sullivan, 'Post-Liberal Judging: The Role of Categorization and Balancing' (1992) 63 *University of Colorado Law Review* 293–317 shows that the dichotomy between rights

rather, that the ECJ does not connect specific doctrinal figures to strict or lenient control standards. It has multiple instruments at its disposal to apply the concepts of restriction, justification and proportionality in ways which can be functionally equivalent despite their doctrinal disparity. It arrives at similar outcomes, albeit on different doctrinal routes.

In order to illustrate the Court's flexible approach it is worth comparing three judgments on public policy justifications arriving at similar outcomes (leeway for Member States) by following a different line of reasoning:[31] first, in relation to Dutch drug policy, the Court found that the free movement of goods does not cover marijuana despite its free availability in the Netherlands, that is, it interpreted narrowly the scope of the fundamental freedoms;[32] second, it considered the sexual abuse of children to amount to an imperative ground of public security when a Member State concludes that the crime might pose a direct threat to the calm and physical security of the population, thereby supporting a generous reading of the justification standard;[33] third, restrictions on gambling were accepted subject to a number of formal caveats in the proportionality assessment.[34] Notwithstanding the similar outcome, the doctrinal argument differed between a rejection of the applicability of the fundamental freedoms over a direct application of grounds for justification and a detailed proportionality assessment. This exemplifies that the doctrinal differentiation between restriction, justification and proportionality need not be the decisive factor whether the outcome of a decision will be more or less lenient. EU law provides for different but functionally equivalent doctrinal channels to fine-tune the impact of individual decisions on domestic legal orders.

E. Goods and Persons

From today's perspective, it appears almost self-evident to apply similar doctrinal standards to the free movement of goods, persons, services and capital. There has been a process of gradual convergence of rules and principles applicable to the economic freedoms. More specifically, they are all construed as prohibitions of restrictions which may be justified by unwritten mandatory requirements.[35]

as trumps and balancing does not necessarily coincide with a stricter control of the legislature in the practice of the US Supreme Court.

[31] See also de Witte (n 29) at 1556–77; and Reich (n 29) at 97–107.

[32] Case C-137/09 *Josemans* EU:C:2010:774 paras 36–42, while scrutinising the Dutch policy in so far as restrictions on access to non-alcoholic beverages in coffee shops selling marijuana are concerned.

[33] See Case C-348/09 *I* EU:C:2012:300 paras 28, 33.

[34] See Cases C-338/04, C-359/04 and C-360/04 *Placanica et al* EU:C:2007:133 paras 53–58; and ch 8 in this volume.

[35] See N Nic Shuibhne, *The Coherence of EU Free Movement Law* (Oxford, Oxford University Press, 2013).

Such convergence has an intuitive appeal in light of the overarching framework of the single market and the parallel structure of the Treaty provisions. It does not mean, however, that the parallelism is persuasive from a broader normative perspective, since the free movement of goods and persons, in particular, may be defined by distinct contextual factors, which are essentially economic in the case of goods, while broader societal factors can have an impact on the free movement of persons.[36] If that is correct, the same doctrinal setting may result in disparate outcomes for the different fundamental freedoms.

It makes a difference, for instance, whether you deny the free movement of drugs in the context of Article 34 TFEU or expel a Union citizen having worked in another Member State for 10 years after a criminal conviction for a serious drug-related criminal offence in accordance with Article 45 TFEU and secondary legislation applicable to the case. An activation of the public policy justification towards citizens after a criminal conviction has human rights implications transcending the essentially economic rationale one may apply to trade-related matters on goods and services.[37] It seems that the ECJ takes account of these differences primarily when deciding individual cases on the basis of parallel doctrinal structures covering all of the fundamental freedoms. This mismatch between synchronised doctrinal standards and disparate contextual factors is another element complicating our analysis. Any rationalisation of the case law is complicated by the ambiguous theoretical foundations of the doctrinal structure and the significance of the circumstances of the individual case for each judgment.

In short, the doctrinal structure for justifying restrictions to the fundamental freedoms is well-established, even though the conceptual foundations remain contested. It was demonstrated that the public policy exception should not be analysed in isolation, since its application to specific scenarios interacts with the ECJ's approach to related doctrinal institutes, such as the concepts of restriction and proportionality. It can be useful, therefore, to step back and to scrutinise the public policy justification at an intermediate level of abstraction from a different angle: the identification of abstract models for how to structure the interplay between domestic policies and judicial review by the ECJ in light of supranational rules. Such broader constitutional outlook may help to identify theoretical arguments explaining the Court's approach to public policy justifications.

[36] See J Snell, 'And Then There Were Two: Products and Citizens in Community Law' in T Tridimas and P Nebbia (eds), *European Union Law for the Twenty-First Century*, vol 2 (Oxford, Hart, 2005) 49, 52–55.

[37] See E Spaventa, 'From *Gebhard* to *Carpenter*: Towards a (Non-)Economic European Constitution' (2004) 41 *CML Rev* 743–73; and F de Cecco, 'Fundamental Freedoms, Fundamental Rights, and the Scope of Free Movement Law' (2014) 15 *German Law Journal* 383, 385–401.

III. THE FEDERAL QUESTION

It is widely accepted that it can be useful to analyse the EU from the angle of federal constitutional theory.[38] Against this background, it is submitted that the interpretation of the public policy exception is not just a technical matter of doctrinal interpretation, but goes to the heart of the federal question about the nature of the EU. Indeed, the ECJ's classic starting point that matters of public policy affect 'one of the fundamental interests of society'[39] provokes the simple question about the fundamental interests of which society the ECJ has in mind: domestic and/or European? It will be demonstrated that the rather specific angle of the public policy exception is a perfect prism to propose an answer this question, thereby deciphering the legal and political infrastructure of the EU. Closer inspection of a classic formula of internal market law may elucidate the constitutional setup of the EU precisely because it has been an essential element of integration through law for several decades.

For all I know, the ECJ has never answered the question in the abstract as to who has the authority to define fundamental interests for matters of public policy. To be sure, any application of the public policy justification remains subject to ECJ oversight, but judges in Luxembourg still have to decide which forum shall be relevant for the identification of fundamental interests. It will be shown in this section that the ECJ's case law on this question is less unidirectional than is sometimes assumed, although the relevant frame of reference remains ambiguous. Judges fluctuate between different solutions, either emphasising a common pan-European understanding or nourishing a certain degree of autonomy on the part of the Member States. This is true, in particular, when we move beyond the realm of goods and services where uniformity has always been defended more eagerly than in matters concerning broader societal or moral issues.

In order to disentangle the puzzle, the analysis below will step back and distinguish two ideal types of how judges conceive of public policy matters. To identify different models of public policy is not to say that the ECJ holds a uniform conception which the collective of judges reflects consciously. Nor do I claim that individual judgments or Commission decisions realise one of the models unequivocally. This does not prevent academic commentators, however, from reconstructing the theoretical infrastructure. Such academic accounts present ideal types modelled upon judgments as legal phenomena and accentuate theoretical features for analytical purposes. They are not mutually exclusive and the positions of policy actors will most likely reflect a blend, combining elements of both models. In this section, I will present two visions of the public policy justification which I shall call the 'conflict of laws model' and the 'federal solution' (III.A and III.B). This section

[38] See S Oeter, 'Federalism and Democracy' in von Bogdandy and Bast (n 2) 55–82; and R Schütze, *From Dual to Cooperative Federalism. The Changing Structure of European Law* (Oxford, Oxford University Press, 2009).

[39] See above n 6 and accompanying text.

will conclude with an attempt to explain the growing acceptance of diversity in the case law on the single market (III.C).

A. Conflict of Laws Model

As the birth certificate of today's EU, the Treaty establishing the European Steel and Coal Community contained a provision on the free movement of workers which stayed short of today's Article 45 TFEU in substance but embraced the notion of 'public policy', referring, in the authentic French language version, to '*ordre public*'.[40] This formulation was taken up during negotiations on the Treaty of Rome that employed the same formula of *ordre public* for all fundamental freedoms constituting the common market.[41] Many readers will be aware that the notion of *ordre public* is much more than a rule of Union law. It was and is the concept of private international law—or conflict of laws—that is probably most widely known. States may reject the application of foreign law whenever it runs counter to their own fundamental principles. For example, Sweden was allowed to grant divorce to a Maltese couple even if the applicable domestic Maltese family law considered, until recently, marriage to be for eternity.[42]

In the world of conflict of laws, *ordre public* becomes relevant only when fundamental choices differ between societies, since country A pursues a different solution than country B. The concept of *ordre public* mediates discrepancies between legal orders—and does not impose its own, quasi-federal vision. This position is taken up, for matters of private international law, in Article 45 of the so-called Brussels I Regulation on jurisdiction and enforcement of judgments in civil and commercial matters, allowing Member States to refuse the recognition of a judgment rendered by a court of another Member State 'if such recognition is manifestly contrary to the public policy (ordre public) in the Member State addressed'.[43]

Interpreting this provision, the ECJ relies on standards mirroring case law on the public policy exception in the context of the single market. It emphasises that the notion of *ordre public* in the Brussels I Regulation on private international law must be interpreted restrictively before continuing, in decidedly general language, that 'while it is not for the Court to define the content of the public policy of a Member State, it is nonetheless required to review the limits within which

[40] Art 69(1) Treaty establishing the European Steel and Coal Community, of which only the French version was authentic in accordance with Art 100.

[41] See Arts 36, 48, 56 and 66 EEC Treaty as established by the Treaty of Rome; the three other authentic language versions of 1957 besides French used the following formulations: *öffentliche Ordnung* (German), *ordine pubblico* (Italian), *openbare orde* (Dutch).

[42] The maintenance of this option was one reason for Sweden not to participate in the adoption of Council Regulation (EU) No 1259/2010 implementing enhanced co-operation in the area of the law applicable to divorce and legal separation [2010] OJ L343/10, which is subject to the mechanism of enhanced co-operation.

[43] Art 45(1)(a) Regulation (EU) No 1215/2012 [2012] OJ L351/1.

the courts of a Member State may have recourse to that concept'.[44] The provision can only be relied upon where recognition or enforcement of a judgment given in another Member State 'would be at variance to an unacceptable degree with the legal order of the State … inasmuch as it would infringe a fundamental principle'.[45]

Examples where EU law followed this road in the context of the single market are the *Omega* and *Sayn-Wittgenstein* judgments, which allowed Member States to adopt country-specific solutions in the application of the fundamental freedoms to domestic measures seeking justification for a restriction of transnational free movement. In both cases, the Court accepted that the national approach was justified, irrespective of whether other Member States or the EU legal order as a whole shared the solution in question. Austria may prohibit aristocratic surnames as an expression of its constitutional identity in the same way as the German reading of human dignity may guide the prohibition of real-life war games.[46] It is not surprising that this recognition of country-specific outcomes was reinforced by the entry into force of the Treaty of Lisbon which stipulated in Article 4(2) TEU that the Union shall respect national constitutional identity, thereby supporting the acceptance of national specificities not much different from the position of various domestic constitutional courts.[47] Member States are allowed to differ—instead of merging into a European superstate.

As a matter of principle, the recognition of differences among Member States is no new phenomenon. In its foundational judgments on the public policy exception, the ECJ found with regard to workers supporting Scientology: 'Nevertheless, the particular circumstances justifying recourse to the concept of public policy may vary from one country to another and from one period to another, and it is therefore necessary in this matter to allow the competent national authorities an area of discretion within the limits imposed by the Treaty.'[48] Along similar lines, there have been judgments throughout the years emphasising that Member States must be recognised as having a definite margin of discretion on matters of public policy, in particular when societal conceptions vary from one Member State to another 'on the basis of, inter alia, moral or cultural views'.[49]

This demonstrates that the Court's supranational control function does not preclude Member States from pursuing their own vision under the umbrella of the public policy exception and similar doctrinal yardsticks. Member States are free, but only to a certain extent. In fact, there is a strand in the case law pointing in a different direction.

[44] Case C-302/13 *flyLAL-Lithuanian Airlines* EU:C:2014:2319 para 47.

[45] ibid, para 49.

[46] See Case C-208/09 *Sayn-Wittgenstein* EU:C:2010:806, which concerned mandatory requirements (not the public policy exception) and Case C-36/02 *Omega* EU:C:2004:614 relying on public policy.

[47] For a comparative overview see M Wendel, 'Lisbon before the Courts: Comparative Perspectives' (2011) 7 *European Constitutional Law Review* 96, 131–36.

[48] Case 41/74 *Van Duyn* (n 5) para 18; and Case 30/77 *Bouchereau* (n 6) para 34.

[49] Case C-244/06 *Dynamic Medien* EU:C:2008:85 para 44.

B. Federal Solution

We may bring together the collection of judgments leaving less leeway to Member States under the heading of 'federal solution'. This ideal type focuses on unity-building aspects in the case law. In extremis, it would replace national decisions by a uniform European understanding of what constitutes a good society—in pretty much the same way as the Court of Justice established, step by step, a pan-European consumer model to the detriment of national cultural or political sensitivities.[50] German beer and Italian pasta are probably among the most renowned examples of the Court promoting its vision of what is right and what is wrong in the context of an economic understanding of the free movement of food in the single market.[51] Again, judgments were delivered on the basis of different doctrinal constellations which resulted in similar outcomes rejecting national attempts to justify restrictions.

It is noticeable that more recent judgments often tend to construe the notion of public policy with reference to other norms of the EU legal order, which has become increasingly complex over the past 20 years. In judgments such as *Josemans* on marijuana from the Netherlands or *I* on the expulsion of a long-term resident after sexual offences against children, the ECJ activated corresponding norms on co-operation in criminal matters, which had entered the supranational legal order with the entry into force of the Treaty of Lisbon[52]—mirroring a parallel development in private international law where European norms have an impact on the definition of the notion of *ordre public*.[53] Similarly, interaction between human rights and economic free movement is increasingly resolved under reference to the supranational standards in the EU Charter on matters such as protection of minors, the right to strike, or freedom of assembly.[54]

This shows that the interpretation of the concept of public policy may benefit from input by rules concerning other domains than the single market, thereby reflecting the growing thematic scope of the EU legal order. Such process of constitutional enrichment suits the federal solution discussed in this subsection in so far as it defines the contents of the public policy justification under recourse to other provisions of Union law. Surprisingly, however, doing so need not result in more uniformity. The judgments on substantive cross-fertilisation

[50] See ch 12 in this volume.

[51] Case 178/84 *Commission v Germany* EU:C:1987:126 on German beer; and Case 407/85 *3 Glocken* EU:C:1988:401 on Italian pasta.

[52] See Case C-348/09 *I* (n 32) paras 38–40; Cases C-338/04, C-359/04 and C-360/04 *Placanica et al* (n 33) paras 25–27; and ch 10 in this volume.

[53] See J von Hein, 'Art 6 EGBGB Öffentliche Ordnung (ordre public)' in *Münchener Kommentar zum BGB*, vol 10 6th edn (München, CH Beck, 2015) paras 144–51, 153–80.

[54] See ECJ (n 49) para 24 on children; Case C-438/05 *The International Transport Workers' Federation and The Finnish Seamen's Union* EU:C:2007:772 para 44 on the right to strike; and Case C-112/00 *Schmidberger* EU:C:2003:333 paras 76–77 on freedom of assembly referring to the ECHR and general principles of Union law.

between different segments of the EU legal order mentioned above all assume, to the contrary, that Member States should have a certain leeway in the context of free movement. Thus, references to the EU Charter or EU criminal law need not result in federal uniformity in terms of public policy. In practice, the ECJ does not always move towards more uniformity. There are few instances in recent case law when Luxembourg developed and imposed its understanding of a just society within the context of the market freedoms. This counter-intuitive development of the free movement case law is in need of explanation.

C. Explaining the Rise of Diversity in Internal Market Case Law

It is widely known that the Court embraced the significance of national discretion in a number of more recent judgments on the fundamental freedoms in the single market which concerned diverse public policy considerations such as advertisement for alcoholic beverages or morally and financially harmful consequences for the individual and society associated with gaming and betting.[55] A certain margin of appreciation is pertinent, as the ECJ recognised explicitly, in areas with moral or cultural implications[56] or whenever there is uncertainty about the impact of certain substances on human health in light of the current state of scientific research.[57] Moreover, Member States have traditionally been granted leeway in foreign policy matters, including questions of war and peace.[58] Even regulatory choices closer to the heart of the single market can be subject to Member State discretion—as the *Commission v Italy* ruling on use restrictions for moto trailers confirmed where the Court emphasised that 'Member States must be allowed a margin of appreciation'[59] in the field of road safety. The same applies to subsidies for renewable energy which Member States may confine to domestic producers under certain circumstances, thereby effectively accepting a factual compartmentalisation of the internal market.[60]

How can we explain this parallelism of more discretion in the single market at a time of a growing constitutional maturity of the European project symbolised by the entry into force of a legally binding Charter of Fundamental Rights? It seems that this asymmetry reflects the subsidiarity of the fundamental freedoms which

[55] See Case C-262/02 *Commission v France* EU:C:2004:431 para 24 on alcoholic beverages; and Case C-243/01 *Gambelli et al* EU:C:2003:597 para 63 on gambling.

[56] See ECJ (n 49) para 44 on protection of minors; and generally R Craufurd Smith, 'European Community Intervention in the Cultural Field: Continuity or Change?' in Smith (ed), *Culture and European Union Law* (Oxford, Oxford University Press, 2004) 28–40.

[57] See Case C-95/01 *Greenham and Abel* EU:C:2004:71 para 37; and J Gerards, 'Pluralism, Deference and the Margin of Appreciation Doctrine' (2011) 17 *ELJ* 80, 94–97.

[58] See ch 10 in this volume.

[59] Case C-110/05 *Commission v Italy* EU:C:2009:66 para 65.

[60] See Case C-573/12 *Ålands Vindkraft* (n 13) para 110; and M Ludwigs, 'Keine Pflicht zur Erstreckung der Ökostromförderung auf in anderen Mitgliedstaaten erzeugten Strom' (2014) *Europäische Zeitschrift für Wirtschaftsrecht* 620, 627–26.

usually become relevant in areas where no secondary legislation has been adopted so far, while the more specific rules in secondary legislation take over in areas which have been subject to legislative harmonisation at EU level. In the absence of harmonisation, the economic freedoms apply precisely because there is no common EU approach. At the same time, it is the corresponding diversity of national rules in the absence of supranational harmonisation that may have motivated the ECJ to adopt a hands-off approach giving Member States more leeway to regulate areas not covered by EU legislation in line with the conflicts of law model discussed above. By contrast, it will apply stricter standards in areas covered by EU legislation, which it tends to submit to much stricter human rights supervision or statutory interpretation.[61]

Forty years ago when the ECJ delivered its foundational judgments on the single market, the economic freedoms were at the vanguard of EU integration. Their significance derived from the ability of the ECJ to prevent protectionist measures in the absence of EU harmonisation.[62] Today's overall picture looks different: after the completion of the single market programme and 20 more years of extensive harmonisation on various issues related to the free movement of goods, persons and services, many questions which would have been resolved on the basis of the fundamental freedoms 40 years ago are subject to EU harmonisation nowadays. It is on these areas of substantive harmonisation by the EU legislature on which the ECJ concentrates and where it develops its vision of good society under recourse, in particular, to human rights in the Charter.[63] By contrast, the ECJ may grant more leeway to Member States in areas not covered by EU legislation to this date,[64] also reflecting continuous calls for subsidiarity and diversity within the EU.[65] It is plausible, therefore, that more recent case law on the public policy exception is defined by a pluralistic outlook complementing the drive for more conformity in areas covered by EU legislation.[66]

This argument fits well into the reorientation of European federalism in recent years, which considers the definition of public goods no longer as a zero-sum issue where a competence should be exercised at either national or European level. Notwithstanding the variety of individual positions, a number of authors emphasise, under the heading of constitutional pluralism, that there need be no contradiction between national singularities and the uniform application of Union law if we

[61] For human rights and EU legislation, see E Muir, 'The Fundamental Rights Implications of EU Legislation: Some Constitutional Challenges' (2014) 51 *CML Rev* 219–46.

[62] See above n 2 and accompanying text.

[63] See S Iglesias Sánchez, 'The Court and the Charter' (2012) 49 *CML Rev* 1565, 1576–82; and T von Danwitz, 'Verfassungsrechtliche Herausforderungen in der jüngeren Rechtsprechung des Gerichtshofs der Europäischen Union' (2013) *Europäische Grundrechte-Zeitschrift* 253, 255–57.

[64] See also Gerards (n 57) 97–99; and Harbo (n 21) at 171 et seq.

[65] *Cf* F-X Millet, *L'Union européenne et l'identité constitutionnelle des États membres* (Paris, LGDJ, 2013).

[66] In applying this conclusion to specific scenarios one may have to distinguish, of course, different levels of intensity of EU legislation: minimum rules at EU level are an intermediate category between strict European standards and national discretion.

perceive different legal orders to be defined by mutual interconnections that may guide the accommodation of diversity in the European legal space.[67] In areas not subject to EU harmonisation, the ECJ may be more willing to hand the final decision back to the national arena, thereby deferring to domestic laws and politics. It might not have developed clear doctrinal standards guiding deference to domestic decision-making,[68] but the overall tendency is tangible and need not contradict a more interventionist approach in areas covered by extensive EU harmonisation on specific policy matters.

IV. THEORETICAL ARGUMENTS FOR NATIONAL DISCRETION

To say that the ECJ leaves Member States discretion when applying the public policy exception does not represent a normative argument whether this should be the case. For that reason, this section introduces a collection of five theoretical arguments why the ECJ should not interfere extensively with non-economic domestic policy choices in areas not covered by EU legislation where the fundamental freedoms continue to apply, since Member States must exercise their residual powers in conformity with Union law. In doing so, I do not deny the responsibility of the ECJ to review domestic policy choices in light of the fundamental freedoms. All I say is that there are good normative reasons why it should leave more discretion to Member States in areas not covered by extensive EU harmonisation measures. In such scenarios, the argument for discretion is particularly strong even if the ECJ will always retain the authority to guarantee that Member States do not behave in a protectionist manner. More specifically, five theoretical arguments for national discretion can be distinguished.

First, it has always been a primary function of the public policy exception to balance the broad thematic scope of the fundamental freedoms, which extend far beyond the realms of the economic and can cover questions with important cultural, social and moral implications. Rules on marijuana, pornography or gambling exemplify the wide scope. Such questions need not be uniform in a single market; similarly, they need not be harmonised fully in a supranational political union, which the EU aspires to be. There are strong arguments that decisions

[67] See A von Bogdandy, 'Common Principles for a Plurality of Orders: A Study on Public Authority in the European Legal Area' (2014) 12 *International Journal of Constitutional Law* 980–1007; L Viellechner, 'Responsiver Rechtspluralismus. Zur Entwicklung eines transnationalen Kollisionsrechts' (2012) 51 *Der Staat* 559–80; and M Kumm, 'The Cosmopolitan Turn in Constitutionalism' in J Dunoff and J Trachtman (eds), *Ruling the World* (Cambridge, Cambridge University Press, 2009) 258–324.

[68] See X Groussot, 'Constitutional Dialogues, Pluralism and Conflicting Identities' in M Avbelj and J Komárek (eds), *Constitutional Pluralism in the European Union and Beyond* (Oxford, Hart, 2012) 319, 338–40; and C Nivard, 'Marge nationale d'appréciation et pluralisme dans la jurisprudence de la Cour de justice de Luxembourg' in M Levinet (ed), *Pluralisme et juges européens des droits de l'homme* (Brussels, Bruylant, 2010) 169, 181 et seq.

relating to cultural, social and moral questions, which have not yet been subject to EU harmonisation,[69] should be left largely to Member States to be taken domestically, thereby giving room for meaningful public discourses on subject matters closely related to the self-understanding of European societies.[70] If that is correct, the ECJ may be right to grant Member States discretion in areas related to important cultural, social and ethical choices[71] even if any delineation between areas with more or less discretion will always be gradual.[72]

Second, it is a general feature of the EU that its institutional set-up and political self-understanding are defined by the mediation of inter-state conflicts and that this predisposition may complicate the ability of EU institutions to sustain prolonged and meaningful debates with the wider public.[73] If that is correct, the ECJ should defer to national laws and politics in particular in areas where the EU legislature has not adopted a uniform European approach,[74] since it may be complicated enough to develop meaningful public discourses on matters where EU institutions have established a uniform position at supranational level.[75] Against this background, the ECJ's widespread focus on proportionality and the need for an individual assessment taking account of the circumstances of each case can be interpreted as a device for relieving pressure from the European project, since the need for an individualised assessment, which often will have been performed by domestic courts, presents an alternative to a uniform standpoint applicable throughout the Union irrespective of differences.[76]

Third, we should acknowledge institutional and procedural limitations. Judges in Luxembourg have to adjudicate in diverse areas of law and they often lack an intimate knowledge of both the factual background and wider political and social implications. This deficit is amplified by rules of procedure, since few social actors

[69] Remember that the ECJ seems to combine leeway for Member States in the context of the fundamental freedoms with a more uniform approach to areas of secondary harmonisation; see above section III.C.

[70] See J Komárek, '*National Constitutional Courts in the European Constitutional Democracy*' (2014) 12 *International Journal of Constitutional Law* 525, 536–41; and A Somek, 'Europe: Political, not Cosmopolitan' (2014) 20 *ELJ* 142–63.

[71] See de Witte (n 29) 1546–51; and C Hilson, 'The Unpatriotism of the Economic Constitution? Rights to Free Movement and their Impact on National and European Identity' (2008) 14 *ELJ* 186–202.

[72] Of course, there can be an overlap between economic and non-economic considerations, such as Case C-341/05 *Laval un Partneri* EU:C:2007:809; in such scenarios, it will often be disputed whether a domestic policy pursues non-economic objective in a non-protectionist manner and the ECJ will have to take its standpoint.

[73] See M Dani, 'Rehabilitating Social Conflicts in European Public Law' (2012) 18 *ELJ* 621, 628–42; and J Neyer, *The Justification of Europe: A Political Theory of Supranational Integration* (Oxford, Oxford University Press, 2012).

[74] See C Joerges, 'Unity in Diversity as Europe's Vocation and Conflicts of Law as Europe's Constitutional Form' in A Greppi and R Nickel (eds), *The Changing Role of Law in the Age of Supranational and Transnational Governance* (Baden-Baden, Nomos, 2014) 127–78.

[75] See A Williams, 'Taking Values Seriously' (2009) 20 *OJLS* 549, 558–62.

[76] See L Azoulai, 'L'autonomie de l'individu européen et la question du statut' in C Kessedjian (ed), *Autonomie en droit européen* (Paris, Editions Panthéon-Assas, 2013) 187, 197–99.

may voice their opinion before the ECJ rules on a matter.[77] Indeed, there are numerous examples in which the ECJ recognised explicitly that it should defer to the assessments of domestic courts, since any final decision 'calls for an analysis of the circumstances of law and of fact which characterise the situation in the Member State concerned, which the national court is in a better position than the Court of Justice to carry out'.[78] You might call this the 'best fit' argument accepting that national institutions may often be better placed than the ECJ to decide certain issues on the basis of legal instructions given by the ECJ.[79]

Fourth, delegation of final decisions back to the domestic arena in ECJ judgments on the fundamental freedoms is no neutral undertaking, since an application of the public policy exception, in particular, does not give Member States carte blanche to do as they please. To the contrary, they remain subject to the legal standards laid down by the ECJ which domestic courts are called upon to apply. This empowerment of domestic judges to apply procedural rules requiring governments and parliaments to justify decisions can change the rules of the game for domestic decision-making.[80] Abstract parliamentary debates about hallmarks of a good society are replaced by national decision-making under the auspices of the principle of proportionality.[81] Doing so is structurally beneficial to the position of individuals and weakens collective identity in decision-making.[82] In doctrinal terms, this may be translated into an argument for a cautious reading of the concept of restriction instead of resolving most cases in the proportionality assessment. By not requiring a justification for unproblematic cases, the ECJ would avert negative side-effects on domestic decision-making without preventing its ability to censor protectionist behaviour.

Finally, we should recognise that the arguments for national discretion in the application of the fundamental freedoms to areas subject to domestic decision-making presented above ought to be reconciled with the need to protect legitimate interests of those not partaking in domestic rule making.[83] When applying the public policy exception, the ECJ has a meaningful role to play to protect these interests, thereby unmasking myths behind national restrictions and preventing

[77] See Gerards (n 57) 85; and J Croon, 'Comparative Institutional Analysis, the European Court of Justice and the General Principle of Non-Discrimination—or—Alternative Tales on Equality' (2013) 19 *ELJ* 153, 163–72.

[78] Case C-405/98 *Gourmet* (n 14) para 33.

[79] See K Lenaerts, 'The Court's Outer and Inner Selves. Exploring the External and Internal Legitimacy of the European Court of Justice' in Adams et al (n 26) 13, 40–45.

[80] See E Spaventa, 'The Constitutional Impact of EU Citizenship' in U Neergaard, R Nielsen and L Roseberry (eds), *European Legal Method* (Copenhagen, DJØF, 2011) 141, 151–54.

[81] See M Everson and C Joerges, 'Reconfiguring the Politics-Law Relationship in the Integration Project through Conflicts-Law Constitutionalism' (2012) 18 *ELJ* 644, 659–62; and Somek (n 70) 155–56.

[82] See JHH Weiler, 'Deciphering the Political and Legal DNA of European Integration' in J Dickson and P Eleftheriadis (eds), *Philosophical Foundations of European Union Law* (Oxford, Oxford University Press, 2012) 137, 155; and A José Menéndez, 'Which Citizenship? Whose Europe?' (2014) 15 *German Law Journal* 907, 917–18, 922–28.

[83] See A Somek, 'The Argument from Transnational Effects' (2019) 16 *ELJ* 315–44 and 375–94.

Member States from clothing protectionist policies in quasi-moral arguments.[84] The tension between national discretion and supranational judicial oversight cannot be dissolved, but may be mitigated by doctrinal instruments focusing on a procedural approach towards justification,[85] including the concept of coherence.[86] Such intermediate approach fits well with the conclusion that ECJ case law on the public policy exception is closely related to other doctrinal enquiries often employed by judges as functional equivalents.[87]

V. CONCLUSION

The public policy exception is an excellent angle from which to identify the constitutional set-up of the EU because it has been an essential element of the case law on the single market for more than 40 years. To this date, the meaning of public policy is defined by the ECJ's foundational judgments, which supported market integration by means of a restrictive approach to justifications. The distinction between the public policy exception and unwritten mandatory requirements appears historically contingent from today's perspective, since most mandatory requirements could equally be construed as a fundamental interest of society. This discrepancy fits well into the overall lack of doctrinal clarity in the construction of the fundamental freedoms. The abstract distinction between the concepts of restriction, justification and proportionality need not coincide with more or less leeway for Member States, since the ECJ treats these topics as functionally equivalent doctrinal channels to adjust the impact of individual decisions. Our focus on public policy presents is closely interrelated, therefore, with the ECJ's approach to the fundamental freedoms more generally.

At an abstract level of analysis, we may distinguish two ideal types of how the ECJ addresses the problem of who decides which fundamental interests of society define the concept of public policy. There are numerous instances where the ECJ emphasised that Member States have a certain leeway as to what they consider significant and that the choice of one country need not coincide with the regulatory position adopted by other Member States or the Union as a whole. At the same time, however, there are also examples of a uniform federal solution adopted by the Court. The novel tendency, on the part of judges, to relate the interpretation of the concept of public policy to other areas of Union law does

[84] See M Everson, 'A Citizenship in Movement' (2014) 15 *German Law Journal* 965, 976; and Azoulai (n 76) 197–99.

[85] See P Popelier and C Van De Heyning, 'Procedural Rationality: Giving Teeth to the Proportionality Analysis' (2013) 9 *European Constitutional Law Review* 230–62; and S Douglas-Scott, 'The Problem of Justice in the European Union: Values, Pluralism, and Critical Legal Justice' in Dickson and Eleftheriadis (n 82) 412–47.

[86] See de Witte (n 29) 1570–77; and G Mathisen, 'Consistency and Coherence as Conditions for Justification of Member State Measures Restricting Free Movement' (2010) 47 *CML Rev* 1021–48.

[87] See above section II.D.

not coincide, paradoxically, with a shift towards more uniformity. This may be explained by today's constitutional context after more than 30 years of extensive harmonisation of various policy fields by the EU legislature. As a result, the fundamental freedoms often apply to subject areas not covered by EU legislation. It is in these areas of residual Member State powers that the normative argument for national discretion is particularly strong. Again, the balance between domestic regulatory autonomy and supranational oversight will be a gradual one with the ECJ applying various doctrinal instruments at its proposal to fine-tune Member States' room for manoeuvre.

10

Public Security Exceptions and EU Free Movement Law

PANOS KOUTRAKOS*

I. INTRODUCTION

QUITE EARLY ON in the life of European integration, Member States assumed that the exceptions from the law on free movement reserved a regulatory space where the exercise of their sovereign powers would be immune to the disciplines imposed by EU rules. This assumption manifested itself in different contexts over the years. A striking example was provided in the area of economic sanctions against third countries. In *Centro-Com*, the British Government argued that it reserved the power to deviate from EU rules imposing economic sanctions against Serbia in order to ensure their effective application, because such a deviation constituted a foreign policy choice which was beyond the scope of the Union legal order.[1]

The Court of Justice accepted that foreign policy was not covered by EU law. However, it added that, 'while it is for Member States to adopt measures of foreign and security policy in the exercise of their national competence, those measures must nevertheless respect the provisions adopted by the Community in the field of the common commercial policy provided for by Article [207 TFEU, ex Article 133] of the Treaty'.[2] The same conclusion was reached in relation to similar claims for reserved powers in other areas.[3] This case law, and the need for Member States

* I am grateful to Niamh Nic Shuibhne and Phil Syrpis for their comments and suggestions and to Niall Coghlan for his research assistance.

[1] Case C-124/95 *Centro-Com* EU:C:1997:8.

[2] ibid, para 27.

[3] These include monetary policy (eg Joined Cases 6 and 11/69 *Commission v France* EU:C:1969:68 para 17; Case 57/86 *Greece v Commission* EU:C:1988:284 para 9; Case 127/87 *Commission v Greece* EU:C:1988:331 para 7), registration of vessels (eg Case C-221/89 *Factortame and Others* EU:C:1991:320 para 14), social policy (eg C-438/05 *The International Transport Workers' Federation and The Finnish Seamen's Union* EU:C:2007:772 para 40), taxation (eg Case C-264/96 *ICI v Colmer* EU:C:1998:370 para 19; Case C-334/02 *Commission v France* EU:C:2004:129 para 21; Case C-446/03 *Marks & Spencer* EU:C:2005:763 para 29; and Case C-524/04 *Test Claimants in the Thin Cap Group litigation* EU:C:2007:161 para 25), health care (Case C-120/95 *Decker* EU:C:1998:167 paras 22 and 23;

to take into account the law of the EU when the policy choices which they deem necessary deviate from EU law, prompted the current President of the Court of Justice, writing in an extra-judicial capacity, to argue that '[t]here is no nucleus of sovereignty that Member States can invoke as such against the Community'.[4]

Of all the grounds for exceptions from free movement, public security is most closely associated with what is traditionally understood as the core of national sovereignty, that is, the sphere of activity within which the State has primary responsibility to protect its territory and citizens. As such, the term is politically charged to an even greater extent than in relation to other grounds of justification. This characteristic not only makes it more difficult to define the scope and content of the term. It also raises questions about the intensity of judicial review and the criteria pursuant to which this should be exercised.

This chapter will examine in a non-exhaustive manner different contexts within which Member States seek to rely upon public security in order to impose restrictions on the application of EU rules. The analysis will explore three main themes: the wide range of different categorisations of public security in primary and secondary law and their implications for the definition of a concept which is already nebulous in its content; the extent to which public security is construed in different terms depending on the legal and policy context within which a Member State seeks to protect it; and the extent to which the Court of Justice provides guidance to national authorities as to how to protect public security in compliance with the substantive and procedural requirements laid down in EU law (and to national courts as to how to monitor such compliance). Given the central role of national courts in the interpretation and application of public security exceptions, the chapter will take into account national case law where possible.[5]

The analysis is structured in three parts. First, it examines public security exceptions provided in EU primary law. Second, it tackles exceptions set out in secondary law by focusing on the principle of sex discrimination in the armed forces and the exercise of rights flowing from EU citizenship. Third, given their special status and extraordinary conditions for their application, it examines separately

Case C-158/96 *Kohll* EU:C:1998:171 paras 18 and 19; Case C-157/99 *BSM Geraets-Smits and HTM Peerbooms* EU:C:2001:404 para 46), and services liberalisation.

[4] K Lenaerts, 'Constitutionalism and the many faces of federalism' 38 *American Journal of Comparative Law* (1990) 205, 220.

[5] For practical reasons, this has been possible only to a limited extent and confined to the courts in the United Kingdom. Given the central role of proportionality review which this chapter will analyse, it is worth pointing out that the UK is a State where the application of the principle of free movement challenged national judges considerably. See, eg, the Sunday trading saga in the UK: Case C-312/89 *CGT v Conforama* EU:C:1991:93; Case C-332/89 *Marchandise* EU:C:1991:94; Case C-169/91 *Stoke-on-Trent and Norwich City Councils v B&Q* EU:C:1992:519 and the analysis in A Arnull, 'What Shall We Do on Sunday?' (1991) 16 *EL Rev* 195 and C Barnard, 'Sunday Trading: A Drama in Five Acts' (1994) 57 *MLR* 449. See also Lord Hoffmann, 'The Influence of the European Principle of Proportionality upon UK Law' in E Ellis (ed), *The Principle of Proportionality in the Laws of Europe* (Oxford, Hart Publishing, 1999) 107.

the exceptional clauses set out in TFEU which enable Member States to deviate from the entire corpus of EU law.

II. PUBLIC SECURITY IN EU PRIMARY LAW—THE CASE OF TRADE

Public security constitutes a ground for exceptions from all four freedoms under the Union's primary rules.[6] The seminal case for the interpretation of this justification is *Campus Oil*.[7] This preliminary reference was about an Irish rule that importers of petroleum products should purchase a certain proportion of their requirements from the only State refinery at a fixed price. The Irish Government argued that the restriction on free movement of goods which that requirement entailed was justified on public security grounds: it was essential that the State should be able to rely upon crude oil at all times, and, to that effect, it ought to ensure the viability of the only Irish refinery.

Three main features of the judgment are noteworthy. The first is the Court's approach to the existence of secondary EU legislation in the area. Where a Member State seeks to deviate from free movement on the basis of a ground of justification recognised under EU law, one of the parameters which the Court examines as a matter of course is the existence of secondary EU legislation and the extent to which this protects the interest which a Member State seeks to protect: if the answer to this question is affirmative, then an exception from EU law is normally not justified as, by purporting to protect an interest already protected at EU level, such a deviation is no longer necessary.[8] Conversely, even in the presence of EU secondary legislation, a Member State would be allowed to rely upon Article 36 TFEU if the substantive content of the former would not protect adequately the public interest mentioned in the latter. In other words, the degree of harmonisation in secondary legislation would have an impact on the scope for national authorities to rely upon the exceptional provisions set out in primary law. In *Campus Oil*, the Union had adopted secondary legislation dealing with difficulties in supplies of crude oil and petroleum products.[9] However, the Court held that, such measures notwithstanding, the Member States do not have 'an unconditional guarantee that supplies will in any event be maintained at least at a level sufficient to meet its minimum needs'.[10] It then held that an interruption of supply of petroleum products was justifiable under the public security exception as such products, 'because of their exceptional importance as an energy source in the modern economy, are

[6] Arts 36 (goods), 45(3) and 52 (persons), 62 (services), and 65 TFEU (capital).

[7] Case 72/83 *Campus Oil* EU:C:1984:256.

[8] See, eg, Case 35/76 *Simmenthal* EU:C:1976:180; Case 5/77 *Tedeschi v Denkavit* EU:C:1977:144; and Case 251/78 *Denkavit* EU:C:1979:252.

[9] Council Dir 68/414/EEC [1968] OJ English Special Edition II/586, Council Dir 73/238/EEC [1973] L 228/1, Council Dec 77/706/EEC [1977] OJ L 292/9, and Council Dec 77/186/EEC [1977] OJ L 61/23.

[10] Case 72/83 *Campus Oil* (n 7) para 31.

of fundamental importance for a country's existence since not only its services but above all its institutions, its essential public services and even the survival of its inhabitants depend upon them'.[11]

The tenor of the judgment suggests that, once public security touches upon the most vital interests of the State, and therefore gives rise to the core of the functions which a State carries out in order to protect its citizens, there is more leeway for autonomous action, the presence of EU secondary legislation in the area notwithstanding. This is not dissimilar to the position the Court had taken in *Chemial* in relation to Italian legislation taxing ethyl alcohol higher than alcohol obtained by fermentation.[12] As the former was based on a petroleum derivative, the objective of the Italian measure was to deter the use of petroleum products for the production of alcohol in order to reserve them for products the use of which would be more important for the State. In subsequent judgments, the concept of public security was interpreted as encompassing both internal and external security.[13]

However, to tolerate and sanction the choices made by the Member States is not tantamount to rendering them beyond the Union legal framework altogether. This is the second noteworthy feature of the judgment in *Campus Oil*. In assessing whether the Irish restriction was proportionate, the Court held that the quantities of petroleum products to which the purchasing obligation referred should not exceed the minimum supply requirements of the State 'without which the operation of essential public services and the survival of its inhabitants would be affected'.[14]

In fact, the Court engaged in quite a detailed examination of what the proportionality test would entail:

> the quantities of petroleum products whose marketing can be ensured under such a system must not exceed the quantities which are necessary, so far as production is concerned, on the one hand, for technical reasons in order that the refinery may operate currently at a sufficient level of its production capacity to ensure that its plant will be available in the event of a crisis and, on the other hand, in order that it may continue to refine at all times the crude oil covered by the long-term contracts which the State concerned has entered into so that it may be assured of regular supplies.[15]

In doing so, it provided guidance to the referring court as to how to play its part in the application of the EU test about exceptions from free movement.

[11] ibid, para 34. See also Case C-503/99 *Commission v Belgium (golden shares)* EU:C:2002:328 para 46.

[12] Case 140/79 *Chemial* EU:C:1981:1.

[13] Case C-367/89 *Criminal Proceedings against Aimé Richardt and Les Accessoires Scientifiques SNC* EU:C:1991:376; Case C-83/94 *Criminal Proceedings against Peter Leifer and Others* EU:C:1995:329; Case C-70/94 *Fritz Werner Industrie-Ausrustungen GmbH v Federal Republic of Germany* EU:C:1995:328 paras 10–11. In the latter case, and with reference to German legislation on external trade, the Court accepted that public security would be undermined by the risk of serious disturbance to foreign relations or to peaceful coexistence of nations (para 27).

[14] Case 72/83 *Campus Oil* (n 7) para 47.

[15] ibid, para 48.

The detailed guidance given to the referring courts about the application of the principle of proportionality is the third main characteristic of the case law of the Court of Justice in the area. There are different ways in which the Court may provide the referring court with detailed guidance and it may do so for different reasons. For instance, it may seek to provide assistance in an area where national courts have found it difficult to apply EU law tests.[16] It may also apply itself an EU law test which it introduced recently in order to illustrate what is expected of national courts or to assuage fears that a newly introduced test may have profound practical implications for Member States.[17] On the other hand, it may provide no guidance at all.[18] Ultimately, there is no discernible pattern which would illustrate hard and fast rules about judicial behaviour.[19] In disputes where public security is invoked, detailed guidance functions as a counterbalance of the central role that national courts occupy not just in their capacity as referring courts but mainly in their task, entrusted by the Court itself, to police the outer limits of the wide discretion granted to national authorities. The more nebulous the public interest and the wider the discretion enjoyed by the Member State, the greater the need to set out with clarity the substantive and procedural conditions within which such discretion ought to be exercised.

Detailed guidance to national courts is also given in other areas where public security is invoked, a case in point being exports of dual-use goods.[20] These are products of both civil and military application. In the light of this characteristic, Member States claimed that exports of such products were beyond the scope of EU law. The Court of Justice rejected this argument[21] and focused, instead, on whether a national restriction on exports might be justified as necessary in order to protect public security. It answered the question in the affirmative and construed the scope for Member States to act in wide terms too. It also left it for the national courts to ascertain whether the national measures are necessary and proportionate. However, in doing so, the Court gave strong indication both as to the justifiability of the national restriction and the criteria on the basis of which the referring courts are to assess the principle of proportionality. For instance, it accepted in *Leifer* that,

> depending on the circumstances, the competent national authorities have a certain degree of discretion when adopting measures which they consider to be necessary in order to

[16] See, eg, Case C-368/95 *Familiapress* EU:C:1997:325 regarding the issues pertaining to proportionality review which the referring court should take into account.

[17] See, eg, Case C-392/93 *British Telecommunications* EU:C:1996:131 on the sufficiently serious test in the context of State liability.

[18] See, eg, Case C-405/98 *Gourmet* EU:C:2001:135 and the criticism in A Biondi, 'Advertising alcohol and the free movement principle: the Gourmet decision' (2001) 26 *EL Rev* 616.

[19] On the different approaches to the construction of the principle of proportionality by the Court in the context of exceptions from free movement pursuant to primary law, see C Barnard, 'Derogations, Justifications and the Four Freedoms: Is State Interest Really Protected?' in C Barnard and O Odudu (eds), *The Outer Limits of European Union Law* (Oxford, Hart Publishing 2009) 273.

[20] For an analysis of this area, see P Koutrakos, *Trade, Foreign Policy and Defence in EU Constitutional Law* (Oxford, Hart Publishing, 2001) ch 6.

[21] Case C-83/94 *Leifer* (n 13) paras 10–11 and Case C-70/94 *Werner* (n 13) paras 10–11.

> guarantee public security in a Member State within the meaning indicated above. When the export of dual-use goods involves a threat to the public security of a Member State, those measures may include a requirement that an applicant for an export licence show that the goods are for civil use and also, having regard to specific circumstances such as inter alia the political situation in the country of destination, that a licence be refused if those goods are objectively suitable for military use.[22]

Similarly, it held in *Richardt* that confiscating goods would be disproportionate if the return of the goods to the Member State of origin sufficed, and also referred to the issues which national courts ought to take into account, such as 'the nature of the goods capable of endangering the security of the State, the circumstances in which the breach was committed and whether or not the trader seeking to effect the transit and holding documents for that purpose issued by another Member State was acting in good faith'.[23]

All in all, in order to assess the construction of the public security exception by the Court, account should be taken of both the detailed analysis and strict application of the principle of proportionality[24] and the clearly narrow terms in which the notion of public security was defined. Indeed, the circumstances in which the notion of public security as construed by the Court would apply would be truly quite exceptional.[25] In a subsequent action against Greece,[26] the Court was asked to deal again with a system of ensuring a minimum stock of petroleum products and the Union measure already mentioned in *Campus Oil*, which imposed such a requirement on Member States.[27] The Greek authorities had, however, enabled the companies bound to store petroleum products to transfer that obligation to refineries based in Greece provided that they had purchased such products from these refineries during the previous year. The Court found this provision contrary to the principle of free movement of goods: it aimed to protect an interest of an economic nature and, in any case, 'the objective of public security could have been achieved by less restrictive measures without it being necessary to make the transfer of the storage obligation to refineries established in Greece conditional upon the obligation to obtain supplies of petroleum products from those refineries'.[28]

The judgment in *Commission v Greece* clearly suggests that the *Campus Oil* principle by no means provides Member States with a *carte blanche* when they claim that necessity related to public security entails a deviation from EU law. In its rather short judgment, the Court merely referred to the arguments made by the late Advocate General Ruiz-Jarabo Colomer in his Opinion, without even

[22] Case C-83/94 *Leifer* (n 13) para 35.
[23] C-367/89 *Richardt* (n 13) para 25.
[24] See T Tridimas, *The General Principles of EC Law* 2nd edn (Oxford, OUP 2007) 226.
[25] See also P Craig and G de Búrca, *EU Law* 6th edn (Oxford: OUP 2015) 699.
[26] Case C-398/98 *Commission v Greece* EU:C:2001:565.
[27] Council Directive 68/414/EEC of 20 December 1968 imposing an obligation on Member States of the EEC to maintain minimum stocks of crude oil and/or petroleum products (OJ, English Special Edition 1968 (II)) 586.
[28] n 26 para 31.

repeating them. He had expressed deep scepticism about the Greek defence, and the absence of a detailed and specific explanation of how public security entailed the adoption of the illegal measure.[29]

Viewed along its strict and elaborate approach to the application of the principle of proportionality, the judgment in *Campus Oil* acknowledges the duty of the Member States to protect their citizens, whilst subjecting its exercise to Union law control. It is noteworthy that the latter is mediated through national courts by the application of the principle of proportionality. All in all, the judgment in *Campus Oil* is not couched in language of deference, but one of balanced co-existence of the rights of Member States as fully sovereign subjects of international law and the obligations imposed under the EU legal order.

In terms of the application of the principles set out in *Campus Oil*, there is no evidence of misuse of this balancing exercise by national courts. For instance, there are very few judgments by courts in the United Kingdom which refer expressly to the judgment in *Campus Oil* and, amongst these, one notices both a narrow interpretation of public security and a considered application of the proportionality test. In *Mabanaft*, for instance,[30] the Court of Appeal in England and Wales dealt with the application of a Directive—replacing the measure with which the Court of Justice dealt in *Campus Oil*—imposing an obligation on Member States to maintain minimum stocks of crude oil and/or petroleum products.[31] In a judgment by Lady Justice Arden, the Court of Appeal was mindful of the criteria set out in *Campus Oil* and the EU law constraints on the exercise of the right of national authorities to protect national security. In doing so, the national court struck the balance between, on the one hand, a strict construction of public security and a detailed analysis of the requirements of necessity and proportionality and, on the other hand, the need to avoid substituting its judgment for the policy choice made by the executive.

The analysis so far has highlighted two main points. The first is about the balancing exercise between the discretion of national authorities to determine how best to protect national security, and the procedural and substantive conditions which EU law requires them to meet. The second is about the central role of national courts and the detailed guidance by the Court of Justice as to how they are expected to carry it out. These points will also emerge below in the examination of how public security is construed in specific contexts of secondary legislation.

[29] See, eg, para 44 of his Opinion, to which the judgment referred, which reads as follows: 'As regards the risk for the distribution system of an industrial unit which is vital for national security, I am of the view that the defendant Government has not shown that, in order to protect national security, it is essential to link the transfer of the storage to the obligation to acquire the products. I myself see no reason why, if under the present system the refineries can store their own products, they cannot, under a system governed by the laws of the market and of free competition, store the products which the marketing undertakings acquire from other Member States.'

[30] *R (Mabanaft Limited) v Secretary of State for Energy and Climate Change* [2009] EWCA Civ 224.

[31] Directive 2006/67/EC [2006] OJ L 217/8, repealed by Council Directive 2009/119/EC OJ L 265/9.

III. PUBLIC SECURITY IN SECONDARY LEGISLATION

Provisions similar to the primary law exception clauses mentioned above are also laid down in secondary EU legislation. For instance, Council Regulation 3285/94 on imports from third countries enables Member States to deviate from its provisions and impose prohibitions, quantitative restrictions or surveillance measures on grounds of public morality, public policy or public security; the protection of health and life of humans, animals or plants, the protection of national treasures possessing artistic, historic or archaeological value, or the protection of industrial and commercial property.[32] Similar provisions are set out in other EU instruments, and they refer to such non-economic interests either expressly,[33] or by reference to the exception clauses set out in the Treaties.[34] Furthermore, there may be special exclusions depending on the subject matter of the set of rules in question.[35]

In its interpretation of such clauses, the Court has adopted the balanced approach which underpins its judgment in *Campus Oil*. This section will provide an outline of this approach in two areas where public security has given rise to interesting issues before national courts, namely equal treatment in the armed forces and the rights granted under EU citizenship.

A. Equal Treatment in the Armed Forces

The prohibition on sex discrimination under primary law is developed further in EU secondary legislation.[36] The application of this principle was the subject matter of three separate cases referred to the Court of Justice in the late 1990s and early 2000s. In *Sirdar*, the Industrial Tribunal (United Kingdom) raised the question of the legality of a British rule preventing women from joining the Royal Marines.[37] In *Kreil*, the Administrative Court, Hannover, raised the question of the consistency with EU law of the German constitutional rule confining the access of

[32] Council Regulation 3285/94 [1994] OJ L 275/1, Art 24(2)(a)(i).

[33] eg Council Regulation 2603/69 on common rules on exports [1969] OJ L 324/25, amended by Regulation 3918/91 [1991] OJ L 372/31 (Art 11).

[34] See, eg, Council Regulation 227/77 on Community transit [1977] OJ L 38/1, Art 10 as interpreted by the Court in Case C-367/89 *Richardt* (n 13) paras 17–18.

[35] See, eg, Directive 2004/18/EC on the coordination of procedures for the award of public works contracts, public supply contracts and public service contracts [2004] OJ L 134/114, Art 14 on secret contracts and contracts requiring special security measures. However, there is also a provision in the preamble (recital 6) according to which '[n]othing in this Directive should prevent the imposition or enforcement of measures necessary to protect public policy, public morality, public security, health, human and animal life or the preservation of plant life, in particular with a view to sustainable development, provided that these measures are in conformity with the Treaty'.

[36] Dir 2006/54/EC on the implementation of the principle of equal opportunities and equal treatment of men and women in matters of employment and occupation [2006] OJ L 204/23. The precursor to this measure was Dir 76/207 [1976] OJ L 39/40. The case law examined in this section refers to the latter.

[37] Case C-273/97 *Sirdar v The Army Board and Secretary of State for Defence* EU:C:1999:523.

women to the armed forces to medical and military-music services.[38] Finally, in *Dory*, the Administrative Court, Stuttgart, focused on the legality of the German constitutional rule which confined compulsory military service to men.[39]

In its judgments in *Sirdar* and *Kreil*, delivered in late 1999 and early 2000 respectively, the Court held that national measures were not excluded from the application of EU law merely because they aimed at the protection of public security or national defence. The public security derogations provided under primary law deal with exceptional and clearly defined cases and by no means introduce an inherent general exception excluding all measures aimed at the protection of public security from the scope of EU law. To assume otherwise would be tantamount to impairing the binding nature of EU law and its uniform application.[40] In the absence of a public security exception in the social provisions of primary law, the Court held that secondary legislation on equal treatment was applicable to employment in the public service[41] and, hence, in the armed forces.

The Court acknowledged that, in order to ensure their security, it was for the Member States to take decisions on the organisation of their armed forces. However, the discretion they enjoy in so deciding should be exercised in a manner which, on the one hand, would genuinely aim at guaranteeing public security and, on the other hand, would be appropriate and necessary to achieve that aim. In *Sirdar*, these criteria were held to be met: the national deviation from the equal treatment principle was confined to a small force and was applied pursuant to the principle of interoperability which required all Royal Marines, without exception and irrespective of their specialisation, to carry out a wide range of activities within the unit and to fight as front-line commandos. The German restriction in *Kreil* was held to be unjustified because, effectively, it excluded the national armed forces *in toto* from the application of the principle of equal treatment.

In *Dory*, the question was different, as the main focus was on the compulsory character of military service. In a paragraph worth citing in full, the Full Court held:

> Certainly, decisions of the Member States concerning the organisation of their armed forces cannot be completely excluded from the application of Community law, particularly where observance of the principle of equal treatment of men and women in connection with employment, including access to military posts, is concerned. But it does not follow that Community law governs the Member States' choices of military organisation for the defence of their territory or of their essential interests.[42]

Certainly, decisions of the Member States concerning the organisation of their armed forces cannot be completely excluded from the application of Community law, particularly where observance of the principle of equal treatment of men

[38] C-285/98 *Kreil v Bundesrepublik Deutschland* EU:C:2000:2.
[39] Case C-186/01 *Dory v Germany* EU:C:2003:146.
[40] See also Case 222/84 *Johnston v Chief Constable of the Royal Ulster Constabulary* EU:C:1986:206.
[41] See also Case 248/83 *Commission v Germany* EU:C:1985:214; Case C-1/95 *Gerster* EU:C:1997:452.
[42] Case C-186/01 *Dory* (n 39) para 35.

and women in connection with employment, including access to military posts, is concerned. But it does not follow that Community law governs the Member States' choices of military organisation for the defence of their territory or of their essential interests.

The Court ruled that '[t]he decision of the Federal Republic Germany to ensure its defence in part by compulsory military service is the expression of such a choice of military organisation to which Community law is ... not applicable'.[43] This conclusion was supported by reference to the importance of the aims of compulsory military service as defined by the German Government in its written observations and at the hearing: in political terms and in terms of the organisation of the armed forces, these consisted of its contribution to the democratic transparency of the military, national integration, the link between the armed forces and the population and the mobilisation of the manpower needed by the armed forces in the event of a conflict. It was in the interests of the territorial security of Germany that military service was compulsory, hence taking precedence over the objectives of policies aimed at the work prospects of young people.

Another aspect of the German rule on which the Court focused was the limited scope of the application of compulsory military service. The Court acknowledged that that 'will generally entail a delay in the progress of [their] career' whilst pointing out that 'military service allows some of [those concerned] to acquire further vocational training or subsequently to take up a military career'.[44] However, it viewed that delay as 'an inevitable consequence of the choice made by the Member State regarding military organisation' and, as such, it 'does not mean that that choice comes within the scope of Community law'.[45] It then concluded as follows:

> The existence of adverse consequences for access to employment cannot, without encroaching on the competences of the Member States, have the effect of compelling the Member State in question either to extend the obligation of military service to women, thus imposing on them the same disadvantages with regard to access to employment, or to abolish compulsory service.[46]

The case law on sex discrimination in the armed forces provides another example of the balance which the Court of Justice is keen to strike between the rights of Member States to protect the interests which are close to the core of their sovereignty and the constraints imposed by EU law on the exercise of these rights. Whilst not uncontroversial,[47] the judgments struck the right balance between the

[43] ibid, para 39.
[44] ibid, para 40.
[45] ibid, para 41.
[46] ibid.
[47] In relation to the judgment in *Sirdar*, for instance, Ellis thought 'the degree of gender-stereotyping contained within [the acceptance by the Court of the principle of operability as a valid rationale for excluding women form the Royal Marines] little short of staggering. Why, it may be asked, is it beyond question that a woman can be a chef but not a commando? And why did the Court not even pay lip service to the examination of this issue?': E Ellis, 'The recent jurisprudence of the Court of Justice in the field of sex equality' (2000) 37 *CML Rev* 1403, 1414–15.

effective application of EU law and the right of Member States to determine how best to protect their security interests. In *Sirdar* and *Kreil*, the Court sought to provide as comprehensive an answer as possible to a difficult problem: the former judgment illustrated how the discretion enjoyed by the Member States in the organisation of their armed forces may be exercised, whereas the latter made it clear that EU law would not grant a blanket exception to national measures regulating that area. As for the judgment in *Dory*, the outer limits of the exception were usefully drawn.[48]

B. EU Citizens' Rights

In secondary legislation governing the free movement of persons, the reference to public security is noteworthy for the grading scale of intensity of public security that the Citizens' Rights Directive introduces in different sets of circumstances.[49] Whilst a Member State may expel an EU citizen or a member of her family on grounds of public security,[50] in cases where the citizen has the right of permanent residence on its territory (that is, she has been resident there for at least five years), expulsion is only justified 'on serious grounds of public policy or public security'.[51] In cases where the citizen has resided in the host Member State for ten years, expulsion is justified only 'on imperative grounds of public security'.[52] The introduction of this grading scale of what constitutes a public security interest reflects two main considerations. The first is related to the severity of the measure which a Member State seeks to justify by relying upon the public security exception: expulsion is a drastic measure with profound implications for both the EU citizen and her family. The second consideration is related to the developing link between the EU citizen and the host Member State: the longer the residence in the territory of the latter, the deeper the link with its society and the more difficult for the national authorities to break that link by expelling the citizen (and her family where relevant).[53]

Whilst sensible in order to reflect the differing links between EU citizens and the host State, the different categories of public security in the CRD add further layers of complexity to the definition of a concept the content of which is already difficult to pinpoint. This is illustrated by the case law on 'imperative grounds of

[48] These issues are analysed in P Koutrakos, 'EC law and equal treatment in the armed forces' (2000) 25 *EL Rev* 433 and 'How far is far enough? EC law and the organization of the armed forces after *Dory*' (2003) 66 *MLR* 759.

[49] Dir 2004/38/EC [2004] OJ L 158/77.

[50] ibid, Art 27(1).

[51] ibid, Art 28(2).

[52] ibid, Art 28(3) where this highly restrictive condition is also imposed on expulsion orders on minors, except where such a measure is in accordance with the UN Convention on the Rights of the Child.

[53] See recitals 23 and 24 of the preamble to CRD.

public security'. In *Tsakouridis*, the Grand Chamber held that it 'presupposes not only the existence of a threat to public security, but also that such a threat is of a particularly high degree of seriousness'.[54] That case was about a Greek citizen whom Germany sought to expel after having been convicted for criminal offences in connection with dealing in narcotics as part of an organised group. The Court had no difficulty finding that such activity constituted 'a diffuse form of crime with impressive economic and operational resources and frequently with transnational connections' and 'could reach a level of intensity that might directly threaten the calm and physical security of the population as a whole or a large part of it'.[55] This conclusion was substantiated by reference to EU secondary legislation which deemed illicit drug trafficking a threat to health, safety and the quality of life of citizens of the Union, and to the legal economy, stability and security of the Member States.[56]

In *PI*, another Grand Chamber judgment 18 months later, the Court dealt with an Italian citizen who had lived in Germany all of his adult life and who, at the age of 41, was sentenced to imprisonment for the sexual assault, sexual coercion and rape of a minor, the daughter of his then partner.[57] What is noteworthy about the case is the approach of the Court to ascertaining the seriousness of the conduct in question. The starting point is EU law itself, both primary and secondary. In relation to the former, reference is made to Article 83(1) TFEU, which provides that the sexual exploitation of children is one of the areas of particularly serious crime with a cross-border dimension in which the EU legislature may intervene. There is, then, reference to Directive 2011/93 on combating the sexual abuse and sexual exploitation of children and child pornography which views sexual abuse and sexual exploitation of children as serious violations of fundamental rights and which provides for minimum prison sentences for specific offences.[58] In the light of the above, the Court concluded that criminal offences amounting to sexual exploitation of children may be covered by the concept of 'imperative grounds of public security' under Article 28(3) CRD provided that they constitute 'a particularly serious threat to one of the fundamental interests of society, which might pose a direct threat to the calm and physical security of the population'.[59] This was a matter for the referring court to decide.

The definition of the term 'imperative grounds of public security' in *PI* has been criticised for its wide scope[60] and has been deemed to undermine the enhanced

[54] Case C-145/09 *Tsakouridis* EU:C:2010:708.

[55] ibid, paras 46 and 47.

[56] First recital of preamble to Council Framework Dec 2004/757/JHA laying down minimum provisions on the constituent elements of criminal acts and penalties in the field of illicit drug trafficking [2004] OJ L 335/8.

[57] Case C-348/09 *PI* EU:C:2012:300.

[58] [2011] OJ L 335/1. The Court refers to the preamble to and Arts 3 and 9 of the Directive.

[59] Case C-348/09 *PI* (n 57) para 28.

[60] See G Anagnostaras, 'Enhanced Protection of EU Nationals against Expulsion and the Concept of Internal Public Security: Comment on the *PI* Case' (2012) 37 *EL Rev* 627.

protection which Article 28(3) CRD is designed to bestow.[61] In his Opinion, Advocate General Bot argued that the high threshold suggested by the term and articulated in *Tsakouridis* was not met. He pointed out the confined context within which the crime in *PI* had been committed (family) and the fact that the applicant had acted alone and independently of any network, and suggested that the risk for the wider society did not necessarily follow from the abhorrence of the crime.

Whilst the scope of 'imperative grounds of public security' in *PI* may appear wide enough to cover interests related to public policy,[62] it should be viewed within its specific context and the scheme set out in the CRD. Integration in the host Member State and social cohesion are central to the logic of the Directive. Criminal conduct of such nature as to attract the interest of the Union's legislature may run counter to what is central in order to 'strengthen the feeling of Union citizenship'.[63] Viewed from this angle, the extent to which EU primary and secondary law is relied upon by the Court in order to assess the conduct which national authorities seek to target is telling. Reference is made in Article 83(1) TFEU to a number of 'areas of particularly serious crime'.[64] In accordance with this provision, the 'cross-border dimension resulting from the nature or impact of such offences or from a special need to combat them on a common basis' triggers the Union's competence to adopt secondary legislation establishing minimum rules concerning the definition of criminal offences and sanctions in these areas. There is, therefore, a curious link which emerges from this line of reasoning: the existence of rules conferring on the EU the competence to legislate is relied upon in order to render a specific activity within the scope of powers of national authorities in order to restrict the application of EU law in cases where, otherwise, the moral underpinnings of EU citizenship might appear to be compromised.[65]

The marginalisation of the distinction between public policy and public security is troubling and by no means conducive to the clarification of these elusive concepts. Nonetheless, the question that arises is whether this contextual construction of public security runs counter to the exceptional nature of the measures laid down in Article 28 CRD. The answer to this question is negative in the

[61] See D Kochenov and B Pirker, 'Deporting the Citizens within the European Union: A Counter-Intuitive Trend in Case C-347/09, *P.I.*' (2013) 19 *Columbia Journal of European Law* 369 and D Kostakopoulou-Dochery and N Ferreira, 'Testing Liberal Norms: the Public Policy and Public Security Derogations and the Cracks in European Union Citizenship' (2014) 20 *Columbia Journal of European Law* 167.

[62] Azoulai and Coutts refer to 'the socialization of the concept of public security': L Azoulai and S Coutts, 'Restricting Union citizens' residence rights on grounds of public security. Where Union citizenship and the AFSJ meet: *P.I.*' (2013) 50 *CML Rev* 553, 559–61.

[63] Recital 17 to CRD. For an analysis of the concept of integration from a different perspective, see ch 5 in this volume.

[64] These are set out in the second subparagraph of Art 83(1) TFEU as follows: terrorism, trafficking in human beings and sexual exploitation of women and children, illicit drug trafficking, illicit arms trafficking, money laundering, corruption, counterfeiting of means of payment, computer crime and organised crime.

[65] See, to that effect, Azoulai and Coutts (n 62) 569–70.

light of the specific conditions under which national authorities are required to apply this interpretation. Two considerations need to be taken into account. The first is the detailed elaboration of what compliance with the principle of proportionality would entail. The sources for this are twofold. On the one hand, there is secondary legislation: the CRD follows up the reference to the principle by setting out a number of factors that need to be taken into account by the authorities of the host Member State considering expulsion, namely the personal conduct of the individual concerned, whether that represents a genuine, present and sufficiently serious threat affecting one of the fundamental interests of society,[66] as well as considerations such as how long the individual concerned has resided on its territory, her age, state of health, family and economic situation, social and cultural integration into the host Member State and the extent of her links with the country of origin.[67] This elaboration on what a proportionality assessment should entail draws upon the case law of the Court of Justice which introduced the principles now laid down in the CRD.[68] This illustration of a direct interaction between the EU legislature and judiciary in the context of the CRD is not confined to the latter's derogation provisions.[69]

On the other hand, the emphasis on what the monitoring of proportionality compliance would entail lies in the Court's own case law. The judgment in *Tsakouridis* is a case in point. It refers to the balance that needs to be struck between the exceptional nature of the threat to public security and the risk of compromising the social rehabilitation of the EU citizen in the State in which he has become genuinely integrated, the latter being not only in her interest but also in that of the EU in general. This balance requires that a range of factors be taken into account: as far as the risk to public security is concerned, these include the possible penalties and the sentences imposed, the degree of involvement in the criminal activity and the risk of reoffending,[70] as well as fundamental human rights, in particular the right to respect for private and family life.[71] As for the proportionality assessment, the Court sets out the factors which the referring court must take into account: the nature and seriousness of the offence committed, the duration of residence of the person concerned in the host Member State, the period which has passed since the offence was committed and the conduct of the person concerned during

[66] According to the Court, this is about the existence in the individual concerned of a propensity to act in the same way in the future: Case C-348/09 *PI* (n 57) para 30.

[67] Arts 27(3) and 28(1) CRD. See also Art 33(2) CRD.

[68] See, eg, Case 67/74 *Bonsignore* EU:C:1975:34 and Case 30/77 *Bouchereau* EU:C:1977:172.

[69] See F Wollenschlaeger, 'The judiciary, the legislature and the evolution of Union citizenship' in P Syrpis (ed), *The Judiciary, the Legislature and the EU Internal Market* (Cambridge, Cambridge University Press, 2012) 302 and, in the same collection, N Nic Shuibhne, 'The Third Age of EU citizenship: Directive 2004/38 in the case law of the Court of Justice' 331.

[70] See also Case 30/77 *Bouchereau* (n 68) para 29.

[71] Case C-145/09 *Tsakouridis* (n 54) para 52 with reference to Case C-400/10 PPU *McB* EU:C:2010:582 para 53.

that period, and the solidity of the social, cultural and family ties with the host Member State.[72]

The second feature of the application of the public security exception is its intense proceduralisation. Article 30(2) CRD refers to the right of the citizen targeted by an EU restriction to 'be informed, precisely and in full, of the public policy, public security or public health grounds on which the decision taken in their case is based'. However, this provision introduces an exception from the principle of full disclosure if 'this is contrary to the interests of State security'. In addition, Article 31 CRD sets procedural safeguards, including the right to appeal of the restrictive measure which should cover the examination of the legality of the decision, as well as of the facts and circumstances on which the latter is based.

These provisions were interpreted by the Court in another Grand Chamber judgment in *ZZ*.[73] This case was about a citizen of dual French and Algerian nationality married to a British citizen and lawfully resident in the UK for 15 years. Following a trip to Algeria, the UK cancelled his right of residence and refused him entry back into the UK on public security grounds. On appeal, the Secretary of State objected to the disclosure of information relied upon against the applicant. Instead, and in accordance with UK legislation, this information was disclosed to the two special advocates appointed to represent his interests. Two hearings took place, an open and a closed one, the latter in the absence of the applicant and his personal advisers, but in the presence of the special advocates who made submissions on his behalf. Similarly, the Special Immigration Appeals Commission rendered two judgments: an open and a closed one, the latter being provided only to the Secretary of State and the applicant's special advocates. The Commission relied on the information set out in the closed judgment and held that the applicant had been involved in terrorist activities and that he represented a genuine present and sufficiently serious threat which affects public security. It also acknowledged that little of the case against him had been disclosed to him and that what had been disclosed did not concern the critical issues of the case. The question referred by the Court of Appeal was whether the non-disclosure of information in the above circumstances was consistent with the right to judicial protection, set out in Article 30(2) CRD and guaranteed by Article 47 of the Charter on the right to an effective remedy and to a fair trial.

The Court articulates the answer to this question with reference to Article 47 of the Charter as well as the provision in Article 52(1) of the Charter according to which any limitations must respect the essence of the fundamental right and be proportionate and necessary in order to genuinely meet objectives of general interest recognised by the European Union. The main focus of the judgment is

[72] The Court points out that in the case of an EU citizen who has spent most or even all of her childhood and youth in the host Member State, 'very good reasons would have to be put forward to justify the expulsion measure': *Tsakouridis* (n 54) para 53.

[73] Case C-300/11 *ZZ* EU:C:2013:363.

the balance that needs to be struck between security and defence rights and, in its effort to bring this home, the judgment oscillates between statements of considerable abstraction and specific issues related to the procedure before the referring court. The Court of Justice held that, in exceptional cases where a national authority opposes precise and full disclosure pursuant to the provisions of Article 27 CRD, the national court 'must have at its disposal and apply techniques and rules of procedural law which accommodate, on the one hand, legitimate State security considerations regarding the nature and sources of the information taken into account in the adoption of such a decision and, on the other hand, the need to ensure sufficient compliance with the person's procedural rights, such as the right to be heard and the adversarial principle'.[74] In practical terms, this is about the provision by national law of 'effective judicial review both of the existence and validity of the reasons invoked by the national authority with regard to State security and of the legality of the decision taken under Article 27 CRD' as well as the provision of 'technique and rules relating to that review'.[75]

In the light of the above, the national court 'must carry out an independent examination of all the matters of law and fact relied upon by the competent national authority and it must determine, in accordance with the national procedural rules, whether State security stands in the way of such disclosure'.[76] If this question were answered in the affirmative, 'judicial review must be carried out in a procedure which strikes an appropriate balance between the requirements flowing from State security and the requirements of the right to effective judicial protection whilst limiting any interference with the exercise of that right to that which is strictly necessary'.[77] In practical terms, this suggests a distinction between the grounds for expulsion and the relevant evidence. As for the former, 'the person concerned must be informed, in any event, of the essence of the grounds on which a decision refusing entry under Article 27 [CRD] is based, as the necessary protection of State security cannot have the effect of denying the person concerned his right to be heard and, therefore, of rendering his right of redress as provided for in Article 31 of that directive ineffective'.[78] As for the evidence, the Court accepts that, [i]n certain cases, disclosure of that evidence is liable to compromise State security in a direct and specific manner, in that it may, in particular, endanger the life, health or freedom of persons or reveal the methods of investigation specifically used by the national security authorities and thus seriously impede, or even prevent, future performance of the tasks of those authorities'.[79]

[74] ibid, para 57 with reference to Case C-415/05 P *Kadi* EU:C:2008:30 para 344.
[75] ibid, para 58.
[76] ibid, para 62.
[77] ibid, para 64.
[78] ibid, para 65.
[79] ibid, para 66.

It is for the national court to assess 'whether and to what extent the restrictions on the rights of the defence arising in particular from a failure to disclose the evidence and the precise and full grounds on which the decision taken under Article 27 [CRD] is based are such as to affect the evidential value of the confidential evidence'.[80] It is also for the national court, 'first, to ensure that the person concerned is informed of the essence of the grounds which constitute the basis of the decision in question in a manner which takes due account of the necessary confidentiality of the evidence and, second, to draw, pursuant to national law, the appropriate conclusions from any failure to comply with that obligation to inform him'.[81]

The judgment in *ZZ* sets out an elaborate analysis of what national courts are required to do in applying the public security derogation under the CRD, as one might expect. In doing so, it follows the path set out in the *Kadi* line of cases (to which it refers expressly).[82] The Court also refrained from deciding the substantive point at issue, a temptation which it does not always resist.[83] When the case went back to the referring court the Court of Appeal, in a judgment by Lord Justice Richards, held that the Court of Justice's judgment in *ZZ* 'lays down with reasonable clarity that the essence of the grounds on which the decision was based must always be disclosed to the person concerned. That is a minimum requirement which cannot yield to the demands of national security. Nor is there anything particularly surprising about such a result in the context of restrictions on the fundamental rights of free movement and residence of Union citizens under EU law'.[84]

Following a detailed and careful assessment of the Court's judgment, the Court of Appeal held that the appellant had not been given the minimum level of disclosure that EU law required. It reached this conclusion having examined both the closed and open judgment of the Special Immigration Appeals Commission and having heard from one of the two special advocates and the barrister acting for the Secretary of State in closed sessions. It did not consider it necessary to render a closed judgment.

The *ZZ* litigation illustrates another aspect of the interpretation and application of the public security derogation, namely the close co-operation between national courts and the Court of Justice. Consistently with the picture which emerged from the analysis of the *Campus Oil* case law in Section II, there is no evidence of misuse of the discretion granted to national courts by the EU's judiciary. In fact, national courts engage actively in a detailed and meaningful assessment of proportionality on the basis of a careful reading of the guidance provided by the Court of Justice.

[80] ibid, para 67.
[81] ibid, para 68.
[82] Case C-415/05 P *Kadi* (n 74).
[83] See, eg, Case C-470/93 *Mars* EU:C:1995:224.
[84] Case No SC/63/2007 *ZZ v Secretary of State for the Home Department* [2014] EWCA Civ 7, [2014] QB 820 para 18.

For instance, in 2012, the Court of Appeal in England and Wales relied heavily on the judgment in *Tsakouridis* and held that committing a serious violent offence against the person justifying a sentence of eight years' imprisonment, along with other offences, did not meet the standards required by the 'imperative grounds of public security' to justify deportation.[85]

In another case, concerning a Dutch national convicted of handling stolen goods and, later, robbery, the Court of Appeal allowed the appeal against a decision of a First-Tier Tribunal which carried out a proportionality analysis without examining the EU law dimension.[86] The Court of Appeal referred specifically to the judgment in *Tsakouridis* and the issues which the Tribunal ought to have examined in the context of the proportionality analysis (namely 'the risk of compromising the social rehabilitation of the Union citizen in the State in which he has become genuinely integrated, which … is not only in his interest but also in that of the European Union in general').[87]

Whilst the discretion of the executive in the host Member State is recognised, national courts also accept that restrictions on free movement are to be interpreted narrowly and have accepted their duty to scrutinise the reasons for any such restrictions. The Court of Appeal in Northern Ireland, for instance, quashed a deportation order of two Dutch sisters which provided no analysis of the reasons for the deportation, such as the risk of reoffending.[88] It held that the decision provided no evidence that it was based exclusively on the personal conduct of the individuals concerned.

The analysis so far highlighted three main points. First, the notion of public security is interpreted in a deeply contextualised manner which has given rise to controversy and may appear to render its definition somewhat elusive. Second, this approach is counterbalanced by a deeply proceduralised understanding of the requirements which national authorities must meet when they rely on the public security exception and a detailed guidance provided to national courts. Third, the limited review set out in this chapter suggests that national courts appear to pay heed to the guidance provided by the Court of Justice.

IV. WHOLLY EXCEPTIONAL CLAUSES IN PRIMARY LAW

The above analysis dealt with the extent to which the Union legal order enables Member States to deviate when they deem it necessary. The exceptional clauses

85 *FV (Italy) v Secretary of State for the Home Department* [2012] EWCA Civ 1199, [2013] 1 WLR 3339.

86 *R (Daha Essa) v Upper Tribunal (Immigration and Asylum Chamber) and another* [2012] EWCA Civ 1718.

87 Case C-145/09 *Tsakouridis* (n 54) para 50, quoted by the Court of Appeal in *Daha Essa*, ibid.

88 *In the Matter of Applications by Siegnerella Elaine Flaneur and Siegnette Elaine Flaneur for Judicial Review* [2011] NICA 72. For an example of a proportionality analysis sanctioned by the Court of Appeal, see *Wolfgang Schmelz v The Immigration Appeal Tribunal* [2004] EWCA Civ 29.

examined above enable national authorities to deviate from specific EU law principles and rules provided that certain conditions are met. However, there are two further clauses in primary law which are defined as 'wholly exceptional'[89] for two reasons: on the one hand, there is no limit to the type of measure which a Member State may adopt and, on the other hand, in adopting such a measure, the State in question may deviate from the entire body of EU law. These provisions are laid down in Articles 346 and 347 TFEU. The former is about trade in and production of arms, munitions and war materials, and the latter is about extraordinary circumstances related to national and international security.

A. Article 347 TFEU

Article 347 TFEU reads as follows:

> Member States shall consult each other with a view to taking together the steps needed to prevent the functioning of the internal market being affected by measures which a Member State may be called upon to take in the event of serious internal disturbances affecting the maintenance of law and order, in the event of war, serious international tension constituting a threat of war, or in order to carry out obligations it has accepted for the purpose of maintaining peace and international security.

The poor drafting of the above provision is striking.[90] The reference, first, to the consultation amongst Member States and then to the national deviation from EU law, as well as the use of the term 'called upon', may suggest that, rather than conferring a right, Article 347 TFEU acknowledges the inherent duty of the Member States to act as fully sovereign subjects of international law. After all, the four sets of circumstances mentioned therein under which Member States may deviate from the entire *corpus* of EU law are exceptional in their significance and touch upon the very core of the function of the State and, therefore, the latter's sovereignty. That they render the action of the State necessary hardly seems worthy of further analysis.

However, the wholly exceptional nature of the circumstances which may necessitate national action and its implications notwithstanding, Article 347 TFEU introduces three sets of conditions which the Member State must meet. The first is substantive: it is only in the circumstances laid down therein that a Member

[89] Case 222/84 *Johnston* (n 40) para 27. See also the Opinion of AG Jacobs in Case C-120/94 *Commission v Greece (FYROM)* EU:C:1995:109 para 46.

[90] For an analysis, see P Koutrakos, 'Is Article 297 EC "a reserve of sovereignty"?' (2000) 37 *CML Rev* 1339, and C Stefanou and H Xanthaki, *A Legal and Political Interpretation of Articles 224 and 225 of the Treaty of Rome: The Former Yugoslav Republic of Macedonia Cases* (Aldershot, Dartmouth and Ashgate, 1997).

State may deviate from EU law. The second set is procedural: the Member State which deems it necessary to act in such circumstances should consult with other Member States in order to adopt a common approach aiming to protect the internal market. In this context, the Commission is also to be involved. According to Article 348(1) TFEU,

> If measures taken in the circumstances referred to in Articles 346 and 347 have the effect of distorting the conditions of competition in the internal market, the Commission shall, together with the State concerned, examine how these measures can be adjusted to the rules laid down in the Treaties.

The above are duties imposed under primary law, and the Member States are bound by the duty of co-operation which is set out in Article 4(3) TEU in terms more elaborate than in the previous constitutional arrangements:

> Pursuant to the principle of sincere cooperation, the Union and the Member States shall, in full mutual respect, assist each other in carrying out tasks which flow from the Treaties.
>
> The Member States shall take any appropriate measure, general or particular, to ensure fulfilment of the obligations arising out of the Treaties or resulting from the acts of the institutions of the Union.
>
> The Member States shall facilitate the achievement of the Union's tasks and refrain from any measure which could jeopardise the attainment of the Union's objectives.

The conditions set out in Article 347 TFEU and implied by the duty of co-operation are not the only reminders that the wholly exceptional role of Member States should be carried out within EU law parameters. Article 348(2) TFEU sets out an extraordinary procedure for judicial review to be relied upon by the Commission or a Member State in cases where another Member state 'makes improper use of the powers provided for in Articles 346 and 347 TFEU. The seriousness of the issues at stake is illustrated by the provision for the Court's ruling to be given *in camera*.

It follows from the above that a course of action deemed by Member States necessary in order to protect public security may not be chosen without any consideration at all for the Union legal order even in cases of extraordinary seriousness. This is entirely consistent with the picture which emerged from the analysis of the exceptional clauses set out in primary and secondary Union law. However, the 'wholly exceptional' nature of the circumstances set out in Article 347 TFEU as well as the Article 348 TFEU procedure raise questions about the enforcement of the EU law conditions outlined above. What is the level of supervision which the Commission and the Member States are prepared to exercise? What is the intensity of control which the Court of Justice deems appropriate? To what extent are Member States free to determine how best to respond to what they deem to be a serious threat to their ability to protect their citizens and their duty to protect their, as well as the international, security?

The record and the practice of the relevant actors so far, or rather the lack thereof, only allude to the answer to this question: there has only been one action brought against a Member State under Article 348 TFEU.[91] Given the maturity of the Union legal order, this suggests reluctance by both the Commission and Member States to challenge choices made by a State in circumstances which the latter deems exceptional. This case was *Commission v Greece (re: FYROM)*, the subject-matter of which was the embargo imposed by Greece against FYROM (the Former Yugoslav Republic of Macedonia).[92] The Commission alleged a violation of the precursor to Article 297 TFEU (Article 297 EC). The Court delivered no judgment on this case, as the embargo was lifted and the Commission withdrew the action early enough. However, Advocate General Jacobs delivered an Opinion which touched upon the most central issues raised when a State deems that a deviation from EU law is necessary in order to protect vital interests.

His analysis is based on a subtle understanding of the complex issues underpinning the case. Whilst he affirmed the existence of the role of both supervision by the Commission and judicial review by the Court in the areas covered by Articles 347 and 348 TFEU, he pointed out that the 'scope and intensity of the review that can be exercised by the Court is ... severely limited on account of the nature of the issues raised'.[93] Advocate General Jacobs referred to the 'paucity of judicially applicable criteria' in the area[94] and 'the extremely limited nature of the judicial review that may be carried out in this area'.[95] He argued that, in essence, such review was confined to determining whether reliance upon Article 347 TFEU involved manifest errors or abuse of power. He concluded that 'the question must be judged from the point of view of the Member State concerned' and elaborated as follows:[96]

> Because of differences of geography and history each of the Member States has its own specific problems and preoccupations in the field of foreign and security policy. Each Member State is better placed than the Community institutions or the other Member States when it is a question of weighing up the dangers posed for it by the conduct of a third State. Security is, moreover, a matter of perception rather than hard fact. What one Member State perceives as an immediate threat to its external security may strike another Member State as relatively harmless.

Choosing his words carefully,[97] Advocate General Jacobs concluded that the imposition of the embargo by Greece could not be said to be 'wholly unreasonable ...

[91] The precursor to Art 347 TFEU was invoked in the late 1960s and 1970s by the Member States in order to impose economic sanctions on third countries: see Koutrakos, *Trade, Foreign Policy and Defence* (n 20) 58–60.

[92] Case C-120/94 *Commission v Greece (FYROM)* (n 89).

[93] ibid, para 50.

[94] ibid.

[95] ibid, para 60.

[96] ibid, para 54.

[97] Further in his Opinion, AG Jacobs points out that 'what matters is not so much that Greece's fears may be unfounded but rather that those fears appear to be genuinely and firmly held by the Greek Government and, it would appear, by the bulk of the Greek people. Where a government and a people are fervently convinced that a foreign State is usurping a part of their cultural patrimony and has long-term designs on a part of their national territory, it would be difficult to say that war is such an unlikely

even if [the threat of war] may be long-term and remote'.[98] In addition to its careful wording, the Opinion in *Commission v Greece* is also characterised by the striking absence of any reference to the procedural aspects of Article 347 TFEU and the failure by Greece to comply with them.[99] If anything, his nuanced and balanced approach struck a balance between State sovereignty and the Union legal order in a manner which left national authorities considerable leeway: the rejection of any claim by the Member States to a *domaine réservé* is accompanied by an acknowledgment of their discretion to determine how best to protect their security; the requirement that reliance upon the notion of necessity, purported to justify a national deviation from EU law, be subject to EU control is followed by an understanding of this notion in sufficiently broad terms to accommodate national concerns; the full application of EU control mechanisms entails the active involvement of national courts which are entrusted with the application of the principle of proportionality.

B. Article 346 TFEU[100]

Article 346 TFEU reads as follows:

> 1. The provisions of the Treaties shall not preclude the application of the following rules:
>
> (a) no Member State shall be obliged to supply information the disclosure of which it considers contrary to the essential interests of its security;
>
> (b) any Member State may take such measures as it considers necessary for the protection of the essential interests of its security which are connected with the production of or trade in arms, munitions and war material; such measures shall not adversely affect the conditions of competition in the internal market regarding products which are not intended for specifically military purposes.
>
> 2. The Council may, acting unanimously on a proposal from the Commission, make changes to the list, which it drew up on 15 April 1958, of the products to which the provisions of paragraph 1(b) apply.

For a long time, this rather obscure provision of the EU Treaty was viewed as placing defence industries beyond the reach of EU law entirely. A broad interpretation of its wording was used to substantiate this: on the one hand, the scope of products which fell within the scope of Article 346 TFEU was viewed as potentially

hypothesis that the threat of war can be excluded altogether. If such matters were to be judged exclusively by what external observers regarded as reasonable behaviour, wars might never occur' (para 58).

[98] ibid, para 56.

[99] See the criticism in Koutrakos, 'Is Article 297 EC "a reserve of sovereignty"?' (n 90) 1356–59.

[100] This section draws upon P Koutrakos, 'The application of EC law to defence-related industries—changing interpretations of Article 296 EC' in C Barnard and O Odudu (eds), *The Outer Limits of European Union Law* (Oxford, Hart Publishing, 2009) 307.

unlimited; on the other hand, the circumstances under which Member States could deviate from EU law were ignored or viewed as merely indicative of the general status of the defence industries as directly linked to national sovereignty. Therefore, the Member States were only too keen to presume that measures regulating their defence industries would be beyond the scope of EU law.[101] This approach was tolerated by the EU institutions.[102] The elusive character of the list mentioned in Article 346(2) TFEU did not help either: it was only published in the *Official Journal of the European Union* 43 years following its adoption in a response by the Commission to a question by the European Parliament.[103]

However, a careful reading of Article 346 TFEU suggests that this approach is misguided. First, the proviso of Article 346 TFEU is confined to the products which are described in the list mentioned in Article 346(2) TFEU. Therefore, the reference to 'the production of or trade in arms, munitions and war material' was not envisaged as an open-ended category of products. This suggests that at no point was it envisaged that dual-use goods, that is products which may be of both civil and military application, should be regulated by national measures deviating from the entire body of EU law. Such an argument is supported both by the content of the list mentioned in Article 346(2) TFEU, and the reference to the effects that such measures should not have on 'products which are not intended for specifically military purposes' in Article 346(1)(b) TFEU.

Second, measures adopted by a Member State under Article 346 TFEU are not ipso facto justified; instead, the deviation from EU law which they entail must be 'necessary for the protection of the essential interests of [national] security'. This is quite an emphatic statement that, rather than being merely a public security clause, Article 346(b) TFEU should be invoked only when the protection of the core of national sovereignty is at stake.

Third, any reliance upon Article 346 TFEU should take into account the effects which its deviation from EU law may have on the status and movement of other products which fall beyond its rather narrow scope. In effect, this provision suggests that national measures deviating from EU law as a whole should not be adopted in a legal vacuum. Instead, Member States are under a duty to consider the implications that such measures may have for the internal market.

Fourth, Article 348(1) TFEU provides for the involvement of the Commission in cases where reliance upon Article 346 TFEU by a Member State would lead to distortions of competition. This provision should be interpreted in the light of the duty of loyal co-operation enshrined in Article 4(3). In other words, a Member State invoking Article 346 TFEU is under a legal duty to co-operate with

[101] In relation to public procurement, see COM (2004) 608 final *Green Paper on Defence Procurement* 6.

[102] See Koutrakos, *Trade, Foreign Policy and Defence* (n 20) 175–82.

[103] Written Question E-1324/01 [2001] OJ C/364E/85. In the meantime, it had only been published in academic analyses: see H Wulf (ed), *Arms Industry Limited* (Oxford, Oxford University Press, 1993) 214.

the Commission in order to adjust any ensuing distortions of competition to the EU law.

Finally, any deviation from EU law under Article 346 TFEU is subject to the jurisdiction of the Court of Justice. The reference to the 'improper use of the powers provided for in Article … 346' in Article 348(2) TFEU refers both to the substantive and procedural conditions which need to be met by a Member State invoking Article 346 TFEU.

It follows from the above that, according to a strict reading of Articles 346 TFEU and 348 TFEU, Member States may regulate their defence industries by deviating from EU law only in so far as such a deviation is confined to a specific class of products, is exercised in accordance with certain principles, and is subject to the jurisdiction of the Court of Justice to ascertain whether it amounts to an abuse of power.

This interpretation has gradually been accepted as a matter of EU law. This has been due to the case law of the Union's judges.[104] In its first judgment on the applicability of Article 346 TFEU, the Court of Justice left no doubt as to the strict interpretation of this provision. In Case C-414/97 *Commission v Spain*,[105] the Court dealt with Spanish legislation exempting from VAT intra-Community imports and acquisitions of arms, munitions and equipment exclusively for military use. It examined the policy objective of the Spanish measure (to determine and allocate the financial resources for the modernisation of the Spanish armed forces) and held that VAT exemptions were not necessary for the protection of Spain's essential security interests. This was because any income from payment of VAT (apart from a small percentage passed on to the EU) would flow into the State's coffers.

This robust approach suggests that Article 346 TFEU does not entail a complete reserve of sovereignty for Member States. Instead, the latter are required to substantiate how the deviation from EU law they deem necessary meets the substantive conditions set out in primary law. Subsequent case law by both the General Court and the Court of Justice[106] has adopted this approach and has also stressed the narrow material scope of Article 346 TFEU.[107]

[104] Another factor has been the gradual adoption of secondary legislation applicable to defence industries in areas such as public procurement and intra-Union transfers. See the analysis in P Koutrakos, *The EU Common Security and Defence Policy* (Oxford, Oxford University Press, 2013) Ch 9 and M Trybus, *Buying Defence and Security in Europe—The EU Defence and Security Procurement Directive in Context* (Cambridge: Cambridge University Press, 2014).

[105] Case C-414/97 *Commission v Spain* EU:C:1999:417.

[106] Case T-26/01 *Fiocchi* EU:T:2003:248; Case C-337/05 *Commission v Italy* EU:C:2008:203; Case C-157/06 *Commission v Italy* EU:C:2008:530; Case C-284/05 *Commission v Finland* EU:C:2009:778; Case C-294/05 *Commission v Sweden* EU:C:2009:779; Case C-372/05 *Commission v Germany* EU:C:2009:780; Case C-409/05 *Commission v Greece* EU:C:2009:782; Case C-461/05 *Commission v Denmark* EU:C:2009:783; Case C-378/05 *Commission v Italy* EU:C:2006:581; Case C-239/06 *Commission v Italy* EU:C:2009:784; Case C-615/10 *Insinööritoimisto InsTiimi Oy* EU:C:2012:324.

[107] In Case C-337/05 *Commission v Italy*, ibid, the Grand Chamber pointed out that 'the purchase of equipment, the use of which for military purposes is hardly certain, must necessarily comply with

There is a thread which brings together the case law on the application of Article 346 TFEU and that on other public security exceptions, namely the absence of specific substantive arguments by Member States. Instead, the defence of national authorities is confined to vague arguments about public security and the national interest. In *Commission v Italy*, for instance, the Italian Government argued that a deviation from the EU public procurement rules was necessary, on the one hand, in order to protect the confidentiality of information about the production of helicopters and, on the other hand, in order to protect the interoperability of the Italian fleet of helicopters.[108] The Court dismissed both. It considered the former disproportionate and pointed out that no reasons were presented to justify why the confidentiality of the information communicated for the production of the helicopters manufactured by the company chosen by the Italian authorities would be less well guaranteed were such production entrusted to other companies, in Italy or in other Member States. Similarly, no reason was provided as to the latter. In the same case, the defences put forward by the Italian Government were staggering in their generality and for the absence of any specific argument whatever which would substantiate, even remotely, their decision. The helicopters that the Italian Government sought to shield from the application of the EU's public procurement rules were envisaged for the use of a wide range of forces, the links of which with the essence of national security were hardly obvious. They included the Corps of Fire Brigades, the Carabinieri, the Coastguard, the Guardia di Finanza Revenue Guard Corps, the State Police and the Department of Civil Protection in the Presidency of the Council of Ministers. Another example of poor defence tactics is illustrated by the series of actions by the Commission against a number of Member States concerning the application of customs legislation on imports of defence equipment and dual-use goods—in the context of which Advocate General Ruiz-Jarabo Colomer described the arguments of the Member States as 'extremely confused' and he stated that he was 'unable to conceal [his] surprise at the manner in which the Member States' approached Article 346 TFEU 'throughout the proceedings'.[109]

Viewed against this paucity of detailed arguments and the tendency of Member States to rely upon vague pronouncements about public security,[110] the rigour with which the Court has interpreted and applied Article 346 TFEU recently is not surprising. The cases on which the Court has rendered the above rulings were

the rules governing the award of public contracts. The supply of helicopters to military corps for the purpose of civilian use must comply with those same rules' (para 47).

[108] ibid.

[109] Opinion in Case C-284/05 *Commission v Finland* EU:C:2009:67; Case C-294/05 *Commission v Sweden*; Case C-372/05 *Commission v Germany*; Case C-409/05 *Commission v Greece*; Case C-461/05 *Commission v Denmark*; Case C-387/05 *Commission v Italy* [2009] I-11705 paras 114 and 113 respectively.

[110] For a similar argument in the context of consumer protection, see the chapter by S Weatherill in this book.

about egregious violations of both the wording and spirit of Article 346 TFEU which exemplified the presumption, widely held by Member States, that primary law reserved for them complete freedom in a domain the scope of which they had the authority to define themselves. Viewed from this angle, it by no means follows that the Court would adopt an intrusive and activist approach once substantive policy choices are explained properly in relation to the requirements set out in Article 346 TFEU.

Finally, there is another theme which emerges from the more recent case law of the Court of Justice on Article 346 TFEU and is about the role of the national courts. In *Insinööritoimisto InsTiimi Oy*, the Court left it to the referring Finnish court to decide whether the conditions laid down in Article 346 TFEU were met in the case of a supply contract of tiltable turnable equipment which the Finnish Government considered beyond the scope of EU public procurement legislation because it was intended for simulating combat situations.[111] The judgment also provided guidance to national courts as to the issues which they needed to assess in order to ascertain the applicability of Article 346 TFEU to the products in question. On the one hand, this role of national courts is an inherent feature of the preliminary reference procedure. On the other hand, and the considerable divergence with which it has been respected by the Court of Justice notwithstanding, it becomes all the more significant viewed within the wholly exceptional context of Article 346 TFEU. After all, the examination of the sensitive matters related to the essential interests of security of the Member States is not to be carried out by a supranational institution which would be removed from the unique political realities which exist in different Member States. Viewed against the analysis of the primary and secondary law public security derogations examined above in this chapter, the role of national courts, as well as the guidance on proportionality review provided by the Court of Justice, emerge as a thread which brings together different strands of the case law.

V. CONCLUSION

This chapter has explored the interpretation and application of public security derogations in different contexts of EU primary and secondary law. It has shown that EU law introduces various distinctions in the definition of public security in different areas, hence complicating further the interpretation of what is an inherently politically charged concept. To distinguish between 'public security', 'serious grounds of public security', 'imperative grounds of public security', 'the essential interests of [national] security' and the interests laid down in Article 346 TFEU would challenge even the subtlest and most discerning of judges.

[111] n 106.

An assessment of the interpretation and application of public security derogations ought to take into account two related practical considerations. The first is about the legal context within which cases reach the Court of Justice and the ensuing function of judgments to provide a specific answer to a set of specific questions aiming to settle a specific dispute. The temptation of legal scholars to expect a comprehensive treatise on EU law concepts every time the Court is called upon to decide a case is to be resisted, and we should expect that judgments may be confined to their specific factual and legal context. The second practical consideration is that the quest for complete certainty in the law of derogations is elusive. The co-existence of national courts and the CJEU, the principle of distinct roles for them and the practice of interlocking functions, as well as the deeply politicised nature of the issues related to public security are only some of the factors which highlight the inherently incremental development of the state of the law in the area.

Taking these considerations into account, a number of interrelated themes about the interpretation and application of public security exceptions emerge from the analysis in this chapter. First, the different formulations of public security in different legal settings have given rise to a contextual analysis of the definition of this concept, at times questioning its distinction from public policy. However, where the content of public security may appear somewhat relativised, it is accompanied by heavy emphasis on the substantive and procedural conditions which national authorities must meet and detailed guidance on the issues that national courts ought to examine in the context of proportionality review. In the definition of public security derogations, guidance on proportionality review and the articulation of a heavily proceduralised framework within which national authorities are expected to exercise their discretion counterbalance the criticism against the Court for lowering the bar for Member States.[112]

Second, in relation to the Treaties' wholly exceptional provisions, the Court has adopted a narrow approach to public security. To do otherwise would have been tantamount to granting Member States a policy area of ill-defined limits within which they could act with no regard for EU law. Viewed from this angle, a process of normalisation emerges which brings the law governing such areas closer to the mainstream of the EU legal order. However, this by no means suggests that the Court is keen to address substantive policy choices which fall within the discretion of national authorities and lie within the political sphere. Instead, the case law examined in this chapter highlights the requirement that such choices are carried out and substantiated with due regard to EU law principles.

Third, the political sensitivity of issues touching upon public security has made Member States complacent when it comes to justifying their choice to derogate from free movement. The absence of substantive engagement with the principles

[112] See C Barnard, 'Free movement of natural persons' in C Barnard and S Peers (eds), *European Union Law* (Oxford: Oxford University Press, 2014) 356, 398.

of necessity and proportionality and the reliance upon vague pronouncements about public interest in some of the cases discussed in this chapter is remarkable. The questionable quality of the arguments put forward by Member States in the context of free movement exceptions is by no means confined to public security cases. For instance, in the early case law on free movement of services and health care, the Court noticed the failure of Member States to adduce any concrete evidence of the detrimental effect that reimbursement of the cost of operations in other Member States would have for the regulation of national health systems.[113]

Fourth, a finely balanced picture emerges: on the one hand, there is no evidence to suggest that the Court of Justice does not take the public security concerns of Member States seriously; on the other hand, there is no evidence to suggest that national courts do not take their duties to comply with the principles set out by the Court of Justice in the area seriously.

The analysis in this chapter has focused on a public interest which lies near the core of national sovereignty. And yet, the interpretation and application of public security in EU legal clauses suggests that the case law in the area is not all that exceptional. Instead, it is based on the main principles of EU substantive law (broad interpretation of free movement provisions, narrow interpretation of exceptions, and intensive review based on proportionality), taking into account the policy framework against which public security is invoked and setting out a deeply proceduralised context within which national authorities are required to exercise their policy discretion and national courts are expected to monitor it.

[113] See the early analysis in P Koutrakos, 'Healthcare as an Economic Service under EC Law' in M Dougan and E Spaventa (eds), *Social Welfare and EU Law* (Oxford: Hart Publishing, 2005) 106.

11

Free Movement, the Quality of Life and the Myth that the Court Balances Interests

GARETH DAVIES

I. INTRODUCTION

THIS CHAPTER IS about the impact of free movement on the quality of life of Europeans, and whether harmful effects on that quality can be used to justify derogations from free movement law. The starting point of the chapter's argument is the observation that in principle such arguments should be possible, but in fact, they are not made, or at least not acknowledged by the Court: a concern for quality of life is absent from the judgments. The ambition of the chapter is then to explore the ways in which quality of life is perhaps different from other interests which appear in the case law, such as consumer protection, the environment, and so on. Can such differences explain the different treatment? The focus is on differences which are relevant to adjudication, which might make quality of life concerns difficult to accept, assess, or justify.

In order to approach this question, the chapter considers how the process of free movement adjudication works. In particular it examines the idea that free movement law is all about balancing interests—those of free movement and integration, and often of a particular individual, on one side, and legitimate public interest objectives on the other, these public interest objectives encompassing all those matters which the Court has acknowledged as actual or potential mandatory requirements, as well as, of course, those exceptions explicitly found in the Treaty.

The suggestion here is that there is no explicit balancing of interests in free movement law. Implicitly it may be present, in that any decision brings some kinds of cost for someone, and so represents a sort of conclusion that the damaged interests weigh less than others at stake. However, the explicit law, the doctrine and principles which found and support the judgments, contains barely a hint of such weighing. On the contrary, the law is quite clear that free movement adjudication is about reconciliation of interests, by one of two possible paths: either the state achieves its public interest objective in a way that permits free movement, or, if that is not possible, the EU is granted authorisation to begin harmonisation, with the goal of a legislative reconciliation of free movement with the public interest at stake. Neither outcome contains even the slightest suggestion that, for example, the interests of the consumer, the environment, or the stability of institutions might have to suffer for the sake of the market. The law is consistent: all good things can be had together within the framework of the Treaty.

This highlights how quality of life concerns are different from others which have been raised. For unlike consumer or environmental matters they are often more fundamentally at odds with the internal market. The quality of life which this chapter will consider is the quality that is contributed by maintaining traditions, shared practices and products, small-scale businesses, and by limiting choice, and by taking decisions together about the shape of society. It is the pleasure which a community may find in communally making and protecting a distinctive kind of society, in which bonds with each other and with the past have a value that may, sometimes, be greater than the value of reduced prices or increased choice. That quality of life concern is inherently at odds with free movement, so that to speak of pursuing it by 'less restrictive and more proportionate' means is to miss the nature of what it is. On the other hand, it is inherently at odds with harmonisation, because to move regulation of such things to the Union level is to take away precisely the social and expressive value of deciding them locally.

Quality of life concerns thus do not fit within the current structure of the law. To recognise them would be to frustrate the current process of adjudication and turn it into something else, so that instead of each judgment being a constructive decision about how to take European integration further, it would become a decision about whether it can go further at all, or must, in the particular context, come to a stop. Quality of life is a cake that cannot be had and eaten.

This does not provide a reason why the Court must or should ignore quality of life arguments. However embarrassing to the integration process, they could nevertheless become part of the law. In that sense the chapter fails to provide a satisfying answer to the question that it sets—why they are ignored—unless one believes that an underlying awareness of how problematic they would be does in fact influence the Court. That is not entirely impossible, but it is not a hypothesis which is further pursued here. Rather, it is hoped that the value of the chapter lies in one of two perspectives that it tries to reveal. Either, the choice to consider quality of life derogations provides an illuminating perspective on free movement law, highlighting how balance is absent and reconciliation is central. This is in fact the path of discovery which the author followed, upon beginning to investigate quality of life and free movement law. Alternatively, one can reverse this, and note that examining how free movement adjudication works, and the centrality of reconciliation, highlights how threatening and troublesome quality of life concerns are for economic law.

II. THE MEANING OF QUALITY OF LIFE

Regulation may have many purposes. Among those which feature prominently in free movement law are the protection of the consumer, of the environment, and of the stability of public institutions. Yet as well as its explicit purposes—the goals which regulators more-or-less consciously want to achieve by adopting or maintaining it—regulation may also have consequences. The English landscape is the product of laws which were explicitly concerned with private property and its delineation, but they led to a distinctively pretty patchwork of hedges and small fields. The shape and size of beer and wine glasses in cafes in many countries is the product of regulation which could be described as consumer protection law, but if those glasses were to change or disappear the concern would be—should be—not that the consumer was now at risk, but that a pleasant tradition was being lost.

Traditions, practices, habits, and aesthetically pleasing side effects can be seen as part of the quality of life. So can other matters, such as the sense of shared identity and belonging which may arise when a community lives and consumes in a common way. Some of these are discussed below in the context of free movement cases which impact on these things.

Of course, the environment and the protection of the consumer and the existence of well-functioning public institutions are also in a sense part of the quality of life. They matter to our contentment. However, when this chapter speaks of quality of life it is concerned with the more second-order concerns described above, those aspects of life which are to some extent the consequence of law, but not its primary purpose. These quality of life concerns have certain characteristics which make them difficult for the law to deal with, despite their importance. Four observations will try to make this clear.

First, consequences tend to be harder for EU law to accept than purposes. Although free movement law is generally considered to be effects-based, when national measures are being reviewed they are usually assessed against their explicit purpose, no doubt because this is less contested and easier to establish. However, consequences may in fact be far more socially important than purpose (however distressing this is to the egos of regulators). The contribution made by a law to quality of life may reside primarily, or to a large extent, in its second-order effects. The importance of the German Beer Purity law to Germany is not really captured by a discussion of consumer protection. What it is like to live in a country without junk beer, and the existence of a shared experience through all strata of society, are the matters at stake.

Second, these quality of life issues tend to be non-quantifiable, and difficult even to assess in any objective way. Because their value lies in the subjective value given to a certain style of life, to objectify them is almost to demean them. Yet adjudication loves objectivity, and in its search for legitimacy and authority will inevitably deal more easily with matters that can be established by data and expertise. How does one distinguish a genuine quality of life argument from an opportunistic attempt at protectionism? The fact that national politics has produced or maintained a rule is an argument that it does represent a genuine subjective preference of the population, and so should be accorded value, yet this is again troublesome for EU law: if 'but we have chosen for this rule and we like it' is a justification for restricting free movement, then free movement law becomes somewhat more complicated, even perhaps residual. Relying on quality of life to restrict free movement can thus seem like an attack on the very essence of the internal market, a point which will be considered again below.

Third, it is often the case that the consequences of a rule for the texture of society arise not because of the particular content of that rule, but simply because there is a rule. It is the fact of standardisation as such which may shape life, by creating shared expectations and experiences. The German Beer Purity law would be no more or less socially important if the actual ingredients permitted were slightly different. The creation of a market is, to some extent, a commitment to protecting and enhancing individual choice, which makes it difficult to know how to deal with rules whose merit is precisely in limiting choice, not because of a market failure or externality, but for its own sake: because a community's self-bondage can make membership of that community a more enriching experience.

This leads to the fourth problem. It is not just the fact of the rule that matters, but also the fact of its authorship. Self-bondage is a very different experience from bondage by another. Where communities define the limits of individualism internally they may enhance the value of membership, but this enhancement would not be the case if the limits were imposed. The value of restrictions and standards for quality of life arises also because they are the product of those limited, an expression of autonomy. It is not paradoxical, but entirely logical, that our greatest expression of autonomy is found in a decision to restrain ourselves in an apparently arbitrary way (the standard might have been different, and no standard is really needed …). That very arbitrariness shows that we are serving no external purpose or master, whether Brussels, the dictates of economic theory or vested interests. It is being silly that is an expression of freedom, not being sensible.

Quality of life, as the term is used here, is thus not amenable to harmonisation. Once a rule becomes European it may be just as effective in protecting parties to transactions and preventing undesirable externalities of the more concrete sort, but it ceases to be a local expression of autonomy, and the constraints on individual freedom which it entails change, at least to an extent, from expressions of membership to expressions of subservience. Where quality of life is tied to identity and a sense of 'we', then in the absence of a similarly thick European identity the rules which shape it cannot be Europeanised without their value being diminished.

This is not to say that more traditional mandatory requirements or Treaty derogations will never have any of the above characteristics. In particular, morality derogations may also be non-quantifiable expressions of particularity.[1] However,

[1] See Case C-36/02 *Omega Spielhallen* EU:C:2004:614; C-208/09 *Sayn-Wittgenstein* EU:C:2010:806.

when rules have significant second-order effects on the texture of public economic life, and when those effects come to be popularly understood as an expression of particularity and identity, and the created texture comes to be appreciated and valued, the internal market law is faced with a problem. Setting aside such rules does harm to welfare that is just as real as that resulting from consumer exploitation or environmental harm, yet treating the preferences at stake as trumps turns free movement into an at-will policy. The traditional ways of finessing these extremes, those of objective measurement of the interests at stake, of harmonisation, of the translation of a particularity into an EU-wide norm, seem to offer no respite. Respecting regulatory choices *merely because people care about them* puts free movement law between a rock and hard place. Yet not respecting things that Europeans care about makes the law a betrayal of those Europeans.

III. FREE MOVEMENT AND QUALITY OF LIFE

It is fairly obvious that free movement of goods, services, persons and companies impacts on the texture of society and on the quality of life for those who live in it.[2] In general, removing barriers to movement brings diversity in some senses, but homogeneity in others—often commercial, but to some extent in values. It increases the opportunities for consumer choice, although not necessarily the importance of the choices, as consumer products often converge to standard forms. It leads to new competition, and often to the replacement of traditional or small-scale commerce by more modern or larger variants. It often weakens collective identities, although it may inspire backlash and a reactionary strengthening of them. It tends to add to economic dynamism, but to increase the subjective sense of insecurity. All these things affect what it is like to live in society. Changing economies have an impact beyond the economic. The globalisation story and the modernisation story are both well known.

More concretely, there may be good reasons, to do with quality of life, why a state might wish to maintain measures which have some restrictive effect on free movement.[3] Most controversially perhaps, for an economist or for the Union policy-maker, it may wish to restrict choice as such, in at least some spheres.

[2] eg JQ Whitman, 'Consumerism versus producerism: A study in comparative law' (2007) 117 *Yale Law Journal* 340; A Bagchi, 'The political economy of regulating contract' (2014) 62 *American Journal of Comparative Law*; G Davies, 'The process and side-effects of harmonisation of European welfare states' (2006) 2 *Jean Monnet Working Paper*; F de Witte, 'Sex, Drugs and EU Law: the Regulation of Moral and Ethical Diversity in EU Law' (2013) 6 *CML Rev* 1545.

[3] G Davies, 'Internal market adjudication and the quality of life in Europe', (2015) 21:2 *Columbia Journal of European Law* 289. Also available as EUI working paper LAW 2014/07; S Timmermans and S Epstein, 'A world of standards but not a standard world: Towards a sociology of standards and standardization' (2010) 36 *Annual Review of Sociology* 69; W Streeck, 'Beneficial constraints: On the economic limits of rational voluntarism' in JR Hollingsworth and R Boyer (eds), *Contemporary Capitalism: The Embeddedness of Institutions* (Cambridge, CUP, 1997) 197.

Choice is not an unconditionally good thing: it is tiring, time-consuming, and can be frustrating, particularly where the choices do not matter very much, as is often the case in consumer goods and services markets.[4] How much choice people should have to suffer in their daily lives, and which particular kinds of choices are more or less offensive or useful, pleasant or unpleasant, are legitimate policy questions to do with how regulation can be used to give populations a better life. To fetishise choice as something to be embraced to the maximum in all circumstances is not only to ignore psychological realities, but to ignore the goal of the Union to increase the well-being of its peoples.[5]

Moreover, in certain contexts, the fact that all people consume the same products or services creates shared experiences which contribute to social bonds, and a sense of belonging.[6] Traditional food products, which have so often been a part of free movement law, are part of the identity of nations, and link populations not just to each other but to the past.[7] A decision that all beer in Germany should comply with traditional regulation is a contribution to the social fabric of Germany.[8] The fact that it means that across other social divisions, from rich and poor to different political groups, all drink the same kind of drink makes it a generator of a certain kind of equality, of a bond between those who may in other ways feel far apart. A decision not to have diversity and choice in that particular product market, or to constrain it within the limits of certain standards, is a choice to do and participate in something together. It is a claim that consumer welfare is not maximised by seeing preferences as purely individual, but that in some cases the subordination of individual desires to collective decisions can be liberating and life-enriching.

There are also good policy reasons to protect certain structures within the economy—the traditional town centre, small shops and businesses, individual ownership rather than chains. The existence of these imparts a certain quality to transactions, and to public space, and it fosters other aspects of the quality of life. In a slow and small-scale economy conversations take place, people have time, and purchasing and consumption become social and human activities as well as just material. There are of course contrary views, and many communities will welcome the virtues of the modern, large and cheap. However, policy decisions about how

[4] G Low, 'The psychology of choice of laws' (2013) 24 *European Business Law Review* 363, 367; B Schwartz, *The Paradox Of Choice: Why More Is Less* (New York, Harper, 2004).

[5] Art 3 TEU.

[6] G Davies, 'Internal market adjudication and the quality of life in Europe' (n 3).

[7] See Case 286/86 *Deserbais* EU:C:1988:434; Case 788/79 *Gilli and Andres* EU:C:1980:171; Case C-12/00 *Commission v Spain (Spanish Chocolate)* EU:C:2003:21; Case C-14/00 *Commission v Italy (Chocolate)* EU:C:2003:22; Case 407/85 *3 Glocken (Pasta)* EU:C:1988:401; Case C-314/89 *Rauh* EU:C:1991:143; Case 178/84 *Commission v Germany (German Beer)* EU:C:1987:126; Case C-184/96 *Commission v France (Foie gras)* EU:C:1998:495; Case 120/78 *Cassis de Dijon* EU:C:1979:42. See also Joined Cases C-158 and 159/04 *Alfa Vita Vassilopoulos AE v Elliniko Dimosio, Nomarchiaki Aftodioikisi Ioanninon* EU:C:2006:562.

[8] Case 178/84, *Commission v Germany (German Beer)* (n 7).

the economy should be organised are not just about protectionism, and trade, and efficiency, and wealth, but also about social bonds and the quality of life. These are legitimate, even essential, concerns to take into account, and to put into the policy balance, if a regulator wishes to improve the well-being of the regulated.

Cases such as those about beer in Germany, or the sole-ownership of opticians in Greece, or the positioning of supermarkets in Spain, are about quality of life.[9] Free movement is involved, and there may be consequences for market access, for efficiency, and for wealth. But there are also consequences for how people in those societies live and relate to each other and experience their daily rituals and the time that they spend in public space. One cannot be serious about policy and think that the entry of Heineken, Specsavers or Tesco is something that brings no social costs, even if it may bring benefits too.

Yet these costs are absent from the case law. The Court professes to consider all legitimate public interest concerns when reviewing national measures. It is a cliché of the law that the list of mandatory requirements which may justify a derogation is an open one.[10] However, concerns about quality of life, such as those briefly discussed above, are neither put forward by the Member States—as far as can be seen from the Opinions and Judgments—nor mentioned by the Court.[11] There is complete silence on the topic. Some examples of the reasoning that results will be discussed below.[12]

The reasons for this silence may well be complex. Free movement law is, in substance, an exercise in freedom of contract, promoting cross-border contract possibilities and removing national regulation which may stand in the way.[13] Traditional views of what is at stake in the regulation of contract tend, however, to focus very much on the parties to the transaction, and their relative positions and capacities. Hence, perhaps, the over-dominance of consumer protection concerns in free movement law. The Court is still trapped in the view of contract as an essentially private matter. By contrast, it is implicit in the argument of this chapter that contracting is a social act, with consequences for wider society, particularly where the contracts take place in public economic space.[14] It should therefore be regulated in that light, with social concerns embedded in the regulation.

[9] *Commission v Germany* (n 7); Case C-140/03 *Commission v Greece* EU:C:2005:242; Case C-400/08 *Commission v Spain* EU:C:2011:172.

[10] Case C-123/00 *Bellamy* EU:C:2001:214; Case C-55/94 *Gebhard v Consiglio dell'Ordine degli Avvocati e Procuratori di Milano* EU:C:1995:411; N Nic Shuibhne, *The Coherence Of Free Movement Law: Constitutional Responsibility And The Court Of Justice* (Oxford, OUP, 2014) 24.

[11] There are intermittent vague hints in this direction, eg the reference to urban decay in *Commission v Spain* (n 9). See also Case C-148/02 *Garcia Avello* EU:C:2003:539; Case C-147/03 *Commission v Austria* EU:C:2005:427; Case 186/87 *Cowan* EU:C:1989:47. See generally G Davies, 'Internal market adjudication' (n 3) at 13–16.

[12] See text following n 25.

[13] G Davies, 'Freedom of contract and the horizontal effect of free movement law' in D Leczykiewicz and S Weatherill (eds), *The involvement of EU law in private law relationships* (Oxford, Hart publishing 2013) 53.

[14] A Bagchi (n 2).

But while attitudes traditional to the law may play a role in the exclusion of social interests, the remainder of this chapter concentrates on the process of adjudication itself. Does the nature of quality of life as a concern perhaps explain why it is neglected in the jurisprudence of exceptions to free movement? How would its contestable, subjective, particularistic nature fit into the framework of free movement law? Two problems arise. One is the problem of reaching objective conclusions, and distinguishing the genuine from the opportunistic argument. The other is that quality of life concerns differ from others in not being reconcilable with the internal market, for the reasons outlined above. To say that rules which are necessary to maintain a certain quality of life 'must be accepted' is a very different legal and integrative act from saying the same about the more concrete and transactional interests in which the case law abounds.[15]

IV. FEEL THE QUALITY, MEASURE THE WIDTH

Quality of life is a somewhat abstract, even vague, matter, certainly in comparison with concrete and measurable concerns such as health and environmental harm, and even in comparison with consumer protection. This does not as such make it impossible to adjudicate, and there are cases where the Court has taken seriously other imprecise matters, such as national identity, the importance of constitutional values to society, and, indeed, morality.[16] Judging the importance of a measure for social cohesion or ways of life may be a challenge, but it is not one that should be a priori ruled too difficult for the Court.

Perhaps the more serious problem is that quality of life would appear to be a very contested and contestable matter, in which it is hard to put forward objective policy arguments. A quality of life argument amounts, in substance, to 'we like it like this'. Again, in comparison with other interests, this may make it seem insubstantial, not so much an objectively important public interest as a mere subjective preference.

Yet the difference is far less than it seems. Measures taken to protect health, the environment, and certainly the consumer are also contestable, and contested. Any such measure embodies both factual and normative assumptions, and even if—which is rarely the case—there may be consensus on the first of these, there is invariably wide diversity of views on the latter.[17] A decision to limit salt in food will attract a certain amount of controversy on the medical science involved, and a great deal of controversy on the question of who should take responsibility for health, or on the role of the state and the individual. That debate is not just in

[15] The quotation is from *Cassis de Dijon* (n 7) para 8.

[16] C-208/09 *Sayn-Wittgenstein* EU:C:2010:806 (n 1); Case C-148/02 *Garcia Avello* (n 11); Case C-36/02 *Omega Spielhallen* (n 1); Case C-258/08 *Ladbrokes* EU:C:2010:308.

[17] See B Wynne, 'Scientific knowledge and the global environment' in M Redclift and T Benton (eds), *Social Theory and the Global Environment* (London, Routledge, 1994) 169, 175–76.

addition to the health question, but also a part of it: what kind of allocation of responsibilities leads ultimately to a healthier society? Thus even questions which seem at first glance 'objective' are filled with arguable assertions about values and society, over which the law usually conveniently skips.[18]

The practical difference between adjudicating health, environmental protection or consumer protection, on the one hand, and quality of life, on the other, is thus that the presence of experts in the field in the former areas makes a faux-objective presentation of the issues possible and even *salonfähig*, in the courtroom at least, if not in the more critical academic world.[19] However, that practical difference should not be taken to represent a deep principled gulf, for it does not. Some issues are more data rich, and some are not: that is all. Moreover, the judgments on identity and morality confirm that courts can cope even without expert support, and can judge social consequence and social importance. Judgments on quality of life would be difficult ones, but they would fall within the kind of work that courts can do.

By contrast, the real problem is less an evidential one than one of ideology. It is very tempting to think that allowing quality of life arguments to restrict free movement is in some sense *wrong*—that it amounts to a rejection of the very essence of the Treaty commitment to an internal market. The argument would be that in signing the Treaty Member States accept the obligation to adapt to free movement. Derogations and exceptions exist to address the usual kinds of market failures and externalities, but quality of life arguments look less like this and more like a rejection of the basic market premises, those of openness, diversity, and individual choice. They are, it might seem, just an attempt to escape the Treaty on no more substantial grounds than that a population does not like its consequences in some particular sphere. That, one might say, is something they should have thought about before they signed.

This perspective makes a plea for quality of life arguments look quite radically anti-market. It is not, however. The argument above is quite wrong. Radicalism is to be found in the suggestion that quality of life arguments are in some sense different in principle from arguments about the consumer, the environment or public health. That represents an implicit commitment to an ideology which is not only rather extreme, but also at odds with the welfare economics which largely prevails in EU policy.

For value is subjective. That is a basic principle of economics, and perhaps one of the few which still might attract widespread support. If things matter it is not because of some objective, inherent worth which they may have, but because people care about them. There is no type difference between health, environment and quality of life. An attempt to deny quality of life concerns in internal market law is

[18] Eg G Davies, 'Morality clauses and decision making in situations of scientific uncertainty: the case of GMOs' (2007) 6 *World Trade Review* 249.

[19] See B Wynne (n 17).

then just the arbitrary designation of one of the preferences of the population as 'illegitimate'. It is at best social engineering, and at worst normative tyranny.

Yet if it is arbitrary from the perspective of welfare policy, it is not necessarily arbitrary from all perspectives. It looks in fact rather like an attempt to dehumanise the internal market. The protection of the environment and the consumer and health all in fact serve smooth market function. They promote transactions, minimise costs, and prevent profitable resources being damaged. Poor regulation in these areas is sand in the machine of the market. If we allow these, but not the less immediately functional quality of life concerns it looks rather as if the European is being instrumentalised to serve the market, and not the other way round. Where his interests do not serve the needs of the market, they are denied.

Such an approach might be associated with a certain kind of right-wing thinking, and feed suspicions of multinational corporate control of policy, but it can also be the product—more plausibly it is suggested—of EU-led thinking, of the traditionalist's approach to the Union, in which integration is the primary good, not welfare. The normative justification for such a view is that the former is an adequate proxy for the latter, an idea which is perhaps at the very heart of the EU and always has been. The rather banal claim made here is just this: it is not always so.

V. RECONCILIATION V BALANCING

Most judicial review processes place the interests of a specific individual against those of the majority, as represented by the legislature. Because of this asymmetry, review is often largely formal, with the individual only being able to oppose measures on substantive grounds in extreme situations.

By contrast, the internal market pits legislature against legislature. While it may be an individual who objects to a national rule, they act as agent of the EU interest in integration, and the EU's policy of free movement is pitted against some conflicting national policy, embodied in national laws. The fact that legitimate policy-makers are represented on both sides is what justifies the Court's characteristically intrusive review, and is what makes a purely formal or marginal approach inappropriate—indeed incoherent, since it glosses the question of which legislator should be prima facie deferred to.

One way of describing the review options available to the Court of Justice is in terms of two techniques: reconciliation and balancing. Balancing interests would entail weighing the matters at stake, coming to some kind of conclusion regarding their relative importance, and coming down on one side (or at least more on one side than on the other). Balancing therefore accepts that there is always a price for every choice. Some interests win, and others lose. Reconciliation, by contrast, would involve looking for the adjudicatory solution which finesses apparent conflict and finds a way in which all interests are protected, perhaps reframing the law, but doing so in a way which takes us to a new place in which interests are no longer at odds.

As will be argued in the next section, the Court is a compulsive reconciler, at least in its explicit reasoning. It may be argued that balance is implicit, but it is not part of the language of the law. That reconciliation is achieved in one of two ways. Either the Court finds, as happens in most cases, that the interest protected by the national rule can be protected in some other way, which no longer conflicts with free movement. It finds, commonly, and explicitly, that the movement restriction is not in fact necessary for what the state wants to achieve. Alternatively, in a minority of cases, it finds that free movement and the national interest cannot be reconciled immediately, because the national measure is in fact necessary, but the reconciliatory aspect of that finding lies in the fact that its very existence provides a legal basis for harmonisation. In the case of the more traditional derogations such harmonisation is another path to reconciliation: the interest put forward by the Member State is not rejected at all, but rather adopted by the EU, for the EU as a whole. The state wins in seeing its concern universalised, while the EU wins in seeing free movement prevail. Such harmonisation will not necessarily happen. That depends on political factors, and perhaps also on economic ones. However, it is authorised. The symbolic importance of this is that it means the Court never in fact sets a limit to the internal market.

The only exceptions to this are where the national interest at stake is of an inherently national type—either it is specific to that state, or it is bound up with autonomy per se, so that harmonisation would harm, rather than protect it. This is arguably the case in *Omega*, and *Sayn-Wittgenstein*, and perhaps a few other cases, where specific national values and preferences were accepted as the basis for limiting free movement.[20]

In those cases the Court emphasised the European basis of the specific national values—human dignity in the one case, and equality in the other. While they had a national interpretation, they could also be placed within a European framework, so that they became examples of EU-wide choices, rather than deviations. The theme of reconciliation is not entirely abandoned.

Quality of life derogations are a step beyond these cases. The relationship between adjudication of interests and their harmonisation which is sketched above is more to do with abstract principle than practice, so that it may seem rather artificial. However, its usefulness here is to highlight a way in which quality of life is different from the run-of-the-mill derogation: harmonisation is not reconciliation. If the Court concedes that quality of life may serve to restrict free movement then it can offer the EU no way out of the cul-de-sac. The decision puts a limit on the market.

The new national identity clause in Article 4 of the TEU may offer some kind of way forward. National identity is not the most obvious peg to hang quality of life issues on, but it becomes more and more plausible, as EU law becomes ever

[20] Case C-36/02 *Omega Spielhallen* (n 1); *Sayn-Wittgenstein* (n 1).

broader. The current crisis of European integration is not about types of act, but about degree: where do we say stop? As the German Constitutional Court has noted, there is a constitutional imperative to retain some kind of local autonomy over the social and economic and cultural conditions of life, and it is that which the EU now seems to threaten, rather than any specific value or institution.[21] If quality of life is to be part of the law then the interests it involves need to be articulated, and perhaps Article 4 can help in that process. It may give the notably inarticulate Member States guidance on how to frame their concerns, and it may also help the Court of Justice play a role in the conversation. There is of course a risk here: by putting national identity in the TEU the Member States made it a concept of EU law, so that the Court of Justice may now adjudicate on what it means. It is, arguably, a small step towards its harmonisation. The first step to neutralising troublesome national policy areas is, as *Rottmann*, *ERT* and *van Duyn* teach us, to recognise the choices to be made, and thereby bring them within EU law.[22] Yet it is not the intention of this chapter to argue that quality of life should always trump free movement. Rather, contrary to the case law, it is suggested that there are real conflicts in the internal market, and they require explicit balancing, and there will always be some give and take. The need is not for quality of life to be fetishised, but for it to be discussed, and in the context of EU law it is quite right that while the voice of the states should be heard, so should the Court-channelled voice of the EU.

VI. THE BALANCING MYTH

The application of free movement law is commonly seen as a balancing process. Indeed, to suggest that proportionality assessment involves balancing interests would attract little dissent in most contexts. The three-part construction of proportionality, derived from German law, provides that a measure is tested for its necessity, its effectiveness, and finally for 'true proportionality'.[23] This last test entails asking whether the impact of the measure is in proportion to what it achieves, which is certainly a form of balancing. The essence of a balance is that interests are weighed, and that the one found less important may have to make concessions, and this could be the outcome of a true proportionality test.

However, the complete and formal proportionality assessment is found more often in books than in judgments.[24] If one looks at the practice of the Court

[21] 2 BvE 2/08 Treaty of Lisbon, Judgment of 30 June 2009, para 249: 'European unification on the basis of a treaty union of sovereign states may, however, not be achieved in such a way that not sufficient space is left to the Member States for the political formation of the economic, cultural and social living conditions.' See also paras 257–59.

[22] Case C-135/08 *Rottmann* EU:C:2010:104; Case C-260/89 *ERT* EU:C:1991:254; Case 41/74 *Van Duyn* EU:C:1974:133.

[23] J Snell, 'True proportionality' (2000) 11 *European Business Law Review* 50.

[24] JH Jans, 'Proportionality revisited' (2000) 27 *Legal Issues of Economic Integration* 39; J Snell (n 23).

when reviewing national measures which are claimed to obstruct free movement, and when measuring them for proportionality, then balancing is a poor way to describe it.[25]

If the Court were balancing interests in a case like *Cassis de Dijon*, its reasoning could take various forms. It might say that both the protection of the consumer and free movement are at stake, and it must therefore make a choice between them, and in the particular context it considers one or the other to be more important, so that measures protecting the other must, alas, be set aside. Alternatively, it might say that a compromise between the two interests must be reached, in which a degree of concession is involved, so that, for example, a lesser degree of consumer protection must be accepted in order to make a reasonable degree of free movement possible. However, the essence of a balancing process is that there is a conflict between the two interests concerned, and a choice must be made, and that the weight of the interests determines how that choice should be made.

By contrast, the reasoning in *Cassis* had a quite different form. The judgment required a national law to be set aside, in order to allow free movement, but this was not, in the view of the Court, a triumph of one interest over another. Rather, the Court found that such conflict could be avoided, because it was possible to protect the consumer interest in another way, which had almost no impact on free movement.[26] The judgment is an exercise in reconciliation, the happy conclusion being an implicit finding that what seemed to be a clash of interests could, through careful and competent law-making, be avoided, so that the EU concern for free movement, and the national concern for consumer protection, could be pursued at once.[27] Similarly, in the *Greek opticians* case, the Greek Government mentioned the importance of personal contact between optician and customer several times, but linked this to public health, trying to justify its restrictive ownership rules in this way.[28] As a result the Court was easily able to find that there was no real conflict. The rules went beyond what was necessary and public health and free movement could be reconciled by having a different ownership regime. This was undoubtedly correct. The judgment does not address, however, the contribution made by that personal contact, by small, non-chain specialist shops, to the character of the Greek public economic sphere.

This is the ubiquitous approach of the case law. In the vast majority of free movement cases the Court finds that Member States must set aside or change their laws in order to remove hindrances to movement. In the vast majority of those it finds that this can be done in a way that imposes no cost on other policies—less obstructive protective techniques are possible.[29] Perhaps we should not be

[25] Jans (n 24); Snell (n 23)
[26] Case 120/78 *Cassis de Dijon* (n 7) paras 13–14.
[27] ibid.
[28] Case C-140/03 *Commission v Greece* (n 9).
[29] eg Case 120/78 *Cassis de Dijon* (n 7); Case 178/84 *Commission v Germany (German Beer)* (n 7); Case C-147/03 *Commission v Austria (Universities)* EU:C:2005:427; Case C-140/03 *Commission v Greece* (n 9).

surprised, given the technocratic bias of the EU as a whole, that one of the most consistent stories in EU law is that the answer to challenging policy situation is greater expertise in legal technique.

In fact, *Cassis* was notable for the way it subordinated free movement to all other interests, at least as a matter of doctrine. The finding of the Court, since often confirmed, is that wherever a legitimate policy interest actually requires that a national law be maintained, the consequences for free movement must be accepted.[30] Fortunately, one might perhaps think, it almost never seems to be the case that obstructive national laws really are necessary. However, the phrase shows that if a measure really is needed for a national interest, it will take precedence over movement. By contrast, there are no cases in which the Court says that given the importance of free movement in a certain context the disadvantageous consequences for consumer protection or the environment 'must be accepted'. Only the opposite.

Thus when a genuine conflict exists the doctrine lays down a priori that the non-economic national interest will always prevail. The function of court adjudication is to see whether such a conflict is actually there. If so, one could argue that a sort of balancing takes place, in that the non-economic interest is found to be more important and free movement makes a concession. The conclusions in the rare cases where Member States win entail a certain weighing and prioritising of the matters at stake, an admission of conflict.

Yet this admission is less than it first seems, given the consequences it has for the possibility of positive harmonisation: when the Court finds that there is a national obstacle to movement that cannot be removed judicially, its judgment serves as a signal that harmonisation would be appropriate, and that there would be a legal basis.[31] For it is quite clear from the Court's own decisions—notably *Tobacco*—that there is competence to take the measures necessary to ensure free movement.[32] The difficult legal and policy question is usually what this allows: what is to be understood as necessary? However, if the Court has found that an obstacle exists, and that it must be accepted, this makes the question simpler. The existence of an obstacle is no longer in doubt, and nor is the need for something beyond litigation in order to remove it.[33] Given that most obstacles to movement, and certainly those in the goods and services field, arise because of differences between national laws, harmonisation is in most cases an effective way of promoting movement. Even cases such as the *Greek opticians* and *Spanish planning rules* can be seen in this light.[34] While it was not directly a difference between laws that was in issue, the expectations of the out-of-state actors who might want to enter

[30] eg Case C-123/00 *Bellamy* (n 10); C-55/94 *Gebhard* (n 10).

[31] G Davies, 'Is mutual recognition an alternative to harmonisation?' in F Ortino and L Bartels (eds), *Regional Trade Agreements and The World Trade Organization* (Oxford, OUP, 2007).

[32] Case C-376/98 *Germany v Parliament and Council (Tobacco advertising)* EU:C:2000:544.

[33] G Davies, 'Can Selling Arrangements be Harmonised?' (2005) 30 *EL Rev* 370.

[34] Case C-140/03 *Commission v Greece* (n 9); Case C-400/08 *Commission v Spain* (n 9).

the markets in question would in practice be conditioned by the legislation in their home states, and the business models that they used. As the Court has acknowledged in several recent cases, having to adjust a business model can be a significant obstacle to movement, so that European legislation which facilitates the use of common business models throughout the EU is prima facie market-promoting.[35] Reconciling consumer, environmental and movement issues in different ways in different states obstructs this. Doing it in a common way throughout the EU makes cross-border business easier.

This casts the free movement case law in a different light. The truly integrative judgments are not those in which the state loses, for in that case the impact may be limited to the particular trader, or sector, in question. Given the variable approaches to judicial precedent in Europe the case may have few ripples outside of those directly involved: that references continue to come to the Court concerning situations which are analytically identical to *Cassis de Dijon* shows that a judicial expression of a principle does not always have the quasi-legislative effect that textbooks suggest. By contrast, where a state wins, the victory may be ultimately greater for the EU, for it opens up a field for harmonisation, with potentially far profounder integration consequences. Such a state victory is in essence a judicial statement that 'this situation is too much for us: it must be passed upstairs to those who deal with more serious problems'. The Court is like a doctor who, having examined a patient, says 'there is nothing I can do except refer you to a specialist'. The patient would be foolish to be relieved that they can go home without any painful injections. The referral suggests that worse is in store.

Yet the weakness of the analogy above is that while doctors cannot cure everything, the EU legislature can, at least on the understanding embodied in the Treaty. Harmonisation does not mean trampling on the interests which were put forward in the case, but rather protecting them EU-wide. The Treaty is quite explicit that the internal market is a market in which not just free movement, but other good things are protected too.[36] Legislation is always intended to reconcile the matters at stake in the market.

The function of courts adjudicating free movement law is therefore to decide at which level reconciliation of interests can best take place: the judicial or the legislative. There is no question of making any interest concede to another. At most, free movement may be temporarily impeded until legislation is in place. But the process which is clearly imagined by the Treaty and the Court is one in which the outcome is ultimately always the same: laws are made in such a way that the policy objectives pursued by national law, and those pursued by the Union, can both be satisfied.[37]

[35] Case C-442/02 *Caixabank France* EU:C:2004:586; Case C-518/06 *Commission v Italy (car insurance)* EU:C:2009:270.

[36] See Arts 7–13 TFEU.

[37] See also G Davies, 'Internal Market Adjudication' (n 3) at 16–18.

Of course, one does not have to believe that this reconciliation is real. It is perfectly arguable—it is very tempting to say perfectly obvious—that *Cassis de Dijon* did in fact result in a lower level of consumer protection, and that most other free movement cases do in fact force Member States to revise downwards their chosen level of protection of the interest at stake.[38] Different is, contrary to the implicit claims of the Court, rarely equal. When the Court says that an interest can be protected in a more proportionate way it is in substance often insisting that a state accept a slightly lower level of protection because of the free movement benefits that this would bring, and that is certainly the result of an unspoken judicial balancing. It is very plausible that discussion between the judges concerns the extent to which it is reasonable to ask a state to make policy concessions, and that the importance of the measures at stake and the degree of their impact on free movement are considered in this discussion. They may well understand their own decisions as the outcome of a balancing. However, the point here is not to engage with judicial psychology or private policy motivations, but with judgments, and the fact remains that the Court does not support or acknowledge policy balancing in the text of the decisions that it delivers. The doctrine supporting those decisions is that all good things can be protected at once and that free movement will not be imposed where that would do harm.

VII. DEVIANT CASE LAW: WHEN DOMINATION CANNOT HIDE

There are exceptions to the rule above. There is a smattering of cases where the Court seems to admit that the internal market entails hard and painful choices. In *Stoke-on-Trent*, *Carpenter*, *Schmidberger*, and *Viking* and *Laval*, the Court actually says in so many words that there is a need to balance free movement against other interests. This is exceptional, and makes it worth looking at these cases in some detail to see what it is about them which may have inspired such openness. What is immediately apparent is that these are some of the most criticised and controversial and simply unusual judgments in free movement law. Without going into cause and effect, there is clearly a correlation between explicit balancing and some of the more difficult and unhappy moments in the life of the law.

[38] See eg HC von Heydebrand, 'Free movement of foodstuffs, consumer protection and food standards in the European Community: Has the Court got it wrong?' (1991) 16 *EL Rev* 391; C Barnard, 'Employment rights, free movement under the EC Treaty and the Services Directive' (2008) *Mitchell Working Paper* No 5/08; N Reich, 'Free Movement v Social Rights in an Enlarged Union: The *Laval* and *Viking* Cases before the ECJ', (2008) 9 *German Law Journal* 125; J Malmberg and T Sigeman, 'Industrial actors and EU economic freedoms: The autonomous collective bargaining model curtailed by the European Court of Justice' (2008) 43 *CML Rev* 1115; T Novitz, 'A human rights analysis of the *Viking* and *Laval* judgments', (2007) 10 *Cambridge Yearbook of European Legal Studies* 541; C Kaupa, 'Maybe not activist enough? On the Court's alleged neoliberal bias in its recent labour cases', in M Dawson, B de Witte and E Muir (eds), *Judicial Activism at the European Court of Justice* (Cheltenham, Edward Elgar, 2013) 56; H Temmink, 'From Danish bottles to Danish bees: The dynamics of free movement of goods and environmental protection—A case law analysis' (2000) 1 *Yearbook of European Environmental Law* 61.

The most striking example is *Stoke-on-Trent Borough Council*.[39] This was one of the Sunday Trading cases that were brought to the Court before *Keck*.[40] It was claimed that British rules preventing shops opening on Sundays were restrictions on trade contrary to the Treaty, because by reducing opening times they reduced sales, and that in turn reduced imports.[41] The Court used quite distinctive language, saying that such measures reflected local 'socio-cultural' characteristics, and that provided the restrictive effect of the measures did not exceed what was 'intrinsic' to measures of that type, they should not be seen as contrary to the Treaty. They went on to say that proportionality assessment involved weighing the interests of free movement against those of national policy, and that since the measures were not excessive in proportion to their goal, they should be permitted.

There are many oddities to this reasoning, not least a certain circularity, or at least emptiness, in the idea of not exceeding the effects that are intrinsic to a goal. One could say that applying standards as in *Cassis* does not exceed what is intrinsic to the goal of creating a marketplace of guaranteed quality goods, but of course that was not the goal that was put forward or accepted. By contrast, in *Stoke-on-Trent* the rule was clearly understood to be not just about the consumer or the fairness of the transaction, but about the wider social consequences of transactions. The aim was to keep Sunday as a commerce-free day, for reasons of quality of life. The UK argued this, and the Court accepted it, and then it became impossible to deny that there was a conflict between the national policy and EU law, and that the rule did not exceed what was intrinsic to its goal, for keeping Sunday free of commerce cannot be done in a way that allows more commerce. Moreover, it was quite clear that this policy preference was not a universal one—some states might not have such rules—but was the result of particular national and local preferences. People in the UK wanted things that way. Once this local nature of preferences is accepted, it is clear that harmonisation does not offer a way towards reconciling interests. Even if there was more or less a European consensus on shop opening times, part of the function of such rules is to allow what the Court called 'socio-cultural' preferences to be expressed in law. The local ownership of the decision is then part of the point. Sunday trading rules contribute to quality of life not just because of their consequences for public economic space, but because they allow a community to express its identity and autonomy.[42]

Such socio-cultural rules are then a particularly unprofitable field for free movement law to enter, because once it is established that they pursue legitimate goals, and that they cannot be overruled or harmonised without harm to those

[39] Case C-169/91 *Stoke on Trent and Norwich City Council v B & Q* EU:C:1992:519.

[40] Joined Cases C-267 and 268/91 *Keck and Mithouard* EU:C:1993:905.

[41] See also Case 145/88 *Torfaen Borough Council v B & Q* EU:C:1989:593. And see also Case C-312/89 *Union Départementale des Syndicats CGT de l'Aisne v Conforama* EU:C:1991:93; Case C-332/89 *Marchandise* EU:C:1991:94.

[42] One might even argue that the value of the rules as expression is despite their concrete consequences for business: being silly (making pointless rules) is a more convincing demonstration of freedom than being sensible.

goals, they will trump free movement law every time—except perhaps where they embody some moral failing so great that it undermines their other virtues, such as perhaps discrimination—and the lawsuit will fail to be a useful trigger for legislation, but merely a waste of time. Hence, after several fruitless lawsuits, the Court abandoned the field in *Keck*, ruling that selling arrangements were not obstacles to movement unless discriminatory. If reconciliation of interests is not possible, then all that is left is balancing (choosing between interests). If the Court is not prepared to choose for the destruction of local socio-cultural preferences, which to its credit it was not, then free movement law, and the EU generally, have nothing to gain from attention to measures of this type.

Keck, and *Stoke-on-Trent*, are therefore examples of the Court conceding the existence of conflicts which this chapter argues are more widely present. Selling arrangements are not the only rules which reflect socio-cultural preferences. So do product standards. Yet these have a far greater effect on trade, so the price for the Union of taking the deferential approach found in *Keck* and *Stoke-on-Trent*, would be far higher. Instead, the law imposes the price of free movement on the Member States, but it does not do so openly. Where the Union loses it is because it has balanced interests and given way.[43] Where Member States lose it is apparently because there is nothing to balance. Quality of life and socio-cultural preferences are implied to be of marginal importance, to be embraced when they bring no price, but ignored if they would get in the way of trade.

Carpenter was not obviously about quality of life, but it also involved a situation where EU law threatened to demand concessions from sensitive areas of national policy.[44] The difference with the above cases is that having admitted a conflict, the Court did not in *Carpenter* then lessen the demands imposed by EU law. What it did instead, in a recent case following *Carpenter*, was stop talking about the conflict.[45]

The case concerned a British man whose non-European wife was facing expulsion from the UK. They successfully resisted that on the grounds that her presence was necessary for his provision of cross-border services under Article 56; she looked after the children while he travelled for work. The Court chose to formulate its result in terms of a fair balance between rights, free movement, and national immigration policy, and found that the latter had to give. The judgment has been maintained in substance, and indeed there are now many citizenship cases which chop holes in national immigration law, but mention of balancing is largely absent.[46] Where family members face expulsion the Court asks whether

[43] At least temporarily, until it harmonises.

[44] Case C-60/00 *Carpenter v Secretary of State for the Home Department* EU:C:2002:434.

[45] Case C-457/12 *S and G* EU:C:2014:136.

[46] ibid. See also Case C-200/02 *Zhu and Chen* EU:C:2004:639; Case C-34/09 *Ruiz Zambrano v ONEm* EU:C:2011:124. *Cf* slightly more ambiguously Case C-413/99 *Baumbast v Secretary of State for the Home Department* EU:C:2002:493 paras 90–91; Case C-184/99 *Grzelczyk* EU:C:2001:458: Where purely financial consequences for the state are involved it is sometimes hard to pretend that no balancing is involved.

their presence is necessary to make EU rights effective, or whether their expulsion would impede those rights. It no longer weighs national immigration interests in the balance.

Partly this is because many of the judgments fall within the citizenship directive or other legislation on free movement of persons, so that the balancing can be said to have been done by the legislature, and the Court's task is merely to interpret the resulting right.[47] However, this is not always the case. There are cases of pure Treaty interpretation, where immigration law obstructs free movement of workers or citizens, and here balancing is also absent.[48] The interests in the balance would of course be hard to formulate: the national interest in excluding non-European family members of migrant citizens is difficult to put in socially acceptable terms. And yet it is real, and it is about quality of life, in that states and populations may wish to limit who becomes part of their community and may feel threatened by a loss of control over their borders, particularly when that loss of control is greater in extent, and far less clearly bounded, than they might have expected from a reading of the Treaty or legislation. It might be better for integration, cathartic perhaps, if these things were discussed within the framework of the law instead of purely by opponents of it. The tension between migrant family rights and social peace and cohesion might, perhaps, be discussable in reasonable and legal terms.[49] Nevertheless, that is not how the Court has chosen to proceed.

Schmidberger, like *Carpenter*, features fundamental rights, but this time they oppose free movement instead of strengthening it.[50] The case is about an opposition between freedom of association and free movement of goods. What was at stake was the right of Austrian demonstrators to block roads in protest against the environmental harm caused by transiting heavy goods traffic. While the case was controversial precisely because of its use of balancing, with the implication that rights might sometimes have to give way to freedoms being found objectionable by some,[51] it is made easier to digest by a number of factors; first, most pragmatically, the demonstrators won. Second, the right of association is itself not absolute, and subject to balancing with other interests, so that the approach taken by the Court is not incompatible with rights-based thinking. Third, rights are a less troublesome limit to EU policy than are local preferences. For a start, they are part of EU policy, making a rights–freedoms balance more of an internal one than a balance between state and Union. Moreover, rights are inherently minority interests. It is not the entire state which will assert a right to speech or demonstration, but a concerned group. Extracting concessions from private interests may be less inflammatory, or less dangerous, than extracting them openly from states.

[47] Directive 2004/38 on the right of citizens of the Union and their family members to move and reside freely; Regulation 492/2011 on freedom of movement for workers.

[48] Case C-457/12 *S and G* (n 45); Case C-370/90 *Singh* EU:C:1992:296. See also n 46.

[49] See for something like this, but in a different context, the French arguments in Case C-265/95 *Commission v France* EU:C:1997:595.

[50] Case C-112/00 *Schmidberger v Austria* EU:C:2003:333.

[51] J Morijn, 'Balancing fundamental rights and common market freedoms in Union law' (2006) 12 *ELJ* 15.

Perhaps this was also in the judges' minds in *Viking Line* and *Laval*, where trade union freedom was in tension with the free movement of services and establishment.[52] Both judgments contain a certain degree of balancing language, suggesting that rights to strike may sometimes have to be balanced against the rights of others to free movement. This imposition on trade union freedom has been one of the most controversial aspects of the cases.[53] In the end the Court retreats from the balancing approach, however, concluding that in fact the industrial action in question was not part of a legitimate campaign of worker protection. This delegitimation enables it to find that the case does not expose any conflict between free movement and worker protection at all—reconciliation again. That reconciliation is not perhaps entirely convincing in fact, but it is the Court's chosen description of the situation, which is to say it is the law.

It remains to be seen where *Viking* and *Laval* will go, or how they will be developed. Trade unions may have seemed like demonstrators, a non-state group who could be safely confined within certain limits, particularly where their behaviour was arguably unmeritorious. However, the trade union behaviour in question was part of a whole 'socio-cultural' approach to industrial relations and economic affairs, which made the judgments particularly sensitive. They amounted to a ruling that Scandinavia had to rethink its consensus and discussion-based industrial relations model.[54] Partly as a result, the cases quickly blew up into one of the greatest judicial controversies of recent years, probably unexpectedly. Hurried attempts to reconcile via harmonisation, with legislation on trade union freedoms, backfired because states regarded this as an unwarranted intrusion into a sensitive and culturally specific field.[55] With hindsight, worker protection, even where officially in the hands of non-state organisations, seems to be as much of an expression of local particularity as are opening hours, and not a private minority concern like demonstrations, and as such to be a field where the Union has little to gain. It would therefore not now be surprising if there were to be, as with selling arrangements, a limited withdrawal. A *Keck* for trade unions would be a judgment that industrial action will only be subject to the Treaty where it is discriminatory on grounds of nationality, but not merely because it may inconvenience those involved in trade, for that consequence, like Sunday trading restrictions, is inherent in the goal that it aims to achieve.

The few cases discussed in this section can hardly display a trend, but what may be said about this little collection of balancing judgments is that they all involve

[52] Case C-438/05 *International Transport Workers' Federation and others v Viking Line* EU:C:2007:772; Case C-341/05 *Laval v SvenskaByggnadsarbetareförbundet* EU:C:2007:809.

[53] See T Novits, 'A human rights analysis of the *Viking* and *Laval* judgments' (2008) 10 *Cambridge Yearbook of European Legal Studies* 541.

[54] J Malmberg and T Sigeman, 'Industrial actions and EU economic freedoms: The autonomous collective bargaining model curtailed by the European Court of Justice' (2008) 45 *CML Rev* 1115.

[55] F Fabbrini and K Granat, 'Yellow card, but no foul: The role of the national parliaments under the subsidiarity protocol and the Commission proposal for an EU regulation on the right to strike' (2013) 50 *CML Rev* 115.

odd situations, and potentially sensitive ones, where existing doctrine does not fit so easily. Having admitted the existence of conflicts the Court abandoned the field in one case (selling arrangements), continued to occupy it in another one where the interests involved are those of a small group rather than a state (*Schmidberger*), and in the remaining two contexts—trade unions and family rights—has apparently decided to stop talking about the conflict of interests that it first admitted. Silence about conflict appears to be associated with progress in developing the law.

VIII. QUALITY OF LIFE AND DEROGATION FROM FREE MOVEMENT: A CONCLUSION

Applying free movement law is a process of reconciling interests and taking integration further. In the rare cases where reconciliation cannot be achieved, the cases generate sometimes unhappy and controversial results, and the Court has sometimes retreated from its initial position.

Bringing quality of life concerns into a judgment would make it a lot more like *Stoke-on-Trent* or *Viking Line* than like *Cassis de Dijon* or another regular goods or services case. The texture of society and the merits of shared experience are not mandatory requirements like any other. If the distinct character of public economic space is a product of the restrictions bounding that space, then the effects on trade are inherent to the goal, and even an expert national legislature cannot pursue them in some more proportionate way that reconciles the restrictions with trade. Nor is the Union legislature likely to be able to address the consequences of a justified derogation, because the capacity to express local preferences and to control one's own environment is a part of the quality of life that is protected by some rules. Harmonisation would destroy what it aimed to protect. Quality of life concerns which reflect local 'socio-cultural' preferences are thus distinctive interests, in that recognising and respecting them does not so much take integration further as highlight where it should stop.

That does not provide a reason why these interests cannot be recognised, nor why they should not be. However, it shows how much the law would be changed if they were. It also displays the dilemma which lies before the Court. If it accepts the importance of these interests, and acknowledges them as mandatory requirements, then it entrenches limits to integration. It erects, within Union law itself, limits to integration which are not just practical, but have a moral status equal to the imperatives of the integration process itself. That is what subsidiarity and the national identity clause try to do too, but the first is ineffective, confined to policing the degree of delegation of Union policy, and it remains to be seen how the second will develop, and whether it can be stretched to encompass quality of life.[56]

[56] See G Davies, 'Subsidiarity, the wrong idea, in the wrong place, at the wrong time' (2006) 43 *CML Rev* 63 (*cf* P Craig, 'Subsidiarity, a Political and Legal Analysis' (2012) 50 *Journal of Common Market Studies* 72); A von Bogdandy and S Schill, 'Overcoming absolute primacy: Respect for national identity under the Lisbon Treaty', (2011) 48 *CML Rev* 1417.

A right of communities to determine the character of their public space and their society, via the recognition of interests such as those described in this chapter, even if not an absolute right, is notably open-ended and far reaching. However, such a right was insisted upon by the Bundesverfassungsgericht in its Lisbon judgment, and it is suggested that it reflects the public mood, so it deserves to be taken seriously.[57]

If the Court, by contrast, ignores these interests in its judgments, then it sends the message that their marginalisation is part of what the EU entails. Any society with self-respect and a sense of identity is then likely to find membership of the Union a poor match with its own values, and a challenge to things that it holds dear. Nevertheless, this is the path that the Court has chosen to date.

However, it is suggested that it has not done so as the result of a fully understood choice. The silence on how free movement relates to the quality of life of Europeans has been shared by Member States, and even by academics, so that it has been easy for the Court, and legislature, to turn a blind eye. Legal thinking about the relationship between quality of life and free movement, and how the law should respond to that relationship, has hardly begun.[58] This chapter has tried merely to outline one way of looking at the problem. The horns of the dilemma are waiting to be seized.

[57] See n 21.

[58] Although see A Somek, *Individualism* (Oxford, Oxford University Press, 2008); F de Witte, 'Sex, Drugs and EU Law' (n 2); M Dani, 'Rehabilitating Social Conflicts in European Public Law' (2012) 18 *ELJ* 621.

12

Justification, Proportionality and Consumer Protection

STEPHEN WEATHERILL

I. INTRODUCTION

THIS CHAPTER DEALS with the protection of the consumer interest as a justification for restrictions on free movement. The cases which have put national measures of consumer protection to the test because they restrict inter-State trade have tended in the past to shine a light on bogus or at best deeply disingenuous claims by the regulating authority. The landmark *Cassis de Dijon* ruling is of exactly this type.[1] Finding violation of the proportionality principle is commonly the Court's way to provoke regulatory renovation at national level. On the face of it this suggests that control of *State* action in the name of proportionality is more aggressive than control of *EU* legislative action, where notoriously few measures are condemned by the Court. Moreover, on the face of it this suggests that control of consumer protection measures which restrict inter-State trade is more aggressive than control of national measures which impede trade but engage richer socio-cultural motivations and the defence of fundamental social and political rights and freedoms. But in fact it is the diet of cases fed to the Court that is the real determining factor.

The Court allowed little margin of appreciation to the regulating authority in the early years because of the poverty of the arguments advanced by way of justification. It was and is more generous to the EU as a legislator and to national authorities pursuing socio-cultural ends because their arguments tend to hold more water. Proportionality is part of the assessment, but under an approach which gives considerable space to the rulemaker to select among competing alternatives. More recently several consumer protection cases have followed this more tolerant model. My argument is that this is not because the Court has chosen to weaken its standard of review or to rethink its understanding of proportionality. Rather what has changed is that what the Court is asked to review is typically a far

[1] Case 120/78 *Rewe Zentrale v Bundesmonopolverwaltung für Branntwein* (*Cassis de Dijon*) EU:C:1979:42.

more coherent set of regulatory practices. And, faced by sincere regulatory choices rather than daft and anachronistic rules of the *Cassis de Dijon* type, the Court responds by adapting its review in the name of proportionality to confine its own intrusive power and to respect the diversity of Member State interventions.

II. THE RISE OF CONSUMER PROTECTION AS A JUSTIFICATION: PUBLIC HEALTH

Article 36 TFEU provides that 'The provisions of Articles 34 and 35 shall not preclude prohibitions or restrictions on imports, exports or goods in transit justified on grounds of ... (inter alia) the protection of health and life of humans, animals or plants.' There is no explicit reference to the consumer in Article 36, but the notion of the protection of the health and life of humans is capable of covering the protection of the physical integrity of the consumer. Accordingly, national rules designed to secure health and safety may be enforced notwithstanding any impediment to integration of markets for goods, provided the conditions under Article 36 are satisfied. The same is true of national rules that restrict integration in markets for services and in relation to the right of establishment. National rules that protect public health are capable of being shown to be justified, pursuant to Articles 52(1) and 62 TFEU. And the early cases that reached the Court were typically examined in this light.

Justification encompasses the compatibility with EU law of both the end in view and the means chosen to achieve that end. This is inherent in the second sentence of Article 36, which declares that 'such prohibitions or restrictions shall not, however, constitute a means of arbitrary discrimination or a disguised restriction on trade between Member States.' Accordingly, it is incumbent on the Member State to show that the national measure adopted is apt to achieve the end in view and the least restrictive of trade necessary to achieve that end.[2] A measure that does not meet these standards is readily condemned as disproportionate.

The Court is not prepared simply to accept at face value submissions that national measures are required to defend domestic health standards. A State may not justify restrictions on the importation of goods from other Member States by relying on mere allegations of health risks which are anyway contradicted by Commission inquiry.[3] In some cases the Court has demonstrated vigorous scepticism. A famous and vivid example is provided by *Commission v United Kingdom*.[4] In this case the UK sought to demonstrate that its restrictions on the import of poultry were justified in the light of the need to tackle the spread of Newcastle disease. The Court remarked on the haste with which the measures had been introduced in the approach to Christmas 1981 at a time when British turkey breeders were appealing

[2] Case 227/82 *Van Bennekom* EU:C:1983:354; Case C-14/02 *ATRAL SA* EU:C:2003:265.
[3] Case C-205/89 *Commission v Greece (pasteurised butter)* EU:C:1991:123.
[4] Case 40/82 *Commission v United Kingdom* EU:C:1984:33.

for protection. There was scant evidence of a seriously considered health policy and the UK, acting in breach of (what is now) Article 34 by obstructing imports, was unable to seek refuge in (what is now) Article 36. In such circumstances the Court is, in effect, identifying national measures as protectionism in favour of home producers. Such a ruling, prohibiting national measures, asserts consumer choice through market integration.

However, this is a fact-specific conclusion. *Eyssen* provides evidence of the Court's sensitivity to the context.[5] Dutch rules banning the use of nisin, a preservative, in processed cheese were presented as measures of health protection, yet other states were prepared to allow the use of nisin, adopting a different view of inconclusive scientific evidence about the safety of the substance. The Court held that a state may take precautions to protect its consumers against health risks in accordance with Article 36 where there is genuine scientific doubt about the safety of the product. EU law does not depress national standards of protection to the lowest common denominator prevailing among the Member States. More recently the Court has adopted the language of the 'precautionary principle' in conceding to Member States the space to maintain rules that restrict trade in goods, especially foodstuffs, on the basis that there is doubt about the effects of particular ingredients on the health of consumers. States enjoy a 'discretion relating to the protection of public health [which] is particularly wide where it is shown that uncertainties continue to exist in the current state of scientific research'.[6] The Court insists, however, that national authorisation procedures shall be targeted at identified risks, rather than applying indiscriminately or in cases of purely hypothetical risk, and that they shall be transparent and open to challenge.[7]

The Court tends to be respectful of a seriously considered health policy—even where other Member States are content with more permissive regimes. As the Court put it in *Ahokainen and Leppik*:

> Member States enjoy a margin of discretion in determining, having regard to the particular social circumstances and to the importance attached by those States to objectives which are legitimate ... such as the prevention of alcohol abuse and the campaign against the various forms of criminality linked to its consumption, the measures which are likely to achieve concrete results.[8]

A comparable permissive approach emerges in the field of free movement of services, where the Court, asked to consider the compatibility of France's *Loi Evin* with (what is now) Article 56 TFEU, concluded that the restrictions on trade consequent on the prohibition of advertisements for alcoholic drinks at sports events broadcast on television were a justified expression of concern to contain alcohol

[5] Case 53/80 *Eyssen* EU:C:1981:35.

[6] Case C-192/01 *Commission v Denmark* EU:C:2003:492 para 43.

[7] Case C-192/01 *Commission v Denmark* (n 6); also eg Case C-41/02 *Commission v Netherlands* EU:C:2004:762.

[8] Case C-434/04 *Ahokainen and Leppik* EU:C:2006:609 para 32.

abuse.[9] The Court, faced by submissions from the Commission and the United Kingdom that the rules were inconsistent, was not impressed. That the rules concerned only television advertising and did not apply to advertising for tobacco fell 'within the discretion of the Member States to decide on the degree of protection which they wish to afford to public health and on the way on which that protection is to be achieved'.[10] In similar vein the Court judged that the failure to extend the rules to cover advertising for alcoholic drinks visible in the background on film sets was an option that lies within the discretion of the regulating Member State.[11]

The Court has gone so far as to declare that the health and life of humans rank 'foremost among the interests' protected by the Treaty.[12] This does not at all permit national measures to escape review when they impede inter-State trade, but it does suggest that the Court will demonstrate a particular sensitivity to justifications rooted in health protection. Perhaps it does, but what matters most of all is the quality of the arguments advanced in defence of obstructive national rules. Whatever type of justification is relied on, the structure of the analysis is identical. So the Court has observed that 'the fact that one Member State imposes less strict rules than another Member State does not necessarily mean that the latter's rules are disproportionate and hence incompatible' with Union law.[13] A regulating State may set tougher standards than its competitors—if it can justify them where they restrict inter-State trade. The Court leaves little scope for implausible justifications dressed up as legitimate policy choices but it is sensitive to genuine regulatory anxiety. Pursuit of an integrated market under EU law does not involve the automatic disabling of national regulatory competence: consumer choice is not the inevitable result of the impact of EU 'negative law'. The next section looks beyond public health to show how other types of justification, which the Court may not rank as 'foremost' among the interests recognised by the Treaty, fall to be assessed against this framework. The key theme is allowing room for recognition of the diversity of regulatory systems and of national values among the Member States.

III. PROTECTION OF THE ECONOMIC INTERESTS OF CONSUMERS: BEYOND ARTICLE 36 TFEU

National measures which are designed to protect the *economic* interests of the consumer, yet which impede trade, such as rules against deceptive marketing practices or misleading product description or rules encouraging or requiring the provision of information to consumers, seem to fall beyond the scope of the justifi-

[9] Case C-262/02 *Commission v France* EU:C:2004:431; Case C-429/02 *Bacardi v TF1* EU:C:2004:432.

[10] Case C-262/02 *Commission v France* ibid, para 33.

[11] Case C-429/02 *Bacardi* ibid, para 40.

[12] eg Case C-170/04 *Rosengren* EU:C:2007:313 para 39; Case C-434/04 *Ahokainen and Leppik* (n 8) para 33; Case C-367/12 *Sokoll-Seebacher* EU:C:2014:68 para 26.

[13] Case C-294/00 *Deutsche Paracelsus Schulen (goods)* EU:C:2002:442; Case C-3/95 *Reisebüro Broede v Gerd Sanker (services)* EU:C:1996:487.

cations envisaged by Article 36. However, provided they are origin-neutral, such rules are capable of being defended despite their restrictive effect on trade. The assessment of the compatibility of such national measures with EU free movement law takes place against the background of one of the Court's most remarkable and celebrated creations, the *Cassis de Dijon* line of authority.[14] This applies where disparity between technical standards in different Member States relating to composition and, more extensively still, relating to marketing are shown to be capable of impeding trade by affecting imported goods more heavily in fact than home-produced goods. This shown, the inquiry turns to the determination of whether the national measures are justified. And famously the Court extended the reach of the available justifications to create a general public interest test: it decided that the requirements relating to the minimum alcohol content of alcoholic beverages imposed by German law did not serve 'a purpose which is in the general interest and such as to take precedence over the requirements of the free movement of goods.'[15]

The consistently rigid reading of Article 36 TFEU is subverted by the Court's creative readiness to admit a wide range of issues to its assessment of the compatibility of national restrictions on inter-State trade in the name of the general or the public interest. Free movement law is *porous*. The protection of the environment is not within the scope of Article 36 TFEU but the Court has long treated it as a concern which may limit the deregulatory bite of Article 34 TFEU.[16] So too may the protection of press diversity pursued by national rules,[17] the preservation of human dignity,[18] protection of the child,[19] and concern for animal welfare.[20]

The protection of the *economic* interests of consumers fits perfectly into the pattern whereby the Court has taken the scope of justification for trade-restrictive barriers beyond that set out in Article 36 TFEU. Indeed it is the first such extension, because it was at stake in *Cassis de Dijon* itself.

However, in close correspondence with public health, which is a justification explicitly recognised by Article 36 TFEU, the Court is not prepared simply to accept at face value submissions that national measures are required to defend the economic interests of consumers. In the *Cassis de Dijon* ruling itself a trade barrier was identified because French blackcurrant liqueur could not be sold in Germany because it fell below the minimum alcohol requirement for such goods under German law. The Court accepted *in principle* that interests beyond the explicit scope of Article 36 might be deployed by the regulator, Germany, but *in*

[14] Case 120/78 *Rewe Zentrale* (n 1).

[15] para 14.

[16] eg Case 302/86 *Commission v Denmark* EU:C:1988:421; Case C-379/98 *Preussen Elektra* EU:C:2001:160.

[17] Case C-368/95 *Vereinigte Familiapress Zeitungsverlags- und vertriebs GmbH v Heinrich Bauer Verlag* EU:C:1997:325.

[18] Case C-36/02 *Omega Spielhallen (free movement of services)* EU:C:2004:614.

[19] Case C-244/06 *Dynamic Medien* EU:C:2008:85.

[20] Case C-219/07 *Nationale Raad van Dierenkwekers en Liefhebbers* EU:C:2008:353.

practice it was unpersuaded. The Court quickly dismissed the preposterous argument that such a rule on product composition—banning weak drink but permitting strong—could be justified as a means to protect public health, and then moved to the slightly stronger claim that the German rule was justified as a means to protect the German consumer from confusion about the qualities of unfamiliar imported products. But here it decided that even if this was a justified end, the means used were unnecessarily restrictive. Labelling would suffice. In similar vein in the well-known *Beer Purity* case German law confined use of the name *Bier* to products brewed using *only* malted barley, hops, yeast and water.[21] Such strict rules governing the permissible ingredients of *Bier* unlawfully restricted the commercial opportunities in Germany of producers brewing elsewhere according to different recipes and traditions. In line with the strong deregulatory impetus in this case law, infused by a preference for the private autonomy of traders and consumers in the market over public regulation, the Court found no justification. German consumers might connect the designation *Bier* to the beverage manufactured solely from the stipulated ingredients, but 'consumers' conceptions which vary from one Member State to the other are also likely to evolve in the course of time within a Member State', and market integration is 'one of the factors that may play a major contributory role in that development'.[22] Any short-term risk of consumer confusion pending development of the market consequent on liberalised cross-border trade could be addressed by compulsory labelling laws, providing detail on the raw materials used in the manufacture of beer. As the Court took the trouble to point out, this pursuit of transparency could be achieved by addressing not only bottles or cans but also casks or beer taps.[23]

In similar vein, in the services sector, *Commission v France* involved French rules obliging tourist guides to obtain a licence.[24] This rule exerted a restrictive effect on the ability of tourist guides from outside France to accompany groups who wished to tour France. The Court did not deny the legitimacy of the objective of ensuring proper cultural and artistic appreciation of the host country, but found the rules in question disproportionately restrictive. The decision is built on an explicit assumption that the licensing requirement is not needed because the market will achieve the desired outcome: the Court considered that in the circumstances which confronted it the tour operator 'who faces competitive pressure from other tour companies' would exercise control over the quality of the services offered by guides in order to protect its reputation.

The rich implications of this approach include a rise in consumer choice and market autonomy; and a rise in the judicial role in making the market at the expense of the legislative role. Prohibiting a national rule contributes to free trade without the need for the EU to adopt legislation in the area. This has the gratifying

[21] Case 178/84 *Commission v Germany* EU:C:1987:126.
[22] ibid, para 34.
[23] ibid, para 36.
[24] Case C-154/89 *Commission v France* EU:C:1991:76.

consequence that diversity—in rules, in products and services—persists.[25] As the Court explicitly observed in the *Tourist Guide* case, the indefensible French rules had the effect that visiting groups would be denied the opportunity to be guided by someone 'who is familiar with their language, their interests and their specific expectations'. A range of national rules that act as impediments to inter-State trade are, if shown to be unjustified interference with the market, replaced by no pre-condition at all.

IV. PROPORTIONALITY AS POLITENESS

There is no doubt that the bulk of the case law dealing with obstructive national rules alleged to protect the economic interests of consumers involves condemnation of national rules that restrict trade. Justification is made out relatively rarely. The argument was presented above in examination of the cases concerning public health that this pattern is not driven by a bias in favour of deregulation but rather amounts to a context-specific rejection of attempts to justify that royally deserve to fail; and that where justification is, in short, more sincere, the Court reacts with appropriate sensitivity. The same inquiry—ideologically aggressive deregulation or context-specific adjudication—is now aimed at the case law that reaches beyond protection of the health of consumers. The same conclusion will be reached.

Commission v Portugal is not a classic consumer protection case but it is richly illustrative of prevailing trends when the Court finds itself confronted with abominably implausible arguments.[26] It involved a measure which prohibited the affixing of any type of tinted film designed to filter light to the windscreen and the windows alongside the passenger seats in motor vehicles. In classic *Cassis de Dijon* fashion, this constituted a technical standard that tended to exclude imported products from the Portuguese market. The Court stated that 'it is for the Member States to show that their legislation is appropriate to ensure the attainment of such objectives and that it is in conformity with the principle of proportionality'.[27] But it noted that Portugal had produced just one argument in support of the challenged measure. This was that it enabled the passenger compartment of motor vehicles to be inspected by means of a simple observation conducted from outside the vehicle. The Court gently pointed out that a visual inspection of this type was only one means among others available as methods to fight crime and prevent offences relating to the obligation to wear seat belts. And the alleged necessity of the measure was fatally wounded when, as the Court remarked, Portugal had admitted at the hearing that it in any event allowed the marketing of motor vehicles fitted *from the outset* with tinted windows. And the Court added—though

[25] This was central to the Commission's '1992' strategy: Commission Communication OJ 1980 C256/2; COM (85) 310, the 'White Paper' on the Completion of the Internal Market, para 61 et seq.

[26] Case C-265/06 *Commission v Portugal* EU:C:2008:210.

[27] ibid, para 39.

the matter surely required no further debate!—that banning tinted film which is transparent went too far since such film would anyway permit visual inspection of the interior of motor vehicles. So the Court concluded that the 'ban must be regarded as being excessive and, therefore, disproportionate with respect to the objectives pursued'.[28]

One may ask which is the more absurd: applying such rules or seeking to defend them in Luxembourg when challenged. The reality here is that this is plain stupid regulation. Proportionality is a polite way of expressing disdain at such over-regulation—more polite than lampooning Portugal for its crass stupidity. EU puts national measures that restrict inter-State trade to the test and in a case like this it slashes away regulatory deadwood.

And many of the early cases on the protection of the economic interests of the consumer are of exactly this type.

In *Cassis de Dijon* there is no explicit mention of the proportionality principle in the judgment, but the structure of the Court's analysis is familiar. The Court dismissed the public health justification brusquely, but, observing that it is 'a simple matter to ensure that suitable information is conveyed to the purchaser by requiring the display of an indication of origin and of the alcohol content on the packaging of products',[29] it used the principle that justification is excluded where there are less restrictive means available to combat consumer confusion about alcohol content than those chosen by the regulator. This is an application of the proportionality principle.

Proportionality appears explicitly in *Walter Rau v de Smedt*.[30] Member States may not prohibit sale of imported margarine in cone-shaped packs where local rules insisted on cube-shaped packaging. Citing *Cassis*, the Court set out what has become widely known as the principle of non-absolute mutual recognition, and added that 'It is also necessary for such rules to be proportionate to the aim in view'; and that 'If a Member State has a choice between various measures to attain the same objective it should choose the means which least restricts the free movement of goods'.[31]

It fully accepted that in principle legislation designed to prevent butter and margarine from being confused in the mind of the consumer would be justified, but achieving that objective through mandatory rules on use of a specific kind of packaging was found 'considerably' to exceed the requirements of the object in view.[32] Labelling would do the job.

Verein gegen Unwesen in Handel und Gewerbe Köln eV v Mars GmbH arose when Mars was the subject of proceedings in Germany aimed at stopping it from

[28] ibid, para 47.
[29] ibid, para 13.
[30] Case 261/81 *Walter Rau v de Smedt* EU:C:1982:382.
[31] ibid, para 12.
[32] ibid, para 17.

displaying a 'flash' on the wrapper of a chocolate bar which advertised the bar as 10 per cent larger in size for the period of a short publicity campaign.[33] The claim was accurate. The bar was 10 per cent bigger. But the 'flash' on the wrapper covered a surface area of more than 10 per cent and it was alleged that it would mislead consumers about the size of the bar. The Court stated that 'reasonably circumspect consumers' are aware that there is no necessary link between publicity markings relating to the size of increase in a product and the size of the increase itself. So Germany's intervention could not be justified. The Court does not reach this conclusion by explicit reliance on the principle of proportionality. In fact, the judgment is remarkably brief. It skips directly from reference to the 'reasonably circumspect' consumer as a benchmark to a finding that the intervention is incompatible with (what is now) Article 34. But the judgment fits perfectly well with an orthodox proportionality analysis. The Court is in effect taking the view that if there truly exist consumers in Germany who are so gullible that they are misled by this type of practice then there must be less restrictive means to address their vulnerability than the imposition of a blanket prohibition on the practice that denies all consumers the benefits of choice in an integrating market.

These cases—and there are heaps more[34]—all involve attempts to use the language of consumer protection to put respectable clothes on protectionist rules that favour local producer interests or rules that simply long ago lost whatever purpose they once have had. The Court will not have it. The aggressive application of EU law is conditioned by the lack of sincerity in the arguments. The Court politely holds (explicitly or by implication) that less restrictive means are available to meet the end in view, but this is a very easy conclusion to reach, since the claimed benefits of the measures in question are so obviously thin and the costs so substantial. Perhaps a consumer here or there will be surprised by and disappointed in the liqueur, the margarine or the chocolate bar that they buy: most consumers will adapt and choose. It is possible to view these as cases involving aggressive application of the proportionality principle but, better, they are cases which condemn State practices as lying beyond the realm of rational regulation when they intervene in a way that assumes that all consumers are gullible.

The chief problem here is not the Court's unwillingness to address justifications advanced by Member States, but rather the Member States' persistent failure to engage constructively in consideration of what degree of regulatory protection a consumer requires in an integrating European market.

Use of the proportionality principle is a type of politeness in these cases. Justification is available in principle to a regulating State wishing to defend tougher standards than its competitors. But it should not come empty-handed to Luxembourg. However, where the Court is presented with arguments to justify sincere

[33] Case C-470/93 *Mars GmbH* EU:C:1995:224.

[34] eg Case 286/86 *Deserbais (fat content of cheese)* EU:C:1988:434. See S Weatherill, *EU Consumer Law and Policy* 2nd edn (Cheltenham, Edward Elgar, 2013) ch 2.

and targeted regulatory choices it does not routinely impose market solutions. This has already been shown above in exploration of the cases dealing with public health protection. Its elaboration in application to cases dealing with the *economic* interests of consumers is explored in the next section.

V. REGULATORY ROOM TO BREATHE

Buet concerned a French rule which went beyond giving consumers the right of cancellation required by the so-called 'Doorstep Selling' Directive, which mandated only minimum rules.[35] France had chosen to apply a ban on canvassing at private dwellings for the sale of educational material. This protected consumers against ill-considered purchases to a degree that the EU legislature had not thought necessary—and moreover to a degree that went beyond what other Member States thought necessary. It was challenged as an obstacle to inter-State trade by a firm that sold English-language teaching material which earned 90 per cent of its turnover by such canvassing at private dwellings.[36] The Court, however, found the rules capable of justification. The centrally important point was that the French rules were, unlike those in *Cassis* and the other peculiar cases considered above, targeted at particular sensitivities and particular products. The Court placed careful emphasis on the greater risk of an ill-considered purchase 'when the canvassing is for enrolment for a course of instruction or the sale of educational material … [because] the potential purchaser often belongs to a category of people who, for one reason or another, are behind with their education and are seeking to catch up.'[37] That, the Court observed, 'makes them particularly vulnerable'.[38] It noted too that the French ban had been enacted 'as a result of numerous complaints caused by such abuses, such as the sale of out-of-date courses'.[39] And it added that 'since teaching is not a consumer product in daily use, an ill-considered purchase could cause the purchaser harm other than mere financial loss that could be longer lasting'.[40]

Accordingly EU free movement law did not serve to deregulate the (French) market. Instead it was interpreted to grant respect to the local regulatory choice designed to protect particularly vulnerable consumers. This is a vision that stretches the sensitivity of EU consumer law beyond a narrow focus on choice and market competition.

[35] Case 382/87 *Buet* EU:C:1989:198.

[36] ibid, para 2. Today there would arise a question whether this is enough to bring the matter within the scope of Art 34 TFEU: for discussion in this context of the impact of Cases C-267 and 268/91 *Keck and Mithouard* EU:C:1993:905 see Weatherill, *EU Consumer Law and Policy* (n 34) 37–39.

[37] ibid, para 13.

[38] ibid, para 13.

[39] ibid, para 13.

[40] ibid, para 14.

In similar vein *A-Punkt Schmuckhandels GmbH v Claudia Schmidt* concerned the prohibition of home jewellery parties in Austria.[41] If this was found to be a barrier to inter-State trade, a matter for the national court to determine,[42] then the Court of Justice was open to the possibility of finding it to be justified despite its restrictive effect on commercial freedom. The Court, using the *Cassis* ruling explicitly as its lodestone, noted that the rule was apt to

> take account of the specific features associated with the sale of silver jewellery in private homes, in particular the potentially higher risk of the consumer being cheated due to a lack of information, the impossibility of comparing prices or the provision of insufficient safeguards as regards the authenticity of that jewellery and the greater psychological pressure to buy where the sale is organised in a private setting.[43]

This is focused—targeted—consumer protection. *Buet* involved a class of consumers vulnerable for want of education, *A-Punkt* concerned consumers who may be vulnerable in a particular setting (at home). In neither case is what is at stake untargeted over-regulation of the type which the Court was asked to examine in *Cassis de Dijon*. Where the national regulator has identified a particular need for protection and crafted a law that is appropriately nuanced and specific, the Court responds by assessing its justifiability with respect for that nuance. *Buet* and *A-Punkt* stand for the limits of consumer choice and market competition promoted by EU free movement law. And the same theme is found in recent cases in the services sector.

In *DKV Belgium* the Court addressed Belgian rules restraining an increase in premium rates for 'individual room' coverage in hospitalisation insurance.[44] The Court found this was a restriction on the right of establishment and the freedom to provide services. But it was receptive to the justification of the particular Belgian rules. It referred to the permissible objective of protecting consumers against sharp, unexpected increases in insurance premiums, though it left it to the national court to ascertain whether or not the chosen system of national regulation went beyond what is necessary in order to achieve that objective.

Citroën Belux concerned a commercial practice engaged in by Citroën consisting of a free offer of comprehensive insurance for six months on the purchase of a Citroën vehicle.[45] This was challenged in Belgium as a prohibited 'combined offer'. This falls within the material scope of Directive 2005/29 on unfair commercial practices, which applies a regime of maximum harmonisation, and so would normally provide a complete answer to the question of whether the practice is fair or not, to the exclusion of Belgian preference. But Article 3(9) of Directive 2005/29 excludes financial services from the maximum harmonisation regime and states

[41] Case C-441/04 *A-Punkt Schmuckhandels GmbH v Claudia Schmidt* EU:C:2006:141.
[42] A delicate 'post-*Keck*' question: *cf* n 36 above.
[43] Case C-441/04 *A-Punkt* (n 41) para 29.
[44] Case C-577/11 *DKV Belgium* EU:C:2013:146.
[45] Case C-265/12 *Citroën Belux* EU:C:2013:498.

instead that Member States may apply more restrictive rules. This is explained by the Directive's Preamble on the basis that:

> Financial services and immovable property, by reason of their complexity and inherent serious risks, necessitate detailed requirements, including positive obligations on traders. For this reason, in the field of financial services and immovable property, this Directive is without prejudice to the right of Member States to go beyond its provisions to protect the economic interests of consumers.

The measure therefore already openly steers thinking towards the particularly pressing need for supplementary protection in this sector, should a Member State choose to provide it. This mirrors *Buet*, which concerned the 'Doorstep Selling' Directive, although in *Citroën Belux* the EU measure does not generally set only minimum standards, but rather it is minimum in character only in its targeting of a particular sector, that of financial services.

Article 56 TFEU was the applicable Treaty provision. The Belgian rule restricted the cross-border provision of services. It was capable of rendering less attractive the provision of financial services in Belgium for businesses established in other Member States who wish to make combined offers of which at least one component is a financial service. So was it justified? The Court concluded that it was. The Belgian choice revealed a sector-specific sensitivity, and the Court was willing to accept that 'financial services are, by nature, complex and entail specific risks with regard to which the consumer is not always sufficiently well informed'.[46] It added that a combined offer of which one component is a financial service tends to lack transparency as regards the conditions, the price and the exact content of that service. So 'such an offer may well mislead consumers as to the true content and actual characteristics of the combination offered and, at the same time, deprive them of the opportunity of comparing the price and quality of that offer with other corresponding services from other economic operators'.[47]

The Court therefore upheld the rule as a contribution to consumer protection. This confirms that the Court is not always aggressively deregulatory in its application of free movement law. A Member State which serves up sincere and targeted arguments for justification can expect to be treated in those terms. There is a match to the approach taken in cases concerning public health such as *Eyssen*, considered above. Public health may enjoy 'foremost' ranking as a justification in the rhetoric of the Court,[48] but in truth the structure of the inquiry applies in common whatever type of justification is advanced by a national regulator. The key is the *quality* of the argument. The more sincere—as an antidote to the poison of anachronistic rulemaking or protectionism—the better. The more targeted—as evasion of blanket over-regulation—the better.

[46] ibid, para 39.
[47] ibid, para 39.
[48] n 12 above.

Article 12 TFEU and Article 38 of the Charter may be expected to act as an increasingly prominent frame for this pro-consumer interpretative approach. Article 12 directs that 'Consumer protection requirements shall be taken into account in defining and implementing other Union policies and activities'; Article 38 simply declares 'Union policies shall ensure a high level of consumer protection'. However, these provisions exert no transformative effect, for the Court's anxiety to treat the law of the internal market as infused with sensitivity to the needs of *genuine* consumer protection is long-standing.[49]

This claim goes beyond consumer protection as a justification for trade-restrictive rules. Article 12 TFEU is just one of several horizontal or cross-cutting provisions in the Treaty that have been added incrementally over time and which mandate policy integration between, inter alia, the internal market and several broader types of regulatory concerns. Provisions in the TFEU such as Articles 11 (environmental protection), 165 (sport), 167 (culture) and 168 (human health) all serve to buttress the argument that free movement law must be applied in this manner sensitive to regulatory values underpinning national measures that restrict trade. Perhaps they might be thought to strengthen that sensitivity, but, at the level of structure, they are confirmation of, not a break with, the Court's past approach. Environmental protection pursued at national level has long been part of the Court's assessment conducted in the name of free movement;[50] sporting bodies were always able to make a case that their legitimate concerns should mitigate the application of free movement law to their practices even before sport became formally recognised by the Treaties with effect from 2009;[51] culture too has been woven into the determination of whether national measures that restrict trade are justified;[52] while health protection formed the meat of most of the very earliest free movement cases decided by the Court, unsurprisingly given its inclusion from the beginning in Article 36 itself.

The Charter too fits comfortably into the well-established analytical structure of free movement law. Its Articles 15 to 17 in the Chapter entitled *Freedoms* correspond to Articles 34 and 56 TFEU, while provisions such as Articles 22 (culture), 35 (health), 37 (environment) and 38 (consumer) are readily aligned with orthodox justifications embraced in free movement law. There is no transformative effect. So in *Commission v Austria*[53] the Court, examining justifications advanced for restrictions on the free movement of goods, simply bundled up (what were then) Articles 2, 3, 6 and 152(1) EC with Articles 35 and 37 of the Charter as

[49] *Cf* S Weatherill, 'Article 38—Consumer Protection' in S Peers, T Hervey, J Kenner and A Ward (eds), *The EU Charter of Fundamental Rights: A Commentary* (Beck, Hart, Nomos, 2014).

[50] eg Case 302/86 *Commission v Denmark* (n 16); Case C-379/98 *Preussen Elektra* (n 16).

[51] Case C-415/93 *Bosman* EU:C:1995:463 especially para 106; Case C-519/04P *Meca-Medina and Majcen v Commission* EU:C:2006:492 especially paras 43, 45, 51.

[52] eg Case C-250/06 *United Pan-Europe Communications Belgium SA* EU:C:2007:783; Case C-531/07 *Fachverband/ LIBRO* EU:C:2009:276 para 34.

[53] Case C-28/09 *Commission v Austria* EU:C:2011:854.

sources of respect for health and environmental protection. The Charter fits easily into the familiar structure of free movement law as an amplification of the relevant material relied on to assess whether a restriction is justified. In *Pfleger* the Court carefully examined the justification for restricting the freedom to provide gambling services within the scope of Article 56 TFEU, and agreed there was room to justify such restrictions in the name of consumer protection and the prevention of both fraud and incitement to squander money on gambling, subject to compliance with proportionality and non-discrimination.[54] The Court then added that the challenged national measures were restrictive not only from the point of view of Article 56 TFEU but also limitations from the perspective of Articles 15 to 17 of the Charter dealing with the freedom to choose an occupation, the freedom to conduct a business and the right to property. But it seems that this adds nothing and changes nothing. The Court simply declared that there was no need for separate examination of the Charter-based claims. Analysis in the case seems to run in perfect parallel to the Court's rather well-established pre-Charter treatment of controls over gambling that restrict inter-State trade.[55] The Charter has not changed free movement law.

Where the State comes empty-handed to Luxembourg it should expect no more generous treatment today than in the past: equally where its regulatory anxieties are sincere and reflected in coherently designed rules it should today, as in the past, expect a Court that is appropriately sensitive. This is a thematic structure that is shared by the Court of Justice's cases dealing with public health protection expressed at national level and by those dealing with the protection of economic interests of consumers. Free movement law is and always has been *porous*.

VI. ALIGNMENT WITH FUNDAMENTAL RIGHTS / MARGIN APPRECIATION CASES

It is well known that cases which have pitted fundamental economic rights against fundamental social and political rights have triggered a noticeably cautious approach by the Court, both to the deregulatory edge of EU free movement law as a control on State regulatory autonomy and to the room for decision of the referring national court. These cases are, I believe, context-driven: the sensitivity of the Court's treatment of claimed justifications is attributable to the complex subject matter and, in particular, to the sensitivity of the calculations it is asked to make. These are the cases which deserve to be read alongside the cases in which the Court has dealt sensitively with sincere and duly targeted measures of consumer protection that obstruct inter-State trade.

[54] Case C-390/12 *Pfleger* EU:C:2014:281.

[55] eg Case C-124/97 *Läärä and Others* EU:C:1999:435; Joined Cases C-338/04 et al *Massimiliano Placanica* EU:C:2007:133; Case C-42/07 *Liga Portuguesa de Futebol Professional and Bwin International* EU:C:2009:519; Case C-258/08 *Ladbrokes* EU:C:2010:308.

It is well known that in *ERT v Dimotiki* the Court for the first time established a clear link between justification for trade barriers and compliance with fundamental rights.[56] It insisted on interpretation of the scope of the freedom to provide services in the light of the general principle of freedom of expression embodied in Article 10 of the European Convention on Human Rights. State restrictions on broadcasting which impeded trade in services had to be justified with reference to the Convention. No adequate justification for the restrictions was demonstrated. Today one would certainly add in a requirement that any such justification would need to be justified with reference to the Charter. Article 11, on freedom of expression and information, would add another thump against the possibility to justify State restrictions on broadcasting which impede trade in services. But in *ERT v Dimotiki* the Court had already in 1991 seized the opportunity to structure the law of free movement in such a way as to accommodate such social and political values.

The case law, driven by EU law's ever-present ingenious and commercially motivated litigants, has grown. It does not deserve exhaustive examination here, because the purpose of this account is only to show structural similarities between it and the consumer cases considered above. *Schmidberger v Austria* is vividly illustrative.[57] The Austrian authorities had permitted a protest to block the movement of transport through the Brenner Pass. The Austrian failure to intervene was in principle capable of falling within the scope of what is now Article 34 TFEU because it led to a temporary obstacle to trade in goods. The justification was rooted in concern to protect the freedom of assembly and freedom of expression of those wishing to draw attention to the environmental damage caused by such trade. In short, economic rights clashed with political rights. The Court declared that:

> since both the Community and its Member States are required to respect fundamental rights, the protection of those rights is a legitimate interest which, in principle, justifies a restriction of the obligations imposed by Community law, even under a fundamental freedom guaranteed by the Treaty such as the free movement of goods.[58]

The economic and the political are both fundamental rights, but they are not absolute rights. The Court stated that 'the interests involved must be weighed having regard to all the circumstances of the case in order to determine whether a fair balance was struck between those interests'; and added that the 'competent authorities enjoy a wide margin of discretion in that regard'.[59] The Court then proceeded actively to assess the balance. Noting a range of factors[60] it made plain that the Austrian (lack of) action against those conducting the protests constituted no violation of EU law, despite the restrictive effect on cross-border trade in goods.

[56] Case C-260/89 *ERT v Dimotiki* EU:C:1991:254.
[57] Case C-112/00 *Schmidberger v Austria* EU:C:2003:333.
[58] ibid, para 74.
[59] ibid, paras 81–82.
[60] ibid, paras 81–94.

The more sensitive and the more remote from commercial considerations the matters advanced in the context of justification of trade barriers, the more generous the Court tends to be to the available scope for justification and also to the breadth of the margin of appreciation enjoyed by the regulator.

A comparable result, but according to slightly different reasoning, may be identified in *Omega Spielhallen*.[61] The case concerned the suppression of games involving simulated killing in Germany on the basis that such practices offended against constitutionally protected standards of respect for human dignity. Imports from the United Kingdom were as a result impeded, and so the Treaty rules on the free movement of services were engaged. Was the German intervention justified? The Court ruled:

> the Community legal order undeniably strives to ensure respect for human dignity as a general principle of law. There can therefore be no doubt that the objective of protecting human dignity is compatible with Community law, it being immaterial in that respect that, in Germany, the principle of respect for human dignity has a particular status as an independent fundamental right.[62]

This is deft. The Court did not frame its analysis as EU free movement law versus German protection of human dignity, but instead as EU free movement law versus *EU* protection of human dignity. The justification was rooted not in German specificity but in EU embrace of a standard of protection comparable with that chosen in Germany (but not found to the same degree in other Member States). In this way the Court ensured that EU law accommodated German anxieties *as EU anxieties*. Today the Charter could and should play a role in this analysis. That human dignity is 'inviolable' is asserted by its Article 1, and this would be readily deployed as part of an argument that restrictions on free movement motivated by concern to protect human dignity are capable of being treated as justified as a matter of EU law. This, however, would be to use the Charter in a decorative rather than a transformative role. *Omega* shows how the Court was already able to convert internal market law into a site where such social, political and cultural sensitivity could be taken seriously.

It is not the Charter alone that may be taken as the Lisbon Treaty's contribution to asserting—in my estimation, confirming—the breadth of values that inform the law of the internal market. According to Article 4(2) TEU the Union 'shall respect the equality of Member States before the Treaties as well as their national identities, inherent in their fundamental structures, political and constitutional, inclusive of regional and local self-government'. This is the more elaborate successor to a provision which pre-Lisbon simply provided that 'The Union shall respect the national identities of its Member States'. The new version could be read as an invitation to show increased respect for national diversity, inter alia in connection

[61] Case C-36/02 *Omega Spielhallen* (n 18).
[62] ibid, para 34.

with free movement law's application to national restrictions. The background to the richly illustrative ruling in *Ilonka Sayn-Wittgenstein v Landeshauptmann von Wien*[63] was an Austrian law from 1919 abolishing the nobility which, inter alia, did away with titles, whereas Germany had done away with privileges but allowed parts of the noble title to be retained in the surname. The applicant was Ilonka Fürstin von Sayn-Wittgenstein in Germany. In Austria she was advised she must be registered instead as Ilonka Sayn-Wittgenstein. This constituted serious inconvenience to her commercial activity. This was selling castles. This was a restriction of the freedom envisaged by Article 21 TFEU, although the matter could also have been readily treated from the perspective of Article 56 TFEU. In the matter of justification, the Court noted that Austria was concerned to abolish titles in the service of equality of citizens before the law. This is recognised under EU law in Article 20 of the Charter. The Court cited *Omega Spielhallen*:[64] these are sensitive issues, where national authorities are permitted a 'margin of discretion'.[65] It then observed that in accordance with Article 4(2) TEU the Union is to respect the national identities of its Member States and that it did not appear disproportionate for a Member State to seek to attain the objective of protecting equal treatment by prohibiting use of titles of nobility.[66]

This is not *exactly* the same as *Omega*. There the Court converted a national constitutional concern into an EU constitutional concern. In *Sayn-Wittgenstein* it used Article 4(2) TEU to show respect for a specifically *Austrian* concern. But the particular trick in *Sayn-Wittgenstein* is to use Article 4(2) to convert a particular substantive national concern, equality, into the EU concern to respect difference where it operates at a sufficiently elevated level, where national identity is engaged. And in any event the difference is slight in practice: free movement law yields to justified national measures on either model. The theme is the Court's concern to take seriously *as a matter of EU law* sensitive matters of social and political concern and of national identity which, as *Omega* and *Schmidberger* demonstrate, is by no means a post-Lisbon innovation.[67]

These cases look different from the classic cases such as *Cassis de Dijon* on the protection of the economic interests of consumers. But I think that the differences relate to quality and sincerity of arguments, not to a fundamental separation of particular areas driven by subject matter. The margin referred to in these cases is exactly the margin also allowed to protect consumers from doorstep selling, home parties, combined offers and so on. States are allowed room to do things differently if they have a sufficiently strong reason.

63 Case C-208/09 *Ilonka Sayn-Wittgenstein v Landeshauptmann von Wien* EU:C:2010:806.
64 Case C-36/02 *Omega Spielhallen* (n 18).
65 ibid, para 87.
66 ibid, paras 92–93.
67 *cf* on mandatory language rules Case C-391/09 *Runevič-Vardyn and Wardyn* EU:C:2011:291; Case C-202/11 *Anton Las v PSA Antwerp* EU:C:2013:239; and the much older ruling in Case 379/87 *Groener* EU:C:1989:599.

So there is a common thread to the case law in which national regulatory intervention is put to the test of EU law where it impedes cross-border trade integration. The key feature that the rulings have in common is sensitivity to the context in which the dispute has arisen. Where justificatory arguments are a sincere reflection of diversity among the Member States in dealing with matters demanding complex and sensitive assessment, the Court leaves room for choice. Compliance with the proportionality principle is necessary but relatively easily achieved: the intensity of review is relatively soft. Where, by contrast, the arguments are thin and reveal incoherent policy choices the Court is much more aggressive, for it scents protectionism or at least anachronistic regulation. In such cases violation of the proportionality principle is readily found but what the Court is really doing is using proportionality as a polite way to condemn Member States for practices that have no place in an integrating market, either because they have been introduced to brake that process in the interest of local traders or simply because they are the lazy remnants of long-standing regimes that need updating but, in the absence of the propulsion provided by EU free movement law, will not receive it because of political inertia.

What the Court does not perform is proportionality review in the strict sense. It does not find that a measure pursues a legitimate objective, forms part of a coherent policy and is the least restrictive means to get to the end result—but find it unlawful because the competing interest in trade integration is more compelling. That would be very intrusive. The Court does not do it.

VII. ALIGNMENT WITH PROPORTIONALITY REVIEW IN THE CONTEXT OF REVIEW OF EU MEASURES

Compliance with the principle of proportionality is a condition of the legality of EU measures. A measure that imposes burdens which go beyond those necessary to bring about its intended objectives is disproportionate and it is therefore invalid. But it is rare to find examples of the Court finding EU acts to be invalid for this reason.

Alliance for Natural Health offers an illustration of the Court's typical approach.[68] An EU Directive permitted the marketing of nutrients only where they had received a favourable opinion from the competent scientific authorities. Nutrients that had not been shown to present a risk to human health, but were not in receipt of a favourable opinion, were prohibited. It was argued that this 'positive list' system was a more burdensome means of regulating the market than the 'negative list'. The Court agreed, but it did not agree that the burden was disproportionate. The chosen legislative measures were appropriate for achieving their objective and the Court, citing the obligation of the EU legislature to pursue a high level of protection of human health which is now contained in Articles 114(3) and

[68] Joined Cases C-154 and 155/04 *Alliance for Natural Health* EU:C:2005:449.

168(1) TFEU as well as Article 35 of the Charter, concluded that they did not go beyond what was necessary to attain that objective.[69] In similar vein the Court decided that imposing strict conditions on authorisation to use heavy fuel oils with a sulphur content of more than 1 per cent by mass entailed substantial costs for some economic operators but that this was justified given the importance of the objectives of environmental protection pursued by the measure.[70]

Typical, too, of the Court's approach is *Vodafone, O2 et al v Secretary of State*, in which the Court conceded a broad discretion to the EU legislature in areas involving political, economic and social choices in which it is called upon to undertake complex assessments and evaluations.[71] This case involved an attack on the validity of the so-called 'Roaming Regulation', Regulation 717/2007. The Regulation caps the wholesale and retail charges terrestrial mobile operators may impose for the provision of roaming services on public mobile networks for voice calls between Member States. It is a measure of harmonisation adopted in the service of the internal market. The Court was faced with the argument that the Regulation infringed the principle of proportionality (and subsidiarity) by covering not only wholesale but also retail charges. But it resisted this on the basis that there is an interdependence between the two levels in the chain which makes the regulation of one but not the other inadequate to meet the task at hand. Legality would be called into question only if the measure is manifestly inappropriate having regard to the objective which the EU is seeking to pursue. There was no such flaw to be found. This is very much the Court's preferred formula. A great many decisions of the Court confirm its willingness to intervene only where a measure is manifestly inappropriate to the objective in view, which reflects its determination to allow the political institutions room to enjoy a sufficient discretionary power in lawmaking.[72]

The package of cases that involve review of EU measures do not include the absurdities of *Cassis de Dijon* and the like. So any inspection of the Court's Reports shows that EU measures tend to escape invalidation, whereas national measures are commonly found to lack justification. But the main reason is not the standard of review but rather the context: the EU may not always be a smart regulator but by definition it, unlike a national regulator, does not come to court to try to defend ancient rules that long ago lost their purpose but not their legal form, nor does it normally deal in rules that exert a protectionist effect between Member States. So the differences relate to quality and sincerity of arguments, not to the identity of rulemaker, EU or national. The margin referred to in these cases involving EU legislative review is functionally the same margin allowed to *national* authorities

[69] ibid, para 111.

[70] Case C-86/03 *Greece v Commission* EU:C:2005:769.

[71] Case C-58/08 *Vodafone, O2 et al v Secretary of State* EU:C:2010:321.

[72] eg Case 331/88 *R v The Minister for Agriculture, Fisheries and Food and The Secretary of State for Health, ex parte Fedesa* EU:C:1990:391; Case C-110/97 *Netherlands v Council* EU:C:2001:620; Case C-94/05 *Emsland-Stärke GmbH* EU:C:2006:185; Case C-558/07 *SPCM and others* EU:C:2009:430.

to protect consumers from doorstep selling, home parties, and combined offers—and to permit green protests and to protect human dignity even where trade is restricted. States are allowed room to do things differently if they have a sufficiently strong reason in circumstances involving complex political, economic and social choices.

The Court is not aggressive in its use of proportionality to discipline measures that are more restrictive than is conceivable where what is at stake is a genuine matter of public concern in respect of which sensitive assessment is called for and in respect of which differing solutions may plausibly be chosen (and typically where national, rather than EU, measures are under review differing solutions *have* indeed been chosen).

VIII. CASES BEFORE NATIONAL COURTS

Even if the Court of Justice's rulings sometimes leave little room for doubt about its view of the proper concrete assessment, as a matter of form the division of function envisaged by the preliminary reference procedure allocates to the national court the final decision on whether a challenged national measure meets the test of proportionality. It is, however, remarkably difficult to find out much about how national courts make the assessment. One splendid but now dated book-length treatment exists,[73] but there is nothing remotely systematic available. Generating such findings would be hugely valuable, though it would require a huge resource commitment too. Cases that come to attention tend to be high-profile events that reach the appellate courts, and, in constructing an explanatory model, there is a real risk of attributing too much weight to the trends visible because counter-trends that might emerge from lower down the judicial hierarchy are simply not known. Cases reaching the appellate courts may not be typical: indeed, since 'the facts assumed or adopted by an appellate court have gone through straining and distortion',[74] their disposal may not have much to do with the dispute that provoked them in the first place. That said, one can make do—warily—only with the material one has.

In the United Kingdom one of the more notable expressions of exasperation about the demands of proportionality under EU law emerged from the notorious 'Sunday Trading' saga, in which it was argued that rules restricting shop opening hours and products that may be sold on a Sunday conflicted with EU free movement law. In *Stoke on Trent Council v B & Q*,[75] a case which ultimately reached the

[73] M Jarvis, *The Application of EC Law by National Courts: The Free Movement of Goods* (Oxford, Clarendon Press, 1998).

[74] K Llewellyn, *The Bramble Bush* (New York, Oceana, 1951) 58. Llewellyn's insights are easily adapted to illuminate the EU's preliminary reference procedure.

[75] [1991] 2 WLR 42.

Court of Justice as a preliminary reference,[76] Hoffmann J (as he then was) sitting in the High Court declared that 'by far the most important question in this case concerns the function of the court in applying the proportionality tests'. He noted that rules governing shop opening hours was a matter 'on which strong and differing views may be held and which has been the subject of frequent parliamentary debate'. He continued:

> In my judgment it is not my function to carry out the balancing exercise or to form my own view on whether the legislative objective could be achieved by other means. These questions involve compromises between competing interests which in a democratic society must be resolved by the legislature. The duty of the court is only to inquire whether the compromise adopted by the United Kingdom Parliament, so far as it affects community trade, is one which a reasonable legislature could have reached.

Part of the legitimating force of EU law lies precisely in its capacity to grant judges a lever capable of prising out anachronistic and protectionist rules that would be left untouched by the political process. It is not in line with EU law to refuse to carry out this inquiry. However, Hoffmann J has a point in his anxiety about what judges are being invited to do, and, finding no violation of EU law, he reaches the right result. Today one would dispose of such a case on the basis that there is no adequate impediment to inter-State trade,[77] but even if one demanded justification then, given the complex socio-cultural issues at stake, it would be relatively straightforward to regard this as a case where respect should be given to the margin of appreciation enjoyed by the rule-maker. So any reform should arrive through the legislative route.[78]

The EU law idea behind *R (Countryside Alliance) v AG* was as ingenious as it was unsuccessful.[79] The Hunting Act 2004 was attacked as an unlawful impediment to inter-State trade in goods—specifically that because horses could no longer be used to carry riders in pursuit of foxes there was a diminution in demand for (inter alia, imported) horses. The speech of Lord Bingham in the House of Lords carried clear echoes of Hoffmann J, in particular in its overt concern not to serve as a judicial route to achieving ends that could not be reached through political means. He insisted on the matter as 'pre-eminently one in which respect should be shown to what the House of Commons decided', being 'a question of moral and political judgment'.

Here too the case would best be decided today as one in which no sufficient obstacle to inter-State trade had been shown to exist and in which therefore there was no obligation on the regulating Member State to show a justification.[80] However, it would be easy to bring the analysis of justification within the margin of

[76] Case C-169/91 *Stoke on Trent and Norwich City Councils v B & Q plc* EU:C:1992:519.

[77] Cases C-267 and 268/91 *Keck and Mithouard* (n 36); Cases C-401 & C-402/92 *Tankstation 't Heukste & JBE Boermans* EU:C:1994:220; Case C-483/12 *Pelckmans Turnhout* EU:C:2014:304.

[78] Which it subsequently did: Sunday Trading Act 1994.

[79] [2007] UKHL 52, [2008] 1 AC 719

[80] Case C-142/05 *Åklagaren v Mickelsson, Roos* EU:C:2009:336.

appreciation permitted in cases such as *Omega*,[81] which is cited in the judgments, and *Schmidberger*,[82] which was cited in argument but not relied on the judgments. Once again, the point would be that if there is to be reform, it should be delivered through the political process.

Both these English decisions reflect a relatively soft intensity of application of the proportionality principle. In neither instance was the national measure perfectly coherent. The rules on 'Sunday trading' were a chaotic mess, the result of pressure on lawmakers over time from the Church and, more recently, trade unions. One could, for example, sell newspapers on a Sunday, but not bibles. Under the Hunting Act one may not hunt foxes and deer, but one may hunt rabbits and rats. The rules were and are odd. But they are not anachronistic, in the sense that they were and are the best that could be extracted from relatively recent attempts to cut a path through a tangled thicket of political disagreement about how to achieve reform, and they were not protectionist either.

Two recent cases in the United Kingdom have reached the higher courts in the field of public health. Both reflect the sense of judicial restraint that pervades the Luxembourg case law when it deals with rules that are motivated by concerns that are—to some extent—coherent and targeted. Here too there is regulatory imperfection, but not an anachronistic or protectionist model.

The Scottish Parliament's introduction of minimum pricing for alcoholic drink was challenged by distillers and importers as a violation of Article 34. It was held by the Court of Session in Edinburgh to be a trade barrier, because it damaged the position of those able to exploit lower costs in the State of production.[83] The Court then held the measure justified as a measure of public health protection. The applicants pressed on the Court of Session that the aims of minimum pricing were confused. Raising the price of cheap alcohol would not tackle hazardous drinking by richer consumers, for example. The Court was also urged to examine with critical rigour the available alternatives. This included an increase in excise duty. But the ruling stressed that EU law allows a margin of appreciation. The judgment finds that 'The fact that there may be controversy, and that the evidence may not be all one way, does not preclude the conclusion that the necessary justification is present'. And it cites the Court of Justice's ruling in *Ahokainen and Leppik*[84] in support of the proposition that EU law affords a measure of respect—'a margin of appreciation'. The challenge failed.

In 2014 the Inner House of the Court of Session agreed to make a preliminary reference to the Court of Justice in Luxembourg.[85] This was lodged in July 2014.[86]

[81] Case C-36/02 *Omega Spielhallen* (n 18).

[82] Case C-112/00 *Schmidberger v Austria* (n 57).

[83] *Petition for Judicial Review by Scotch Whisky association and others* (Court of Session, 2013) www.scotcourts.gov.uk/opinions/2013CSOH70.html.

[84] Case C-434/04 *Ahokainen and Leppik* (n 8).

[85] [2014] CSIH 38.

[86] Case C-333/14 *Scotch Whisky Association* EU:C:2015:845.

The questions referred push the Court to explain the nature of the inquiry which the national court is required to undertake in such circumstances.

Sinclair Collis involved an attack on rules preventing the sale of tobacco products from automatic vending machines.[87] The proper intensity of the Court's scrutiny was at the heart of the analysis.[88] The Court of Appeal was split 2:1, and the pains to draw fine distinctions taken at length and separately by all the three members of the court prompt a sense of yearning for the flawed but usually condensed style of the Luxembourg single collegiate judgment.

Arden LJ looked for a manifest error, and did not find one. She took the view that in matters of public health it is enough to conclude that the decision-maker's conclusion that there was no less intrusive measure was not a manifestly inappropriate conclusion.[89] This was not to drop her judicial guard: she warned against letting this 'cloak' permit a State to achieve a quite different objective from its stated (and legitimate) aim.[90] But it did mean a readiness to accept that States may choose to do things differently without violating EU law. So she referred to 'the flexibility of the principles of proportionality'.[91] That flexibility, in her view, enabled recognition of the diversity of regulatory systems and national values—*in casu*, in the protection of public health—among the Member States. EU law controls national regulatory autonomy 'but with a much less intensive level of scrutiny than under a strict test of proportionality'.[92]

The Master of the Rolls got to the same result—that the measure was lawful—but by a slightly different route. He too was concerned to permit the rule-maker a margin of appreciation. But he considered that the margin granted to the Secretary of State should be narrower than that granted to a national legislature or to EU-level lawmaking.[93] He thought the justification for the ban 'not very convincing' but 'not so weak nor so illogical as to justify a court interfering'.[94]

Laws LJ, who dissented, focused on the margin of appreciation and found its scope relatively broad where what is at stake in claimed justification is 'the promotion of a benefit of great general importance such as public health, or a general policy of the European Union'.[95] However, having yielded this, he found that there had been no adequate consideration by the Minister of less restrictive alternatives and so the ban was unlawful. Having granted a margin of appreciation he treated the application of the least restrictive means test as of particular importance.[96] This, however, is a difference which is largely procedural. Laws LJ demands fuller

[87] [2011] EWCA Civ 437, [2012] QB 394.
[88] Laws LJ, paras 24–25.
[89] paras 164, 173.
[90] para 124.
[91] para 127. See also paras 134, 135.
[92] para 127.
[93] para 214: *cf* para 181 (Arden).
[94] para 237.
[95] para 23.
[96] paras 48–51, 80.

articulation of the available choices as a condition of legality than do Arden LJ and the Master of the Rolls, but all three are more or less agreed on the standard of review that should be imposed on the substantive decision.

It is slightly surprising that *Ahokainen and Leppik* is mentioned only *en passant*, in an extract from the ruling in *Rosengren*.[97] But in general the Court of Justice's case law is treated with care by all three judges. It is striking that throughout, the analysis runs together cases involving review of EU measures and of national measures. Arden LJ pauses to reflect on this convergence.[98] She is correct to note that the type of justification advanced by the rulemaker has an influence on the way in which the proportionality test is applied. Complex assessment in an area where genuine public health issues have arisen militates against judicial use of 'the heavy-handed hammer of the strict test of proportionality'[99]—and this is true whether the matter deals with national or EU intervention.

I have no quarrel with either *Scotch Whisky* or *Sinclair Collis*. Neither measure can be defended as part of a perfectly realised and entirely rational regulatory scheme. They are one element in the overall and incrementally developed pattern of regulation of alcohol and tobacco. For centuries lawmakers have been deprived of the luxury of starting from scratch where regulation of these products are concerned. One might be critical of inconsistencies and oddities at the edge of the regulatory design, but to hold the measure unlawful on that basis would be to use EU law to 'correct' national choices in far too intrusive a fashion. The Court of Justice's *Loi Evin* decisions considered above[100] are of exactly this type. At stake are political, economic and social choices which require complex assessments and evaluations. It would be different if what was at stake was a residue of ancient regulation with no contemporary value or reliance on public health protection as a cover for protectionism. In the background lies the level of diversity in regulatory preference that is and should be permitted within the EU. The more lenient the review conducted in the name of proportionality, the wider the scope of that permitted diversity. *Scotch Whisky* and *Sinclair Collis* are broadly in alignment with the Court of Justice's relatively generous treatment of national measures that pursue sincere regulatory objectives in a targeted way and they are in line too with the Court's treatment of EU measures.

IX. CONCLUSION

In the case law concerning consumer protection as a justification for trade-restrictive measures, the principle of proportionality plays a less prominent role than may initially be supposed. A large number of cases accuse Member States

[97] para 121. Case C-434/04 *Ahokainen and Leppik* (n 8); Case C-170/04 *Rosengren* (n 12).
[98] Especially paras 129–34.
[99] para 133.
[100] n 9.

of applying rules that are more restrictive than necessary to achieve the end in view, and therefore deny that the impugned national measures meet the demands of proportionality. On closer inspection, however, proportionality is frequently a polite way of condemning the Member State rules as incoherent, poorly designed, anachronistic, deviously or openly protectionist and/or plain daft. *Cassis de Dijon* itself is a perfect example. Proportionality as an analytical tool plays a part in the finding that banning weaker alcohol drink as a means to protect consumers from confusion caused by the availability of new products is unduly restrictive, because the end in view can be reached by mandatory labelling requirements. This is not without significance, for it reveals an assumption loaded into EU free movement law about the virtues of choice in the deregulated market and the capacity of consumers to read and respond to disclosed information. But it is hard to see this as a difficult or controversial conclusion in the case itself and, more generally as a means to attack market-fragmenting national measures which have no place in an interdependent EU-wide economy, it seems fully in line with the internal project mapped by the Treaty. And proportionality plays no part in the dismissal of the arguments based on public health, which were plain daft.

The truly controversial application of the proportionality principle would involve acceptance that a measure is the least restrictive available to meet the end in view, but that the end in view itself is simply not important enough to prevail over the interest in promoting market integration in the EU. This would be a vigorous assertion of judicially driven market deregulation. It would be a far more substantial incursion into national regulatory autonomy than is achieved through the more orthodox 'softer' version of proportionality. But in the consumer protection cases the Court does *not* do this. It is receptive to sincerely expressed and designed justifications. The margin of discretion or appreciation permitted to the rule-maker is functionally equivalent to a refusal to use proportionality in a strict sense as a curtailment of regulatory competence. Much the same comment is applicable in the context of *EU* legislative activity to the Court's admission that only a manifestly inappropriate measure will fall foul of its scrutiny. And so the dividing line between cases that involve review in the name of proportionality that assert an aggressive judicial intervention and those that are more deferential is not formed by the identity of the rulemaker—EU or Member State—nor by the particular category of justification being advanced, but instead by the quality and plausibility of the arguments advanced. Daft arguments are treated as such, and the reason that more daft arguments, attracting consequently aggressive review, are advanced by Member States is that they, unlike the EU, have centuries of regulatory deadwood that has lost its purpose and needs cleansing in order to promote the internal market project. But where the regulation has a proper targeted purpose—at national or EU level—the Court treats it and its maker with respect.

13

The Proportionality Test: Constructive Dialogue between the English and Scottish Courts

MALCOLM JARVIS

IN ADJUDICATING ON the proportionality of exceptions from EU movement law, national judges act as 'judges of the European Union legal order'.[1] The contribution of, and responsibility conferred on, national judges in that capacity has long been appreciated.[2] However, analysis of how national judges discharge that responsibility in practice is too often neglected. That is a pity. The experience of national courts applying exceptions from EU movement law provides rich and instructive lessons for the development of EU movement law in general, and the application of the proportionality test in particular.

This chapter seeks to address the latter by reference to English and Scottish case law adjudicating on challenges to the compatibility of bans on tobacco-vending machines with EU law on the free movement of goods.[3] Those cases provide a fascinating example of a dynamic dialogue between the Scottish and English courts as to the scope and proper application of the proportionality principle in the context of the public health protection under Article 36 TFEU.

[1] *R (Sinclair Collis Ltd) v Secretary of State for Health* [2011] EWCA Civ 437, [2012] QB 394 paras 133 and 182 per Arden LJ. See also Case T-51/89 *Tetra Pak Rausing SA v Commission (Community courts of general jurisdiction)* EU:T:1990:41 para 42 and Case T-219/95R *Danielsson, Largenteau and Haoa v Commission (ordinary courts of Community law)* EU:T:1995:219 para 77.

[2] J Steiner, 'The Application of EEC law in National Courts: Problems, Pitfalls and Precepts' (1980) 96 *LQR* 126; I Maher, 'National Courts as European Community Courts' (1994) 14 *Legal Studies* 226, JT Lang, 'The duties of National Courts under Community Constitutional Law' (1997) 22 *EL Rev* 3 and M Jarvis, *The Application of EC Law by National Courts: The Free Movement of Goods* (Oxford, Oxford University Press, 1998).

[3] *R (Sinclair Collis Ltd) v Secretary of State for Health* (n 1) (Court of Appeal) and *Sinclair Collis Ltd v Lord Advocate* (2013) SC 221, [2013] SLT 100 (Court of Session (Inner House, Extra Division)).

Three themes, or questions, emerge from the foregoing dialogue:

1) First, what is the status of the 'manifestly inappropriate' test when a national court is applying the 'less restrictive alternative means' limb of the proportionality test?
2) Second, should the identity of the author of a national measure affect the scope and application of the proportionality test under Article 36 TFEU?
3) Third, what is the relationship between Article 36 TFEU, on the one hand, and the European Convention on Human Rights (the Convention) and the Charter of Fundamental Rights, on the other?

Each theme will be addressed in turn following brief consideration of the proportionality test itself and the relevant English and Scottish legislation banning tobacco vending machines.

I. LEGAL CONTEXT: THE PROPORTIONALITY PRINCIPLE

There is, of course, much learning on the subject of proportionality.[4] For present purposes it suffices to note that national measures which restrict the free movement of goods will only be justified under one of the exceptions in Article 36 TFEU if they are shown to be proportionate. That means that the relevant national measure must be shown to be (a) appropriate (suitable) and (b) necessary for the purpose of achieving its legitimate aim. As part of the 'necessity' limb it must be shown that the least intrusive means of interfering with the free movement of goods has been employed (the 'least restrictive alternative means' test).[5]

II. ENGLISH AND SCOTTISH LEGISLATION BANNING TOBACCO VENDING MACHINES AND THE EU LAW CHALLENGES TO THOSE BANS

The sale of tobacco from automatic vending machines was prohibited in England and Wales, with effect from 1 October 2011, by the Protection from Tobacco (Sales from Vending Machines) (England) Regulations 2010 made by the Secretary of State for Health pursuant to the power conferred on him by section

[4] See T Tridimas, *The General Principles of EU Law* 2nd edn (Oxford, Oxford University Press, 2006) 136*ff*; G de Búrca, 'The Principle of Proportionality and its Application in EC Law' (1993) 13 *Yearbook of European Law* 105; N Emiliou, *The Principle of Proportionality in European Law* (London, Kluwer Law International, 1996); T Harbo, 'The function of the proportionality principle in EU law' (2010) 16 *European Law Journal* 158; P Craig, 'Proportionality, Rationality and Review' [2010] *New Zealand Law Reports* 265; and W Sauter, 'Proportionality in EU law: A Balancing Act?' (2013) 15 *Cambridge Yearbook of European Legal Studies* 439.

[5] The *locus classicus* with respect to Art 36 TFEU is Case 104/75 *De Peijper* EU:C:1976:67 paras 16–17. For a more recent application see eg Case C-108/09 *Ker-Optika bt v ANTSZ Dél-dunántúli Regionáliss Intézete* EU:C:2010:725 paras 57–76.

3A of the Children and Young Persons (Protection from Tobacco) Act 1991 as amended by the Health Act 2009. The latter empowered the Secretary of State, at his discretion, to introduce regulations imposing a total ban on sales from tobacco vending machines.

A separate prohibition was enacted by the Scottish Parliament, pursuant to powers devolved under the Scotland Act 1998. Section 9 of the Tobacco and Primary Medical Services (Scotland) Act 2010 makes it an offence for a person having the management or control of premises to have a vending machine available for use on those premises.

The English and the Scottish bans were challenged in, respectively, the English and Scottish courts. In both sets of proceedings it was assumed that there was restriction on the free movement of goods contrary to Article 34 TFEU: the bans impeded importation of tobacco vending machines (and spare parts) manufactured in other Member States.[6] In neither set of proceedings did the applicants contend that the bans impeded importation and sale of cigarettes which would otherwise be sold from vending machines. No issue therefore arose as to whether the bans constituted a 'selling arrangement' outside the scope of Article 34 TFEU.[7]

In each case, the justification deployed for the restriction on the free movement of goods was the protection of public health under Article 36 TFEU and, in both cases, the legislation was found to be justified.[8]

III. THE STATUS OF THE 'MANIFESTLY INAPPROPRIATE' TEST AS PART OF THE PROPORTIONALITY PRINCIPLE

The CJEU has long held that where the court is concerned with the proportionality of acts adopted *by the EU institutions* that involve political, economic and social choices, the legality of such measures can be affected only if they are 'manifestly inappropriate' having regard to the objective which the competent institution is seeking to pursue.[9] The CJEU has not applied the same 'manifestly inappropriate' test when the proportionality of *national* measures that involve such choices are at

[6] In the English *Sinclair Collis* case a 'prima facie' breach of Art 34 TFEU was assumed: see paras 19 and 115. In the Scottish *Sinclair Collis* case the Court of Session accepted that the ban hindered trade in vending machines between Member States but expressed doubts as to whether Art 34 TFEU could be invoked to preserve a market in a particular product where no such market exists in several Member States (paras 52–53).

[7] Cases C-267 and 268/91 *Keck and Mithouard* EU:C:1993:905.

[8] In the English *Sinclair Collis* case, Laws LJ dissented on this point.

[9] See Case 331/88 *R v Minister for Agriculture, Fisheries and Food ex parte Fedesa* EU:C:1990:391 para 14; Case C-189/01 *Jippes and Others* EU:C:2001:420 para 82; Case C-491/01 *R v Secretary of State for Health, ex parte British American Tobacco* EU:C:2002:741 para 123; Case C-434/02 *Arnold André GmbH v Landrat des Kreises Herford* EU:C:2004:800 paras 46 and 56; Case C-343/09 *Afton Chemical Ltd v Secretary of State for Transport* EU:C:2010:419 para 46 and Case C-309/10 *Agrana Zucker GmbH v Bundesminister für Land-und Forstwirtschaft, Umwelt und Wasserwirtschaft* EU:C:2011:531 para 43.

issue (at least where the national measure was not enacted to implement EU law). Further, CJEU case law offers little guidance as to how the 'manifestly inappropriate' test is to be applied in practice. In particular, when does the inappropriateness of a measure become 'manifest' and how is that to be determined?

Against that uncertain background, English and Scottish judges have expressed sharply divergent views on the application of the 'manifestly inappropriate' test to the proportionality of English and Scottish legislation banning tobacco vending machines. As will be seen, the views expressed by the English and Scottish judges went beyond mere disagreement. Each judgment referred to, and engaged constructively with, the others.[10] The disagreement thus took the form of a conversation about where the uncertainties in the CJEU's case law lie, how they should be resolved and how they fall to be applied to the facts in these cases.

In *Regina (Sinclair Collis Ltd) v Secretary of State for Health*[11] Laws LJ rejected the 'manifestly inappropriate' test as having any application when considering the proportionality of a public health justification.[12] In his view the 'less restrictive alternative means' test means that there is no scope for the 'manifestly inappropriate' test when assessing the proportionality of a national measure under Article 36 TFEU. If it were otherwise, the value of the former test would be 'critically undermined'.[13]

Arden LJ disagreed because, in her view, the 'manifestly inappropriate' test is a statement of the level of intensity of review that is applicable to any of the constituent elements of the proportionality test, including the 'less restrictive alternative means' test.[14] In her view, where the proportionality of a measure of discretionary power in the field of public health is at issue, the 'less restrictive alternative means' test either does not apply or, if it does, applies 'with the lower level of intensity of scrutiny consistent with the "manifestly inappropriate" level'.[15] In that way, the 'manifestly inappropriate' test can, in Arden LJ's judgment, 'either form part of, or appear side-by-side with, a conventional statement of the core principle of proportionality'.[16] A measure therefore complies with the principle of proportionality in the context of public health protection if the decision-maker's conclusion that there was no less intrusive measure was 'not a manifestly inappropriate conclusion'.[17]

Lord Neuberger MR charted a middle course between Laws and Arden LJJ stating that the obligation to opt for the alternative which is less restrictive of trade

> should not be applied by a court in such a way as to usurp the role of the primary decision-maker. So, where there is an alternative possible measure, there may be a

[10] In the English *Sinclair Collis* case, see in particular Laws LJ's judgment at para 82, Arden LJ's judgment at paras 83, 130, 131, 154, 157, 180 and 181 and Lord Neuberger's judgment at para 185. In the Scottish *Sinclair Collis* case see para 57 of the Court of Session's judgment.

[11] n 1 above.

[12] ibid, paras 39–41 and 47–48.

[13] ibid, para 40.

[14] ibid, para 116.

[15] ibid, para 126.

[16] ibid, para 116.

[17] ibid, para 164.

> difference of view as to which measure would be less onerous, and unless the view of the member state's government that its measure is the more appropriate is manifestly wrong, the court should not substitute its own view for that of the government.[18]

By contrast, in delivering the opinion of the Court of Session in *Sinclair Collis Ltd v Lord Advocate*,[19] Lord Carloway agreed with Laws LJ, but for different reasons.[20] In his view, the 'manifestly inappropriate' test does not apply where a national court is testing the proportionality of national measures against the fundamental principles contained in the EU treaties.[21] Lord Carloway based that on a distinction drawn by Prof Takis Tridimas between:

(a) the proportionality of EU legislation and the proportionality of national measures implementing EU law, on the one hand, for which the 'manifestly inappropriate' test applies; and
(b) the proportionality of national measures restricting the fundamental freedoms, for which the 'manifestly inappropriate' test does not apply.[22]

Lord Carloway explained that distinction by reference to the fact that where the proportionality of EU legislation is challenged the balance is between private and public interests, whereas the balance when assessing the proportionality of national measures that restrict the fundamental freedoms is between EU and state interests.[23] Laws LJ had rejected the latter distinction stating: 'I find it difficult to see why … the distribution of public legal authority between legislature and judiciary should differ from the one case to the other'.[24] Lord Carloway said that he did not share Laws LJ's misgivings, but did not elaborate further.[25]

Lord Carloway also expressed agreement, in part, with Arden LJ. He agreed that the core principle of proportionality required that the measure be 'suitable and necessary' and that it must be shown that 'the least intrusive means' have been employed. However, he expressed difficulty 'in reconciling that approach with [Arden LJ's] adoption … of "manifestly inappropriate" as a test for determining whether the least intrusive means could have been selected'.[26]

The foregoing dialogue between the English and Scottish courts as to the status of the 'manifestly inappropriate' test is instructive because it informs the debate, at EU level, as to where, and how, the CJEU's case law on the proportionality of exceptions to EU free movement law needs to be clarified or refined. As will be evident, the two principal areas of disagreement were as to: (a) Whether the 'manifestly

18 ibid, para 203.
19 n 3 above.
20 The two other judges sitting with Lord Carloway in the Inner House, Court of Session, were Lord Bonomy and Lord Osborne.
21 ibid, para 56.
22 Tridimas, *General Principles* (n 4) 137–38.
23 n 1 above, para 56.
24 ibid, para 47.
25 ibid, para 57.
26 ibid, para 57.

inappropriate' test applies where a national court is testing the proportionality of national measures against the fundamental principles contained in the EU treaties; and if so (b) What the proper scope of the 'manifestly inappropriate' test is and how it is to be reconciled with the 'least restrictive alternative means' test.

As to the first point, as noted above, CJEU case law applying the 'manifestly inappropriate' test has been concerned with the proportionality of EU legislation.[27] Indeed the only CJEU case cited in which the 'manifestly inappropriate' test *appears* to have been applied to the proportionality of a national measure is *Aragonesa*,[28] which concerned a Catalan restriction on the advertisement of alcohol above a certain strength. The CJEU stated that the application of the national provision to beverages having an alcoholic strength of more than 23 degrees 'does not appear to be manifestly *unreasonable* as part of a campaign against alcoholism' (emphasis added).[29] Since that is an isolated reference to words approximating to the 'manifestly inappropriate' test, it is an uncertain basis for concluding that it applies when testing the proportionality of national measures.[30]

But if the 'manifestly inappropriate' test applies only when the proportionality of EU legislation is at issue (as the Court of Session concluded) it is difficult to see (as Laws LJ commented) why it should not also apply when national provisions are at issue. The fact that, in the latter case, the balance to be struck is between EU and state interests is not an explanation for why a different approach is warranted. On the contrary, the CJEU has emphasised, on a number of occasions, that the prohibition of quantitative restrictions and measures having equivalent effect in Article 34 TFEU applies to measures adopted by the EU institutions as well as national measures.[31] If, as the CJEU has held is the case,[32] the 'manifestly inappropriate' test applies when the compatibility of EU measures with Articles 34 to 36 TFEU is challenged, it is difficult to see why it should not also apply when the

[27] See cases cited in n 9.

[28] Cases C-1 and 176/90 *Aragonesa de Publicidad Exterior SA v Departamento de Sanidad y Seguridad Social de la Generalitat de Catalunna* EU:C:1991:327.

[29] ibid, para 17 of the judgment.

[30] In other cases the CJEU has recognised that Member States must be given a 'margin of appreciation' in selecting the appropriate level of protection, but without referring to the 'manifestly inappropriate' test: see Case C-110/05 *Commission v Italy* EU:C:2009:66 para 65 and Case C-434/04 *Ahokainen and Leppik* EU:C:2006:609 para 32. Note also that the 'manifestly inappropriate' test was recently applied by the English High Court when assessing the proportionality of English legislation regulating gambling operators in prima facie breach of the freedom to provide services: *Gibraltar Betting & Gaming Association Ltd v The Secretary of State for Culture, Media & Sport* [2014] EWHC 3236 (Admin), [2015] 1 CMLR 28 paras 99–102.

[31] Case 15/83 *Denkavit Nederland v Hoofdproduktschap voor Akkerbouwprodukten* EU:C:1984:183 para 15; Case C-51/93 *Meyhui NV v Schott Zwiesel Glaswerke AG* EU:C:1994:312 para 11; Case C-114/96 *Kieffer and Thill* EU:C:1997:316 para 27; Case C-434/02 *Arnold André GmbH* (n 9) para 57; and Joined Cases C-154 and 155/04 *R (on the application of Alliance for Natural Health and Others) v Secretary of State for Health* EU:C:2005:449 para 47.

[32] Case C-434/02 *Arnold André GmbH* (n 9) paras 46, 56 and 59; Case C-210/03 *Swedish Match* EU:C:2004:802 paras 48, 58 and 61; and Joined Cases C-154 and 155/04 *Alliance for Natural Health* (n 31) para 52.

compatibility of national measures with those same Articles has to be determined (at least where complex political, economic and social choices are involved).

Turning to the proper scope of the 'manifestly inappropriate' test, it is suggested that Laws LJ was right to point out that that test is, on its face, incompatible with the 'least restrictive alternative means' test. As he noted, the 'least restrictive alternative means' test requires that where there is a choice between several 'appropriate' measures, recourse must be had to the least onerous, even if a more onerous alternative would not itself be 'manifestly inappropriate' in relation to the relevant objective. Despite that apparent contradiction, the CJEU has referred to the 'manifestly inappropriate' test *as part of* judicial review of compliance with the proportionality principle[33] and has applied the 'manifestly inappropriate' test and the 'less restrictive alternative means' test in one and the same case without explaining how they are to be reconciled.[34] In some cases (albeit not ones concerning the compatibility of EU legislation with EU movement law), the CJEU has gone so far as to state that what must be ascertained 'is not whether the measure adopted by the legislature was the only measure possible or the best measure possible, but whether it was manifestly inappropriate'.[35] As Advocate General Kokott has warned, that statement is liable to be misunderstood.[36] Quite how it is to be reconciled with the 'least restrictive alternative means' test is left unexplained.

That the present uncertainty is such as to have led Arden LJ to suggest that the 'least restrictive alternative means' test does not (or at least may not) apply *at all* where the 'manifestly inappropriate' test is in play is a matter of concern. The core principle of proportionality requires that a measure be shown to be necessary for the purpose of achieving its legitimate aim and a corollary of the latter is the 'least restrictive alternative means' test (as Arden LJ accepted).[37] With respect, Laws LJ was surely correct to observe that 'the court cannot altogether be absolved of its responsibility to look for the "less restrictive alternative", since that is surely a condition of necessity'.[38]

One way in which the 'manifestly inappropriate' test may be reconciled with the 'least restrictive alternative means' test is to treat the former as a statement of the level of intensity of review (as Arden LJ suggested). Thus the 'manifestly

[33] See eg the cases cited at n 9 above. See also Joined Cases C-154 and 155/04 *Alliance for Natural Health* (n 31) para 52.

[34] See eg Case C-210/03 *Swedish Match* (n 32) paras 48 and 56–58 and Case C-434/02 *Arnold André GmbH* (n 9) at paras 45–46 and 54–56.

[35] Case C-189/01 *Jippes* (n 9) para 83; Case C-309/10 *Agrana Zucker GmbH* (n 9) para 44; Case C-58/08 *R (on the application of Vodafone Ltd, Telefónica O2 Europe et al) v Secretary of State for Business, Enterprise and Regulatory Reform* EU:C:2010:321 para 52.

[36] Case C-558/07 *R (on the application of SPCM SA, CH Erbslöh KG, Lake Chemicals and Minerals Ltd and Hercules Inc) v Secretary of State for the Environment, Food and Rural Affairs* EU:C:2009:142 para 74 of the Opinion. See also the reservations expressed by Advocate General Trstenjak in C-213/09 *Barsoum Chabo v Hauptzollamt Hamburg-Hafen* EU:C:2010:372 para 80.

[37] para 115.

[38] para 47. See also *Gibraltar Betting & Gaming Association Ltd v The Secretary of State for Culture, Media & Sport* [2014] EWHC 3236 (Admin), [2015] 1 CMLR 28 para 184.

inappropriate' test means that the court will only interfere if the decision maker's conclusion as to what is the 'least restrictive alternative means' if that conclusion was manifestly wrong. That approach (which was the one effectively adopted by Lord Neuberger MR) focuses on the appropriateness of the decision-maker's conclusion rather than the measure itself. But attention may be re-focused on the measure itself by asking not only whether the measure is 'manifestly inappropriate' (under the first limb of the proportionality test) but also whether it is 'manifestly unnecessary' (under the second limb of the proportionality test).[39]

If, as is submitted is the case, the 'manifestly inappropriate' test is to be treated as a statement of the level of intensity of review, the differences between Arden LJ and Laws LJ may be more apparent than real. Indeed, Laws LJ's description of how the proportionality principle is to be applied in practice comes to much the same thing as treating the 'manifestly inappropriate' test as a statement of the level of intensity of review. Thus Laws LJ explained that when the decision maker is accorded a broad margin of appreciation

> the court leaves a wider space for the decision-maker's own judgment as to the application of the standards [within the proportionality test]. The questions the standards represent must still be asked and answered, first by the decision-maker himself; but the broader the margin of appreciation, the less inclined the court will be to strike an autonomous balance of the material factors.[40]

The lively discussion between the English and Scottish courts, and the difficulties they encountered in applying the proportionality test, mean that Arden LJ was right to observe, extra-judicially, that '[t]he question whether the "not manifestly inappropriate" test applies in EU law and, if it does, its scope is important and it is clearly one which the [United Kingdom] Supreme Court should now address'.[41] The Supreme Court did so in *R (Lumsdon) v Legal Services Board*,[42] describing the adoption of the 'manifestly inappropriate' test by the majority in the English *Sinclair Collis* case as 'open to criticism'.[43] In the meantime, in *Scotch Whisky Association v Lord Advocate* the Court of Session referred questions to the CJEU arising out of a public health justification for the restriction on the free movement of goods resulting from Scottish legislation on minimum alcohol pricing. One of those questions was whether a national court was required,

[39] As suggested by Advocate General Trstenjak in C-213/09 *Barsoum Chabo* (n 36) para 80.

[40] para 50.

[41] M Arden, 'Proportionality: the way ahead' (2013) *Public Law* 497, 506.

[42] [2014] EWCA Civ 1276, [2015] 3 WLR 121 paras 33-82. See also *Kennedy v Charity Commission* [2014] UKSC 20, [2014] 2 WLR 808 para 54; *Bank Mellat v HM Treasury (No 2)* [2013] UKSC 39, [2013] 3 WLR 179 para 94; *R (on the application of Nicklinson) v Ministry of Justice* [2014] UKSC 38, [2014] 3 WLR 200 paras 170, 189, 232 and 346 and *R (on the application of Rotherham Borough Council) v Secretary of State for Business, Innovation and Skills* [2014] EWCA Civ 1080, [2015] 1 All ER 242 paras 47 and 54–56.

[43] Ibid, para 82.

when determining whether national rules are justified by an object provided for in Article 36 TFEU, to form an objective view on the availability of any less restrictive alternative means to achieve that object.[44] The Court of Session specifically drew the CJEU's attention to the divergent views on the application of the 'manifestly inappropriate' test expressed by appellate courts in the United Kingdom.[45] In its response, the CJEU held that the national court was bound 'to examine objectively whether it may reasonably be concluded from the evidence submitted' that there were no less restrictive alternative means.[46] It is not clear whether that objective-reasonableness test differs from the Supreme Court's approach in *Lumsdon*. It certainly implies a stricter test than one of 'manifestly inappropriate' and it is the test which the English courts have sought to apply in subsequent cases.[47]

IV. DOES IDENTITY OF THE AUTHOR OF THE NATIONAL MEASURE MATTER?

A related point on which there was an equally lively difference of views is as to whether the identity of the author of a national measure which restricts the free movement of goods has any bearing on the application of the proportionality test. On this issue too, there was a dialogue between the English and Scottish judges.[48]

Laws LJ expressed the clear view that '[a]cts of the primary legislator attract a broader margin [of appreciation]; acts of the secondary legislator, a narrower'.[49] Whilst Arden LJ agreed that the primary legislator tends to attract a lower level of scrutiny, that will not inevitably be the case when all the relevant factors are taken into account. Arden LJ concluded that there is 'no bright line rule that the "secondary legislator"… attracts a narrower margin than the "primary legislator"'.[50] On this issue too, Lord Neuberger MR adopted a position somewhere between the two, concluding that the identity of the decision-maker was but one relevant factor influencing a broad or narrow margin of discretion, along with 'the nature of the decision, the reasons for the decision and the effect of the decision'.[51]

The Court of Session adopted a different approach stating:

> It may be that, in situations where EU policy is being implemented, a wider margin is given to measures passed by the central state legislature rather than those created by

[44] See the fourth question referred.

[45] See Advocate General Bot's Opinion (EU:C:2015:527) at para 80.

[46] EU:C:2015:845 at para 56.

[47] *R (on the application of British American Tobacco and others) v Secretary of State for Health* [2016] EWHC 1169 (Admin) at paras 677-678.

[48] In the English *Sinclair Collis* case, see in particular Laws LJ's judgment at para 23, Arden LJ's judgment at paras 137, 148 and 152 and Lord Neuberger's judgment at paras 210 and 212. In the Scottish *Sinclair Collis* case see para 59 of the Court of Session's judgment.

[49] para 23.

[50] para 137.

[51] para 200.

executive order (*R v Secretary of State for Health, ex parte Eastside Cheese Co* [1999] 3 CMLR 123, Lord Bingham CJ at para 48). However, in determining whether a measure contravenes Article 34 or is justified by Article 36, the court has reservations about whether the margin can vary in accordance with the nature of the particular organ of the state which creates or implements the measure. It might appear strange if the manner in which a European Union member state elects to organise government within its borders were capable of increasing or decreasing the margin of appreciation available to that state relative to measures challenged as infringing one of the EU Treaties' fundamental principles. The legality of a measure ought not to depend upon whether a measure is passed by a central, national, provincial or local government legislature or determined by an official or subsidiary body under delegated authority from such a legislature.[52]

Again, the foregoing dialogue between the English and Scottish courts is instructive. As a matter of principle, it is respectfully suggested that the Court of Session is right that the identity of the author of a national measure ought not to affect the application of the proportionality principle in general, and the 'less restrictive alternative means' test in particular. The analysis, and outcome, should be the same irrespective of whether the restriction on free movement was imposed by the legislature or a single state official.[53] Since statements made by a single government official can give rise to a breach of Article 34 TFEU,[54] it is difficult to see why the standards by which the proportionality of such measures are to be assessed should be different from that which would apply to measures adopted in primary or secondary legislation.

As a matter of practice, however, measures involving political or social choices are more likely to be enacted by the primary legislator so that the wider margin of appreciation, discussed in the previous section, will apply to such measures. However, that is a function of the measure adopted, not the identity of its author. Moreover, many measures are enacted by government ministers pursuant to power given by primary legislation. In such cases the relevant minister and the primary legislator are engaged in a 'common enterprise'[55] and it may not be possible to identify a single 'author'. For those reasons, it is submitted that Arden LJ is right to point out that there can be no hard-and-fast rule in relation to this question.[56]

[52] para 59.

[53] Or indeed organisations or bodies which regulate an economic activity in a 'collective manner', assuming the judgments in Case 36/74 *Walrave v Union Cyclise Internationale* EU:C:1974:140; Case C-438/05 *ITF v Viking Line* EU:C:2007:772; and Case C-341/05 *Laval v Svenska Byggnadsarbetareförbundet* EU:C:2007:809 can and will be transposed to the free movement of goods.

[54] See eg Case C-470/03 *AGM-COS.MET v Finland and Lehtinen* EU:C:2007:213.

[55] Arden LJ para 151.

[56] It is perhaps for this reason that the Supreme Court left the issue open in *Lumsden* (n 42) at para 81. Note also that where the Court is required to assess evidence that was not before the author of the national measure at the time it was enacted, it is somewhat artificial to treat the author as having exercised any margin of appreciation over that evidence: see *R (on the application of British American Tobacco and others) v Secretary of State for Health* (n 47) at para 454.

V. THE RELATIONSHIP BETWEEN ARTICLE 36 TFEU AND THE CONVENTION/CHARTER

It is common for national legislation to be challenged both on the grounds that it breaches EU free movement provisions and on the grounds that it is incompatible with the Convention. The Convention right most frequently invoked along with the free movement of goods is the right to property (Article 1 of Protocol 1). However, challenges to national measures on the grounds that they restrict the free movement of goods have also been accompanied by reliance on the right to respect for private and family life, the right to peaceful assembly and freedom of expression.[57]

The approach adopted by the English courts in *Sinclair Collis* was to treat Article 36 TFEU and the relevant Convention right as alternatives but to deal only with the former. That was in part because it had been conceded that since it was more difficult for a Member State to justify a measure under Article 36 TFEU than under Article 1 of Protocol 1, there was no need for separate consideration of Article 1 of Protocol 1. Laws LJ was happy to follow that approach and he therefore undertook no separate analysis of Article 1 of Protocol 1.[58]

For his part, Lord Neuberger MR considered that there was no reason to address Article 1 of Protocol 1 because more guidance was available in the CJEU's jurisprudence on Article 36 TFEU than in European Court of Human Rights jurisprudence on Article 1 of Protocol 1,[59] a proposition with which Arden LJ agreed.[60]

By contrast, the Court of Session undertook separate analysis of both Article 36 TFEU and Article 1 of Protocol 1.[61] Thus in analysing proportionality of the ban on vending machines under Article 1 of Protocol 1 the Court of Session applied the three-part test identified by Lord Hope in *R v Shayler*,[62] namely (1) whether the objective which is sought to be achieved (viz the 'pressing social need') is sufficiently important to justify limiting the fundamental right; (2) whether the means chosen to limit that right are rational, fair and not arbitrary and (3) whether the means used impair the right as minimally as is reasonably possible.

It is submitted that the Court of Session's approach is to be preferred. The English court's approach was pragmatic, but unprincipled. First, justifications for restrictions to EU free movement law must themselves be interpreted in

[57] See *R (Countryside Alliance) v Attorney General* [2007] UKHL 52, [2008] 1 AC 719; and Case C-368/95 *Vereinigte Familiapress v Bauer Verlag* EU:C:1997:325.

[58] *Sinclair Collis* (n 1) paras 53–54. A similar approach was adopted by Beatson J in *R (Petsafe Ltd) v The Welsh Ministers* [2010] EWHC 2908 (Admin), [2011] Eu LR 270 para 77. In *Countryside Alliance* (n 58) Lord Brown adopted the opposite approach stating (at para 165): 'In my judgment, if the Hunting Act 2004 is not to be declared incompatible with the appellants' Convention rights, it is certainly not to be disapplied by virtue of EC law'. The difference may be explained by the fact that *Countryside Alliance* concerned so called 'core' Convention rights (Arts 8 and 10).

[59] para 194.

[60] para 147.

[61] paras 54–62 and 63–65 respectively.

[62] [2002] UKHL 11, [2003] 1 AC 247 para 61. See now the four-part test in *Bank Mellat v HM Treasury (No 2)* (n 42) at para 20.

the light of general principles of law and, in particular, fundamental rights.[63] That can only be achieved if there is separate analysis of the compatibility of the measure with Convention rights. Indeed Lord Neuberger MR's assumption that it is theoretically possible for a measure to violate Article 1 of Protocol 1, without also violating Articles 34 to 36 TFEU,[64] is difficult to reconcile with the CJEU's judgment in *ERT*.[65]

Second, the fact that CJEU jurisprudence on Article 36 TFEU provides more guidance than ECtHR jurisprudence on Article 1 of Protocol 1 is not, it is respectfully suggested, a good reason not to apply the latter provision. What matters is the substance of the available guidance, not its volume.

Third, it is not safe to assume that the more stringent test will include the lesser. The proportionality tests under, respectively, Article 36 TFEU and Article 1 of Protocol 1 ask different questions. In particular, application of the latter will not involve consideration of whether there are alternative means less restrictive of trade between Member States.[66]

For these reasons, the Scottish court's approach, undertaking analysis of both Article 36 TFEU and Article 1 of Protocol 1, is safer and more principled.

VI. CONCLUSIONS

National courts are at the 'coal face' when they are called upon to adjudicate on the proportionality of exceptions to EU movement law. The constructive dialogue between the English and Scottish courts in the cases considered here should, it is suggested, be regarded as making a positive contribution to the development of EU movement law. The divergent views expressed in the various judgments on the points identified above went beyond mere disagreement. Each judgment referred to, and engaged constructively with, the others in order to tease out the uncertainties in the practical application of the proportionality principle. The practical issues that emerged are instructive and inform the development of the proportionality of exceptions to the free movement of goods. Moreover, they show the English and Scottish courts discharging the responsibility conferred on them as 'judges of the European Union legal order' with care and sensitivity.

[63] Case C-260/89 *ERT v DEP* EU:C:1991:254 para 43.

[64] para 192.

[65] n 64 above.

[66] Indeed, in *Lumsdon* (n 42) the Supreme Court pointed out (at para 26) that although there was some common ground, 'the principle of proportionality in EU law is neither expressed nor applied in the same way as the principle of proportionality under the [Convention]'. In *R (on the application of British American Tobacco and others) v Secretary of State for Health* (n 47) Green J noted (at para 426) that that was not particularly helpful in cases where overlapping proportionality challenges are made under EU law (including the Charter of Fundamental Rights) and the Convention, in relation to the same facts. Since under EU law the Charter is to be construed in accordance with the Convention, a certain amount of 'intellectual gymnastics' is required if the two tests are different but to be construed as consistent with one another.

An inevitable question is whether the issues discussed in this chapter should have been referred to the CJEU for a preliminary ruling under Article 267 TFEU. Such a reference, at least on the issue of justification, was not mentioned in the judgments of either court. As indicated above, the status of the 'manifestly inappropriate' test when a national court is considering the proportionality of *national* measures for the protection of public health was (and to some extent remains) unclear. The discretion to refer questions on that issue could, and perhaps should, have been exercised, particularly since disagreement over it led (at least in part) to a dissenting judgment by Laws LJ. It does not appear, however, that any party requested that a reference be made and since the English appeal was determined with expedition, the delay that a reference to the CJEU would have entailed is likely to have been a consideration militating against such a reference.

Subject to that, and so long as there is no risk of irreconcilable judgments, the cases discussed in this chapter show that a constructive dialogue *between* national courts can be just as valuable as the dialogue between the national courts, on the one hand, and the CJEU on the other.

14

EU Secondary Legislation and its Impact on Derogations from Free Movement

PHIL SYRPIS

I. INTRODUCTION

THE INTENSIFYING APPLICATION of a broad market access-type approach to EU free movement law—the result of the Court of Justice's interpretation of the text of the Treaties—means that, at least under the main strand of the Court's case law, almost any national law or practice is capable of being conceived as a restriction to the Treaty freedoms. The consequence of this is that States have to justify an increasing range of national measures. In order to do so, they must frame their justifications of discriminatory rules so as to fit one of the categories of derogation expressly mentioned in the Treaties (in the case of the free movement of goods, those found in Article 36 TFEU; and in the case of the other freedoms, the grounds of public policy, public security and public health). In the case of indistinctly applicable rules, the mandatory requirements and imperative requirements in the general interest developed via the case law of the Court of Justice are also available. In addition, they must show that the national rule or practice, adopted on legitimate grounds, satisfies a proportionality test. These requirements are imposed as a result of a combination of the wording of the Treaties and the case law of the Court of Justice.

The substantive chapters in this book analyse that Treaty framework and the way in which it has been interpreted by the Court. While the structure of the law relating to the various freedoms is well established, the law itself is far from clear. The relationship between various categories of justifications (in particular, those in which Member States raise 'economic' arguments, and those in which the arguments are based on the protection of fundamental rights) remains unclear. So too is the application of the proportionality test, in particular as regards the extent of the burden on Member States to demonstrate the need for, and suitability of, restrictive rules which differ from those in other States. Institutionally, there are also complexities. Actions challenging Member State failure to fulfil EU legal obligations may be brought (by the Commission under Article 258 TFEU; or, rarely, by another Member State under Article 259 TFEU) directly before the Court of Justice. Alternatively, and more commonly, challenges will be heard before national courts charged with applying directly effective Union law. Such national courts may or may not choose to refer questions on the interpretation of EU law to the Court using Article 267 TFEU.

The resulting law explains how far difference and diversity are permissible within the EU internal market, and indicates to States how arguments in favour of difference and diversity may best be formulated. The relationship between uniformity and harmonisation on the one hand, and difference and diversity on the other is, notwithstanding the prevalence of glib phrases such as 'united in diversity', a difficult one, with huge political salience. These difficulties have only increased as a result of, first, the eastward expansion of the EU and the increased heterogeneity of the Union, and, second, the economic crisis, which has heightened the protectionist reflexes of the Member States, and resulted in an increase in the amount of national measures capable of restricting free movement. Debates, in particular about the free movement of people and migration, with access to jobs and benefits to the fore, have become increasingly toxic.

Part of the burden of many of the contributions to this volume has been to demonstrate that the language of the Treaties is open-textured and contextual, leaving courts at both the European and the national level with a range of difficult choices. In interpreting the Treaties, it is not easy for the Court either to interpret the bare words of the Treaties, or to navigate the tensions between the underlying arguments for, on the one hand, uniformity and free trade, and on the other, diversity and the preservation of national regulatory autonomy. Both of these are, unambiguously since the adoption of the Treaty of Lisbon, protected at the constitutional level within the European Union.

This chapter has a different focus. It examines the extent to which the adoption of secondary legislation by the EU institutions affects the nature and form of the argumentation relating to derogations. In those areas in which secondary legislation has been adopted, the political institutions have supplemented the Treaty framework with more specific rules, typically providing some extra guidance to the Court about the nature of the relationship between uniformity and diversity. David Edward is right to conclude that the dominant role of the Court is, at least in part, 'due to the failure of the others to fulfil the obligations assigned to them by the Treaty'.[1] And yet, while it is true to say that the presence of secondary legislation, which puts flesh on the bones of the Treaty text, is capable of steering policy makers and courts, it is also true to say that it is apt to introduce extra layers of complexity into what is already a murky legal picture. My task in this chapter is to attempt to point towards the many different ways in which the Treaties and secondary legislation interrelate in order to attempt to explain the parameters of the role of the EU legislature in the development of the EU internal market.

The first section of this chapter relates to the role of the EU legislature in the EU internal market context. Thus, it explores the constitutional structure established

[1] See ch 1 in this volume.

by the Treaties, in order to determine the potential for the legislature to seek to steer the internal market in particular directions. While the legislature is able to intervene in a range of ways, the rationale for particular interventions is often, usually for predictable political reasons, left unstated, or less than fully developed, with the consequence that many legislative interventions have less of an impact on the direction of internal market law than many in the Council, European Parliament and Commission might expect.

The second section turns the focus onto the role of the Court. Essentially, the question here is whether the Court has allowed the EU legislature sufficient scope to play its part in the development of the internal market. The activism of the Court has been the focus of much academic attention, but activism in the context of Treaty interpretation has a rather different constitutional flavour to activism in a context where there is EU legislation in place. This contribution aims to shed some light on the Court's reactions to legislative interventions of different types, and to seek to explain some of the reasons underlying its choices.

First, however, in order to frame the discussion in this chapter, I begin with two examples of legislation adopted by the EU legislature; and discuss the way in which they have been interpreted by the Court.

II. TWO TYPES OF LEGISLATIVE INTERVENTION AND THE REACTION OF THE COURT

Directives 70/311/EEC and 2007/46/EC relating to the steering equipment of passenger vehicles are, in many respects, unexceptional. Directive 70/311/EEC was based on Article 100 EEC (now, Article 115 TFEU); and Directive 2007/46/EC was based on Article 95 EC (now, Article 114 TFEU). Thus, they are both internal market measures. The directives were considered by the Court of Justice in March 2014, in the context of enforcement actions against Poland and Lithuania.[2]

In the case, the Court pointed out that the directives establish a 'harmonised framework', creating 'a uniform-type approval procedure for new vehicles, based on the principle of total harmonisation'.[3] The aim was 'the establishment and functioning of the internal market, while seeking to ensure a high level of road safety'.[4] The main point of disagreement between the Commission and the Polish Government was on whether the determination of the position of the driver's seat of a vehicle was or was not within the scope of that harmonised framework.

[2] See Case C-639/11 *Commission v Poland* EU:C:2014:173. Case 61/12 *Commission v Lithuania* EU:C:2014:172 is materially identical. The focus here is on the Polish case. See Directive 70/311/EEC on the approximation of the laws of the Member States relating to the steering equipment for motor vehicles and their trailers, repealed by Directive 2007/46/EC establishing a framework for the approval of motor vehicles and their trailers, and of systems, components and separate technical units intended for such vehicles, 2007 OJ l263/1.

[3] See Case C-639/11 *Commission v Poland* ibid, para 34.

[4] ibid, para 35.

The Court's conclusion was that it was: '[t]he European Union legislature granted in that regard a freedom to motor vehicle manufacturers that may not be cancelled or impeded by national legislation'.[5] It reasoned that the legislature 'took account of that potential risk' resulting from having steering equipment on the same side as the direction of the traffic, when it added Article 2a to Directive 70/311 at the time of the accession of the UK to the EU without supplementing the list of requirements in the Annex to the Directive,[6] and that it was therefore clear that 'the position of the driver's seat, an integral part of the steering equipment of a vehicle, comes within the harmonisation established by [the] Directives'.[7]

Poland obliged vehicle manufacturers to reposition the steering equipment of passenger vehicles to the left hand side, for reasons connected to the ensuring of road safety and the protection of the health and lives of people.[8] This created problems for those seeking to register vehicles originating in the UK and Ireland. The Commission argued that the repositioning requirement was contrary to EU law. It should be noted that the legal framework is different in relation to *new passenger vehicles*, in respect of which the harmonised framework established by the Directives applies; and in relation to *vehicles previously registered* in another Member State, in respect of which Article 34 TFEU applies.[9]

In relation to *new vehicles*, once the Court had established, via a process of interpretation of the Directives, that the position of the steering wheel of new vehicles fell within their scope, and once it had characterised the legislation as being based on the principle of total harmonisation, it was able, with sole reference to the Directives in question, to conclude that national rules obliging vehicle manufacturers to reposition the steering equipment were contrary to EU law.

My main focus here is not on the interpretation of the Directives, but rather on the possible impact that the harmonised framework they establish has on the way in which the Court approached the task of Treaty interpretation. In relation to passenger *vehicles previously registered* in another Member State, the Directives do not apply. Those are instead governed by Article 34 TFEU. The Court was clear that the contested legislation constituted a measure having equivalent effect to a quantitative restriction, in so far as its effect was to hinder access to the Polish market for vehicles lawfully constructed and registered in other Member States.[10] The question was then whether the national legislation may be justified in order to meet imperative requirements, and whether it was proportionate. The Court had little difficulty in accepting that, in principle, the legislation at issue was

[5] ibid, para 38.

[6] ibid, para 42.

[7] ibid, para 47.

[8] ibid, para 25.

[9] ibid, para 28. This was also emphasised by Advocate General Jääskinen who stated, at para 67 of his Opinion, EU:C:2013:728, that 'it is clear from the first paragraph of Article 1 of Framework Directive 2007/46 that that directive harmonises only the administrative provisions and general technical requirements for approval of all *new* vehicles within its scope'.

[10] See Case C-639/11 *Commission v Poland* (n 2), para 52.

appropriate for reducing the risk of accidents on Polish roads.[11] Attention then turned to the proportionality of the legislation; that is 'whether the legislation at issue goes beyond what is necessary in order to attain the objective pursued'.[12] For a number of reasons, the Court felt able to conclude that the legislation was not proportionate.

First, the Polish legislation tolerates the risk involved in tourists driving in Poland in vehicles equipped with a steering wheel on the right. According to the Court, the risk is 'the same, particularly as the flow of visitors in Polish territory is continuous, and the risk cannot be considered to be less important on the ground that the visitors visiting Poland for a limited period with such a vehicle drive more carefully than those whose vehicle is registered in that Member State'.[13] Second, the Court refers to the fact that 'the legislation of 22 Member States, that is to say a large majority of the Member States, either allows explicitly the registration of vehicles which have their steering equipment on the same side as the direction of the traffic, or tolerates such'.[14] Third, and here the Court is frustratingly brief, it notes that 'the statistical data relied on by the Polish Government do not prove to the requisite legal standard the relationship between the number of accidents put forward and the involvement of vehicles with the driver's seat on the right'.[15] Fourth, the Court points out that 'there exist means and measures less restrictive of free movement of goods than the measure at issue', and capable of significantly reducing the risk of accidents; for example, imposing other measures that would be capable of ensuring sufficient rear and forward visibility for the drivers of cars with the steering-wheel positioned on the same side as the direction of traffic.[16]

This pattern is familiar. National measures are found to restrict trade, and to be capable of justification. Thus, as so often, the legality of the national measure depends on the application of the proportionality test. In this case, it is particularly disappointing not to have some fuller elaboration of either the impact of the fact that 'a large majority of Member States' feel able to ensure road safety without imposing the same restrictions as Poland and Lithuania (discussed in para 61), or of the requisite standard of proof demanded by the Court (mentioned in para 62). In relation to the latter point, the Advocate General makes the point that the burden of proof falls on the Member States to show that 'the possible risks associated with the vehicles concerned in their territory differ considerably from those involved in the territory of the other Member States'.[17]

[11] ibid, paras 54–57.
[12] ibid, 58.
[13] ibid, para 60.
[14] ibid, para 61. The Advocate General makes the point, at para 93 of his Opinion (n 9), that the rules in force in Poland and Lithuania are 'relatively isolated'.
[15] See Case C-639/11 *Commission v Poland* (n 2) para 62.
[16] ibid, para 63.
[17] Case C-639/11 *Commission v Poland* Opinion of Advocate General Jääskinen (n 9), para 99.

For the purposes of this chapter, a final reason given by the Court is particularly interesting.[18] The Court states that 'the risk arising from the use in the Polish territory of vehicles with the steering wheel on the right is the same, whether those vehicles are new or previously registered in another Member State'; new vehicles are covered by the legislative framework, and by this stage in its judgment, the Court had already concluded 'that the legislature took account of that potential risk when it adopted Article 2a of Directive 70/311'.[19] We know that, taken together, the above reasons are enough to render the Polish rule disproportionate. However, we do not know whether one, or some, taken in isolation, would have the same effect. In particular, we do not know whether, given the Court's assertion that new and previously registered vehicles represent the same risk, the legislature's assessment of the risk in relation to new vehicles also automatically applies to previously registered vehicles; or whether it applies to previously registered vehicles only as a result of the coincidence of the various factors referred to in paragraphs 59 to 64 of the judgment. In the event that the former is correct, the legislation on new vehicles effectively also applies to previously registered vehicles. This amounts to a substantial increase in the scope of the legislation in question, and a clear indication that the passage of secondary legislation is able to have an influence on the Court's interpretation of Article 34 in this context.

The case is, in many respects, straightforward and unremarkable. The legality of the Directives was not in question. An issue of interpretation—whether the position of the steering wheel fell within the scope of the Directives—needed to be addressed, but was nevertheless settled relatively easily (and without recourse to the Treaties). The characterisation of the Directives as 'based on the principle of total harmonisation' was also straightforward, as the recitals were explicit on this point. Thus, it is clear that the legislature is able to adopt measures which in effect replace, or supplant, the Treaties. The Treaties do remain relevant—they may be used in order to assist the Court in its interpretative task, and in the event of any challenge to the legality of directives—but, typically, as in this case, they fade into the background.

However, in other situations, the impact of legislation may be very different. Where legislation is not based on the principle of total harmonisation,[20] the legal situation is rendered more complex, simply as a result of the fact that legislation

[18] It is perhaps worth noting that this was in fact the first reason given by the Court; though it is impossible to know whether to attach any significance to the order in which reasons were listed by the Court.

[19] See Case C-639/11 *Commission v Poland* (n 9), para 59. Advocate General Jääskinen did not make any such connection between the parts of his Opinion in which dealt with new cars, and with those already registered in another Member State.

[20] This may be the result of the limits of EU legislative competence, the result of a simple failure to reach agreement on a regime of total harmonisation, the result of a clear statement by the legislature that something other than total harmonisation is the objective, or the result of judicial interpretation of a particular piece of legislation.

will not supplant, but instead coexists with, the Treaties.[21] Where, for example, a regime of minimum harmonisation applies, the competence of the Member States is not straightforwardly pre-empted. Instead Member States are obliged to abide by the EU minimum standard, but remain free to set standards above the EU minimum, but only provided that they comply with the Treaties.[22] Thus, it is a combination of Treaties and EU legislation, as interpreted by the judiciary, which determines the extent to which States have freedom to act. Similarly, where the EU measure is a 'framework measure' which affords Member States some scope for manoeuvre, it is clear that Member States are obliged to remain within the parameters set by the legislation. However, they are also obliged to act in conformity with the Treaties.

I focus here on the recent judgment of the Court in *RegioPost*.[23] The case, one of a series relating to the legality of social conditions in public procurement contracts,[24] concerned the interpretation of Article 26 of Directive 2004/18, which provides that

> contracting authorities may lay down special conditions relating to the performance of a contract, provided that these are compatible with [Union] law and are indicated in the contract notice or in the specifications. The conditions governing the performance of a contract may, in particular, concern social and environmental considerations.[25]

The key question was whether EU law precludes a provision, adopted by the municipality of Landau, which made it mandatory for a contracting authority to award contracts only to undertakings which pay their employees a minimum wage (set out in the Law of the *Land* of Rhineland Palatinate).

The Court had no difficulty in saying that the condition laid down by the municipality was a 'special condition' within the scope of Article 26 of Directive 2004/18;[26] that it met the criteria of transparency laid down in the Article;[27] and, more controversially, that it was not directly or indirectly discriminatory.[28] Thus, the remaining question was whether the social condition was compatible with Union law.

[21] It is important to note that neither the distinction between regulations and directives, nor whether the measure in question was adopted under an internal market or other legal basis, can be determinative of the extent to which the national legislator retains autonomy. It is necessary in each case to interpret each Treaty provision, and each legislative intervention.

[22] See M Dougan, 'Minimum Harmonization and the Internal Market' (2000) 37 *CML Rev* 853.

[23] Case C-115/14 *RegioPost v Stadt Landau in der Pfalz* EU:C:2015:760.

[24] See Case C-346/06 *Rüffert* EU:C:2008:189 and Case C-549/13 *Bundesdruckerei* EU:C:2014:2235.

[25] Directive 2004/18/EC on the coordination of procedures for the award of public works contracts, public supply contracts and public service contracts, 2004 OJ L134/114.

[26] Case C-115/14 *RegioPost* (n 23) para 54.

[27] ibid, para 55.

[28] ibid, para 56. The special condition would be indirectly discriminatory if it imposed a requirement which it would be harder for undertakings established outside, rather than inside, Germany to satisfy. As the Court itself notes, at para 51, it is 'by no means inconceivable' that undertakings established in MS other than Germany, 'in which the cost of living and the minimum rate of pay in force are significantly lower than those prevailing in the *Land* of Rhineland Palatinate' might be dissuaded from participating in the tender process. Such undertakings are surely likely to find the special condition more difficult to satisfy than undertakings established in Germany.

The Court began by stating that, as Article 26 of Directive 2004/18 does not lay down exhaustive rules, the regional law 'may be assessed in the light of the primary law of the EU'.[29] Paragraphs 57 to 59 provide some welcome clarification as regards the relationship between primary and secondary law in the EU. As the Court points out, it is clear that where an EU measure exhaustively harmonises a field, as for example was the case for Directives 70/311/EEC and 2007/46/EC relating to the steering equipment of passenger vehicles discussed above, national measures falling within that field 'must be assessed in the light of the provisions of the harmonising measure *and not* in the light of primary law'.[30] Conversely, where EU measures do not exhaustively harmonise, the legality of national measures is dependent on what is likely to be a complex analysis of primary and secondary law.

At this stage the Court did not, as one might have expected, assess the Law of the *Land* of Rhineland Palatinate with reference to Article 56 TFEU. Instead, it relied on the Posted Workers Directive (PWD).[31] In some respects, this is explicable. There have, for a number of years, been indications in the case law of the Court that the limits of national autonomy in the field of the provision of services are set by the Court's controversial interpretation of the PWD, rather than by its interpretation of the text of Article 56 TFEU.[32] The Court has essentially held, in *Laval* and *Rüffert* for example, that national measures and conditions which go beyond what is envisaged in Article 3 of the PWD, breach the Treaties. It adopted the same approach here; albeit with a different result. The Court held that the law of the *Land* of Rhineland Palatinate 'may prohibit, impede or render less attractive' the provision of services, and that it may, in principle, be justified by the objective of protecting workers.[33] One would expect the next stage of the analysis to be about the proportionality of the measure. The Court's focus was, however, on whether the measure at issue was in conformity with the PWD. In reaching the conclusion that the national measure was not precluded by Article 26 of Directive 2004/18, the Court relied on the fact that the measure

[29] Case C-115/14 *RegioPost* (n 23) para 59.

[30] ibid, para 57 (my emphasis).

[31] ibid, para 60: 'it is necessary to determine whether … the minimum conditions laid down in Directive 96/71 are observed in the host member State in respect of posted workers'. It should be noted that Advocate General Mengozzi took a different turn here. He argued (at para 53 of his Opinion) that the PWD did not apply, but this was only on the ground that there was no cross-border element in the factual scenario in *RegioPost*. He thus took the view (at para 60 of his Opinion) that 'the *renvoi* made to EU law by Article 26 of Directive 20014/18 relates exclusively to Article 56 TFEU'. Directive 96/71/EC concerning the posting of workers in the framework of the provision of services, 1997 OJ L18/1.

[32] See Case C-346/06 *Rüffert* (n 24), para 33: 'As regards the matters referred to in Article 3(1), first subparagraph, (a) to (g), Directive 96/71 expressly lays down the degree of protection for workers of undertakings established in other Member States who are posted to the territory of the host Member State which the latter State is entitled to require those undertakings to observe.'

[33] ibid, paras 69 and 70.

was in conformity with the stipulations in Article 3 of the PWD. The minimum rate of pay imposed was 'laid down by a legislative provision', 'which applied generally to the award of any public contract', and it conferred 'a minimum social protection', since national legislation did not impose 'a lower minimum wage for the postal services sector'.[34]

This reliance on the PWD is constitutionally interesting, especially in the light of the statements in paragraphs 57 to 59 of *RegioPost*. The PWD is a provision of secondary, and not primary, law. It is, moreover, not a measure which exhaustively harmonises the field, as the Court itself made clear in *Laval*.[35] Nevertheless, the interpretation of Article 26 of Directive 2004/18 ends up depending on the Court's interpretation of primary law; and the Court's interpretation of the relevant primary law provision—Article 56 TFEU in this context—is dictated by its (controversial) interpretation of the PWD.[36]

In this chapter, the intention is not to go into the rights and wrongs of the Court's interpretation of Article 56 TFEU. It is simply to make the point that the passage of secondary legislation is apt to affect the nature and form of the argumentation relating to derogations from fundamental freedoms. In some situations, the effect of the change is simple, as in the case of the Directives relating to the steering equipment of passenger vehicles; here the provisions of secondary law essentially displace or supplant the provisions of the Treaties though, as noted above, it may be that the existence of the Directive influences the argumentation in cognate areas in which the Directive does not apply. In other situations, things are apt to become much more complicated. For example, in the public procurement field, the legality of social conditions, which seem to be authorised by one piece of secondary legislation, ends up being dependent on the Court's interpretation of Article 56 TFEU, which itself depends on the interpretation of another piece of secondary legislation. Primary and secondary law rules coexist; the meaning of each rule is up for interpretation, the scope of each rule may be a matter of controversy, and the constitutional relationship between rules at various levels may also be conceptualised in a number of different ways.

With these case studies in mind, it is now time to turn to a closer analysis of the role of first the legislature, and then the Court, in the EU internal market context.

[34] Case C-115/14 *RegioPost* (n 23) paras 75 and 76.

[35] Case C-341/05 *Laval* EU:C:2007:809 para 60: 'Nevertheless, Directive 96/71 did not harmonise the material content of those mandatory rules for minimum protection. That content may accordingly be freely defined by the Member States, in compliance with the Treaty and the general principles of [Union] law.'

[36] See further P Syrpis and T Novitz, 'The EU Internal Market and Domestic Labour Law: Looking Beyond Autonomy' in A Bogg, C Costello, A Davies and J Prassl (eds), *The Autonomy of Labour Law* (Oxford, Hart, 2015) 299–300.

III. THE ROLE OF THE EU LEGISLATURE IN THE INTERNAL MARKET CONTEXT

The EU Treaties envisage roles for both the judiciary and the legislature in the creation of the EU internal market. As the various chapters in this book have shown, the judiciary has played a huge role in the development of the EU internal market. This chapter explores the additional contribution made by the legislature, and reflects on the impact that legislative interventions have on the judicial role.[37]

One obvious way in which the Member States can influence the development of European integration is via amending the text of the Treaties. In fact, the text of the Treaties has been frequently amended; so much so that, since the passage of the Single European Act in the mid-1980s, the EU has been in a state of almost constant constitutional flux. It is clear that changes to the wording of the Treaties can have a profound impact on the case law of the Court, but that they do not necessarily do so. Niamh Nic Shuibhne's chapter in this volume discusses the impact of the changes made at Lisbon,[38] and in the chapters by Sara Iglesias Sanchez and Diego Acosta, Eleanor Spaventa and Aidan O'Neill,[39] the impact of the introduction of EU citizenship by the Maastricht Treaty is discussed.

However, it is also possible for States to influence the development of the internal market via the adoption of secondary legislation. There are a number of legal bases under which the EU legislature is afforded the competence to adopt a variety of measures 'with the aim of establishing or ensuring the functioning of the internal market, in accordance with the relevant provisions of the Treaties',[40] together with a number of others which afford the EU legislature what is often a more restricted competence to adopt legislation to serve other (for example social or environmental) goals. As we shall see, these legislative interventions may pursue a number of different objectives. They typically involve a desire on the part of the legislative institutions to afford greater clarity and specificity to the bare text of the Treaties, and should be read in the light of pre-existing judicial elaborations of the meaning of the text of the Treaties.

The complexity of the EU legislative process is well known to all students of EU law. The Commission, Council, European Parliament, and potentially a number of other institutional actors combine, in a bewildering variety of ways, to produce EU legislative acts.[41] There are concerns about the transparency and accountability of

[37] This section is based on P Syrpis (ed), *The Judiciary, the Legislature and the EU Internal Market* (Cambridge, Cambridge University Press, 2012).

[38] See ch 15.

[39] See chs 5, 4, and 3 respectively.

[40] The wording is taken from Art 26 TFEU. There are specific provisions in relation to non-discrimination, citizenship, and the free movement of persons, services and capital. There are also more general powers to approximate laws in Arts 114 and 115 TFEU, and a residual competence to adopt measures to attain one of the objectives of the Treaties in Art 352 TFEU.

[41] See Arts 288–99 TFEU.

the legislative process, which manifest themselves more generally as concerns with a 'democratic deficit' within the EU.[42]

The Treaties (as interpreted by the Court) create the framework within which the EU legislature operates. The Treaties, as most recently amended at Lisbon, organise the functioning of the Union and determine the areas of, delimitation of, and arrangements for, the exercise of competence.[43] They designate particular competences as 'exclusive', 'shared', and 'supporting'. The internal market is designated as an area in which the Union shares competence with the Member States.[44] The Treaties introduce, and describe the effect of, the principles of subsidiarity and proportionality,[45] and outline—albeit only in broad terms—the permissible objectives of EU action under particular legal bases.

There are a number of specific legal bases which afford the EU institutions the competence to act in the internal market arena. Most provide for the adoption of directives and/or regulations, though some limit the competence of the EU institutions to the adoption of particular measures. Article 26(1) TFEU states that the Union 'shall adopt measures with the aim of progressively establishing or ensuring the functioning of the internal market, in accordance with the relevant provisions of the Treaties'. Article 27 specifically calls upon the Commission to 'take into account the extent of the effort that certain economies showing differences in development will have to sustain for the establishment of the internal market', authorising the proposal of derogations, provided that they are 'of temporary nature' and that they 'cause the least possible disturbance to the functioning of the internal market'.

The main provisions for the approximation of laws are Articles 114 and 115 TFEU (on which the Directives relating to the steering equipment of passenger vehicles discussed above were based). Article 114 authorises the European Parliament and the Council, acting in accordance with the ordinary legislative procedure, to adopt 'measures for the approximation of the provisions laid down by law, regulation or administrative action in Member States which have as their object the establishment and functioning of the internal market'.[46] There are a number of substantive and procedural limitations in the remaining paragraphs of Article 114. It is worth noting that paragraphs 4 and 5 of Article 114 TFEU create a system whereby Member States are able to either maintain or introduce national provisions, provided that they have been notified to, and approved by, the Commission. A more restricted range of justifications is available to the Member States.

[42] See eg P Craig, 'Democracy and Rule-Making within the EC: An empirical and normative assessment' (1997) 3 *European Law Journal* 105; and C Lord, 'Assessing democracy in a contested polity' (2001) 39 *Journal of Common Market Studies* 641.

[43] Art 1 TFEU. Categories and areas of Union competence are outlined in Arts 2–6 TFEU.

[44] Art 4(2)(a) TFEU.

[45] Art 5 TEU.

[46] Art 114(1) TFEU.

Under paragraph 4, national provisions may be maintained 'on the grounds of major needs referred to in Article 36, or relating to the protection of the environment or the working environment'. Under paragraph 5, national provisions may be introduced where 'based on new scientific evidence relating to the protection of the environment or the working environment on grounds of a problem specific to that Member State arising after the adoption of the harmonisation measure'.[47] Article 115, which is expressed to be without prejudice to Article 114, authorises the Council, acting unanimously, to adopt directives 'for the approximation of such laws, regulations or administrative provisions of the Member States as directly affect the establishment or functioning of the internal market'. Beyond those general provisions, there are a number of more specific legal bases, each with their own legislative procedures. Among the most significant are: Article 18 TFEU, which provides for the adoption of rules to prevent discrimination on grounds of nationality; Article 19 TFEU, which provides for the taking of action to combat other forms of discrimination; Article 21 TFEU, which provides for the adoption of provisions facilitating the exercise of the free movement and residence rights of citizens; Article 46 TFEU, which provides for the issuing of directives and regulations setting out the measures required to bring about freedom of movement for workers; Article 48 TFEU, which provides for the adoption of measures in the social security field to provide freedom of movement for workers; Article 50 TFEU, which provides for action, by means of directives, in order to attain freedom of establishment; Article 53 TFEU, which provides for the issue of directives for the mutual recognition of diplomas etc; Article 59 TFEU, which provides for the issue of directives for the liberalisation of specific services (under which both the Public Procurement and Posted Workers Directives discussed above were enacted); and Article 64 TFEU, which provides for the adoption of measures on the movement of capital to or from third countries.

Alongside these 'internal market' legal bases, there are other legal bases in other parts of Treaties (for example, in the Titles of the Treaties dealing with Employment, Social Policy, Public Health, Consumer Protection, and the Environment) which afford the EU legislature what is often a more limited competence to act in order to further the Union's objectives in those policy fields. In these fields, it is not uncommon for harmonisation to be specifically excluded,[48] and/or for it to be made clear that EU legislation is not to prevent any Member State from maintaining or introducing more stringent protective measures compatible with the Treaties.[49]

There are important differences between these legal bases. Much of the academic analysis has focused on the different legislative procedures involved—particularly on whether the European Parliament has the status of co-legislator

[47] See Case T-234/04 *Netherlands v Commission* EU:T:2007:335; and Case C-439 and 454/05P *Land Oberösterreich and Austria v Commission* EU:C:2007:510.

[48] See eg Art 149 TFEU, Art 153(2)(a) TFEU, Art 165(4) TFEU and Art 168(5) TFEU.

[49] See eg Art 153(4) TFEU, Art 169(4) TFEU, Art 193 TFEU.

with the Council; and whether the Council may adopt measures via qualified majority, or only via unanimity. Legislative procedures of course have a big impact on how easily secondary legislation may be adopted, and on the form of such legislation—it is, for example, likely that legislation will be more flexible where its adoption depends on the agreement of each and every Member State. But, for present purposes, the more important questions concern the nature of the relationships between the Treaties, EU legislation, and measures subsequently adopted at the national level; and in particular centre on the extent to which the adoption of EU legislation is able to affect the autonomy of the national legislator.

One of the problems is that, as noted above, the language of the Treaties is open-textured; so that the legal bases outlined above afford significant room for manoeuvre for the legislative institutions.[50] Second, much of the legislation adopted by the legislative institutions is itself unclear. The tensions between uniformity and diversity, which are a feature of the Treaties, are often all too apparent not only in the preambles, but also in the text of the legislation which is adopted. The result of this lack of clarity is, as David Edward suggests in Chapter 1, that much ends up depending on the interpretive stance adopted by the Court.

The nature of the relationship between the judiciary and the legislature is, in constitutional law terms, intriguing. In the EU, as in other systems in which the legislature operates within a constitutional frame, it is possible to view the relationship between the judiciary and the legislature in two (rather extreme) ways; the first privileging the position of the judiciary, the second privileging that of the legislature.[51]

The first, and in constitutional law terms rather hierarchical and traditional approach, involves privileging the position of the Treaties over legislation, and as a result, privileging the position of the judiciary over that of the legislature. Under this first approach, the Treaties are the primary law of the EU. All legislation is secondary. The Court's interpretation of the Treaties should not be influenced by the passage of legislation. In deciding on the legality of legislation in the internal market context, the Court should not hesitate to use judicial review to annul legislation which is contrary to the Treaties. In its interpretation of EU legislation, the Court should use the Treaties as its touchstone, and be prepared (within the limits of judicial propriety, however defined) to strain the meaning of legislation so that it most closely corresponds with, and indeed furthers, the Court's conception of the dictates of the Treaties.

[50] See M Pollack, 'Creeping Competence: The Expanding Agenda of the European Community' (1994) 14 *Journal of Public Policy* 95. Allan Rosas, in the Foreword to this book, makes the point that 'the scope and content of such secondary law may vary greatly'.

[51] The literature on 'political' and 'legal' constitutions and constitutionalism is also relevant here; see eg G Gee and G Webber, 'What Is a Political Constitution?' (2010) 30 *OJLS* 273. Seen from this perspective, the EU Treaties create a legal, rather than a political, constitution; with the result that it falls to the courts to determine the extent to which the political institutions are able to play their part in the elaboration of the dictates of the constitution. See further G Davies, 'Legislative Control of the European Court of Justice' (2014) 51 *CML Rev* 1.

The second, rather more organic approach affords the legislature more of a meaningful role in the development of the internal market. Under this approach, the influence of the political institutions on the meaning of the key concepts introduced in the Treaties cannot sensibly be limited to their role in Treaty revision. The argument here is that the internal market concept should not be left solely to the Court's interpretation of the open-textured text of the Treaties, but that it is a political matter on which national governments, the Commission, the European Parliament and a range of other stakeholders have relevant and valuable input. This approach appears particularly attractive in the internal market context, in which it has, at least since the Single European Act, been accepted that negative (judiciary-driven) and positive (legislature-driven) integration are complementary routes towards the creation of the internal market.[52] Granted, there are limits imposed by the Treaties (and policed by the Court); but the Court should, in its case law, strive to reflect the will expressed by the political institutions. This has implications for the way in which the judiciary should approach its tasks. The Court should only exercise its power to review the acts of the Union institutions in extreme circumstances, where, for example, the legislature has 'manifestly', or 'manifestly and gravely', exceeded the limits of its powers. It should read secondary legislation literally. It should even, perhaps, be prepared to adjust its own interpretation of Treaty texts in the light of the stance adopted by the legislature (an outcome clearly at odds with the more hierarchical first approach).[53] Those who subscribe to this approach would agree with Paul Craig, who has argued that 'where the [Union] legislature has given considered thought to the more particular meaning to be accorded to a right laid down in a Treaty article and expressed this through [Union] legislation, the [Union] courts should treat this with respect'.[54] They would also agree with those writers who call for deference, or self-restraint, on the part of the courts, so as to 'avoid intrusion on the perceived proper domain of political judgment'.[55] Where the Court is filling in gaps left by the legislature, it should try to behave as a good legislator behaves. Where, however, the legislature has spoken, the question for the Court is whether to unmake, or respect, the legislature's choice; and in that situation the Court should be sensitive to the institutional balance and the discretionary powers of the legislative institutions.[56]

[52] See eg K Armstrong and S Bulmer, *The Governance of the Single European Market* (Manchester, Manchester University Press, 1998).

[53] A good example is Case C-158/07 *Förster* EU:C:2008:630, in which the Court accepted the legality of a five-year minimum residence criterion for a student's equal access to maintenance grants; on the basis of 'a rather dubious bow before the Citizenship Directive', which had been passed but which was not yet applicable in the case at hand; and which represented an advance of its pre-existing case law (Case C-209/03 *Bidar* EU:C:2005:169, which had held that the UK's three-year requirement was in line with Union law); see F Wollenschläger, 'The judiciary, the legislature and the evolution of Union citizenship' in Syrpis (ed) (n 37) 323.

[54] P Craig, *EU Administrative Law* (Oxford, Oxford University Press, 2006) 520.

[55] S Weatherill, 'Supply of and demand for internal market regulation: strategies, preferences and interpretation' in N Nic Shuibhne (ed), *Regulating the Internal Market* (Cheltenham, Edward Elgar, 2006) 38.

[56] See J Ely, *Democracy and Distrust* (Cambridge, Harvard University Press, 1980) 68.

These two approaches are very different. The first sees the Treaties in formal terms, and leaves questions of interpretation in the expert and independent hands of the judiciary. The Court's task is to police the limits of what is constitutional, and to rule on whether the legislature has infringed those limits. In the EU internal market context, the Court's interpretation of the Treaties becomes crucial, and influences the ability of the legislature to act so as to shape the internal market. Under this first approach, one would expect to see a clear distinction between the way in which the Court deals with amendments to the Treaty text (which might properly be expected to have a great influence on the Court's jurisprudence) and the mere adoption of secondary legislation within the existing Treaty framework. The second approach is less hierarchical. One of the effects of Court decisions is to 'concretise' the constitution—so that, over time, the Court contributes to the creation of a tighter framework affecting the legality of State (and also private) conduct. Crucially, however, legislative interventions also play a part in this concretisation process, leading one towards the conclusion that it is via a dynamic interaction between the judiciary and the legislature that the internal market concept evolves.

IV. THE ROLE OF THE COURT OF JUSTICE

It is not a surprise that the case law of the Court does not conform to either of these two extreme approaches. The provisions on judicial review are open-textured, and 'do not on their face tell one anything about the test or standard of review in relation to matters of law, fact or discretion'.[57] The Court is, albeit on rare occasions, prepared to annul EU legislation which, in its view, infringes the Treaties and/or general principles of EU law. It also, rather more commonly, shows itself willing to interpret EU legislation creatively, so that its scope and meaning come to correspond to the Court's view of the demands of the internal market.[58] However, on other occasions, the Court seems to give more weight and respect to EU legislation, showing itself to be reluctant to annul it (even when it seems possible to argue that it is in breach of the Treaties), and interpreting it literally (even when a literal interpretation goes against the main thrust of its case law).[59]

[57] Craig, *EU Administrative Law* (n 54) 266. See further Lord Mance, 'The interface between national and European law' (2013) 38 *EL Rev* 437, 451: 'It is not the Court of Justice's role to act as a legislator, or to extend or "improve" legislation in respects which the actual EU legislators might have agreed, but could not or did not on the fact of it agree'; and '[t]he Court of Justice should not lightly discount the policy decisions, interests and compromises which have influenced the Council to a particular legislative conclusion; nor should it give the appearance that it attaches little significance to them.'

[58] This creativity, so critics of the Court's reasoning argue, is apt to damage the legitimacy of the EU.

[59] For a fuller analysis, see P Syrpis, 'The Relationship between Primary and Secondary Law in the EU' (2015) 52 *CML Rev* 461. See also the comments by Allan Rosas in the Foreword in relation to Case C-333/13 *Dano* EU:C:2014:2358. Rosas states that 'we may deplore this requirement [to have sufficient resources as a condition of residence] established in the Directive but the Court is not empowered to remove it, unless it was held that it is in violation of Article 21 TFEU'.

What becomes apparent from an analysis of the Court's jurisprudence is that the Court rarely, if ever, gives an overt rationalisation for its choice of approach. This is perhaps indicative of the fact that it has yet to articulate the 'proper' relationship between the judiciary and the legislature in the internal market context. It is sensitive to its own institutional position and, much like other courts which operate in a constitutional context, it has to define the boundaries of its own role, and to come to decisions about how far to exercise deference, or self-restraint, in the face of interventions by the legislature. The Court is faced with such decisions not only in the context of judicial review, but also in relation to its interpretive role:

> Some self-restraint or deference is required to ensure that judges do not simply take over the role of ministers and officials in determining and applying government policy. But too much self-restraint or deference will prevent the judges from fulfilling their own constitutional role of ensuring the lawfulness, fairness and justifiability of administrative action.[60]

In the final analysis, the relationship between the judiciary and the legislature, and the boundary between issues which are 'legal' and those which are 'political', is very difficult to draw.[61] The key elements in the analysis are a combination of democracy, legitimacy and expertise. Those who emphasise democracy tend to advocate a more limited role for courts.[62] On the other hand, those who emphasise legitimacy and expertise are rather more prepared to allow courts to have the decisive say more often.[63]

One feature of the EU Treaty framework is that the Court of Justice 'operates in an unusually permissive strategic environment. When it interprets the treaties, for instance, its zone of discretion is virtually unlimited'.[64] Since the early years of market making, the Court has held that the free movement of persons provisions of the Treaties are capable of having direct effect, notwithstanding the provision they make for the adoption of EU legislation, stating, for example in *Thieffry*,[65] that 'a person subject to [Union] law cannot be denied the practical benefit of that freedom solely by virtue of the fact that, for a particular profession, the Directives

[60] See A Davies, 'Judicial Self-Restraint in Labour Law' (2009) 38 *Industrial Law Journal* 278, 284.

[61] See also T Horsley, 'Reflections on the Role of the Court of Justice as the "Motor" of European Integration: Legal Limits to Judicial Lawmaking' (2013) 50 *CML Rev* 931. Horsley understands the Court as an institutional actor, and deals (at 933, and then 956–63) with the way in which the Art 13(2) TEU principle of mutual sincere co-operation might oblige 'the Court to engage in a more constructive process of inter-institutional policymaking with the Union legislature'.

[62] See eg J Waldron, 'The Core of the Case against Judicial Review' (2005–06) 115 *Yale Law Journal* 1346; and A Kavanagh, 'Defending Deference in Public Law and Constitutional Theory' (2010) 126 *LQR* 222.

[63] See A Fritzsche, 'Discretion, Scope of Judicial Review and Institutional Balance in European Law' (2010) 47 *CML Rev* 361.

[64] A Stone Sweet, 'The European Court of Justice' in P Craig and G de Búrca (eds), *The Evolution of the EU Law* 2nd edn (Oxford, Oxford University Press, 2011) 127.

[65] Case 71/76 *Thieffry* EU:C:1977:65.

provided for by [Article 53 TFEU] have not yet been adopted'.[66] Similarly, since *Dassonville*,[67] the Court has interpreted the free movement provisions expansively, bringing a broad range of national measures within their scope, and putting the onus on states to justify (restrictive) national rules and show them to be proportionate.[68] National courts also have a role to play in this interpretive endeavour, but are, under the *CILFIT* guidelines,[69] expected to refer all difficult questions of interpretation to the Court of Justice.

The discretionary powers of the Court remain intact in situations in which the text of the Treaties has been supplemented by secondary legislation. The Court of Justice has a broad jurisdiction to rule on the legality or validity of acts of the EU institutions; and has, albeit on relatively rare occasions, annulled legislative acts which exceed the competence of the institutions under particular legal bases, or which are held to infringe the Treaties or any rule of law relating to their application.[70] This is a judicial review function, and it is the Court's task, either in direct actions brought via Article 263 TFEU, or when dealing with Article 267 TFEU references from national courts on the validity of an act of the institutions of the Union, to assess the compatibility of legislation with the Treaties. Second, the Court has the task of interpreting the Treaties and secondary legislation. The relationship between the Court and national courts is significant here; while the interpretation of the Treaties is primarily the task of the Court of Justice, it is, in most cases, for national courts to decide whether national rules infringe EU law.[71] Much depends on the interpretive methodologies the Court employs,[72] and on the extent to which the Court is prepared to defer to the interventions of the legislature. Secondary legislation can, for example, as shown in both cases discussed in

[66] The Court accorded direct effect to the free movement of capital provisions of the Treaties much later, in Joined Cases C-163, 165 and 250/94 *Sanz de Lera* EU:C:1995:451. Note, however, that, in other cases, the absence of EU level legislation does affect the Court's analysis: see eg Case 81/87 *Daily Mail* EU:C:1988:456 para 14; and Case C-210/06 *Cartesio* EU:C:2008:723 para 109.

[67] Case 8/74 *Procureur du Roi v Dassonville* EU:C:1974:82.

[68] The Court's framework has been aptly described as 'highly intrusive' and also 'maximally flexible'. See A Stone Sweet, 'The European Court of Justice' in P Craig and G de Búrca (eds), *The Evolution of EU Law* 2nd edn (Oxford, Oxford University Press, 2011) 137.

[69] See Case 283/81 *CILFIT v Ministry of Health* EU:C:1982:335. The case makes it clear, at paras 13–20, that national courts against whose decision there is no judicial remedy under national law are not obliged to refer questions of interpretation to the Court where the correct application of Union law is 'so obvious as to leave no scope for any reasonable doubt as to the manner in which the question raised is to be resolved'.

[70] See, for a high profile recent example, Joined Cases C-293 and 594/12 *Digital Rights Ireland Ltd* EU:C:2014:238.

[71] Where cases are brought directly before the Court of Justice under Art 258 or 259 TFEU (by the Commission or another Member State) it falls to the Court to assess whether or not a State has failed to fulfil an obligation under the Treaties. In other cases, which come to the Court under Art 267 as a result of preliminary references by national courts, the Court of Justice's task is to interpret EU law, while that of the national courts is to apply that law to the factual scenario at hand.

[72] See Lord Mance, 'The interface between national and European law' (2013) 38 *EL Rev* 437, 450: 'free-ranging interpretive activity involves courts in decisions which ought to be taken by the legislature'. See further G Conway, *The Limits of Legal Reasoning and the European Court of Justice* (Cambridge, Cambridge University Press, 2012); G Beck, *The Legal Reasoning of the Court of Justice of the EU*

detail in this chapter, impact on the way in which the justification and proportionality tests operate, and can therefore operate so as to supplement the Treaties, and affect the regulatory competence of the Member States. This depends on the Court affording a significant amount of weight to the interventions of the legislature, in line with political rather than legal conceptions of the EU constitution. However, there are also many examples in which the Court seems to be more eager to use the Treaties in order to impose limits on the reach of secondary legislation. One prominent example is in the case of *Baumbast*.[73] There, as is well known, national action apparently in conformity with EU secondary legislation was held to breach the principle of proportionality, in the particular circumstances of the case before the Court. The result of this approach on the part of the Court is 'an appreciable decrease' in the 'effective regulatory competence' of the EU legislature,[74] as a direct result of the activism of the Court.

V. CONCLUSION

The Court has used the power which it is afforded via the EU's constitutional framework in rather unpredictable ways; appearing deferential to EU legislative interventions in some cases, while in others showing little appetite for allowing the interventions of the EU legislature to deflect it. The cases seem to be decided on the basis of little more than intuition,[75] and the Court appears to lack a clear sense of where the boundary between the legal and the political is, and ought to be, located. It has a variety of techniques available to it, both in relation to the stance it adopts towards judicial review and in relation to the criteria it deploys when interpreting provisions of EU law (be they Treaty provisions, general principles of EU law, or secondary legislation). It deploys combinations of those techniques in order to reach its conclusions in any given case, employing what Beck terms 'its distinctive flexible approach to legal reasoning'.[76] It is, as a result, very difficult to predict the impact which the existence of secondary legislation may have on the Court's analysis of the free movement provisions of the Treaties; and this lack of

(Oxford, Hart, 2012); and H-W Micklitz and B de Witte (eds), *The European Court of Justice and the Autonomy of the Member States* (Cambridge, Intersentia, 2012).

[73] See Case C-413/99 *Baumbast* EU:C:2002:493.

[74] M Dougan, 'The Constitutional Dimension to the case law on Union Citizenship' (2006) 31 *EL Rev* 613, 640.

[75] See, albeit in a different context, J Snell, 'The Notion of Market Access: A Concept or a Slogan?' (2010) 47 *CML Rev* 437, 469.

[76] G Beck, 'The Court of Justice, legal reasoning and the Pringle case—law as the continuation of politics by other means' (2014) 39 *EL Rev* 234, 234. Beck is scathing about the decision in Case C-370/12 *Pringle* EU:C:2012:756, on the legality of the European Stability Mechanism, in which he claims that the Court exploits 'the vagueness and norm uncertainty in its general approach to the maximum, probably to a point where legal reasoning no longer imposes any constraints on judicial law-making. At this point, the legal becomes political'.

legal certainty has damaging consequences for both the legislature and for potential litigants.[77]

It appears that the EU Treaties give the Court an almost free rein to decide how much weight to attach to the interventions of the legislature, affording the Court an almost unlimited power to exercise its powers of judicial review and, more importantly, creative interpretation—in relation to the meaning of the Treaties, the meaning of EU level legislation, and the nature of the relationship between the two. The Court has used this power in unpredictable ways, illustrating perhaps the difficulty it has with locating the proper boundary between the legal and the political, and with identifying the proper weight which it should attach to the interventions of the legislature. The result is that the impact of EU secondary legislation on free movement law is uncertain; and that the ability of the legislature to influence the development of internal market law is dependent on the vagaries of the case law of the Court. It is therefore very much, to return to the words of Allan Rosas in the Foreword, to be hoped that fairness and reasonableness, and common sense, prevail.

[77] See also Lord Mance, 'The interface between national and European law' (2013) 38 *EL Rev* 437, 451: 'legal certainty is only achieved if the outcome of litigation on EU legal themes is predictable'.

15

Primary Laws: Judging Free Movement Restrictions after Lisbon

NIAMH NIC SHUIBHNE*

I. INTRODUCTION

THE JUSTIFICATION STANDARD normally applied in free movement law—that is, restrictions of free movement rights that are not directly discriminatory may be justified by overriding reasons in the public interest—does not require a static conception of public interest. Legitimate reasons in the public interest can change over time. Crucially, they can also differ across the Member States. For example, in the case law on betting and gambling restrictions, the Court of Justice acknowledges that 'there are significant moral, religious and cultural differences between the Member States'; therefore, '[i]n the absence of harmonisation on the issue at EU level, it is for each Member State to determine in those areas, in accordance with its own scale of values, what is required in order to ensure that the interests in question are protected'.[1] Similarly, even for situations that connect to the Treaty-circumscribed derogation grounds, which apply when restrictions are directly discriminatory, the Court has accepted that 'the specific circumstances which may justify recourse to the concept of public policy may vary from one country to another and from one era to another'.[2]

In parallel, however, the Court has also been careful to delimit the exercise and extent of permitted national discretion within boundaries that are pitched and controlled by EU law. For example, it matches recognition of national differences with the demanding threshold that 'public policy may be relied on only if there is a genuine and sufficiently serious threat to a fundamental interest of society'.[3] In

* School of Law, University of Edinburgh. Thanks to my co-editors for their insightful comments on the draft chapter. An early version was presented at the Annual Leiden-London Meeting held at Leiden University in June 2014; I am grateful to the participants for their comments and suggestions.

[1] Case C-463/13 *Stanley International Betting and Stanleybet Malta* EU:C:2015:25 para 51. For detailed analysis of the relevant case law, see D Doukas, 'Morality, Free Movement and Judicial Restraint at the European Court of Justice', ch 8 in this volume.

[2] Case C-36/02 *Omega* EU:C:2004:614 para 31; citing Case 41/74 *Van Duyn* EU:C:1974:133 para 18 and Case 30/77 *Bouchereau* EU:C:1977:172 para 34. See similarly Case C-244/06 *Dynamic Medien* EU:C:2008:85 para 44 and Case C-208/09 *Sayn-Wittgenstein* EU:C:2010:806 para 91.

[3] Case C-36/02 *Omega* ibid, para 30.

this way, the Court evaluates public interest reasons in a way that is both adaptive and bounded: protecting a fundamental essence for free movement rights on the one hand, while striving also to assign meaningful public interest credit to legitimate restrictions of those rights on the other.[4] Proportionality review then probes further into how that legitimacy dimension manifests in practice.

Thinking about what should, in turn, guide the Court, this chapter examines the changes to primary EU law effected by the Lisbon Treaty and asks if they have altered how public interest justification arguments are, or should be, assessed. In section II, why free movement law might have benefited from some revision is first briefly outlined, followed by an overview of the main Lisbon amendments that can be linked with the protection of public interest. When these changes are looked at together, an impression of public interest that is focused on the protection of national as well as Union public interest initially emerges. At one level, that perception is strengthened by the fact that most of the Lisbon amendments have barely featured in the Court's recent considerations of free movement restrictions (section III) with the exception, in relative terms, of respect for national identity as protected by Article 4(2) TEU (section IV).

The chapter pursues two further questions through the course of that analysis. First, why has the degree of primary law change realised through Lisbon actually had such limited effect on the interpretation of free movement law in EU judicial practice? Several of the chapters in this volume have identified where and/or how Lisbon amendments could make a difference. It will be argued here that how the Treaties were amended is a significant part of the answer. Second, what are the implications of an apparently growing focus on issues connected to national public interest for the complex challenge of accommodating diversity appropriately on the one hand, while securing not just the boundaries but also the aims and purposes of free movement on the other? This is a more difficult question to answer, not least because of the paradoxically compound and deferential nature of the national interest framework that some of the contributions also reveal—and which the Lisbon Treaty and its interpretation seem, contrary to the initial impression referred to above, in fact to have intensified.

II. FREE MOVEMENT AND PUBLIC INTEREST IN PRIMARY EU LAW: AN OVERVIEW OF THE LISBON AMENDMENTS

This section provides three central parts of context: first, a brief outline of why the restriction/justification framework applied in free movement law might be

[4] These dual aims were conveyed in *Van Duyn* as follows: 'the concept of public policy in the context of the Community and where, in particular, it is used as a justification for derogating from the fundamental principle of freedom of movement for workers, must be interpreted strictly, so that its scope cannot be determined unilaterally by each Member State without being subject to control by the institutions of the Community. Nevertheless, the particular circumstances justifying recourse to the concept of public policy may vary from one country to another and from one period to another, and it is therefore necessary in this matter to allow the competent national authorities an area of discretion within the limits imposed by the Treaty' (para 18).

questioned in the first place; second, changes to primary law put in place by the Lisbon Treaty that reflect elements of Union public interest; and third, Lisbon amendments that convey public interest more as concerns rooted in national interest.

A. Background: Did the Legal Environment of Free Movement Need to Be Revised?

Treaty change is at once an exceptional and standard mode of EU law making. Revising existing provisions or adding new ones either catches the Treaty up with a policy agenda already under way, or can set a new agenda entirely. In other words, Treaty change both reflects and produces how the purposes, objectives and tasks of the Union advance, retreat and multiply. Treaty change also represents the regulatory sphere in which the Member States can expect to have their greatest impact on the case law of the Court of Justice, noting unresolved debates about the capacity of secondary legislation in that respect.[5]

The basic Treaty provisions on free movement rights, where we also find corresponding derogations, were not substantively changed through Lisbon. Nevertheless, questions that feed into long-standing debates about the expansive reach of these rights—and the proper functioning of justification and proportionality arguments in consequence—had further intensified during the extended period of preparation for the Treaty establishing a Constitution for Europe and then Lisbon. First, the perception that the law on how (easily) a restriction of free movement rights could be established had reached a justify-by-default stage became virtually conventional—that is, pretty much any national policy choice could be conceived as a potential restriction of free movement rights, requiring Member States almost always then to demonstrate both a relevant public interest defence as well as the specific measure's suitability and necessity for achieving that aim (that is, its proportionality). But if pretty much any national policy choice can awaken the strictures of EU legal supervision, then the constitutional assignment of the internal market as a *shared* Union/Member State competence is largely negated. Relatedly, conceptualisation of justification arguments as an expression of subsidiarity in the operation of that shared competence is diminished. The decisions made by the Court—as the institution of the Union called on to evaluate national policy choices where challenged—then fall as much into political as judicial analysis.[6]

[5] See further P Syrpis, 'EU Secondary Legislation and its Impact on Derogations from Free Movement', ch 14 in this volume.

[6] See T Horsley, 'Reflections on the role of the Court of Justice as the motor of European integration: legal limits to judicial lawmaking' (2013) 50(4) *CML Rev* 931. Davies highlights the particular character of judicial review at EU level by noting that 'the internal market pits legislature against legislature. While it may be an individual who objects to a national rule, they act as agent of the EU interest in integration, and the EU's policy of free movement is pitted against some conflicting national policy, embodied in national laws. The fact that legitimate policy-makers are represented on both sides is what justifies the Court's characteristically intrusive review' (ch 11, this volume).

These concerns open up, in turn, questions about the very point of free movement rights, perfectly illustrated by the contrasting approaches of the Advocate General and the Court in *CaixaBank France*. Addressing whether or not the contested national rule was a restriction of freedom of establishment, AG Tizzano urged caution, on the basis that 'the Member States remain as a matter of principle competent to regulate the pursuit of economic activities, by means of non-discriminatory measures' in the absence of harmonisation by the EU legislator.[7] The logistical challenge of pushing 28 sets of national rules through the filter of harmonisation forces us to be realistic about just how much internal market space remains—and will remain—un-legislated at EU level. In that light, the Advocate General's disquiet about the reach of free movement law in *CaixaBank France* concerned 'national measures that regulate the pursuit of an economic activity *without directly affecting access to that activity* and *without discriminating* either in law or in fact between national and foreign operators as restrictions contrary to the Treaty *for the sole reason that they reduce* the *economic attractiveness* of pursuing that activity'.[8] In his view, to determine that EU law extended to catch such rules:

> would permit economic operators—both national and foreign—to abuse Article [49 TFEU] in order *to oppose any national measure that, solely because it regulated the conditions for pursuing an economic activity*, could in the final analysis narrow profit margins and hence reduce the attractiveness of pursuing that particular economic activity. However, *that would be tantamount to bending the Treaty to a purpose for which it was not intended*: that is to say, not in order to create an internal market in which conditions are similar to those of a single market and where operators can move freely, but in order *to establish a market without rules*. Or rather, *a market in which rules are prohibited as a matter of principle*, except for those necessary and proportionate to meeting imperative requirements in the public interest.[9]

On that analysis, the internal market moves considerably further away from the essentials of free movement. However, the Court further ascended its broad understanding of market access as the driving dynamic of the Treaty, stating that '[a]ll measures which prohibit, impede or render less attractive the exercise of [freedom of establishment] must be regarded as … restrictions' and thereby progressing to a review of the contested measure's justification and proportionality.[10]

Second, pushing the work forward onto the justification and proportionality stages of free movement law was compounded by the fact that while it is relatively

[7] AG Tizzano in Case C-442/02 *CaixaBank France* EU:C:2004:187, para 61 of the Opinion.
[8] ibid, para 58 (emphasis in original).
[9] ibid, paras 62–63 (emphasis added).
[10] Case C-442/02 *CaixaBank France* EU:C:2004:586 para 11. For comprehensive analysis of criticisms on the nature and reach of market access, see J Snell, 'The Notion of Market Access: A Concept or a Slogan?' (2010) 47(2) *CML Rev* 437.

easy to establish a legitimate public interest in principle, it remained extremely difficult for States to succeed in reality. The reasons for this ranged from the exigencies of the less restrictive measure part of proportionality review to intensifying scrutiny of the evidence and proof that States presented when defending their public interest claims.[11] The result was a thinning out of the substance of public interest reasons, reducing justification to a veneer beneath which the reach of free movement rights still advanced largely unimpeded.

Third, how public interest grounds that also constitute fundamental rights should be managed within the structure of free movement law was especially tested ahead of the ratification of the Lisbon Treaty. In *Viking Line*, AG Poiares Maduro pointed out that

> [n]either the Treaty rules on freedom of movement, nor the right to associate and the right to strike are absolute. Moreover, nothing in the Treaty suggests that the [Union]'s social policy objectives must always take precedence over the objective of having a properly functioning common market. On the contrary, the inclusion of both policy objectives in the Treaty signifies the aim of the [Union] to bring these policies together.[12]

In reality, however, both the practice of and discourse on reconciling fundamental freedoms and fundamental rights was characterised by the language of clash, collision and conflict. The fact that primary Union law appears to protect several objectives at the same normative level is an important contributing factor that will be returned to in more detail below. More generally, we can remember that the Court's perceived privileging of economic freedom over fundamental rights—and especially over differing national conceptions and means of protection of fundamental social rights—was a particularly sore discussion point at the time of the Lisbon negotiations.[13]

[11] See D Edward, 'Introduction—The Exceptions to the Four Freedoms: The Historical Context', ch 1 in this volume; N Nic Shuibhne and M Maci, 'Proving Public Interest: The Growing Impact of Evidence in Free Movement Case Law' (2013) 50(4) *CML Rev* 965; C Barnard, 'Derogations, Justifications and the Four Freedoms: is State Interest Really Protected?' in C Barnard and O Odudu (eds), *The Outer Limits of European Union Law* (Oxford, Hart Publishing, 2009) 273.

[12] AG Poiares Maduro in Case C-438/05 *Viking Line* EU:C:2007:292, para 23 of the Opinion.

[13] eg on *Viking Line* (EU:C:2007:772) and Case C-341/05 *Laval un Partneri* EU:C:2007:809 see ACL Davies 'One Step Forward, Two Steps Back? The *Laval* and *Viking* Cases at the ECJ' (2008) 37 *Industrial Law Journal* 126; S Sciarra, '*Viking* and *Laval*: Collective Labour Rights and Market Freedoms in the Enlarged EU' (2007–2008) 10 *Cambridge Yearbook of European Legal Studies* 563; P Syrpis and T Novitz, 'Economic and social rights in conflict: political and judicial approaches to their reconciliation' (2008) 33 *EL Rev* 411. More generally, see J Morijn, 'Balancing Fundamental Rights and Common Market Freedoms in Union law: *Schmidberger* and *Omega* in the Light of the European Constitution' (2006) 12 *European Law Journal* 15; and E Spaventa, 'Federalisation versus centralisation: tensions in fundamental rights discourse in the EU' in M Dougan and S Currie (eds), *50 Years of the European Treaties: Looking Back and Thinking Forward* (Oxford, Hart Publishing, 2009) 343.

B. Overview of the Lisbon Amendments I: Public Interest as Union Interest

Starting with the provision that mandates the establishment of the internal market, Article 3(3) TEU as amended by Lisbon rephrases the goal-like language of Article 2 EC[14] with a series of harder-edged prescriptions:

> The Union shall establish an internal market. It shall work for the sustainable development of Europe based on balanced economic growth and price stability, a highly competitive social market economy, aiming at full employment and social progress, and a high level of protection and improvement of the quality of the environment. It shall promote scientific and technological advance. It shall combat social exclusion and discrimination, and shall promote social justice and protection, equality between women and men, solidarity between generations and protection of the rights of the child. It shall promote economic, social and territorial cohesion, and solidarity among Member States. It shall respect its rich cultural and linguistic diversity, and shall ensure that Europe's cultural heritage is safeguarded and enhanced.

The horizontal character of this list recalls AG Poiares Maduro's observation that 'the Treaty signifies the aim of the [Union] to bring these policies together', supported by Article 7 TFEU's statement that '[t]he Union shall ensure consistency between its policies and activities, taking all of its objectives into account and in accordance with the principle of conferral of powers'.

The tasks bundled together in Article 3(3) TEU are then unpacked more distinctly in the TFEU. Article 8 TFEU requires the Union to 'aim to eliminate inequalities, and to promote equality, between men and women'. Next, an updated set of mainstreaming clauses requires the Union to take certain interests into account in the definition and implementation of its policies and activities more generally: a 'high level of employment, the guarantee of adequate social protection, the fight against social exclusion, and a high level of education, training and protection of human health' (Article 9); combatting 'discrimination based on sex, racial or ethnic origin, religion or belief, disability, age or sexual orientation' (Article 10); protecting the environment, 'in particular with a view to promoting sustainable development' (Article 11); and consumer protection (Article 12).[15]

[14] 'The Community shall have as its task, by establishing a common market and an economic and monetary union and by implementing common policies or activities referred to in Articles 3 and 4, to promote throughout the Community a harmonious, balanced and sustainable development of economic activities, a high level of employment and of social protection, equality between men and women, sustainable and non-inflationary growth, a high degree of competitiveness and convergence of economic performance, a high level of protection and improvement of the quality of the environment, the raising of the standard of living and quality of life, and economic and social cohesion and solidarity among Member States.'

[15] Additionally, Article 13 TFEU provides that '[i]n formulating and implementing the Union's agriculture, fisheries, transport, internal market, research and technological development and space policies, the Union and the Member States shall, since animals are sentient beings, pay full regard to the welfare requirements of animals, while respecting the legislative or administrative provisions and customs of the Member States relating in particular to religious rites, cultural traditions and regional heritage'.

Read together, these TEU and TFEU provisions arguably showcase the public interest reasons to which the Union attaches particular significance, constituting the pivots of *Union* public interest. But while these policies will almost certainly conflict with each other in reality, the Treaty does not offer guidance on or a blueprint for how to prioritise or choose between them where this becomes necessary. Even *one* of the stated objectives in Article 3(3)—achieving a 'highly competitive social market economy'—is, as Snell points out, 'far from self-defining and may not be free from internal tensions'.[16] The Treaty establishing a Constitution for Europe might have made a difference in this respect since it separated out the core intention of offering Union citizens 'an area of freedom, security and justice without internal frontiers, and an internal market where competition is free and undistorted'.[17] But Article 3(3) TEU as enacted, mapping the structure if not the tone of Article 2 EC, seems instead to equalise the significance of the objectives and tasks listed, and also to thread the additional goals of the mainstreaming clauses through them.

Explicitly stating that the achievement of the internal market was a Union activity privileged above others would have erroneously reduced the nature and purpose of the contemporary Union. But what we have instead—with numerous objectives and tasks listed without an internal priority—has just complicated the already unreadable code that obscures, conversely, what the purpose of the internal market is within the contemporary Union. It is also unclear how the justification of restrictions on free movement rights should be managed in light of the expanded articulations of Union public interest: what if anything might have changed from before? A paradox therefore emerges here: the more articulate that primary law becomes as to what the EU should be doing, the less clear it becomes as to how the EU should actually go about it. In consequence, the role of the Court is enhanced all the more—an issue returned to in section III below.

C. Overview of the Lisbon Amendments II: Public Interest as National Interest

Other Lisbon amendments are more consciously framed around protecting elements of *national* public interest. First, Article 48 TFEU introduces an emergency brake in the field of new social security legislation affecting the free movement of workers, allowing a Member State to suspend the ordinary legislative procedure and refer the issue to the European Council on the basis that the proposed

[16] J Snell, 'Economic Justifications and the Role of the State', ch 2 in this volume.

[17] Article I-3(2) of the Treaty establishing a Constitution for Europe, OJ 2004 C310/1; with the other objectives now listed in Article 3(3) TEU following separately in Article I-3(3). See also, Article I-4(1): '[t]he free movement of persons, services, goods and capital, and freedom of establishment shall be guaranteed within and by the Union, in accordance with the Constitution.'

legislation would 'affect important aspects of its social security system' or 'the financial balance of that system'.[18] Second, Article 168(7) TFEU requires that 'Union action shall respect the responsibilities of the Member States for the definition of their health policy and for the organisation and delivery of health services and medical care'.[19] Furthermore, Article 152 TFEU, which amplifies previous Treaty statements about the autonomy of the social partners, can also be noted since it expressly incorporates 'taking into account the diversity of national systems'. These examples indicate specific priorities (or anxieties) held by the Member States at the crucial Treaty settlement point; and also that they worked to have agreed responses welded into primary EU law.

But explicitly construing some public interest reasons in the language of national interest also resonates with a much wider objective: the fact that the Lisbon Treaty was strongly aimed at refining the division of powers between the Union and the Member States at a more general level too. From that perspective, four thematic emphases characterise the Lisbon amendments as a complete package: first, the principle of conferral, including explicit classification and delimitation of Union and Member State competences;[20] second, the principle of subsidiarity, including a novel function for national parliaments in the EU law-making process;[21] third, principles of and mechanisms for enhancing participatory and representative democracy;[22] and, fourth, the significance of fundamental rights in the EU legal order. A unifying theme here suggests the objective of greater decentralisation, reflecting an ambition to preserve or restore the footing of the *national* in EU governance. On the significance of fundamental rights more specifically, Article 2 TEU makes it clear that respect for human rights is one of the values on which the Union is founded; Article 6(1) TEU confers on the Charter of Fundamental Rights 'the same legal values as the Treaties'; and Article 6(2) TEU requires that the Union 'shall accede' to the ECHR. But here, once again, the 'same legal value' formula perpetuates the absence of guidance or priority mechanisms that would help to

[18] 'Where a member of the Council declares that a draft legislative act referred to [Article 48(1)] would affect important aspects of its social security system, including its scope, cost or financial structure, or would affect the financial balance of that system, it may request that the matter be referred to the European Council. In that case, the ordinary legislative procedure shall be suspended. After discussion, the European Council shall, within four months of this suspension, either: (a) refer the draft back to the Council, which shall terminate the suspension of the ordinary legislative procedure; or (b) take no action or request the Commission to submit a new proposal; in that case, the act originally proposed shall be deemed not to have been adopted'. This provision is underpinned by Declaration 22 attached to the Lisbon Treaty.

[19] The provision continues: '[t]he responsibilities of the Member States shall include the management of health services and medical care and the allocation of the resources assigned to them. The measures referred to in paragraph 4(a) shall not affect national provisions on the donation or medical use of organs and blood.'

[20] Esp Art 4 TEU and Arts 2–6 TFEU.

[21] Esp Art 5(3) TEU, Protocol on the Role of National Parliaments in the European Union, and Protocol on the Application of the Principles of Subsidiarity and Proportionality.

[22] Esp Art 10 TEU.

determine the choices that need to be made *between* these norms of primary law in concrete cases.[23]

Broader public interest as national interest signals can also be tracked from the policy areas still protected by the requirements of the special legislative procedure and from policies for the realisation of which Union action must confine itself to 'support[ing], coordinat[ing] or supplement[ing] the actions of the Member States' (Article 6 TFEU). On the first point, the policy areas assigned to the special legislative procedure—requiring the agreement of every Member State if legislation is to proceed—are:

— discrimination on grounds other than nationality;[24]
— social security and social protection;[25]
— EU citizenship;[26]
— retreating from the liberalisation of capital movement;[27]
— regulation of the family;[28]
— regulation of crime;[29]
— fiscal policy;[30] and
— language rules.[31]

On the second point, Article 6 TFEU lists the competences for which the Member States retain primary regulatory responsibility, namely protection and

[23] eg AG Trstenjak in Case C-271/08 *Commission v Germany* EU:C:2010:183, para 81 of the Opinion: 'In the case of a conflict between a fundamental right and a fundamental freedom, both legal positions must be presumed to have equal status. That general equality in status implies, first, that, in the interests of fundamental rights, fundamental freedoms may be restricted. However, second, it implies also that the exercise of fundamental freedoms may justify a restriction on fundamental rights.'

[24] Art 19 TFEU, ie 'sex, racial or ethnic origin, religion or belief, disability, age or sexual orientation'—notwithstanding the prohibition on these and other forms of discrimination by Art 21(1) of the Charter and the mainstreaming obligation in Art 10 TFEU.

[25] Art 21(3) TFEU on social security or social protection measures to facilitate free movement and residence rights for EU citizens; additionally, Art 153 TFEU on social security and social protection of workers, protection of workers where their employment contract is terminated, representation and collective defence of the interests of workers and employers, including co-determination, and conditions of employment for third-country nationals legally residing in Union territory.

[26] Arts 22 (voting procedures for municipal and European Parliament elections), 23 (diplomatic or consular protection in third countries), 25 (strengthening the rights of EU citizens, including an indication that national constitutional requirements may be triggered), and 77 ('provisions concerning passports, identity cards, residence permits or any other such document' that might also facilitate movement and residence rights for EU citizens) TFEU.

[27] Art 64(3) TFEU, concerning capital movement to or from third countries only.

[28] Art 81 TFEU on 'measures concerning family law with cross-border implications'.

[29] Arts 83, 86, 87 and 89 TFEU, including the definition of criminal offences and sanctions for effective implementation of harmonised areas of EU law, operational co-operation between police and other law enforcement authorities in the Member States, and the establishment of a European Public Prosecutor's Office for crimes affecting the financial interests of the Union.

[30] Art 113 TFEU, ie 'provisions for the harmonisation of legislation concerning turnover taxes, excise duties and other forms of indirect taxation to the extent that such harmonisation is necessary to ensure the establishment and the functioning of the internal market and to avoid distortion of competition'; and Arts 192(2) and 194(3) TFEU for fiscal measures relating to town and country planning, the environment and energy.

[31] Art 118 TFEU on language arrangements for European intellectual property rights.

improvement of public health; industry; culture; tourism; education, vocational training, youth and sport; civil co-operation; and administrative co-operation.[32]

The wider scheme of the Treaty is often referred to in order to flesh out public interest concepts at the justification and proportionality stages of free movement law.[33] But the public interest grounds listed above are arguably of *special* concern to the Member States. Has that been taken into account at the justification and/or proportionality stages of free movement law following the coming into force of the Lisbon Treaty? Should it?

III. INTERPRETING THE LISBON AMENDMENTS

Weatherill has written that 'defining the scope of the Treaty provisions on the internal market is clearly a logically distinct issue from determining whether rules that fall within their scope are justified. And yet the issues cannot be sensibly kept fully separate. The broader the scope of application, the more crucial the *receptivity* under EU law to justification, for once the matter is wrenched out of the autonomy of the national regulator, practices may be maintained only where EU law standards of justification are met.'[34] Commenting on the likely impact of the Lisbon Treaty in that context, the European Parliament's Committee on Constitutional Affairs considered that there is now 'a greater emphasis on policies that visibly benefit citizens', citing many of the objectives listed in Article 3(3) TEU by way of illustration.[35] In paragraph 3.3 of the Explanatory Statement, it was noted that '[t]hese objectives thus make up a basic political programme which was the well-spring for the establishment of the Union'. But, once again, discussion of how to prioritise or choose between the relevant virtues (as a matter of law) is completely absent.

In his 2010 report on the single market for the European Commission—drawn from by Snell as a report that acknowledges 'a general disenfranchisement among citizens'[36]—Monti first placed the Lisbon Treaty in its wider context:

[32] Additionally, more specific Treaty provisions preclude harmonisation in these policy areas; see generally Art 2(5) TFEU and, eg, on education, Art 165(4) TFEU. See also Arts 4(3) (research, technological development and space, and providing that 'the Union shall have competence to carry out activities, in particular to define and implement programmes; however, the exercise of that competence shall not result in Member States being prevented from exercising theirs') and 4(4) (development co-operation and humanitarian aid, providing that 'the Union shall have competence to carry out activities and conduct a common policy; however, the exercise of that competence shall not result in Member States being prevented from exercising theirs') TFEU.

[33] See eg the discussion on Case C-145/09 *Tsakouridis* EU:C:2010:708 and Case C-348/09 *I* EU:C:2012:300 in P Koutrakos, 'Public security exceptions and EU free movement law', ch 10 in this volume.

[34] S Weatherill, 'The Court's Case Law on the Internal Market: 'A Circumloquacious Statement of the Result, Rather than a Reason for Arriving at It'?' in M Adams, H de Waele, G Meeusen and G Straetmans (eds), *Judging Europe's Judges: The Legitimacy of the Case Law of the European Court of Justice Examined* (Oxford, Hart Publishing, 2013) 87, 105 (emphasis added).

[35] EP Committee on Constitutional Affairs, 2008 Report on the Lisbon Treaty (A6-0013/2008) www.europarl.europa.eu/sides/getDoc.do?type=REPORT&reference=A6-2008-0013&language=EN.

[36] Snell (n 16).

> [T]ensions between market integration and social objectives are even more vividly exposed, now that the Lisbon Treaty has introduced, even formally, the objective of achieving a 'highly competitive social market economy'. If the market and the social components do not find an appropriate reconciliation, something has to give in. Following the crisis, with the declining appetite for the market and the increasing concern about inequalities, it is by no means clear that it would be the market, i.e. the single market, to prevail.[37]

Then, commenting expressly on the rulings in *Viking Line* and *Laval*, and noting the binding effect of the Charter conceived through Lisbon since then, he argued that '[t]hese elements should *shape a new legal context*, in which the issues and concerns raised by the trade unions should hopefully find an adequate response'.[38]

How might that 'adequate response' manifest in free movement law? In his Opinion in *Santos Palhota*, AG Cruz Villalón transposed the Lisbon factor directly to the justification stage:

> As a result of the entry into force of the Treaty of Lisbon, when working conditions constitute an overriding reason relating to the public interest justifying a derogation from the freedom to provide services, *they must no longer be interpreted strictly*. In so far as the protection of workers is a matter which warrants protection under the Treaties themselves, it is not a simple derogation from a freedom, still less an unwritten exception inferred from case-law. To the extent that the *new primary law framework* provides for a mandatory high level of social protection, it *authorises the Member States*, for the purpose of safeguarding a certain level of social protection, *to restrict a freedom, and to do so without European Union law's regarding it as something exceptional and, therefore, as warranting a strict interpretation*.[39]

The Advocate General's proposal would turn decades of free movement law's rights broadly/exceptions narrowly paradigm on its head. Could such a radical reorientation be rationalised by the Lisbon amendments detailed in Section 2—amendments that have, as the Opinion underlines, created a 'new primary law framework'?

Returning to Weatherill's work, however, he rightly tempers our expectations of truly significant transformation on the basis of Treaty change alone. Writing shortly after the coming into effect of the Lisbon Treaty, he argued:

> [There] are aspects of the Lisbon Treaty that serve to strengthen the argument that free movement law must be more attentive to (in short) non-economic objectives—the Charter of Fundamental Rights, the Treaty's horizontal clauses, defence of constitutional identity and the relegation of the commitment to undistorted competition in the internal market. But one's assessment of the significance of any such potential adjustment

[37] M Monti, *A New Strategy for the Single Market: At the Service of Europe's Economy and Society* 9 May 2010, prepared at the request of the European Commission President http://ec.europa.eu/bepa/pdf/monti_report_final_10_05_2010_en.pdf, 26.

[38] ibid, 70 (emphasis added).

[39] AG Cruz Villalón in Case C-515/08 *Santos Palhota* EU:C:2010:245 para 53 of the Opinion (emphasis added).

depends heavily on whether one reckons the Court in the past to have been sincerely anxious to respect social and cultural concerns expressed through (trade-restrictive) national measures; and any prediction as to the future also entails engagement with Europe's judges, for *the ambiguity of the relevant legal material* ensures that *considerable power has been delegated to the Court to choose between competing interpretations ... The Lisbon Treaty does not make a qualitative change to the structure and scope of the law governing free movement.*[40]

Weatherill's initial instinct has been confirmed in his contribution to this volume; in particular, his analysis of consumer protection as a public interest objective concludes that the TFEU's mainstreaming clauses evidence 'confirmation of, not break with, the Court's past approach'.[41] Importantly, he reminds us that free movement law has always had the capacity for sensitivity to other interests. But he also brings out the institutional angle of continuity—the decisive control held by the Court of Justice in the making of these decisions, both pre- and post-Lisbon. Additionally, Syrpis demonstrates that the Court exercises this crucial function whether there is EU legislation in the area or not.[42]

These statements challenge conventional assumptions that primary law change is and should be enough to bring about substantive legal change. However, in the area of free movement law, the still-predominant contribution of judicial interpretation is directly linked to *how* public interest provisions were amended or drafted at Lisbon, especially since no corresponding editing attention was paid to the free movement provisions. Ultimately, the Court can—and has to—do this because, as Snell argues, '[t]he balance between the differing interests is not set in the Treaty, but needs to be established in political and judicial arenas'.[43] This assertion is borne out by the scant attention actually paid to relevant amendments in the case law since Lisbon, on the one hand; and the pliability of their interpretation when they do feature, on the other.

The second point can be illustrated by reflecting on the contrasting uses to which Article 2 TEU was put by AG Kokott and the Court respectively in *Opinion 2/13* on EU accession to the ECHR.[44] There has been significant discussion of the primary law effects of the Charter post-Lisbon. However, what the Court requires is that '[w]here several rights and fundamental freedoms protected by

[40] S Weatherill, 'From Economic Rights to Fundamental Rights' in S de Vries, U Bernitz and S Weatherill (eds), *The Protection of Fundamental Rights in the EU After Lisbon* (Oxford, Hart Publishing, 2012) 11, 35–36 (emphasis added).

[41] S Weatherill, 'Justification, Proportionality and Consumer Protection', ch 12 in this volume. Exploring the theme of pre-/post-Lisbon continuity in the field of fundamental rights protection, see S Iglesias Sánchez, 'The Court and the Charter: The Impact of the Entry into Force of the Lisbon Treaty on the ECJ's Approach to Fundamental Rights' (2012) 49(5) *CML Rev* 1565.

[42] P Syrpis, 'EU Secondary Legislation and its Impact on Derogations from Free Movement', ch 14 in this volume.

[43] Snell (n 16).

[44] *cf* para 164 of the View of AG Kokott (EU:C:2014:2475) and paras 162–68 of the Opinion of the Court (EU:C:2014:2454), reaching very different conclusions on the desirability of external supervision of the EU as a result.

the European Union legal order are at issue', the aim must be to 'reconcil[e] the requirements of the protection of those different rights and freedoms and a fair balance between them'.[45] But we remain at square one as to how, more concretely, we should prioritise the multiplicity of objectives that might be relevant. A discourse based on balance and reconciliation—even noting Davies' caution to distinguish between rather than collapse these terms—cannot escape the fact that concrete choices between values have to be made to resolve the practical questions at the heart of pertinent disputes.[46] Moreover, the further we drill into proportionality—where most of the balancing and reconciling takes place—the further we move away from the sphere of legal analysis. The insights provided by Judge Rosas in the Foreword—which also suggest recognition of the distinction between balancing and reconciling—reflect the reality of proportionality review very plainly:

> Here is an example where the result of reconciling, or as the case may be, balancing of different interests will not depend so much on the actual formulation used in the judgment but rather on perceptions among the sitting judges of what is fair and reasonable, based on an overall assessment of all relevant factors and whether the problem for the proper functioning of the internal market is deemed to be minor or more serious. It almost goes without saying that the final outcome could be different had the case been decided by another chamber of the Court than the one to which the case has been referred.

A linking point for present purposes is that the dynamics outlined by both contributors are made possible by the Treaties' normative symmetry.

Interestingly, Article 3(3) TEU is rarely cited in post-Lisbon case law.[47] Where it is, it is normally as one of a string of provisions mentioned to convey that the Lisbon Treaty had effects right across primary EU law. For example, in *Las* and also in *Runevič-Vardyn*, the Court confirmed the explicit primary law status of a public interest reason previously protected in a more amorphous way: '[a]ccording to the fourth subparagraph of Article 3(3) EU and Article 22 of the Charter of Fundamental Rights of the European Union, the Union must respect its rich cultural and linguistic diversity. Article 4(2) EU provides that the Union must also respect the national identity of its Member States, which includes protection of a State's official national language'.[48] This linkage between the text of the Treaties

[45] Case C-283/11 *Sky Österreich* EU:C:2013:28, para 60.

[46] This question is explored more fully in N Nic Shuibhne, 'Fundamental rights and the framework of internal market adjudication: is the Charter making a difference?' in P Koutrakos and J Snell (eds), *Research Handbook on EU Internal Market Law* (London, Edward Elgar Publishing, forthcoming 2016). See generally Davies (n 6).

[47] eg for the sole judgment reference to the aim of combating social exclusion and discrimination in Art 3(3) TEU, see Case C-236/09 *Association belge des Consommateurs Test-Achats and Others* EU:C:2011:100; on the aim of combating social exclusion and poverty in the context of social and housing assistance under Art 34(3) of the Charter, see Case C-571/10 *Kamberaj* EU:C:2012:233 para 80.

[48] Case C-391/09 *Runevič-Vardyn* EU:C:2011:291 para 86. See similarly Case C-202/11 *Las* EU:C:2013:239 para 26; see previously eg Case 379/87 *Groener* EU:C:1989:599 para 19; Case C-222/07 *UTECA* EU:C:2009:124 para 27. For discussion, see B de Witte, 'Cultural Policy Justifications', ch 7 in this volume.

and the narratives of the case law underscores the point about pre-/post-Lisbon continuity, and so contributes something mainly at a formal or symbolic level on the whole. Can any change in emphasis, more substantively, be discerned?

Building on the observation above, it is clear that the newer ideas embedded in Article 3(3) have yet to catch on. For example, the aim of achieving a 'social market economy' has been referred to in the substantive part of one judgment of the General Court[49] and in a handful of Advocate General opinions.[50] But it has never even been mentioned in a judgment of the Court of Justice to date. The mainstreaming clauses have made a similarly thin imprint on judicial reasoning, in express terms at least.[51] This is regrettable in two senses: that the values prioritised by these provisions have not been discussed more substantively; but also that the obligations that primary law provisions place on the Court itself, as an institution of the Union, have not been experimented with either.[52] Article 152 TFEU on the role of the social partners has been referred to in two judgments—*Commission v Germany*[53] and *Erny*.[54] But tellingly, the judgments in both cases went on to emphasise the limits that can legitimately be placed on the exercise of collective action: referencing *Viking Line* and *Laval* in *Commission v Germany* (paras 41–44); and asserting that 'although it is apparent, in particular from [Article 152(1) TFEU], that the European Union respects the autonomy of the social partners, the fact none the less remains, as is stated in Article 28 of the Charter ... that the right of workers and employers, or their respective organisations, to negotiate and conclude collective agreements at the appropriate levels must be exercised in accordance with European Union law' in *Erny* (para 50).

Compliance with Union law also emerges as the ultimate standard being checked for by the Court from the reference to Article 168(7) TFEU in *Ottica New Line di Accardi Vincenzo*:

> [T]he Court notes that, in accordance with Article 168(7) TFEU, as interpreted in its case-law, European Union law does not detract from the power of the Member States to adopt provisions aimed at organising their health services. *In exercising that power, however, the Member States must comply with European Union law*, in particular the provisions of the TFEU on the freedom of establishment, which prohibit the Member States from introducing or maintaining *unjustified* restrictions on the exercise of that freedom in the healthcare sector.[55]

[49] Case T-565/08 *Corsica Ferries France v Commission* EU:T:2012:415, para 82.

[50] eg AG Kokott in Case C-557/12 *KONE and Others* EU:C:2014:45, para 66 of the Opinion.

[51] eg Art 9 TFEU has been cited in one judgment to date, Case C-544/10 *Deutsches Weintor* EU:C:2012:526 para 49: 'the Court has already recognised on several occasions that measures restricting the advertising of alcoholic beverages in order to combat alcohol abuse reflect public health concerns and that the protection of public health constitutes, as follows also from Article 9 TFEU, an objective of general interest justifying, where appropriate, a restriction of a fundamental freedom.'

[52] eg on the implications of mainstreaming the protection of cultural and linguistic diversity, see de Witte (n 48). On the Court and institutional obligations, see Horsley (n 6).

[53] Case C-271/08 EU:C:2010:426, para 39.

[54] Case C-172/11 EU:C:2012:399, para 50.

[55] Case C-539/11 EU:C:2013:591 para 24 (emphasis added).

The Court re-centralises freedom of establishment here too.[56] So, yes, Member States have some discretion over the national policy choices that are important to them; and the policy areas that are especially important to them have now been flagged more prominently in the Treaties. But compliance with free movement law continues to erect a stubborn super-boundary and, whatever Article 3(3) TEU and other provisions might suggest, the Lisbon Treaty has not yet produced either a conceptual or structural shift in that position.

How can such a burst of primary law amendments make so timid an indent on the judicial shaping of legitimate public interest reasons? At one level, recalling the continuity factor demonstrated by Weatherill, it is not necessarily alarming that the Lisbon-amended provisions barely feature in judicial adjudication if the values underpinning them had always featured in the case law anyway. But should significant adjustments of emphasis through explicit primary law revision make quite so little difference? For example, as Barnard has argued,

> [t]he horizontal provisions in Articles 7–13 TFEU are not merely decorative baubles on the top of the EU Christmas tree. They need to be considered in respect of all decision-making at EU level, and at national level too when national policy makers are acting in the sphere of EU law. While they might not reverse the policy choices themselves, the execution of the policy might well need to be adapted to accommodate some of the horizontal interests.[57]

The justification of restrictions of free movement rights surely constitutes 'execution of the policy' in that respect.

A key point to return to is therefore the actual mode of Treaty change. More activities, policies, aims, values, tasks and objectives have been added with every process of Treaty revision—but they have been added around what is already there, without reflection on or resolution of a more explicit *system* for public interest(s) determination when various interests pull inevitably in different directions. In other words, the Lisbon Treaty did not rectify the poverty of primary law interpretative instructions for the Court. It did not, in substantive legal terms, re-engineer the relationship between primary law-conferred free movement rights and primary law-protected public interest derogations. And it did not introduce a more granular framework for justification and proportionality. Since the distant days of *Dassonville, van Binsbergen* and *Cassis de Dijon*,[58] we have absorbed the prolonged fiction that national restrictions on free movement rights are controlled

[56] See similarly eg Joined Cases C-171/07 and C-172/07 *Apothekerkammer des Saarlandes and Others* EU:C:2009:316, para 18 ('Community law does not detract from the power of the Member States to organise their social security systems and to adopt, in particular, provisions intended to govern the organisation of health services such as pharmacies. In exercising that power, however, the Member States must comply with Community law, in particular the provisions of the Treaty on the freedoms of movement, including freedom of establishment').

[57] C Barnard, 'The Protection of Fundamental Social Rights in Europe after Lisbon: A Question of Conflicts of Interests' in de Vries, Bernitz and Weatherill (eds) (n 40) 37, 56.

[58] Case 8/74 *Dassonville* EU:C:1974:82; Case 33/74 *Van Binsbergen* EU:C:1974:131; Case 120/78 *Cassis de Dijon* EU:C:1979:42.

and delimited by the Treaty's free movement provisions—a fiction that falls quietly apart even, in some cases, where restrictions are directly discriminatory.[59] And since most restrictions discriminate either indirectly or not at all, the substance of public interest justification remains Court-led, not Treaty-led.

However, the Treaties are Member States-led. It is not surprising that the Lisbon amendments offer more of a something-for-everyone compromise than a system recognising *agreed* harder choices. But the Member States then have to accept that if over-reliance on judicial exegesis is what follows in consequence, it is their own over-reliance in reality. Snell's point about the incoherence of case law on economic justifications—that having expanded the reach of free movement law beyond protectionism, the Court is now 'caught in a trap of its own making' since these choices '[force] the Court to decide the legality of a very large number of national rules without a clear theory to guide it'[60]—is more generally relevant too. On top of this, the Court does not have a clear *Treaty* to guide it either. If the Member States intended that the Court should confine its review of policy choices to questions about competence limits post-Lisbon, they needed to do far more work on the overall scheme of the Treaty than was undertaken, non-adopted treaties aside.

Another factor to bear in mind is that it may still be considered early days, since the Lisbon Treaty has only been in effect since late 2009. On that view, case law that engages more substantively with the full range of the Lisbon amendments may yet be on the way. However, the slowness of any push in that direction thus far makes the comparatively rapid engagement with one amendment—Article 4(2) TEU on respect for national identity—all the more striking. What might that be about?

IV. ARTICLE 4(2) TEU AND RESPECT FOR NATIONAL IDENTITY: NATIONAL OR UNION PUBLIC INTEREST?

Prior to the adoption of the Lisbon Treaty, the Working Group on Complementary Competences (established under the auspices of the Convention on the Future of Europe)[61] considered an elaboration of the statement in ex Article 6(3) TEU that the Union should respect the national identities of its Member States. The Group sought 'to provide added transparency of what constitutes the essential elements of national identity, which the EU must respect in the exercise of its competence'.[62] It conceived of two areas of 'core national responsibilities': (1) '[f]undamental structures and

[59] eg on protection of the environment, see Case C-2/90 *Commission v Belgium (Walloon waste)* EU:C:1992:310 and Case C-28/09 *Commission v Austria* EU:C:2011:854.

[60] Snell (n 16). On the question of protectionism, see K Lenaerts and JA Gutiérrez-Fons, 'The Constitutional Allocation of Powers and General Principles of EU Law' (2010) 47(6) *CML Rev* 1629, 1666; for extended analysis, see S Arrowsmith, 'Rethinking the Approach to Economic Justifications under the EU's Free Movement Rules' (2015) 68(1) *Current Legal Problems* 307.

[61] See http://european-convention.europa.eu/EN/bienvenue/bienvenue2352.html?lang=EN.

[62] Final Report of Working Group V, 2002, CONV 375/1/02 REV 1 http://european-convention.europa.eu/pdf/reg/en/02/cv00/cv00375-re01.en02.pdf, 10.

essential functions of a Member State';[63] and (2) '[b]asic public choices and social values of a Member State'.[64] However, while the central purpose of an elaborated national identity clause concerned 'safeguarding the role and importance of the Member States in the Treaty while at the same time allowing the necessary margin of flexibility', the Group did not envisage it as a 'derogation clause':

> The Member States will *remain under a duty to respect the provisions of the Treaties*. The article would therefore not constitute a definition of Member State competence, thereby wrongly conveying the message that it is the Union that grants competence to the Member States, or that Union action may never impact on these fields. The purpose would be to *render more visible and more operational the existing principle* that the Union, in the exercise of its competence, is under an obligation to respect the national identities of the Member States. The clause would send an important message to the citizens as well as provide useful guidance for the Union institutions in the fulfilment of its tasks.[65]

Article 4(2) TEU, as adopted,[66] provides that '[t]he Union shall respect the equality of Member States before the Treaties as well as their national identities, inherent in their fundamental structures, political and constitutional, inclusive of regional and local self-government. It shall respect their essential State functions, including ensuring the territorial integrity of the State, maintaining law and order and safeguarding national security. In particular, national security remains the sole responsibility of each Member State.'[67]

In *Michaniki*, construing national identity as including the constitutional identity of a Member State, AG Poiares Maduro considered the reach of ex Article 6(3) TEU in the context of justification just before the Lisbon Treaty (and therefore

[63] ibid, 11, providing the following examples: '(a) political and constitutional structure, including regional and local self-government; (b) national citizenship; (c) territory; (d) the legal status of churches and religious societies; (e) national defence and the organisation of armed forces; (g) choice of languages'.

[64] ibid, providing the following examples: '(a) policy for distribution of income; (b) imposition and collection of personal taxes; (c) system of social welfare benefits; (d) educational system; (e) public health care system; (f) cultural preservation and development; (g) compulsory military or community service'.

[65] ibid (emphasis added).

[66] The Working Group's final recommendation was that '[t]he provisions contained in TEU Article 6(3) that the Union respects the national identity of the Member States should be made more transparent by clarifying that the essential elements of the national identity include, among others, fundamental structures and essential functions of the Member States notably their political and constitutional structure, including regional and local self-government; their choices regarding language; national citizenship; territory; legal status of churches and religious societies; national defence and the organisation of armed forces' but it was added that 'no specific mentioning of basic policy choices of the Member States in the identity clause would be required' (ibid, 11–12).

[67] These ideas are also reflected in the preamble to the Charter of Fundamental Rights: 'The Union contributes to the preservation and to the development of these common values while respecting the diversity of the cultures and traditions of the peoples of Europe as well as the national identities of the Member States and the organisation of their public authorities at national, regional and local levels.' Drawing from the principle of the equality of the Member States also expressed in Art 4(2), see AG Kokott in Joined Cases C-144/13, C-154/13 and C-160/13 *VDP Dental Laboratory* EU:C:2014:2163, para 84 of the Opinion; and AG Wahl in Case C-44/14 *Spain v Parliament and Council* EU:C:2015:320, para 35 of the Opinion.

Article 4(2) TEU) came into effect. In his view, the Member States *could* deploy protection of national identity to defend restrictions on free movement rights, in two senses. Underscoring the view that Article 4(2) is a justiciable provision,[68] and differing from the expectations of the Working Group, he argued that a State 'may, first of all, explicitly rely on it as a legitimate and independent ground of derogation'.[69] Alternatively, 'preservation of national constitutional identity can also enable a Member State to develop, within certain limits, *its own definition of a legitimate interest* capable of justifying an obstacle to a fundamental freedom of movement' (emphasis added)—illustrating the second point by referring to *Omega*, a decision in which the Court initially ruled out the relevance of the specific German constitutional conception of human dignity when discussing public interest reasons but then found a place for recognising it when reviewing proportionality.[70] On that view, it could be argued that the post-Lisbon decision in *Sayn-Wittgenstein*—returned to just below—is arguably a 'better' *Omega*, in the sense that using Article 4(2) to underpin *why* the Court will accept the legitimacy of distinctive national interpretations of an otherwise broadly shared principle (equal treatment and human dignity in these cases respectively) is more convincing than trying to say that the German understanding of human dignity both was (proportionality) and was not (justification) a relevant factor in the *Omega* ruling.

However, AG Poiares Maduro cautioned against conceptualising respect for national constitutional identity as 'an absolute obligation to defer to all national constitutional rules' with the attendant risk that 'national constitutions could become instruments allowing Member States to avoid [Union] law in given fields'.[71] The general concern evoked by his remark re-engages comments made in Section 3 about the ultimate futility of a model that over-estimates the capacity of balance and reconciliation. The real challenge is this: how can the Court find a way to make the Lisbon-upgraded national identity clause substantively meaningful without dissolving decades of case law that instead aims to level out the sources

[68] See further LFM Besselink, case comment on *Sayn-Wittgenstein* (2012) 49 *CML Rev* 671; D Sarmiento, 'Who's Afraid of the Charter? The Court of Justice, National Courts and the New Framework of Fundamental Rights Protection in Europe' (2013) 50 *CML Rev* 1267, 1292.

[69] AG Poiares Maduro in Case C-213/07 *Michaniki* EU:C:2008:544 para 32 of the Opinion; referring to Case C-473/93 *Commission v Luxembourg* EU:C:1996:80 para 35. This point was implicitly confirmed by the Court for Art 4(2) TEU in Case C-51/08 *Commission v Luxembourg* EU:C:2011:336 para 124. In *Rottmann*, AG Poiares Maduro had also argued that the composition of the national body politic was also 'clearly an essential element' of national identity (Case C-135/08 *Rottmann* EU:C:2009:588 para 25 of the Opinion).

[70] Case C-36/02 *Omega* (n 2) discussed by Weatherill (n 41).

[71] AG Poiares Maduro in *Michaniki*, para 33 of the Opinion. See similarly, AG Bot in Case C-399/11 *Melloni* EU:C:2012:600, para 142 of the Opinion: 'a concept demanding protection for a fundamental right must not be confused with an attack on the national identity or, more specifically, the constitutional identity of a Member State. The present case does indeed concern a fundamental right protected by the Spanish Constitution, the importance of which cannot be underestimated, but that does not mean that the application of Article 4(2) TEU must be envisaged here.'

of national law vis-à-vis compliance with Union law and thereby to reinforce the ideal of uniform application of Union law across all of the Member States?[72]

The Advocate General saw the critical dynamic as one of synergy: '[j]ust as [Union] law takes the national constitutional identity of the Member States into consideration, national constitutional law must be adapted to the requirements of the [Union] legal order'.[73] This is undoubtedly true; and it finds reflection in the responsibilities placed on Member States by Article 4(3) TEU and the principle of sincere co-operation. But we are no further forward in resolving the stubborn problem of how to cut through apparently equalised interests. Put plainly, something will always have to give. And perhaps it is not surprising that, aiming to reconcile national discretion with the requirements of EU law, AG Poiares Maduro placed his faith in the conventional capacity of proportionality.[74]

Importantly for present purposes, the Court has followed the general path identified by AG Poiares Maduro in its post-Lisbon case law, by expressly linking respect for national identity with public interest reasons to justify free movement restrictions: with protection of a State's official language(s);[75] a State's political status (in *Sayn-Wittgenstein*, the status of Austria as a Republic);[76] and the organisation of a State's internal governance structures (in *Digibet and Albers*, the division of competences between the *Länder* in Germany).[77] However, the remuneration of judges, assessed in the light of EU equal treatment standards, has been excluded from the scope of Article 4(2)'s protective effects.[78] It will be important to watch how the Court develops this exclusion dimension in future case law—that is, to see when and why it decides that certain interests do not, in its view, come within the scope of national identity—because these determinations suggest a centralised supervisory function that brings a sharp angle to the idea of multilevel constitutionalism.

In his contribution, Thym examines that challenge through the premises of federalism.[79] From a different starting point, Davies reaches essentially the same point with respect to prospects for the centralisation of power: 'by putting national identity in the TEU the Member States *made it a concept of EU law*, so that the Court of Justice may now adjudicate on what it means', remarking that this is 'arguably, a small step *towards its harmonisation*'.[80] Thym does remind us that 'the ECJ does not always move towards more uniformity'. And the recurring need

[72] Case 11/70 *Internationale Handelsgesellschaft* EU:C:1970:114 para 3; confirmed in eg Case C-409/06 *Winner Wetten* EU:C:2010:503 para 61 and *Melloni* EU:C:2013:107 para 59. On similar questions in the domain of public policy, see D Thym, 'The Constitutional Dimension of Public Policy Justifications', ch 9 in this volume.

[73] AG Poiares Maduro in *Michaniki*, para 34 of the Opinion.

[74] See similarly AG Jääskinen in *Runevič-Vardyn* EU:C:2010:784, paras 80–81 of the Opinion.

[75] See n 48.

[76] *Sayn-Wittgenstein* (n 2) paras 90–93.

[77] Case C-156/13 *Digibet and Albers* EU:C:2014:1756 para 34.

[78] Case C-393/10 *O'Brien* EU:C:2012:110 paras 47–49.

[79] Thym (n 72).

[80] Davies (n 6) (emphasis added).

for the Court at least to provide clear guidance for Member States (including for national courts) can be reinforced as case law on Article 4(2) continues to develop. The danger is, though, that the very motivation behind protecting national identity in the first place will become subsumed by the centralisation of substance that occurs through the centralisation of interpretation.

Back in the foundational case law era of *Dassonville, van Binsbergen* and *Cassis de Dijon*, the justification options created by the Court were premised on mutual recognition. Importantly, this conceptual framing required that imported goods were to be accepted on a national market *unless* a legitimate overriding public interest reason could be demonstrated. Does Article 4(2) alongside other Lisbon amendments now swap the conceptual starting point?[81] Apprehension about chronic recourse to respect for national identity would anticipate a problematic fragmentation of public interest along national lines, and a problematic erosion of the worth of free movement rights in consequence. The Court has been alert to this, reiterating, for example, that respect for national identity involves a State's most '*fundamental* constitutional objectives'.[82] Moreover, justification that is premised on respect for national identity does not displace proportionality review, and it does not seem to compel softer proportionality review as a rule either. For example, as Chapter 7 discusses, this occurred in *Sayn-Wittgenstein* but not in *Las* (if we measure softness of review in terms of the degree of discretion that remained with the State).

However, in different ways, Davies and Thym highlight a less obvious but potentially lethal consequence of the merging of Union and national public interest that Article 4(2) effects: Article 4(2) transforms respect for *national* identity into a *Union* public interest reason. Conversely, as a means to shape other legitimate interest arguments, it provides a constitutional basis for the carving out of distinctive understandings of public interest arguments. In the case law to date, Article 4(2) has been referred to mostly in this second understanding of its role at justification stage. That the grasp of Article 4(2) might be contained there is, however, challenged by Davies in particular. His concern about the harmonising of national difference in the pursuit of Union public interest is well demonstrated by the decision in *Josemans*—suggesting that Article 4(2) does not necessarily provide a way out when the policy realised distinctively at national level departs very obviously from the more mainstream societal choices made by other Member States.[83]

The circularity of trying to separate out Union public interest and national public interest post-Lisbon is further exposed by Weatherill's analysis of *Sayn-Wittgenstein*: because of Article 4(2), what the Court can now do is 'convert' national public interest reasons into an 'EU concern to respect difference where

[81] eg mapping some problematic consequences that occur when State interest is brought to the fore in an economic sense, see Snell (n 16); and E Spaventa, 'Economic Justifications and Union Citizenship: Reallocating Welfare Responsibilities to the State of Origin', ch 3 in this volume.

[82] Case C-208/09 *Sayn-Wittgenstein* (n 2) para 93 (emphasis added).

[83] Case C-137/09 *Josemans* EU:C:2010:774; discussed in Doukas (n 1).

it operates at a sufficiently elevated level, where national identity is engaged'.[84] So Iglesias Sánchez and Acosta Arcarazo are right, on the one hand, that '[t]he doctrine of justifications is not premised upon the need that the public interests raised by the States are also protected as a Union interest'.[85] Ironically, however, Article 4(2) has the potential to subsume *the most important* national public interest reasons as Union public interest. Therefore, what these authors demonstrate in the specific case of social justifications—that 'recognition of a legitimate interest of the States converges with the need to ensure the protection and promotion of values that are placed among the core objectives of the Union itself'—has been diffused, not counteracted, by the Lisbon Treaty. This point renews the original conception that public interest arguments simply do not come first per se. Instead, they sometimes override the pursuit of free movement rights, which the case law evidence to date would suggest have remained the starting point, for good or ill. Drawing Article 4(2) into the analysis would further suggest that conceiving justification arguments as national public interest reasons is possibly a decoy—and, ironically, all the more so post-Lisbon. It would be astounding if the authors of the Treaty amendments were perfectly aware of this.

V. CONCLUSION

Where within free movement law can we live with or tolerate difference and divergence; and more than this, respect and proactively promote it; and where can—and should—we not? The Lisbon Treaty takes us no closer to answers. Instead, it amplifies a chorus of them. But if nothing much changes in law after considerable Treaty revision—ostensibly the biggest clout that the Member States possess as a means of EU law making—then something is wrong. It seems odd, in other words, that we need to investigate the prospects of a 'parallel evolution in the … case law', using de Witte's phrase in Chapter 7. Some solutions lie in the Court's own choosing. And it is unrealistic to think that Treaty words could be impervious to judicial interpretation. The proliferation of objectives and values around existing text without serious reflection on their interaction is also understandable as a reflection of the compromises and deliberately eschewed decisions that underpin the political reality. But it is flawed in terms of shaping a route to greater legal clarity.

Meanwhile, we persist in packing too many free movement problems into proportionality review, where the vast majority of claims are won or lost. But proportionality is also the most difficult stage of analysis to render into law. We can discern from some of the contributions to this volume that consensus among Member States on a particular public interest reason has sometimes delivered

[84] Weatherill (n 41).

[85] S Iglesias Sánchez and D Acosta Arcarazo, 'Social Justifications for Restrictions of the Right to Welfare Equality: Students and Beyond' ch 5 in this volume.

tougher proportionality review. Conversely, a less settled value landscape has sometimes induced national policy relief. However, we saw just as many examples that do not fit these trends.[86] A more systematic approach would avoid accusations of arbitrariness; and would be more helpful for national courts—which normally apply proportionality in relevant cases themselves, without a preliminary reference being made[87]—and for national legislatures and executives, who make the policy choices in the first place. Enhanced constitutional protection of respect for national identity may provide an improved alignment between primary law and case law dynamics that were already in play. However, if the Member States shaped Article 4(2) TEU in hopes of more transformative protection of national difference, then they did not do enough elsewhere in the Lisbon Treaty to ensure that they might actually achieve it.

That is not necessarily a bad thing from the perspective of the aims and purposes of free movement rights, since the underlying diversity questions would be better tackled through processes of change that manage *both* parts of the complex free movement/justification equation together. But the wider Union context suggests waning political and public appetite for the conventional ideology of integration. The consequences of this are not just a growing interest in governance ideas that engage co-operation, flexibility, pluralism and differentiation. We also now find ourselves at the edges of 'renegotiating' core Treaty ideas: not just a recalibration of the space for public interest arguments that might legitimately restrict free movement rights; but the possible re-visioning of free movement as an objective of the Union much more profoundly. The fact that the extensive Lisbon revisions of primary law have had very little impact in practice leaves a sour impression. And that may make how the next adventure in Treaty change is tackled—where renegotiation of the very legacy of free movement may itself be on the table—a lot more worrying.

[86] eg discussing the application of margin of appreciation language in the *Trailers* case law, where one might expect that road safety as a public interest reason should be relatively straightforward from the perspective of consensus, see Thym (n 72); discussing Case C-110/05 *Commission v Italy* EU:C:2009:66. Discussing the unpredictability of post-Lisbon case law on cultural policy justifications, see de Witte (n 48).

[87] See generally Jarvis, 'The Proportionality Test: Constructive Dialogue between the English and Scottish Courts', ch 13 in this volume; see also Weatherill (n 41), who cautions: 'Cases that come to attention tend to be high-profile events that reach the appellate courts, and, in constructing an explanatory model, there is a real risk of attributing too much weight to the trends visible because countertrends that might emerge from lower down the judicial hierarchy are simply not known. Cases reaching the appellate courts may not be typical.'

Index

abortions 146, 154
absence of harmonisation 184, 297, 300
abuse, sexual 177, 201
acquisition and loss of nationality 73
acquisition of films 139–40
acquisition of the right of permanent residence 82, 90, 99
active citizens 22, 51, 88, 90–91
activism 280, 295
addiction 162, 168
administrative action 288, 293
adoption of secondary legislation 279, 287, 292
advertising 121, 137, 165, 183, 242–43, 270
  revenue 137–38
Advocates General 24, 27, 87, 89, 96, 99, 300–301, 313–15
alcohol 108, 146, 153, 163, 168, 193, 263, 270
  abuse 163, 242
  content 108, 247
alcoholic beverages 183, 242–44, 261
alcoholism 153, 270
allocation of responsibilities between Member States 40
application of public security exceptions/derogations 191, 215–16
appropriateness 10, 83, 93–95, 103, 164, 272
arbitrary discrimination, prohibition 4, 149–51, 164, 167, 241
archaeological value 135, 197
armed forces 13, 63, 191, 197–200, 213
arms 208, 211–13
audiovisual media services 158
Austria 47, 49, 101, 103, 250, 252, 254, 256
autonomy 221, 228, 234, 290, 295, 304, 306, 310
  national regulatory 189, 262, 264, 279
  private 26, 245
AVMS Directive 158

balance 139, 141–42, 203, 205, 228–29, 235–36, 269–70, 308–9
  fair 235, 254, 309
  financial 17, 19, 22, 45, 87, 89, 92, 95
  right 138, 199
balancing exercise 10, 176, 196, 260
balancing of interests 218–39
  deviant case law 233–38
  myth 229–33
  v reconciliation 227–29
barriers to trade 2, 7, 171

Baumbast 37, 97, 295
beer 120, 220, 223–24, 245
Belgium 2, 19, 42, 74, 113, 117, 124–25, 250–51
benefit tourism 22, 39, 81
Bidar 22, 38, 88, 91, 96–97, 99, 101
blanket rules 48, 99
bogus self-employed persons 113, 125
Brexit referendum, franchise 53, 62–74, 77–78
Brey 47–50, 82, 88, 101
British citizens 53, 63–64, 68–69, 75–77
British nationals 53, 64–65, 67, 69–72, 74, 78
budgetary considerations 36–39, 44, 47, 88
burden, unreasonable 35, 38, 43, 46, 83, 86–88, 90, 95
burden of proof 154, 166, 282

Campus Oil 192–93, 195–97
cannabis 147, 157
capital 1–2, 4–5, 21–25, 27, 120, 122–23, 149, 151
  movements 2, 25, 305
Carpenter 233, 235–36
Cassis de Dijon 5–7, 108, 172–73, 175, 232–33, 240–41, 244, 246–47
centralisation 315–16
CFR, *see* Charter of Fundamental Rights
Charter of Fundamental Rights (CFR) 57, 133–34, 139–40, 182–84, 204, 252–56, 307, 309–10
children 41, 45, 10[illegible], 160, 173, 177, 182, 235
  of frontier workers 47, 91
  of migrant workers 91, 104
  sexual exploitation 201
choices, social 258–59, 263, 267, 271, 274
citizens 13–15, 29–30, 32–33, 42–43, 50–72, 74–78, 102–5, 200–201
  British 53, 63–64, 68–69, 75–77
  Commonwealth 53, 59, 62–63
  Union 36, 38, 40–42, 44, 46–47, 49–50, 67, 206–7
Citizens' Rights Directive 200
citizenship 21, 23, 32–52, 56, 74, 76–77, 80–81, 197
  cases 44, 92–93, 102, 235
  national 56, 59, 74
  rights 56, 71
  Union 33–35, 37, 40, 52, 56, 73, 202
CJEU, *see* Court of Justice of the European Union
closed judgments 204, 206

coherence 17, 24–25, 30, 188
collective action 20, 27, 126, 310
commercial transactions 6–7, 135, 173
Commission 7–8, 67–68, 113–17, 122, 127, 209–14, 280–81, 287–88
common market 2–4, 106, 109, 171, 180, 301
freedoms 131, 136–37
Commonwealth citizens 53, 59, 62–63
companies 4, 25, 120, 122–23, 125, 127, 195, 214
competence 130, 132, 134, 199, 202, 287–88, 312–13, 315
legal 60, 66
national 133, 190
regulatory 243, 264, 295
shared 148, 299
competing interests 10, 257, 260
competing public interest objectives 144–45, 166
competition 21, 26, 28, 108, 121, 125, 209, 211–13
distortions of 125, 212–13
international 14–15, 20
law 26, 106, 108–9
market 249–50
undistorted 14, 19, 307
competitive social market economy 29, 84, 302–3, 307
compliance 3, 191, 203, 253–54, 257, 271, 310–11, 315
comprehensive health insurance 36, 39, 41
compromises 10, 21, 26, 39, 51, 151, 230, 260
confidentiality 206, 214
conflict of laws model 179–80
consensus 30, 169, 225, 237, 317
consistency 18, 93, 151–52, 155–56, 164, 166–67, 197, 302
requirement 151, 165–66, 169
test 157, 165, 167
constitutional framework 131, 133–34, 139, 295
constitutional identity 181, 307, 313–15
constitutional phenomena 13–15
constitutions, national 23, 154–55, 314
constructive dialogue 276–77
consumer choice 222, 242–43, 245, 250
consumer protection 7, 109–12, 128–29, 173–74, 224–26, 230–31, 240, 250–53
alignment with fundamental rights/margin appreciation cases 253–57
alignment with proportionality review 257–59
case law 108–9
cases before national courts 259–63
high level of 108, 252
justification 108, 112, 128
and proportionality 240–64
rise as justification 241–43
consumers 6–7, 108–10, 120–21, 129–30, 219–20, 225–27, 241–43, 247–52
economic interests 243–46, 249, 251, 253, 256
welfare 108–11, 120, 129–30, 223
content 89, 94, 180, 182, 191, 200, 212, 216
social 83, 92
contracts 124, 140, 224, 284
employment 124–25, 140
contributions 32, 37–38, 49–50, 115, 220, 223, 315, 317
control 165, 172, 177, 209, 211, 236, 238, 240
co-operation 154, 182, 209, 318
administrative 306
close 206
loyal 212
costs 17, 25, 94, 217–18, 224, 230, 248, 258
Court of Justice of the European Union (CJEU) 8–13, 58–61, 75, 131–35, 140–46, 215–17, 267–73, 277–78; *see also cases subheadings*
role 292–95
crime 61, 162, 177, 201–2, 305
prevention 167–68
criminal offences 201–2
criminality 153, 165, 242
cross-border trade 148–49, 152, 254
crude oil 192–93, 196
cultural diversity 133–34, 136, 141–42
value 131, 134, 141–42
cultural goods 135
cultural heritage 131, 133, 302
cultural policy 131, 133–37, 139–40
case law before Lisbon 135–38
justifications 131–42
national 134, 138–39, 141
as ordinary legitimate interest 135–38
post-Lisbon case law 139–41
cultural products 135–36
culture 131–35, 252, 306
constitutional framework 132–34
customs, enforcement 3
customs union 2–4
Cyprus 55, 63, 70

Dano 41–43, 48–50, 82, 101–2
Dassonville 4–5, 294, 311, 316
data processing centres (DPCs) 123
defence industries 211–13
deference 144–45, 154–55, 157, 161–62, 168, 185, 291, 293
increasing 145, 163, 166–67, 169
degree of integration 46, 88, 90–91, 95, 101
democracy 54, 56, 78–79, 293
democratic society 10, 260
democratic Union 54–55, 79
demonstrations 236–37
Denmark 5, 55

deportation 207
derogations 82, 99–100, 148–49, 151–54, 158–61, 163–64, 167–68, 278–79
dialogue 265–66, 269, 273–74, 277
constructive 276–77
dignity, human 54, 154–55, 181, 228, 244, 255, 259, 314
diplomas 96–97, 103, 289
direct actions 8, 10, 294
direct universal suffrage 57–58, 60
Directive 2004/38 35–43, 46–48, 50–51, 82, 88, 90, 92–102, 104–5
disability 44–45, 302
disclosure 204–6, 211
discretion 152–58, 160–62, 167–69, 181, 185–86, 194, 206–7, 242–43
national 158, 162, 164, 166, 170, 183, 185, 187–89
discretionary powers 268, 291, 294
discrimination 6, 9–10, 32–33, 70, 72, 163, 289, 302
arbitrary, *see* arbitrary discrimination, prohibition
on grounds of nationality 9, 70, 289
discriminatory rules 27, 174–75, 278
disenfranchisement, *see* enfranchisement
disguised restrictions 3–4, 149, 241
disproportionality, *see* proportionality
distortions of competition 125, 212–13
diversity 184–85, 222–23, 225–26, 241, 243, 255, 262–63, 279
cultural, *see* cultural diversity
linguistic 133, 139–41, 173, 302, 309
domaine réservée 171
domestic courts, *see* national courts
domestic legislation, *see* national legislation
domestic *ordre public* 157–58, 160, 167–68
Doorstep Selling Directive 249, 251
DPCs (data processing centres) 123
drugs 147, 156–57, 167, 178
dual-use goods 194–95, 212, 214
dumping, social 113–14, 125–26
duty-free allowances 152–53

ECHR, *see* European Convention on Human Rights
economic activities 1–2, 4, 39, 46, 91, 171, 174, 300
economic considerations 15, 21, 27, 36, 46, 51–52, 87, 172
as function of social objectives 86–88
economic freedoms 22, 33, 136, 174, 177, 184, 301
economic interests of consumers 243–46
economic justifications 12–35, 37, 42–44, 48, 51, 83, 86–87, 312
bigger picture 23–30
cases 15–23, 40–44
economic objectives 19, 87
economic operators 94, 135, 251, 258, 300
economic reasons 12–13, 18, 20, 26–27, 32
economic risks 14–15, 31
economic sanctions 190
economic security 13–14, 29–30
economic space, public 224, 230, 234, 238
economy 15, 25, 50, 103, 223–24, 288
education 14, 39, 46, 83–84, 97, 249–50, 302, 306
education grants 45–46, 66
elections 56–62, 75
general 57–58, 63, 68
local 55, 59, 62
municipal 56–59, 62
national 53, 55, 67–68, 76
electoral roll 55, 67–68
employees 63, 111, 113, 122–24, 127, 140, 284
employers 107, 110, 115, 120, 125, 140, 310
employment 20, 29–30, 33, 84–86, 91–92, 98, 198–99, 302
contracts 124–25, 140
markets 38–39, 89, 97, 114
enforcement 3–4, 130, 180–81, 209, 280
customs 3
proceedings 111, 116, 119
enfranchisement 53–79
English and Scottish Courts 265–77
environment 7–8, 218–20, 225–27, 231, 238, 244, 289, 302
environmental harm 222, 225, 236
environmental protection 7, 133–34, 173, 226, 252–53, 258
equal treatment 35–36, 38, 40–41, 43, 46, 81–82, 92, 197–98
principle 38, 61, 81–82, 99, 102, 198
equality 54, 56, 70, 80, 223, 228, 256, 302
of Member States 105, 255, 313
essential interests 198–99, 211–12, 215
EU citizenship, *see* Union citizenship
EURA, *see* European Union Referendum Act
European Convention on Human Rights (ECHR) 11, 76, 78, 169, 254, 266, 304, 308
European Council 54, 303
European integration, *see* integration
European *ordre public* 157, 168
European Parliament 54, 56, 159, 212, 287–89, 291
right to vote in elections to 59–62
European Union Referendum Act (EURA) 62, 74–76, 78
evidence 10, 110, 114, 117, 133–34, 165–66, 205–7, 217
exceptional clauses 192, 207–15
exclusive rights 18–19
expertise 220, 231, 293
exports 3–4, 6, 21, 45, 104, 194–95, 241

express derogations
  of public morality 163–64
  of public policy 151, 153–54, 156, 159, 164, 167–68
expulsion 156, 182, 200, 203, 205, 235–36

factors of production 33–34
fair balance 235, 254, 309
fairness 6–7, 103, 173, 234, 293, 296
family life 203, 275
family members 22, 42, 49, 235
federal question 179–85
federal solution 170, 179, 182
films 136, 139–40, 247
financial balance 17, 19, 22, 45, 87, 89, 92, 95
financial services 16, 145, 149, 160, 163, 250–51
financial solidarity 37–38
financial sustainability 87, 89
Finland 20, 93, 152
Förster 85, 90–92, 99–100
four freedoms 1–11, 18, 25, 28, 30, 93, 107–8, 119–20
France 45, 61, 71, 243, 245, 249
franchise 53, 60–61, 64, 66, 68–69, 72, 77, 79
  parliamentary 68
  referendum 53, 62–63, 67, 70
fraud 156, 162, 167–68, 253
free movement of services 122, 128, 154, 156, 159–61, 164, 237, 242
freedoms
  four 1, 3, 5, 7–9, 11, 28, 107–8, 119–20
  fundamental 9–10, 143–45, 149, 170–72, 174–78, 180–81, 183–85, 187–89
frontier workers 91, 94, 99
  children 47, 91
fundamental freedoms 9–10, 143–45, 149, 170–72, 174–78, 180–81, 183–85, 187–89
fundamental interests 172, 179, 188, 297
  of society 151, 153–54, 173, 188, 201, 203
fundamental rights 68, 78, 168–69, 253–54, 276, 278, 301, 304
fundamental social rights 84, 301

gambling 145, 161–68, 177, 185, 253
games of chance 146–47, 149, 161–66
GATT 2–4, 6
general elections 57–58, 63, 68
general interest 7, 9–10, 17, 25, 114, 122, 137, 148
  objectives 19, 173
genetically modified organisms (GMOs) 152
genuine and sufficient connection 45
genuine link 38–39, 43–44, 86, 89, 94–95, 100, 102
Germany 41–43, 66, 116–17, 122, 127–28, 223–24, 244–45, 255–56
  law 9, 127, 229, 244–45

Gibraltar 59, 62–63, 77
Giersch 47, 85, 91, 94, 104
GMOs (genetically modified organisms) 152
goods 1–2, 4–7, 120, 135–38, 149–50, 176–79, 195, 265–67
  cultural 135
  dual-use 194–95, 212, 214
  imported 6, 149–50, 244, 246, 316
grants, education 45–46, 66
Greece 16, 107, 195, 210–11, 224

harmonisation 132, 184–86, 219, 221–22, 228–29, 231–32, 234, 237–38
  absence of 184, 297, 300
  measures 152, 170, 185, 258, 289
  total 280–81, 283
health 121–22, 152–53, 201, 203, 205, 225–27, 241, 252–53
  care 16, 30, 32, 217
  human 183, 252, 257, 302
  insurance, comprehensive 36, 39, 41
  public, *see* public health
  risks 241–42
  services 24, 304, 310
home Member States 67, 146–47, 161, 163, 167
home nationals 151, 155, 157, 168
host society 37–39, 41, 43
host States 35, 37–43, 48–49, 101–2, 115–16, 126–28, 200, 202–4
host welfare society 37, 44, 46, 51
human dignity 54, 154–55, 181, 228, 244, 255, 259, 314
human rights 54, 78, 169, 182, 184, 266, 275, 304
Human Rights Act 11
Hunting Act 260–61

identity 221–23, 226, 234, 239, 258, 264, 266, 273–74
  constitutional 181, 307, 313–15
  national, *see* national identity
imperative grounds of public security 200–202, 207, 215
imperative requirements 9, 154, 278, 281, 300
imported goods 6, 149–50, 244, 246, 316
imports 3–6, 120, 150, 153, 161, 176, 197, 241
imprisonment 23, 61, 201, 207
inactive citizens 37, 40, 44, 46, 48–49, 51, 97
inactive migrants 35, 39, 42
inadmissibility 13–14
institutions 11, 133, 142, 144, 186, 267, 288, 294
  legislative 287, 290–91
  political 279, 291
integration 50–51, 88–92, 94–96, 101–5, 218–19, 227, 238, 241
  assessment 104–5
  link 88–89, 93, 102, 105

market 134, 141–42, 148, 171, 173, 242, 245, 264
notion 88, 94, 103–4
objective 83, 86, 90, 94, 97
requirements 88–89, 96
intensity of review 93, 145, 257
interests
balancing 218–39
consumer 230, 240
producer 26, 248
public, *see* public interest
vested 79, 221
interference 72, 109, 144–45, 169, 205
internal market 32–34, 50–51, 225–29, 279–80, 287–89, 291–92, 299–300, 302–3
context 279, 286–87, 290–93
law 17, 30, 176, 179, 222, 226, 255, 280
international competition 14–15, 20
International Covenant on Civil and Political Rights 71–72
interpretation 101–2, 171–73, 191–92, 215–17, 281, 285–86, 290–92, 294
narrow 196, 217
strict 29, 171, 213, 307
inter-State trade 240, 243–44, 246–47, 249–50, 253, 260
invalidity benefits 95, 98, 104
Ireland 5, 55, 62–63, 70, 154, 281
Italy 74, 117, 123, 130, 214

jobseekers 82, 86, 89, 92, 97, 99, 102
Josemans 147, 156–57, 167, 182, 316
judicial deference, *see* deference
judicial restraint 132, 144, 158–59, 161, 168, 261
judicial review, *see* review
judicial scrutiny 135, 158, 162, 165
judiciary 78, 82, 144–45, 203, 206, 284, 287, 290–93
jurisdiction 10, 24, 102, 158, 180, 213, 294
justifiability 194, 250, 293
justification 16–19, 83–85, 111–19, 173–77, 187–88, 240–41, 243–63, 306
cultural policy 131–42
economic, *see* economic justifications
moral 149, 159, 161–62, 168
objective 81–84, 92–93, 103
public policy, *see* public policy, justifications
social, *see* social justifications
stage 17–18, 307, 316
worker protection, *see* worker protection, justification

Keck 121, 234–35, 237

labour lawyers 109, 113
labour market 50, 86, 92, 94, 100, 107, 113–14
language rules 159, 305
languages, official 124, 139–41, 309, 315
Laval 126, 130, 233, 237, 285–86, 307, 310
lawful residence 47, 50
legal bases 134, 228, 231, 287–90
legal certainty 99, 156, 168, 296
legal order 73–74, 170, 172, 180–83, 185, 190, 207, 209–11
legality 20–21, 145, 197–98, 204–5, 257–58, 282–83, 285, 290
and morality 145–49
legislative institutions 287, 290–91
legislature(s) 10, 20–21, 257–58, 260, 274, 279–81, 283, 286–96
EU legislature role in internal market context 287–92
national 79, 238, 262, 318
legitimacy 14–15, 29–30, 78–79, 87–88, 93, 104, 220, 245
legitimate interests 20–21, 27, 81, 84, 88, 135, 314, 317
legitimate objectives 83, 86–87
legitimate public interest 137, 218, 224, 301, 311, 316
linguistic diversity 133, 139–41, 173, 302, 309
linkage 16–19, 309
Lisbon Treaty 29, 60, 131–35, 139, 142, 181, 279, 287–88
and public interest 298–306
interpretation 306–12
Lithuania 141, 280, 282
local preferences 234, 236, 238
long-term residents 53, 73, 182
loss of nationality 73
lotteries 146–47
loyal co-operation 212
Luxembourg 41, 113–15, 117, 124–25, 127, 247–48, 253, 261–62
Luxembourg Compromise 5

mainstreaming clauses 134, 302–3, 310
maintenance costs of students 46, 88, 90
maintenance grants 39, 46–47, 82, 90
Malta 55, 63, 70
mandatory requirements 6–7, 137, 141, 160, 172–73, 175, 188, 238
and public policy 172–74
manifestly inappropriate test 266–73, 277
margin of appreciation 157, 161, 163, 166–69, 183, 260–62, 272, 274
margin of discretion 153–54, 160, 162, 242, 254, 256, 264
market access 174–75, 224, 300
market competition 249–50
market economy, competitive social 29, 84, 302–3, 307
market freedoms 83, 131, 136–37, 147, 183
market integration 134, 141–42, 148, 171, 173, 242, 245, 264

marketing 6, 16, 147, 150, 157, 161, 244, 246
markets 107, 227–28, 232, 241, 245–46, 248–49, 300, 307
  employment 38–39, 89, 97, 114
  labour 50, 86, 92, 94, 100, 107, 113–14
  national 16, 129, 316
migrant workers 47, 85, 91, 107, 120, 124, 128
  children 91, 104
military service 198–99
minimum standards 158, 168, 251
minors 41, 148, 158–59, 163, 168, 182
mobility 46, 81, 104–5, 135–36, 138, 140
  students 84–85
monopolies, state 163, 165–66
moral considerations 143–49, 154–55, 158–59, 161–62, 167–69
  moral justifications as judge-made public interest exceptions 159–67
moral regulation 143, 147, 168
morality 132, 143–69, 225–26
  and legality 145–49
  and public policy 153–59
Morgan and Bucher 85, 93, 97–98, 100, 104
motor vehicles 246–47
municipal elections 56–59, 62
munitions 208, 211–13

national authorities 162, 165, 191–92, 194, 202–3, 205, 207–8, 216–17
national citizenship 56, 59, 74
national competence 133, 190, 243
national constitutional identity 181, 314–15
national courts 118, 186–87, 194–97, 205–7, 215–17, 259, 276–77, 294
  referring 20, 253
national cultural policy 134, 138–39, 141
national discretion 158, 162, 164, 166, 170, 183, 185, 187–89
  theoretical arguments for 185–88
national elections 53, 55, 67–68, 76
national identity 139, 225, 228–29, 238, 255–56, 298, 309, 312–18
  clause 228, 238, 313–14
  respect for 298, 312, 316, 318
national interest 109, 214, 228, 231, 236, 299, 303–4
national legislation/law(s) 40–41, 55, 65–66, 68, 115–16, 164, 230–32, 281
national legislatures 79, 238, 262, 318
national markets 16, 129, 316
national measures 240–41, 243–44, 252–53, 263–64, 266–71, 273–75, 277–79, 285
national policy 30, 134, 147, 165, 170, 178, 227, 234–35
national public interest 298, 303, 316–17
national regulation 109, 129, 164, 166, 243, 248, 250, 260
national regulators 250–51, 258, 306
national regulatory autonomy 189, 262, 264, 279
national restrictions 6, 30, 187, 194, 244, 256, 311
national rules 16–17, 107–8, 120–21, 129, 227–28, 241, 244–46, 294
  obstructive 243, 246
national security 4, 196, 206, 214, 313
national social security systems 45, 89, 95
national sovereignty 68, 191, 212, 217
national treasures 3, 135, 197
national values 228, 243, 262
national welfare systems 34, 80, 83, 86, 88
national workers 107, 119–20, 122–24, 126, 128
  cases 120–23
nationality 28, 35, 44–46, 54–56, 60, 72–73, 98–100, 104–5
  acquisition and loss of 73
  discrimination on grounds of 9, 70, 289
  loss of 73
  state of 33, 43, 45, 49, 51–52, 90
nationals 37, 53, 55–56, 59–61, 64–68, 70, 100–103, 155–57
  home 151, 155, 157, 168
  non-resident 55, 66
necessity assessment 95
Netherlands 16, 18, 22, 24, 60–61, 95–96, 147, 149
non-discrimination 54, 78, 135, 145, 151–52, 161, 164, 166–68; *see also* discrimination
non-discriminatory measures 51, 174–75, 300
non-discriminatory rules 28
non-economic interests 197, 231
non-economic migration 33, 36
non-economic public interest objectives 152–53, 169
non-economically active citizens 22, 51, 88
non-residence 64, 68–69, 72, 104
non-resident nationals 55, 66

objective justifications 81–84, 92–93, 103
objectives 8, 83–85, 87, 89, 246–47, 299, 301–3, 309
  core 84, 317
  general interest 19, 173
  legitimate 83, 86–87
  policy 112, 132–33, 142, 175, 232, 301
  social 86, 94, 307
obstructive national rules 243, 246
official languages 124, 139–41, 309, 315
oil, crude 192–93, 196
Omega 154, 160, 228, 255–56, 261, 314
openness 83, 92, 226, 233
ordre public 180, 182
  domestic 157–58, 160, 167–68
  European 157, 168

Organisation for Economic Co-operation and Development (OECD) 2
Organisation for European Economic Co-operation 2
over-regulation 247, 250–51
overriding requirements 10, 12, 122, 126, 137, 148–49, 159, 161

parliamentary elections 59, 62, 68
passenger vehicles, steering equipment 280–82, 285–86, 288
pensioners 47, 50, 102
pensions 45, 47–48, 93, 95, 101
permanent residence 66, 82, 90, 99, 200
  acquisition of the right of 82, 90, 99
personal circumstances 38, 47–49, 101
petroleum products 192–93, 195–96
physical security 177, 201
pluralism, constitutional 184
Poland 280–82
policies, national 30, 134, 147, 165, 170, 178, 227, 234–35
policy choices 85, 185, 191, 196, 215–16, 299, 311–12, 318
policy objectives 112, 132–33, 142, 175, 232, 301
political institutions 279, 291
political rights 71–72, 240, 253–54
pornography 146, 150, 158–59, 185
Portugal 107, 246
posted workers 110–11, 114, 117, 120, 124–29
Posted Workers Directive (PWD) 128, 285–86, 289
powers 209–10, 213, 266–67, 291, 295–96, 302, 304, 310
  discretionary 268, 291, 294
precedence 109–10, 199, 231, 244, 301
preliminary reference procedure 8, 215, 259
prices 19, 136, 227, 235, 250–51, 261
primary law 191–92, 197–98, 207–9, 213, 215, 285–86, 290, 297–318
  public interest Lisbon amendments 298–306
  public security in 192–96
Prinz 65, 89–90, 95, 98, 100, 104
private parties 12, 21, 24, 26–27
privatisation 24–25
procedural conditions 194, 213, 216
procedural rules 187, 205
producer interests 26, 248
profits 19, 25, 147, 166
proportionality 9–10, 151–55, 161–64, 176–78, 194–96, 245–49, 257–59, 261–71
  analysis 93, 207
  Art 36 TFEU and Convention/Charter rights 275–76
  assessment 42, 92–102, 171, 176–77, 187, 203, 229, 234
  and consumer protection 240–64
  identity of author of national measure 273–74
  manifestly inappropriate test 266–73, 277
  as politeness 246–49
  principle 240, 247–48, 257, 261, 264–67, 271–72, 274, 276
  and public policy 175–77
  review 75, 77, 215–16, 257–59, 298, 301, 309, 316–18
  test 160, 163–64, 176, 193, 196, 260, 263, 265–78
proportionate control measures 127–29
proportionate restrictions 72, 156, 159
protection of public health 6–7, 242, 249, 253, 261–63, 265, 267–68, 277
protectionism 27–28, 30, 32, 34, 124–28, 174, 221, 224
public economic space 224, 230, 234, 238
public goods 18–19, 184
public health 5, 7, 19, 230, 241, 243–46, 251, 261–62
  protection 6–7, 249, 253, 261–63, 265, 267–68, 272, 277
public interest 111–15, 143–45, 151–54, 159–69, 217–19, 297–309, 311–12, 314–18
  grounds/reasons 143–45, 148, 161, 298, 301, 303–4, 306, 314–16
  Lisbon amendments 298–306
  national 298, 303, 316–17
  objectives 144, 151–53, 156, 159, 161–67, 218
    competing 144–45, 166
    non-economic 152–53, 169
  requirement 81, 107, 109, 111
public morality 144–45, 149–54, 158–59, 161, 163, 167–68
  as express derogation 149–53
  express derogation 163–64
  grounds of 149–50, 197
public ownership 24–25
public policy 144–45, 153–56, 158–59, 161, 172–74, 179–83, 188, 202
  doctrinal basics and conceptual foundations 171–78
  exception 157, 170–76, 178–81, 184–85, 187–88
  express derogation 151, 153–54, 156, 159, 164, 167–68
  federal question 179–85
  foundational judgments 171–73, 181, 184, 188
  goods and persons 177–78
  interplay between justifications and restrictions 174–75
  justifications 170–89
  and mandatory requirements 172–74
  and morality 153–59
  and proportionality 175–77

theoretical arguments for national discretion 185–88
public procurement rules 214
public security 5, 10, 19, 191–98, 200–204, 207, 209, 214–17
exceptions 190–217
application 191, 215–16
imperative grounds of 200–202, 207, 215
notion 195, 207
in primary law 192–96, 207–15
in secondary legislation 197–207
trade 192–96
public services 87, 198
public space 223–24, 239
PWD, *see* Posted Workers Directive

quality of life 201, 218–39
arguments 219, 226
and free movement 222–25
meaning 220–22
quantitative analysis 110–11, 119, 127
quantitative restrictions 3–5, 149, 197, 270, 281
quotas 3–4

real link 38, 41, 44–45, 86, 89, 97, 101, 103–4
reconciliation 219, 230, 233, 235, 237–38, 309, 314
v balancing 227–29
referendum franchise 53, 62–74, 77–78, 130
referring courts 20, 141, 193–94, 201, 203, 205–6, 215, 253
refineries 193, 195
regulation
double 17, 28
national 109, 129, 164, 166, 243, 248, 250, 260
regulators, national 250–51, 258, 306
regulatory competence 243, 264, 295
reliance 69, 94, 102, 105, 146, 154, 210–12, 217
residence 33, 35, 39–40, 52, 54, 56–57, 67–68, 97–101
conditions 66, 68, 94, 98, 100, 102
permanent 66, 82, 90, 99, 200
requirements 47, 76, 85, 90–92, 95–96, 100, 103, 127
right of 36–37, 45, 48, 50, 88, 102, 204, 289
uninterrupted 66, 90, 98
residency, directives 37–38, 40, 99
respect for national identity 298, 312, 316, 318
restraint 143–69
judicial 132, 144, 158–59, 161, 168, 261
restrictions
disguised 3–4, 149, 241
disproportionate 163–64
national 6, 30, 187, 194, 244, 256, 311
proportionate 72, 156, 159
restrictive measures 10, 12, 20, 93, 96, 195, 204
restrictive rules 112, 230, 251, 278
retirement pensions, *see* pensions
review 144–45, 154–55, 168–69, 209–10, 257–59, 263–64, 271–72, 290–93
intrusive 227
level of intensity 268, 271–72
proportionality 75, 77, 215–16, 257–59, 298, 301, 309, 316–18
right of residence 36–37, 45, 48, 50, 88, 102, 204, 289
right to vote 53–61, 63, 67–72, 76–77
in elections to European Parliament 59, 59–62
in municipal elections 57–59
UK's EU referendum 62–74
right to welfare equality 80–105
risk 17–18, 42–43, 87, 125–26, 162–64, 202–3, 251, 282–83
road safety 183, 280–82
Rottmann 60, 73, 229
rule of law 54, 78, 148, 294
rules 5–7, 16, 24–26, 107–10, 221–22, 233–35, 242–51, 258–62
blanket 48, 99
general 3, 5, 56, 157, 174–75
national, *see* national rules
procedural 187, 205
restrictive 112, 230, 251, 278
tax 17–18, 32

safety 13, 201, 241–42
road 183, 280–82
sanctions, economic 190
Sayn-Wittgenstein 228, 256, 314–16
Schmidberger 233, 236, 238, 254, 256, 261
Scotland 58–59, 265, 267–69, 272–74, 276
Scottish Courts 265–77
Scottish Parliament 58–59, 261, 266–68, 272
scrutiny 24, 47, 162, 168–69, 262, 264, 268, 273
judicial 135, 158, 162, 165
secondary law 54, 82, 99, 191, 202, 215, 285–86
secondary legislation 37, 40, 42, 46, 184, 192–93, 196–98, 200–203
impact on derogations 278–96
two types of legislative intervention and Court reaction 280–86
security 13–14, 195, 198, 201, 205, 209–12, 215, 303
economic 13–14, 29–30
international 208
national 4, 196, 206, 214, 313
physical 177, 201
public, *see* public security
state 204–5
self-employed persons 82, 113, 125
self-restraint 291, 293
selling arrangements 30, 150, 235, 237–38, 267

service providers 28, 112, 115, 124–25, 127, 147
self-employed 113, 125
services 4–6, 114–15, 117, 122–23, 135–40, 146–47, 159–61, 254–56
financial 16, 145, 149, 160, 163, 250–51
Services Directive 29, 112, 146, 159
sexual abuse 177, 201
shared competence 148, 299
Shindler 74–78
Single European Act 3, 8, 287, 291
single market 106, 108–10, 129, 170–72, 178, 180–85, 188, 306–7
social assistance 35–36, 38–39, 48, 82, 97, 99–100
systems 35, 42, 48, 87–88, 101
social benefits 73, 83, 94, 96, 99, 102, 105
social bonds 223–24
social choices 258–59, 263, 267, 271, 274
social content 83, 92
social dumping 113–14, 125–26
social exclusion 84, 302
social justice 84, 302
social justifications 80–105, 156, 317
and social mandates of Treaty 83–86
social objectives 94, 307
and economic considerations 86–88
social order 144, 154, 160, 162–63, 165, 168
social partners 304, 310
social policies 47, 91, 96, 112, 289
social progress 84, 302
social protection 30, 84, 133, 302, 305
level of 22, 29, 307
of workers 29, 111–12, 126
social rights 44, 84, 107, 301
social security 127, 303, 305
fraud 113, 125
systems 17, 22, 27, 45, 89, 95, 98, 104
financial balance of 113, 125
social values 158, 168, 313
society 85–86, 88, 90–91, 179–80, 182–84, 219–22, 224–26, 238–39
fundamental interests of 151, 153–54, 173, 188, 201, 203
solidarity 36, 51, 54, 81, 88, 92, 302
financial 37–38
obligation of 86, 89, 95
sovereignty, national 68, 191, 212, 217
Spain 10, 44, 59, 66, 130, 136, 139, 213
law 136, 139–40
stability 96, 201, 219–20
standards 149, 168–69, 221, 223, 241, 243, 272, 274
minimum 158, 168, 251
moral 148, 159, 167–68
state interest 110, 119, 269–70
state monopolies 163, 165–66
state role 12–31
state security 204–5
states of nationality 33, 43, 45, 49, 51–52, 90
states of origin, and welfare responsibilities 32–52
steering equipment of passenger vehicles 280–82, 285–86, 288
Stoke-on-Trent 233–35, 238, 259
strict interpretation 29, 171, 213, 307
students 38, 45–46, 85–86, 88, 90–91, 93–94, 96–99, 104
maintenance costs 46, 88, 90
mobility 84–85
subsidiarity 183–84, 238, 258, 288, 299, 304
sufficient resources 36, 41–42, 47–49, 88, 102
Sundays 121, 137, 234, 259, 261
supervision 6, 59, 124, 209–10
supranational citizenship 51–52
sustainability, financial 87, 89
sustainable development 302
Sweden 180

tax restrictions 18, 21, 27
tax revenue 15, 18–19, 21
tax rules 17–18, 32
taxation 27, 38, 105, 134
technological change 14–15, 31
TFEU, *see* Treaty on the Functioning of the European Union
Thiele Meneses 85, 100, 104
threat of war 208, 211
tobacco 146, 231, 243, 263, 266–67
total harmonisation 280–81, 283
trade 2–4, 121, 211–12, 234–35, 237–38, 240–44, 252, 254
barriers 244, 254–55, 261
and public security 192–96
trade union freedoms 237
trade unions 20, 26, 118, 126, 237–38, 261, 307
traders 195, 232, 245, 251, 257
transactions 221, 223–24, 227, 234
commercial 6–7, 135, 173
transformative effect 52, 252
transitional period 3, 5–6, 171
Treaty change 299, 307, 311, 318
Treaty of Maastricht 34, 81, 131, 134, 138, 287
Treaty of Rome 108, 112, 180
Treaty on European Union (TEU), Article 4(2) 181, 255–56, 298, 312–18
Treaty on the Functioning of the European Union (TFEU) 117–22, 149–54, 208–15, 241–44, 251–54, 265–68, 273–81, 288–89
Art 36 275–76
Tsakouridis 201–3, 207

UK, *see* United Kingdom
undistorted competition 14, 19, 307
unemployment 34, 87
involuntary 102

uniform application 142, 184, 198, 315
uninterrupted residence 66, 90, 98
Union citizens 36, 38, 40–42, 44, 46–47, 49–50, 67, 206–7
Union citizenship 33–35, 37, 40, 52, 73, 202
Union interests 84, 109–10, 121, 302, 317
Union of Democracies 54
United Kingdom 38, 44–45, 53, 58–60, 62–79, 150, 234–35, 241–43
  English and Scottish Courts 265–77
  European Union Referendum Act (EURA) 62, 74–76, 78
  Human Rights Act 11
  Hunting Act 260–61
universal suffrage, direct 57–58, 60
unjustified restrictions 66, 69, 75, 139
unreasonable burden 35, 38, 43, 46, 83, 86–88, 90, 95
unwritten mandatory requirements 173, 175, 177, 188

value judgements, fundamental 155, 157, 168
values 54, 84–85, 104–5, 140–42, 219–22, 226, 309–11, 317
  archaeological 135, 197
  national 228, 243, 262
  social 158, 168, 313
vested interests 79, 221
Viking 20, 118, 126, 130, 233, 237–38, 301, 307
voting 55–56, 59, 61–62, 69–70, 74–75, 79
  rights 58–59, 61, 68, 122; *see also* franchise

war materials 208, 211–12
welfare
  community 36, 42, 44, 51
  consumer 108–11, 120, 129–30, 223
  resources 36–37, 43, 52, 103
  responsibilities 33, 43, 51–52
    reallocation to state of origin 32–52
  worker 109–11, 119, 121, 124–30
welfare equality, right to 80–105
welfare state 33–34, 36, 39, 42–43, 87
welfare tourism 43, 81
women 54, 198–99, 302
work permits 41, 125
work visas 77, 127
worker protection 20, 27, 237, 307
  cases 116–20
  justification 106–31
    limits 111–16
  methodology 111
  and worker welfare 109–10
worker welfare 119, 121, 124–30
  prioritisation 124–26
  and worker protection 109–10
working conditions 109, 121, 307
work-seekers 35, 39, 50

www.ingramcontent.com/pod-product-compliance
Ingram Content Group UK Ltd.
Pitfield, Milton Keynes, MK11 3LW, UK
UKHW020133290926
15471UKWH00003B/457